AF478046

The Art of Contact

The Art of Contact

Comparative Approaches to Greek and Phoenician Art

S. Rebecca Martin

PENN

University of Pennsylvania Press

Philadelphia

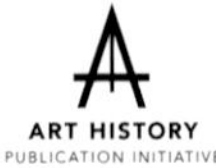

This book is made possible by a collaborative grant from the
Andrew W. Mellon Foundation.

Published by
University of Pennsylvania Press
Philadelphia, Pennsylvania 19104-4112
www.upenn.edu/pennpress

Printed in the United States of America on acid-free paper
10 9 8 7 6 5 4 3 2 1

A Cataloging-in-Publication record is available from the Library of Congress
ISBN 978-0-8122-4908-8

Contents

Color plates follow page 150

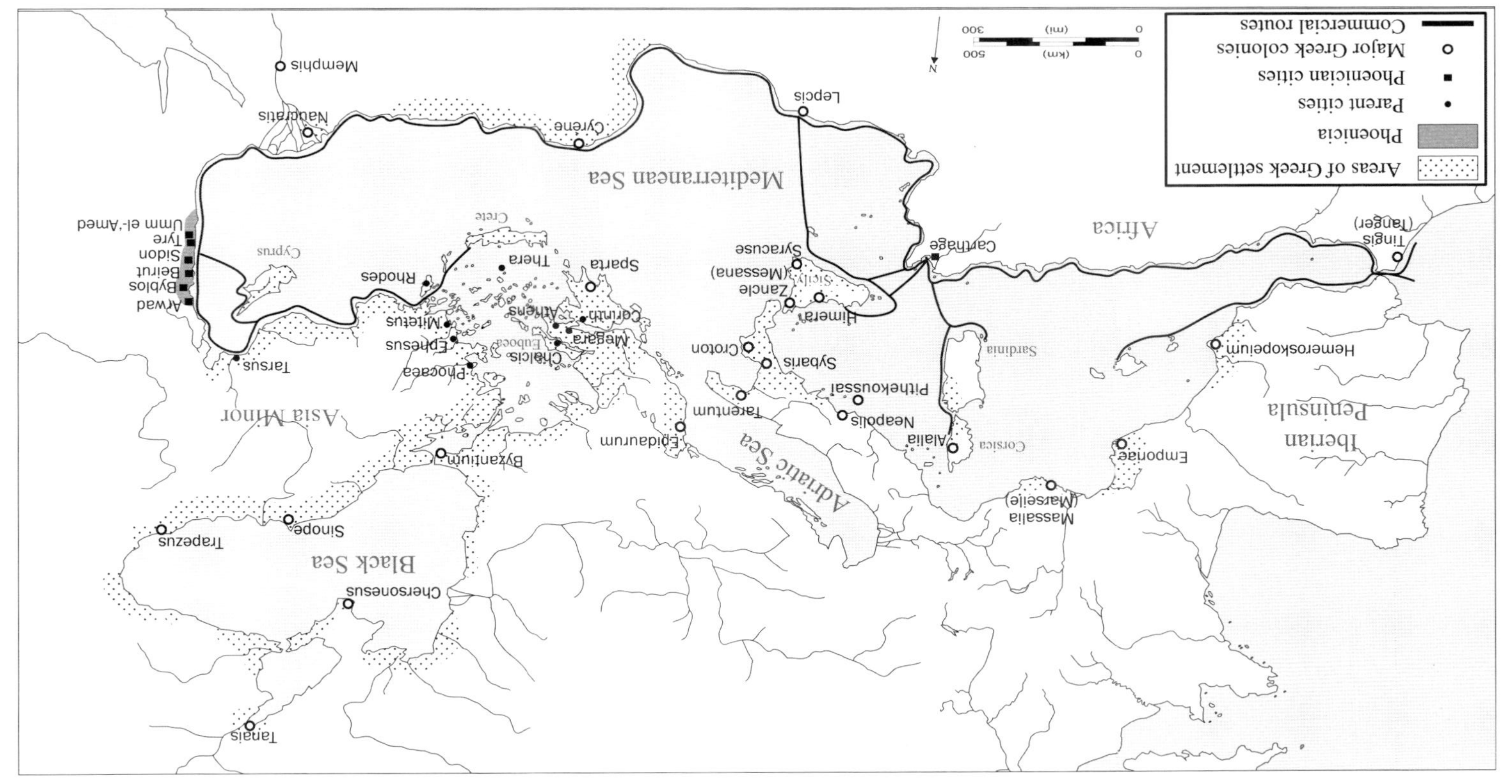

Map 1. The Mediterranean, showing a simplified reconstruction of Phoenician and Greek colonies and trading areas. By Sveta Matskevich.

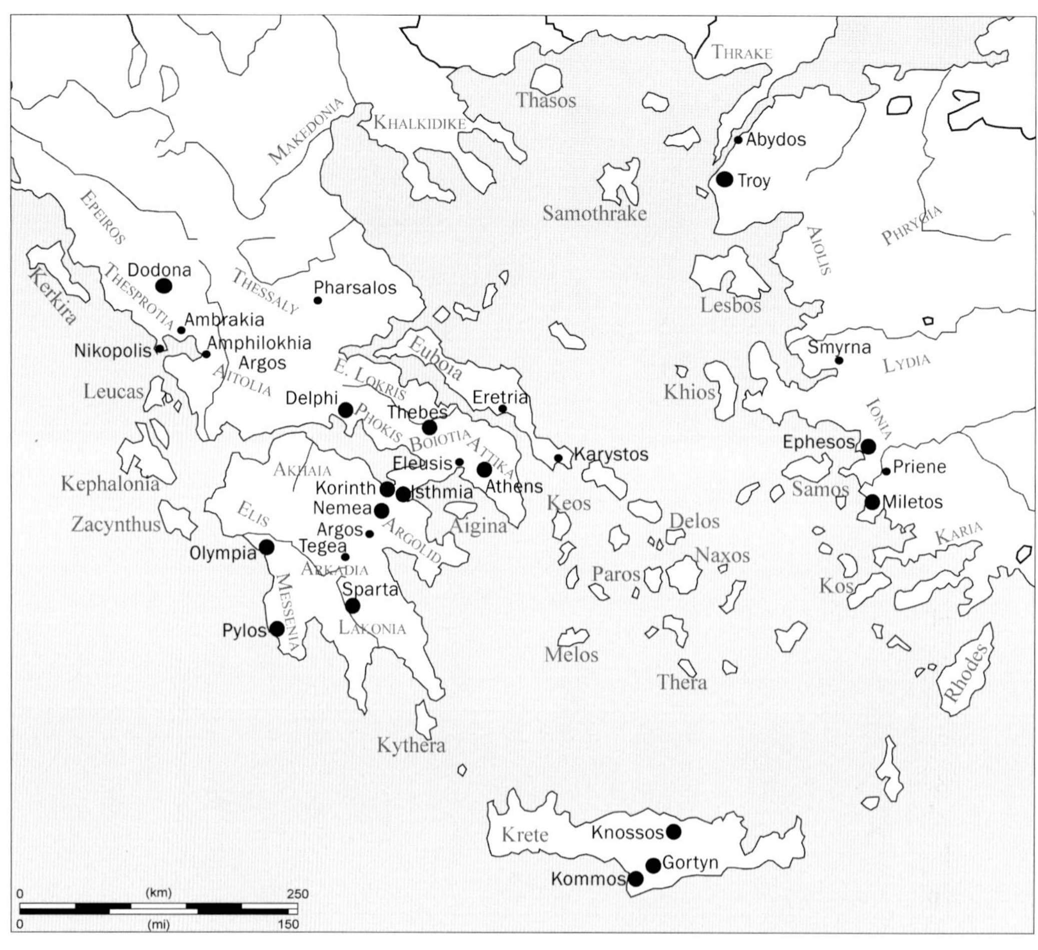

Map 2. Greece and the Aegean. Redrawn by Sveta Matskevich after Hall 2002, map.

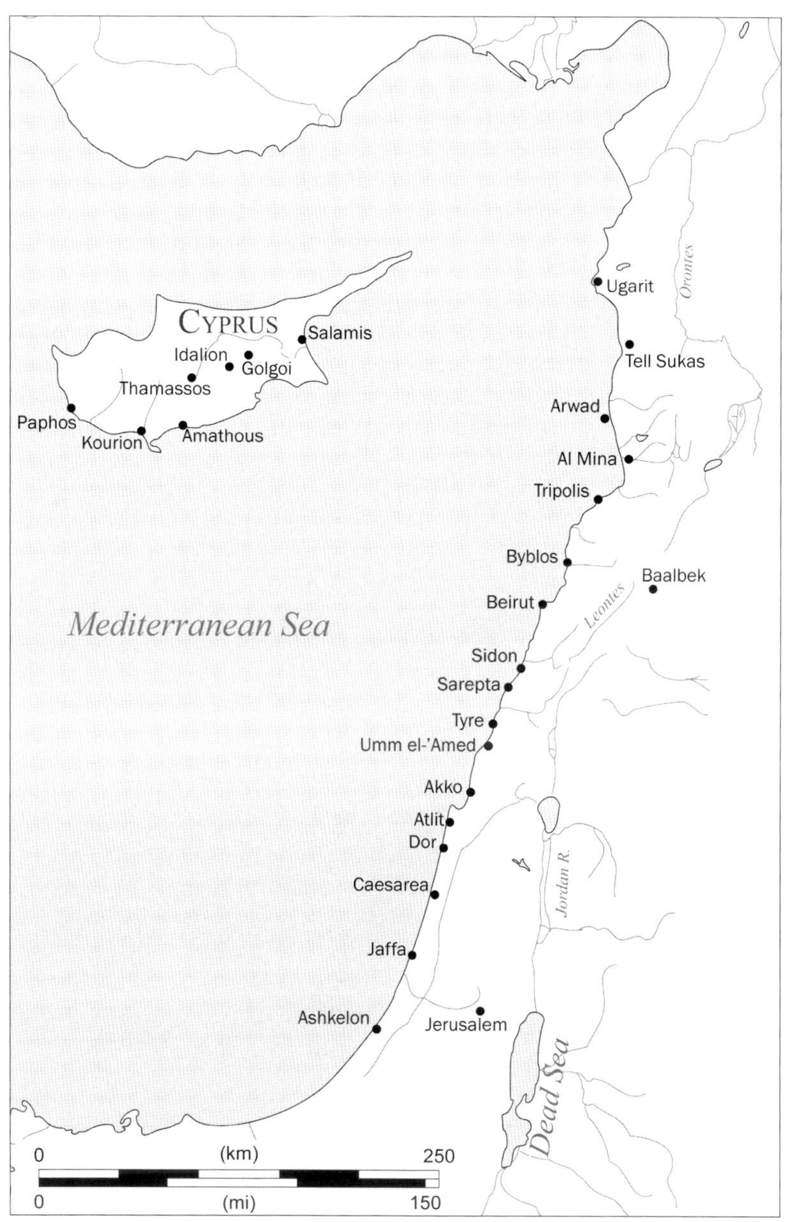

Map 3. Phoenicia and Cyprus. Redrawn by Sveta Matskevich after http://ngm.national geographic.com/ngm/0410/feature2/images/mp_full.2.jpg.

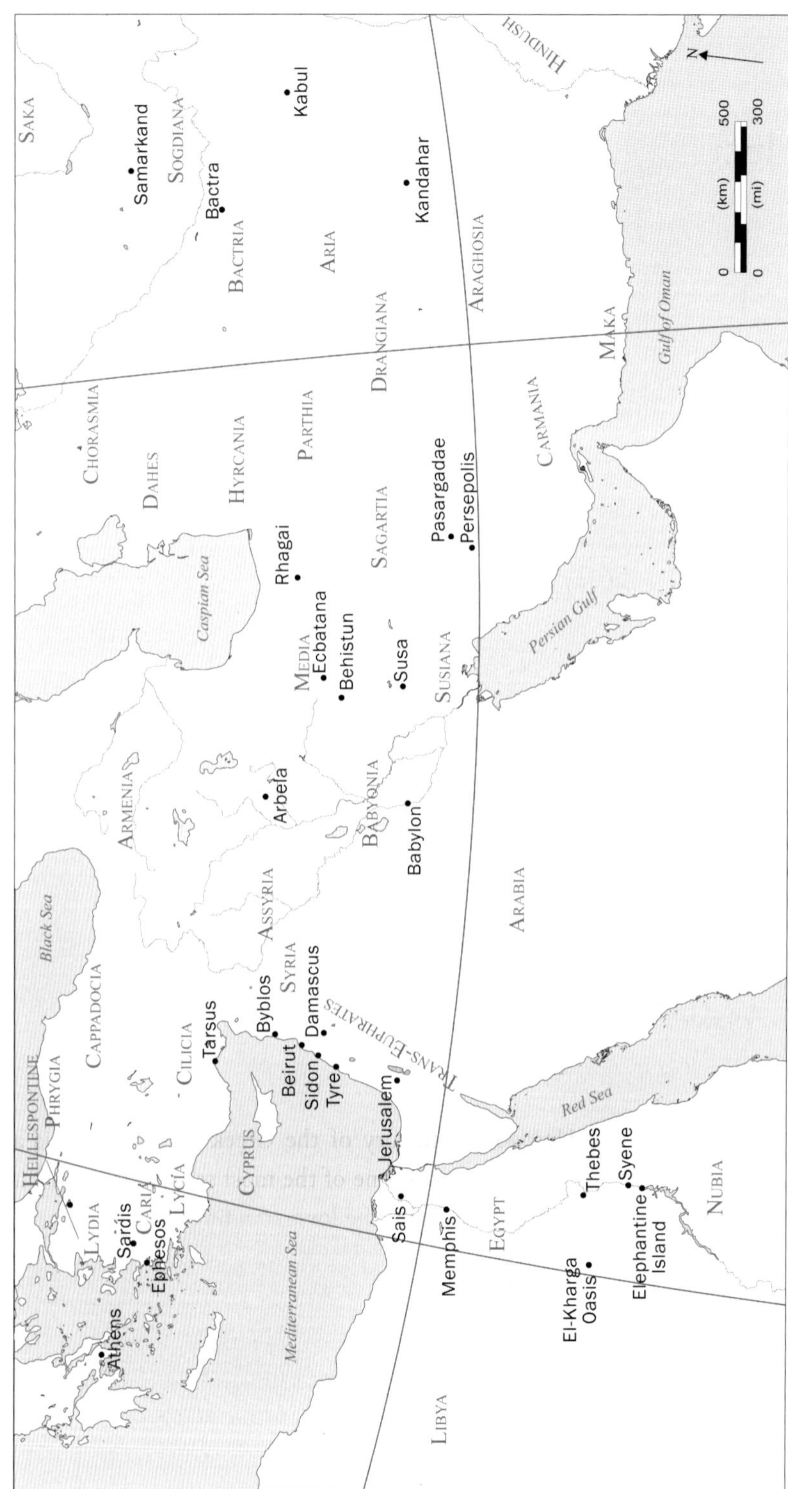

Map 4. The Achaemenid Empire. Redrawn by Sveta Matskevich after Briant 2002, 366, map 2.

Introduction

Ἡροδότου Ἁλικαρνησσέος ἱστορίης ἀπόδεξις ἥδε, ὡς
μήτε τὰ γενόμενα ἐξ ἀνθρώπων τῷ χρόνῳ ἐξίτηλα
γένηται, μήτε ἔργα μεγάλα τε καὶ θωμαστά, τὰ μὲν
Ἕλλησι τὰ δὲ βαρβάροισι ἀποδεχθέντα, ἀκλεᾶ γένηται,
τά τε ἄλλα καὶ δι' ἣν αἰτίην ἐπολέμησαν ἀλλήλοισι.
Περσέων μέν νυν οἱ λόγιοι Φοίνικας αἰτίους φασὶ
γενέσθαι τῆς διαφορῆς.

Here is the inquiry of Herodotus of Halicarnassus so that
things done by man not be forgotten in time and that
great and marvelous deeds, some by the Hellenes, some
by the barbarians, not lose their glory; and especially that
the causes may be remembered for which these waged
war with one another. Those of the Persians who have
knowledge of history declare that the Phoenicians were
the cause of the dispute.

The proem (1.1.1–1.5.4) to Herodotos's history of the Greek-Persian Wars is a discussion of causation. For good reason it is one of the most studied passages in classical history.[1] Herodotos begins by relating the long-standing conflict between Europe and Asia from the points of view of the Greeks' chief antagonists, Persian and Phoenician barbaroi (barbarians, foreigners; see Maps 1–4). He is characteristically balanced and skeptical about these accounts: "Among the Persians, the learned men say that the Phoenicians were the cause of the dispute." According to Herodotos's Persian sources, Phoenician traders kidnapped Io, among other Argive women, and carried them off to Egypt. No particular reason is cited for this deed. Perhaps Io's kidnapping occurred, simply, because both were there? In revenge, some Greeks[2] then kidnapped the king of Tyre's daughter Europa.

Despite the clear fragmentation of these episodes, they set off a chain of female abductions, including Medea's and Helen's, that in turn led to the sometimes ruinous pursuit of the abductees. The Persians say they only got involved when Greeks made incursions into Asia with the invasion of Troy (1.4.4). The Phoenicians of course denied their part (1.5). They claimed that Io had ingratiated herself to the Phoenician captain, became pregnant, and ran off on his ship to Egypt in shame and "of her own free will" (cf. 1.4.2). To Herodotos, all this attention paid to the kidnapping and attempted recovery of women was folly. Critique of the "cherchez la femme" cycle of fate is implied.[3]

As far as Greek-Phoenician contact studies go, there is something to learn in these Persian tales. At first it is surprising that Herodotos's Persian sources do not blame the Greeks from the outset, or not directly;[4] rather they blame their own subject-allies, the Phoenicians, using Greek mythology to do so. It is interesting how the Phoenicians are said to have turned the tables on the story. In claiming that Io left Argos of her own free will, they frame the Greeks as jealous, impudent, and thoroughly guilty. In this tale, the rapes of Europa and Medea, not of Io, set off the cycle of fate. Whereas the Persian account promotes Phoenician desire for Greek women, the Phoenician account suggests instead the desirability of a foreign ship captain to a well-born Greek girl. It is hard to deny the humor in this part of the prologue as seen through the eyes of barbaroi (compare it to Xerxes's incredulous reaction to the naked, hair-combing Spartans in book 7).[5] I agree with those who do not see in these tales genuine history writing. Yet we should take the passage seriously for what it says about the perceived differences between Greeks and barbaroi, especially when the "Persian tales"—not Io's journey to Egypt—are given the responsibility of articulating the separation of Europe and Asia. By placing the story in the context of these conflicts, however they are parodied, the difference between Europe and Asia is framed in political, not "natural," terms, as something "*historically determined rather than essential.*"[6] It is a compelling idea with which to begin.

Many attempts have been made to sort through and characterize just this kind of intense interaction in the eastern Mediterranean in which the coastal Levant was a regular participant.[7] The tension in the ancient accounts between the accidental, coincidental, or historical and the essential, structural, or inevitable carries on, although, as I argue in this book, most scholarship draws at least a little bit from both sides. Greek-Phoenician studies are typically concerned with the idea of influence resulting from physical proximity and the abstract notion of "culture contact." Common topics are colonization and two intense periods of interaction in the Iron Age and in the Classical and Hellenistic eras, referred to as "Orientalizing" and "Hellenization," respectively. Critique of the latter is where this study began.[8]

Hellenization is a problematic and dissatisfying term thought to describe an acculturation process through which people become more Greek.[9] Notwithstanding the recent emphasis on conscious choice, Hellenization is frequently presented as the inevitable result of culture contact—the result of the use of Greek-made *objects* by a non-Greek *person*—nearly always without addressing the agency of the human actors or the influential objects (compare the Persian account of the abduction of Io).[10] Hellenization presupposes that interaction with Greeks or their art leads to acculturation and assimilation, which are characterized by changes to non-Greeks with different, limited, or no impact on Greeks themselves. A similar Hellenocentrism is apparent in studies of the earlier Orientalizing phenomenon that tend to generalize external "input" and frame the Greek art that responded to it as exceptional. I wish to emphasize at the outset that my criticisms of Hellenization and Orientalizing are not just critiques of these terms, although that discussion matters very much,[11] but in fact are fundamental critiques of the concepts' merits. As I will argue, Hellenization and Orientalization by any other names are just as flawed.

Although its proponents now tend to describe it as an active process on the part of the Hellenized,[12] Hellenization nevertheless assumes a center-to-periphery model. It relies on the idea that cultures or ethnicities are delineated clearly—a debatable notion, and one that is undermined further by some striking behavioral parallels manifest in Greeks and Phoenicians that complicate up front the understanding of how they changed in response to contact.[13] To the idea that contact results in acculturation and assimilation may be added the outcomes of bilingualism, syncretization, hybridity, and creolization, which have had some traction in the many book-length studies and anthologies about the relationship of Greece and the East.[14] Of these alternate models, hybridity is currently the most popular in ancient Mediterranean studies, though, as I will argue, it can serve as another proxy for acculturation. Hence this book requires at least brief reconsideration of the ideas of culture and acculturation; of what it meant to be, become, or behave like a Greek or Phoenician; and of modern scholars' ability to define their boundaries and interactions from the available evidence. The discussion will avoid the idea that Greek cultural imperialism was inevitable.

The Art of Contact is written with a classical audience in mind, particularly for those interested in Greek–Near Eastern contact studies, art history, and historical methods. Its premise is straightforward: the methods we use to study ancient history shape our perceptions of it; art histories of the first millennium BCE Mediterranean are dominated by misleading primordialist narratives; and, while these narratives have been effectively critiqued since at least the 1980s, the fields of classical and Phoenician art history have not really moved on. Many scholars are willing to embrace some hard-won ideas (such as Greek receptivity to Near Eastern craft) and terminology (such as agency, hybridity, and networks), but much Greek art history remains essentialist and chauvinistic. Why? The reasons, I argue, can be found in our basic understanding of what "Greeks" and "Greek art" were and how both concepts are used to prefigure the presumed political and cultural triumph of Greece.[15] Core characteristics of the field of classical art history, one of which is evident in its very name, encourage its resistance to methodological change—a criticism of classics made already by Edward Said in the late 1970s. One result is that the rise of culture studies in classics has mostly *increased* Hellenocentrism and helped fix racial ideas about ancient Greeks. Recent interest in Punes and Phoenicians has only somewhat shifted this discourse and certainly has not undone the East/West dichotomy.[16] Yet I neither call for an end to positivism nor espouse a new, overarching theoretical model. Rather, *Art of Contact* takes a long but selective view of Greek and Phoenician art and artistic interaction, and a holistic view of their modern study, in order to advocate for greater awareness of the relationship between theory and the writing of ancient (art) history.

It should be clear, I hope, that I am not following *longue durée* approaches that deemphasize events over long-term processes.[17] Rather I am trying to use a handful of works of art ("events") over a reasonably long stretch of time to critique still-popular dichotomies, evaluate terminology, and destabilize ideas about fixed long-term processes. Geographically and chronologically diverse case studies are preferred to the sustained study of a particular time, place, or class of objects, because the problems of interpretation I wish to address are, I believe, pervasive. A comprehensive study would not suit. Of course it would be idle to deny that the decisions I have made are personally intriguing. I work in the eastern Mediterranean and so have favored the region with which I am most intimately familiar. Yet I think it is important to avoid emphasizing the "Mediterranean context" as a perfect route to understanding, because the idea of a single Mediterranean context, no matter how connected, is false, and the complementary notion of a Greek or Phoenician context is in itself often quite problematic. Since culture and context are always problematic in the study of Phoenicia, "Phoenicia" is an important idea to study, not least of all in comparison to our much more comprehensive notions about "Greece."

Some of the particular objects that make up the case studies come from quite clear contexts, such as coins minted in fifth- and fourth-century Sidon and Tyre. Others—from Hellenistic Delos, for example—were selected precisely because of the difficulty (often impossibility) of assigning a clear-cut cultural context to their site of manufacture, display, or deployment. Through these case studies, I hope to balance the familiar with the less known, to underscore that problems of interpretation are not particular to only some objects of contact some of the time, such as objects made in "contact zones," but rather to all arts of contact every time they appear. Accordingly, the discussion moves in time and space to keep it from growing too comfortable with any one area or idea, to maintain a healthy critical attitude as much as possible. Ultimately I find the case studies representative of the kind of challenges that we face in contact and comparative studies. In selecting them, I hope to show how art can contribute to the understanding of Greek and Phoenician identities as well as Greek-Phoenician relationships.[18] Thus, while critical and to some extent minimalist, this book is not pessimistic about the possibility of writing Greek and Phoenician art histories.

My claim that art is a key tool in the understanding of Greek-Phoenician contact is not in itself new, and in several respects it reflects traditional priorities in the field of Greek art history, notably the theory of style. I am attempting to espouse an alternate approach to this fundamental issue, however, one that proceeds from criticism of grand narrative contact histories, and one that sees no important distinctions for historians between the terms "art," "craft," and "material culture." Although many of the examples that follow are recognizable as "art," I am not concerned here with the problem of fine arts (les beaux arts) versus minor arts or crafts, as it seems to me that we can use the term "art" in the sense of *expressive object.* It is nonetheless important to keep in mind that ancient people could and did distinguish between arts and crafts, artists and craftsmen, some being held in higher esteem.[19] Likewise, if we were to think of "craftsmen" in our sense of laborer,[20] they should be distinguished from "artists," because art is expressive in a way that other utilitarian objects that constitute a material culture might not necessarily be. I am not interested in all the kinds of artifacts that compose material culture. I write here about metal bowls, not hammers; marble statues, not chisels; coins, not dies. While it would be possible to make the case that metal- and stone-working tools are expressive objects, I do not necessarily see them as such. They do not fit my understanding of art and are not as interesting to me in terms of what they express about responses to contact.[21]

But as James Porter and others have pointed out, all arts and crafts result from material manipulation, suggesting that, as in the contest of line drawing between Apelles and Protogenes (Pliny *HN* 35.81–83), all artists are craftsmen—are makers—of some sort.[22] So one might argue that not all craftsmen are artists, but that certain practices, such as signing works of gems and sculpture, *and* mosaics and pottery, transcend genre distinctions (cf. Hephaistos, *Il.* 18.478–614).[23] Put simply, the lines between these categories are blurry and not always important. I subscribe to the claim that "works of art are a form of address," and, "like most forms of address, they demand a response."[24] This kind of expressive object is at the center of the case studies used here.

Principles and Aims of the Project

The story of the interaction of Greeks, Phoenicians, and their neighbors is as challenging as it is compelling. It must be assembled from a variety of sources—historical and literary, archaeological and art historical—each of which offers its own, limited, perspective. Only occasionally does any one of the four support the others. The often-recognized imbalance of the written evidence—overwhelmingly Greek—encourages us to take on a Hellenic literary perspective even when the focus, as here, is on objects. It is, therefore, important to state at the outset that any classicist will approach the Near East through the varied stereotypes of the Greek record, and Phoenicia offers little to a discussion thus defined. So, in addition to pursuing the question of what it is we mean when we speak of "Greeks" and "Phoenicians," a major goal of this book is to articulate what is signaled by their respective artistic labels. The advantage of focusing on a theme—art and behaviors that seem to be produced by contact—is that it allows us to compare our methods, reveal biases, and explore different theories. By locating the study in the first millennium,[25] the book takes a view of these artistic traditions in a way that engages the classical canon and the impact of the "non-Western" world on Western visual conventions.[26] I will stress that acknowledging interaction and mixing is only a place to begin, not an explanation or argument in itself.

Four principles guide the project. The first principle is simple: *barbarians matter.* Direct contact between Greeks and others—in particular the peoples of the Near East—is the main reason Hellenists find themselves studying non-Greek people. Non-Greek peoples contextualized Greek behaviors, contributed to Greek patterns of thought, and, especially through colonization and conflict, provoked the self-fashioning of the Hellene. Following Walter Burkert, we understand that the so-called Orientalizing phenomenon was attributable not only to the trade in raw goods and cultural products but also to the migration of people from the Near East; following Sarah Morris, we know that the effect of the Near East on Greek art and literature of the Iron Age was profound; following Ann Gunter, we understand how to locate this process in history; and following Margaret Miller, we know that the emulation of Persians was a real phenomenon even in a Classical Athens "obsessed" with ethnic difference.[27] Yet, foreign peoples—here Phoenicians—should matter to us not only for what they can tell us about Greeks but also because they are interesting and important in their own right. Their artistic traditions show what other choices were made by people experiencing similar "global" events and employing similar materials. I do not wish to imply falsely that Phoenicians and Punes are unpopular; quite the reverse, especially in Italy.[28] Rather I am suggesting that in Greek-Phoenician comparative studies it is incumbent upon Hellenists to take the Phoenician component seriously. Accordingly, I juxtapose the Greek and Phoenician artistic traditions to elucidate both. One goal of doing so is to challenge the very canons that delineate them.

Throughout this book I attempt to distinguish between "Hellenes" as an ancient ethnocultural group and "Greeks" as a group forged by modern scholarship, and "Hellas" as regions inhabited by Hellenes and "Greece" as the scholarly idea of ancient Greece that correlates to a great extent with the modern nation of Greece. Such distinctions are not always clear and can be fraught, but the attempt serves, I hope, to emphasize that the convenience of referring to a loose, largely nonnationalistic, and, especially in Alexander's day, mixed group of people as "Greeks" from "Greece" obscures a rather complex picture. The monolithic term "Greeks" encourages polarization and facile contrast with "others." The term "Phoenician" is, of course, at least equally problematic as an entirely etic term.[29] The Greek record suggests that "phoinikes" is an "all-embracing [term], enveloping the whole range of Semitic peoples from the Levantine region, without distinction."[30] The name really cannot map on to the region in any meaningful way or on to our modern usage of the term "Phoenician" to refer to a people whose mainland was bounded, approximately, by the geography of modern Lebanon.

The second guiding principle of the project is rather less simple: *proper use of theory is our responsibility.* In juxtaposing Phoenician and Greek art, we can compare different reactions to similar historical, social, and economic stimuli. The comparison gives us the opportunity to reexamine our patterns of thinking about ancient people as well—to reexamine our methodology or theoretical principles. This self-consciousness is important because the field of classics is not a discipline, per se, but a commitment to the study of ancient history primarily through Greece and Rome. Training is rigorous, especially as concerns languages and source criticism, but while it does enshrine institutional perspectives, classics does not tend to articulate particular *approaches* to thinking about the past. It is not a methodology.[31] Training in adjacent disciplines is often expressly theoretical, allowing its practitioners to identify with schools of thought or major theorists. There are Boasian anthropologists, processual archaeologists, Gombrichian art historians, and so forth. There is a healthy number of theorists working in classics, with pioneering work appearing in areas such as prehistory; memory and symbol cognition; phenomenology and landscape; postcolonialism; the expressly theoretical cultural journal *Arethusa*; and so on.[32] Yet theory itself is not now pervasive in the Anglo-American tradition of classical studies, nor has it ever been.

If the term "theory" itself provokes discomfort, we can replace it with a variety of euphemisms, as I do here: approaches, points of view, and so on. But in these more friendly phrases we lose, I think, the constant reminder that inquiries about the past rest on a series of decisions we have made, not on incontestable truths. Because so much remains of the historical record of Greco-Roman antiquity—because classics is, relatively speaking, spoiled for choice—no study can or should attempt to engage all available data in any given area. Such a task is impossible and undesirable; we must be selective—but selective how? Here is the point where theory comes in, or should come in, because methods are shaped by theoretical perspectives whether or not we acknowledge them.[33] While other periods of art history might be more or less (but rarely not at all) expressly theoretical, it is not unusual for Greek or Roman art history to consider itself unconcerned with theory, to frame "doing theory" as a choice, or to praise work for being free of jargon. Most classical art and archaeology is proudly atheoretical or theoretical only on a systems level, rarely on the level of the object. I believe that it is a mistake to deny the critical role of theory to all forms of object-centered or social history writing.

Through the juxtaposition of current approaches to Greek and Phoenician art history, I argue that theory is a responsibility that must be taken more seriously. Our main framework for studying the classical past is culture, and *culture is a theory.*[34] Further, a major framework for the study of ancient art is style, and *style is also a theory.*[35] Some art historians believe that even the act of looking is guided by theory.[36] In other words, if we are writing cultural history or using formal analysis to date an object, we are already doing theory. One person's jargon is another person's critical terminology, and it is impossible to claim that classics or Near Eastern studies should strenuously avoid using terms and ideas unfamiliar in everyday discourse in order to increase their accessibility to nonspecialists. As I hope to demonstrate here, a number of theories have the potential to make deeper inroads into classics because they form clear bridges between the empirical and the interpretative. Contextual-based middle-range theories and hermeneutics offer interpretive structures for moving from artifacts to interpretation of behaviors and processes to evaluation of those interpretations.[37] They can also lack some of the irrational dogmatism that many people tend to associate with the term "theory," and disdain.[38] Whatever approaches are used, I believe it is important to retain the term "theory" as a vivid reminder that not everything we consider important about the past was or can be measured scientifically (for which, some would say, see already Beazley).[39]

The third and fourth principles guiding the project are: *contact makes critical contributions to the expressions of identity in art,* and *art is where we might learn the most about Phoenician collective identity.* This book is a call to use theoretically informed approaches to better understand what we mean by collective identity, context, and contact and how these key contributors to the human experience operated in antiquity. I show that interaction can have a variety of effects on art and behavior, from little discernible impact to significant, if sometimes subtle or unanticipated, changes. Again we can see that *Art of Contact* is not attempting to replace universalizing acculturation with a new theory; rather it eschews universalism in favor of theories of interaction and art history that challenge the status quo. Art history is important for this relationship, as it offers a legitimate and intellectually rigorous set of approaches even for the study of objects that have suffered from radical recontextualization and decontextualization. Social theories are among the most popular ways to study objects at present, but I do not believe they are always the best (or only) ways to understand how art objects were made, valued, or functioned. Art history and art criticism encourage the study of connections between the immaterial (such as aesthetics) and their expression in the object. And while objects can be used to talk about various social processes (such as interrelationships), I am certain that we should also talk about art itself.

Each chapter that follows contains a methodological study of limited scope, bounded by genre, chronology, and context. Each slowly builds the case that interaction affects art in a way not fully explained by current models. The chapters are arranged in thematic, roughly chronological, order. Chapter 1 serves as an introduction to the main stakes in the book. It begins with critiques of major terms and concepts—Orientalizing and Hellenization, culture, material culture and art, culture contact—before offering brief introductions to Greek and Phoenician art history as they relate to this study. Chapter 2 shows how the apparent advantages of traditional approaches are often instead limiting. It focuses first on Greek art history by juxtaposing the kouros and the Hellenistic picture mosaic. It aims to expose the double standard of Orientalizing and Hellenization in eastern Mediterranean art history. I conclude that an original, and possibly lasting, goal of the kouros was to emulate Egyptian art, whereas the Hellenistic picture mosaic should be understood as a Mediterranean—not "purely Greek"—craft produced by interaction and elite patronage. The chapter concludes by introducing a category of Phoenician art, the anthropoid sarcophagus, that is caught in the crosshairs of Orientalizing and Hellenization. I show how various attempts to make these objects derivative of foreign art have impaired the understanding of how and why the first Phoenician monumental art form came to be.

Chapters 3, 4, and 5 explore how we came to understand the meanings of "Greek," "Phoenician," and their artistic traditions. Chapter 3 builds on Chapter 2's conclusions to show how essentialism shapes our perceptions of ancient people. I argue that race was and is a major factor in the drawing of Greeks as exceptional relative to their neighbors, a truth that we must acknowledge rather than disguise as culture. The chapter attempts to set out some main characteristics of Greek art but suggests that there is no evidence of a "Phoenician art" in the Iron Age. Instead, I follow those who see Phoenicia and Phoenicians of this period as literary constructs rather than ontological categories. Nonetheless it is clear from the ancient record that beginning in the later Iron Age, the city-states we associate with Phoenicia grew together politically. It is under Achaemenid rule that Phoenician identity most clearly emerges in the archaeological record. Following on that claim, Chapter 4 uses examples of monumental and portable art to show how Phoenician collective identities were represented. I conclude that Phoenicianism (the term I use to describe collective Phoenician identity) does exist after all; but it is evident archaeologically only beginning in the late sixth and fifth centuries when the rise of the Achaemenid Empire created the conditions for the growth of regional identities. In Chapter 5, I scale down the discussion further, by considering the value of two theories—hybridity and Richard White's middle ground—to our understanding of two specific works of sculpture, one each produced in Sidon and Delos: the "Alexander Sarcophagus" and the "Slipper Slapper," respectively. I argue for the limited and cautious use of hybridity and middle ground theory for understanding eastern Mediterranean art and show how neither work can be understood fully until it is approached as part of Phoenician art history. The chapter closes by sketching the persistent challenges of Phoenician art and cautiously beginning to define it.

The book's Conclusion reflects on the art of contact through two lenses: originality and the idea of the artwork as an agent, perhaps a quasi-autonomous one.[40] I review the examples that have come before to emphasize the relationship between theories, methodologies, and outcomes achieved in an effort to further characterize Phoenician art and challenge the idea that Greek art, although indebted to other traditions, was exceptional. I stress that originality is not an objective feature of ancient art and suggest that the now-popular theory of art agency is not novel, because art history has been interested in critical object-centered methodologies since at least the late nineteenth century. Nonetheless, I conclude that the current version of art agency is an important tool to understanding artistic interaction; it might be a useful way to reinvigorate the study of works of Iron Age art called (carelessly, in my view) "Phoenician." Finally, I call for a few objectives for future studies of Greek and Phoenician art history that respond to the principles outlined in this Introduction.

CHAPTER 1

Culture, Contact, and Art History: Framing the Theoretical Landscape

One implication of the study of culture contact is that cultures otherwise exist in separate spaces, spaces that can be distinguished because of certain features thought to belong to specific groups in specific periods. Such thinking is fundamental to much archaeology and art history; it manifests itself expressly in the theory of style and thus shows the intimate relationships between culture and its physical manifestations, referred to variously as material culture or art. Yet cultural distinctiveness should not be taken for granted, however necessary classification of specific traits and objects might seem. Walter Burkert has pointed to this tension, saying, "Probably we should not even insist on separating neatly what testifies to interconnections," while himself insisting that pointing to "interconnections" is not enough.[1] When several aspects of a context are shared, as in colonial environments, determining what objects or behaviors fall within or outside a cultural group can be difficult.[2] My understanding of culture, which is discussed below, allows for the possibility that people we might wish to separate into Greek and Phoenician cultural categories did indeed sometimes share a number of traits that make it difficult or impossible to always distinguish them according to their archaeological traces.

Since culture is not an "unchanging, primordial substrate" but a lived and dynamic experience,[3] the less the evidence at hand reporting perceptions of that lived experience, the less one can claim to know about a culture. Greek beliefs and values are well represented in the written sources, whereas Phoenician beliefs are obviously not. For Phoenicians the material record must make the case, yet archaeological finds are often wanting or hard to understand. In other words, the difficulty of defining Phoenician culture through its material record—not to mention the problem of defining its unique properties—is compounded by the lack of textual evidence explaining what Phoenicians thought about themselves (or much of anything else, for that matter). These limitations should be taken very seriously when one speaks in general terms of a Phoenician culture or changes to it. Ironically, these very limitations mean that it has become too easy to ascribe to Phoenicians motivations and actions that have very little support—but that of course also lack outright contradictory evidence. It is plain that Phoenicians and vague processual notions such as diffusion go hand in hand in modern scholarship.

How, then, shall one go about understanding contact between Greeks and Phoenicians? What boundaries were being strengthened or transgressed through their interaction? In the wake of postcolonialism, globalization, and self-conscious multiculturalism, borders are increasingly contested spaces. Rather than viewing them as barriers, some prefer to understand ancient cultural boundaries as permeable, unstable, in flux, or fuzzy points of contact. Figuring out how to employ those ideas in historical studies is hard, as is recovering individuals within cultural groups who exhibit different behaviors (subcultures and countercultures).[4] These subcultures and pluralities are the internal elements that make a cultural system dynamic. Yet, in order for cultural history to work, it would appear that the basic unit—a culture—must be recognizable according to some common factors: shared behaviors (of which language may be one), customs, and artifacts. Likewise, it seems that there must be some recognition of difference to distinguish, however tentatively, one cultural group from another, so that we may speak about the cultures we call Greek or Phoenician.

In sum, it is very difficult to distinguish between historic groups of Hellenes and Phoenicians and the use of "Greek culture" and "Phoenician culture" as heuristic (experiential, investigative) systems.[5] In the pursuit of clarity, the impulse to calcify culture is very strong, no matter how much we acknowledge that the concept is an abstraction. And so we begin by acknowledging the difficulties inherent in some of the basic terms and concepts that inform this study: culture, models of culture in contact, and the relationships between culture, material culture, and art. It is not my wish to use this discussion to justify monolithic usage of such terms, "Greek" and "Phoenician" most of all. At the same time, I still find them convenient so long as we use the terms carefully and agree that they are our own.

The Critical Terminology: Culture, Material Culture, and Art

I believe that study of artistic production, representation, patronage, display, and reception—the study of, in other words, the particular issues that concern historians of art—is one of the best means to tackle the Greek-Phoenician relationship anew. Before considering the respective Greek and Phoenician art historical traditions, it is important to think about what Greek and Phoenician mean. As ideas about Greek culture and Phoenician culture were developed in the eighteenth and nineteenth centuries, respectively, they evolved in parallel with major developments in art history and culture theory.[6] Although Greek literature has always played a role in the conception of both peoples, art—now sometimes called material culture—is a key element in the understanding of Greek culture and, often, the only emic evidence of Phoenician culture. The goal of the discussion that follows is to position this project in the history of culture studies and to avoid the (common, certainly not universal) problem of discussing Greeks and Phoenicians with dated ideas about culture itself.[7] While this material can be found in a variety of sources, I present it with the explicit goal of illuminating the study of Greek and Phoenician art history.

Culture

How can it be, as some have claimed, "easier to express why we want to study 'culture' . . . than to define the term itself"?[8] Because the concept of culture is not only inherently complex but is also engaged in the description of very different things. It can indicate broad processes, such as human development, or very narrow phenomena, such as elite funerary practices in a particular area. The anxiety provoked by culture is signaled by its frequent encasement in scare quotes,[9] showing a desire to create distance from the term while acknowledging the lack of an easy alternative. Culture is used to characterize various kinds of human behaviors and fabrications, from the development of language, philosophy, and rituals to the making of tools, literature, and art. Another way of looking at the term "culture" is as a collective category that encompasses social, political, and ideological production.[10] As with the related word "civilization," culture often carries with it an implication of biological life cycles or evolutionary processes that allow it to be described as early, mature, or declining (as Cic. *Tusc.* 2.5.13). The culture concept is a core value of humanism; understandably, those who work in the Near East and classical worlds have a keen interest in understanding these "cradles" of Western civilization. Beyond those general notions there is not much agreement among humanists or social scientists about what culture is.[11]

According to the father of American anthropology, Franz Boas, the constitutive elements of cultural behavior were developed accidentally and had to be learned, a point of view that was meant to distinguish culture from race while also challenging prejudicial cultural universalism. Boasian culture is permeable, fluid, and to some extent always an admixture because of contact and diffusion.[12] The impact of Boasian cultural relativism was enormous. Cultural, Marxist, and processual archaeologists in the Anglo-American and German traditions had varied responses, some of which led, ironically, to more bounded and static ideas of archaeologically evident cultural groups. Archaeological culture—in which *objects* are understood as *culture* and so as trace elements of a *people*—is associated especially with the work of V. Gordon Childe. It is not difficult to see how the distinction between archaeological culture (traces of a people through objects) and race might be murky. In practice culture has become a frequent proxy for race and a tool of racism in both academic and public discourse.

In his final book, *Global Transformations*, anthropologist Michel-Rolph Trouillot discusses this problematic trajectory of the culture concept.[13] The difficulty with culture, in his estimation, came about because a term once used experimentally was reified, and soon was treated as though autonomous. Trouillot says, "As culture became a thing, it also started doing things . . . culture shifted from a descriptive conceptual tool to an explanatory concept."[14] The movement from description to explanation is common in classical art history, as, for example, Orientalizing shifted from a label of a style or period to become a teleological process.[15] Trouillot insists that there is nothing inherently essential about culture. Instead, culture is structuring and learned consciously. It is a legitimate way to investigate "human activity."[16] What happened to the culture concept between Boas and Trouillot is of course quite complex, and no brief summary (or single book) can do the subject justice.[17] Yet a few points are needed here to situate what has occurred theoretically speaking, especially in the study of culture in Anglo-American classical archaeology and, to a lesser extent, art history.

While Boasian cultural archaeology was pioneering and really quite remarkable for its resistance to racial ideologies, some of its flaws were quickly detected. The theoretical culture concept was complex and fluid, but in practice it encouraged taxonomies, historical particularism (unique cultures), and diffusionism—shortcomings that are still thriving today in classical studies. Around the middle of the century, a Weberian school of archaeology became established, especially in Anglo-American anthropology. In this school, culture is approached sociologically and objects, symbolically.[18] By the 1960s the "new" archaeology (processualism) was gaining traction. It espoused more dynamic adaptive models, anthropological approaches, and an expanded idea of which objects should be studied to understand culture. Since the 1960s, cultural studies have emphasized adaptation within cultural groups rather than variations among them. Processual and postprocessual archaeologists have distanced themselves further from ideas of bounded archaeological cultures, ultimately pushing beyond the "static" and "cellular" model of culture, spread to classical studies by Moses Finley, to ever-increasing interest in the "fluidity and connectedness" of cultures in the manner of social anthropologist Fredrik Barth.[19]

The impact of these mid-century developments has been quite significant in some circles. The symbolic approach to culture became important to postprocessualists, including Ian Hodder, arguably the most popular theorist in archaeology since the 1980s.[20] Hodder's work is relatively well read among classical archaeologists, a number of whom he has trained. That is not to say that the field lacks other theorists. James Wiseman and Anthony Snodgrass were among the first classical archaeologists to point out that the new archaeology had something to offer.[21] Wiseman founded a department of archaeology in 1982 at Boston University (where much of this book was written, in the Department of History of Art and Architecture) on the idea of a united discipline. Yet the potential of archaeology to continue to operate as a unified field has more prominent adherents on the other side of the Atlantic. As Stephen Dyson, writing in 1993, put it, "The bad news for Classical archaeologists hoping for a return to the good old days of empirical positivism is that old, reliable England has spawned a whole generation of quarreling, trendy young theoretical archaeologists, who have plunged the discipline into the postmodern age."[22] Postprocessualism has been embraced by a healthy number of British, many Cambridge-affiliated, classical archaeologists and art historians. Jeremy Tanner is explicit about the extent to which his formative work—his dissertation, first book, and related essays—draws on sociology's founding father in the United States, Talcott Parsons, to espouse a sociology of art. Others, such as Mary Beard, John Henderson, Robin Osborne, and Michael Squire, some of whom work with art only occasionally, are less easy to associate with specific strains of postmodern thinking.

It has been suggested lately that some of the most provocative postprocessualists are coming to a kind of consensus about—or at least showing a greater interest in—taking a holistic theoretical approach to archaeology, a perspective explored in this book. A holistic approach can be understood as one focused on the benefits of different methods, "in which many flowers can bloom and ideas and approaches interact rather than fight to the death."[23] While postmodern theory may be coming into a new, more settled phase, the idea that *classical* archaeology was or is in danger of being torn asunder by sustained theoretical debate is pretty absurd. Why? We can recall Colin Renfrew's 1980 centenary address to the Archaeological Institute of America in which he famously and succinctly described "the great divide." The great divide was born in the decades leading up to his address, when Old and New World archaeology began moving apart, geographically and conceptually. Anthropological archaeology went one way, to theory and to the Americas, while Old World archaeology was taken up by classical and Near Eastern studies to continue along another trajectory, one that privileged taxonomy and interpretations focused by the lens of literature over process-oriented approaches.[24] While Renfrew's points were made more than thirty-five years ago, in many ways they still hold. Classical archaeology has been only moderately affected by the archaeological trends across the great divide. Just over a decade ago, Jonathan Hall claimed, "The conventional understanding of culture among classical scholars is informed by anthropological theories that were dominant in the early decades of the twentieth century."[25] I agree that many studies present cultures in essentialist terms, as discrete and rigidly divided, for a variety of reasons, habit surely ranking high among them.[26] In recent decades, however, the topic of early Greece (to cite one example) has been approached with increasing sensitivity, with less emphasis on hunting down the origins of Greek objects and behaviors and more emphasis on their contextual use.[27] This trend has made only marginal inroads into the study of the Classical era.

Bearing in mind these challenges, a working definition of culture is a must. I try to conceive of culture as a dynamic structuring system in which individuals participate to a greater or lesser extent in "shared beliefs, values, customs, behaviors, and artifacts," which are used by, "members of a society . . . to cope with their world and with one another, and that are transmitted from generation to generation through learning."[28] This definition frames culture as practice.[29] The guiding idea is that adaptive behavior—psychological, functional, ecological, and so forth—is in conversation with, and not strictly determinative of, social behavior, including language, art, and symbolism. Culture is shaped by historical circumstances and by its constituents (individual behaviors, art, and so on).[30] The study of culture, then, is dependent on both observation and theorizing.

To some, this definition might lack sufficient address to phenomenology, in which culture is understood through human experience. Human experience is part of what makes the concept of culture appealing: what makes us who we are and what links us to and separates us from distant people.[31] Phenomenological and cognitive archaeology address this need for human agency in archaeological inquiry. The idea of studying "the human experience" can be taken too far, however, when empathy becomes the key to understanding the past, a historically dangerous proposition in classical studies.[32] Nevertheless, emphasis on human agency remains a necessary component of an archaeological approach to the past, since it grounds the discussion of systems in lived experience. It thereby provides an important challenge to the idea of the system as an entity independent of human agents, without making the idea of the system necessarily impossible.[33] After all, it is people who make art, who travel, and who come into contact—not culture itself. Within this structuring conception of culture, I believe it important to understand that changes have varied causes and results, some progressive, some seemingly random, and can affect one part of the system or certain participants in that system more than others.[34] These qualifications notwithstanding, I maintain that cultural changes—and the components of culture—were always more the concern of people who felt they created the social system than those believed to stand outside it.[35]

Material Culture and Art

"All art is material culture. . . . Classical art history therefore is archaeology or it is nothing," asserted James Whitley in 2001.[36] The revival of such pronouncements from the early days of new archaeology—like "American archaeology is anthropology or it is nothing"[37]—suggests the material culture concept of new archaeology has had a significant impact on the field of Greek archaeology. The number of recent studies of material culture is impressive.[38] Its popularity is evident especially in certain intellectual corners, such as University College London (UCL). UCL is where editors of the *Journal of Material Culture* (*JMC*, est. 1996) reside, in the Department of Anthropology. *JMC*'s tagline sums up some current thinking about material culture studies: "*JMC* is concerned with the relationship between artefacts and social relations irrespective of time and place and aims to systematically explore the linkage between the construction of social identities and the production and use of culture." In other words, *JMC* subscribes to a theoretical position in which human-made items are studied socially, social processes being understood as the generators of identity and culture. *JMC*'s studies resist disciplinary constraints, geographical, chronological, or otherwise. Psychology and hard sciences, although not named in the tagline, are also important. Studying the broad category of material culture through social processes rewards us with a better understanding of context, encourages sensitivity to methods, and focuses research on what objects were doing—that is, on their social function.

Of course not everyone uses the material culture concept in this way. Once again it is possible to see many Near Eastern and classical archaeologists and art historians on the other side of the divide. Some employ the phrase "material culture" to signal a robust category of made objects in contrast to the seemingly narrower term "art"[39] and without indicating a theoretical approach, either anthropological or sociological. The divide is replicated to some extent in *JMC*, which, at the time of writing, contains only a handful of articles that address Roman or Greek material and almost nothing addressing Phoenician, Levantine, or Egyptian material. A similar situation is found in recent anthologies, such as Peter van Dommelen and A. Bernard Knapp's 2010 volume, *Material Connections in the Ancient Mediterranean*. Despite its broad title, the text has only one essay that speaks (in part) about the Classical period in Greece and none on the Hellenistic period. Of course edited volumes must be selective. The point is, for many classical archaeologists and art historians, especially those working in the Classical period, material culture can mean simply "objects," whereas recent anthologies and the

JMC are increasingly signaling a particular *theory* of culture: culture as material-ity.[40] The two views are difficult to reconcile. In classics, the cultural system is understood as inclusive of significant practices—literature, theater, music, and so on—that for the most part are studied without regard for their (often no longer preserved) physical qualities. In art history, the idea that art is material culture is often taken for granted, as I have done on occasion, whereas the idea of material culture as a theory or process is relatively rare. It is unfortunate that art history and material culture studies have had limited engagement despite sometimes totally overlapping intellectual interests.[41]

The idea that material culture *must* be studied through "the relationship between artefacts and social relations" deserves scrutiny, too. Many Greek and Phoenician objects have been radically re- or decontextualized through deliberate destruction (the melting down of marble sculpture to produce lime), looting (both ancient and modern), and the ongoing antiquities trade. Art historians regularly work with copies and fragments, objects found in farmers' fields or fishermen's nets, or paintings now known only through their description. The study of Iron Age Phoenicia suffers acutely from the rupture of art history and archaeology, and I do not wish to suggest that ancient art history is improved by ignoring archaeo-logical context. Yet, while material culture studies can and do say very interesting things about material found in primary deposition, it is less clear how to approach metal bowls or ivory inlays that were never used or even viewed once they were stacked in a room in Ashurbanipal's palace. Although they are evidence of culture contact, these bowls and ivories were not "culturally redefined and put to use."[42] While some bowls and ivories were valued in Assyria for their intrinsic and aes-thetic properties, storage implies the amassing of wealth or potential use without incorporation into Assyrian society. Dwelling upon how Assyrians dealt with their recontextualization will produce few insights.

While, of course, that limitation is interesting in itself, nonsociological ap-proaches, even art historical and critical ones employing seemingly old-fashioned theories of style, aesthetics, or intentionality, can say many things about what these objects were and are doing. Close inspection of an object can also reveal something about the choices made by its maker, that is, about process and what the artist did through his or her skilled movement.[43] Still more relevant to these decontextual-ized objects is art criticism's alternative ways to consider the formal properties of the object itself and not only as a way to get to the subject (in the anthropological sense) or to event-driven history.[44] Further, some of these objects are representa-tional, and art history and criticism have a long and rich discourse on images and visuality that stretches from Wölfflin's day to today's departments of visual stud-ies.[45] Bowls and ivories can be studied with a variety of other emphases, too, not all of them visual.[46] In sum, art history and criticism allow us to infer connections between the immaterial (aesthetics, processes) and its expression in the object, even when the connective traces are faint or, in the case of decontextualized objects, hypothetical. Art can be used to talk fruitfully about other things, but it is important to remember that it is equally possible and important to talk about the object itself.[47]

Interpreting objects that now exist outside specific social systems does not seem so dangerous to me, so long as we remain aware of what we are doing. There are limits to studying things without "social lives" or, put differently, to studying material without culture, objects without frames.[48] And of course one wants to avoid using art criticism to increase the market value of objects, although there are many examples where "age value" seems to trump aesthetic value in the antiquities market.[49] The study of decontextualized objects can almost serve as a corrective to the tendency to reify society (as one might accuse British anthropologists of doing) or culture (as one might accuse American anthropologists of doing) while underscoring that art historians must engage in the conversation about theories of material culture.[50] While it is unwise—even impossible, as I claim in Chapter 3—to attempt to reconcile decontextualized objects with original Phoenician contexts, ivories and metal bowls still exist and demand attention. This is something art history and criticism can do, and well, even if approaches that reject or transcend materiality or context are not to everyone's taste.[51]

And so, while it is possible to claim that all art belongs to the category material culture, I do not support the claim that the only valid way to interpret objects is through a *sociological* or *anthropological theory* of material culture. Objects record human transactions, but if it is ever possible to interpret the meaning or action of an object that has been appropriated, it is impossible to conclude that the true expression of an object is fixed. Such sentiments have been expressed by art historians many times over. Accordingly, although I do not wish to make the point too forcefully, I see some advantages to calling the objects that I study art.

A Very Brief Introduction to the Practice of Greek Art History

"Historians of classical art," writes Alice Donahue, "occupy a no-man's-land that exists uneasily among the fields of art history, classics, and archaeology."[52] Greek art and Greek art history are well known, so I do not try to offer here an even-handed historiography, which is available in the recent work of especially Donahue and Tanner.[53] Rather I aim to make a few points that are especially relevant to my comparison of Greek and Phoenician art. The approach to the study of Greek art is both broad and narrow. It is inconsistently ecumenical in terms of what it admits from outside the Aegean basin—Magna Graecia, much of the Hellenistic world—and from patrons that were not Hellenes, such as the Karian Mausolos. It is consistently narrow in terms of what it favors: monumental art and architecture and vase painting, especially Athenian. The study of even some very fine and highly valued works, such as jewelry, exists mainly on the fringes of Greek art history.[54] Terracottas and humbler objects likewise occupy mainly the margins, in their case, in an awkward space between and within the disciplines of art history and archaeology.

To some extent the scholarly approach to Greek art follows ancient genre biases and to some extent it contradicts them, with the most obvious contradiction being our intense study of vase painting—a craft that did not merit significant commentary in antiquity. When it comes to the approach to art history, however, very much is shared between the early ancient accounts found in Pliny's *Natural History* and modern ones. Through his Hellenistic sources, Pliny emphasizes attribution to named artists (what would become connoisseurship) and analysis of formal approaches (what would become various theories of style).[55] The neoclassicist Johann Joachim Winckelmann (1717–1768) was the first to develop a theory of style in Greek and Roman art in his 1764 *Geschichte der Kunst des Altertums*.[56] Winckelmann was unapologetic when it came to admiring certain works of art and not others. Classical Athenian art was held in his highest esteem; after Alexander, Winckelmann claimed, art declined (compare the description of art's decline after the 121st Olympiad in Plin. *HN* 35.52).

Major contributions to the theory of style were made by other German-language historians. The aforementioned Swiss Heinrich Wölfflin (1864–1945) was the most influential of all formalists. Wölfflin championed formalism in all of his writings, including the 1899 *Klassische Kunst*.[57] The German-born Adolf Furtwängler (1853–1907) did foundational work in Greek vase painting and sculpture. His 1893 *Meisterwerke der griechischen Plastik* promoted his connoisseurship-based approach. His influential Italian (but German-trained) counterpart Giovanni Morelli (1816–1891) was a Renaissance art historian who promoted a forensic method to detect in minute details the traces of artistic activity.[58] When Furtwängler's *Meisterwerke* text was translated into English in 1895, just two years after the original was published in German, his translator Eugénie Sellers Strong revised the text to make it more Morellian.[59] Thus the "scientific connoisseurship"[60] approach spread from German to Anglo-American scholarship. It was used to rediscover lost Greek masters (*Meisterforschungen*) and masterworks in the Roman sculptures that copied them (*Kopienkritik*) or to identify in even small fragments of painted pottery the hands of its artists.

The most famous practitioner of this approach in classical archaeology, although he did not draw on Morelli explicitly, is John Davidson Beazley.[61] From the 1910s to the 1960s Beazley employed a combination of rigorous formal analysis, connoisseurship, and an evolutionary theory of style to bring order to bear on Athenian painted vases.[62] Beazley's method led to the identification of more than a thousand artists and workshops, which established the chief priorities for the study of painted pottery and paved the way for establishing the seriation of undecorated fine wares (black glaze pottery). Attribution continues to be of paramount importance even though it and Beazley's method are sometimes "trivialized,"[63] notably with the rise of culture history and social archaeology. Yet Beazley's method and relative chronology remain the standard in the analysis of Attic vase painting.[64] Without Beazley's classifications, we would be hard pressed to make meaningful connections among the pots found in enormous numbers in excavations all over the Mediterranean and well beyond.[65] The chronological precision of these items, even if subject to slight modifications, is unsurpassed by almost any other class of object besides coins and inscriptions. The field archaeologist therefore rightly values its attribution. Moreover, Beazley, while he never espoused a theory, and even openly eschewed it, developed an as yet unrivaled method of visual perception.[66] His Morellian approach is now unpopular, and his critical understanding of vision passé, but no one can claim to have inspected more works of art in an effort to understand the Greek artist.[67] That is not a small gift.[68]

While also a formalist, the Austrian Alois Riegl (1858–1905) gives us a better idea about what can be done when theories of style are probed consciously. Riegl's 1893 *Stilfragen* was dedicated to the history of the style of ornament. One of *Stilfragen*'s important, and difficult, theories is *Kunstwollen*, approximately "will to art."[69] Kunstwollen provides a vital conceptual frame for style. Its central idea is that styles change because they must, as art restlessly seeks solutions for its own flaws. Kunstwollen clearly draws on the Hegelian and psychoanalytic thinking of Riegl's contemporaries, but it recasts changes in art as transformation rather than progression or decline. "All art possesses intentionality, or purposiveness"[70] and is driven to express the ideology of its time. Riegl's 1901 *Spätrömische Kunstindustrie* further developed the Kunstwollen concept through its positive presentation of late antique art,[71] providing the postclassical periods refuge from the disdain of Winckelmann and his followers.[72] While Riegl is arguably one of the most important formative theorists of art,[73] two aspects of his approach are especially relevant here. First, his presentation of art as an active agent is prescient, as Kunstwollen has echoes in visual studies and the anthropologically oriented theories of art/object agency explored by Douglass Bailey, Alfred Gell, Janet Hoskins, Richard Lesure, and others.[74] Second, Riegl's interest in and ability to extract from the particular to shape the general, to theorize *from art to culture*, has implications for the comparative study of art.

A recurring theme in the work of these theorists is style. Style connects their work to today's art history, even if most now use style in a matter-of-fact way. But as Ann Gunter has recently argued, the labels "Greek art," "Greek style," and so on rest on the uneasy idea that art and ethnicity are related and recognizable in style.[75] The link between ethnicity and style has long been criticized, most vociferously by anthropologists. These scholars concede that it is really very difficult to know when an object's style consciously signals group identity versus individual preferences, or when it is concerned with neither. The interpretation of style becomes even more difficult in complex and mobile societies with rich and varied artifact records and with artists that we think might have recognizable personal approaches or "hands." Even while there is disagreement on how best to exploit style in anthropology, style remains the chief structuring element of classical art and archaeology. Richard Neer has been outspoken on this topic.[76] He points out that assigning objects to cultures and locating them chronologically—the goals of most stylistic analysis—is in fact a high-stakes undertaking. Refusing to think about how connoisseurship works is thus perilous. Certainly Phoenician art history provides an example of what can go wrong when scholars do not come to terms with the difficult relationships between style, culture, and ethnicity.

The often-critiqued, sometimes even reviled, formalism that is without doubt foundational to classical art history must be understood as equally fundamental to classical archaeology.[77] Although it is the special task of art historians to make objects their chief subject, it is impossible to sustain the idea that classical archaeologists do not study art or use style.[78] A takeaway point, and one that underpins this book, is that studies of Greek art, whatever their goals and however they use objects, rely on an understanding of the category "Greek art" that is completely intertwined with the forensic systems developed in the earliest days of the discipline. Some of the most prolific twentieth-century authors of Greek art history—Martin Robertson, Robert Cook, and John Boardman—reinforced these systems and, through their handbooks, have created generations of classicists who have adopted similar points of view.[79] Publications like the *Lexicon iconographicum mythologiae classicae*, Pauly-Wissowa, and the *Corpus inscriptionum graecarum* are as helpful and necessary to research as they are programmatically reinforcing dated priorities. On the one hand, decades of *Altertumswissenschaft* have left classics with unsurpassed databases, incredibly sensitive understanding of an amazing range of things (texts, objects, makers, patrons, and so forth), very high standards of publication, and a vivid sense of the ancient past from which any number of groundbreaking analyses could proceed. On the other hand, it is possible to argue that classics has not been much interested in doing new things with its great tradition of data. Deep connections to the field's antiquarian roots have consequences: while Greek art history and archaeology continue to grow through excavation and continue to refine their data—adding to it, for example, relatively recent scientific tools such as dendrochronology and C14 testing—both prioritize new discoveries and revised interpretations over new theories.[80] I think it is fair to say that we have not taken full advantage of our many and unparalleled advantages.

An Introduction to Phoenicia, Its Art, and Its Art History

Phoenician studies, by contrast, lack almost all of those advantages. What should be called "Phoenicia" and who should be called "Phoenicians" is still more vague than what is meant by "Greece" and "Greeks" (see Maps 1 and 3).[81] Of course the name Phoenicia is known only from Greek sources. In Herodotos Phoenicia is a part of Syria, and it is distinguished from another Syrian area inhabited by Palestinians—Philistines—to the south.[82] In the clockwise periplous of Ps.-Skylax (104), Cilicia is followed by Coele-Syria, which is inhabited by Syrians and, at the coast, Phoenicians (both are described as *ethnē*). Although more systematic in his description than Herodotos, Ps.-Skylax omits the important city-state of Gebal/ Byblos altogether.[83] In Persian sources the region geographically described as "Beyond the River," the Transeuphrates or *'br nhrh*, conforms loosely to what Greeks called Syria or Herodotos's fifth satrapy (3.91).[84] In the biblical texts Phoenicians are not described as a people. *Kn'n* (Canaan) appears a few times in the Bible as a term for merchant, as in the so-called oracle of Tyre (Isa 23:8). The same passage appears to use "merchants of Sidon" to refer generally to traders from the region (Isa 23:3). In Isaiah 23:11, "Canaan" seems to refer to the region.

It is often asserted that the Phoenicians called themselves Canaanites. The evidence is Augustine's unfinished commentary on Paul's letter to the Romans.[85] Recent analysis of the commentary's extant manuscripts questions the textual and historical value of the passage. The passage begins with Valerius, then bishop of Hippo, contemplating the providential relationships between the Phoenician word for three, *šlš* (*tria* in Latin), and the Latin word *salus* (salvation). It is likely, although admittedly uncertain, that the original text continued to make inquiries regarding *language* rather than identity: "In the woman's language *tria* is said as *salus*. For it was Canaanite, for which reason our rustics, when asked what it is (*quid sit?*), reply in Phoenician 'Chanani.'"[86] The earliest and only extant example of a historical person's self-identification as "a Phoenician" dates to the third or fourth century CE, in the last line of the novel *Aithiopika* by Heliodoros of Emesa.[87] This evidence shows that what the people we call Phoenicians called themselves collectively, if they ever had cause to do so, is not known. While the classical sources seem to conflate language and people, we should be skeptical that Greek and Latin speakers distinguished what they called Phoenician or Canaanite from other Semitic languages. Near Eastern source material lacks evidence of a corollary to Greek Phoenicians, which only intensifies the confusion.[88]

Modern scholars nevertheless find "Phoenicia" useful as a way to describe a territory on the eastern Mediterranean littoral whose chief city-states stretched from Arwad (Arados in Greek) and 'Amrit (Greek Marathos), both in what is now Syria, to Ṣūr (Greek Tyros, hereafter Tyre) in southern Lebanon. Seemingly related people are found well beyond this territory. Colonies stretched westward beginning in the ninth century, reaching as far as the Iberian Peninsula.[89] Archaeologists believe that sites from Tell Sukas (in the northern reaches) to Tel Dor (toward the south) were inhabited in the Iron Age by people with similar languages and material cultures.[90] Greek and Phoenician sources dating to the Persian period (ca. 525–333) attest to Phoenician political control in the eastern Mediterranean as far north as Myriandos (in Cilicia) and south to Ashkelon (in what is now southern Israel).[91] A number of these sites were unoccupied during at least the majority of the sixth century. The circumstances of their reoccupation are not fully known.[92] Some have argued that urban growth in the Iron Age and later periods led to the spread of Phoenician settlements inland, into, for example, the lower Galilee.[93] Yet it is necessary to stress here that the relationships between language, material culture, and geography, as well as the ancient sources and modern archaeology, can be murky.

Phoenicia's most famous and lasting cultural contribution is thought to be its alphabet. The shared use of this writing system is a fine example of Mediterranean connectivity. By the ninth century it was used by Aramaic and Hebrew speakers and by some Cypriots and Cretans; later, in the eighth century, it was adopted elsewhere and in Greece was tied to the legend of Kadmos (Figure 1).[94] Several Phoenician dialects were known in different periods and regions, some of which seemed to have been used only in specific city-states, notably Gebal (hereafter Byblos, following the Greek and the common English usage). Standard Phoenician is associated with the dialects of Tyre and Sidon. Punic was a distinct dialect from the sixth or fifth century, although very close to Tyrian and Sidonian.[95] Phoenician epigraphic habits are not well represented in the archaeological record by comparison with the corpus of Greek inscriptions. No great store of archival material, alluded to in various accounts from Wen-Amun to Roman sources, has been found in the mainland.[96] Including Carthage and its environs, there are only around ten thousand Phoenician "texts," many quite brief.[97]

However limited our source material, we should not assume it is evidence of limited Phoenician literacy. The use of Phoenician on humble gravestones shows that, as for Greeks,[98] the materiality of writing was important to Phoenician speakers. The extant texts indicate that Phoenician enjoyed a long history, from the

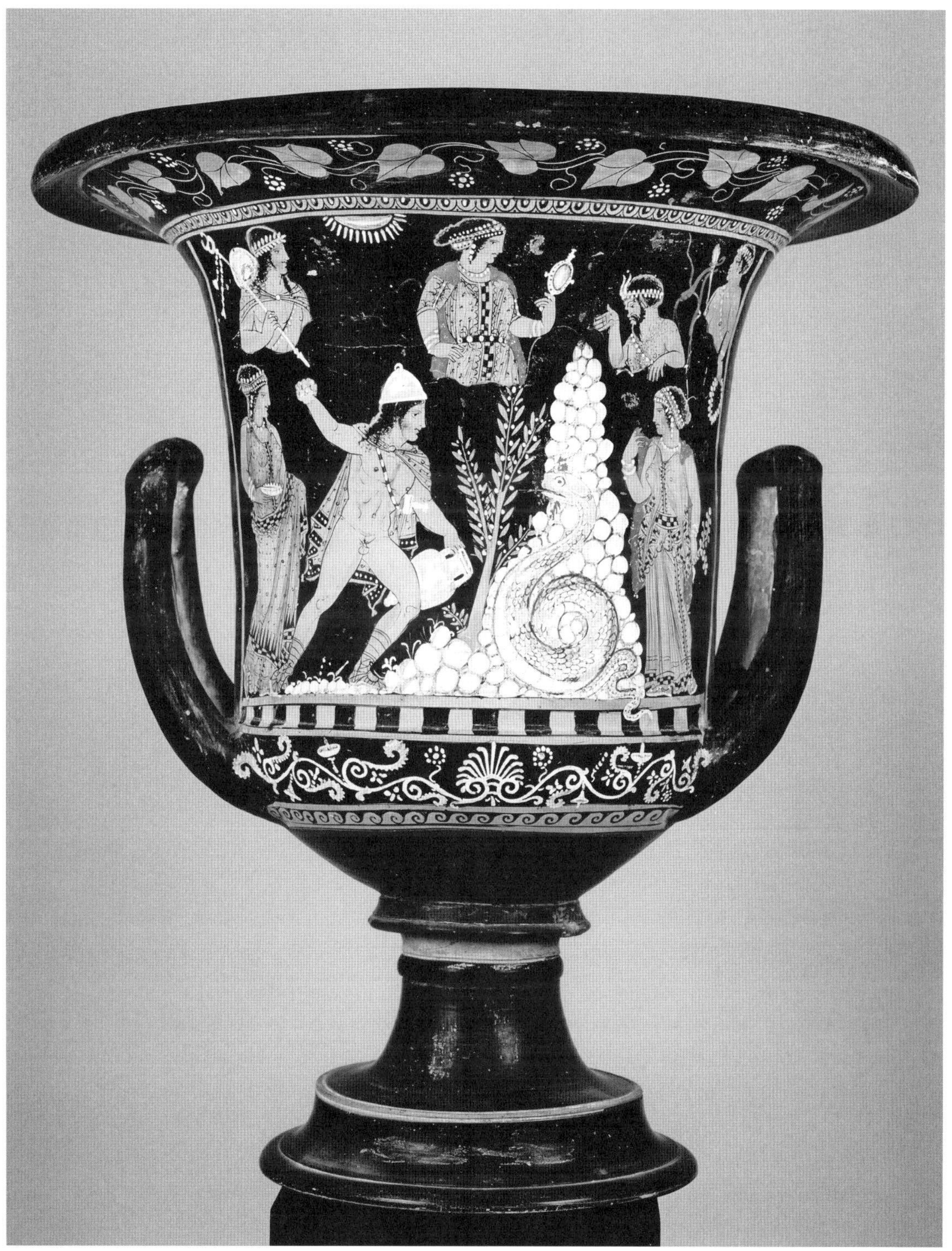

Figure 1. Campanian red-figure krater with Kadmos and the dragon (side A) from Sant'Agata de'Goti, Paestum attr. to the Python Painter, ca. 350–340. Paris, Musée du Louvre N 3157 (K 33). Ceramic. Ht. 0.56 m. Photo: Art Resource, N.Y.

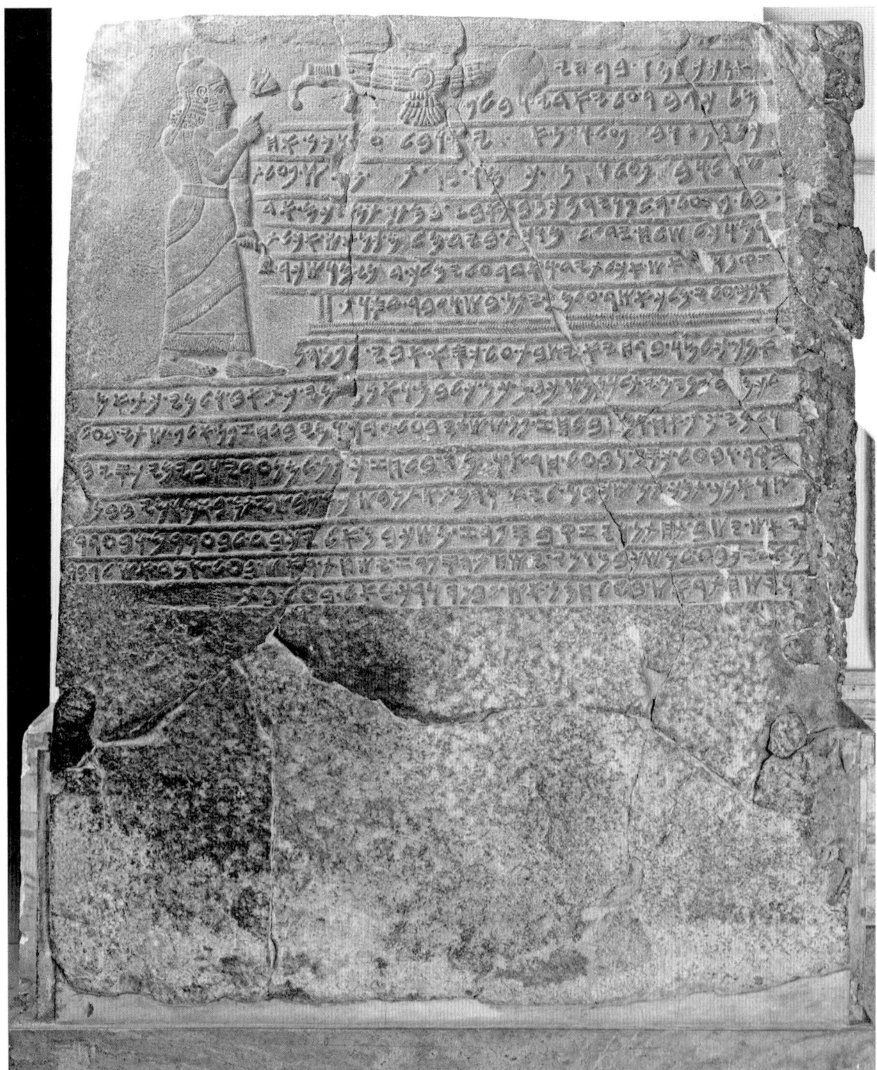

Figure 2. Kilamuwa Inscription from Sam'al (Zincirli), ca. 835 (=*KAI* 24). Berlin, Vorderasiatisches Museum der Staatlichen Museen S 06579. Basalt. Ht. 1.55 m. Photo: Art Resource, N.Y.

late eleventh century BCE into the Roman imperial era (and in some cases, beyond). In the ninth to eighth centuries BCE, Phoenician was used briefly as a diplomatic or prestige language in southern Asia Minor. The famous Kilamuwa Inscription shows that at this time Phoenician was already a rhetorically sophisticated language suitable for the boasting of the kings of Sam'al (modern Zincirli; Figure 2).[99]

In contrast to Greek art and art history, Phoenician art and its history are not especially well known. While Greek art history emerged even during the period in which Greek art was being produced, Phoenician art history did not exist until

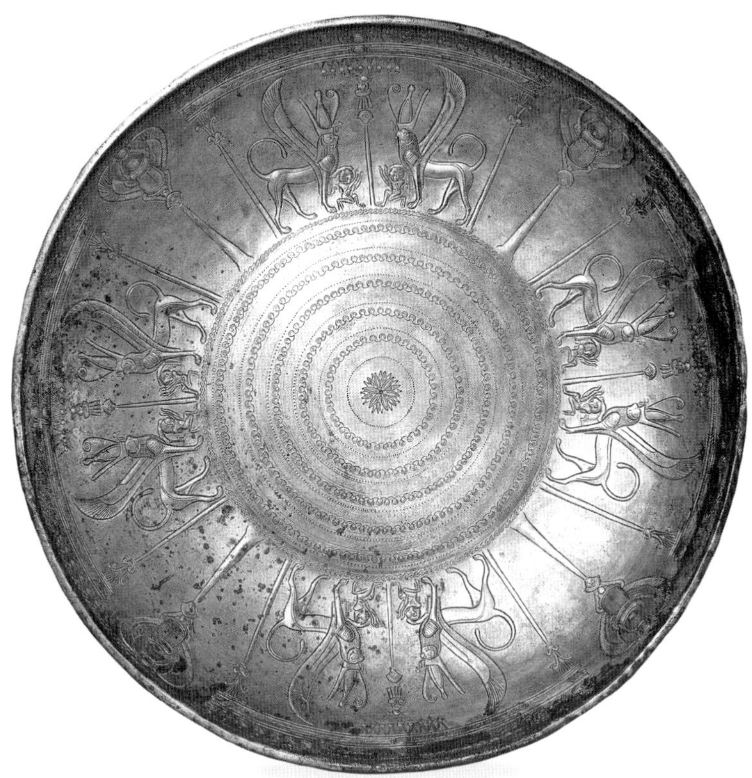

Figure 3. Bowl from Nimrud, 8th c. London, British Museum WA 115505. Bronze. Diam. 0.21 m. Photo: © The Trustees of the British Museum.

the 1850s.[100] The first three discoveries of what would be known as Phoenician art occurred in the 1830s and 1840s at Etruscan Cerveteri, Assyrian Nimrud, and Cyprus.[101] Each findspot produced decorated metal bowls. These use different metals and techniques, some incised or chased, some embossed. They show a mix of hunting, battle, and animal motifs that draw from Assyrian and Egyptian art. The bowls were soon tied to the Levant, in part because their physical properties and wide distribution recalled Homer's Phoenicians. One bowl was inscribed in Phoenician, confirming the association; other bowls soon followed.[102] While according to biblical sources (e.g., 2 Chr 2:13–14) areas of Phoenicia, such as Tyre, were producing luxury arts already in the tenth century, these bowls do not seem to date before the eighth century.[103] A variety of regional labels has been applied to the more than one hundred examples, many fragmentary, of the metal bowls that are now known.

A brief reading of the bowl from Nimrud in Figure 3 will highlight some characteristic features of this group and its reception.[104] The bronze bowl is shallow and broad; only its interior is decorated. The overall approach to the decorative scheme is highly symmetrical, with first geometric then figural concentric bands arranged around a central floral motif. The widest band is at the exterior and contains figural work, including four pairs of opposing sphinxes rendered with falcon heads and wings. They wear the Egyptian double crown and raise their paws over diminutive enemies. Between these groups are winged scarabs on upright poles. The bowl's Egyptian imagery raises an interesting question: in employing *exclusively* Egyptian (and not Assyrian or other) iconography and style, why do we not consider it, simply, an Egyptian object? The question is legitimate, and its answer can follow a familiar colonialist rationale: "Among all these hybrid pieces, one bowl from Nimrud is curiously exclusive in the use of Egyptian motifs . . . winged scarabs and correctly drawn falcon-headed sphinxes trampling their enemies. Yet even this has no Egyptian parallel, the geometric design is quite un-Egyptian, and the whole decoration is jejune and over-elegant, like those which Napoleon's cabinetmakers produced after the return of the Egyptian expedition. Once again we are led to Phoenicia."[105] While Henri Frankfort's chauvinistic language might no longer be the scholarly norm, the substance of what he describes regarding this bowl—that, although it employs Egyptian iconography and at least to some extent Egyptian style, it is on the whole "quite un-Egyptian"—is characteristic of the usage of "Egyptianizing" in Phoenician art.[106] Such questions concerning authenticity and originality of Phoenician style are very important when it comes to the study of this art from a practical standpoint. Phoenician art history tends to operate in a space between the more easily recognizable and valued artistic traditions around it.

The essence of Frankfort's words has been applied to a number of ivories we associate with Levantine craftsmen, including some from Nimrud that are specifically called Phoenician (Figure 4). Those assigned to as yet unknown Phoenician workshops are the ivories with more strongly Egyptianizing iconography and style. General support for this approach can be found in archeologically retrieved material that shows continuous interest in Egyptian art and architecture from at least the later Iron Age until the Hellenistic and Roman eras.[107] The winged disk, the sphinx, the uraeus, and the naiskos (meaning in this context a small temple or shrine) are Egyptian in origin and make regular appearances in works of art and architecture found in Phoenicia. Some portable objects, such as faience amulets, seals, and coins, show a similar strong and lasting interest in motifs of Egyptian origin. Reading this evidence onto the corpora of Iron Age ivories and metal bowls is problematic, however, as we simply cannot associate those objects with Phoenician manufacture and can hardly assume that only Phoenician art had ties to Egypt.

The two greatest challenges of Phoenician art history are thus highlighted by these critical early discoveries: none of the metal bowls and hardly any ivories were

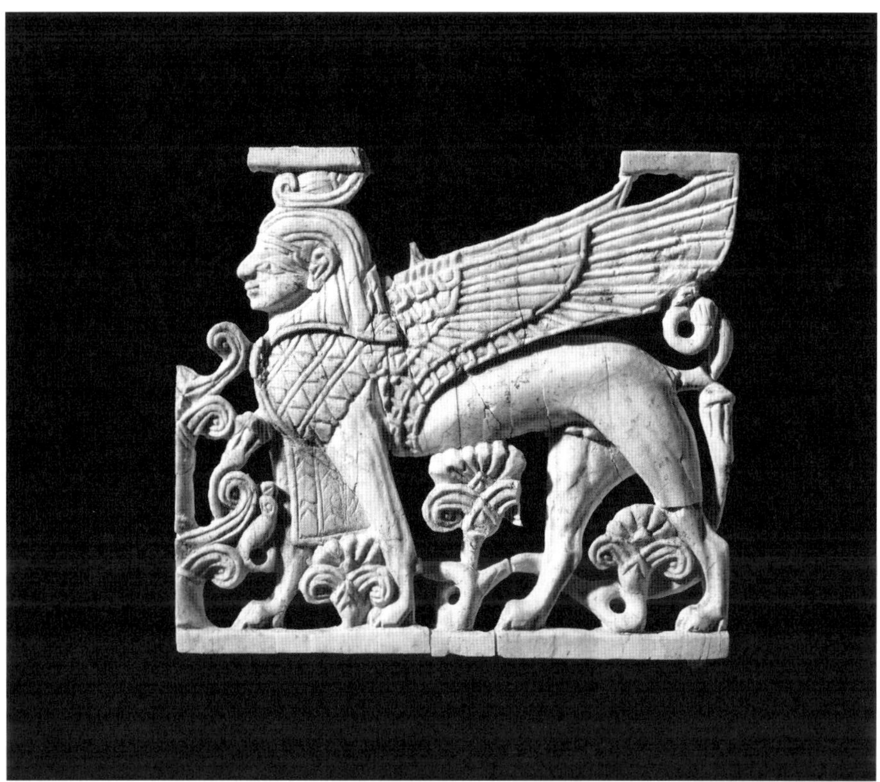

Figure 4. Openwork panel from Nimrud, 8th c. London, British Museum 134322. Ivory. 0.69×0.77 m. Photo: © The Trustees of the British Museum.

found in Phoenicia, and the portable objects that we assign to Phoenician manufacture do not necessarily share stylistic or iconographic features with one another or with material excavated in Phoenicia.[108] Yet it is almost universally believed that these two genres, metal bowls and carved ivories, mark the inception of Phoenician fine art. It is really no surprise that the Hellenist George Perrot declared in 1885 that Phoenicia had no "national art."[109] However simplistic the view, it, too, is revealing of the challenges faced in studying Phoenician art to this day.

Sabatino Moscati (1922–1997), a scholar and important public figure, was hugely influential in shaping modern perceptions of Phoenicians and highlighting priorities of their study.[110] His 1966 publication, of *Il mondo dei Fenici*, initiated the study of Phoenician colonization just two years after the publication of John Boardman's *Greeks Overseas*.[111] Moscati's efforts to bring his passion to the masses culminated in the 1988 exhibition at the Palazzo Grassi in Venice, *I Fenici*. The show was wildly popular, with nearly a million visitors coming to see its thousand-plus artifacts.[112] Reviews of *I Fenici* take their cues from Moscati, lauding the recognition of an "enigmatic" and "forgotten civilization" and defining the Phoenicians as "a people that lived a millennium from the days of the Old Testament's Canaan to the Punic Wars between Rome and Carthage."[113] The exhibit's title certainly implies a comprehensive approach, but one of the most active regions of eastern Phoenician research, from modern Israel, was seriously underrepresented.[114] Moreover, reviewers and contributors to the 765-page exhibition catalogue seemed unconcerned that Phoenicians could hardly be called a forgotten or mysterious people in what many consider to be the Phoenician "mainland"—modern Lebanon—an irony made more palpable owing to the show's billing as "the first general exhibition that examines the Phoenicians' full geographical scope, from Lebanon to Spain."[115]

Among the many implications of *I Fenici* was the idea that Phoenicians were a cohesive if regionally varied people. The exhibit showed the "evolution" of their culture in material form, presenting it as "an original synthesis," both diverse and distinctive. Yet only a few objects that we think were made by Phoenicians are found across different Phoenician sites. In the Iron Age—predating the ivories and metal bowls—is Cypro-Phoenician bichrome pottery (see Plate 1, top). The red and black geometric decoration that gives bichrome its conventional name appears in the mid-eleventh century and persists into the ninth century. The bichrome technique stands at the beginning of a ceramic sequence that includes some other distinctive pottery, such as black-on-red (see Plate 1, bottom).[116] From the later Iron Age and into the late Hellenistic period come other terracotta objects, such as "Astarte plaques" or "plaque figurines" (Figure 5), "pregnant female" figurines, masks, and protomai.[117] Contrary to the sentiment expressed in Frankfort's quotation above, Egyptian motifs are only one part of this Phoenician artistic tradition.

Two observations can be made from this evidence. First, pots, terracottas, and other relatively humble objects provide some of the best support for the idea of a Phoenician material culture in the Iron Age. And, second, they have very limited connections to the luxury arts discussed above or to the remaining hodgepodge of portable luxury objects typically associated with Iron Age and Persian-period Phoenicians, such as painted ostrich eggs and carved tridacna shells (Figure 6), both of which can be connected to the Levant only loosely.[118] The disconnection is attributed to the difference between arts made for local consumption and those made for export.[119] But that conclusion is not very satisfying, as it is impossible to support it using the available evidence.[120] Moreover, excavations of sanctuaries and nekropoleis in "mainland Phoenicia" reveal still more diversity in monumental art and architecture.[121]

I think it should be admitted that "Phoenician art" is a tenuous idea, mostly a fantasy. It is possible that some day we will have evidence that people from Byblos or Tyre produced ivories and used painted ostrich eggs, but at the present stage of research it is misleading to use these objects to paint a gradual development of

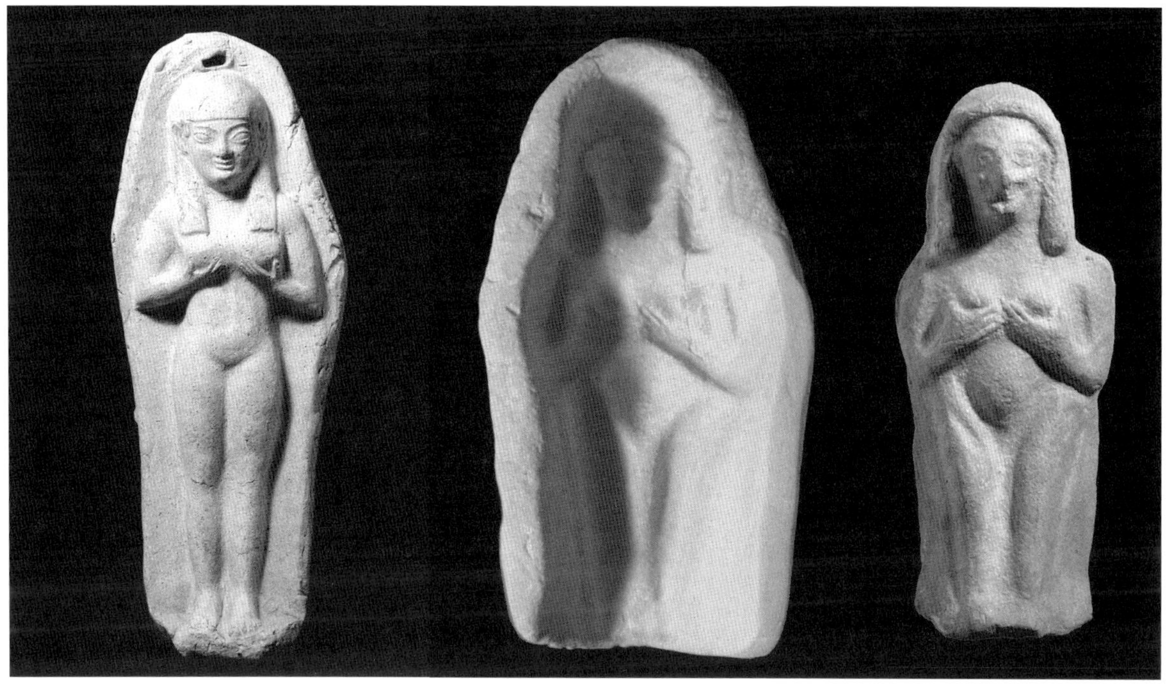

Figure 5. Left: plaque figurine from Tharros (Sardinia), 6th c. London, British Museum ME 133132. Ceramic. Ht. 0.17 m. Photo: © The Trustees of the British Museum. Center: figurine mold from Tel Dor (Israel), later Iron Age II. Tel Dor no. 38397, L3952. Terracotta. Est. ht. 0.12 m. Right: modern figurine made from that ancient mold. Photo: Professor Ephraim Stern and the Tel Dor Excavation Project.

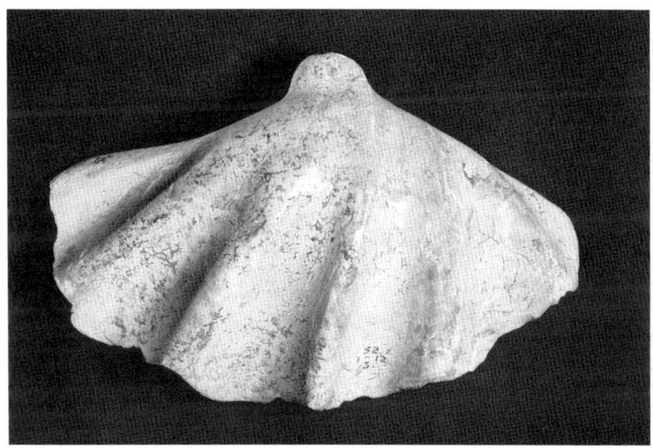

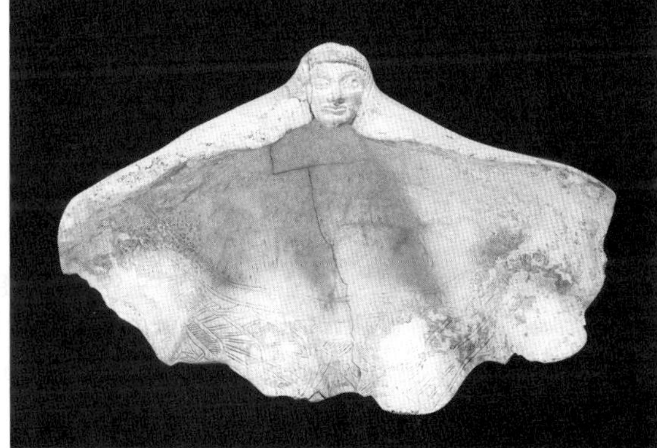

Figure 6. *Tridacna squamosa* shell cosmetic container thought to be from Vulci, 700–650. Assembled from fragments. London, British Museum 1852,0112.3. Shell. 0.21 × 0.13 m. Photo: © The Trustees of the British Museum.

"Phoenician art" beginning in the late Bronze Age.[122] The problem is exacerbated by the visual splendor of these objects, which are rendered with such confidence that one cannot help but wish to associate them with particular artists, workshops, or at least peoples. The temptation to tie them to Homer's Phoenicians is strong. Yet classification is a core value of art history that these luxury objects resist. And so the question of *what* should be called Phoenician art is a major feature of its history. A second major question, one that is often left unanswered in Phoenician studies, expands upon the aforementioned difficulty of associating style and ethnicity and concerns what has been called the difference "between identification *with* and identification *as*."[123] We must pay attention to the differences between use of an object, style, or motif and the idea that these items signal a particular ethnic or cultural group or a cohesive collective identity.

Part of what makes the study of Phoenician art compelling are the very limitations and paradoxes introduced here.[124] The presentation of Phoenician art in *I Fenici* and most other surveys is biased toward the Iron Age and the western Mediterranean, with the peculiar result that interest in the subject of Phoenician art fades at the very point that archaeologically retrieved evidence from "mainland Phoenicia" picks up. At the same time, the Iron Age objects presented in *I Fenici* as though made by mainland and Cypriot Phoenicians seem to have almost no relationship with the numerous objects from the west.[125] Accordingly, although I treat here objects and institutions that span the first millennium, my emphasis will be on the fifth to second centuries, periods that are underrepresented in synthetic works on Phoenicia, and on Phoenician art found in the eastern Mediterranean, in the Phoenician littoral, and in Greek territories.

Greek-Phoenician Contact Studies: An Introduction

I am able to focus on the Persian/Classical and Hellenistic periods thanks to recent scholarship that has reanalyzed or published for the first time the results of the colonial phase of Phoenician archaeology conducted by Osman Hamdi-Bey (1842–1910), first director of the Ottoman Museum in Constantinople, who was involved with the excavation of sites from Nemrut Dağı to cemeteries in Sidon; Theodore Macridy Bey (1872–1940), second director of the Ottoman Museum, who followed in Hamdi-Bey's footsteps and participated in the excavation of a number of sites, including Hittite Hatusha and the Eshmun sanctuary outside Sidon; and Maurice Dunand (1889–1987), director of the Mission archéologique française in Lebanon. Key authors of important art histories include Eric Gubel, Katja Lembke, Glenn Markoe, and Rolf Stucky. The efforts of Lembke and Stucky to publish Phoenician sites and sculpture are all the more admirable because of poor record keeping by colonial archaeologists and the heavy losses of material sustained in the Lebanese civil war.

Nicholas Vella and Josette Élayi have made critical contributions to our understanding of Achaemenid Phoenicia. Élayi has indefatigably investigated all aspects of this period, and established a conference and proceedings dedicated to its study, *Transeuphratène,* in 1989. Recent archaeological work in Lebanon by Maria Aubet, Helene Sader, and again Élayi has been refreshingly committed to swift publication. Finally, a generation of scholars trained in the United States (many trained, as was I, at the University of California, Berkeley, with other cohorts from the University of Michigan, Ann Arbor, and Harvard University) has been outspoken in its critical approach to Phoenician studies of the Persian-Roman periods: Helen Dixon (mortuary practices), Brian Doak (aniconism), Vadim Jigoulov (Achaemenid-period Phoenicia), Jessica Nitschke (dispensing with Hellenization, for which one should also see the important work on Phoenician religion by Corinne Bonnet), and Jo Crawley Quinn (Punes and Phoenician identities). As is clear, much of this work has engaged and critiqued the ways that previous scholarship approached the results of Punic and Phoenician interaction with Greeks, Romans, and Persians. It is with those critiques in mind that we turn to the approaches that concern this book, Orientalizing and Hellenization.

Orientalizing

The term "Orientalizing" first appeared in classical scholarship in 1870 when Alexander Conze (1831–1914) used it to describe an art historical style seen especially in Greek pottery that borrows motifs from metalwork, ivories, and textiles—the very three media most associated with Iron Age Phoenician artistic production. Orientalizing is now also known as a cultural phase that follows the late Geometric period, dating from circa 700 to the mid-sixth century. Orientalizing has long signaled more than an isolated phenomenon in scholarship that considers, for example, the adoption of the Phoenician alphabet in Greece mythologized in the legends of Kadmos (see Figure 1).[126] The term is applied, generally, to the Eastern impact on the cultures of several Mediterranean regions (including Etruria), sometimes as far back as the Bronze Age and extending at least into the first half of the first millennium.[127] Orientalizing is widely presented as the catalyst for Greek culture,[128] which, until very recently, was framed consistently in romantic and nationalist terms.[129]

In 1978 Edward Said's *Orientalism* (most recently republished in 2003) appeared with its now well-known critique of Eurocentrism in the academy. Its second chapter took aim directly at the French Orientalists Baron Silvestre de Sacy (1758–1838) and Ernest Renan (1823–1892), the latter a major figure in the development of Phoenician studies.[130] Some of Said's critical work was already being done, and so he can be understood as extending, not quite anticipating, a period of sustained interest in culture contact, specifically Eastern influence on Greece. In the French tradition one finds the work of such famous (post)structuralists as Jacques Lacan (1901–1981) and Michel Foucault (1926–1984), and especially Jean-Pierre Vernant (1914–2007), Pierre Vidal-Naquet (1930–2006), and other members of the Paris school who were interested in "the Other" and "refused to endorse any form of totalization" or master narrative about the classical world.[131] Their approach, much influenced by the work of Claude Lévi-Strauss, has been very influential. For example, François Hartog's 1980 *Le miroir d'Hérodote: Essai sur la représentation de l'autre* argues that Herodotos's description of non-Greeks, especially Skythians, tells us more about Greeks than about foreigners.[132] Walter Burkert's 1984 *Die orientalisierende Epoche in der griechischen Religion und Literatur* was also influential.[133] Object-oriented study was important in the United States, as demonstrated by Jane Carter's *Greek Ivory-Carving in the Orientalizing and Archaic Periods* and Sarah Morris's *The Black and White Style*, both from the mid-1980s. Burkert's work especially can be seen as a critical predecessor of more conceptually oriented Anglo-American scholarship, including, among others, Sarah Morris's 1992 *Daidalos and the Origins of Greek Art* and Martin West's 1997 literary study *The East Face of Helicon*.[134]

Despite this impressive body of scholarship, one clear drawback of Orientalizing is that its very study threatens to reify the premise that Said was contesting, the manufactured polarity between Orient and Occident. The tension is as obvious at it is seemingly unresolvable, because the problem is innate to the very idea underpinning this episode of culture contact, that is, the idea of discrete precontact and postcontact cultures. However we label them, it would seem that contact studies are predicated on *difference* and are accordingly inclined to draw paradoxical conclusions about connectivity. It follows that one can support the idea of an Orientalizing period while also thinking that Greece became separate from the East because of its conflict with the Achaemenid Empire. Standard textbooks of art history agree, presenting the origins of the Western artistic canon in the Orient: Mesopotamia, the Levant, and Egypt. In the early 2000s, Nicholas Vella and Corinna Riva organized a conference to probe the contradictions of Orientalizing, asking if it was "a valid heuristic term for interpreting dynamics of cultural contact and change within the ancient Mediterranean."[135] As one would expect, the volume provided no definitive answer. On the one hand, the study of Orientalizing can illuminate an important period of artistic receptivity and production in Greece. On the other, it tends to present Greece as a coherent entity, one standing apart from an undifferentiated mass of Easternness that is hardly historically viable.

The Orient, as many have observed, does not exist. Even if that fact did not matter to Greeks,[136] it should matter to modern scholarship.

One of the problems underscored by Vella and Riva's conference volume is the assumption that sustained contact with the Orient (the Near East, Phoenicia) is sufficient cause for change. Put another way, Near Eastern peoples, especially Levantines, and Phoenicians most of all, are ways of *"explaining change,"*[137] which shows a connection between the conception of Phoenicia(n) and the troubled trajectory of the culture concept. The idea that Phoenicians might change things simply by being present is suggested—humorously—in Io's abduction in the proem to the *Histories* (Hdt. 1.1.1–1.5.4). But it is important to separate out description, if Orientalizing is truly a good descriptor, from causation.[138] As James Whitley has said, "We can no longer take for granted that the Aegean was the crucible of the Iron Age Mediterranean, or explain the extensive borrowings that Greeks took from their Near Eastern neighbors as somehow being natural and inevitable."[139] I would add to this statement that we must not take for granted that Phoenicians explain change. Again following Whitley, one of the responsibilities that attends use of the Orientalizing concept is that it "needs to be *theorized*."[140] It is a mistake to allow culture contact to stand in as a neutral explanation of change. Moreover, Orientalizing is not an unbiased contact model, even if one restricts its definition to art produced in seventh-century Greece and Etruria.[141] In this version of Orientalizing, as Greeks appropriated iconography (such as the Master of Animals), technologies (such as the lost-wax technique), and ideas from the Near East (which here includes Egypt), they generated what would become their own, uniquely Greek, Archaic and Classical culture. The mechanism of Orientalizing so conceived is appropriation fueled by Greek exceptionalism. The promotion of Greek initiative in the Iron Age assures that Greece is at the center of this phenomenon, Whitley's sentiment notwithstanding. As a consequence, Greece is characterized as "Orientalizing" but never "Orientalized."[142]

Hellenization, Modern and Ancient

Hellenization is a different animal. Commonplace definitions such as "the diffusion of [Greek] culture, a process usually seen as active" (offered by the *Oxford Classical Dictionary*),[143] describe the encounter between a discrete Greek culture and various non-Greeks in three ways: through trade; the movement of people, especially craftsmen; and political subjugation. Hellenization can result from the export of Greek goods and artists; from Greek merchants, mercenaries, or colonists trading, settling and intermarrying abroad; and from Alexander's conquest and the establishment of the successor kingdoms in the East. Hellenization is evolution, and once contact with Greeks or Greek culture begins, it leads to ever-greater acculturation.

Much modern interest in Hellenism and Hellenization can be traced back to the mid-nineteenth century and the work of Johann G. Droysen. Droysen's notion of *Hellenismus* is derived from the term *hellēnismos* (ἑλληνισμός), which, with its cognates derived from the verb *hellēnizein* (ἑλληνίζειν), conveyed the sense of speaking correct Greek and having Greek habits (as at 2 Macc 4:13).[144] Although he "gets blamed for so much" that is wrong with the approach to the period following the death of Alexander to the rise of Rome, Droysen's aim was not to describe the general idea of Hellenism or Hellenization.[145] Droysen's idea of what constituted the Hellenistic world was rather broad, more inclusive and Mediterranean in its approach than nearly any modern study of the period. Droysen reasoned that, in Hellenismus, Greek and non-Greek might be fused in some way (*Verschmelzung*). The idea that cultural fusion was a conscious Greek goal has been well refuted, most prominently by Arnaldo Momigliano.[146] The idea that Greeks were culturally dominant in their relationships with their neighbors persists.

Greek geographers and ethnographers frequently discuss foreigners who are in various stages of what we would call acculturation. Language is a prominent theme.[147] Attitudes about the term "barbaroi" seem to vary over time and space and among individual writers. Strabo's (14.2.28) lengthy discussion of the Karians and the term "barbaroi" is interesting for what it says about this study because, like Phoenicians, Karians intermingled frequently with Greek speakers in various settings.[148] Strabo argues that barbaroi was once meant to describe those who spoke in a harsh tongue, then came to refer generally, and incorrectly, to all non-Hellenes. He contrasts Karians, who had lasting interactions with Hellenes as their neighbors and fellow mercenaries, to other non-Hellenes who had less recourse to speaking Greek or to adopting the Hellenic way of life. Barbaroi who do not adopt Hellenic customs are those not "interwoven" with Hellenes ("τῶν γὰρ ἄλλων οὔτ' ἐπιπλεκομένων πω σφόδρα τοῖς Ἕλλησιν"). From the perspective of hindsight— in this case, from the Augustan age—Strabo's passage highlights several key points in understanding different attitudes toward barbaroi. It shows that acculturation was logical for interwoven groups (*epiplekomena*), but less so for those that did not live and work among Hellenes. Through the example of language, Strabo suggests a process in which barbaroi could become increasingly better at "being Hellenic." Hellenes and barbaroi are perceived not as antithetical but as different points on the same continuum.

In fact the idea of movement along a continuum was explicit as early as the fifth century in the word "mixellēnes."[149] Although the precise meaning of mixellēnes is opaque, it seems to refer to barbaroi in the process of becoming Hellenes.[150] While Thucydides does not employ the term "mixellēnes," his evolutionary description of Hellenic civilization (1.6) has some parallels. When he points out that, even in his day, some Hellenes were more civilized than others, he makes a direct parallel between less civilized Hellenes and barbaroi.[151] In fact Thucydides (2.68.5) is one of the first Greek authors to describe Hellenization.[152] What he meant by the verb "hellēnizein" is not altogether clear. Take for example the Amphilochian Argives, who he says were "ἡλληνίσθησαν τὴν νῦν γλῶσσαν" by the Ambracians (see Map 2). The phrase may be translated rather literally as "learned to speak Greek, the tongue they now use," or "became Hellenic with regard to the speech they still use."[153] So although Amphilochian Argos was founded by a mainland Argive hero, Amphilochos, and although Amphilochia is within Hellas, to Thucydides Amphilochians were not necessarily Hellenes by birth. To return to the Augustan period, we can see how Strabo dealt with the same subject (7.7.1): he refers to all Amphilochians as barbarians. It is unlikely that Strabo had forgotten Thucydides's account, since he had clearly mined his text for references to barbaroi.[154] Rather, he offers by way of explanation that the Amphilochians were barbaroi because they were ethnically Epirote. In Strabo's assessment, ethnicity is separate from language and negates acculturation.

In sum, a plurality of Greek models existed, even in the fifth century when we might expect that interest in articulating the differences between Greek and non-Greek was high and prone to rhetorical flourishes. These models seem to have been quite fluid and could be interpreted and reinterpreted at will, even by the same author in the same book. It is perhaps a poor idea, then, to imagine barbaros and Hellene only as different stages on a single, continuous line, since the continuum may be used to support an evolutionary approach to identity not borne out by our evidence.[155] The evidence suggests not only that there were more possibilities than the either/or opposition of barbaros and Hellene but also that participation in and movement between groups only sometimes related to simple ideas of progress, making them impossible to record in a linear fashion.[156] The main lesson to be learned from these passages is in the awareness signaled by mixellēnes and the various cognates of hellēnizein that not all human characteristics were fixed, especially language.[157] We can compare these views to the perspective of modern scholarship, where language is an important indicator of those we call Greeks and Phoenicians. Yet it is clear that language has different social values in different contexts. From Strabo we can see that the ability to speak Greek did not make one a Hellene, even though, eventually, it might change one's status somewhat.[158] Yet whatever the extent of the Hellenization of the Amphilochian Argives, it did not keep the Amphilochians from being referred to collectively as barbaroi.[159] The term "mixellēnes" suggests some other kind of process.

If speaking or behaving like a Hellene did not necessarily make someone a Hellene, we must consider the implications. It appears that ancient sources sometimes differentiated between Hellenic behaviors that could be learned and modified and those that were fixed. For modern scholars this may be understood as a distinction between an evolving Greek culture (Hellenism) and the Greek ethnicity, the Hellenic ethnos. But over the past few decades or so the idea that ethnicity is a static or objective category has been disproven,[160] and the presumption that Hellene and barbaros always represented opposing ethnic poles is misleading. Appeals to Ionian and Dorian kinship were, for example, critical to the respective Athenian and Spartan hegemonies. Kinship ties were even allegedly used by the Persians to ensure Argive neutrality in the Persian Wars.[161] Consequently there is no clear recipe for the archetypal Hellene against which the non-Hellene—in our case, the Phoenician—can be measured. It follows that, as a descriptor, "Hellene" is unstable, selectively applying some combination of cultural behaviors, kinship ties (ethnicity) and general genealogical ties ("descendants of Doros"), civic identity ("Spartans"), intra-Hellenic identity ("Dorians"), and so on, dependent on context.[162] Most difference was located *within* such categories in a fashion that "serve[d] to underscore, not to undermine" individual and collective identities.[163] It is important to resist succumbing to absolutes to explain what was meant by hellēnizein and its cognates. One could speak Greek, behave in some respects like a Hellene, or be tied ethnically to some Hellenes while still maintaining an Amphilochian, Karian, Persian, or Phoenician identity. While it was possible to summon ethnicity as a countermeasure to Hellenization, as did Strabo regarding the Amphilochians, ethnicity could provide a common ground while other factors were recognized as (quite) different, as with the Persian ethnic hero Perses.

Hellenization has been used in a different, but related, way in modern scholarship. Views of Hellenization related to Droysen's Hellenismus can assume that "administrative and political changes were the framework and prerequisite for further-reaching cultural and mental processes."[164] But both the Greek term "hellēnizein" and the regular appearance of "Greek art" outside areas occupied by Greeks exist well before Alexander's conquest. Contrary to the approach of Hellenismus, the idea that the Hellenization of Phoenicia began before Alexander has been viable for quite some time, at least since it appeared in Fergus Millar's 1983 study of Phoenician cities. For the most part Millar presents a balanced picture of Phoenicia according to our limited source material, but he overstates the acculturation of the fourth-century Phoenician kings whom, he suggests, were critical contributors to the eventual process of widespread Phoenician Hellenization. Pre-conquest Phoenician Hellenization represents a substantial departure from the hellēnizein examples discussed above because the idea must be explored principally through the archaeological record. Once we are careful to recognize the subjectivity and self-promotion of ethnicity, however, we must acknowledge that the primary—though not the only—means of retrieving ethnic identity in historic periods is through the written sources, meaning that it is very difficult to reconstruct the particular ethnic identities of Phoenicians.

Fundamental Problems in Greek-Phoenician Contact Studies

Notwithstanding recent attempts to understand contact and behavioral change with greater nuance, there are some persistent methodological problems. There is a tendency to judge earlier evidence by later outcomes. Studies of Hellenization reify a theoretical process by promoting the idea of gradual, but inevitable, evolution.[165] There is an equally faulty tendency, however, to pursue "origins" uncritically, as Orientalizing makes all too clear. The groups we have come to call Greeks and Phoenicians came into contact at least as early as the ninth century. Contact is understood to have been initiated by Aegean—especially Euboean—and Phoenician traders, whether directly through maritime trade or through various trading settlements and colonies, of which Pithekoussai and Al Mina are among the best known in the west and east, respectively. The early evidence of contact comes primarily through art, especially pottery and metal wares, such as Greek ceramics at Tell Sukas and Levantine bronzes, ceramics, and weapons in graves at Lefkandi. Both examples are understood through Aegean initiation: Sukas is interpreted as another Greek emporion, and a particularly rich Lefkandi grave with north Syrian, Cypriot, and Phoenician objects is assigned to a Euboean trader.[166] There is no apparent paradigm here for Hellenization, since acculturation is not considered a result of the earliest contacts. Instead, Greek pots are equated with Greek settlements, and Levantine goods are understood as Greek prestige items, with some exceptions. The parallel with Hellenization is found only in the emphasis on Greece.

To risk oversimplification, there are three possible behavioral outcomes of interaction: that one or both parties are apparently unaffected by contact; that one or both change their behaviors to some degree; or that one or both participate in a particular set of behaviors only within the "contact zones."[167] There are many ways to explain the changes that might result from contact: as aggregate, which is how Orientalizing is generally framed; as oppositional, an idea fundamental to much scholarship about Greek identity, particularly in Classical Athens; as emulation, which underpins most theories about the origins of the symposion; as adaptive survival, which is one way to understand Romanization; as subjugation or assimilation—Romanization again or Hellenization after Alexander; as rejection or resistance, as in Maccabean anti-Hellenism; very often as violent, such as the destructions of Tyre and Carthage;[168] and so on.

Most of these reactions frame contact in "the dualism of conflict and consensus."[169] A conflict model assumes displacement; a consensus or collaborative model assumes some degree of assimilation or acculturation. The main problem with the latter is the presentation of acculturation as consensus. Acculturation is a bilateral process of interaction related to its conceptual cousin, diffusion. According to its traditional definition, it has two, very different, possible results: either the increasing similarity of both cultures in contact or the destruction of one culture.[170] In practice, acculturation is used consistently as a euphemism for an asymmetrical process in which one culture dominates the other.[171] One does not hear much about bilateral Greco-Phoenician acculturation even when some evidence, such as the Slipper Slapper discussed in Chapter 5, might suggest the possibility. In the terms of the conflict-consensus model, acculturation and assimilation are really degrees of cultural displacement. The model is focused entirely on outcome; it cannot account for either the cause or the result of aggregate change, in which local agents pursue, co-opt, and redefine external input. Instead, the model shows all change as to some extent destructive.

Modern usage of Hellenization is a consequence of this kind of conflict-consensus approach to contact. To repeat, the concept does not signal an aggregate process, like Orientalizing, but signals an evolutionary one in which a culture's or an individual's original characteristics fade into something more Greek. It appears that Hellenization has become a multilayered euphemism. In its *Oxford Classical Dictionary* definition mentioned above, we can see how the attempts to update the idea have created confusion. Hellenization is "the *diffusion* of [Greek] culture, a process usually seen as *active*."[172] The term conceals the fact that the proposed outcome of contact—acculturation—signals the end of another culture in its pre-contact form. It promotes acculturation through local agency, which is the active component, while simultaneously advocating its inevitability as expressed through the idea of diffusion. The contradictions just pile up.

It seems reasonable at this point to ask why terms like Orientalizing and Hellenization, if so deeply flawed, continue to be used. There are many reasons. I do not think that it is excessive to acknowledge chauvinism on the part of classical scholars (to which I cannot claim to be immune). To some extent, chauvinism is institutionalized, since classicists tend to approach subjects through the lens of Greece and Rome.[173] But the terms are used with enthusiasm by nonclassicists, too, because the eastern Mediterranean *seems* to be more "Near Eastern" early in the first millennium and more "Greek" the later we move through it. Still another reason is linguistic: while it is the Phoenician alphabet that is disseminated in the ninth-century Mediterranean, it is Greek that becomes the lingua franca of the Hellenistic and Roman eras. (When language does not change, it is always possible to deny acculturation.[174]) In sum, Orientalizing and Hellenization are appealingly tidy ideas.

Through our need to create history out of unruly and sometimes disappointing evidence, what is simplest or neatest can often seem best. The problem, however, with this Occam's razor approach to Mediterranean history is that it is far too easy to confuse what is simple and correct with what we value. I believe that Orientalizing and Hellenization cannot be modified adequately to justify their continued use as terms of convenience. Their use is a barrier to understanding the outcomes of Greek-Phoenician contact. For similar reasons, Romanization has likewise undergone withering critiques: "The very structure of the word [Romanization], however ingeniously defined, forces Mediterranean cultural and economic history to be about Rome. It puts Rome in the centre of immensely complex social and cultural processes that . . . may have only a tangential relationship with Roman activity. . . . The problem is that it *dictates* a field of research."[175]

Arts of Contact

To get to the heart of how we approach cultural and artistic contact, this chapter compares the two most widely used models in Greek art history, namely, Orientalizing and Hellenization. Most Orientalizing studies concentrate on specific media—metal work, ivories, and pottery, especially—all of which might implicate Phoenician art and traders. Hellenization studies differ because they can focus on a number of different topics and subjects and are not at all restricted to Greek-Phoenician contact. Both topics have attracted a good deal of excellent scholarship in the past few decades, some of which was introduced in the previous chapter; I do not intend to duplicate here what has been done elsewhere. This chapter focuses instead on the discourses surrounding what we consider Greek art, about which we know so much relative to Phoenician art, through the kouros and the picture mosaic. I aim to comment on persistent, fundamental problems in our ways of thinking about arts produced and disseminated by contact and how they contribute to our understanding of art's expressiveness. Accordingly, it is important to touch upon the roles played in art making by patrons and viewers as well as artists.

I believe the kouros is a straightforward, although not uncontroversial, example of external contributions to Greek art of the Archaic period. It is a useful, if atypical, case study of the Orientalizing period because of the relatively good state of preservation of both the Egyptian prototype and the kouros itself. Hellenistic picture mosaics are likewise relatively well preserved by the standards of their genre and period. The idea that they are an outgrowth of culture contact is, however, my own, so I will make the case for it below. Juxtaposition of the kouros and the picture mosaic underscores the double standards that pervade thinking about Greek art relative to other arts of the eastern Mediterranean. The goal is to explore the tendency to distinguish the Greek tradition as exceptional, sui generis despite its obvious indebtedness to other traditions. I argue that the problems of interpretation stem from the habit of presenting each of these art forms as purely Greek.

I have chosen this unintuitive pairing deliberately in order to underscore the different ways one goes about discerning the "cultural identity" of an art object. The comparison starts with the invention of each art form, what is known, surmised, or proposed about its origins; how each is studied; and what debates arise in its scholarship. From there, I explore the cultural origins of both genres, which includes some comments on the roles of artists, patrons, and contexts. Oftentimes the question of origin is not itself very compelling or even very important to understanding an art form because "the medium of exchange of culture does as much or more to explain the cultural from."[1] But I will show that origins are important in each of these cases to consider—and to correct—our impression of what these art forms are trying to express in social terms. Finally, the double standard apparent in these different contact scenarios will be considered in its own right. I argue that these apparent extremes of art, one original and geographically particular, the other pluralistic and diffuse, cannot be understood as discrete cultural products, which raises again the question of culture's relationship with art. At this point, Phoenicia is brought into the discussion through the invention of its monumental sculpture. The anthropoid sarcophagus is a type caught in an awkward space between Egyptian and Greek art. It allows us to think through different ways of characterizing arts produced by contact, especially the roles of artist and patron in the varied reactions to elite Egyptian funerary art.

On Origins: The Kouros and the Picture Mosaic

The Kouros, Part 1

The kouros is a well-known type of approximately life-sized or larger, sometimes colossal, Greek Archaic sculpture invented in the second half of the seventh century and produced until around 500. Most of the preserved votive dedications (*agalmata* and *anathēmata*) or tomb markers (*sēmata* or *mnēmata*) were made in marble; small-scale versions were often in bronze, terracotta, or gypsum. The ancient name of the statue type is not known. The word "kouros," from the Greek term for "boy," began being used in the late nineteenth century. The name became synonymous with the type only in 1942, however, when Gisela Richter entitled her influential study *Kouroi*.[2] How and where the kouros type was invented is debated, as is the extent of its dependence on Egyptian or Near Eastern models. The earliest extant kouroi seem to have been made in the Cyclades, on Naxos.[3] These are found in sanctuaries in Boiotia and Delos and in both sanctuary and funerary contexts in Thera and Samos.[4] Some areas, such as Attika, develop the type later on, from circa 600. In situ, the kouros operated within the visually charged religious context of the sanctuary or the cemetery.[5] Kouroi pleased the gods while pointing to their donors or the deceased, functioning simultaneously as *agalmata* and *mnēmata*, that is, as "delights" and "memorials."

The most widely influential narrative about ancient art and the kouros comes from the Viennese-born art historian Ernst Gombrich (1909–2001). In his 1950 *Story of Art* and 1959 *Art and Illusion,* Gombrich drew inspiration from Richter's 1942 monograph to show how the kouros embodied the priorities of the Western art historical tradition. He admired the kouros's will to progress toward ever-increasing naturalism that would allow, eventually, the Greek sculptor to surpass his Egyptian teacher. To Gombrich, a key characteristic of the kouros was that it *evolved* in terms of its anatomic realism, an idea that fits well with modern Western ideals of cultural and artistic progress. This virtuous evolution was rooted firmly in empiricism and mimesis in the sense of emulating the natural world. And so, while Egyptians produced art analytically, in order to repeatedly express knowledge of an ancient formula, Greeks produced art through vision, experience, and a willingness to push boundaries, moving from Egyptian *schēmata* to something superior. This model of Greek art was both moral and highly political. As befits the post–World War II context in which his ideas emerged, Gombrich presents the invention of democracy in Athens as a part of the classical artistic revolution.[6] Hence a brief moment of inspiration from Egyptian art led to experimentation and the "Greek revolution" that gave birth to the enduring Classical period, the acme of Greek art. Gombrich's reading is passionate, its idealistic and historical flaws as obvious as its impact was long-lasting.[7] Gombrich's work demonstrates that the interpretation of the kouros says a lot about the conception of Greek art and its fundamental place in the canon of Western art. The "ideological stakes" of the kouros are high.[8]

The decision to focus on the kouros, rather than the more complex history of female stone statuary, is telling.[9] Unlike its female counterparts in stone, the kouros has remarkably consistent formal features over its wide distribution. Its resemblance to striding Egyptian male statuary is striking (Figure 7): both figures stand frontally, a position that emphasizes their broad shoulders and narrow waists; both have elaborate hair or wigs, usually long; both stand with arms at their sides and clenched fists; both deliberately ignore their viewers; and both, despite having their left legs forward in a striding pose, are flat-footed and "fundamentally immobile"—that is, they are represented in a kind of energetic stasis.[10] Much has been made of the kouros's nudity or near nudity. As many have pointed out, the formal similarity between the kouros and its Egyptian model helps to highlight this choice made by Greeks. There is no evidence of artists working out different ideas about the type. The kouros emerges fully formed. Thus concludes Rainer Mack: "The invention of the kouros [was located] within a material pro-

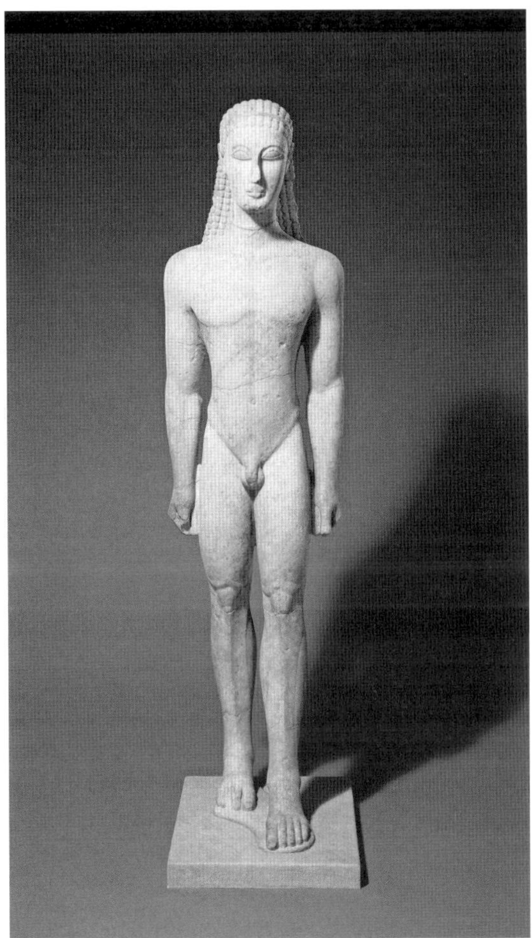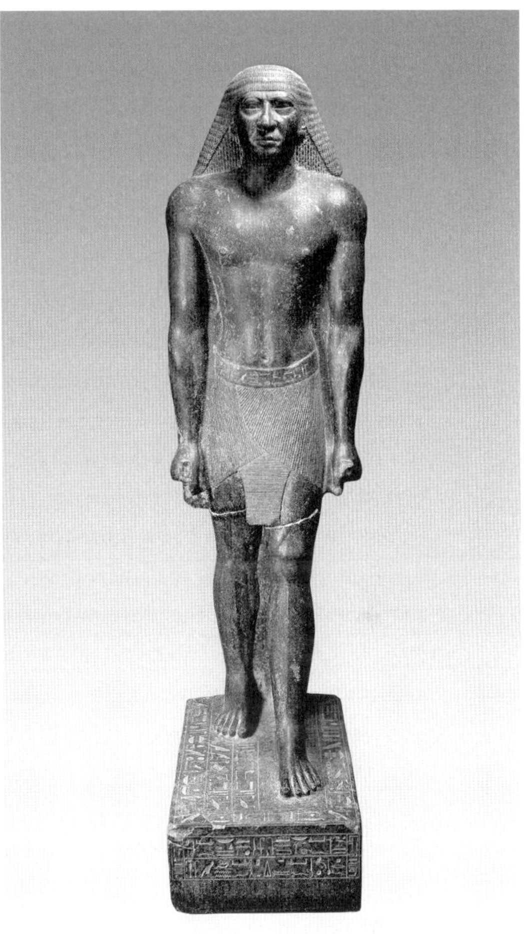

Figure 7. Left: kouros from Attika? early 6th c. New York, Metropolitan Museum of Art 32.11.1. Marble. Ht. 1.94 m. Photo: Art Resource, N.Y. Right: statue of Mentuemhet from Karnak, ca. 650. Cairo, Egyptian Museum. Granite. Ht. 1.34 m. Photo: Jürgen Liepe.

cess of setting-off or distinguishing, that is within a practice of differentiation."[11] This is an important claim that requires further consideration below.

First, let us look squarely at our evidence of the kouros. Nearly four hundred examples of the kouros type survive (compared to the approximately 250 surviving korai). This is truly an extraordinary number given what we believe are typical survival rates of other ancient Greek artworks, hovering at or below 1 percent of ancient production.[12] Should a rate of even 5 percent preservation hold for the kouros, it is possible that tens of thousands of kouroi once existed. Given that around fifty are known from Attika, several thousand might have once stood in just that area. In a recent study, Nora Brüggemann has shown that, of those kouroi with known provenance, around 70 percent (n = ca. 270) were votive dedications, 13 percent (n = 50) were grave markers, and 17 percent (n = 65) were found abandoned in Cycladic quarries.[13] Over the lifespan of the type, its main findspots were Attika (as usual), Boiotia, the Cyclades, and Ionia. In a funerary context, the kouros is found almost exclusively in Attika, the Cyclades, and Ionia. Attika is unusual, as a matter of fact, for having more funerary kouroi than votive ones (by contrast, fifty korai have been found on the Athenian acropolis).[14] The largest concentration of votive kouroi by far is in the sanctuary of Apollo at the Ptoion in Boiotia, which counts some 120 examples.[15] Although the kouros type is known in North Africa and Italy, it is clear that the Greeks' neighbors were almost totally uninterested in it.[16]

Thus another advantage of studying the kouros type is that it is found almost exclusively in areas where we believe Greek speakers lived, and neither its distribution nor its manufacture is concentrated in only one or two sites. It is important to point out, however, that there are not many examples from western, central, and northern Greece or the Peloponnese and a number of islands, including Crete (and in this context we must remember that the *sphyrelaton* or "hammered bronze" male figure from Dreros of circa 700 did not foreshadow Cretan interest in the monumental stone kouros).[17] In other words, the type is mostly Aegean in a narrow sense—Athenian, Boiotian, Cycladic, and Ionian—and not much at all a part of the life of Doric Greeks.[18] More than 80 percent of votive kouroi with inscriptions are dedicated to Apollo. Understandably, scholars were initially inclined to view them as representations of Apollo as well, even though the type was dedicated to several gods, both male and female. Yet in vase painting from the seventh-century Cyclades, home to the earliest known kouroi, Apollo was shown bearded and fully clothed.[19] For this and other reasons many now believe that kouroi show ideal male youths, aged probably in their late teens.[20]

A few characteristics of the kouros seem to encourage identification with the statues by onlookers. The form seems to be somatically indistinct.[21] The kouros smiles to signal its elite status, shining (*aglaos*) and happy, just as aristocrats could refer to themselves as *geleontes*, the "smiling ones." The smile further indicates the statue's magical life force, an expression of the kind of vitality that Greeks admired in Egyptian art and had valued already in their own artistic production since the Daidalic period.[22] Tanner has argued that sanctuary kouroi represented the deity whom they were meant to delight as *agalmata*.[23] Slippage between the divine and the statue was not only allowed but expected, even though care seems to have been taken not to upstage Apollo.[24] Kouroi sometimes received offerings, further strengthening connections to the gods.[25] In the sanctuary and in the funerary setting—the latter deliberately invoking the former with its statuary, naiskoi, and offerings—the kouros reinforced the proximity of elite and god. Representing the youthful form in dynamic stasis, outside human time,[26] heightened its special status.

The social function of the kouros was to thematize a specific kind of ideal sameness, what later Greeks called *kalokagathia*, meaning "beautiful and good." The ideal of kalokagathia guarantees the endless youth of Olympians and heroes such as Theseus. It is also what causes Memnon, despite his Ethiopian origins, to be somatically indistinguishable from Greek-born heroes. Like these divine and heroic figures, the kouros remains forever in its *akmē*, its "jeweled springtime," beautiful, *isotheos* ("godlike"), and sexually appealing.[27] At the same time, this ideal underscored the critical social differences between the favored realm of the aristocracy and the other members of the demos.

Comparison of the New York kouros from Richter's early Sounion Group (Figure 7, left) to kouroi from her "modeled" Tenea-Volomandra Group and "graceful" Melos Group shows how much styles of kouroi are varied by region.[28] At the same time, the pose and schema of kouroi are remarkably consistent. In Egypt sculpture was made in more-or-less centralized royal workshops and from there was distributed and emulated by Egyptian elites. There was certainly no equivalent system in the Aegean. Yet the pose and schematic attention to certain passages of the sculpted body approach the visual stability of the Egyptian striding male figure from which the kouros borrows, counteracting the clichés of originality that have been used to separate Greek sculpture from Egyptian. If it is correct to think that attribute-free kouroi are heroic youths that can but do not necessarily represent any youth in particular—the kouros as Youth—here is a key difference from the Egyptian prototype, which was used to represent individuals. In this reading, the kouros's *lack* of humanism and individuality might be the biggest conceptual contrast.[29] I suspect, however, that the anonymity of the kouros has been exaggerated in modern scholarship. Egyptian statuary reminds us how art that appears formulaic should not be confused with the generic. If we understand Mentuemhet as a portrait (Figure 7, right), surely the New York kouros and other funerary kouroi should be portraits (*eikones*) as well, even if they do not seem like true likenesses to modern eyes.

Further, although the problem has been recognized for a long time, poor preservation of paint and perhaps other added features are creating a false impression that the kouros lacked specificity. Colorful jewelry and hair ornamentations would have enhanced the statue's *poikilia* ("adornment," "variegatedness")[30] and masculine *charis* ("beauty"),[31] thus increasing its particularity. The kouros excavated with Phrasikleia once had a painted necklace and pubic hair. The New York kouros and the Dipylon head—thought to be by the same sculptor—have sculpted necklaces. The Sounion kouros of circa 590 had a painted *tainia* (long head band). The colossus dedicated by Isches in circa 580 was painted all over in reddish-brown ochre; paint was found also on the hair, eyes, lips, nipples, and pubic area. That statue might also have had a painted moustache or even a beard, traces of which are found on other kouroi (see Plate 2).[32] These particular features have contributed to the idea that certain kouroi represent heroes.[33] Ian Jenkins even suggests clothing might have been painted on to some kouroi. This is possible, but kouroi that preserve carved genitals indicate that at least that part of the body was exposed.[34] Bearing these examples in mind, it is possible to imagine that other, or perhaps many, kouroi had distinguishing features that further challenge the idea that the type was meant to show undistinguished, teenaged Youth.

Since the discovery of the Thera kouros in the 1830s, the connection between the kouros and Egyptian statuary has been noted; by the early twentieth century, it had become a regular part of the scholarly discourse.[35] Egyptian sculpture was known to Greeks long before the first kouros was made, however, which suggests that a specific, perhaps new, cause should be sought. Brunilde Ridgway claims that a new way of representing Apollo resulted from new thinking about him: "Perhaps the aftermath of the colonization movement, and a renewed wave of influence from the Orient, stressed a new conception of the god as a figure of action."[36] A similar claim has been made regarding dedications at the Samian Heraion and the learning of the lost-wax technique from Egyptians.[37] It does seem that Greeks had a new interest in monumentality, as the kouros type appears near the beginning of monumental stone sculpture; interest in work of this scale might be connected to ideas about divinity, if not always to Apollo himself.[38]

For more than thirty years, scholarly consensus has held that the kouros was not only modeled after Egyptian statues but also sometimes employed their proportional system. Eleanor Guralnick, in an important series of articles based on her doctoral dissertation, argued that some kouroi were made throughout the sixth century using the so-called Egyptian second canon of proportions.[39] If Guralnick's thesis were correct, one would have thought that the possibility the kouros was a type developed first in Egypt or by Egyptian craftsman would have been taken seriously, but it was not. Instead, the kouros was and is presented as a product of "influence" or "inspiration."[40] The recent statistical analysis of the kouros by Jane Carter and Laura Steinberg argues that an overall ideal proportional approach does exist in preserved kouroi, and the kouros ideal is, indeed, similar to the ideal Egyptian approach. Yet these authors have proved that, contra Guralnick, kouroi do not reveal particular fidelity to an Egyptian proportional system (one that is, according to Egyptologists, not especially consistent).[41] They can be more accurately divided according to regional styles (Carter and Steinberg's Naxian/Attic and Parian/Attic groups) with independent chronological development.[42]

Nevertheless, there are other reasons some scholars favor the idea of Egyptian artistic "influence" over more direct artistic interaction. Recalling the emphasis on difference mentioned earlier, to us the kouroi *look* Greek, not Egyptian. First there is the nudity. Then there is the removal of stone from between the arms and torso and between the legs. There is also the appearance of the sources of inspiration, late Twenty-fifth Dynasty (Kushite) sculpture and Saïte sculpture, which was alternately more naturalistic or cartoonishly exaggerated in comparison to kouroi.[43] In other words, despite its clear reliance on an Egyptian model, it is possible to understand the kouros as a Greek invention expressing the Archaic style (as Ridgway suggested), thereby stressing the originality of Greek artists from the very beginning of Greek monumental sculpture. Echoing Gombrich, Boardman explains the process thus: Greek artists "chose carefully, never merely copied"; what they chose, he claims, they turned into something "wholly Greek."[44]

The Picture Mosaic, Part 1

The invention of the picture mosaic seems like a complete inversion of the invention of the kouros. The earliest and finest tessellated mosaics, especially those picture mosaics produced in the technique we refer to as *opus vermiculatum*, are not concentrated in one part of the Mediterranean. The picture mosaic in particular, as a creation of the Hellenistic period, is to a significant extent detached from the Greek "mainland."[45] The ideological stakes of the mosaic would appear to be rather low compared to the kouros, although, as we will see, that does not necessarily follow. Because it lacks a clear nucleus of development, several competing ideas have arisen regarding mosaic's invention.[46] Much of the difficulty surrounding the question of mosaic's origins stems from a familiar set of problems: limited preservation, a reluctance to excavate below floors (or otherwise damage them with scientific testing), and modern mishandling. Altogether these challenges encourage the dating of mosaics according to a theory of style that is difficult to corroborate.

Contra Pliny's *Historia naturalis* 36.184, Greeks were not the first people to make paved, decorated floors, and no site, Greek or otherwise, has evidence of the transition from pebble, chip, and other early pavements to tessellation and thence to opus vermiculatum picture mosaics.[47] Two main theories about the development of tessellation have been proposed. Echoing the origin theories of the symposion, one argument puts forward an eastern Mediterranean origin, and another favors the West.[48] Neither is totally convincing at this stage. Tessellation does appear early at the site of Morgantina in Sicily. The Ganymede mosaic from the eponymous house at Morgantina is dated to the third century on firm evidence, making it one of the earliest examples of fully realized tessellation (Figure 8).[49] The floor uses tesserae and some larger pieces of cut stone to create an energetic composition showing the boy's abduction by Zeus. Ganymede's expression is

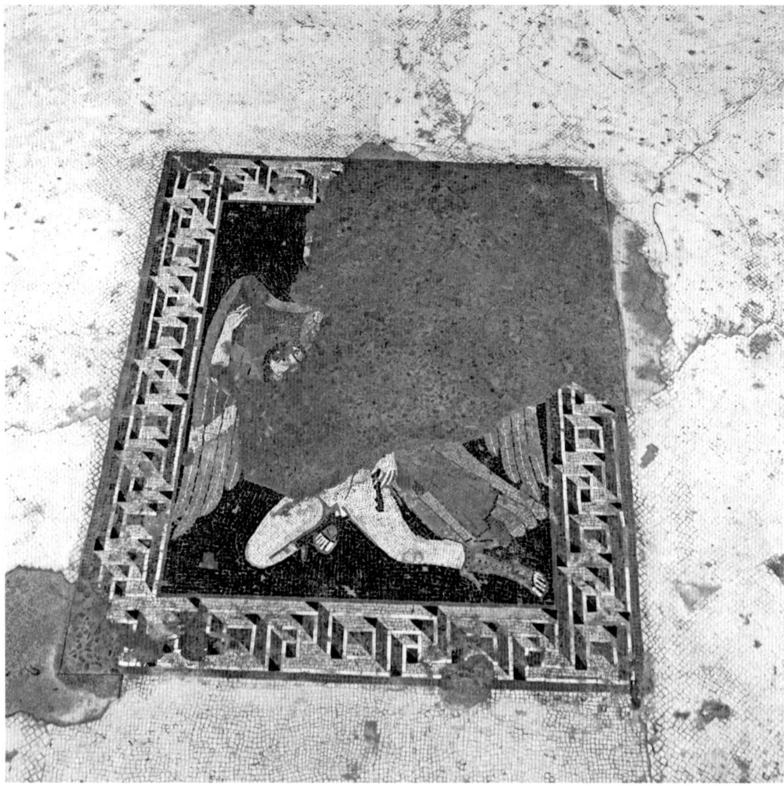

Figure 8. Mosaic from the House of Ganymede, Morgantina (Sicily), 3rd c. Various materials. 10.5 × 13.0 m. After Phillips 1960, fig. 4. Photo: courtesy of the Princeton Expedition to Morgantina.

vivid, his body well modeled and foreshortened, showing mosaic's illusionistic potential.

Of course some pebble mosaics are highly illusionistic, too. Pella provides good examples, including Gnosis's stag hunt, from probably the last quarter of the fourth century (Figure 9). As Katherine Dunbabin has noted, the approach to modeling at Pella can be compared favorably to the tessellated Ganymede mosaic despite the difference in technique.[50] An anecdote about Hieron II, the tyrant of Syracuse, is sometimes taken as confirmation of mosaic's early development in Sicily (Moschion ap. Ath. 5.206d–209e). According to the tale, Hieron presented the galley ship *Syracusia* to Ptolemy III Euergetes as famine relief after the failure of the Nile flood. The *Syracusia* was large, luxurious, and decorated with mosaic panels (*abakiskoi*) showing stories from the *Iliad*.[51] If we understand that these panels were constructed in Syracuse, the passage offers further support that tessellation was developed in Sicily by the middle of the third century.[52] The story is also noteworthy in that it presents mosaic as a valuable object in elite gift-exchange.[53]

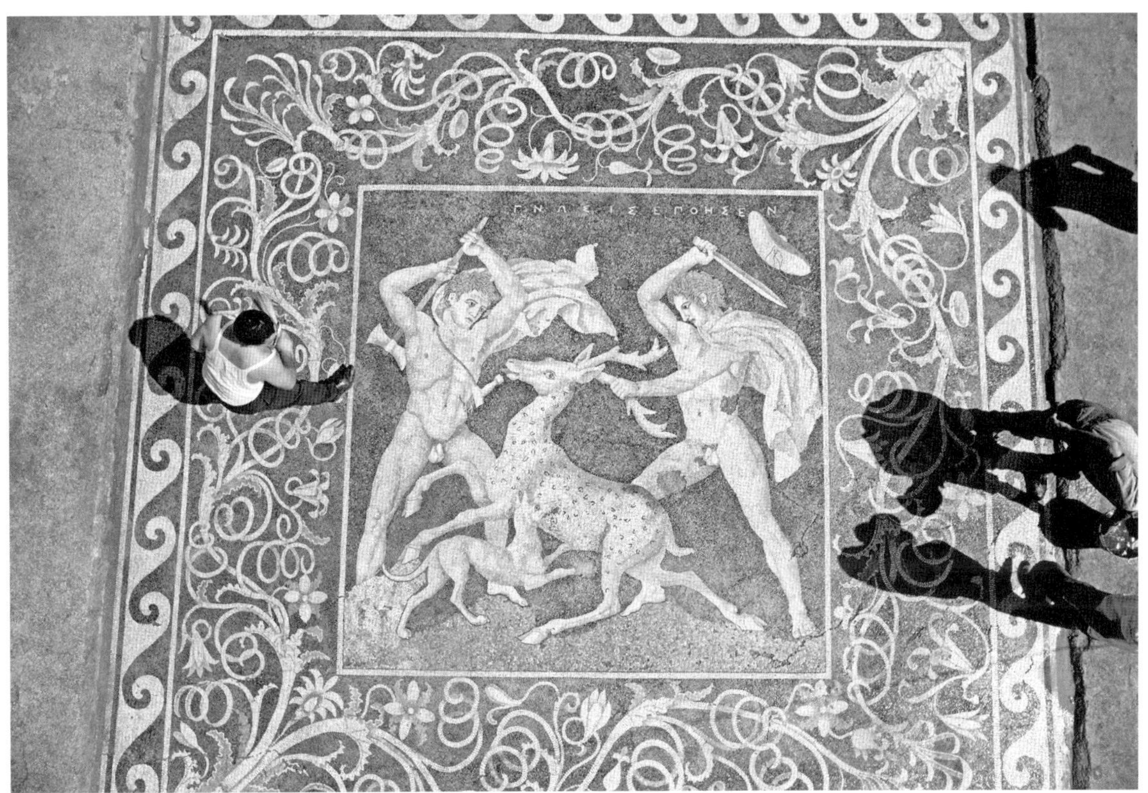

Figure 9. Mosaic from Pella house I.5 signed by Gnosis, probably last quarter of the 4th c. Pella, Archaeological Museum. Pebbles, lead. 3.24×3.17 m. Photo: Frank and Helen Schreider/National Geographic/Getty Images.

Although they lack firmly dated early tessellated mosaics, the eastern royal courts were also significant sites of mosaic development and patronage.[54] Pliny (*HN* 36.184) suggests that Pergamon was admired for its mosaics, and its most famous practitioner, Sosos—the only mosaicist mentioned in Pliny's history (36.184–89)—made two generic mosaics there showing drinking doves and a floor dirtied by feasting (the *asarōtos oikos*), versions of which are known at Delos, Pompeii, Hadrian's Tivoli villa, and elsewhere.[55] Egypt's importance in at least the dissemination of mosaics and subjects is suggested by papyrological evidence and attested by the lasting popularity of Nilotic themes, especially in mosaics from the Bay of Naples region.[56] The well-known business contract, the Zenon papyrus 59665 (256–46 BCE), provides the sole extant example of how Hellenistic decorative floors were arranged. The contract describes in detail the plan of mosaics in two baths, one for each sex, for a villa in Egyptian Philadelphia. The *paradeigma* ("model") for the men's floor comes from a royal workshop,[57] proving that the influence of royal workshops extended beyond the palatial centers to locations lacking resident craftsmen, in this case, from the tip of the Nile Delta into the Fayyum.

Egypt is also where evidence of mosaic's potential to rival monumental painting is found for the first time. The mosaic said to be from Tell Timai (Thmuis) signed by Sōphilos is generally considered to be the earliest extant opus vermiculatum; it is dated to circa 200–150 (see Plate 3).[58] At the center of the mosaic is a vivid female figure in red tunic and silver cuirass holding a ship's flagstaff (*stylis*) and wearing an elaborate headdress in the form of a warship. A golden anchor fibula secures her chlamys. She is identified sometimes as a personification of Alexandria and sometimes as Ptolemaic Queen Berenike II (r. 246–221), though neither interpretation is certain.[59] The overall impression of bust and headdress is of vibrant intensity. The signature "Sōphilos epoiei" appears at the upper left of the central field. The subject is rendered as though viewed at eye level, and it is thought that this mosaic and a second version (also said to come from Thmuis) are copies of the same painting.[60] Here, and in other Hellenistic mosaics from the delta region—the mixed technique Shatby stag hunt or the vermiculatum wrestlers and "guilty dog" from the palaces area in Alexandria—we have precious evidence of technical virtuosity and a clear interest in illusionism.[61] The urge to associate these works with lost Greek paintings is understandable. But neither Greek iconography nor a precedent in Greek painting was required to create illusionistic mosaics, as attested by the popularity of black and white floors, hunting and Nilotic scenes, and the famous *asarōtos oikos* of Sosos most of all.[62] In fact, explicitly mythological or political scenes are relatively rare in Hellenistic mosaics, whereas theatrical, landscape, and generic scenes were very popular.[63]

In the interpretation of the picture mosaic, one notes a willingness to sever context and patronage from the cultural identity of a work of art and to associate *technical* virtuosity with a Greek *style*. The evidence points to a more complex history. The preceding discussion of tessellation's early emergence in Sicily underscores the extent to which the marginalization of the western Mediterranean in histories of Greek art might be limiting our understanding of mosaic's origins. We know that Italian artists were very important to the development of mosaic, especially black and white illusionistic floors.[64] If the development of illusionistic pebble mosaics, tessellation, and opus vermiculatum occurred in several Mediterranean contexts in the fourth to second centuries, the extent to which all such floors should be collapsed into a single category of "Greek art" must be reconsidered. One can ignore patron and context in favor of iconography or argue that Greek craftsmen or members of the Macedonian court helped spread the demand for decorated floors to places like Pergamon and Alexandria, but the point remains that vermiculatum was achieved in Egypt only once Greeks, Macedonians, and various non-Greek-speaking people came into contact. Tessellated mosaics, we should note, have not been found in the Antigonid capital.

Further, in the few vermiculatum floors preserved in the delta, we find subjects ranging from the apparently Hellenic (wrestlers) to the universal (portraits, a dog). According to the available, though certainly imperfect, evidence of experimentation in multiple third-century locations, it is not clear that vermiculatum would have occurred without these contacts. Certainly we should avoid thinking that the popularity of mosaics in Egypt or Italy is a sign of Hellenization. There is no evidence of tessellated mosaics moving out from an imaginary core in the Balkan Peninsula to equally imaginary cultural peripheries.[65] Instead, the appearance of picture mosaics in domestic contexts in Pompeii, in baths in the Egyptian Fayyum, and in houses in the mixed milieu of Hellenistic Delos underscores the idea that culture contact was essential to the genre's development.

I believe that the origins of the kouros and the development and spread of the picture mosaic must be understood fundamentally as responses to the movement of people and ideas. The juxtaposition of these two genres exposes contradiction in the evaluation of arts of contact, first, in the uneven importance placed on origins of motives and techniques versus findspots of objects. Traditional interpretations of the kouros encourage the conclusion that sites of manufacture and display are most important when it comes to understanding an art form's cultural identity or intended social function. Traditional views of the picture mosaic argue just the opposite, making the unconvincing claim that the site of manufacture and display are less important than the origins and style of motifs.

Art and Identity

The Kouros, Part 2

In order to do more than simply point to connectivity, we must now take a closer look at the way these objects functioned in context, putting aside for the time being Burkert's warning that an object that points to "interconnections" cannot be parsed.[66] While dedicatory inscriptions on kouroi or kouros bases are common, very few retain what might be artist signatures.[67] One of the bases of the Delphic "Kleobis and Biton" (possibly the Dioskouroi) preserves a partial signature of [Poly]medes of Argos.[68] Despite the paucity of signatures, which are in themselves no guarantee of artistic identity, the Greek identity of the artists and patrons of all kouroi is taken for granted. Indeed, the kouros is understood as an expression of Greek culture, leading Guralnick in 1978 to ask what, when looking at Figure 7, would seem an extraordinary question: "One persistent question, since the visual evidence has been subject to conflicting interpretations, is whether there is Egyptian influence on early Greek sculpture. There is at present no generally accepted theory of what would constitute such an influence, nor any objective proof of it. Thus some scholars have concluded that similarities are accidental or coincidental and common to the arts of primitive societies."[69] Others, Guralnick adds, see the Egyptian connection and believe that it testifies to the "observation of prototypes and the learning of techniques in established schools . . . of stone carving."[70] Thus the kouros is presented as a product of mimesis, in the sense of observation and imitation, and of education. Even this more plausible scenario reveals how our understanding of the invention of monumental sculpture by Greeks is framed by modern ideologies.

Following Ian Morris, we can characterize the kouros as an example of deliberately eastward-looking behavior, art created for internal conversation and elite competition.[71] Given pervasive, though now seriously challenged, ideas about the symposion as an emulation of eastern luxury, and given the clear evidence that even Classical-era Athenians emulated their sworn enemy Persia in a number of ways, it seems curious to me how little notice is given to the idea that the impetus for the kouros was *emulation* of Egypt and elite Egyptians, one that made a profound, lasting, and structural change to Greek art.[72] Only a few art historians, notably Rhys Carpenter, have been open and supportive of the idea of emulation. Compare the views of another classical art historian, Robert Cook, who was able to insist seriously that no Greek sculptor had even seen an Egyptian statue and that any similarities, if they existed, "might have been transmitted by hearsay."[73] It comes perhaps as little surprise that, rather than supposing a direct connection with Egypt, some scholars posit a Levantine connection (that better fits pervasive ideas about the Orientalizing period's Syro-Levantine connections) supported in part by the style and iconography of the problematic carved ivories.[74] But the claim that the similarity of the kouros to Egyptian statuary is coincidental stretches credibility to the breaking point.

No one is suggesting, however, that the kouros and its Egyptian prototype are indistinguishable—they are different stylistically from the start—or that all of the characteristics of kouroi over time resulted from a single episode of contact in the mid-seventh century.[75] While it is of course impossible to prove exactly how the kouros came about, there is much better evidence of cultural and historical events that coincide with its invention than one will find for most ancient art. There already was awareness and admiration of Egypt and Egyptian art as indicated by earlier imports, anecdotes about Daidalos training in Egypt, and Greek art itself.[76] Emulation of the Egyptian wig begins circa 700, as seen, for example, on subgeometric terracottas at Argos and Sparta,[77] proving that Greek art had an established practice of selective emulation of Egyptian art prior to the Archaic period and the invention of the kouros.

The kouros's invention likely arose following military, settlement, and trading activity in Egypt, rather than through imitation of imports or imports alone. In the seventh century, Psamtik (Psammetikhos, r. 664–610) hired Ionian and Karian mercenaries to help him reconquer and reunify Egypt, expel Assyria in the process, and usher in a brief period of Egyptian political domination. Some of these mercenaries were garrisoned in camps such as Tahpanes (Daphnae) in the northeast delta.[78] Despite Cook's suggestion to the contrary, we know that mercenaries saw Egyptian statues on campaign. Grave stelai inscribed in Greek and Karian have been excavated at Saqqara, and in the sixth century a few soldiers even inscribed their names on the legs of statues of the thirteenth-century pharaoh Ramses II (Ozymandias in Greek) at Abu Simbel, some seven hundred miles up the Nile.[79] A handful of soldiers left polis ethnics naming Teos, Kolophon, and Rhodes. Psamtik also opened Egypt to Greek merchants.[80] In the mid to late seventh century, Greeks established what would become a polis or emporion (Greek sources call it both) at Naukratis in the western delta.[81] When Herodotos later visited the Temple of Neith ("Athena") at Saïs (2.28), he was only twenty-five kilometers from Naukratis. It is impossible to deny that these experiences were hugely influential to Greek art and architecture, even while acknowledging that some techniques were likely learned from migrant Egyptian artisans. Exposure to Egyptian art in situ seems to have led directly to the rise of monumental and colossal stone architecture and stone sculpture, as was put forth freely by Greeks.[82]

The debated part of this prehistory of the kouros concerns how much Egyptian technology matters versus Greek originality, and how excess attention to the latter has shaped art history.[83] Bearing in mind that the Egyptian precedent is clear, what makes scholars so certain that only Greeks produced kouroi? In truth, thanks to the circulation of skilled workers in the Mediterranean, it is much harder to know the particular cultural or ethnic identity of artists than some admit.[84] We cannot really ever know about the identity of most artists, though it is possible to point out that the preserved signatures on kouroi, as well as the preserved dedicatory inscriptions, are written in Greek. Gypsum kouroi found at Naukratis (and elsewhere) offer different evidence. They bear a striking resemblance to Cypriot statuary, and it seems that Cypriot-trained sculptors made them.[85] Although male nudity was not a common feature of Cypriot art, these nude statuettes show how Cypriot artists tailored their work for Hellenic patrons. It follows that Egyptian sculptors could have made kouroi, too, although one might expect that these would look more like Egyptian statues—in stylistic and technical terms, in the treatment of facial features, the overall approach to the body, the removal of stone, or the distribution of weight.[86] Regardless, we must not take for granted that only Greek artists could produce the kouros. Bearing in mind the conventions of Archaic art for aristocrats, the expression of kalokagathia, we should not assume that all the kouroi represent Hellenes, either.[87]

Our evidence suggests that patronage was the most important factor in determining the formal features of the kouros, whereas artists had a significant amount of input into its style. But we have still not answered the question of why the type was invented in the first place. Does the kouros exist to represent a Greek identity in opposition to an Egyptian one? Does this priority explain its particular features, its nudity and its tendency toward naturalism? As Andrew Stewart and others have pointed out, one curiosity about nudity in Greek art is that, with the exception of the Knidia, our source material does not comment on it.[88] Male and female nakedness is shown in some Egyptian art, too. It is generally perceived by Hellenists as a rare phenomenon, however, especially among the elite adult male statuary that kouroi were emulating. And so, the thinking goes, nudity emphasizes the conscious distinction of Hellenes through the body of the kouros.[89]

Greek art had already established a convention of male nudity before the emergence of the kouros. While nudity of both sexes is a feature of some late Geometric art (e.g., on the Dipylon krater of ca. 750), from the late eighth century women are typically clothed, while nudity becomes popular, if not a "default setting," for males.[90] What these examples show is that a major function of clothing or nakedness in Archaic art was to mark gender, that is, to mark difference between the sexes, not difference between Greeks and non-Greeks. Several contend that the nudity of the kouros is more than an artistic practice, however, thinking that it stems from a particular Greek interest in the anatomy and proportions of the human body. Richter, Gombrich, Boardman, and others date kouroi according to their increasing success at imitation of the *eidos* ("form") of the body. Such thinking fits with the idea that nudity can be tied also to the Greek interest in improving the body through athletics and training without clothing. Both ideas are flawed. First, nudity in art cannot be only an imitation of social practice, because it is employed in artistic contexts where it never was in life.[91] Second, nudity in art predates widespread nudity in athletics according to several ancient sources, which place its advent at the Olympics in 720.[92]

Further, Robin Osborne, following *On Ancient Medicine* 4.2 and other sources, has recently argued that the goal of athletics was not to train the body to make it more beautiful but to make it stronger. Beauty, Greeks believed, was the cause of athletic achievement, not its result.[93] Greeks were hardly interested at all in the development of muscles themselves, Osborne has shown, but instead focused attention on the joints and hard or soft flesh.[94] Thus the attention paid in sculpture to the cuirass-like abdomen, to the knees, and to the scapulae stemmed not from naturalistic concerns but rather from a particular ideology of the body. For example, Simmonides (fr. 542 *PMG*) wrote in the late seventh to early sixth century: "It is difficult for a man to become truly noble (*agathos*), foursquare (*tetragōnon*) in hands, feet, and mind, crafted without flaw."[95] We can infer that the "conventional irrealism"[96] of the kouros's body was as intentional as the emphases on its schema and bronze hardness.[97] The kouros deliberately evokes visual properties very similar to those of bronze armor, both the cuirass and the greave.[98]

Even within the development of different regional types, this ideology of the body was highly valued, probably more valued than anatomical realism. One notes even in the most naturalistic kouros, Aristodikos, that mimesis was not the chief motivation for its formal properties. The goal of kouroi, then, was to look like other kouroi. It follows that their naturalism must be understood in relation to other kouroi, not to the real.[99] As the "signifying relations among kouroi are fully 'horizontal'" and "non-hierarchical,"[100] Mack accordingly presents the kouros not as a generic entity but as a kind of simulacrum that was always part of a social network, one that embraced community while striving for personal differentiation. Seen this way, the somatic naturalism of some kouroi represents a choice, not an evolutionary achievement. I would take Mack's reading a step further to argue that, like most social entities, the kouros's impetus and evolution was almost entirely internal even though it never could have emerged without contact. Its nudity was symbolic, a marker of gender and the kind of beauty that was divinely given, not earned through training.[101]

So, although the nudity of the kouros represents a conscious choice not found in its prototype, I think it is a mistake to interpret that choice as motivated by a desire to articulate cultural difference—that is, to sculpt Hellenism in opposition to Egyptianism (if the idea of Hellenism even existed ca. 650). I would claim just the opposite of that now well-established view. The various structuralist approaches to the kouros misinterpret its symbolic nakedness by emphasizing the "removal" of the Egyptian kilt over the nearly identical use of the male body. Egyptian elite art was modest about male genitalia but not about the rest of the male body, which it used, nearly fully exposed, to promote vigor, virility, and divinity. One clear aim of the kouros was to retain the pose of its model, which suggests that the importance of Egyptian elite art—the particulars of which most Greeks were at least vaguely aware (Diod. Sic. 1.98.9)—continued to matter long after the Greek tradition was well established. In retaining this pose for the exposed male body, the kouros evoked precisely the same qualities as its Egyptian predecessors, albeit within the conventions of Greek art in which male genitalia played an important role, and the kilt none.[102]

Some have speculated in practical terms about the type's invention. Greek artists might have apprenticed in Egyptian workshops, for example, an idea that comes from the assumption that artists could not simply "improvise" monumental stone sculpture, "nor [could stone sculpture] spring spontaneously expert from instinctive talent and innate skillfulness."[103] Carpenter concludes that the first kouroi sculptors must have been from poleis with traders in the delta, probably Ionians from Miletos, Samos, and maybe Chios.[104] Jeffrey Hurwit suggests more than one origin and draws the reasonable conclusion that the inspiration for monumental stone work came from observation of, especially, New Kingdom *kolossi* in Egypt.[105]

In specific terms I think it likely that the first kouroi were made by craftsmen who had visited Egypt itself, not as Greek artists seeking an education (although that did, apparently, happen) but as bronze workers who traveled with the troops.[106] The relationship between bronze body armor—the cuirass and the greaves—and the schematic representation of bone and musculature in kouroi encourages this idea, from the single line of the pectoral ridge to the attention paid to the anatomy of the knee. In both we see the play between naturalism and artifice, the general and the particular, all of which was meant to glorify the divinely wrought masculine body.[107] It is possible the earliest kouroi were made in Egypt itself, but we lack evidence. Certainly the eastern Aegean islands, most of all Samos, were important sites for regular interchange with Egypt and developed art that looked toward Egypt even while the Cyclades supplied at least the raw material for the earliest kouroi.[108] (The colossus in the Heraion dedicated by Isches is notably Egyptian looking.) Whatever its means, the transfer of technology and ideology from Egypt to the Aegean in both bronze and stone had a profound effect.

Early monumental female stone statues such as the Cretan "Lady of Auxerre" of circa 650–625 and the contemporary "Nikandre" from Delos illustrate key differences in the development of female statuary.[109] Both works share a number of formal properties we associate with Orientalizing stone statuary, including the so-called Daidalic flatness and a triangular wig or wig-like treatment of the hair. As with much of what we call Orientalizing, the borrowing of these features and the technical skill to execute them is clear, even if the precise source material and means of transmission are disputed. Proximity of these works to Assyrian art is explicit.[110] Nikandre, standing at 1.75 meters (to the Lady of Auxerre's 0.65 meters), marks the beginning of life-sized and over life-sized korai and thus marks the transition from the Daidalic to the Archaic style. While early male figures such as the 0.8 meter sphyrelaton of Dreros of circa 700 could have taken a similar path, they did not. The Dreros male shares some qualities with the kouros, notably the schematized pectoral ridge, but not its wig, pose, or scale. Unlike the kore, and contra Cook, the stone kouros did not evolve out of even later Daidalic art. We can conclude that although monumental stone sculpture would still have been a part of Greek art without direct contact with Egypt, the kouros type as such would not exist without its Egyptian prototype. This conclusion should encourage us to reject once and for all Gombrich's obviously overblown and ahistorical narrative of the kouros as transcendent.

The Picture Mosaic, Part 2

Retuning now to picture mosaics, we see another approach to the significance of origins. Mosaics made in situ in various Mediterranean locations imply the movement of skilled artists. Scholars regularly claim these artists were Greek. For example, in relation to the Egyptian tholoi designs described in the Zenon papyrus, Wiktor Daszewski wrote: "It is perhaps the enterprising sprit of the first generation of Greeks in a new country . . . that stimulates small experiments, improvements and adjustments of the older Greek prototypes and techniques to the realities and requirements of the new environment. . . . Most likely the mosaicist was of Greek origin."[111] This romantic reconstruction of events recalls claims about the independence of the kouros from Egyptian prototypes. It can be compared to this statement about tessellated mosaics in Hellenistic Italy: "We may safely assume either the actual presence of Greek craftsmen . . . or the importation of works ready-made from the Greek East."[112] And to this one regarding the Alexander Mosaic: "The mosaic was laid on the spot by a team of craftsmen, who may safely be taken to have been Greek."[113] There is some evidence about the identity of mosaicists that complicates this picture. Eight pre-imperial mosaics are inscribed with what seem to be artist signatures (Table 1). Here again all the signatures are written in Greek. Yet the accompanying ethnics and findspots suggest that mosaic was an art form that transcended the Greek cultural identity it has been ascribed.

A few comments can be made about the corpus. The signatures come from disparate areas, from Segesta, the Elyminian capital in northwest Sicily, to Pergamon, demonstrating that the practice was widespread and not at all common.

Table 1. Pre-imperial Mosaics with Possible Signatures

Findspot	Name	Ethnic
Athens pebble mosaic	[. . .] ōn	
Thmuis	Sōphilos	
Delos, House of the Dolphins	[Askle]piadēs	Arados (Arwad)
Delos, Sanctuary of the Syrian Gods	Antaios son of Aischriōnos	
Euesperides	Euk[leidēs?]	
Pella pebble mosaic	Gnosis	
Pergamon, Palace V	Hēphaistiōn	
Pompeii, Villa of Cicero	Dioskouridēs (twice)	Samos (twice)
Segesta	[D]ionysios son of [Hē]rakleidēs	Alexandria

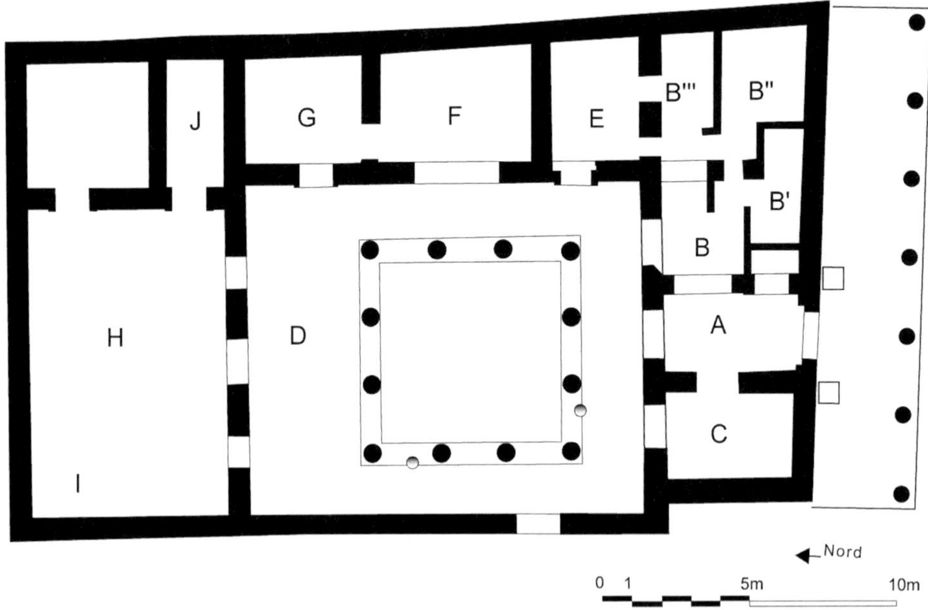

Figure 10. Plan of the House of the Dolphins, Delos. Photo: courtesy École française d'Athènes.

Two are found on pebble mosaics in Athens and Pella (see Figure 9). The rest are tessellated, such as Plate 4. Fewer than half of the signatures include ethnics that identify individuals from Phoenician Arwad, Samos, and a place called Alexandria (we cannot be sure which one).[114] These signatures were found on mosaics from Delos, Pompeii, and Elyminian Segesta, meaning that findspots and ethnics never match.[115]

Asklepiadēs of Arwad merits further consideration. In circa 100, he signed the mosaic in the House of the Dolphins on Delos (see Plates 4 and 5).[116] Delos is the most important site for our understanding of Hellenistic picture mosaics.[117] More than 350 have been found there in domestic contexts that postdate the island becoming a free port in 166. As I discuss in more detail in Chapter 5, Delos is known as a site of intense engagement of people from different parts of the Mediterranean. The house's plan, with a vestibule leading to a Doric peristyle, is an Italian arrangement popular there.[118] Its main entrance contains a tessellated image of the so-called sign of Tanit (Figure 10, room "A," and Figure 11).[119] The motif is characterized by a circle interpreted as a "head," a cross-bar interpreted as "arms," and a triangular "body" (a schematized dress). The origins of the form are not clear. Many possibilities have been proposed, ranging from the ankh to an anchor, palmette, or "bottle" motif.[120] The identification of the "sign" with the Phoenician goddess Tanit might be supported by dedications naming the goddess

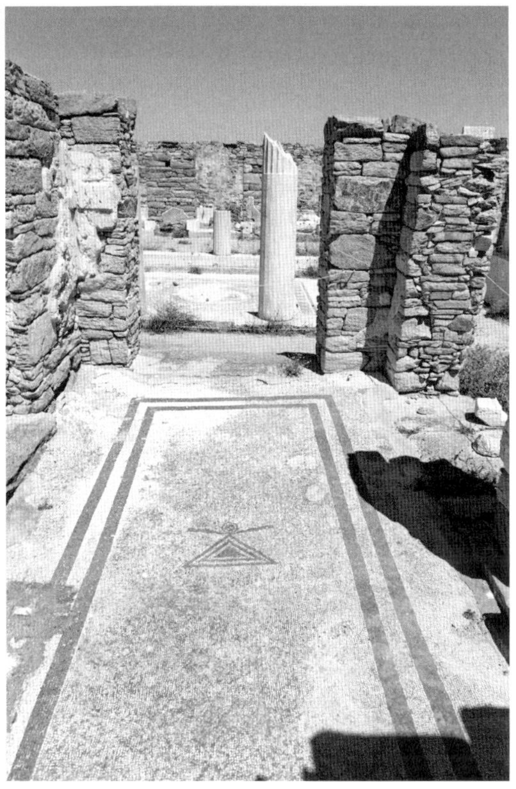

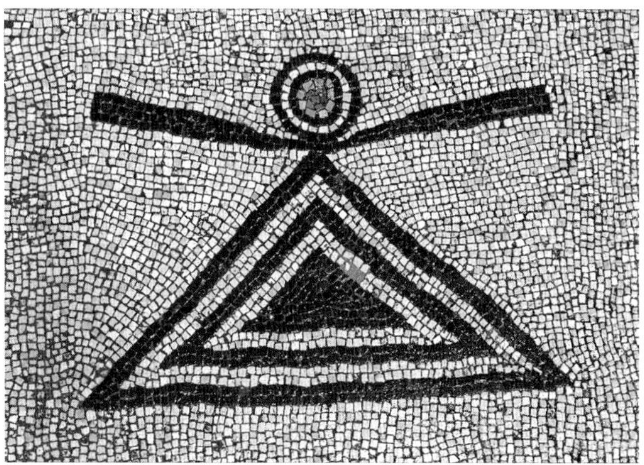

Figure 11. Left: sign of Tanit mosaic from the entrance to the House of the Dolphins, Delos. Various materials. 3.27 m × 1.24 m. Photo: courtesy Sklifas Steven/Alamy. Right: detail of the mosaic. Various materials. Photo: École française d'Athènes.

and showing the motif, although the scholarship—much of it very conjectural— lacks consensus.[121] On floors, the "sign" might have an apotropaic function,[122] and it was very popular on grave stelai in Punic tophet cemeteries.[123] The motif thus raises the possibility that a "Phoenician" patron employed a "Phoenician" mosaicist, perhaps intentionally.

The house's eponymous mosaic is found in its open peristyle (Figure 10, room "D," and Plates 4 and 5), whose main entrance passes through the Tanit vestibule (see Figure 11, left). The floor is framed by a series of black, white, and red rectangular bands and crenellations. At the floor's center is a series of circular bands and patterned areas in opus vermiculatum, including crest waves, meander, guilloche, astragal, and a marine-inspired tendril with alternating lion and griffon heads, all surrounding a damaged rosette set on a dark floral ground. The small and fragmentary inscription lies between two patterned bands near the central motif: [ΑΣΚΛΕ]ΠΙΑΔΗΣ ΑΡΑΔΙΟ[Σ] ΕΠΟΙΕΙ (see Plate 4, bottom). Each of the floor's four triangular corner areas contains a winged male figure, usually identified as Eros, riding a dolphin like a horse and leading a second on the rein. Each holds an attribute (see Plate 5): at northwest a caduceus, at southwest a thyrsos, at southeast a trident, and at northeast perhaps a club (it is very damaged), symbols of

Hermes, Dionysos, Poseidon, and Herakles, respectively. The thyrsos-bearing figure seems to be the winner of this little race, as his dolphin carries a crown.

While the iconography of the vestibule mosaic seemingly identifies the patron as Phoenician, nothing about the peristyle mosaic's virtuoso quality or iconography indicates that the patrons or artist were Phoenician. Or at least not until it is read in combination with the sign of Tanit, which can be paired in Phoenician art with one or more dolphins or the prow of a ship in allusion to seafaring, perhaps here a reference to the homeowner's livelihood.[124] The dolphins of the peristyle mosaic are stylized, with their tails intertwined and their postures aggressive. Their alert eyes and toothy jaws recall the similarly zoomorphic bows and long, pointed bronze battle rams of Phoenician triremes.[125] These might be intentional references to naval power. When filled with rainwater, this mosaic would become more vital as the dolphins and their riders bearing symbols of divine power seemingly raced around the dynamic circular bands of crest waves, meander pattern, and sea creatures evocative of Ocean encircling the *oikoumenē* (the "known world"). Hallie Franks has shown that floor mosaics could function as virtual *periploi*, and here the illusion of movement around a body of water is clear.[126] The implied movement might also have other seafaring overtones, encirclement being a naval tactic—one that was used, unsuccessfully, by the Persian fleet at Artemision.[127] Three of the divine symbols on the Asklepiadēs mosaic have roles in Phoenician art and religion (the thyrsos does not). The club and the trident appear on coins ranging from the mainland to Spain, sometimes alongside dolphins.[128] The caduceus is especially popular in Punic funerary stelai from the fifth century, where it is often shown near or held by the "sign of Tanit."[129]

Without speculating as to the meaning of any one of these motifs, it is possible to read the mosaic iconography of this house as part of a single socioreligious program, one that is Phoenician in design, even if it appears to us Greek in terms of its technique and style and in most of its iconography. Yet even if the allusion to maritime prowess had personal meaning, it is likely that the Dolphin mosaic was generic, like most Delos mosaics. Marine themes were popular on the mercantile island.[130] Thus in a number of different ways the Dolphin mosaic underscores the danger of assuming that iconography, and even style, are always good indicators of an artist's or patron's identity. Asklepiadēs's work is indistinguishable from that of Sōphilos. (Of course we do not know that Sōphilos was a Hellene, either.) Lacking the ethnic "of Arados," Asklepiadēs would be presumed a Greek with an appropriate theophoric name. Without the vestibule's reference to Tanit, the patron and the program might have been viewed as Greek, too, or at least "fully Hellenized." We must accept that many mosaicists, even those like Asklepiadēs who produced some of the genre's finest works, would not have considered themselves Hellenes. The artist signature in the House of the Dolphins proves that the work of non-Hellenic mosaicists was acceptable. Perhaps it was even unremarkable. Further, because the Tanit mosaic, not the Dolphin mosaic, was in the most public area of the house, we must reject the idea that picture mosaics were intended to make their patrons appear more sophisticated in a particularly Greek manner.

The deployment of Greek iconography and style, the exclusive appearance of Greek in artists' signatures, and the pro-Greek perspective of mosaic's one appearance in literature have contributed to the idea that picture mosaics were invented and made by Greeks. Yet these assumptions cannot stand: there is no direct continuity between Greek pebble mosaics and tessellated ones; Hellenistic centers at Delos, Alexandria, and Pergamon were not populated exclusively by innovative Hellenic artists; the appearance and popularity of mosaics in Sicily and Italy cannot be explained only in terms of acculturation; Punes, Sicilians, Italians, Anatolians, Levantines, and Egyptians made clear contributions to the development of paved floors; and we cannot, with our current knowledge, propose meaningful or direct connections between Greek iconography, technique, and the origins of an artist or patron. Altogether these observations suggest that the cultural milieu of picture mosaics was not Hellenic, certainly not exclusively.

Moreover, the origins of tessellation itself upset the idea that tessellated mosaics were once Hellenic and later became part of the Mediterranean koine. Rather than signaling Hellenic culture, these mosaics seem to promote some other kind of status. Probably they should be read as a sign of participation in an ever-greater Mediterranean elite environment, one that in this case downplays or even lacks cultural specificity. It makes sense to think about what was new in this period in order to contextualize the invention of picture mosaics. While monumental painting was long established in parts of the Balkan Peninsula by this period, painted pavements were rare after the Bronze Age; the same can be said of Egyptian painted floors.[131] The greatest concentration of preserved mosaics are in Pompeii, Delos, and Pergamon (we can only speculate about the Seleukid courts), that is, both in Hellenistic courts and in Hellenistic/Republican domestic contexts with known wall painting traditions. It seems likely that vermiculatum mosaics were a technological development stemming from the desire to increase the painterly qualities of durable floors. Although the evidence is entirely circumstantial, I think it is probable that, like the kouros, the picture mosaic was first created through contact between artists trained in Greek and Macedonian regions with Egyptian arts and artists, in this case, in the context of the Ptolemaic royal court.

While we should not assume all mosaics were patronized for the same reason, and while mosaics did serve practical purposes (Vitr. *De arch.* 7.1), conspicuous consumption was a key impetus. Ruth Westgate has discussed conspicuous consumption in the domestic sphere of the sort on display at Delos. A greater square area was used for circulation and entertainment in Hellenistic homes than in their counterparts from the Classical period. One result was the appearance of decoration in more rooms, especially those suited to receiving guests. A corresponding likelihood is that greater numbers of people saw their decoration, as suggested by the extensive mosaic program in the House of the Masks at Delos or the baths of the Philadelphian villa mentioned in the Zenon papyrus.[132] Once again, caution should be taken in equating such status markers with Greekness. The signatures themselves remind us of this point: "of Alexandria," "of Samos," "of Arados." Viewed in this light, individual mosaics might say, "like the royal court," "from a distant island," or "by an artist from our homeland."

We do not know if Asklepiadēs ever worked on the Phoenician mainland or if the decorated floors in the House of the Dolphins mirror, in some way, what was happening in Phoenician cities. But I think it is accurate to say that some contexts, such as Hellenistic Delos, had specific social conditions that generated demands for ever more lavish and creative mosaic programs. Like these floors, the signatures may be expressing not the objective ethnic or cultural identity of an ancient artist or patron but rather civic or social identities particular to such contexts. Picture mosaics might have served a number of social functions. Their style and iconography signal they were generally decorative and playful, a physical manifestation of good taste derived from the strong connections that gave rise to tessellation, spread innovations in tessellation and vermiculatum far afield, and helped shape the very Mediterranean perspectives of which they were a part.

Arts of Contact

Greeks were quite interested in their cultural origins, and Egypt ranked highest among all sources (e.g., Hdt. 2.35). Yet because of fixed perceptions about the exceptional qualities of Greek art, the kouros is almost always presented as a response to Egyptian art that was eager to distance itself from its source. This oppositional reading seems to be an inversion of the function of the type. The connection between the divine, the elite, and the cultural authority of Egypt is constantly replicated in and reinforced by the form.[133] The kouros operates in a way similar to its prototype insofar as both are signs that, for example, use walking to demonstrate vivacity.[134] This point is evident when we remind ourselves that, for all the individuality, experimentation, and regional diversity seen in the type, the point of reference is not abandoned because of its lack of expressive naturalism. Instead, the type persists until a major political and social upheaval *required* that it be changed,[135] which helps us understand that the most important role of the kouros within the polis was to demonstrate the power and privilege of elites.

Conversely, the popularity of the picture mosaic beyond the Hellenistic courts is regularly cast as emulation or acculturation. In order to maintain the idea that picture mosaics are evidence of Hellenization, scholarship, perhaps unwittingly, continually asserts the Hellenism of mosaics and their makers regardless of the lack of explicit evidence or evidence to the contrary. It should be clear that this reading cannot hold either. One of the chief social functions of the mosaic was to signal participation in the elite Mediterranean milieu, by which I mean costly signaling through art without cultural specificity. I do not claim, however, that the picture mosaic does not belong to the history of Greek art. Rather, unlike the case of the kouros, we possess direct evidence that neither its artists nor its patrons (and certainly not its contexts) were exclusively Greek, even in the broader sense in which one might employ that term in the Hellenistic era.

Although only rarely transported, the picture mosaic shares a number of similarities with objects that circulated. The later Iron Age Mediterranean provides a number of examples, such as the Lyre-Player Group of scaraboid seals. There is familiar debate about precisely where these objects were made and how to associate their iconography with any place in particular. They date to the second half of the eighth century.[136] As their conventional name suggests, many show anthropoid figures playing the lyre.[137] There is general agreement that the seals were made in the eastern Mediterranean, likely Syria, but their distribution spreads across the Mediterranean as far west as Huelva, Spain (Figure 12).[138] The seals' functions differ by region. At sites farthest west (with the possible exception of Huelva), they are found in burials and, at some of these sites, including Pithekoussai, mounted on silver hoops or thread for personal adornment or protection; nearly all come from sanctuaries in "mainland" Greece and Cyprus; and, in the Near East, they are found in occupational debris. So at Euboean Lefkandi, the Lyre-Player Group seals were used principally as dedications, whereas those from the Euboean colony of Pithekoussai were personal protective amulets found in funerary contexts.[139]

While such uses are not mutually exclusive, the regional division even among Greeks (although identity is complicated at Pithekoussai) suggests significant difference in beliefs while at the same time offering indisputable proof of widespread receptivity to the seals. We should pay attention to what the Lyre-Player seals tell us. They show how the function of similar-looking objects can vary in ways that are socially determined, even by people we imagine are closely related. All of these objects might be understood as art forms produced and sustained by ongoing interaction, although in the case of picture mosaics it seems to have been the artists, rather than the objects, that circulated. Each testifies to the art of contact's resistance to easy definition. We should not expect arts produced by contact to belong exclusively to one region, cultural or ethnic group, or visual tradition.

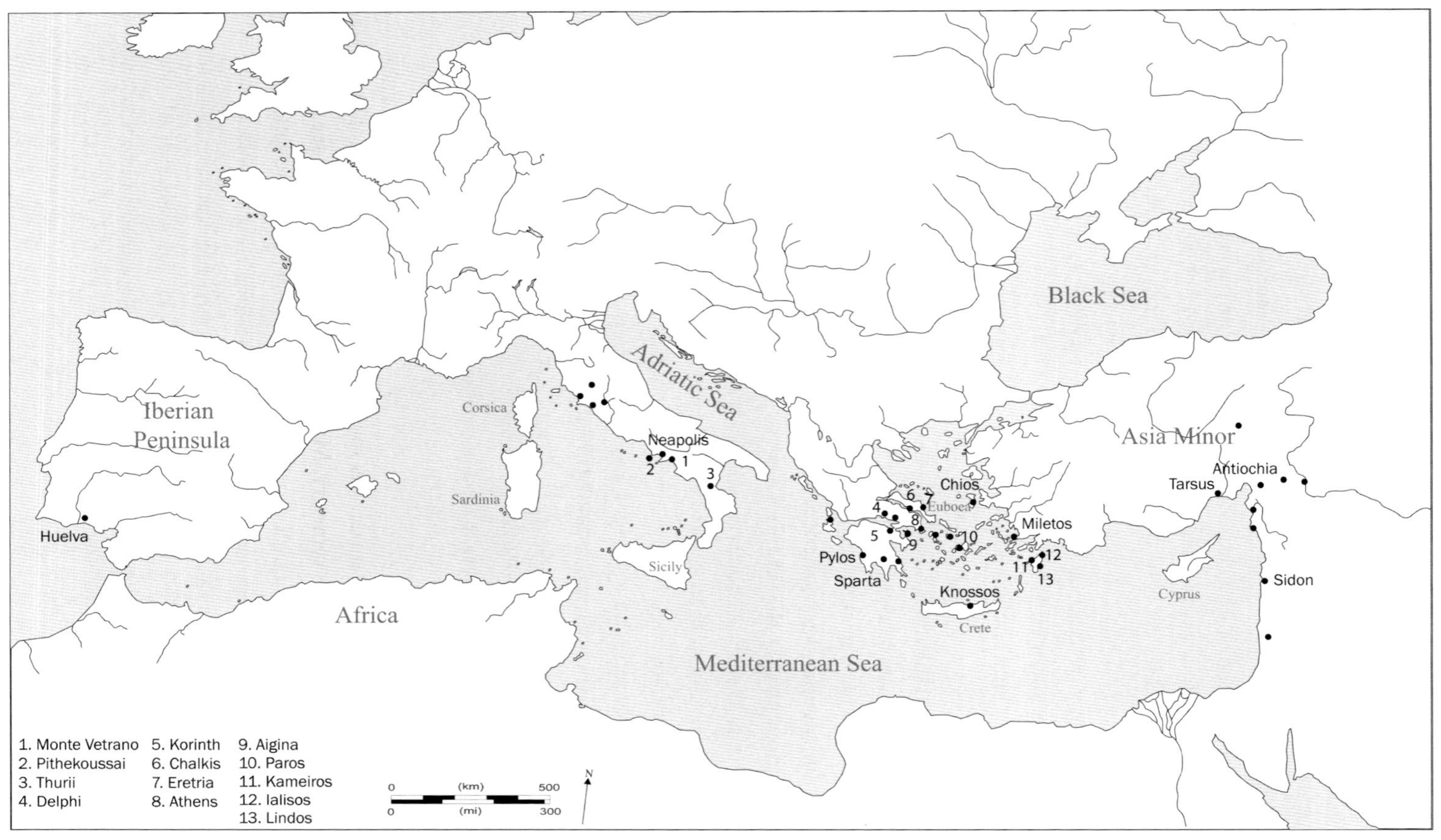

Figure 12. Distribution of Lyre Player Group seals. Map redrawn with minor changes and additions by Sveta Matskevich after Boardman 1990, fig. 20.

The approach to these objects should be different from the approach to those with single sites of manufacture informed by a fairly cohesive visual tradition, such as Athenian pottery, even if the latter were also distributed broadly.[140] Something quite different is happening with the kouros, as its consistency must be important to its function. It seems that the movement of patrons spread the type to specific sanctuaries and poleis. In suggesting that the kouros was an emulation of Egyptian art—and was not fundamentally interested in distinguishing the "homemade" from the "foreign," least of all the "Hellenic" from the "barbarian"—I have challenged ideas about Orientalizing Greeks and the inherent originality of Greek art. A brief discussion of the origins of Phoenician monumental sculpture will show how entrenched and limiting these views can be in the discourse of Phoenician art as well.

What we know of Phoenician art of the Iron Age shows that it was openly engaged with Egyptian art, but there was no major tradition of monumental stone sculpture in this period.[141] Once again military activity in Egypt seems to have been the key to the invention of a monumental sculpture industry. According to Herodotos (3.10–19), Phoenicians accompanied Cambyses (r. 529–522) on his Egyptian campaign. A careful reading of the source material suggests that the navy played an important role in this conflict.[142] After the circa 525 Persian conquests of several cities, including Memphis, Cambyses made plans to advance on other areas (3.17).[143] At some point when they were in Egypt, Sidonians took from a sculptor's workshop, or perhaps directly from a Saïte nekropolis, three stone anthropoid sarcophagi made for local elites.[144] The sarcophagus in Figure 13 already had an Egyptian inscription naming its occupant, a general named Pa-en-Ptah. Pa-en-Ptah's sarcophagus was excavated in the 'Ayaa nekropolis east of Sidon. It was interred with a new occupant, the king Tabnit, identified by a Phoenician inscription added to the foot of the figure (Figure 13; see Figures 21 and 23). Tabnit's mummified corpse was found inside on a wooden plank.[145]

With Tabnit's sarcophagus was found the second looted one, incomplete and lacking an inscription; a female was found inside.[146] The third sarcophagus was found in another Sidonian cemetery, Magharat Abloun (Figure 14; see Figures 22 and 24). It was not yet complete when stolen, and a Phoenician inscription naming its occupant was added to the front of the body. This epitaph of Tabnit's successor King Eshmunazar II is twenty-two lines long and well preserved.[147]

It is widely agreed that these looted sarcophagi were the progenitors of a peculiar Phoenician sculptural type known conventionally as anthropoid sarcophagi (Figures 15 and 16). Around one hundred and twenty of the sarcophagi are known. They come almost exclusively from Phoenician areas, the majority from Sidon (fifty-nine) and Arwad (twenty-eight). None has been found so far in Tyre.[148] Unfortunately, no anthropoid sarcophagi have identifying inscriptions,

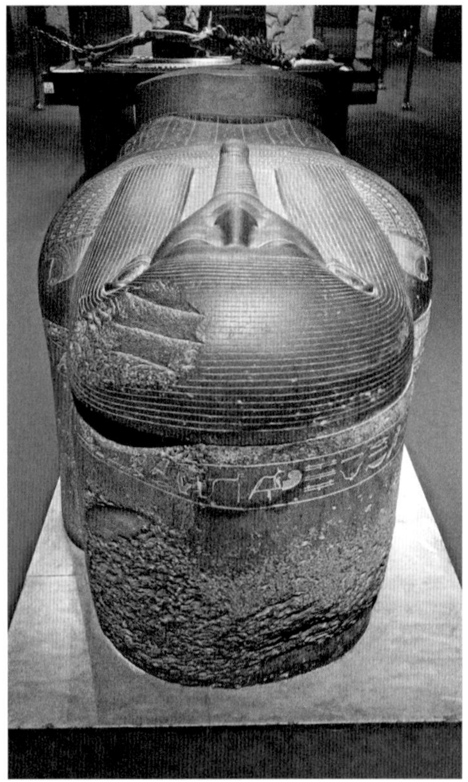

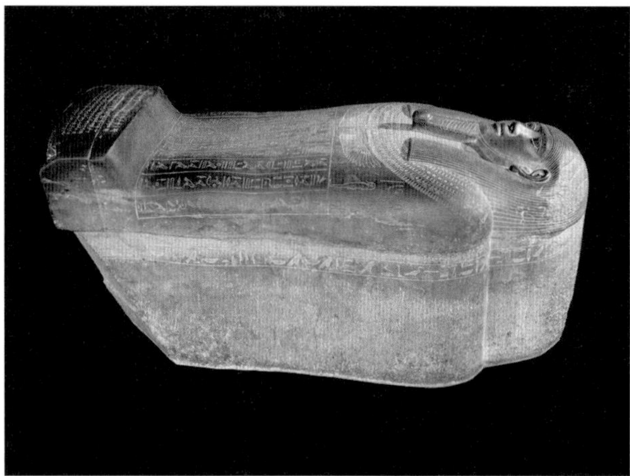

Figure 13. Sarcophagus and mummy of Tabnit from the 'Ayaa Nekropolis near Sidon, ca. 525. Made in Saqqara or Giza. Istanbul, Archaeological Museum 800. Amphibolite. Ht. 2.32 m. Detail photo: author's own. Overview photo: Art Resource, N.Y.

although traces of paint are visible on some examples, suggesting there might once have been.[149] Many were made of Parian or other Cycladic marble, and so Aegean quarries and, likely, Greek craftsmen were important parts of the production.[150] The earliest anthropoid sarcophagi are thought to date to around 480 or 470; the latest are usually dated to around the time of Alexander, but probably the type persisted into the Hellenistic period.[151] Their chronology within that range is also disputed and rests on several criteria concerning archaeology, changes in the overall form, and rightly disputed ideas about their relationship to Egyptian and Greek art.[152]

The anthropoid sarcophagus shares with its Saïte prototype its basic form and emphasis on the representation of the head. Occasionally other parts of the body are shown—feet, hands, knees, and so forth—or indicated on the lower half, such as the calves or buttocks. Some heads have Egyptian features, but they differ from the exaggerated and stylized features of the looted sarcophagi. As with the kouros, we lack for these objects a working out of the type in reaction to its Egyptian predecessor. The picture is only complicated by the sarcophagi that draw upon Greek art, both Archaic and Classical, in the approach to the hair or face (Figure 16, center and right).[153] Some sarcophagi even combine features from Egyptian and Greek art, pairing a visage and hairstyle that recall Greek sculpture with

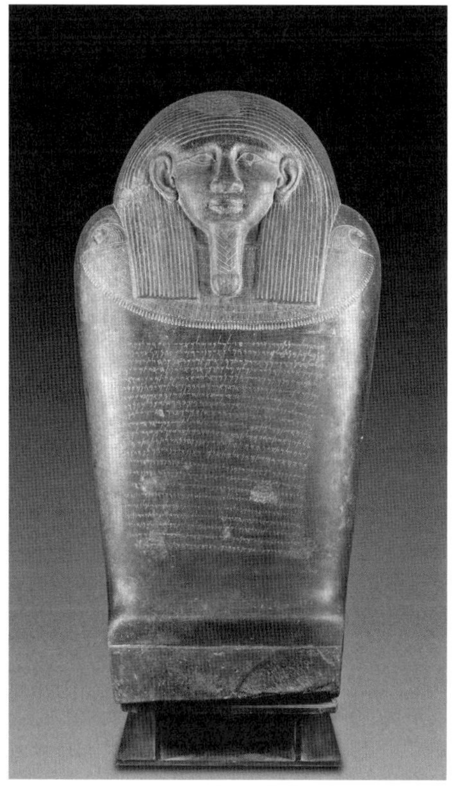

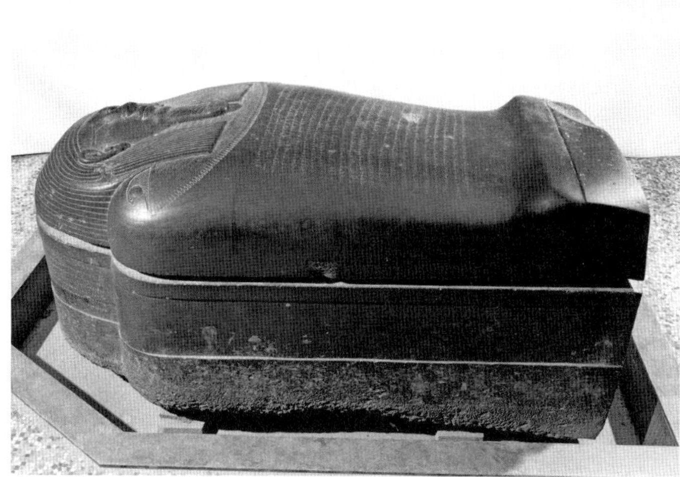

Figure 14. Sarcophagus of Eshmunazar II from the nekropolis of Magharat Abloun near Sidon, ca. 525. Made in Saqqara or Giza. Paris, Musée du Louvre AO 4806. Amphibolite. Ht. 2.56 m. Photos: Art Resource, N.Y.

the Egyptian box beard and klaft headdress (Figure 16, left).[154] According to the accepted date for the invention of the type in around 480, sarcophagi with Archaic features such as snail curls might best be understood as Archaizing. The classical Greek sources upon which other sarcophagi draw, from Severe Style sculpture to Attic grave stelai to Pheidias and Polykleitos, have great longevity in Hellenistic and later sculpture.[155] It is possible that those features are Classicizing. If so, the stylistic criteria used to date these objects must be reviewed.

As one should by now expect from Phoenician art history, nearly every argument about the sarcophagi can be contested. Especially problematic, given the general agreement on their Egyptian origin, is the claim that the sarcophagi were manufactured by Greek workshops in Sidon and accordingly are evidence of the Hellenization of the Phoenician elite.[156] Somehow these monuments are caught in the crosshairs of Orientalizing and Hellenization. The presumed lack of Phoenician agency is not surprising given how difficult it is to recover Phoenicians from the material record, yet the numerous parallels in the invention of the kouros and the anthropoid sarcophagi show how much these agential perceptions are ideological. If Phoenicians were eager to emulate Greek monumental sculpture, anthropoid sarcophagi would be a poor choice. Even putting aside the Egyptian features,

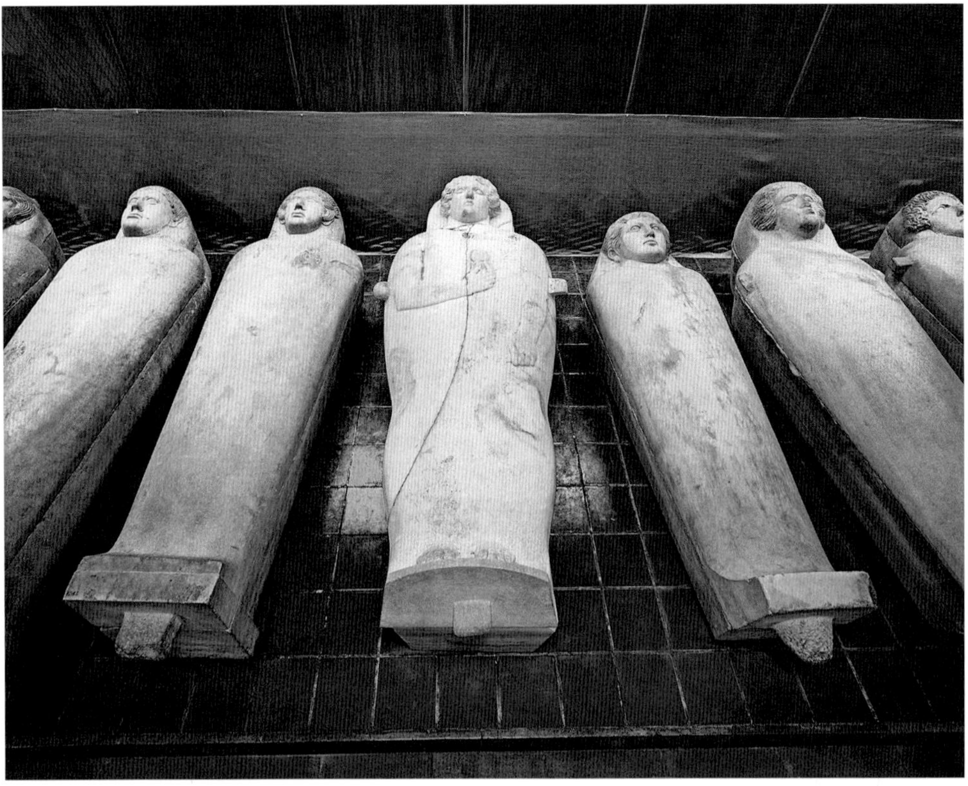

Figure 15. Anthropoid sarcophagi in the Beirut National Museum. Marble. Various sizes. Photo: Erich Lessing.

this stone sarcophagus type is unique to Phoenicians. The two typical approaches to these objects, one emphasizing the important role of Greek sculptors in the invention of the type, the other stressing their gradual Hellenization away from the Egyptian type, are not supported by extant evidence.[157] The peculiarity of the type and the experimentation evident in its many variations reinforce the idea that these attempts to assign ethnocultural identities to the objects' makers is unwise. The final artistic result only seems to us a pastiche, one that is surely indicative of specific, if unknown to us, Phoenician ideologies.

Those who insist that Greek sculptors carved the first kouroi have little grounds to deny the possibility that Phoenician sculptors made these sarcophagi (compare Figures 7 and 15 and 16). The types share similarities beyond their use in funerary contexts. Both emerge from Egyptian sculpture that is reconfigured according to new artistic conventions (it would not be hard to make the case that the Phoenician result was the more creative of the two). We see in both a lasting interest in the prototype and a desire to set the individual apart or not from other elites. Neither type can be dated on the basis of style without controversy, although

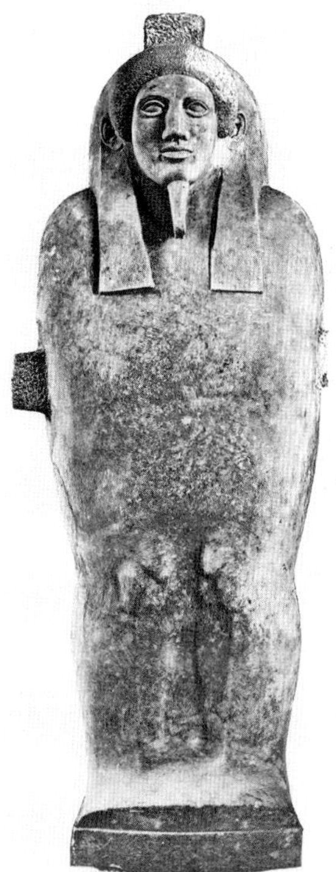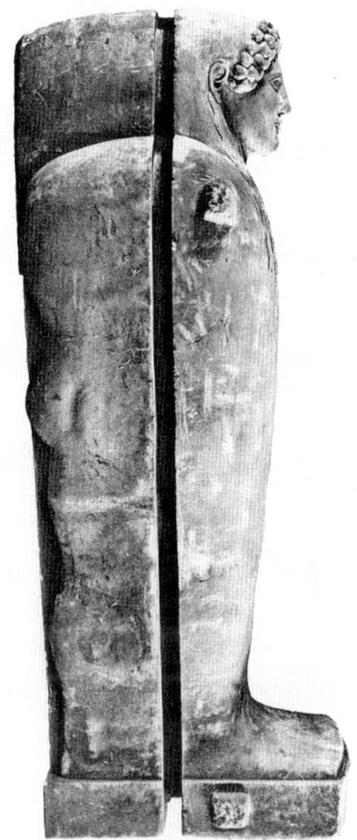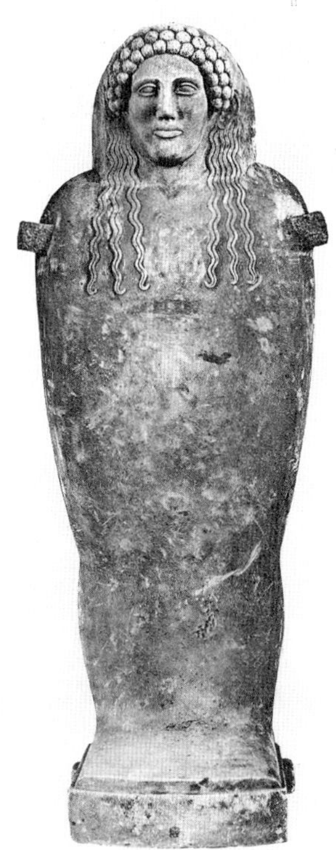

Figure 16. Left: anthropoid sarcophagus from the 'Ayaa Nekropolis near Sidon, 475–450. Istanbul, Archaeological Museum 799. Parian marble. Ht. 2.16 m. Photo: Heidelberg University Library. Center, right: anthropoid sarcophagus from the 'Ayaa Nekropolis near Sidon, 475–450. Istanbul, Archaeological Museum 798. Parian marble. Ht. 2.22 m. Photo: Heidelberg University Library.

this problem is much more acute on the Phoenician side of things, as usual.[158] Finally, neither is found outside its cultural sphere. Through a favorable lens, inconsistences or variations in the kouros—nudity for a kilt, for example—have been seen as virtuous expressions of the Greek individual spirit. Yet similar variations—the combination of Archaic snail curls with a box beard, for example—could be interpreted as weaknesses or misunderstandings by more critical interpreters of Phoenician art.[159] The "Greek spirit" does not explain the appearance of early kouroi, just as artistic fecklessness cannot explain the Sidonian theft of monumental sculpture from Egypt. It is more plausible to suppose that sixth-century Sidonians stole those sarcophagi from a freshly conquered Egypt *because they could*, whereas seventh-century Greeks in a newly stable Egypt had to make their own sculptures from the beginning. When Sidonians no longer had access to Egyptian sculpture, they innovated.

In sum, the first kouroi and first anthropoid sarcophagi can be placed into refreshingly specific historical contexts, both of which emphasize the immense religious, political, and social capital of Egypt and Egyptian art. In clear contrast to the picture mosaic, each of these sculptural forms was found only in certain locations, ones that we would call Greek and Phoenician, respectively. I would again emphasize, however, that the cultural specificity we detect in these works of sculpture does not mean that either was interested primarily in expressing culture itself—as is easily demonstrated by the kouros that was not even patronized by all elite male Hellenes. To that end, it is not unimportant that neither the kouros nor the anthropoid sarcophagus has been found everywhere in areas inhabited by Greeks and Phoenicians, even in areas with other forms of monumental sculpture or stone architecture. Far from it. What each of these case studies shows is how much conventions of interpretation—which are so often shaped by the cultural capital of Greece in modern times—shape our perceptions of works of art, from how and why art was made to what it meant to express and to whom. Many have discussed the difficulty of moving past entrenched ideas of Greek exceptionalism and modern nationalism.[160]

Of course, Greek exceptionalism was a feature of some ancient thought, too, notably in Pliny's presentation of Greek art for a Roman audience. There is some evidence that Greeks believed in their artistic exceptionalism. Pausanias comes to mind, as does, more obliquely, the funerary speech of Perikles, in which the statesman famously called on Athens to be "an education to all of Greece" for its appreciations of "grace" and "beauty" (Thuc. 2.41–43). But there is no reason for us to take this self-aggrandizing mythology at face value; indeed, we are obligated to critique it at least as much as we are obligated to critique scholarship that relies on it. One means of doing so is to change our approach, to consider what happens when we refuse to leave unchallenged the Hellenocentric logic of Orientalizing and Hellenization contact models. If we frame the kouros, picture mosaic, and anthropoid sarcophagi more neutrally as arts of contact, we can consider anew how connectivity even between the same areas can have very different artistic results. While these objects are material expressions of particular ideologies, those ideologies should not be understood as deliberately and consciously cultural, and certainly not at all "Western" or "Eastern." They are much more limited in scope and historically and socially specific in their intent.

CHAPTER 3

Exceptional Greeks
and Phantom Phoenicians

It is a basic premise of this book that contact can make critical contributions to the expression of identity in art, whether interaction is in the form of armed conflict or trade, cooperation, competition, artistic migration, emulation, or from elsewhere. Yet it is clear that the idea of "interaction" itself is tangled up in the problematic way that we divide what we call Greece from the Near East. While it is convenient and justifiable to separate what we study geographically or chronologically, the last chapter demonstrated that it is more problematic to present Greece and the Near East, or Greek, Egyptian, and Phoenician art, as *fundamentally* different. We have seen that qualities most often associated with Greek art in the later Archaic period and beyond—its superior execution, innovation, naturalism, and so forth—are openly chauvinistic. One result is that much other Mediterranean art thought to be of comparable excellence is understood as the product of Greek artists or the imitation of Greek art. Works such as picture mosaics or the Sidonian relief sarcophagi (see Chapter 5) attract attention from classical art historians who engage in a discourse largely uninterested in Near Eastern arts, a discourse that presents these works as a part of Greek art history and perpetuates stereotypes of each tradition. This way of thinking is so deeply entrenched that "one does not have to be an advocate of [the] particular theory in order to propagate it."[1] Belief in the idea of fundamental difference between Greece and "the East" is implicit in Orientalizing and Hellenization. The terms imply temporally bounded interactions of otherwise discrete traditions. For this and many other reasons Orientalizing and Hellenization are really quite easy to criticize, even while they continue to have a solid grip on scholarship.

One major hurdle is a reluctance to give up on the idea of "East and West" language that continuously reifies and reaffirms the very problematic points of view most scholarship ostensibly wishes to overcome.[2] Of course, comparative studies of broad geographical scope will always lack the refinement we might find elsewhere, in, say, the history of specific persons (biography, agency, or cognitive archaeology), individual monuments, or even a single city. But the problem is not only one of scale or particular terminology. Rather, generalization is a constant threat in comparative studies because, just like "West" and "East," "Greeks" and "Phoenicians" are arbitrary categories. They are ideal, not real, entities, imagined communities of modern scholarship most of all.[3] Ideas about "the Greeks" and "the Phoenicians" were and are malleable, contextually based, and subject to regional, disciplinary, and temporal variation. Further, the people we call Greeks in the first millennium BCE did not always conceive of themselves as a collective, and, even when they did, Hellenism in the sense of "behaving like a Greek" was only occasionally the most important part of their identity.[4] The idea of a culturally defined Hellenism is as stubbornly vague as it is commonly held.

A still greater challenge is that we have trouble recovering information that might tell us what—or *if*—Phoenicians thought of Greeks or of themselves as a collectivity.[5] So before we turn to the rise and expression of Phoenician collective identity in the following chapter, the way scholars use evidence to define and interpret these groups must first be explored in this one, in order to think about how we came to create Greek and Phoenician collectivities and assign to them artistic traditions. We will do so by following through on the problems raised in the previous chapter concerning the limitations and abilities of art to signal collective identity. In thinking through how scholarship has drawn identity on a large scale to arrive at the ideas of "Greeks" and "Phoenicians," I will show how tacit attachment to essentialism—race, most of all—encourages us to resist changing our fundamental ideas about identity. The final step is to show how we have come to apply these labels to art. I argue that while it is possible to rely on textual evidence to understand Greeks and Greek art, the very ideas of Phoenicians and Phoenician art are problematic.

Collective Identity and the Role of Race
in the Discipline

From Hesiod (especially at the end of the *Theogony*) to Herodotos and the Hellenistic geographers we learn that first-millennium Greek texts were interested in the makeup of different groups and that non-Hellenes were always an important part of the oikoumenē. Even so, Hellenes were deeply self-interested, meaning the roles played by others in their self-perceptions were usually peripheral.[6] By contrast, Phoenician histories that date before the Roman era are lacking, leaving us with no narrative to guide our understanding of their attitudes about identity or reactions to the events of the first millennium.[7] We must be content to work primarily with the rich Greek sources, both written and visual, while the Phoenician reaction can be sought in its artistic output and corpus of inscriptions. These sources indicate that the first half of the first millennium was marked by periodic connectivity and receptivity among eastern Mediterranean elites, suggesting that aristocratic mores and aspirations were driving forces encouraging contact and the expression of group identity. Identity transgressed some of the limits of geography, as made clear in gift exchange, the spread of the Lyre-Player Group seals, and perhaps also in social phenomena, such as the Greek adoption of the Phoenician alphabet.

The "Phoenicians" whom Greeks encountered would not have been members of the princely class, however, as the scattered Greek evidence assures us. Given this testimony and what we can infer from the archaeological record, it is likely that mobile Phoenicians were artisans, traders, merchants, and sailors.[8] Possibly even literacy was transferred via this group.[9] These transnational developments connected some members of Greek, Phoenician, and other societies while, at the same time, leading to deep structural changes in Hellas. Ethnic distinctiveness seems to have played an increasingly important role in the formation of the political communities that gave rise to and solidified the city-state.[10] Precisely when or if we can pinpoint transpolitical or common Greek or Phoenician identities is debatable.[11]

Some see colonization as an important catalyst for Hellenism. Most scholarship agrees that Greek self-awareness was cemented in, or at least was developed by, its confrontation with the Persians. This idea is deeply rooted in our understanding of the Classical era, specifically, and Greek history in general.[12] The Persian Wars, it is said, mark the recognition of the fundamental (cultural? ethnic? racial?) difference between Greeks and Near Eastern peoples, which in turn made various Greeks aware of their similarities. From this point, the complex idea of the supraethnic, culturally defined Hellene emerged.[13] According to this way of thinking, it was on the field of Marathon that exceptional Hellenism really took shape. The idea is too neat and has been rightly criticized. But there is no disputing the importance of the Persian Wars to Greek identity in several areas. To some Greeks of this period, anti-Persian sentiment was driven by the physical consequences of the conflict—war casualties, ruined cities, and desecrated sanctuaries. Ostentatious opposition to Persia was useful for poleis with imperial aspirations, notably Athens, a tool that could be deployed strategically and, apparently, without fear of its obvious hypocrisy.[14]

Some of the Phoenician city-states were, of course, deeply involved in this conflict from the time Cambyses created a navy out of his maritime territories. Our only sources for their involvement are Greek, and they have the familiar terminological and conceptual problems.[15] Herman Wallinga argues that Cambyses created the fleet, likely in response to the invention of the trireme and its potential to add to the strength of the Saïte navy. Our sources report that Phoenician naval service for the king began with his mostly successful Egyptian campaign in circa 525. Phoenicians were active in the war against the Greeks as early as the battle of Ladē in 494 (Hdt. 6.6, 6.14). They constructed one of the bridges over the Hellespont (Hdt. 7.34) and appeared at key battles, including Artemision (Hdt. 7.89), Salamis (Hdt. 8.85, 8.90), and Eurymedon (Thuc. 1.100; they were dismissed at Mykale according to Hdt. 9.96). In Herodotus (3.19.3) one gets the impression that Phoenicians make up most of Cambyses's fleet or were the most important part of it.[16] Phrynikhos's 476 *Phoenissae*—for which Themistokles was *chorēgos*—shows that Athenians thought Phoenicians made up the bulk of Xerxes's navy, too. Thucydides refers to the Persian navy as simply the "Phoenician fleet." Yet a Corinthian war monument erected on Salamis names both Persian and Phoenician ships,[17] and we have testimony of the use of Greek and Egyptian ships as well (such as Hdt. 3.13.1, 3.14.5, 5.33.2; Diod. Sic. 11.3.7, 11.17.2).

The fleet was part of the ongoing naval conflicts with and among Greeks throughout the fifth century (e.g., Thuc. 1.110, 1.116), even operating as an extension of Spartan power through Sparta's alliance with Tissaphernes in the Peloponnesian War (e.g., Thuc. 8.87–88). And yet, Phoenicians were rarely the specific focus of Greek antipathy in literature or in art, even in Athens where naval defense formed the basic justification for its empire.[18] (We can recall that Herodotus claims it was the Persians, not any Greeks, who blamed Phoenicians for the wars.) In this respect Phoenicians were similar: there are no examples in text or in art that I am aware of expressing antipathy toward Greeks. This does not mean, however, that the Achaemenid campaigns in which the Phoenicians participated left them feeling neutral toward Greeks. Greek sources indicate that the Phoenicians suffered some very heavy losses. These conflicts could have contributed to a Phoenician sense of collective identity, an idea I explore in the next chapter.

Collective identities can be formed around any kind of common characteristic—class, gender, age, place of birth, language, physical ability, and so forth (for the difficult idea of culture, see Chapter 1). Here the concern is what was Greek or Phoenician, individually or collectively. The question, however innocent, presupposes that these categories were significant in antiquity. There is some ground to cover first. It is prudent to begin with questions about what we mean by terms such as Greek and Phoenician: What kind of identity do they signal and what do they exclude? How are they meaningful labels of groups of people? And to what extent can we associate those terms or groups with art? The discussion that follows considers how scholarship arrived at general ideas about Greek and Phoenician identity—about Hellenism and what I call, after Jo Crawley Quinn,

Phoenicianism.[19] Neither of these identities should be confused with ethnicity, as both could encompass more than one ethnic group. But neither are these synonyms for culture, as there are many who participated in Greek or Phoenician cultural spheres that were little concerned with Hellenism and Phoenicianism. Rather, taking a page from ethnic studies, and from those who believe in the self-ascription of ethnicity, I understand each of these terms to refer to a conscious collective identity that draws from both social (artistic, linguistic) and ethnic (religious, kinship) identities but is not synonymous with either.

The path to understanding art's expression of Hellenism or Phoenicianism takes us through some tricky, but important, territory, beginning here with the roles played in classical scholarship by ethnicity and its difficult conceptual companion, race. We begin with ethnicity, as it has a clear ancient pedigree. Ethnicity comes from *to ethnos*, "band," "tribe," "people," "flocks (of animals)." It signaled a self-conscious and subjective expression of a commonality, sometimes coexisting with polis identity, and sometimes on a still greater scale (as Thuc. 1.18).[20] It follows that an individual could have multiple ethnicities: according to his or her deme, polis, region, or tribe, with regional ethnicities being by far the most common.[21] These ethnicities shifted, sometimes according to ephemeral factors such as an individual's location. So Alcibiades might be "of the Skambonidai" in Athens but simply "Athenian" when abroad.[22] In the oft-cited passage in Herodotos (8.144.2), Athenians define "to Hellēnikon [ethnos]" as common blood, language, religion, and customs. This description is deceptively straightforward, particularly when cited outside its rhetorical context. The varied usages of ethnē in Greek literature defy a single definition, not least of all within Herodotos's own history.[23] An ethnos might take shape for a variety of reasons. It is popular now to think of ethnicity as a largely aggregate ideological phenomenon that centers on perceived sameness and difference, some of which was not particularly historical. As mythical kinship was an important part of the ethnic group, the basis of a given ethnos was grounded in fictions and memories expressed through, to cite two examples, toponyms and rituals. Ethnicity could be expressed also through the material record that concerns us here, in dress and hairstyle, prestige goods (sometimes imported), symbols, and cuisine.

However appealing the open-ended idea that ethnicity is an expression of commonality over time—what can be called, generally, a common past—it is a very difficult thing to observe. Moreover, ethnic markers are unstable. Greek speech, as discussed in Chapter 1, may have been an important marker of a growing sense of Hellenic ethnicity in the Archaic era, but by the Hellenistic period, it does not reflect even a collective identity. Not only did ethnic markers vary because of changes over time or space, they varied also through deliberate manipulation in order to gain particular advantage. Ethnicity formation was a continuous and subjective process with constantly shifting criteria, which makes its study both very compelling and incredibly difficult. We cannot fully reconcile the existence of ethnē against the imprecision of the term "ethnos" and the ambiguity—sometimes apparently deliberate—of the ideas underpinning it. Of the many scholars working on ethnicity, few approach the topic in the same way or value the different kinds of evidence equally—notably, the archaeological evidence.[24] When Isokrates (*Paneg.* 50) claimed that the name Hellene was no longer a designation of ancestry (*genos*) but had become a way of thinking—a system of education (*paideia*)—he seems to challenge the idea that ethnicity and culture are independent.[25] Although these tensions are not the subject of this book, I believe that ethnicity can be expressed through the material record even though ethnicities are not stable "culture-bearing units." There is no such thing as a stable ethnic style.[26]

In contrast to ethnicity, the term "race" is not Greek in origin, but it is nevertheless very important to our understanding of ancient people. The etymology of "race" prior to the fifteenth century is disputed. It is widely believed that the concept of race was not known in antiquity, which makes race's prominence in classical scholarship that much more intriguing. The term appears in a few key places. In the LSJ, "race" is offered as a translation of genos, a definition familiar from the word "genocide" and a translation used frequently in modern scholarship, such as the Hesiodic "myth of the races" in *Works and Days*.[27] While the term and concept of race are apparently modern, the use of race to discuss ancient Greek identity might be justified, to some extent, by the biological aspect of ancient Greek self-perception. As Herodotos (8.144.2) and Isokrates (*Paneg.* 50) show, shared blood was a component of the understanding of ethnicity, even when ethnic kinship was used to trace an ultimately fictive lineage.

Clearly the Greek understanding of these ideas was quite entangled. Yet ethnos and genos were different, and both might be important to collective identity. Modern scholarship would seem to distinguish the two terms more precisely, with ethnicity expressing who you *think* you are in a subjective manner and race/tribe/people indicating *what* you are in a primordial or biological sense. But the entanglement of these ideas is a major component of modern scholarship as well, one that is dangerous to ignore, since the idea of clearly bounded races is unscientific.[28] It is because of these problems, not in spite of them, that I agree with Denise McCoskey's claim: "The concept of race remains essential to the study of antiquity."[29]

Most investigations of collective identity that concern ancient Greeks and Phoenicians engage race on some level, even, or perhaps especially, when essentialism is not overt. The tendency to view Greeks and easterners ("Orientals") in axiomatic terms is explicit in art history classifications. The field's desire to move past the idea of Greece as the birthplace of Western civilization lags behind its ability to let go of or challenge concepts rooted in Greek exceptionalism. Hellenization is explicitly about the power of the Greek origins of things, whether a stylistic and cultural superiority or, I would argue, a tacit biological one. To call a group "Hellenized" is to imply the existence of a people that is very close to a Greek one but is still, at its core, somehow not identical. In the perceived difference between a Greek and, say, a "fully Hellenized" Phoenician, I do not detect a difference in subjective collective identity but rather detect a categorical difference, one that seems difficult to distinguish from the kind of essentialism that drives the theory of race, and one that dredges up the unfortunate traditions of anti-Semitism and Orientalism in classical scholarship.[30] This is not to deny the adoption of Greek things and behaviors by Phoenicians, of course, but rather to challenge the way we characterize that adoption as change that is simultaneously fundamental *and* superficial and altogether less authentic than the *real Greek thing.* It does not matter to this way of thinking that very many of these real Greek things are also perceived to have come to Greece from the Levant during the Orientalizing period. While this selective commitment to origins seems to contradict the field's clear shift to discussing Greeks in Mediterranean terms,[31] our reluctance to let these ideas go is revealing.

I believe that "Greek" is often employed in an essential or racial sense. Greekness is associated first and foremost with language but fleshed out with a certain flexibility in geographic range and the various qualities associated with culture that still somehow draw a hard line between it and non-Greekness. Ancient Hellenes only very rarely saw themselves this way, as a group defined by certain unchangeable characteristics. "Greek" is also used in modern scholarship to signal an ethnicity, that is, the conscious subjective identity of the Hellene that coexists with ethnic identities on the level of regional, polis, and still smaller scales. It is very difficult to pin down how this idea might have worked, as the maintenance of such a large ethnic consciousness would have required tremendous intellectual effort. It was difficult enough on the level of the polis.[32] While the emphasis on paideia to structure identity in Isokrates or during the Second Sophistic comes to mind, those Hellenic identities were clearly class based.[33] Surely the differences between Hellenes were nearly always more numerous, apparent, and important than the similarities between them: in common kinship (on many scales), language (dialects do not map neatly onto Dorian or Ionian ethnic identities), and customs (clearly varied).[34]

Hellenism in other words, was not primordial, nor necessarily sustainable outside political rhetoric and poetic ideology (e.g., Pin. *Ol.* 10). Further, Panhellenism as a political or religious ideal seems to have been far more important in the Roman era than previously, although there certainly are earlier examples to be found.[35] I tend to agree with Jonathan Hall's claim that Hellenism in his sense of Hellenicity was a supraethnic idea, one that only mattered to some Hellenes some of the time, even while I dispute the idea of a stable "Greek culture." If Hellenism is a cultural identity, it is impossible to argue that it is fixed or tied directly to ethnicity or geography, which opens up interesting questions about the difference between Hellenism and what we mean by Greeks.

Like "Greek," and like many other terms we employ to signal ancient collective identities, "Phoenician" is often used in an essentialist, racial sense. Phoenician is a difficult idea for several reasons, a few of which require mention here. The fact that the word is etic and Greek is of course a great challenge (compare the so-called Skythian archer, Plate 6). Modern use of the term is no less fraught.[36] The pioneers of Phoenician studies—Renan, Perrot, and others—were unapologetic Orientalists who sometimes expressed ideas that many would now consider racist. Our simple awareness of that fact has been an established part of the academic discourse since Said's 1978 critique of de Sacy, Renan, and their legacies. Yet it has not changed the way classicists continue to characterize Phoenicia as Eastern by studying it through a colonialist lens. Further complications come from the fact that, despite gradual improvements in our knowledge, many gaps in the basic understanding of Phoenicianism persist, such as when in history Phoenician might be distinguished from Canaanite, or distinguished as a group at all.[37] No Assyrian, Achaemenid, Egyptian, or biblical texts settle the matter, either.[38] A straightforward example of the confusion can be found in the Peoples of the Past handbook series, in which Jonathan Tubb's *Canaanites* and Glenn Markoe's *Phoenicians* overlap in time and place even though each author presents his subject as a discrete ethnocultural entity.[39]

How we arrived at these ideas about Greek and Phoenician needs consideration. From its emergence in the eighteenth century, the field of classical studies, which then encompassed various subdisciplines, pursued with passion the idea of the particular, exceptional qualities of the peoples that inhabited Greece and Rome.[40] These qualities might be presented in cultural terms. Yet, as Winckelmann's pioneering 1764 *Geschichte der Kunst des Altertums* shows, they were widely understood to have emerged from essential genetic and geographical factors that distinguished Greeks and Romans from other Mediterranean peoples. These studies appeared at the very time human taxonomy became popular and European imperialism was forging qualitative differences between imperial rulers and their subjects.[41] Classics is fundamentally teleological,[42] and the field was from the start conflated with imperial, nationalist, and racial ideologies that make it difficult to this day to approach ancient Greece in dispassionate terms.

At the same time, it is important to acknowledge classical scholarship's lasting commitment to exploring the relationships between Greeks, Romans, and their neighbors. Some of the greatest achievements in early art history and archaeology were classifications that underscore the kinds of similarities and differences on which identity studies are based: Winckelmann began the process of distinguishing Greek and Roman art, Heinrich Schliemann (1822–1890) coined the descriptor "Mycenaean," and Arthur Evans (1851–1941) gave us "Minoan." Classics has been interested in identity and contact studies long before they had these names.

Persistent interest in the "classical character"[43] has taken many forms, however, the lowest and most notorious of which was its use in Nazi propaganda and eugenics. Understandably the racial approach to classical history became unpalatable during this time, as Ashley Montagu's 1942 *Man's Most Dangerous Myth: The Fallacy of Race* forcefully articulates.[44] Fleeing the specter of prejudice, other aspects of collective identity such as language became more popular scholarly topics, although often these, too, were—and still are—presented in essentialist terms that fail to distinguish them from racial or other determinisms. A generation later, however, a revised understanding of ethnicity in the field of anthropology yielded a way of understanding subjective and permeable social organization that made ethnic studies legitimate again. The work of Fredrik Barth is critical to understanding this sea change.[45] For much of the later 1970s, the 1980s, and the 1990s, studies of collective identity, often characterized specifically as ethnicity, were very much in vogue in classics. Great strides were made in recognizing the subjectivity of Greek history, and interest in the Greek perception of the oikoumenē—barbaroi, "Greek homosexuality," women, children, and other "Others"—was high.[46] Some works focused expressly and carefully on the Near Eastern impact on Greece with great sensitivity to the visual arts.

Despite the success of much of this work, or perhaps because of it, problems arose. Some of this scholarship's focused interest on Others contributed to a false impression of large-scale static binaries between Greek and barbarian (ethnicities?) that do not reflect well the complexity of the evidence and increasing sophistication of available methodologies. Much of this discussion depends on arbitrary selections of Athenian art, often without addressing their specific approaches to representation. The meaning of the term "ethnicity" and its relationship to identity seemed to become increasingly elusive as these studies proliferated.[47] Such problems have arisen from a combination of two powerful factors: the fear or refusal to talk about the extent to which racial ideologies continue to underpin our ideas about the ancient world, and the insufficient attention paid to the point that culture and ethnicity, like race, are *theories*, not ontological categories. Understandably, there are those who believe that the time for ethnicity studies has passed and who now prefer to speak instead more generally of identity. The term "identity," too, is rather problematic, however, when it serves merely as a way to elude precision.[48]

Beginning in the late 1990s and early 2000s, more classical scholars were willing to engage directly the idea of race.[49] Again classics was following on broader trends and the increased popularity of other taboo or seemingly passé topics, such as environmental determinism.[50] Global politics in this period—the end of apartheid, ethnic cleansing and genocide[51] in the Bosnian Wars and Rwanda, the Kurdish independence movement, the Afghan and Iraq wars, the debates concerning immigration and terrorism—have helped race stay in the spotlight. In the United States the fascination with race is persistent even as it maintains its ability to provoke discomfort. Although in 1997 the American Anthropological Association called unsuccessfully for the United States Census to do away with race as a category, the Census and equal-opportunity surveys signal that race and ethnicity are still among the most valued metrics of American identity.[52] A similar commitment to and confusion about the meaning of race and its relationship to identity, physical appearance, institutions, and behaviors is an ongoing issue in classics as well, especially in classical art history.

To illustrate these points I will turn briefly to the intellectual setting and reception of Martin Bernal's three-volume *Black Athena* series (1987, 1991, 2006),[53] which engages many of the very same topics as this book. The first volume appeared nine years after Said's *Orientalism* and just four years after the publication of Frank Snowden's *Before Color Prejudice*.[54] Bernal's work has clear similarities to both. Although it can be compared to Said's postcolonial critique of classical Eurocentrism,[55] *Black Athena*, while also very unforgiving of traditional discourse, was not interested in theory. Bernal was a positivist, like Snowden. In *Before Color Prejudice* and its 1970 predecessor *Blacks in Antiquity*, Snowden demonstrated that skin-color prejudice was not a feature of classical art. What his argument means in terms of collective identity is rather confused by the focus on skin color, however, because skin color was not a major interest of Greeks and Romans in their perceptions of themselves or others.[56] As Snowden admits, while Greeks and Romans were certainly aware of the existence of black skin,[57] and of the difference between it and their own, lighter skin color, they did not consider themselves to be, in contrast, white.[58]

John Dee has shown that Greeks and Romans had no specific vocabulary to describe their own skin color. By contrast he cites evidence that Greeks did not consider themselves "λευκοί by nature."[59] Odysseus is once described as black or at least very dark in appearance (*Od.* 16.175). Elsewhere Homer describes Achilles shining in his dark bronze armor, an aesthetic comparison that speaks to the visual appeal of bronze statuary.[60] White skin was associated sometimes with women as an unnatural feature and with some non-Greek people, such as Persians, who lacked *andragathia*—manly virtue—as conveyed through swarthiness (see Plates 21 and 22).[61] Such passages suggest that both relatively light and relatively dark skin could be remarkable to Greeks. In art, skin-tone colors were varied according to the conventions of the medium. For example, while women were often painted white on pottery, Vinzenz Brinkmann has shown that the skin of korai such as Phrasikleia was painted "a very light ochre brown, or orange-brown" (see Plates 7 and 8).[62] Although it began to emerge in the late antique and medieval periods, the idea of "whiteness" did not exist fully before it was invented in the sixteenth to eighteenth centuries in concert with the beginning of the African slave trade and, later, the creation of scientific racism. Whiteness was first understood as a meaningful feature of antiquity only when Winckelmann (1717–1768) mapped it onto Greek ideal beauty and the perfect, unified surfaces of marble sculpture.[63]

Tanner has pointed out that "no field better illustrates" Bernal's critique of systemic prejudice in ancient studies than art history.[64] As a white Englishman with newly discovered Jewish ancestry, Bernal arguably shared with many others—including at times Burkert, Droysen, Momigliano, and Snowden—an interest in "working out his own cultural issues on the canvas of antiquity."[65] But unlike the texts of any of these other scholars, *Black Athena* sparked the popular imagination, while much of its scholarly reaction can be characterized as outrage.[66] Bernal was trained as a Sinologist, and although autodidacticism is a tradition long established in classics, his work does not rise to the high level of the work of notable amateurs like Michael Ventris (1922–1956). *Black Athena* is prone to errors of fact and interpretation. It relies on problematic, and by most accounts false, theories of Egyptian and Phoenician colonization of Greece and takes for granted the historicity of debunked ideas like the "Dorian Invasion." Bernal's use of sociology is inconsistent; his ideas are often contradictory or opaque. His claim that nineteenth-century classicism was the root of racism in the Western tradition is selective and exaggerated.[67] So not only are many of the facts wrong, the approach, too, is poor.

Why, then, did what appears to be a mediocre scholarly project incite such a strong response? Bernal struck a nerve. It is clear that he embraced his status as an alternative historian, drawing inspiration from others who made their own very bold, diffusionist claims on the basis of flawed linguistic and archaeological evidence.[68] His project has a deliberately pugilistic tone, and he reached out to Afrocentrists for support for his work.[69] These strategies shifted the discourse away from scholarly self-critique and the innovative use of data to position *Black Athena* and its supporters as judges of the failings of the modern university. The marketing and popular perception of Bernal's text, more than the obvious weakness of his scholarship, drove his detractors.[70] The strength of the response to *Black Athena* was both more vigorous and more palatable because Bernal was a tenured faculty member at an elite American institution, Cornell; because he had an elite pedigree, his Cambridge degree; and because, unlike most Afrocentrists, he was white.[71]

Bernal's "insider" status lessened the sense, to some, that critique of *Black Athena* was overtly racist or another episode in the so-called culture wars waged between social conservatives and various opposing groups.[72]

There are also lessons to be learned from the project itself. While the title *Black Athena* equates a black skin color to Egyptianness, Bernal does not present race as an ontological category. He understood race correctly as an ideological construct. He argued that racism was systemic and might be perpetuated unwittingly, a point that seems to have been missed by some of his harshest critics. For these reasons, his work continues to be useful not only for self-identifying Afrocentrists but also for those who engage the ideological basis of race in order to explore the "institutional patterns and social practices" that contribute to racism.[73] Bernal's greatest contribution might be how openly he showed that race was integral to classical scholarship's perception of the past—such as the belief in the whiteness of Greeks—when most scholars are content to tiptoe around these issues, preferring to cloak the particular classical "character" in the cover of culture.[74]

The explanations for the hesitancy to address race head-on are complex. The use of classics in racist discourse is clearly important, but the distaste for race has only increased in recent decades, and not only in classical studies.[75] Another is the popular idea that neither race nor racism was part of the classical worldview. The argument underpins both Snowden's and Bernal's projects, albeit in divergent ways. Yet it is easily refuted by even a cursory read of the environmentally deterministic *Airs, Waters, Places* and, according to Susan Lape, the Athenian citizenship law.[76] Still another challenge is the fear, one that I share, that the discussion of race will bolster a belief in race as a valid human classification. While recent studies do not try to assert the axiomatic existence of Greek, Ionic, or Athenian races, with some disputing outright the existence of race,[77] they do run the risk of revivifying the racial ideologies lingering in the legacy of classicism or perpetuating the unacceptable prejudice in the ancient source material by presenting it neutrally. Benjamin Isaac's important 2004 study *The Invention of Racism in Classical Antiquity* is notable for its care in handling these very issues.

Representation in Greek Art

Thus far we have seen that probing the modern terms of convenience "Greek" and "Phoenician" reveals that they rest on some difficult essentialist ideas that have an uneasy relationship with ancient Hellenes and "Phoenicians" and modern racial modes of thinking. Now it is necessary to consider briefly the representational strategies of Greeks and Phoenicians, to describe, in other words, what we mean by Greek and Phoenician art. The discussion starts with Greek art, because it offers, as usual, a richer record. In Greek art the visual expression of identity takes multiple forms, as the arts were used to construct ideal and, to a lesser extent, negative character, both emic and etic. It can be argued that all Greek representation is a form of self-representation, including also art that makes foreigners its subject.

Greeks are not by any means the first people to show foreigners in their art. Monumental Near Eastern and Egyptian art frequently shows foreigners, usually through imagery of conflict, conquest, and propitiation in relief, sculpture, and wall painting.[78] Phoenician art is less interested in the subject of conflict between different visually marked people, though examples, such as the Alexander Sarcophagus, can be cited and are discussed in Chapter 5's consideration of hybridity. State-sponsored art is one seemingly clear context for the expression of collective identity; it could be used to promote civic identity, as seen, famously, in the Parthenon. Of course, not all visual expressions of official civic identity were made on such a large scale; horoi and other inscription-bearing stelai, official weights and measures, and coins were important small-scale sociopolitical markers.

Greek art's commitment to natural subject matter and animation is balanced by its preference for rich materials, pattern, tendency toward virtuoso display, and use of arbitrary techniques to stipulate its object. Like the use of silver for teeth and quartz for eyes in works of bronze, *technē* itself ultimately underscored artifice. Conventional symbols (such as Alexander's *anastolē*) and denotation ("I am the *sēma* of Phrasikleia") were just two of Greek art's arbitrary representational tools. Our evidence suggests that nearly all sculpture honoring people required denotation—writing of some sort—to identify the honorand, votary, or deceased.[79] All of these tendencies indicate that Greek art operated in a manner at once more sophisticated and more ambiguous than mimesis in the Platonic (*Resp.* 10.596e–597e) or Aristotelian (*Poet., Metaph.*) sense of copying.[80] Here we can recall the value of the kouros as a recognizable type and how the schematic formal approach to the human form seen also in the Classical era's Doryphoros is a key component of its admiration, both modern and ancient.[81]

Greek art of the Classical period may be explicitly engaged in the discussion of what it means to represent.[82] Monumental anthropomorphic and zoomorphic painting and sculpture were celebrated for their ability not only to please but also to persuade, even fool, the eye by using a combination of anatomical accuracy and implied action. The bronze cow sculpted by Myron and dedicated on the Athenian akropolis in circa 450 was lauded especially for its pleasing and skillful naturalism (Pliny *HN* 34.57–58).[83] Yet even highly naturalistic art was not very much concerned with representing individual objects (see Xen. *Mem.* 3.10.1–5), unless we believe that Myron's cow was representing one cow in particular. Nor did naturalistic art have a straightforward relationship with verisimilitude, meaning that some artistic conventions, such as nudity, have a logic all their own, one that is neither internally consistent nor, as discussed in the previous chapter, possible to map directly on Greek behaviors.

The astonishment expressed at such length in the more than thirty epigrams on Myron's cow, and in Pliny's description of the competition between the painters Zeuxis and Parrhasios (*HN* 35.61–66), draws attention to their artists, to their technē, and thence to the pleasing disingenuousness of the works.[84] The same can be said for portraits of this period that express simultaneously an individual, a generic archetype (athlete, hero, statesman), and a portrait type (standing male nude, standing draped female). Such thinking allowed reinscription of portraits of even famous individuals with no alteration to the likeness (e.g., Paus. 1.18.3).[85] Some famous portraitists, such as the late classical master Lysippos, were especially adept at wrestling specific traits, whether real physical features or deliberately constructed ideal ones, into typologically appropriate portraits that gave the impression or effect of somatic realism.[86] The evidence of artists working from live models and casts is first attested in the fourth century, but even then, as with Lysippos's portraits of Alexander, the final result was very much a manipulation (Plut. *Mor.* 335b).[87]

Greek artwork was not necessarily concerned with originality, either, in the sense of the unique—a point to which we will return. The two Riace bronzes, for example, likely either came from the same model or one was cast from a mold made of the other.[88] The practices of reusing models and replicating types were standard in both major sculptural media because Greek art was highly conventional. Our difficulty in agreeing on who is represented in works such as the Riace Warriors or the Doryphoros is further revealing of the complexities of representation and underscores how unimportant specific physical features could be to the understanding of what was seen. In both cases, attributes, context, or inscriptions were needed to lend the works the particularity that their highly naturalistic bodies lacked. Naturalistic representations functioned also as symbols and allegories, as, for example, Lysippos's Kairos, "Point of Decision." Standing on one toe as if running, stretching its wings, and balancing scales on the tip of a razor blade, the Kairos underscores the intimate relationships between physical naturalism, conceptual abstraction, and meaning in allegorical art. The point is made elegantly in Poseidippos's third-century epigram in which the statue speaks to an inquisitor.[89]

Much Greek art is interested in communicating ideal traits, as evinced by the proliferation of certain somatic and character types and themes rich with metaphorical value. Yet Greek art is interested also in contrast—in difference—in both the physical and the ideological sense. The kouros embodies both, balancing its typological consistency with individual poikilia, which together put the world of the kouros in the realm of the aristocratic and divine and at some distance from that of the middling and lower classes. The kouros shows how contact could be a very important contributor to the expression of identity in art. But given the complex relationship between representation and "the real" sketched briefly here, it is somewhat puzzling that works of Greek art, both monumental sculpture and, especially, vase painting, are often treated as documents of Greek observations of historical Others. Representations we know to be fictitious continue to be identified as though documentary, as when the archer in Plate 6 is identified as "a Skythian" through vague associations of costume and character.[90] This does not mean that art has no value as a record of physical appearances or behaviors. Rather images, like the written record, are only more pieces of evidence deserving scrutiny. The study of representation, like the study of identity, should not be allowed to languish in essentialism.

The complex logic of representation is evident in heroic archetypes, which, excepting beefy Herakles or child heroes, are usually physically indistinguishable from one another and from humans, contributing to our inability to determine whether the Doryphoros represents a man or Achilles. Memnon is a good example of a foreign figure who was somatically indistinguishable from a Greek (see Plate 9).[91] He is a generic, aristocratic hero, his Ethiopian origins suggested sometimes not at all, as in Plate 9, and elsewhere by pairing him with one or more attendant figures with coarse, curly hair and other physiognomic features that recall Egyptian art's conventions for Nubians.[92] He is almost never shown with Ethiopian physical markers, though examples exist, such as the red-figure krater of circa 490–480 where his hair is rendered in relief dots (see Plate 10).[93] Rarely is he shown in foreign costume, though we do have the Attic red-figure column krater of circa 450 on which Memnon battles Amazons on horseback while clad in a *chitōniskos cheiridōtos*, patterned trousers, and Greek helmet.[94]

As discussed above, color was very important to painting, sculpture, and architecture, yet color was not necessarily naturalistic. The technical limits of black-and red-figure vase painting usually make it impossible to know the extent to which black skin alone sometimes signaled "Ethiopian." There are a few examples, however, where black is used deliberately for skin color, as on the plastic drinking horn of circa 460 showing a boy battling a crocodile (see Plate 11).[95] His black skin would have played off the once-green crocodile and contrasts the visual logic of the red figure on the horn itself. Antiheroes, such as the Egyptian pharaoh Bousiris, on the other hand, could be represented in a variety of non-Greek ways. Miller has demonstrated how Bousiris was shown by Athenian vase painters in different costumes in the late Archaic and Classical periods, from Egyptian pharaoh to generalized tyrant to Persian great king.[96] In other words, even when Bousiris's dress was rendered with specificity, it was not necessarily concerned with ethnic accuracy. There is a kind of parallel here with naturalism.

Already in the late sixth century the long-lapelled cap (*kidaris*) and patterned costume were generalized as what has been called "Oriental," "Eastern," or "Skythian" dress. This costume was used for some Amazons, as seen in the skyphos of circa 510–500 shown in Plate 8, and for Trojan Paris (a rendering common in the later fifth century and ubiquitous in the fourth). Soon these costumes would be extended to a variety of other characters, sometimes inconsistently, as with Andromeda in Athenian pottery.[97] The only Phoenician to appear in Greek art is Kadmos, the founder of Thebes and father of the Greek alphabet (see Figure 1). He is never Orientalized. On Athenian, Lakonian, and south Italian vases, Kadmos is shown in standard heroic ways, in full armor or wearing some combination of chitōniskos, chlamys, pilos or petasos, and sandals or boots but otherwise nude. His identity is made clear through inscription or context, usually battling the dragon of Thebes, which is also how he appears in Etruscan funerary art, or sowing its teeth.[98] This is the same way Kadmos appears on Roman coins of Tyre.[99]

Representation in Phoenician Art

It is more difficult still to summarize the approaches to representation in Phoenician art, because, simply put, "Phoenician art" as a category is difficult. Even though objects are on record as early as the 1624 discovery of a terracotta anthropoid sarcophagus on Malta, sustained academic and museological interest in Phoenician art history began only in the mid-nineteenth century.[100] From these early days, the corpus of Phoenician art was drawn widely from the Mediterranean and characterized comparatively, often in opposition to the classical. As Vella has suggested, for Grand Tourists and academics such as Winckelmann, "who often made the crossing to Malta from the port of Girgenti (modern Agrigento) after having been to see the Greek temples . . . 'Punic' came to represent what 'Greek' clearly was not."[101] The idea of a Phoenician artistic style first emerged through study of discoveries of metal bowls by Layard and others. The sometimes dismissive and prejudicial attitudes toward Phoenicians and Phoenician art found in these early publications has persisted, and not only from outside Near Eastern studies.[102]

The context in which the archaeology of Phoenicia began was likewise colonialist. One must travel to Istanbul and Paris to see the most famous Sidonian sarcophagi. There are parallels here with Greek art history, but a major difference is that relatively few North American and European scholars make the trip to Lebanon and Syria, whereas Athens has some twenty foreign schools and a number of active foreign excavations. A lack of personal familiarity with the terrain, people, and institutions in Syria and Lebanon, and to a lesser extent northern Israel, as well as the ongoing political instability of that region contribute to the idea that Phoenicia is peripheral. Although Phoenician art history and archaeology have developed substantially in recent years, a clear picture of a Phoenician artistic tradition remains elusive.[103] Weak support for a collective Phoenician identity in the Greek and Near Eastern textual sources seems to be verified by what remains of Phoenician art, making the use of "Phoenician" to describe a style of art quite problematic. As I claim in the Introduction, the disconnect between Phoenician art history and Phoenician archaeology is one of the most pressing issues facing our understanding of Phoenicianism. Ironically, the problem is quite acute in the Iron Age, meaning that the worked ivory and metal bowls that formed the basis of our initial understanding of Phoenician art are suspect (see Figures 3 and 4).

One clear solution is to deal directly with material that has been excavated in Phoenicia. The archaeological record is poorly known in mainland Phoenicia for the Iron Age, however. While it is tempting to ascribe to lack of excavation the problem of discovering the "true" Phoenician origins of worked ivory and metal bowls, the idea is probably fantastical. We have very little direct evidence of metal working or ivory working on the mainland.[104] Published areas of the well-excavated Sarepta (Sarafand, Lebanon) yielded fewer than ten ivory objects, only three of which are figurative, and not even one scrap of a "Phoenician" metal bowl.[105] And, as Hans Niemeyer and others point out, neither bowls nor ivories appear in the main colonies, not at Carthage, Malta, Sicily, or elsewhere.[106] Even Markoe, the foremost expert on "Phoenician" metal bowls, admitted regarding those from Assyria, "we simply do not know where these vessels were produced."[107] The contrast with widely exported objects from Greek poleis, such as sixth-century Corinthian pottery, is clear and significant. Several other scholars have pointed out the keen problems of settling on sites of manufacture, suggesting the bowls were traded or moved as booty, were made by itinerant craftsmen, or were made in a variety of locations by local craftsmen.[108] Each theory is speculative, though the idea that these objects should be assigned to specific cultural or ethnic groups is perhaps the thorniest problem.

Marian Feldman has recently argued that the worked ivories and bowls should not be assigned to specific Syrian or Phoenician workshops.[109] She believes that it is so difficult to assign these objects to particular regions because doing so is an academic exercise doomed by the connectivity, decentralized networks, and, as she calls it, "mobility of style" that created demand for ivory inlays and metal bowls among members of a shared habitus.[110] In other words, in using the terms "Phoenician," "North Syrian," and "Etrurian" to classify these objects, we have, in effect, fixed imperfect evidence into false categories, presenting cogent ethnically and geographically determined groups for objects that were in fact produced in a number of locations that cannot be divided ethnically or geographically according to their findspots, styles, or iconographies.[111] For Feldman, following Bourdieu's idea of taste, "style *constitutes* community identity rather than simply *reflects* it."[112] She argues that the ivories are best called generally Levantine, although she does not, of course, deny that stylistic differences within them are apparent and important. With the bowls, the very objects first used to identify a "Phoenician style," even that loose Levantine designation is probably too narrow. Vella has arrived at a similar conclusion, reframing the metal bowls as "boundary objects" composed of the "encoded knowledge of connections between landscapes and practices far and wide, bridging old traditions and dissimilar places."[113] I agree that the impetus for the metal bowls and worked ivories was most likely ongoing Mediterranean contact in a fashion comparable to the Lyre-Player Group seals and foreshadowing the Hellenistic picture mosaic. Assigning manufacture of these objects to phantom Phoenicians seems spurious.[114] Even if we are to do so, we cannot argue that such objects were important to them: we do not have evidence that Phoenicians used them.

If we are to cleave these objects from Phoenicians, what remains of Iron Age "Phoenician art"? One class of excavated object that can be associated with the "incipient Phoenician culture" of this period is bichrome pottery, which is succeeded by black-on-red and, later still, red slip (see Plate 1).[115] These objects are not made exclusively on the Phoenician mainland, however, and do not continue seamlessly, or at all in some cases, into later periods. Circulation of pottery and change in ceramic production is, of course, natural even if it frustrates efforts to isolate Phoenicians in the archaeological record. There are still more challenges.[116] Several key sites, such as Arwad, have not been systematically excavated (see Map 3). Others, such as Tyre, have impressive but uneven excavations owing to dense modern occupation. In Tyre's case, the modern city stretches from the mainland over the mole originally constructed by Alexander in 332 and onto the former island. So while exposure of Roman and later periods is fairly extensive, the best published information to date about the Iron Age city comes from a sounding.[117] It is not unusual to see scholars summon images and descriptions of Tyrian tribute to the Assyrians to flesh out this picture, but it is not possible to use these sources to separate items of Tyrian manufacture from other amassed wealth.[118]

Sidon likewise has dense modern occupation limiting archaeological activity, although the ongoing "College Site" excavations carried out by the British Museum in collaboration with the Department of Antiquities of Lebanon have contributed much to our understanding of the city. Some impressive finds—such as a forty-meter-high mound of used murex shells for the making of purple dye—offer a window on to what was once a great center of commercial activity. Most impressive of all in Tyre and Sidon are the cemeteries. Tyre's al-Bass cemetery has yielded a number of inscribed and iconic Iron Age tombstones of nonelites.[119] South of Sidon is the Dakerman cemetery with hundreds of tombs dating from the Bronze

Age to the Roman period. Recent excavations at Beirut have added to our poor knowledge of the early city, including the tenth- or ninth-century glacis. At Sarepta, a shrine was excavated that dates to the second half of the seventh century. Offerings were presented on a table near a cutting thought to be for an incense altar or standing stone (in this case, a cut stone) that seems to have been associated with the cult of Aštart.[120] More than any other major city-state, Byblos has produced very impressive finds, especially from its Bronze Age tombs and its "Obelisk" and Ba'alat Gebal temples that continued in use into the Hellenistic period.[121] Iron Age Byblos is still poorly understood, however, even though this period coincided with the city's greatest power.[122]

In sum, we do not have a clear picture of what these city-states looked like in the Iron Age, although we have a better understanding of mortuary spaces and sanctuaries. Finds include the aforementioned Cypro-Phoenician pottery as well as figurative terracottas and masks, the occasional carved ivory or gold object, imported Greek pottery (especially at Tyre), and very few monumental objects. These include the sarcophagus of Ahiram of Byblos (thirteenth century or later; the inscription is tenth century), the relief of a storm god from 'Amrit or Tell Kazel (ninth or eighth century), an eighth-century Egyptianizing striding figure in high relief from Tyre, and the statue of Pharaoh Osorkon I given to Eliba'al of Byblos, the last certainly a gift imported from Egypt.[123] By comparison to these monumental arts and elite offerings, nonelite Iron Age funerary stelai can seem cohesive. Fifty-two stelai from the Khaldé (near Beirut), Dakerman (Sidon), Tell el-Burak (Sidon), and al-Bass (Tyre) cemeteries were recently surveyed by Sader.[124] These are generally crude affairs bearing inscriptions and simple linear decorations: ankhs that may or may not be related to Tanit (discussed in Chapters 2 and 5), crescent moons, disks, uraei, heads, standing stones, and other symbols. Those that could be dated on archaeological or paleographic grounds range from the tenth to the sixth centuries, which fits well with the chronology of the Tyre al-Bass cemetery proposed by its excavators. The distribution of the stelai is, however, erratic, with none coming from north of Beirut—so, none from Byblos—and with the largest cemetery of all, Dakerman, yielding only one, compared to the many from al-Bass. The Iron Age tombstones might be a mostly Tyrian phenomenon.[125]

Our understanding of the archaeology of mainland Phoenicia in the Persian, Hellenistic, and Roman periods is usually better, if still woefully incomplete. Excavations at Beirut have revealed whole Persian period insulae (Figure 17).[126] Sidon's Persian and Hellenistic elite cemeteries of Magharat Abloun and 'Ayaa once held the looted Egyptian, anthropoid, and relief sarcophagi. Near Tyre, Kharayeb's Persian and Hellenistic sanctuary deposit yielded more than a thousand terracottas.[127] The Persian and Hellenistic sanctuaries at Umm el-'Amed and Bostan

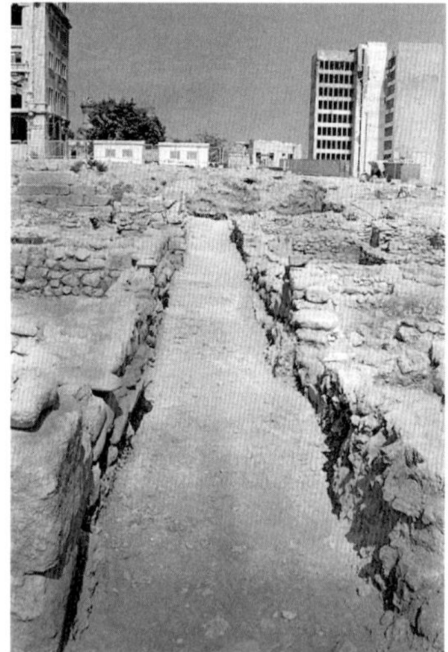
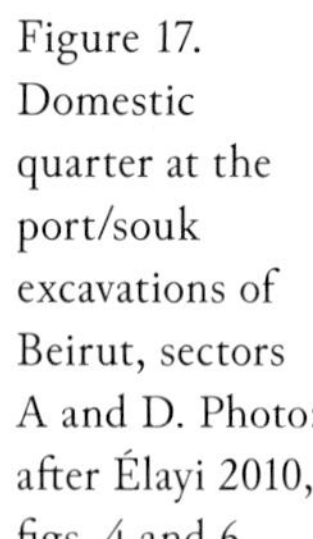
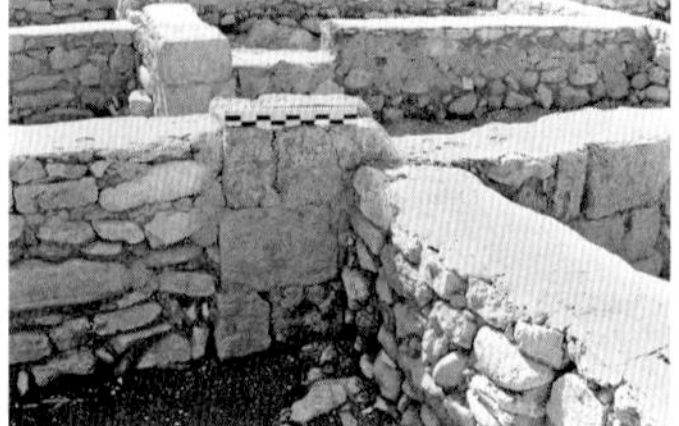

Figure 17. Domestic quarter at the port/souk excavations of Beirut, sectors A and D. Photo: after Élayi 2010, figs. 4 and 6.

esh-Sheik (near Sidon), both of which are discussed in the next chapter, were loaded with dedications of different genres, techniques, and styles. At the other extreme of the mainland is 'Amrit, the mainland port of Arwad, well known for its Persian and Hellenistic remains.[128] Its most famous finds are a sanctuary, two monumental stone tombs, and smaller naiskoi. No pre-Roman Phoenician temple is better preserved than the so-called Ma'abed, a porticoed courtyard with a stone shrine at its center set in basin cut from bedrock (Figure 18). A nearby offerings pit contained hundreds of fragments of limestone sculpture. Although some scholars are keen to privilege various external influences on its design, the sanctuary is demonstrably Levantine.[129] The statues from the offerings pit that could be typed, however, are Cypro-Archaic.

Even this brief look at archaeological remains suggests it is unwise to attempt to circumscribe Sidonian, Tyrian, or other architectural or artistic *styles*, and incredibly difficult to assemble even a general "Phoenician" one.[130] We are not yet able to delineate precise phases of artistic activity in Phoenician art history, and archaeological remains are inconsistent from site to site, making it is nearly impossible to talk about developments over time across genres. Rather, we must look within them. First, there are some architectural features and decorations that are found in disparate sites from the Iron Age and well into the Hellenistic period, such as crenellations and uraei, as well as the ashlar pier wall construction technique (seen in Figure 17).[131] The Yehawmilk and Umm el-'Amed stelai (see Figures 19, 33–34), and Egyptianizing/Phoenician and Cypriot/Cypriot-type sculpture in the round from Sidon, Umm el-'Amed, and 'Amrit (see Figure 32) show that there were many approaches to sculptural representation available at around the same time in

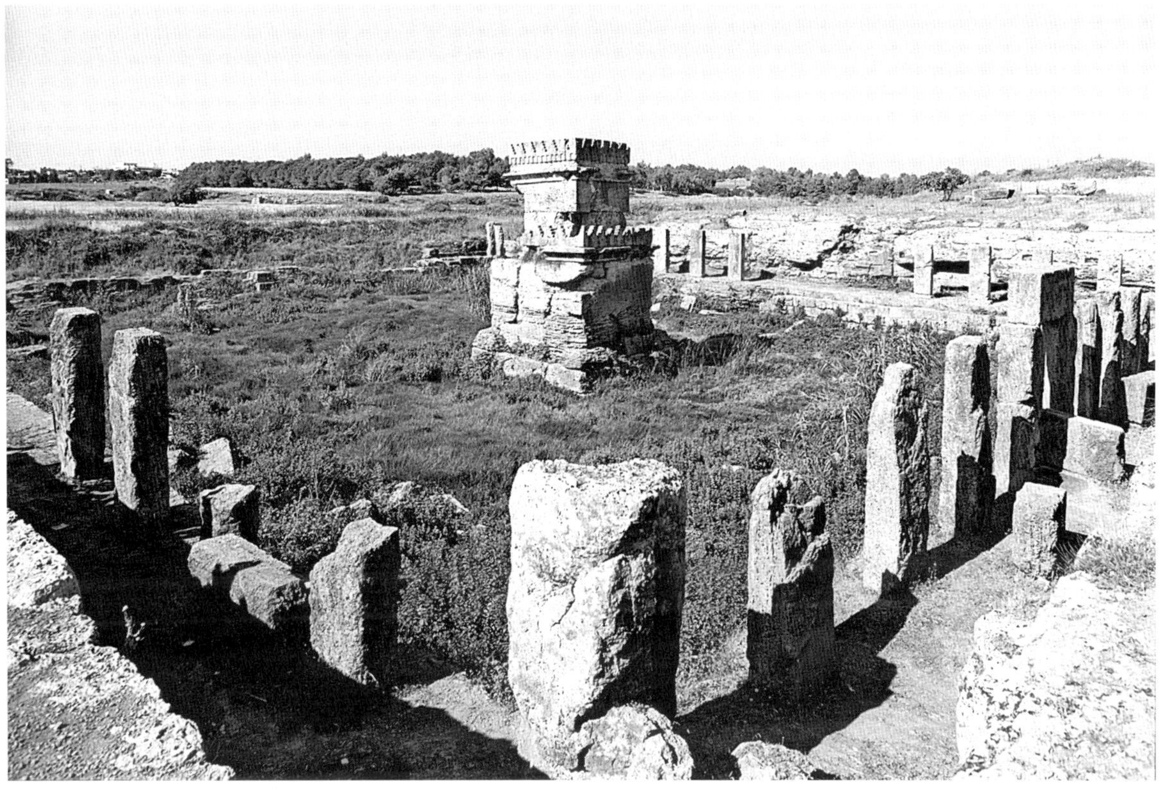

Figure 18. The sanctuary at 'Amrit. Photo: Jerzy Strzelecki, available under the terms of the GNU Free Documentation License.

the Phoenician mainland, even among the Sidonian elite. Only certain genres of sculpture, such as the anthropoid sarcophagi or Aštart thrones,[132] are unique to Phoenicia or Phoenicians, the former including Punic areas.

From there things get more difficult. There are the genres of art in which Phoenicians might have played a role that should be instead understood as generally Levantine or broader still, such as the worked ivories, metal bowls, Lyre-Player Group seals, painted ostrich eggs, and carved tridacna shells. There are other artistic traditions to which Phoenicians are thought to have contributed that includes glass, faience (sometimes imitation faience), and metal amulets, scarabs, and other seals; metal and terracotta figurines and masks/protomes/plaques; ceramic and bone vessels and small objects; and a variety of metal objects from gold jewelry to bronze votive razors to silver coins. Although imported painted vases, primarily from Athens, are a component of the Phoenician material record from the first half of the fifth century, there is no contemporary Phoenician figurative pottery tradition. (Some painted ostrich eggs have anthropomorphic features.) Traces of color are found on reliefs, naiskoi, and monumental sculpture, and Hellenistic era tombs show that at least by that time wall painting was part of Phoenician art, but it is difficult to know how extensive the monumental painting tradition was.[133] "Tyrian purple" was, of course, famous (Pliny *HN* 9.127), although archaeological evidence shows that other people made blue, red, and purple dye from the murex snail.[134] Garments woven from dyed fabrics might have been finished at the point of final sale, so they cannot be associated absolutely with Phoenician craftsman. There is no evidence of illusionism in Phoenician art before the later Hellenistic era when it is found in, for example, a few preserved mosaics that can be associated with Phoenicia or Phoenicians, such as the dolphin mosaic at Delos discussed in the previous chapter (Plates 4–5).

There are some observable similarities to Greek art that are probably coincidental. For example, Phoenicians are thought to have put a premium on rich materials, but Phoenician art had a lively tradition in the cheaper ones, especially terracottas. Both artistic traditions are anthropomorphic, sometimes schematizing the human form, sometimes exploring it naturalistically, and nearly always relying on iconography, context, or inscriptions to identify individuals. Both traditions valued pattern (and presumably the skill it took to achieve it) and made judicious use of symbol (such as the ankh and caduceus) and allegory (such as the Master of Animals). Both have a tradition of aniconic representation as well. In sum, we do not yet have a handle on what constitutes a Phoenician style of art or what belongs or not to Phoenician art history.

A few different approaches to art from the Persian-Hellenistic periods are currently being explored. Some publications concern the scientific presentation of excavated material, as in the aforementioned work of Sader. Rolf Stucky's publications of the Eshmun sanctuary at Bostan esh-Sheik are invaluable for our overall understanding of the site and for organizing the approach to specific monuments. Stucky is interested in culture contact, but he neither takes a critical approach to the idea of "Greek influence" nor to the terminology we use to distinguish Greek from Near Eastern.[135] Katje Lembke's monographs of the anthropoid sarcophagi and sculpture from 'Amrit are essential reading.[136] In both, she stresses the gathering of information from archaeological context, especially important with art resistant to easy stylistic analysis, as well as scientific testing. Like Stucky, Lembke's interest in this material, and in who made what and when, does not necessarily encourage reflection on how we move from style and technique to the ethnicity of the artist. Josette Élayi's strategy to promote the study of Persian period Phoenicia is relentless publishing. Her work emphasizes Phoenician initiative while remaining fairly conservative in its framing of Phoenicia's eventual Hellenization.[137]

Some recent publications pursue new interpretive strategies. Vadim Jigoulov has stressed the importance of treating Persian period Phoenicia as part of the

Achaemenid empire, using coin imagery especially to make his case.[138] Jessica Nitschke's critiques of Hellenization ask scholars to pay more attention to what makes sanctuaries and monumental sculpture Phoenician.[139] Jennifer Stager's publication of a Greek-Phoenician funerary stele from Athens (discussed in the next chapter) explores visual and textual bilingualism as well as the importance of Phoenician patronage in shaping art.[140] What all of these studies have in common is their focus on objects that were or are thought to be excavated in Phoenicia, or were made or patronized by Phoenicians. Altogether they suggest that the art history of the Persian-Hellenistic periods has a promising future.

Improbable Collectivities: Exceptional Greeks and Phantom Phoenicians

Racial and colonial modes of thinking led directly to the construction of Greeks, Phoenicians, and their art histories in the eighteenth and nineteenth centuries. Yet these modes are not located only in the past; they continue to encourage resistance to structural changes in thinking about their subjects. Art history from the eighteenth century has had a profound impact on ideas about the Greeks. Winckelmann's work on Greek art was an important expression of emerging Western values, qualities that were lacking, in his opinion, in Egyptian and Phoenician art.[141] The consequences of this mindset are arguably greater still for the way we have constructed Phoenicia and its artistic traditions. It will not do to call Phoenicia "a Mediterranean state of mind"[142] or to use "Phoenician" to describe a category of objects that coalesce loosely around the coastal Levant and the objects conveyed by "men in boats."[143] Such perspectives do not fit even the limited evidence we have, and they serve to reduce the idea of Phoenician culture to Orientalism itself.[144]

Important as Phoenicians seem in the Iron Age Mediterranean, from the development of trade to colonization to the transmission of culture, we do not really know who they were or *if* they were as a collective entity.[145] They did not seem to share a pantheon.[146] Of the more than forty mentions of Phoenicians in Herodotos, only one or two seem concerned with a region in the Levant. We cannot be certain that even Greeks had cause to view these people collectively, although when they did so, the reasons seem to have been linguistic. In Near Eastern sources we find more persuasive evidence of some of these same people using a common language and associated with maritime prowess, control of strategic ports, and natural resources. Domination of some city-states over others is attested, as in the ninth century when Tyre's power grew under Ithoba'al I (r. 887–856) to eventually encompass Sidon. These episodes might be evidence of political confederations,[147] and it is through Tyre's maritime expansion that use of Phoenician was spread to Anatolia.

What we seem to have in the Iron Age is evidence of what we call, following Greek literary sources, Phoenicians, but no conclusive evidence of Phoenicia as a place or a Phoenician collective identity.[148] The existence of Phoenicia as a particular, even if dynamically interpreted, place would seem a prerequisite to the existence of "a" Phoenician culture. In this period, it is one for which we have only tentative evidence. While it might be tempting to dismiss such problems as unfortunate gaps in the historical record, or to suggest that Phoenician history suffers merely from very "limited chronological resolution,"[149] I believe it is preferable to avoid creating Phoenicians where none can be shown to exist. To be clear, I do not deny that there were Levantine people who used the language we call Phoenician inhabiting the region from Nahr 'Amrit to the Carmel coast, nor that these people were involved in trade and colonization that brought them to the Balkan Peninsula and into contact with Greek-speaking colonists in the western Mediterranean. But I maintain that the "Phoenician art" of the Iron Age is an invention of modern scholarship and insist that it does us little good to continue to study ivories and metal bowls as examples of it. Portable objects of course have a place in the discussion of what might have constituted a Phoenician art or visual culture, especially those that come from controlled excavation. Excavated material from Cyprus and the western Mediterranean fits, too, but scholarly emphasis *must* shift as much as possible to monuments and objects retrieved from Iron Age Byblos, Sidon, Tyre, and other sites to ground future discussions in reality.

Whatever the complex of causes, the archaeological record suggests that something different happens in this region after the significant political upheavals of the later Iron Age. Following the early Persian period, that is from around 530 BCE, we begin to find many more monumental works of art and architecture that can be ascribed without hesitation to Phoenician patronage and use contexts. I think it is both historically tenable and intellectually responsible to talk about Phoenician art and identity in the Persian, Hellenistic, and Roman periods. The seeds for this development were planted in the Iron Age, but, as I argue in the next chapter, they bloomed after the Persian Wars encouraged sustained, large-scale collective thinking—peer-polity interaction. Literature and coinage of the Roman imperial era suggest that this was not a one-time event, although it is impossible to say whether these were merely episodes or part of broader trend.

CHAPTER 4

The Rise of Phoenicianism

From the very beginning of the Achaemenid era there is evidence of cross-Mediterranean Phoenician group consciousness. Herodotus (3.19) reports that the Phoenician fleet on campaign in Egypt refused Cambyses's demand to advance on the Carthaginians:

> Φοίνικες δὲ οὐκ ἔφασαν ποιήσειν ταῦτα: ὁρκίοισι γὰρ μεγάλοισι ἐνδεδέσθαι, καὶ οὐκ ἂν ποιέειν ὅσια ἐπὶ τοὺς παῖδας τοὺς ἑωυτῶν στρατευόμενοι

> But the Phoenicians said they would not do it; for they were bound, they said, by strong oaths, and if they advanced on their own children they would be doing an impious thing.[1]

The relationship with Carthage was not one-sided. According to several Greek sources (Arr. *Anab.* 2.24.5; Curt. 4.2.10–11; Diod. Sic. 20.14; Polyb. 31.12.12), the Carthaginians sent a delegation annually to their mother city with offerings of first fruits to their patron deity Baʿal Ṣūr, the god of Tyre—Melqart. Tyre hoped for Carthaginian support during Alexander's siege (Diod. Sic. 17.40.3; Just. *Epit.* 11.10.12), although Quintus Curtius reports that Carthage was overwhelmed by war at home and could only take wives and children to safety (Curt. 4.3.19–20). Carthage's response to her 310 siege by Agathokles of Syracuse was to renew offerings to the mother city, having lapsed in the effort and angered Melqart (Diod. Sic. 20.14.1–3). We are reminded periodically in other accounts of the connectivity of Phoenicians, as when the Sidonians who helped Alexander lay siege to Tyre are said to have secreted away fifteen thousand Tyrians to safety (Curt. 4.4.15–16). Greeks, at least, saw connections between Phoenician city-states in the Persian and Hellenistic eras.

All the same, we must recognize that it is inherently problematic to seek Phoenician collective identity through Greek and Roman textual evidence. The same passage describing the siege of Carthage in Diodoros gives us one reason why: it describes a mass child sacrifice (Diod. Sic. 20.14.4–6). While there is good evidence that Carthaginians practiced child sacrifice in the tophet sanctuary, there is no evidence (yet?) of this practice at home.[2] Moreover, Diodoros's account is sensational in its description of the magnitude and callousness of the rites. Other reasons to be skeptical of Greek and Roman source material were articulated by Irene Winter, who showed that the supposed ethnonym *phoinix* was in fact principally literary, and by Jonathan Prag, who demonstrated *poenus* was as well.[3] The same can be true for "Sidonian," a sometime metonym for Phoenician (as at *Il.* 23.743). Homer's Phoenicians are most explicitly literary; Herodotos's are more historical, although still often vague (we have seen how the periploi can be confusing, too); and Thucydides's repetition of the threat of the "Phoenician fleet" turns the very real power of the Persian navy into a looming off-stage character. The Hellenistic historians inherited these views.

Rather than survey this evidence, a project that has been undertaken several times before,[4] this chapter seeks to understand the emic evidence. I argue that the Persian period is the first time one can point to explicit archaeological evidence of a self-conscious Phoenician identity, one that continues and grows even as imperial control over the Phoenician city-states changes hands from the Achaemenids (530s–330s) to Alexander (330s) and thence to a chaotic period in which various successors battled for control over Alexander's empire.[5] The process by which Phoenician identity emerged certainly began in the Iron Age, and it is likely that the crucible of the Persian Wars helped shape it. Greek sources suggest that the period between Alexander's conquest and the eventual Ptolemaic takeover, a period in which the Phoenician city-states were frequently besieged and suffered great losses, could have helped this group consciousness along.

I want to acknowledge from the beginning that this kind of thinking is somewhat conventional, even if it has not been pursued seriously on the Phoenician side of things, and the arguments that follow stem from a conservative approach to historical analysis, source criticism. I hope to demonstrate that we can take the lessons of the previous chapter and apply them in a number of ways, here, by highlighting the Phoenician evidence and entertaining the possibility that some Phoenicians and some Greeks reacted to the events of the late sixth and fifth centuries in similar ways. The reasons for the rise of Phoenicianism are of course more complex than an upwelling of nationalism through armed conflict and occupation. I suggest that they must be understood in terms of fifth-century political changes that reshaped eastern Mediterranean economies. These changes never led to the creation of a Phoenician state, however, nor of a monoculture, and it remains difficult even in this period to pin down "a" Phoenician culture or artistic style.

To illuminate Phoenician self-ascription, this chapter discusses monumental art, including inscriptions, and portable art—coins—from the Persian and Hellenistic periods. The advantage of considering monumental art is that we can be reasonably certain of its intended context of display. It offers considerable insight into elite, often royal, self-presentation. This section closes with two bilingual inscriptions from Attika that allow for the comparison of emic and etic representational strategies. Coins flesh out the picture by showing how state identity was constructed and conveyed in portable form. Altogether the written and visual evidence reveals glimpses of a sophisticated self-consciousness and autonomy rarely acknowledged in Persian-and Hellenistic-period Phoenicians or their art. The stability of identity and evidence of independence are all the more remarkable for enduring through this often-turbulent period.

Monumental Evidence: Epigraphy, Art, Architecture

The compelling corpus of Phoenician epigraphy is for the most part published, but our understanding of the language's vocabulary, grammar, and syntax is limited. There are around ten thousand texts in the extant corpus,[6] and we know only about two thousand words total.[7] Phoenician is a sometimes difficult, largely consonantal, language, in which small differences in the interpretation of letter forms can lead to major differences in translation or date. When inscriptions are not formulaic, experts can disagree about them to such an extent that the navigation of their arguments can seem nearly impossible.[8] It is clear that we must proceed with caution and be wary of aligning inscriptions with historical events recorded in other sources. Difficulties of interpretation notwithstanding, these texts, as well those written in Greek by or for Phoenicians, are precious. Most Phoenician language inscriptions of the Persian and Hellenistic periods are votive and funerary, written in the varied dialects of the regions in which they were found.[9] Inscriptions from these periods have turned up in all the major city-states and sites, with the fewest coming from Tyre. Byblos has only a handful, but they are important. The sanctuary of Umm el-'Amed has a number of inscriptions, but Sidon (including the Eshmun sanctuary) is the richest source.

Evidence of a Phoenician approach to expressing identity begins with simple onomastic formulae.[10] For both males and females, common folk and royals, theophoric idionyms were popular. In Phoenician-language inscriptions, family and civic identities are expressed, the former sometimes concerning multiple generations, the latter through toponyms (rarely ethnonyms as in Greek).[11] Bilingual inscriptions likewise emphasize ancestry and use civic toponyms. Take for example the inscription on the Yehawmilk stele from Byblos, dated to the mid-fifth century on paleographic and archaeological grounds (Figure 19).[12] It begins:

> *ʾnk yḥwmlk mlk gbl bn yḥrbʿl bn bn ʾrmlk mlk gbl ʾš pʿltn ḥrbt bʿlt gbl mmlkt ʿl gbl*

I am Yehawmilk king of Byblos, son of Yeharbaʿal, grandson of Urimilk king of Byblos whom the lady Gebal Baʿalat made ruler over Byblos.[13]

The remaining lines describe Yehawmilk's construction of a shrine or portico (*ʿrpt*) in honor of the city's principal deity, Baʿalat Gebal, familiarly known as the "Lady of Byblos"; a request for her to reciprocate; and warnings about violating her temple. The image on the upper portion of the round-topped limestone stele expands upon the text and the implied intimacy between goddess and king. At the top is carved a winged disk, a long-lived symbol of religious significance for Phoenicians and perhaps here a reference to Baʿalat Gebal's temple gateway inlaid with a golden winged disk (lines 5–6).[14] A mark for a metal peg remains in the stone to surmount the stele with a metal attachment, raising the alternate possibility that the golden disk in the inscription refers to the stele itself.[15] The carved disk stretches over an enthroned Baʿalat Gebal fashioned as Hathor. She holds the *wadj* (papyrus scepter) and wears a headdress with horns flanking a sun disk. Before her is the robed king with a cylindrical crown, extending an offering cup with one hand and making a gesture of supplication with the other.

Yehawmilk's costume is similar to the cylindrical hat and ceremonial costume found in Persian art.[16] In concert with the representation of Baʿalat Gebal as Hathor, the stele tempts scholars to emphasize external "influence" and emulations.[17] There is no reason to see this particular combination of features as "foreign," however. The selective use of Egyptian iconography and architectural elements is already familiar to us from the few extant examples of Phoenician Iron Age art, including gravestones, as well as the Persian period anthropoid sarcophagi and naiskoi at ʿAmrit. Use of Persian costume to signify state power is also found on coins of Sidon (see Figure 37, discussed below).[18] Further reference to Persian-granted authority is found in other inscriptions, including the Eshmunazar sarcophagus (referencing *ʾdn mlkm*, "the lord of kings").[19] The result on the Yehawmilk stele is not disjointed but seamless, as self-assured as the content of the inscription itself (the letters are somewhat clumsily carved, however). We should not read the imagery in a totally different way from its inscription. The stele is evidence of self-fashioning in terms that are simultaneously interconnected and, like the Byblian dialect itself, distinct.

A funerary inscription from Byblos is found on the sarcophagus of Batnoam, dated to around 400 (Figure 20). It indicates that Byblian funerary practices were consciously conservative:

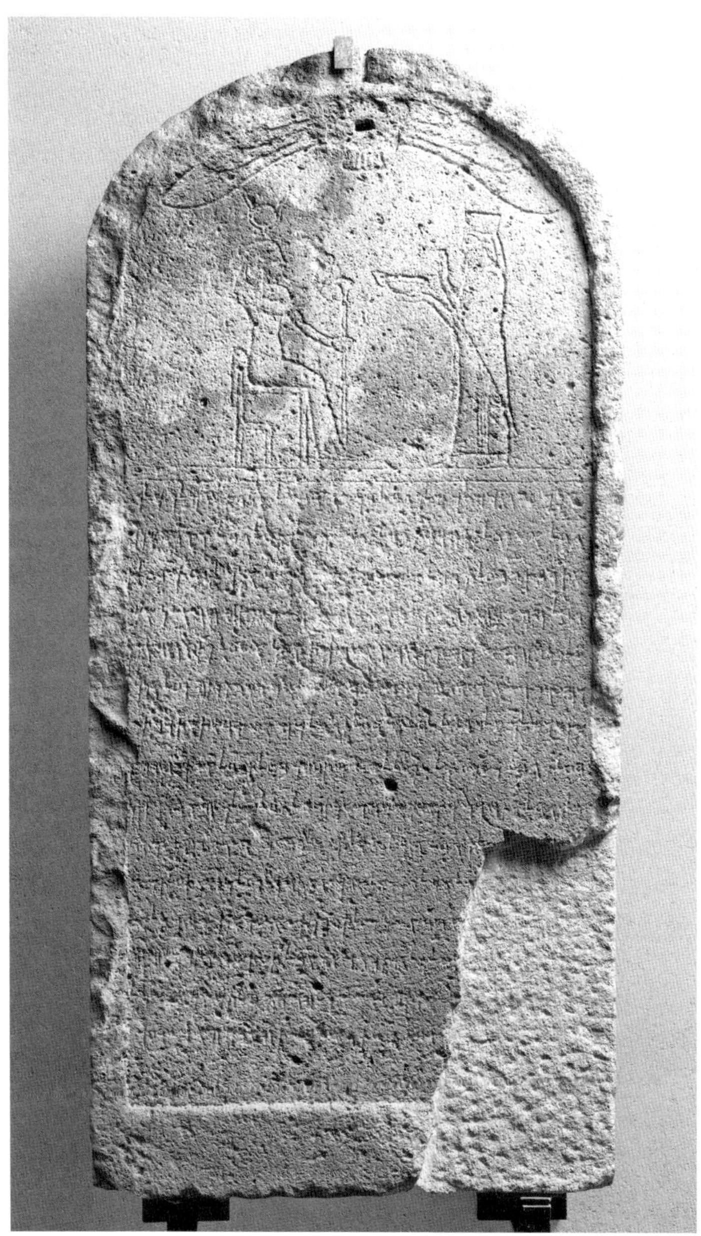

Figure 19. Yehawmilk stele from Byblos, ca. 450 (= *KAI* 10). Paris, Musée du Louvre AO 22368. Limestone. Ht. 1.12 m. Photo: Art Resource, N.Y.

Figure 20. Detail of inscription on Batnoam sarcophagus from Byblos, ca. 400 (= *KAI* 11). Beirut, National Museum. Marble. 0.94 m (length of inscription). Photo: author's own.

bʾrn zn ʾnk btnʿm ʾm mlk ʿzbʿl mlk gbl bn plṭbʿl khn bʿlt škbt bswt wmrʾš ʿly wmḥsm ḥrṣ lpy kmʾš lmlkyt ʾš kn lpny

In this coffin lie I Batnoam, mother of king Azbaʿal, king of Byblos, son of Palitbaʿal, priest of the Lady, in a robe and with a tiara on my head and a gold bridle on my mouth, as was the custom with the royal ladies who were before me.[20]

Here as on the Yehawmilk stele is the onomastic formula tying together lineage with theophoric names (iterations of Baʿal), city-state, and city deity, in this case shortened to just her honorific title, Baʿalat. Batnoam's ceremonial clothing is described as well as the "gold bridle" used to prepare her body for burial. Continuity of custom is emphasized in the final part of the inscription. While bearing in mind

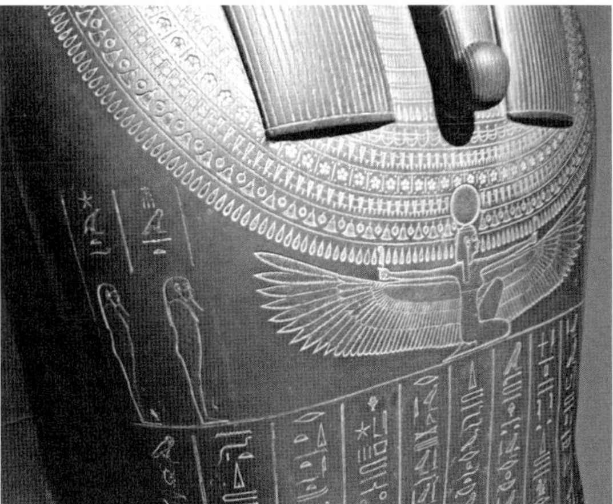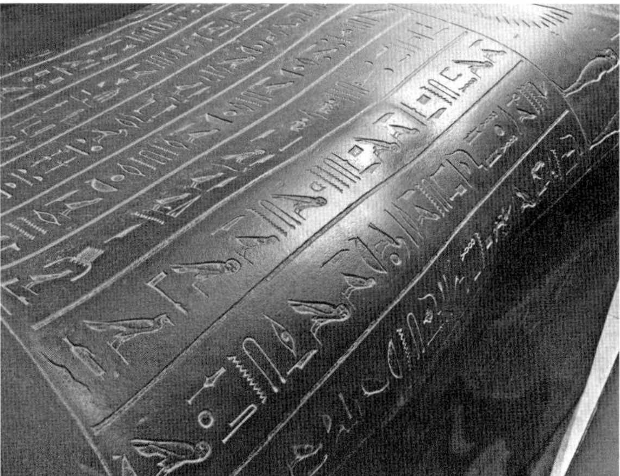

Figure 21. Details of Sarcophagus of Tabnit (Figure 13).

this is a funerary inscription, not a votive stele, and for a royal mother, not a king, it is nonetheless important to note how the accompanying visual properties are much different from those of Yehawmilk's stele. Batnoam's sarcophagus is in imported white marble, not limestone, and the surface is otherwise plain. It is not clear that it was meant to be plain, however, as tool marks are still apparent on all visible surfaces, proving that at least the fine smoothing was never done. Perhaps it was intended to take an anthropoid form,[21] but it is usually presented as a deliberately rectilinear sarcophagus (called a *thēkē*, or "chest," by scholars) of the type found also in Sidon. Unfortunately our evidence is insufficient to speculate further.

Three Sidonian royal funerary inscriptions can be used for comparison. Two were introduced in Chapter 2, the looted basalt sarcophagi of King Tabnit and his son Eshmunazar II (Figures 13 and 14; Figures 21 to 24). The lids of both sarcophagi represent the deceased wearing a funerary mask, wig, stylized beard, and broad collars terminating in falcon heads. Tabnit's has a representation of a kneeling Isis with sun disk crown, wings outstretched in protection (Figure 21, left). While the two sarcophagi are similar stylistically, they are not by the same hand.

There are a number of differences in the approach to the facial features and hair (Figure 22). Eshmunazar's overall form is squat, with virtually no articulation of the body (see Figure 14), which seems to be the intended result for the unfinished third looted sarcophagus holding an unidentified female, perhaps his mother, Amotaštart. Tabnit's is slimmer, with more articulation of the form near the knees, the muscle and bones of the knees and shins being clearly visible below the hieroglyphs (Figure 21, right). For reasons that cannot be known to us, the extant hieroglyphic inscription on the cover for General Pa-en-Ptah was not removed from Tabnit's sarcophagus. The eight-line inscription honoring Tabnit was

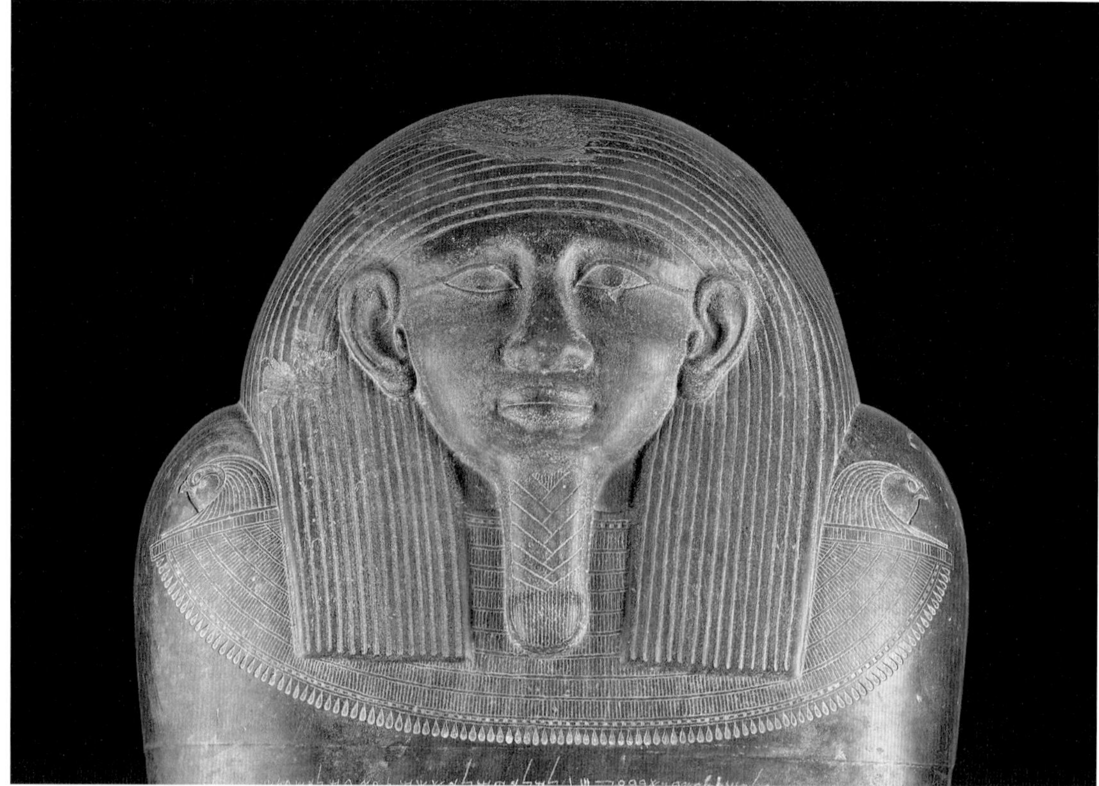

Figure 22. Detail of Sarcophagus of Eshmunazar II (Figure 14).

written on the feet instead (Figure 23; see also Figure 13). It begins with the now familiar onomastic formula of name, city, and city goddess:

ʾnk tbnt khn ʿštrt mlk ṣdnm bn ʾšmnʿzr khn ʿštrt mlk ṣdnm škb bʾrn

I Tabnit, priest of Aštart, king of Sidon, son of Eshmunazar, priest of Aštart, king of Sidon, am lying here in this coffin.[22]

The following lines concern warnings about violating the burial similar to those found on the Yehawmilk stele, although for a different context.[23]

Similar warnings are found on Eshmunazar II's sarcophagus (Figures 14, 22, and 24).[24] Eshmunazar's inscription is in the expected location, on the lid of the sarcophagus, and is, fittingly, much longer (Figure 24). The twenty-two lines tell of his status, lineage, and untimely death; his mother Amotaštart's regency; and their dedications to Aštart and Eshmun. Lines 18–20 give us the best extant information about Sidon's political position in the early Persian period:

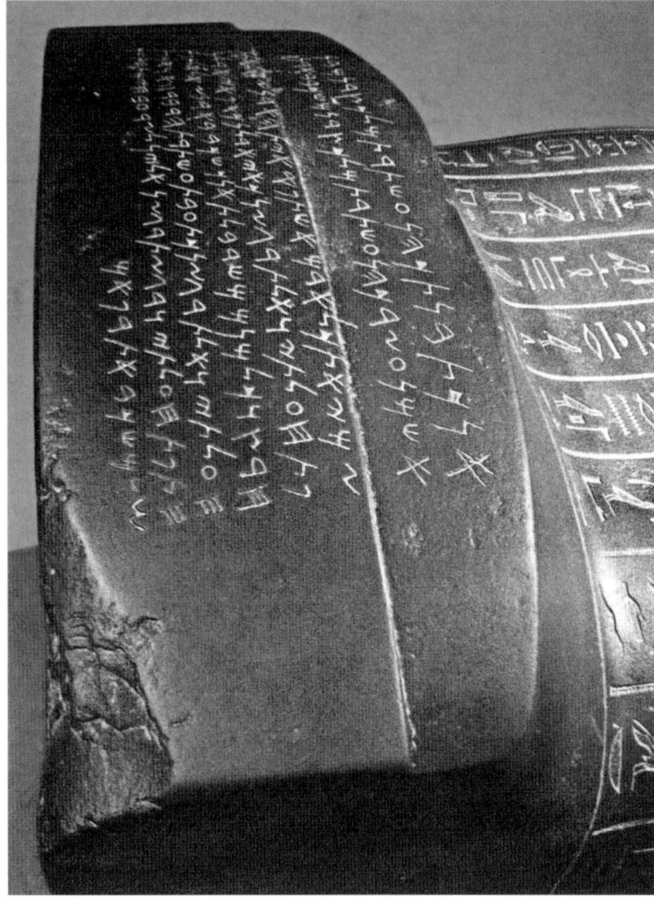

Figure 23. Detail of
Sarcophagus of
Tabnit (Figure 13).

[18] . . . *wᶜd ytn ln ʾdn mlkm*
[19] *ʾyt dʾr wypy ʾrṣt dgn hʾdrt ʾš bšd šrn lmdt ṣmt ʾš pᶜlt wyspnnm*
[20] *ᶜlt gbl ʾrṣ lknnm lṣdnm lᶜl[m]* . . .

[18] . . . furthermore the lord of kings gave us
[19] Dor [*dʾr*] and Joppa [*ypy*], the rich lands of Dagon/corn that are in the
plain of Sharon, as a reward for the striking deeds that I performed; and
we added them
[20] to the borders of the land, that they might belong to Sidon forever . . . [25]

The towns mentioned in line 19, Dor and Jaffa, have been identified in the north
and south of the Sharon Plain, respectively, and prove that Sidon's control south-
ward was considerable.[26]

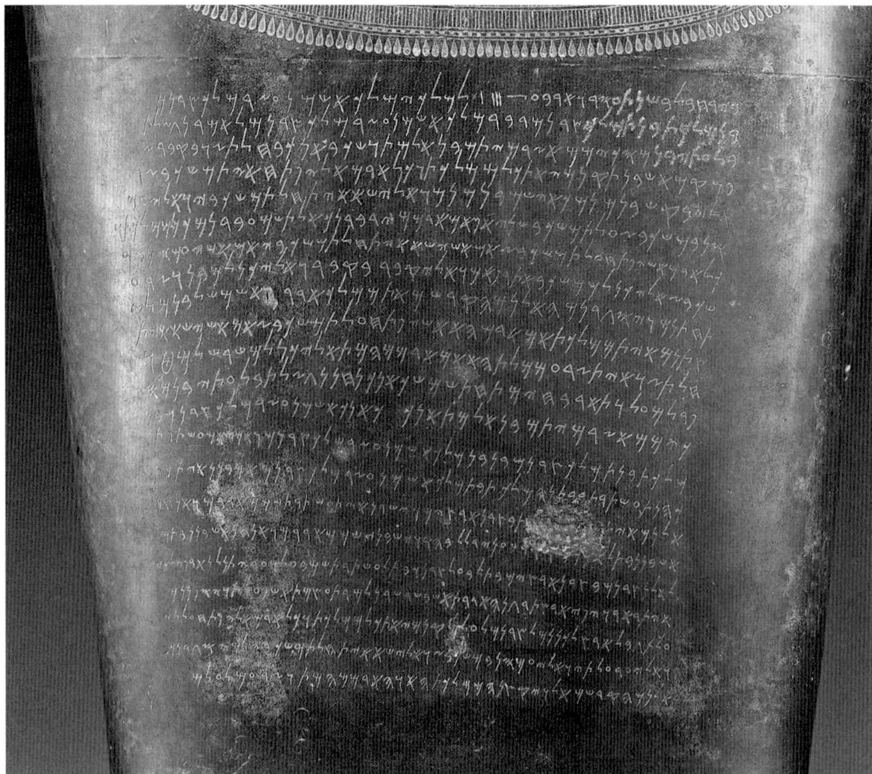

Figure 24. Detail of Sarcophagus of Eshmunazar II (Figure 14).

Neither Eshmunazar II's name nor any other name among the kings in his dynasty is recorded in Greek or other sources. The vague language of these inscriptions has led to a debate over the date of the dynasty. I follow what is called the "high chronology" by those who have worked on the date of the sarcophagus. In the high chronology, the inscriptions are thought to date to the late sixth or early fifth century. A conservative reading of the extant information suggests that the Sidonians obtained these sarcophagi on campaign in Egypt, possibly with Cambyses.[27] I think it possible that Tabnit died on campaign and was prepared there for burial at home.[28] This scenario might also explain why his funerary inscription was hastily put on the feet on the sarcophagus and why Eshmunazar II became king when still a child, perhaps an infant, and was richly rewarded for service to the king.[29] If so, Cambyses or Xerxes would be the "lord of kings" mentioned in line 18, perhaps having granted power to Sidon for assistance with the Egyptian or Greek campaigns, respectively. This is, of course, just speculation, though it complements nicely the visual information. These prototype sarcophagi seem especially poignant in this historical moment, as they refer to Egypt and her domination by the Persians that was brought about, in part, by Sidonians.

Another royal inscription comes from the Eshmun sanctuary found near an orange grove just outside Sidon referred to as Bostan esh-Sheik (Figures 25 and 26).[30] It was inscribed on the base of a marble child statue in the late fifth to mid-fourth century (Figure 27).[31] The one-line inscription is for a prince Ba'alshillem from another Sidonian dynasty:

hsml z 'š ytn b'lšlm bn mlk b'n' mlk ṣdnm bn mlk 'bd'mn mlk ṣdnm bn mlk b'lšlm mlk ṣdnm l'dny l'šmn b'n ydl ybrk

This (is the) statue [*sml*] that Ba'alshillem son of king Ba'na, king of Sidon, son of king 'Abdamun, king of Sidon, son of king Ba'alshillem, king of Sidon, gave to his lord Eshmun at the Ydl-Spring. May he bless him![32]

While the inscription is formulaic, the statue and its context are intriguing. The Ba'alshillem II statue is one of a popular type at the sanctuary made of marble and limestone. These are sometimes referred to as "temple boys" after the conventional name for the Cypriot prototype.[33] The earliest child statues at Bostan esh-Sheik are in limestone and stylistically Cypriot. Soon thereafter some statues are made of marble and are stylistically Greek. The Ba'alshillem II statue is an example of the latter. We do not know exactly how these statues were used or where precisely they were originally displayed.[34] The Ba'alshillem II inscription indicates that this statue was meant to represent the prince himself as a gift to Eshmun in exchange for protection.

How we interpret this work in terms of Sidonian royal identity very much depends on understanding its general context. The Eshmun temple complex had a long use from the seventh century to the Byzantine period. In the early Persian period Bodaštart, grandson of Eshmunazar II, built its monumental platform.[35] Owing to its long use, erratic excavation, and modern looting, very little is known about the structures that once stood on this platform, if any. The hundreds of architectural fragments recovered from the site, many of which have since been lost, show that builders drew on a variety of elements, most explicitly (and logically) Achaemenid royal architecture.[36] A few features of the later Persian and Hellenistic sanctuary are especially relevant to this discussion. One is a structure northeast of the monumental platform of unknown function containing water basins, offerings, and a number of small rooms (Figure 28). In plan, the building's closest extant parallels, although they are only general, come from Levantine-built structures on Delos, the clubhouse of the Poseidoniasts of Beirut (see Figure 39) and the sanctuary of the Syrian gods Atargatis and Hadad.[37]

The building's decorative friezes are poorly preserved. They show children engaged in various activities and are original to the structure. Their style supports a

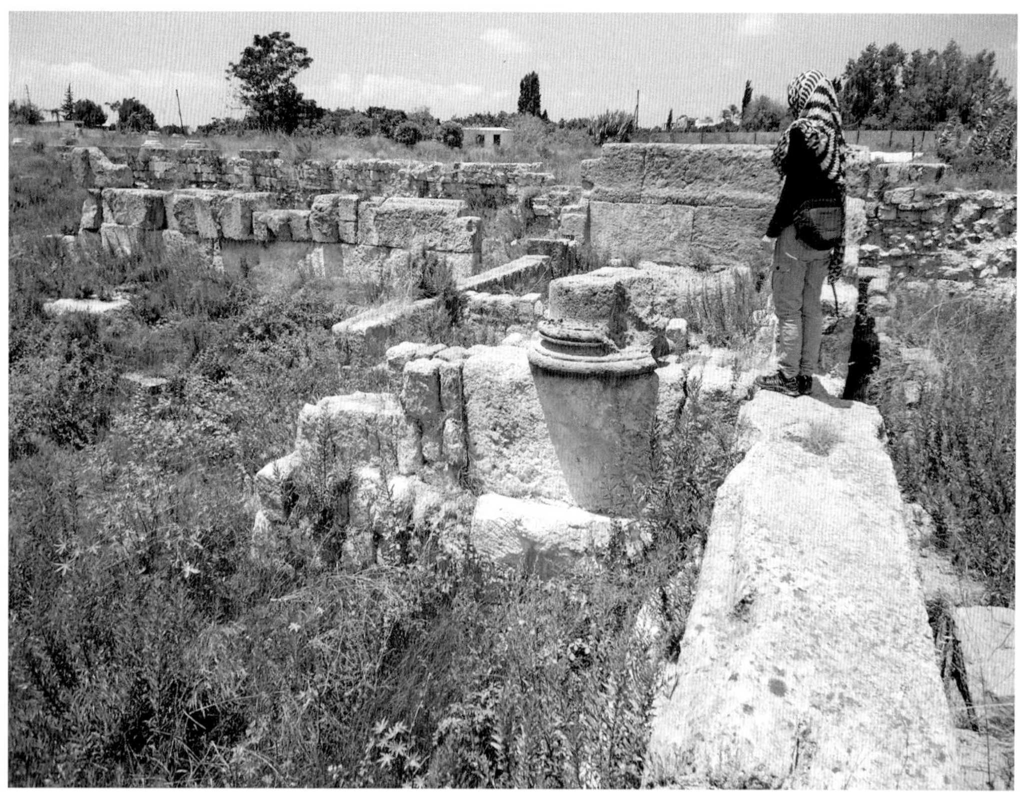

Figure 25. View of Bostan esh-Sheikh taken in 2013. Photo: author's own.

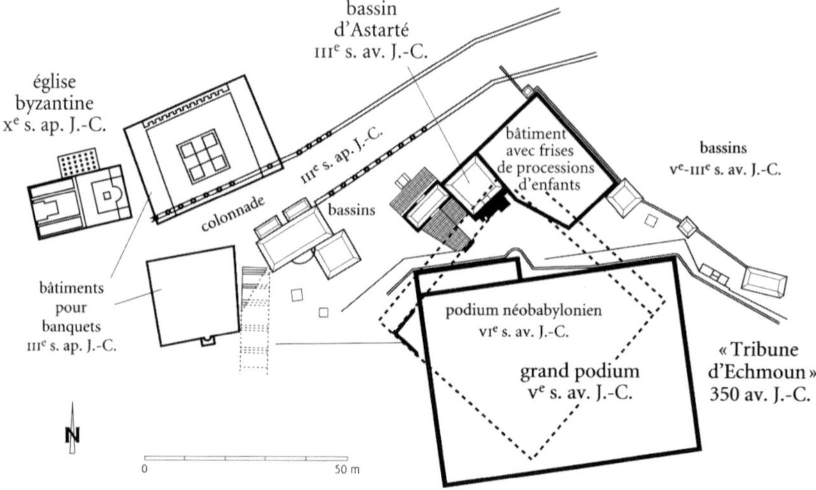

Figure 26. Site plan of the Sanctuary of Eshmun at Bostan esh-Sheikh. Plan redrawn
by Sveta Matskevich after *Liban, l'autre rive*, 135.

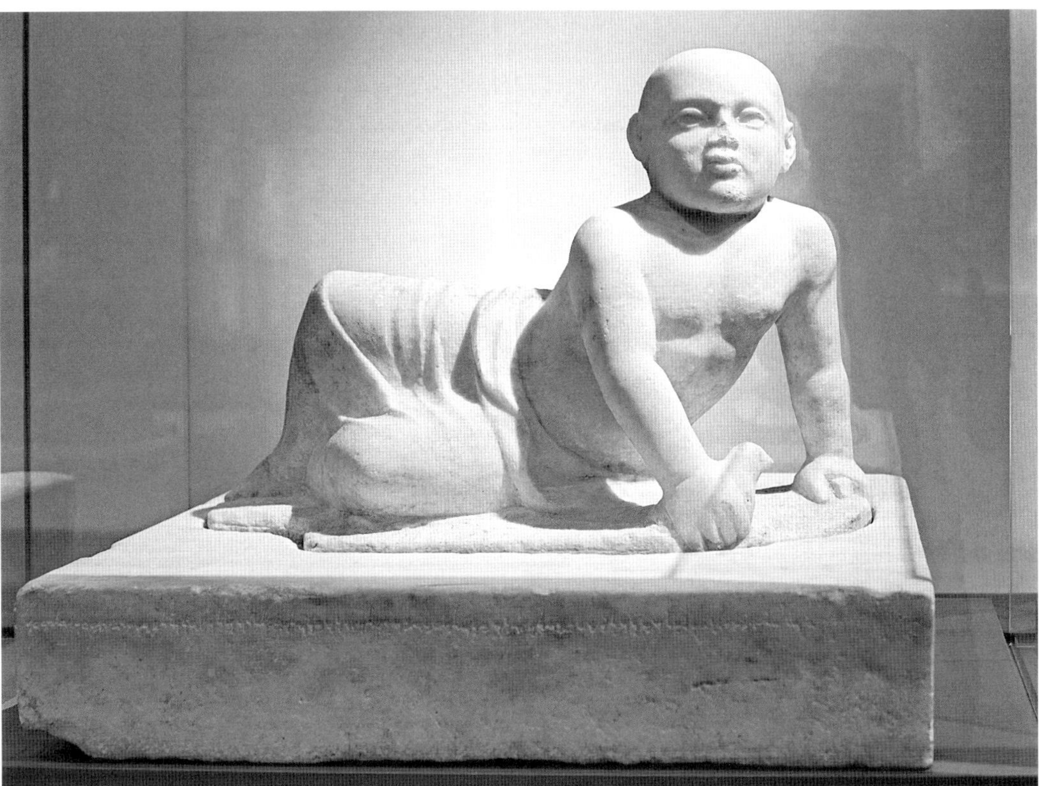

Figure 27. Statue of Ba'alshillem II found near the Eshmun complex at Bostan esh-Sheikh, ca. 425–350. Beirut, National Museum. Marble. 0.50 m (length of inscription). Photo: Jessica Nitschke.

Hellenistic date.[38] The friezes are further proof of the activity of sculptors trained in Greek workshops. Sharing a wall with this building is a structure in front of the main platform, the so-called Bassin d'Astarté (Figure 26). The rectilinear building was once flooded. The back wall had a frieze of children engaged in a hunt and a niche in which was set a so-called Aštart throne, a quasi-aniconic object type found in Sidon, Tyre, and related sanctuaries that was composed of a throne flanked by lions or sphinxes. One throne from Tyre dated to the second century is inscribed with a dedication to the goddess.[39] The functions of these adjacent buildings are not known, though water seems to have been important to both at different points in their use, recalling the 'Amrit temple (see Figure 18).

Finally, at the base of the monumental platform was found the most famous object from the sanctuary, the so-called tribune of Eshmun that is said to have "enormous bearing on the 'Hellenization' of Sidon during the period of Persian domination" (see Plates 12 and 13; its findspot is indicated in Figure 26).[40] It was set into a semicircular stone area, the centerpiece of which was a standing stone in

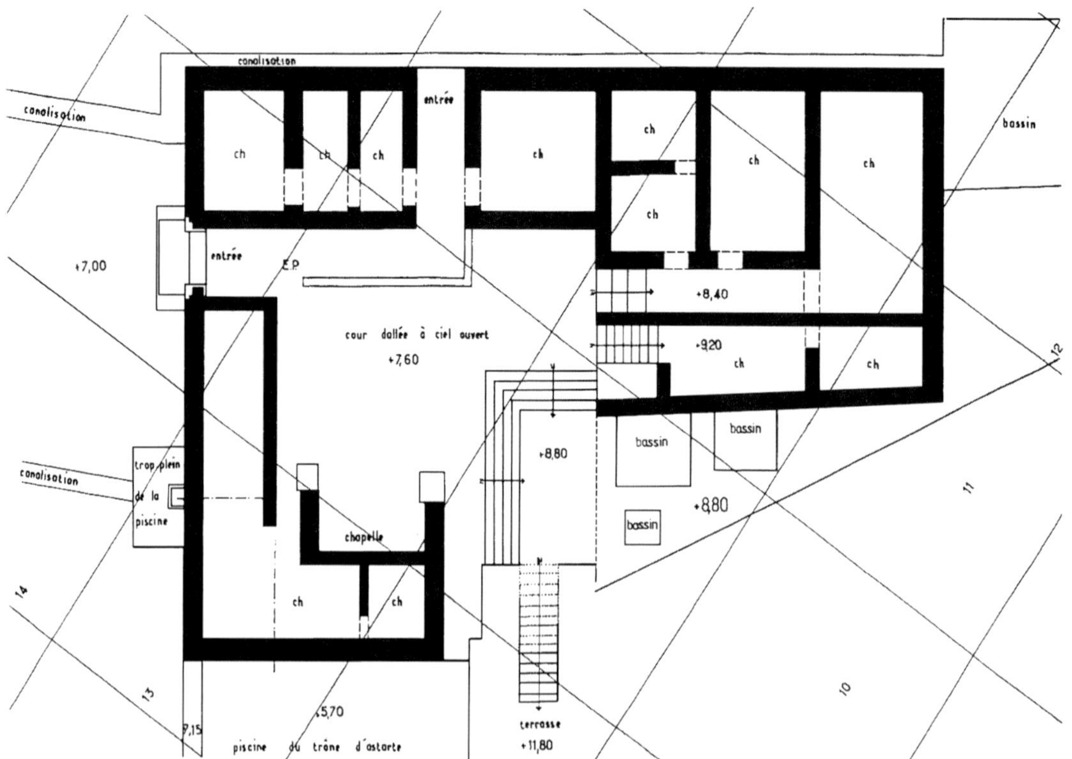

Figure 28. Plan of the building of uncertain function with children friezes at Bostan esh-Sheikh, probably of early Hellenistic date. Plan redrawn with minor changes by Sveta Matskevich after Stucky 1997, fig. 3.

the form of a pillar. To the right of the pillar was found the limestone foundation on which the marble "tribune" once stood. It was surely made by Greek-trained sculptors and takes the form of a Greek monumental altar in-antis. Because its moldings are similar to those used on the Alexander Sarcophagus and those sarcophagi found with it, possibly the same sculptor or workshop made all these works in the early Hellenistic period.[41] Its two friezes show a gathering of the gods and, below, a revelry. This iconography is Greek, and although attempts have been made to tie the program to Eshmun, no connection is really detectable (that does not mean Sidonians made no connections, of course).[42] The object's function is debated. The fine marble Aštart throne seen in Figure 29 once sat on top of it, as seen in the reconstruction in Figure 30.[43] Because it was set with its open side facing a retaining wall, it could not have functioned as an altar. The circumstances in which it was found suggest either reuse, misunderstanding, or rejection of its intended function.

The combination of elements—aniconic standing stone, Greek altar with reliefs, and an Aštart throne—offers a fascinating window into the world of Sido-

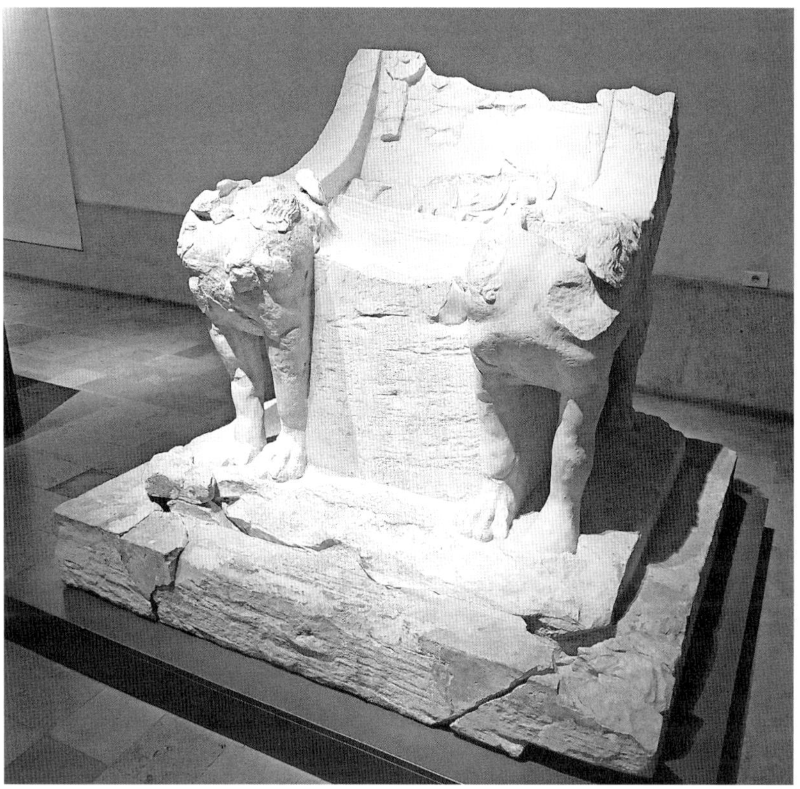

Figure 29. Marble Aštart throne from Bostan esh-Sheikh that once sat on top of the so-called tribune (altar) (Plates 12 and 13). Beirut, National Museum 2067. Marble. Ht. 1.44 m. Photo: author's own.

nian art and religion of the early Hellenistic period. The use of this altar-as-statue base for an Aštart throne could only happen in the repertoire of Phoenician art. It is certainly poor evidence of acculturation. The Greek style of the late fifth-century statue of Ba'alshillem II does not, therefore, signal a clear shift in the style of dedications at the sanctuary or a gradual loss of Sidonian religious practices to Greek ones. In fact, children statues appear in Greek sanctuaries in smaller numbers and only about a century after the Ba'alshillem statue was dedicated in Sidon.[44] In the second century and later, marble statues of Greek and Roman deities begin to appear at the site, mainly of Asklepios, Hygeia, and Dionysos and his retinue.[45] These statues, too, might best be framed in terms of the complex aggregations that were long established in the sanctuary. Although Vella has shown that there is no single plan or style in Phoenician sanctuaries of the Persian and Hellenistic periods,[46] it is possible to detect a number of conceptual parallels between the Eshmun sanctuary complex and the 'Amrit sanctuary, from the stress placed on water in religious contexts to the strategic use of Achaemenid, Cypriot, or Greek imagery

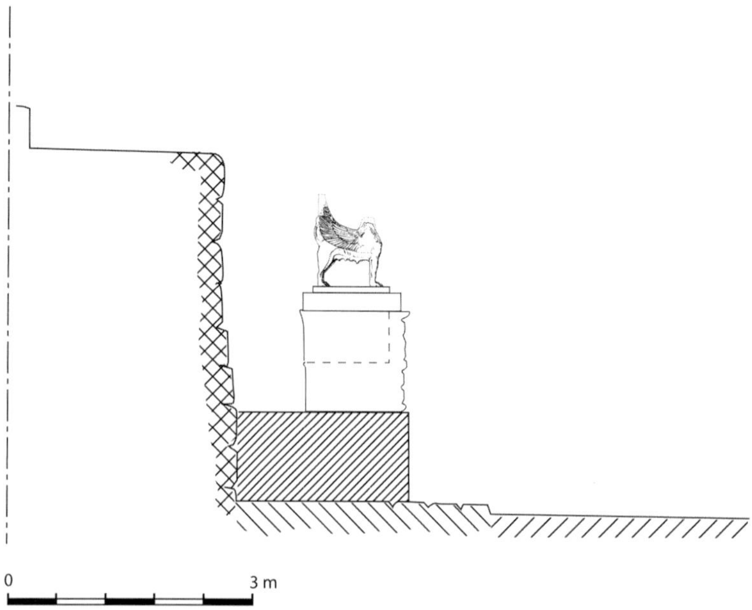

Figure 30. Reconstruction of the arrangement. Plan redrawn by Sveta Matskevich after Kawkabani 2003, fig. 8.

to the peculiar combinations of those traditions with extant (local, Phoenician) traditions of art and architecture.

The sanctuary at Hammon, now called Umm el-'Amed and located less than twenty kilometers south of Tyre, offers yet another opportunity to consider the approach to Phoenician self-representation in a religious context (see Map 3 and Figure 31).[47] Although there is evidence of earlier occupation at the site, the initial phase of construction of the large sanctuary complex dates to the late fourth to early third centuries. The sanctuary was active until its decline in the first century BCE. It has two sacred enclosures, one dedicated to Milk 'Aštart, a god related to Aštart and Melqart,[48] and another to an unidentified deity in the so-called East Temple. In plan, both enclosures are courtyards surrounding their respective temples, a long-lived arrangement for sacred space in the Levant. Each has a number of other features, such as porticoes, various smaller rooms, and, in the Milk 'Aštart enclosure, a colonnaded hall.[49] The hall is a good example of the kind of combinations seen elsewhere at this and other sanctuaries. The form is found in ceremonial use in a number of locations, from Anatolia to Egypt and Achaemenid Persia. But the hall's appearance here in a sacred enclosure is unique, as is its use of Greek-style columns, Ionic on the exterior and Doric on the interior. Additional structures including a portico in the Milk 'Aštart complex also selectively employ Greek architectural orders, whereas other features are embellished with the long-popular disk and uraei.

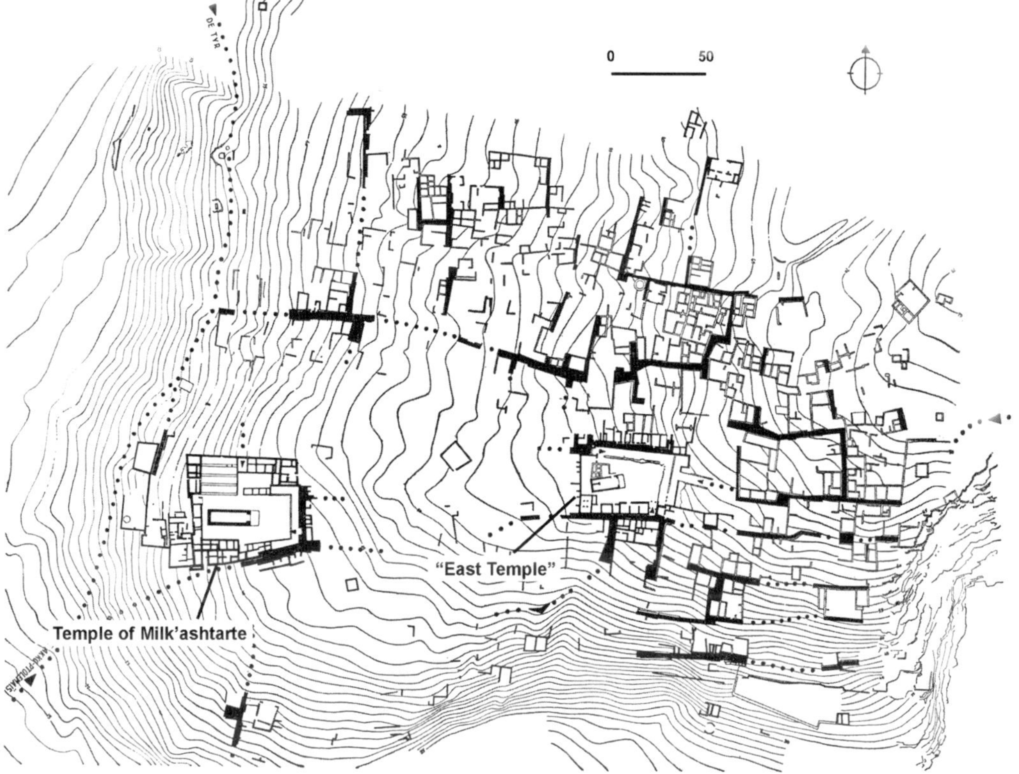

Figure 31. Plan of the sanctuary at Umm el-'Amed. Plan: after Dunand and Duru 1962, fig. 20 modified by Nitschke 2007, fig. 136. Courtesy of Jessica Nitschke.

Two fragmentary orthostats found in the Milk 'Aštart complex show young bulls on the attack, one of which charges at a stylized tree.[50] Their poses and style have drawn comparison to some of the carved ivories as well as a stele from the Eshmun sanctuary.[51] Two other fragmentary orthostats show a cultic scene in which the human figure interacts with a column topped by a volute ("Aeolic") capital, an architectural element also found in some ivories and, from a variety of periods, at sites in the upper Galilee (Hazor), Judah (Ramat Rachel), and Cyprus (Golgoi, Tamassos). A limestone block with reliefs on three of its four sides of uncertain function was also found in this complex.[52] It shows male figures engaged in various cultic activities: interacting with a tree of life, carrying a censer, and making gestures of supplication. Stylistically and in terms of content, all of these reliefs seem to fit with Iron Age Levantine portable objects or preexisting art and architectural practices, though it is not clear how specific or significant these relationships might be. The small amount of sculpture recovered thus far from Phoenicia makes it difficult to say whether or not we should associate the reliefs with a monumental "Phoenician style" of Hellenistic art. The damaged state of these objects only makes that task more difficult.

There are works in the sanctuary that are exclusively Phoenician, however, such as the Aštart throne found in the East temple.[53] Another example of Phoenician monumental art is the well-preserved statue of one ʿAbdosir that was found near the main entrance of the Milk ʿAštart temple (Figure 32).[54] It is inscribed in Phoenician, as are all the inscriptions from the site:

Pdny lmlkʿštrt ʾlḥmn ʾš ndr ʿbdk ʿbdʾsr bn ʾrš zkrn kšmʿ ql[y] ybrk

To my lord, to Milk ʿAštart, god of Hammon, that which your servant ʿAbdosir, son of Arish, vowed as a memorial when he heard (his) voice. May he bless him![55]

The statue shows ʿAbdosir in the familiar striding pose wearing a short kilt. His right arm was once bent upward, likely in a gesture of supplication. The statue is dated to the third or second century and shows the use of a type known in the Iron Age and popular in some sanctuaries in the Persian period.[56] There are other Egyptian/izing elements in the sanctuary that are new as well, such as the Egyptian- (not Levantine-) type sphinxes that Nitschke has interpreted as

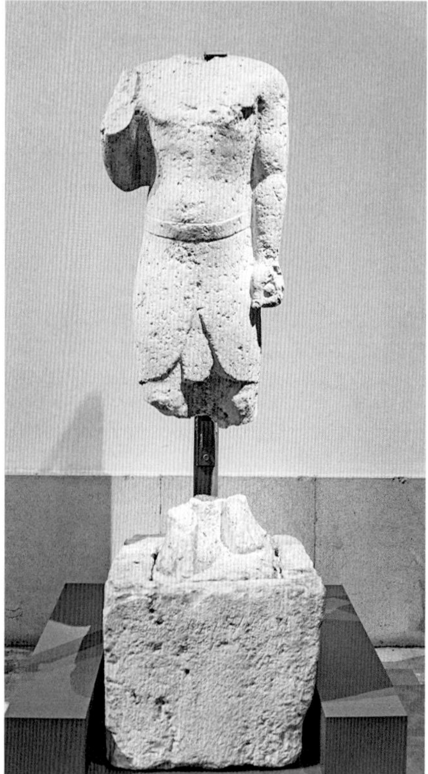

Figure 32. Statue of ʿAbdosir from Umm el-ʿAmed, 3rd or 2nd c. Beirut, National Museum 2004. Limestone. Ht. 1.02 m (preserved body), 0.45 m (base). Photo: Jessica Nitschke.

Ptolemaic portraits.[57] A few marble dedications were executed in Hellenistic Greek styles.

A group of sixteen Hellenistic limestone stelai from the site and its vicinity adds to this intriguing assemblage.[58] These stelai show males and females engaged in ritual activities (Figures 33 and 34). Their precise function, votive or funerary, is debated.[59] The best-preserved male reliefs have a number of parallels to the earlier Yehawmilk stele (see Figure 19): a winged disk with uraei is stretched out on the usually curved top of the stele. Below is a figure, barefoot and clean-shaven, gesturing in supplication with one hand and holding an offering or cult object, such as a box or a sphinx, in the other. The figures are typically identified as priests, but we cannot always be certain.[60] Like Yehawmilk, most wear Persian ceremonial robes and cylindrical hats (Figure 33, left).[61] One well-preserved stele shows instead a figure in a different costume, a long himation with sleeves that hit at the elbow and a soft, rounded head covering secured with a band that scholars call the *kausia* (Figure 33, right).[62] It is inscribed:

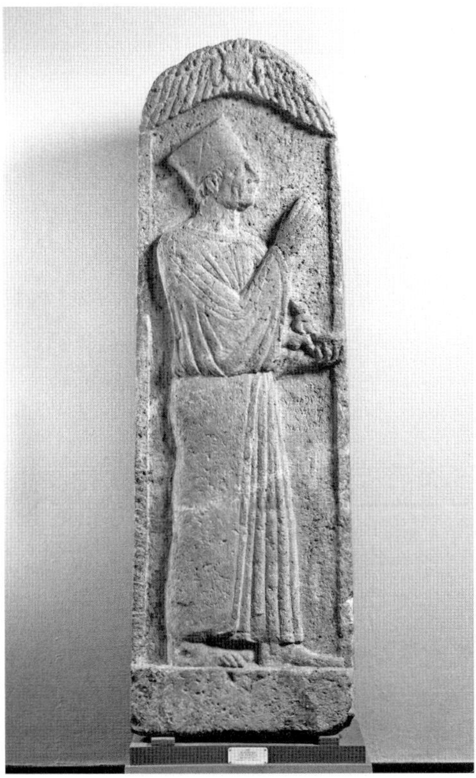
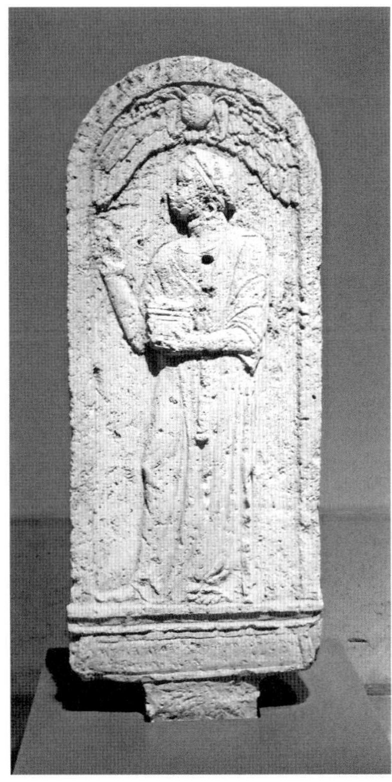

Figure 33. Stelai from Umm el-'Amed, 3rd or 2nd c. Left: Stele of Ba'alyaton. Copenhagen, Ny Carlsberg Glyptotek 1835. Limestone. Ht. ca. 1.81 m. Photo: Ny Carlsberg Glyptotek, Copenhagen/Ole Haupt. Right: Stele of Ba'alshamar. Beirut, National Museum 2072. Limestone. Ht. 1.27 m. Photo: author's own.

lbʿlšmr rb šʿrm bn ʿbdʾsr skr
ʾš ṭnʾ lʾb ʾš ly ʿbdʾsr rb šʿrm

To Baʿalshamar chief of the gate, son of ʿAbdosir, a commemoration
which has been set up for his father ʿAbdosir, chief of the gate.[63]

The recipient, Baʿalshamar son of ʿAbdosir, might be related to the same ʿAbdosir
who is represented by the kilt statue.

The well-preserved female stelai follow the same format, usually rounded with
a winged disk outstretched over a worshipper in similar pose (Figure 34).[64] In their
case, however, the figures consistently wear what appears to be Greek ritual attire,
the chiton and himation. Stylistically some these reliefs look more Greek in the
softer treatment of the face, hair, and drapery folds. The example on the left shows
the himation worn over the head. On the stele at right, an attempt is made to
carve the himation's folds tightly across the figure's right-hand side. The stelai show

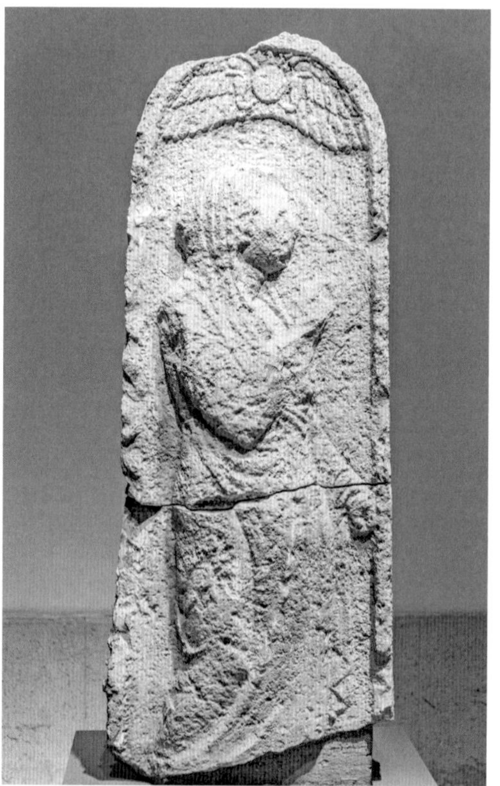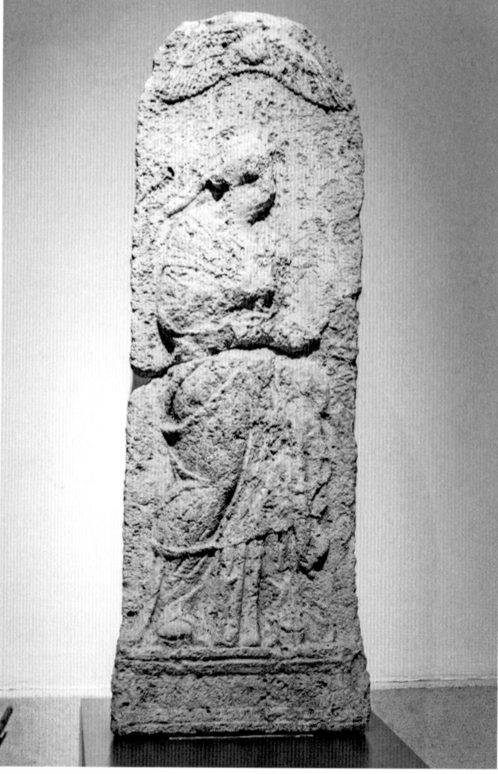

Figure 34. Stelai from Umm el-ʿAmed, 3rd or 2nd c. Left: Beirut, National Museum 2071.
Limestone. Ht. 1.62 m. Right: Beirut, National Museum 2075. Limestone. Ht. 1.21 m.
Photos: Jessica Nitschke.

that some of the types seen in votive terracottas, such as those from the Kharayeb votive deposit, were becoming desirable in monumental art as well.[65] By comparison, most of the male figures' drapery is somewhat stiff. The body positions in both males and females can be awkward as well.

Umm el-ʿAmed offers further proof that selective use of Levantine, Egyptian, Greek, and Achaemenid imagery was a way that at least some Phoenicians represented themselves to themselves. Again we see that these combinations cannot be divided neatly into successive episodes of Egyptian, Achaemenid, and Greek acculturation. Not only are some of the Egyptian elements at this site new, such as the Ptolemaic sphinxes, it also would appear that the Persian male dress on the limestone stelai is conservative, a tradition that began in the Persian period and by the Hellenistic period had become part of Phoenician elite representation (whether or not people actually dressed this way is separate matter, however). The coexistence of these elements marks the sanctuary in general terms as Phoenician, but it seems impossible given this evidence to decide what visual elements here might signal particular civic or broader Phoenician collective identities.

Although we have such compelling evidence of contact in visual art, we lack evidence that many Greeks or Macedonians immigrated to Phoenicia in the Persian and Hellenistic eras. The earliest known Greek monumental inscription dates only to circa 200, and not many more inscriptions are known before the Roman era.[66] Some Phoenicians, however, did use Greek and lived or worked in Greek cities. Their perspectives are very important for thinking about differences in self-presentation at home and abroad. For example, a bilingual inscription from the port of Athens known as the "Piraeus Inscription" describes honors for a member of the community:

[1] *bym 4 lmrzḥ bšt 14 lʿm ṣdn tm bd ṣdnym bn ʾspt lʿṭr* [2] *ʾyt šmʿbʿl bn mgn ʾš nšʾ hgw ʿl bt ʾlm wʿl mbnt ḥṣr bt ʾlm* [3] *ʿṭrt ḥrṣ bdrknm 20 lmḥt k bn ʾyt ḥṣr bt ʾlm wpʿl ʾyt kl* [4] *ʾš ʿlty mšrt ʾyt rʿt z lktb bʾdmm ʾš nšʾm ln ʿl bt* [5] *ʾlm ʿlt mṣbt ḥrṣ wyṭnʾy bʿrpt bt ʾlm ʿn ʾš lknt gw* [6] *ʿrb ʿlt mṣbt z yšʾn bksp ʾlm bʿl ṣdn drkmnm 20 lmḥt* [7] *lkn ydʿ hṣdnym k ydʿ hgw lšlm ḥlpt ʾyt ʾdmm ʾš pʿl* [8] *mšrt ʾt pn gw* [9] τὸ κοινὸν τῶν Σιδωνίων Διοπείθ(η)ν Σιδώνιον

[Phoenician] [1] On the fourth day of the *marzeah*, in the 14th year of the people of Sidon, it was resolved by Sidonians (*ṣdnym*) in assembly (*ʾspt*):—to crown [2] Shemaʿbaal, son of *Mgn*, who (had been) a superintendent of the community (*gw*) in charge of the temple and in charge of the buildings in the temple court, [3] with a gold crown worth 20 full-weight darics, because he (re)built the temple court and did all [4] that was required by him by way of service;—that the men who are our superintendents in charge of the temple should write this decision [5] on a chiseled stele, and should set it up in the portico of the temple before the eyes of men;— (and) that the community (*gw*) should be named [6] as guarantor. For this stele the people from Sidon shall draw 20 full-weight drachmae from the temple treasury. [7] So may the Sidonians (*ṣdnym*) know that the community (*gw*) knows how to requite the men who have rendered [8] service before the community (*gw*).

[Greek] [1] The community of Sidonians (honors) [2] Diopeithes the Sidonian.[67]

The inscription points to a wealthy Sidonian community that was both independent of and conversant in Athenian civic matters. The Phoenician portion follows the model of Greek dedications.[68] In it, the honorand is identified as one Shemaʻbaal son of Magon. Following a common Phoenician practice, an equivalent for his name is given in the Greek portion, Diopeithes, and the typical patronym is dropped in favor of the Greek ethnic.[69] No god is mentioned outright, though scholars assume that Baʻal, as the chief god of Sidon, is the intended recipient. It is not clear whether the temple in the inscription was in Attika or Sidon itself. Either way, the ties between this community (*gw, koinon*) to the Phoenician city-state are represented as ongoing. "Sidon" and its cognates appear here six times. In the Phoenician portion, Sidon is used to date the inscription ("in the 14th year of the people of Sidon") and to specify the group ("the Sidonians in assembly"). In the Greek portion it is again used to describe the group and as a personal ethnic ("Diopeithes the Sidonian").

The dating strategy in the inscription underscores the difficulties laid out in the beginning of this section about correlating even detailed Phoenician inscriptions with historical events. Although the formula is found also at Umm el-ʻAmed,[70] the meaning of *bšt* 14 *lʻm ṣdn* on the Piraeus Inscription has generated a lot of different interpretations. Edward Lipiński and other specialists assure us that the Greek inscription dates to the third century on paleographic grounds. Indeed "year one" of Sidon cannot be any later because of the monetary terms mentioned, Persian darics, whose use did not continue past the first quarter of the third century.[71] Year one is sometimes counted from Alexander's conquests in 333/2 or from the appointment of Alexander's supposed client king, Abdalonymos.[72] Lipiński points out that the inscription does not mention a king of Sidon, and he accordingly prefers to associate year one with the beginning of the Seleukid era in 312/11. Because we know hardly anything about the political organization of the Phoenician city-states in this or any period, including exactly how long the monarchies of different city-states were left in place, this is speculation.[73] Whatever moment is marked by "year one," it testifies to the existence of Sidonian collective identity in what was probably a very confused period.

Attika provides other examples of Phoenician self-presentation abroad. One especially rich example is a funerary stele from the Athenian Kerameikos that has recently been carefully studied by Jennifer Stager and again by Olga Tribulato.[74] The stele has three inscriptions, Greek and Phoenician epitaphs followed by a longer Greek epigram. It probably dates to the early third century.[75] In the epitaphs we learn the Greek and Phoenician names of the deceased and the man who paid for the stele:

Ἀντίπατρος Ἀφροδισίου Ἀσκαλ[ωνίτης]
Δομσαλὼς Δομανὼ Σιδώνιος ἀνέθηκε
ʾnk šm . bn ʿbdʿštrt ʾšqlny
ʾš yṭnʾt ʾnk dʿmṣlḥ bn dʿmḥnʾ ṣdny

[Greek] Antipatros, son of Aphrodisios, the Ashkel(onite)
Domsalōs, son of Domanō, the Sidonian, dedicated (this stele)

[Phoenician] I Shem . son of ʿAbdaštart the Ashkelon(ite)
(This is the stele) which I, Domseleh, son of Domhano the Sidonian set up.[76]

Here we see a juxtaposition of onomastic strategies, one opting for translation in Greek (Antipatros/Shem) and the other transliteration (Domsalōs/Domseleh). As Stager and Tribulato argue, these practices suggest degrees of linguistic and cultural bilingualism. The "cultural duality" of the deceased, Antipatros/Shem, is greater by comparison with his friend Domseleh.[77]

The accompanying imagery shows the deceased on a bier being attacked by a lion, which is, in turn, energetically repelled by a male figure in front of ship's prow and naval standard. Stager argues persuasively that what we see here is a Phoenician funerary practice executed in Athenian style. The epigram goes some way to spelling out what is seen to Greek speakers but does not explain its full meaning. Tribulato argues that its *hapax legomena*, rather than its grammatical mistakes, are a key to understanding that a Phoenician, presumably Domseleh, closely supervised the language of the epigram.[78] The stele's imagery addressed two audiences, an Athenian one that might have had particular reactions to the male figure fighting a lion, and a Phoenician one that would understand its visual language differently. Stager argues that a Phoenician observer would have associated a lion and ship's prow with astral navigation, Phoenician maritime religion, and Antipatros/Shem's home city of Ashkelon.[79]

The compelling final line of the epigram reads:

Φοινίκην δ' ἔλιπον τεῖδε χθονὶ σῶμα κέκρυνμαι

I left Phoenicia and I am, in body, here hidden in the earth.[80]

There are only half a dozen instances in which phoinix and its cognates appear in Greek-language inscriptions.[81] On the Kerameikos stele's epigram, "Phoenicia" is being substituted for the specific Ashkelonite and Sidonian identities in the epitaph. Stager argues that Phoenicia means something that was both different from and broader than a civic identity. Because the epigram and the epitaph are written in different hands, the epigram could have been part of the original dedication by Domseleh or it could have been added later. Accordingly, we cannot know if this Phoenicianism was internally expressed or externally imposed. But even without the epigram, the epitaphs and the image show a collectivity that coexisted with distinct civic identities—Ashkelon and Sidon are distinct *and* related, as are the Greek and Phoenician languages and the imagery on the stele.

The use of the Phoenician language, an important choice in this context, privileges a Phoenician audience while showing command of Greek and knowledge of an Athenian type of monument, as does the imagery despite its Athenian style. This last point is very important to the way that we react to Greek style or imagery in other contexts, such as the Eshmun sanctuary in the patron Domseleh's home city. In fact, Stager and Tribulato disagree on how to interpret this monument's aggregations, if they indicate that Antipatros/Shem died at sea en route to Athens (Stager's view) or are proof that he lived in Athens (Tribulato's view). Their close studies show how much we have to gain from taking the Phoenician components of such objects seriously. The Kerameikos and Piraeus inscriptions are representative of the Phoenician inscriptions in Attika, Thebes, and Corinth as a whole, which balance different degrees of bilingualism, civic heterogeneity, and Phoenician community.[82]

A few preliminary points can be drawn from this evidence. First, to get to the most obvious one, phoinix and its cognates are rare in the Greek epigraphic record. Explicit claims to be "a Phoenician" in Greek literature are more rare still. In Achilles Tatius's second-century CE romance, the character Klitophōn identifies himself as a Phoenician from Tyre (1.3.1):

ἐμοὶ Φοινίκη γένος, Τύρος ἡ πατρίς, ὄνομα Κλειτοφῶν, πατὴρ Ἱππίας, ἀδελφὸς πατρὸς Σώστρατος

I am a Phoenician, my homeland is Tyre; my name is Klitophōn, my father is called Hippias, my uncle Sōstratos.[83]

Hints of self-adoption of phoinix are found elsewhere in the imperial period, in Herennius Philo of Byblos's so-called *Phoenician History,* which was written in Greek in the second century CE, and the aforementioned single line of Heliodoros's *Aithiopika* (10.41.4).[84] There are more examples, which together speak to new, revived, or increasing interest in Phoenician identity in the imperial period,[85] an interest that, however compelling, cannot be read as entirely emic or ethnic and cannot be pushed retroactively into the first millennium BCE. Just as important is the parallel evidence of the persistence of strong civic identities, some of which, such as the Piraeus Inscription, show no indication whatsoever of a broader Phoenicianism.

While iconography such as the disk and uraei was in use in the coastal Levant from the Bronze Age into the second half of the first millennium, what we see beginning in the Persian period are classes of monumental objects that are particular to Phoenicians. We also find in Phoenicia combinations of styles, iconographies, and types that are not found elsewhere, as Umm el-'Amed and the Eshmun complex at Bostan esh-Sheik demonstrate. Most often the Greek and Phoenician points of contact are emphasized, such as the combination of Aštart throne and Greek altar, but that is only one small part of what was happening even in the Eshmun complex. Greek style was not a feature of the 'Amrit sanctuary or even a factor in the limited evidence we have from Byblos. Instead we see evidence of various responses to tradition and to new contacts with different results. We should not necessarily conclude, however, that the city-state was the "chief horizon of identity"[86] for the people we call Phoenicians. Hints of Phoenicianism are found in theophoric names that cannot be assigned to specific city-states, in anthropoid sarcophagi from multiple locations, and, in more general terms, in the approach to sacred spaces. Phoenicianism is explicit in the Kerameikos inscription that brings together Sidonian and Ashkelonite.

Portable Evidence: Coins

The earliest known Mediterranean coins come from late seventh- or early sixth-century western Asia Minor. Although the impetus for the invention of coinage is debated, early coins had very limited circulation, suggesting local needs were being met.[87] The first coins to circulate more widely were minted in the silver-rich regions of Thrace and Macedon in the late sixth century. Aegina was the first Greek polis to mint, beginning in the mid-sixth century. These issues were not much to look at, "dumpy pieces with a turtle" on the obverse, and a crossed-line punch on the reverse.[88] Yet even crude decorative schemes served as visual reminders of a coin's value and issuing authority. Aeginitan turtles were the first coins to circulate in the Near East. Shortly after the full exploitation of the silver mines at

Laureion began in 483,[89] they were eclipsed in popularity by the Athenian silver tetradrachm—the Athenian owl—an overtly civic coin evoked in this choral passage from Aristophanes's *Birds*:

γλαῦκες ὑμᾶς οὔποτ᾽ ἐπιλείψουσι Λαυρειωτικαί,
ἀλλ᾽ ἐνοικήσουσιν ἔνδον, ἔν τε τοῖς βαλλαντίοις
ἐννεοττεύσουσι κἀκλέψουσι μικρὰ κέρματα

Never shall the Lauriotic owls from you depart,
But shall in your houses dwell, and in your purses too
Nestle close, and hatch a brood of little coins for you.[90]

The owl spread throughout the eastern Mediterranean, becoming synonymous with coinage itself. It was widely imitated.[91]

The coin's design is both elegant and straightforward (see Plate 14). On the obverse is the helmeted head of Athena, facing right. Beginning with the Classical issues (from post ca. 480–475) she is also laureate, surely to celebrate the victory over Xerxes, and a floral scroll is added to her helmet. On the reverse is Athena's owl, standing with the body facing right, face front, large eyes upon the beholder.[92] Athena's olive branch is in the field over the back of the bird; a small crescent moon is between them, the latter another feature added in the Classical era. To the right of the owl is the legend with the polis ethnic ΑΘΕ for *Athēnaiōn*, "of the Athenians." These elements are found on Athenian silver coinage, with some interruptions and many small die variations, until the mid-third century BCE. The style is kept Archaic deliberately, moving in small stages from the profile eye, to the three-quarter eye, to the early fourth century, when Athena's naturalistic makeover was complete, her eye rendered in profile and her Archaic smile softened.

While Athena shows up on the coins of many states, this combination of Athena plus her owl points clearly to the city that bears her name and to their shared military strength and wisdom.[93] The coins were minted throughout the fifth century (fewer in the first few decades after the wars) as Athens expanded its empire and brought the Delian League treasury home. Eventually Athens demanded use of its coinage by her subject-allies.[94] Whereas major civic structures such as the Parthenon defined the Athenian identity at home for an audience composed of citizens, metics, and visitors, the Athenian tetradrachm distilled essential features of the state over incredible distances, declaring the stability and power of Athens as guaranteed by its patron deity and the remarkable purity of its coins.[95]

Although there is ongoing debate about the extent to which users paid attention to coin imagery, it is clear from imitation owls minted elsewhere that people at a remove from Athens understood the Athenian owl as the eastern Mediterranean's primary coinage and an important commercial tool. It remains to be explored how much the coins projected a particular Athenian or even Hellenic identity and to whom. No mainland Phoenician cities imitated the owls directly. One reason for not doing so was practical, as imitations upset the confidence in a coin's value.[96] There is a time lag between the popularity of coinage in Greek poleis and the minting of coinage in Phoenicia and Egypt, one that has contributed to the idea that the minting of coins is symptomatic of Hellenization. There is no real support for this view. As Jigoulov points out in his brief review of the state of the field, Phoenician numismatics began as an offshoot of Greek numismatics. Only very recently has the study of Phoenician coins become a field in its own right, meaning that the approach to the topic is still Hellenocentric or in the early stages of reacting against Hellenocentrism.[97] For this reason the discussion below concerning imagery is detailed, though not comprehensive. The goal is to emphasize the great extent to which the coinage of the Phoenician city-states from its inception operated with a visual logic all its own, a pattern that has been established already in the preceding discussion of monumental art and inscriptions. Like monumental stone sculpture, the coins' standards and imagery are evidence of the independence of and competitive relationship between city-states that coexisted with elements of connectivity.

The fact remains that the Achaemenid Empire adopted coinage second hand from Lydia, just as Greek states did (Hdt. 1.94.1; see Map 4). The main mint seems to have been at Sardis. The first coins were lion and bull Croesus staters ("Croeseids") minted after 546.[98] Although the date of the introduction of the Achaemenid gold darics and silver sigloi (shekels) is debated, there is good evidence they were first minted by Darius I in the last decade of the sixth century as part of his major economic reforms.[99] It is quite likely that payment for naval service, for the building and manning of ships, was an important motivation.[100] The move to coinage in Phoenicia—where Persian coins hardly circulated, according to our available evidence[101]—was probably similarly motivated but must be understood also in the context of the increasingly important role of coins, Athenian owls chief among them, in eastern Mediterranean commerce.

Just before the middle of the fifth century, in the midst of ongoing conflict with Athens and perhaps owing to a dip in the production of and access to owls after 480,[102] the four major Phoenician city-states begin minting coins. The traditional view is that the first city to mint was Byblos in circa 460, followed in succession by Tyre, Sidon, and Arwad (Figures 35–36, Plate 15).[103] Probably the first silvers were made by melting down Greek coins, thus transferring the added value of the coin—on top of its raw material—to the Phoenician states.[104] It appears that these coins did not circulate widely before the fourth century, although our understanding of their use is meager owing to limited publication of coins from controlled excavations. Their impetus is debated, sometimes attributed to a desire to participate in the coinage economy. No hoards of Phoenician coins have been found in Hellas, however.[105] Beyond Arwad, which minted Persian-standard sigloi and staters, the main denominations of these coins deliberately but not exclusively employed an independent standard, what we call the "Phoenician standard," tied to a silver stater or shekel of circa 13.9 grams that was divided into many smaller values.[106]

As Colin Kraay has argued for Athenian coins, the relatively large silvers were probably not minted for use in local markets, even though their circulation was initially rather limited. Kraay argued payments made to and by the state were the motivation for minting, although it must be emphasized that the minting of coins for such a purpose presupposes that both the state and its members would find coinage useful. Clearly the question of the origin of Phoenician coins is complex, though I favor the idea of internal factors brought about by external events. Beginning in the late sixth or early fifth century, Darius's aforementioned reorganization of the Achaemenid Empire promoted changes in civic structures throughout Phoenicia. Accompanying these changes were new financial and tax systems and, critically, coin payment for military and naval service.[107] Many of the very same conditions leading to the creation of Athenian owls were shared by the Achaemenids and Phoenicians, which led to their decision or ability to mint self-promoting coins. Even in Anatolia the importance of coinage grew under Achaemenid rule.[108]

Leslie Kurke has made an eloquent argument that Athenian coins were valued for what she calls essential and functional/symbolic factors. She places emphasis on the Athenians' near-exclusive use of silver, a metal she associates with the middling identity and the polis in contrast to the golden ideology of elites.[109] The primary use of silver for Phoenician coinage deserves attention, too. It is doubtful the Achaemenids would have allowed Phoenicians to mint in gold, and it is likely that the Phoenician states would not have had much use for such high-denomination coins. Achaemenid darics were informally called *toxotai*, or "archers," by Greeks owing to their standard iconography of a striding figure in a long robe and crown carrying a bow and sometimes other weapons (as Plut. *Artax.* 20.4, *Ages.* 15.6). They were minted in a very pure (98 percent) gold.[110] Greek sources suggest the idea of gold coinage was virtually synonymous with darics, which was one more reason Greeks associated gold with the East.[111]

Following on this idea and Kurke's line of thinking, it is possible to infer ways that the materiality of Phoenician coinage was perceived in ideological terms. The use of silver for the highest denominations could have articulated the difference between Sidon and Tyre and their suzerain even while both of these cities employed some Achaemenid imagery on their coins (discussed below). The fact that most Phoenician city-states did not adopt the Persian silver denomination, the siglos, adds to the idea that these choices were in part ideological. Although their motivations were different from those of Athenians, Phoenicians could have perceived a similar dialectic of metals, with, in this case, gold as an emblem of Persia and silver as civic and quasi-independent. I follow Kurke in concluding that the civic coins constructed and controlled value, thereby increasing the authority and power of city-states tangibly (economically) and symbolically.[112] Iconography reinforces this general picture.

Skill in miniature work is plain from the coins' execution. Gubel has shown that some of their visual content stems from glyptic arts. The contextual study of seals is made difficult by their popularity in the art market, however, and some of his broader claims regarding seals of the Persian period have been criticized accordingly.[113] Recalling what we have already seen in monumental arts, it is clear that the iconography of different civic issues was developed through a local tradition in combination with the selective use of reinterpreted foreign motifs. Our understanding of what is shown is often hampered by our generally poor grasp on Phoenician religious and state symbolism. For example, the early coins of Arwad show a fish-tailed deity with a warship on the reverse.[114] There is no consensus on the identity of the ichthymorphic deity, and even the meaning of the warship is not straightforward—it might be a general reference to maritime prowess or a reference to or appropriation of Sidonian or Persian iconography. In the early part of the fourth century, the iconography on silver coinage changes. Some shows bearded faces (of the ichthymorphic deity?) or sea horses (Figure 35). In circa 380–350, waves are added to the reverse with the ship, and the eye of the bearded figure gets a naturalistic makeover—that is, after Athena does on her owls—as in the example illustrated here.

The coinage of Byblos is quite different.[115] The earliest issues show a sphinx wearing a double crown and a number of reverses, some of which are seemingly generic (head of a helmeted figure), others expressly Egyptian (scepter, vulture, and ram). Circa 400 the obverse iconography becomes bellicose: a galley and soldiers. Some reverses are kept, and others, such a sitting lion, are added. The lion likely represents Aštart and might be a reference to the growing power of Sidon, where her cult was long established (compare the Shem stele from Athens). Changes again occur in the beginning of the fourth century when obverses are loaded with imagery (Figure 36). They show, from top to bottom, a galley, a winged sea horse (sometimes referred to in the literature as a *hippocamp*), and a shell. Reverses often show a lion attacking a bull, as in the illustrated example, a long-lived image that was embraced by Achaemenids and here seems to be a deliberate reference to Persia.

Sidonian coinage is consistent on its obverse: a galley with small variations in the details, sometimes with fortifications in the background, that recalls Herodotos's

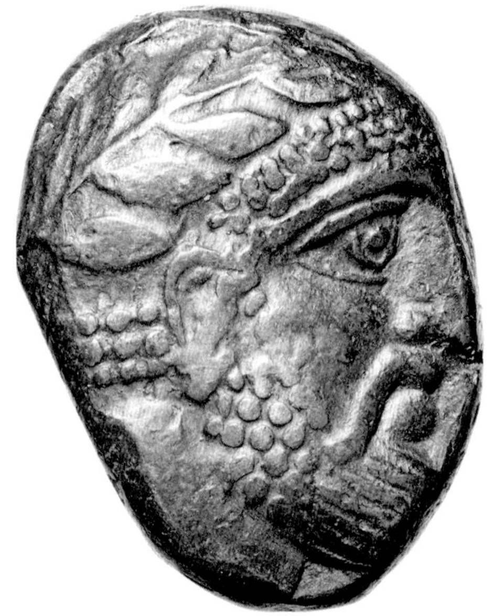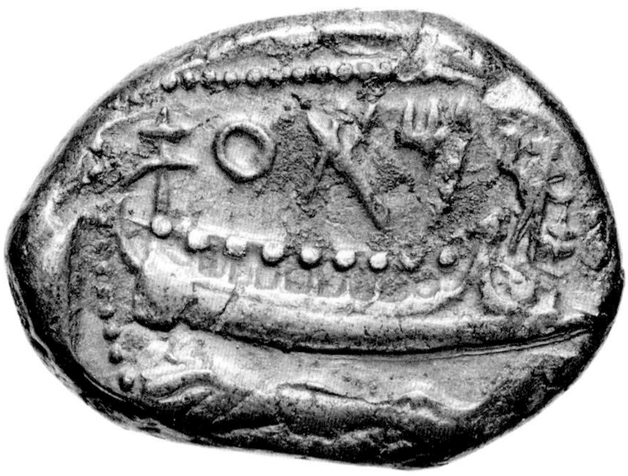

Figure 35. Silver stater minted in Arwad, later 4th c. Obverse: bearded male; reverse: ship and Phoenician inscription. Paris, Bibliothèque nationale de France FRBNF41741201. Silver. 10.7 gr. Photo: Bibliothèque nationale de France.

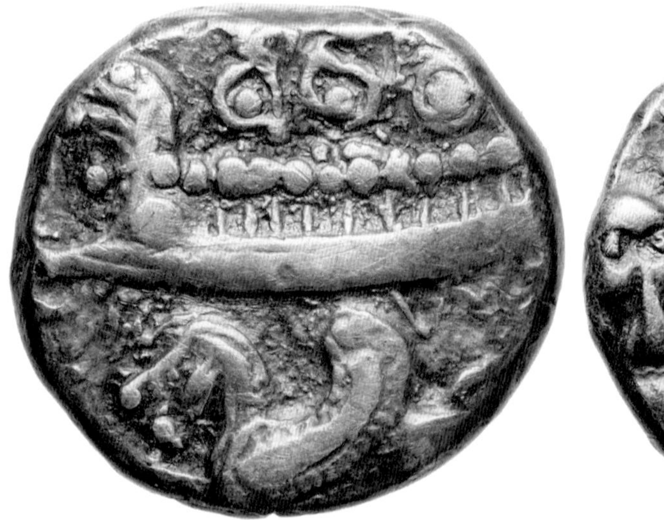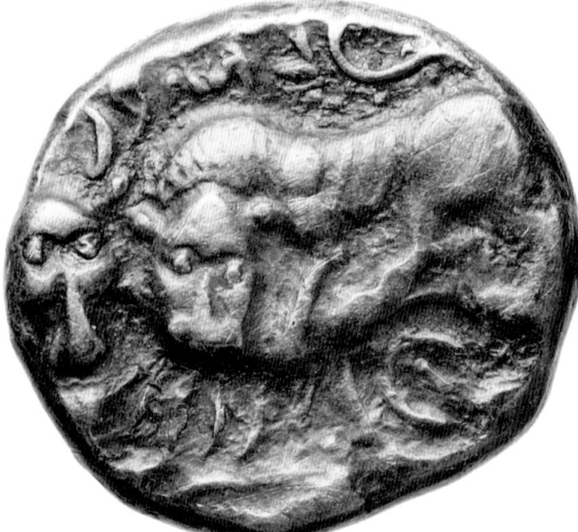

Figure 36. Silver drachma of Elpa'al, minted in Byblos, 4th c. Obverse: galley with soldiers, winged sea horse, shell; reverse: lion attacking bull. Paris, Bibliothèque nationale de France FRBNF41741215. Silver. 2.92 gr. Photo: Bibliothèque nationale de France.

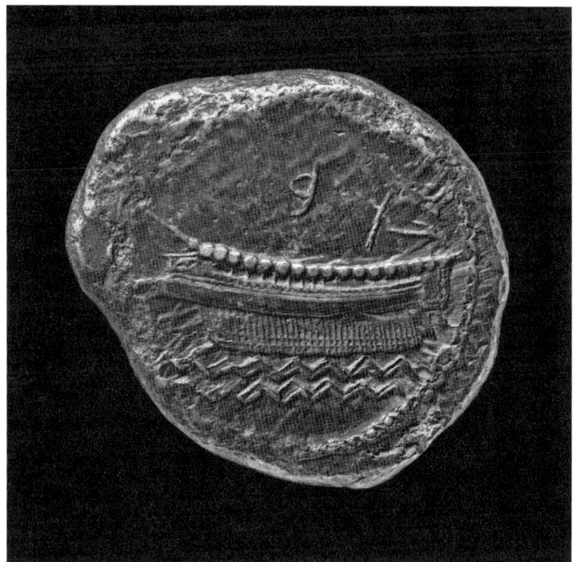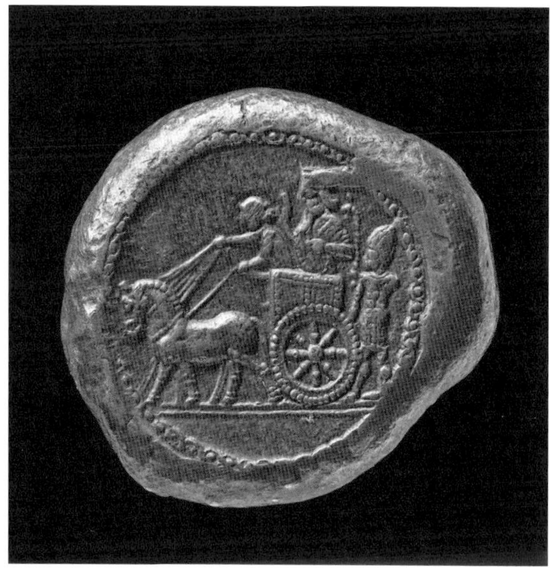

Figure 37. Silver coin of Baʿalshillem II, minted in Sidon. Obverse: ship; reverse: chariot carrying a royal figure followed by attendant, late 5th or earlier 4th c. London, British Museum 1918,0204.157. Silver. 28.3 gr. Photo: © The Trustees of the British Museum.

statement that Sidonians were the best of the fleet (7.96–100; Figure 37).[116] Reverses are varied, but they mostly relate to imperial Achaemenid imagery. They begin with a nod to Persian coinage, an archer. The use of this motif is somewhat remarkable because, despite its wide circulation in the Western Empire, only one Persian coin has been excavated so far in Phoenicia proper, a silver from Byblos.[117] Our knowledge of the circulation of darics is poor, and only about 160 examples of Persian coins are known in all of the Transeuphrates.[118] Nonetheless, it is clear the imagery was familiar to Phoenician kings, and it was an important part of Sidonian (and, as we will see, Tyrian) self-representation on coinage. From circa 430, the reverse shows a chariot with driver and royal rider, which from the end of the fifth century is followed by an attendant on foot (as in Figure 37, right). The rider, sometimes interpreted as a statue, is shown in Persian ceremonial dress. As on Arwadian and Byblian coinage, inscriptions of the king appear on Sidonian coins shortly thereafter, from circa 400. In the fourth century several changes occurred, including more denominations and the reappearance of an archer figure as well as a standing lion. The coins of ʿAbdaštart I (in Greek Straton I, r. ca. 365–352) stand out in this period, as they show further standard and iconographic changes. ʿAbdaštart minted bronzes with a bearded and diademed head and a galley on the reverse. Stylistically his coins look like other Sidonian issues, but they were minted on the Attic standard. A relationship between the king and Athens is attested also by a Greek inscription from the Athenian akropolis telling how 'Abdaštart assisted an Athenian delegation to the Persian court.[119] Sidonian traders were awarded tax breaks in return.

Some see this coinage as evidence of Sidon's increasing resistance to Achaemenid rule. It is important to this argument that Abdaštart's successor, Tennes, openly rebelled against Persia.[120] In Diodoros's account of the so-called Tennes Rebellion of circa 350, Sidon is presented as instigator, but other city-states seem to be involved, too. Tyre and Arwad are implied participants.[121] It is in this period that Sidonian and Tyrian standards are closest, a move that might have been meant to reinforce political unity.[122] A parallel situation is found in Anatolia, where in the fourth century silver sigloi production slows and is replaced by different satrapal issues, including those with tiarate heads on the obverse. Elspeth Dusinberre has argued against this change as evidence of growing independence, however, because the tiara headgear shown on the coins is the same as what Persians wore into battle. Thus this type and other new issues functioned in a symbolic fashion that fit the original sigloi, even while the iconography changed and the style of their execution became Greek.[123] In both cases, we have good evidence that standards and imagery were meaningful to the issuing kings, Persian imagery most of all.[124] Sidon's Persian-looking coins have been downplayed in most treatments of Phoenician art of this period, a consequence of the desire to see Sidon as leading the way in Phoenicia's Hellenization. In fact, Arwad is the only city-state to produce coinage that responds to the style of Greek art, and only Tyre's coins have iconographic similarities.

Tyre's popular owl reverses are found on seven different Persian-period series (see Plate 15).[125] The earliest Tyrian coins were minted with a variety of themes on their obverse: a dolphin over waves and a shell or a bearded figure on a winged sea horse flying over waves and also above a shell or dolphin (see Plate 15, top). Although we lack independent corroboration of his appearance in this period, the bearded figure is usually identified as Melqart, under the assumption that pride of place on Tyrian coinage belongs to the city god. The Melqart bowman becomes the standard imagery of Tyrian obverses in the fourth century. The winged sea horse, like the one on Byblian coinage, seems to stem from Phoenician seal imagery,[126] while the pose of the bearded figure is derived from the Persian archer motif.[127] Like the Persian archer, the Tyrian one holds a bow in his left hand. His costume is different, however, and he does not wear a crown. Instead of holding attributes in his right hand, the Tyrian figure holds the reins of his sea horse. As Nitschke has shown, the similarities and differences are both important to the presentation of Tyrian identity. Whereas the Persian archer shows the empire's dominance over the land, the Melqart figure on his flying sea horse rules over the sea.[128]

It is in this context that we must turn to the owl reverses and their relationship with the Mediterranean's dominant coinage. Like its Athenian counterpart, the

Tyrian owl stands with its body usually to the right and its head facing front, looking out at the viewer. Both owls have their left foot in front of their right. Both have dots (sometimes lines) on their bodies to indicate mottled feathers, leaving the wings and tail feathers smooth. But that is where the similarities end. Whereas the Classical Athenian owl seen in Plate 14 is Archaizing, the Tyrian owl is just as clearly derived from an Egyptian prototype.[129] In the fifth century, the Tyrian owl has a compact body and a long and wide wing that stretches from breast to back; a small head; a strong brow line plunging into the beak; squared tail feathers of equal length that descend all the way to the ground; and ear tufts.[130] Many of these features are found also in the owl hieroglyph, the sure source of the Tyrian image (compare the many owl hieroglyphs on the Tabnit sarcophagus seen in Figure 21, right). Key similarities include the pose, shape of the body and tail, and emphasis on the V-shaped brow.[131] Along with the owl on the coin's reverse are the crook and the flail, symbols of Egyptian divinity and kingship. These attributes are arranged behind the owl's body from upper left to lower right so that the owl is in chiastic superimposition.

Just because it is clear that these motifs were appropriated from Egypt, we should not forget to ask why. Why an owl, and why the crook and flail? Owls are not mentioned in any Phoenician inscriptions, and they hardly appear in Phoenician art before they become a standard image on these early Tyrian coins. They do not make frequent appearances afterward.[132] It is possible that the owl had an apotropaic or magical role in Tyrian funerary rites, but the evidence is thin.[133] While apotropaic imagery is known on coins, probably this is not the right connection in this case. The crook and the flail are curious, too. In Egyptian hieroglyphs, neither is shown together with the owl. When paired in art, they are usually held one in each hand, arranged in a chiastic or "V" shape. Examples can be found in funerary imagery of pharaohs and Osiris.[134] When the crook and flail are aligned, as on the coins, it is because they are held in one hand. Examples include some images of Anubis, pharaohs, and Horus the Child.[135] The flail also appears in chiastic juxtaposition with two common bird hieroglyphs, the vulture and the falcon. The falcon seems to be the link with Phoenician art. On seals thought to be of Phoenician manufacture, the crook and flail are attributes of Egyptian-type hawks or falcons in an arrangement similar to that on the Tyrian coins (see Plate 16).[136] What we see on the coins are two elements of Egyptian visual art that are combined for the first and only time. The arrangement may have meant to evoke images of the Horus/falcon-flail hieroglyphs that seem to be the progenitors also of the seal imagery seen here.

The Tyrian owl image is equal parts appropriation and innovation, like the Melqart archer on a sea horse with which it was often paired. Both images show Tyre's authority through their respective appropriation of Egyptian and Achaemenid symbols of leadership. Yet the particular choice of the Egyptian owl can only be explained in terms of Athenian owls.[137] Rather than imitating or appropriating Athena's owl as one might expect, the Tyrian owl is deliberately rejecting its visual qualities in favor of Phoenician ones. With its prominent ear tufts, small head, and particular body, the Tyrian owl even seems to be interested in representing a different species.[138] As a construct of the Tyrian state, the owl issues are very sophisticated. At once they stake a claim to the growing coin-based economy, negotiate with three major powers through their own symbols of authority, and produce something unique—something Tyrian. The Tyrian owls appear as late as 275. The consistency of the imagery made them "more easily recognisable within and without the minting city."[139] Possibly the predatory owl was as synonymous with Tyre as the Melqart archer. Unlike the winged sea horse, shell, and dolphin, the owl is never found on the coins of other states.

The general message of the various Phoenician coins is clear enough. Power is expressed in economic, religious, and political terms by appropriating, recombining, and generating iconography. While there is evidence that golden archers were synonymous with Persia, we have less evidence about what Athenian owls signaled to users. Were they seen specifically as Athenian? Or were they read as Greek? The Athenian owls quite deliberately construct an identity for their city: the owl is Athena, and Athena is Athens. It would be a mistake to argue against the coins' political particularity. It would be a further mistake to think that Phoenicians were incapable of understanding at least some of what the coins were trying to say. As the Tyrian owls ably demonstrate, the Athenian owl was seen as a major symbol of power. Changes to the owl—its species, attributes, and style—underscore an awareness that all of these visual components were significant.

Athenians were well known by Tyrians in the era of the coins' emergence, as Athens was the main power in the Greek navy that opposed the combined Phoenician forces. Sidon, Tyre, and Arwad all contributed ships in service of Persia.[140] At the same time, we should acknowledge that direct contact between Athenians and the Phoenician fleet did not inspire Greeks to discuss Phoenicians in a careful way. We must accept the possibility that Phoenicians showed the same degree of uninterest in Greeks or the parallel tendency to conflate a city-state with a larger collective, a point of view perhaps encouraged by the formation of the Delian League in 478. Further, the ubiquity of the Athenian owls might support the idea that, however particular their visual properties, they had superseded the scale of their particular minting polis.

Nonetheless, it seems plausible that the Athenian owls projected Athenian identity in Phoenicia, but there is no way to know the extent to which "Athenian" also meant "Greek" there. The identities associated with Tyrian coins, and Phoenician coins as a class of objects, are still more difficult to recover. Here again we will find reasons to argue for and against art's expression of collective identity on a level exceeding the state. There is no reason to think that Phoenician coinage began as part of a unified effort, just as it is unlikely that the Phoenician fleet began as any sort of collective force. From our admittedly imperfect evidence, it appears that the major mints started up at different times, beginning, paradoxically, with the weakest of the four city-states, Byblos. These mints were not operating at the behest of Persia, as most employed their own standards and all clearly had free rein to choose their iconography. Further, no city-states minted coins identical in terms of their design.

Yet there are points of connectivity. Some coins share iconographic elements, such as the shell or the sea horse; they are made in silver or bronze but never gold; and they circulated primarily within Phoenicia. Importantly, Byblos, Sidon, and Tyre make an effort in this period to employ a similar weight standard, the afore-mentioned Phoenician standard, for some issues. In the mid-fourth century, it was employed also in Carthage.[141] This standard not only set the Phoenician economic system apart from that of the Greeks and the Persians, it also distinguished Phoenicia from its closer neighbors, some of which, like Judah, had a special status within the Achaemenid Empire (Neh 5:15–18).[142] The coins may be a rare state-ment of Phoenician political, or at least economic, unity that persists for some seventy years.

Phoenicianism and the Fifth Century

To conclude, we may reconsider what is at stake in the idea of an emerging Phoe-nician collective identity and what conditions might have shaped it. It is impor-tant to situate this discussion in the very small scale of mainland Phoenicia (see Maps 1, 3, and 4). From what can be determined, cities were small and surely densely populated: bigger city-states, such as Arwad and Sidon, are estimated to have measured between forty and sixty hectares at their largest extent; Beirut and Sarepta were considerably smaller. Even Tyre may have measured no more than sixteen hectares in its urban core.[143] The distance between the two mainland mints at farthest remove—Tyre and Arwad—is only about two hundred kilometers. Tyre and Sidon are separated by about fifty kilometers, Sidon and Beirut by a mere forty or so. Corinth and Athens, by contrast, are about eighty-five kilometers apart; Ath-ens and Delphi are separated by about 175 kilometers, Sparta and Delphi by some 320 kilometers (overland). While there is disagreement about how they developed, the Phoenician language and writing system suggest easy communication between different city-states. Moreover, members of these maritime cities were on the move and frequently traded with one another. These factors—scale, trade, mobility, and communication—mean that it is quite possible a collective Phoenician identity existed at some points in the Iron Age, even if we lack much evidence to support it.

All the same, the events of the late sixth and fifth centuries had a major impact on Phoenicia and the entire eastern Mediterranean. The incorporation of the Levant into the Achaemenid Empire drove many of these events. Major Phoenician city-states began fighting alongside one another in opposition to Greek forces at the 494 battle of Ladē. The Eshmunazar sarcophagus suggests that this type of service sometimes had handsome rewards, certainly among the main protagonists on the Phoenician side, the neighboring states of Sidon and Tyre. The anecdote regarding Carthage recorded in Herodotos might be a Greek projection, but legends on Hellenistic bronzes of Sidon and Tyre demonstrate the continuity of their close, yet very competitive, relationship. While second-century Sidonian coins were inscribed "Sidon, mother of Carthage, Hippo, Kition, and Tyre" (cf. Just. *Epit.* 18.3.5), contemporary Tyrian coins proclaimed that Tyre was the "mother of the Sidonians."[144] In these legends we see a deliberate doubling of meaning, a proclamation of one state's superiority over her neighbor(s), notably her greatest regional rival, in Hellenic terms, a strategy that has echoes in the bilingual inscriptions from Athens and, more explicitly, in Persian-period Tyrian coinage.

In fact, Tyre was the state that most often expressed its Phoenicianism in the long run, even after it became a free port in 126 BCE. As late as the third century CE, Tyre minted coins showing Kadmos handing the Greeks their alphabet[145] as well as coins commemorating the founding of Carthage.[146] This evidence might suggest that Phoenician identity got *stronger* as the second half of the first millennium unfolded, reaching its acme in the first and second centuries CE, a phenomenon that can be compared to Michael Scott's argument concerning the late development of Panhellenism.[147] But, as I said previously regarding the self-ascription of phoinix, we cannot read these tantalizing late examples back onto the fifth century. Any attempt to plot a clear trajectory of Phoenician art or culture and identity is mired in unknowns.

Nevertheless, we can observe how the city-states' coins show a remarkable degree of economic independence from their suzerain.[148] Here, as in Egypt, the Persians seem to have ruled with "as light a hand as possible" and with better results.[149] As a class of objects, the coins promote the viability of the Phoenician economic system versus an Athenian (or Greek or any other) one through the deployment of the Phoenician standard and particular motives. The imagery on the coins guaranteed their value not only to and among members of individual Phoenician city-states but also to those with whom they traded. Circulation of this imagery within the city-state was not restricted to elites, a point that has been underplayed in Phoenician numismatics. I believe that Phoenician coin production is further evidence of group consciousness emerging through a type of peer-polity interaction,[150] the conditions for which were created in the period from the rise of the Achaemenid Empire to the Persian Wars and their aftermath. As we have seen, Phoenicia has many characteristics of this model. It was composed of small city-states—polities of comparable scale—in the same region that, because of Achaemenid political and economic policies, experienced simultaneous organizational change. Interaction within and among polities led to competitive innovation.

It is not, of course, strictly necessary to frame these events in terms of peer-polity interaction. Nor is it advisable to forget that texts figure heavily in similar arguments made on the Greek side of things. Miller has shown, however, that even in Athens, a vociferous opponent of Persia, interest in "Perserie" was widespread in the fifth century.[151] Furthermore, "oppositional" thinking is not found in Herodotos. As I stressed in the previous chapter, we should be critical of the idea that Greeks considered themselves a national group in any period and must be open to challenging the Greek/anti-Greek approach so often associated with the Persian Wars and their aftermath.[152] Hellenism, like Phoenicianism, is still mostly a modern construct.[153] The point remains, however, that we have some evidence in the fifth century of collective "Phoenician" action. Coinage focuses our attention on artistic products we can confidently assign to specific groups, an opportunity as rare in Levantine portable art as it is commonplace in Athenian art. It follows that the Persian Wars could have shaped Phoenician as well as Greek collective identity, even while we recognize that these events had greater political and economic impact on some city-states, such as Athens, Tyre, and Sidon, than on others. When Sidon and some other Phoenician states moved their coinage to the Attic standard for a time in the fourth century, their motivations are unclear.[154] Possibly different uses of the Attic standard, however short lived, signaled movement away from Persia. Whatever its impetus, the move serves to underscore the collective (although not universal) decision to otherwise use an independent standard.

The new political and economic realities of the Persian period had a major impact on trade that goes some way to explaining why more Greek elements appear in Phoenician art at this time and why there is altogether more Phoenician monumental art in the archaeological record, some of which was made in imported basalt or marble. It is popular to think that, by this time, mainland Phoenicians did not dominate the western Mediterranean. That role was increasingly assumed by Carthage where the increase of population and prosperity is well attested in the archaeological record.[155] Mainland and southern Phoenician traders were thereby limited to the eastern Mediterranean, bringing them in ever-closer contact and competition with Cypriot and Greek merchants.[156] Peter van Alfen has conducted a thorough study of Mediterranean commodities, in which he suggests that the Persian-Greek rivalry was a key factor affecting trade. He argues that trade in strategic goods—timber, pitch, and agricultural products—may have been restricted by both Persians and Greeks for obvious political reasons.

One important implication of this thesis is the idea that traditionally defined necessities were not traded freely, so that Phoenicia's most famous natural resource, cedar, did not figure as prominently in trade with Greeks of this period as we might assume.[157] At the same time, we have ample evidence of a dramatic increase in trade and prosperity in the Aegean and throughout the eastern Mediterranean. Van Alfen is careful to point out that this prosperity is not restricted to the elites commonly associated with "luxury" goods. Mostly these products did not function as they did in Homeric times, as badges of exclusive status, with the likely exception of expensive purple dye, textiles, and monumental works of art. Instead, both written testimonia and archaeological evidence show that prosperity was enjoyed by a far greater portion of the population than ever before. 70 percent of what was exported from the Aegean was manufactured or refined, like Attic pottery, suggesting that a good deal of what ended up in Phoenicia would leave an archaeological imprint.[158] By contrast, spices or metals sent west from the Levant would be used up or reprocessed, and often lost. In other words, the exchange of goods between Greeks and Phoenicians might be misrepresented by the archaeological record. Aegean finewares, finished marble products, and terracottas, all of which are durable and highly visible in the archaeological record, make it appear as though the Greek contribution to the exchange was particularly cultural as opposed to commodity based. It is in this light that Tyrian owls might be seen as another imitation of the Athenian ones, when, as has been shown here, they are evidence of a much richer, and more interesting, conversation among rivals.

What of the commodities that flowed in the other direction? The maritime people of the Levantine coast, it is worth remembering, specialized in trade, not only in the export of locally made or locally grown products. In the Persian period they could have exported Levantine goods, such as cinnabar, pomegranate, and sumac, as well as goods from Arabia and even southeast Asia, including exotic spices, like cinnamon and nutmeg, or balms, such as frankincense.[159] Many of these items are hard to detect empirically, yet their quantity and importance should not be underestimated. In fact, textual evidence indicates more classes of goods were flowing westward than in the opposition direction, at a rate of 3:1. Frankincense, for example, was used in Athenian religious rites (Pl. *Leg.* 8.847b–c), reminding us that a number of these westward-moving ephemeral products were socially significant.

What contributed to the commodification and increased production of goods is not well understood. Archaeologically we can see that some cities prospered more than others. In part, we can attribute increased prosperity to a general increase in trade and the profits made from taxation, money changing, and minting itself. The Phoenician city-states that thrived were major ports, and the city that manufactured the Greek goods found most often in the archaeological record of Persian-period Phoenicia—we may speak specifically of Athens and Attic pottery—built up its port at the Piraeus early in the fifth century (Thuc. 1.93).[160] Coinage also played a role by allowing nearly anyone with cash to purchase once-exclusive products.

A better understanding of Mediterranean trade does not in itself explain why certain goods were exchanged, however.[161] But, by recasting Greek "cultural" products as commodities, we can begin to correct some of the bias encouraged by the archaeological record and art histories written from it.[162] This more balanced picture of Greek-Phoenician exchange puts pressure on the assumed asymmetry of their relationship. It also reminds us that other sources visible in the Phoenician material record—from Persia, Egypt, and Cyprus—were involved in the overall discourse of contact. It is clear from portable and monumental evidence that Greek art was not more important to or esteemed by Phoenicians than the art of these other regions, even long into the Hellenistic period. And so we can return to the idea that this period was one of political and economic development with the power to change relationships between polities. Phoenician monumental art and coins offer evidence of two simultaneous trends, one in which individuals and individual city-states prospered and vied with one another, the other in which at least some members of some city-states emphasized connectivity. While we have almost no way of knowing what sort of language was used to express such points of connectivity, if any, and can debate the extent to which it mattered to most of those we call Phoenicians, it is nonetheless critical to our understanding of Mediterranean history that Phoenicianism is evident in material form for the first time in the Persian and Hellenistic periods.

CHAPTER 5

Hybridity, the Middle Ground, and the "Conundrum of 'Mixing'"

The previous two chapters had three major claims. First, I argued that essentialism is still a feature of classical studies, one that is fundamentally racial in its outlook despite being presented in a variety of different "cultural" ways. Arguably, this thinking has created Greeks and Phoenicians and their art histories. Moving away from essentialism without rejecting these categories is, understandably, very difficult. Second, I affirmed the idea that there is as yet precious little evidence of Phoenician collective identity in Iron Age artworks. Taken together, these claims show how problematic are the ideas of "the Phoenicians" and "Phoenician art" in modern scholarship. The imaginary category of "Phoenician art" of the Iron Age is, however, one more factor contributing to the claim that Phoenicians and Phoenician art were Hellenized in their contact with Greeks and Greek art beginning in the fifth century. I offer an alternative view, my third point, arguing that naval service to the Achaemenids against the Egyptians and Greeks and changes in Mediterranean commodities exchange created for the first time the right conditions for peer-polity interaction, one that could have encouraged the development of a collective identity extending across individual states and vertically through social strata. Although Phoenicianism was surely important only to some Phoenicians some of the time, it is from this period that we can speak about a robust category of "Phoenician art."

We have seen that Phoenician monumental art and coinage show a sophisticated awareness of Achaemenid, Egyptian, and Greek art in the fifth century, an awareness that, I believe, does not favor the Greek over the others. Rather than imagining the Macedonian conquest as the moment when Phoenician culture was "mutilated beyond repair," it is accurate to recognize the Hellenistic period as a time of intense artistic productivity.[1] As we have seen, in this period the sanctuary sites of 'Amrit, Bostan esh-Sheikh, and Umm el-'Amed were loaded with stone dedications, especially reliefs, in addition to large temples that follow conceptually, sometimes stylistically, from the art and architecture of the Persian period. Turning squarely to the Hellenistic period, we will scale down further, focusing on only two specific works of sculpture, one each found in Sidon and Delos. These objects were chosen specifically to challenge the idea of a gradual loss of Phoenician identity following Alexander's conquests. Accordingly, the Sidonian work is from the early Hellenistic period and the Delian work from late in the period. The case studies are paired with two currently popular heuristics, hybridity and the middle ground, as a way to begin to unpack their complications. Both of these postcolonial theories aim, borrowing a phrase from Annie Coombes and Avtar Brah, to make sense of interaction and the "conundrum of 'mixing.'"[2]

I begin with the so-called Alexander Sarcophagus, a magnificent funerary monument and arguably the most famous work of Phoenician art, because I believe that it exemplifies well the appeal and the shortcomings of hybridity. The sarcophagus's visual ambiguity has encouraged a host of contradictory readings. I recast it as an example of Sidonian art that follows from Persian-era funerary sculpture, while suggesting through hybridity theory that its expression of Sidonian identity might have been at the expense of Achaemenids and Macedonians. From there, we move on to Delos and Richard White's middle ground, another theory developed for the study of colonial encounters.[3] I suggest that the theory has wide, if perhaps unintended, applicability and use it to read the so-called Slipper Slapper sculptural group.[4] Middle ground theory reveals that the work expresses a particular identity in a fashion analogous to the island's famous portraits of Italians. Neither the Alexander Sarcophagus nor the Slipper Slapper can be classified as only Greek or Phoenician art. Each shows what happens when we dispense with Hellenization and instead acknowledge that the relationship between Greek and Phoenician sculpture of the Hellenistic period was negotiated on small scales that require context-appropriate theorizing to interpret. The chapter closes with an introduction to the themes of the book's Conclusion by asking how we might use the Alexander Sarcophagus and the Slipper Slapper to refine the academic category "Phoenician art."

Hybridity and the Alexander Sarcophagus

It is impossible to deny that colonialism has informed our perceptions of ancient history, sometimes explicitly, such as the parallels drawn between the British Raj and imperial Rome. Critique of the colonial view of the Hellenistic world has already taken place in many circles,[5] though, as I show in this chapter, that critique has yet to fundamentally alter the conversation. Greek art history is still mostly conservative in our conception. A case in point is Syracuse, the home of Hieron II and his luxurious mosaic-bearing ship.[6] Considered in antiquity to be among the richest and most beautiful of Hellenic cities (Cic. *Verr.* 2.4.117; Livy 26.32), Syracuse is noticeably absent from the standard discussions of Greek art and architecture.[7] Why has Syracusan art been (nearly) excluded despite the city's lively history, its high profile in the Mediterranean, and ongoing research of its archaeological remains? Carla Antonaccio suggests, pointedly, "Hellenists are uncomfortable with colonial new money and the sense that colonial culture is not original, but derivative, and that the material culture, especially monuments, of places like Syracuse can be uncomfortably uncanonical."[8] Colonialism is evident in Orientalizing scholarship, too, although the usual relationship has been inverted through Orientalism, framing Near Eastern input as less interesting than the Greek result. It is clear that the approach to and the results of understanding interaction in these ways betray systematic bias in favor of Greece or Rome that interferes with our understanding of contact and its consequences.

Postcolonial approaches to the ancient world have some clear appeal in that they allow us to study these complex scenarios with more nuance than diffusion, core-periphery, or conflict-consensus approaches.[9] Though they do not always succeed in doing so, postcolonial theories strive to give a voice—agency—to those without hegemonic power. They allow for the possibilities of receptivity and reciprocity that might result in changes to both parties.[10] To those who work in regions where hegemonic narratives threaten to drown out other, often indigenous, voices—in places like Spain, France, Sicily, Cyprus—postcolonialism's inclusivity offers an important countermeasure to regional and disciplinary marginalization and a corrective to the problem of conflating history itself with the recorded events and monuments we prioritize.[11] As the example of Syracuse shows, one curious consequence of colonialism in Greek art and archaeology is that it serves to homogenize—one could say Hellenize—the Greek canon, while the "uncanonical" is free to reap the benefits of critical theory.

Another, and very important, contribution of postcolonialism is its determination to question neutrality in historical narratives. As Gayatri Spivak insisted, even those using postcolonial theory can fail to recover or understand the motives and thoughts of subordinates. Antonio Gramsci called these people the "subaltern," a concept that is complex and variously defined, even in Gramsci's own writings (compare Bhabha and hybridity below).[12] A key point here is that it is very difficult to write histories of the subaltern even with the best of intentions and even when using methodologies we believe to be objective and fair. Spivak's warning underscores how objectivity is itself subjectively conceived and perceived. In this critique of objectivity, postcolonialism can seem uninterested in solutions in an unsettling way, especially for fields that laud groundedness and empiricism. But this is not necessarily a claim that truth is elusive or its pursuit futile. Rather, it is a belief that multiple truths exist and claims to the contrary—in support of absolute historical authenticity—are inherently false. Here is yet another reminder of the limitations on accuracy imposed by our source material and the perspectives we bring to it.

What many postcolonial theories are trying to get at is how best to approach the encounters of people and the resulting conundrum of mixing in social, political, and religious spheres. Studies of the eastern Mediterranean have embraced postcolonial theory for quite some time, notably in the work of Amélie Kuhrt and Susan Sherwin-White.[13] In the Mediterranean, hybridity is a popular postcolonial approach to study culture mixture. As is often the case, in hybridity we encounter a theory not developed first for Mediterranean studies or for archaeology and culture specifically.[14] In its most famous, but by no means original, postcolonial usage by the literary theorist Homi Bhabha, hybridity explained behavior in the negotiated "third space" created by the colonial encounter. Bhabha conceived of hybridity as a political strategy between parties holding unequal status,[15] though now the concept is used more broadly by Bhabha and others to describe different kinds of "in-betweenness." "Hybrid" is an adjective frequently applied to cultural identity as well as to archaeology that resists monolithic definition.[16] It has been presented as an effective way to describe the art of the Hellenistic East.[17] Many have found the term helpful to label behaviors or objects that do not quite fit ideas about the culture or art of a single group. In short, hybridity is employed for processes and behaviors; it is a way to study the "how" as well as the "what" of mixing.

The term is Latin in origin, *hybrida* or *hibrida*. It was used to denote biological admixtures of animals and to insult people of some kind of mixed heritage (e.g., Pliny *HN* 8.213).[18] We can compare both to the fascination with mixtures (*Mischwesen*) in composite animals in Greek art and myth, which are, for the most part, thought to be imports from Egypt and the Near East.[19] Some hybrid animals, such as centaurs, could have positive portrayals in Greek art and myth, but the transgressive power of most hybrids, especially the female ones such as gorgons, sphinxes, and sirens, is a major theme. We can compare hybrida also to the Greek mixellēnes and related terms that suggest another epistemological precedent for our interest in cultural and biological mixture. These words seem to "indicate the recognition of separate Greek [and Roman] and native identities, and the hybridization that results from their combination."[20] In modern times, hybridity was not in frequent usage until the nineteenth century, when it featured prominently in questions probing humanity as one or many species. The leap from polygenesis to scientific racism, and thence to miscegenation and mongrelization, was short.[21] Hybridity's "objectionable" history is shared with many other terms now used to describe culture mixture.[22] For example, Portuguese *crioulo*, from which we get "creole," was used to describe African slaves in the New World. Terms denoting displacement and difference lend themselves easily to prejudice, and creole was no exception.[23]

Modern theory aims to reappropriate these more recent usages of hybridity, creolization, and the related term "syncretism." Today hybridity is mostly understood as a positive term in a variety of contexts, from its social scientific usage in globalization to plant science's "hybrid vigor." It is important to ask how these uses of hybridity are not simply another way of indicating biracialism, multiculturalism, or, in the case of objects, emulation and appropriation. For theorists the difference lies in power relations among people and institutions. While multiculturalism "masquerades as a solely cultural descriptor"—one that is autonomous and apolitical—hybridity "is constituted and contested through complex hierarchies of power."[24] This is a significant distinction that suggests hybridity is a theory suited expressly for encounters that are negotiated through power hierarchies. It cannot be used apolitically or without human or institutional agents, just as art and culture cannot act autonomously (for which see Chapter 1). As Philipp Stockhammer, a supporter of hybridity theory, has said: "Depriving Bhabha's terminology of its political dimension brings us back to the biological connotations of the term 'hybridity.' There is no doubt that hybridity as a biological metaphor is highly problematic . . . and its translation into an apolitical concept for the cultural sciences is questionable."[25] I wonder most of all about hybridity's utility for understanding the outcome of mixing among people of relatively equal status or among people operating freely, without a shared central authority.[26] Other models of behavior, for instance peer-polity interaction discussed in the previous chapter, or middle ground theory, which is discussed below, might be more suitable in such situations.

Despite the popularity of hybridity, it is often criticized. A frequent objection is to the dialectical implications of the hybrid.[27] The unmixed or "pure" antithesis to hybridity would seem to be just another example of the judgmental language and xenophobic modes of thinking postcolonialism means to avoid. (While language about purity is not applied to Phoenician art—far from it—it is not uncommon to see it used to describe Greek art.)[28] Some argue that hybridity is best framed as a scholarly category, an answer to a very real problem that we have created with our classifications. The taxonomic interests that drive our work—what is Greek *or* Phoenician—create a demand for descriptive language for things that fall in between. Proponents of hybridity theory might frame its artificiality in a positive light, as just one more scholarly tool. It requires only that we acknowledge that two traditions we perceive to be different have come into contact.[29] While this view of hybridity as a tool is compelling, as soon as we leave the theoretical to attempt its application, problems inevitably arise.

One problem is easy to predict: hybridity's in-betweenness still lends credibility to our flawed taxonomies and to the reliance on taxonomy in general when other approaches might better suit. Stephanie Langin-Hooper has explored this problem in the terracotta figurines of Hellenistic Babylonia, which appear to posses some Hellenic and some non-Hellenic traits. Langin-Hooper argues that disaggregating the figurines' features into Greek and Babylonian types is an exercise that reinforces modern colonial tensions between East and West, while missing out on what makes these objects interesting, namely, how they functioned. As she points out, there are limits to what can be learned even from labeling these objects as hybrids. Hybridity, Langin-Hooper concludes, is not an end in itself but "a starting point for questions of purpose and agency."[30] Used too casually, hybridity can turn into a force of essentialism, working as "an *inversion*, rather than a *negation*" or *rejection* of hegemonic categories.[31] Moreover, since the use of hybridity in historical Mediterranean scholarship now tends to be conceptual, not theoretical, and cultural (not political), it is in real danger of disregarding the term's critical contingencies.[32] Hybridity used to construct alternative narratives with rigid historical certitude—as though using humbler archaeological evidence, recognizing social heterogeneity, or employing a new term can fix the situation on its own—misses the point.

Hybridity is especially problematic as a way to distinguish between Greek and Phoenician art, as it threatens to characterize them as fundamentally pure and eclectic, respectively, when, in objects such as the Alexander Sarcophagus, it is difficult or impossible to disaggregate Greek and Phoenician elements. Indeed, Edward Said and Bruno Latour have argued that just about everything can be perceived as some kind of aggregation,[33] although in a scenario of first contact it is certainly easier to point out fundamental precontact differences, even if both parties were already some kind of other hybrid. Ptolemaic Egypt has been presented as a hybrid, for example, a state that was neither Egyptian nor Greek but drew on both identities, as well as Macedonian and Persian practices.[34] The proposition is much more precarious for my present study, however. As the previous chapters have shown, by the time we can talk about Greeks and Phoenicians some of their behaviors and arts appear to us to be already aggregated. Part of the conundrum of mixing, then, is determining whether or not what we are witnessing is a historical mixture or a scholarly one.[35] For it to be meaningful, we must be careful to distinguish hybridity as something specific, not merely as a synonym for "interaction." It is neither a universal theory nor the only way to point to heterogeneity. We must also avoid using hybridity as a new, less obviously judgmental, way to keep discussing stages of acculturation.

We turn now to our first case study, a work of art widely cited as an expression of the hybridization or Hellenization of the Sidonian court.[36] The Alexander

Sarcophagus poses a number of challenges, from how its various iconographic and stylistic elements work together to whether or not it is a material expression of the "radical heterogeneity"[37] one might associate with hybridity (see Plates 17–22).[38] Indeed, the superbly carved sarcophagus raises a number of more fundamental questions: who was shown on it, who made up its intended audience, who sculpted it, and who was represented by it. The facts of its 1887 discovery in the 'Ayaa nekropolis east of Sidon elucidate the answers only a little (Figure 38, which shows chamber A). 'Ayaa was one of Sidon's three elite nekropoleis. Included among the rich finds in its rock-cut tombs was the Tabnit sarcophagus (found in chamber B;

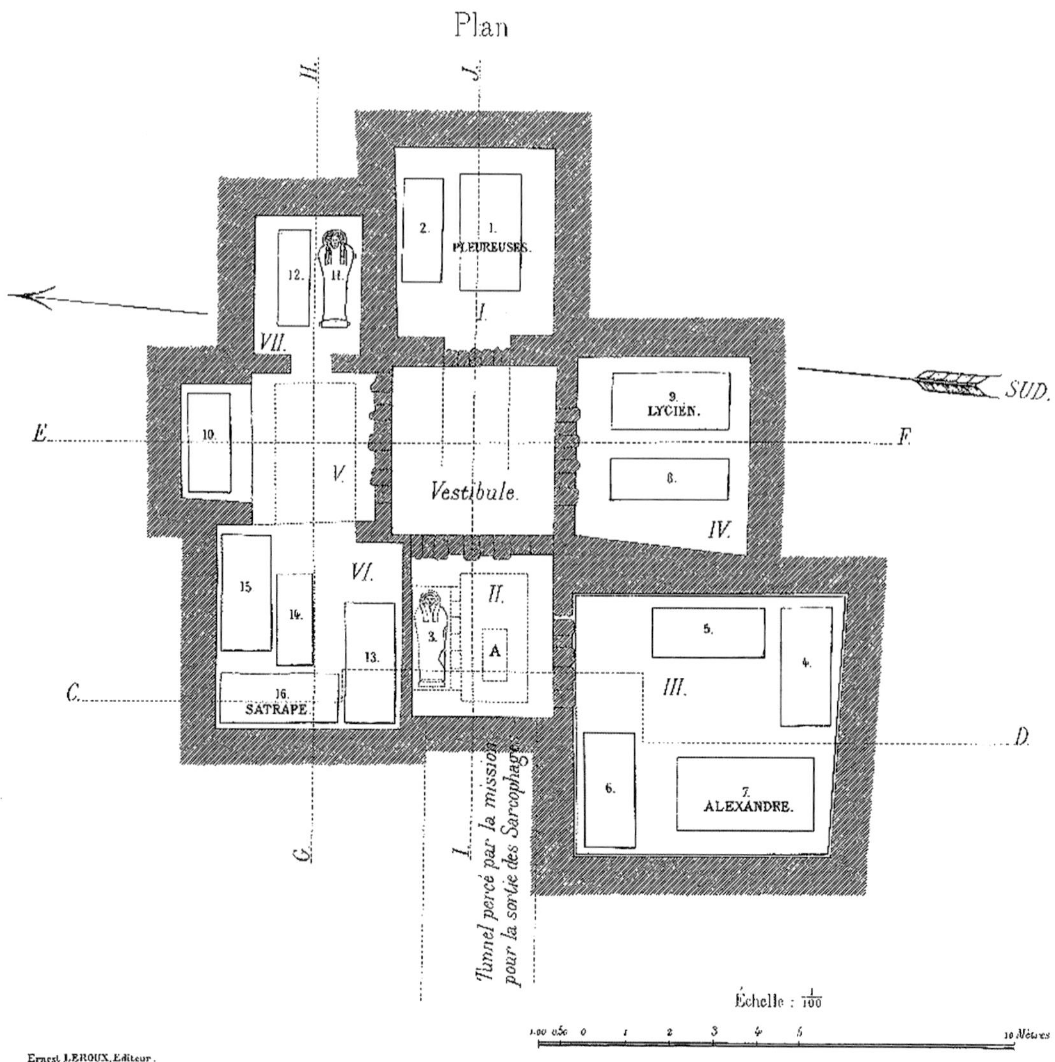

Figure 38. Plan of chamber A at the 'Ayaa Nekropolis near Sidon. Plan redrawn by Sveta Matskevich after Hamdi Bey and Reinach 1892, pl. III: plan.

see also Figures 13, 21, 23). (The Eshmunazar sarcophagus was discovered in 1855 at the Magharat Abloun nekropolis southeast of the city.)[39] Its most famous monuments are the four, high-quality relief sarcophagi, each decorated with panel reliefs and architectural features. The others are known as the Satrap, Lycian, and Mourning Women sarcophagi.[40] These are thought to date approximately to a one-hundred-year period, from the Satrap and Lycian sarcophagi in the late fifth century (their relative relationship is debated) to the Alexander Sarcophagus in the later fourth.[41] As one would anticipate from their names and broad chronological range, the sarcophagi are not consistent in their iconography or style. Because of this, their dating is tied to the problematic chronology of the Sidonian kings. As one would anticipate in the study of Phoenician art, they are not particularly well understood despite each having at least one dedicated monograph.

To set up the right expectations for the Alexander Sarcophagus, brief mention of some features of the earlier three tombs is necessary.[42] All are carved in marble and have what to our eyes are mixed programs, including figures that are dressed according to the conventions of Greek art in Greek and Persian costume. They are stylistically Greek as well. Each has some relief decoration on all of its four sides. Each also has Ionic architectural features, at minimum moldings and akroteria or antefixes. Finally, each sarcophagus has at least one other clear quotation of an artistic tradition or subject previously unknown in Sidonian art: the Satrap Sarcophagus's panther hunt; the Lycian tomb's eponymous "Gothic" pointed lid and scene showing the myth of the Lapith king Kaineus (Pind. fr. 128f); the heavily clad females on the Mourning Women Sarcophagus that recall Athenian gravestones; and, of course, Alexander, who appears on the latest tomb.

The relief sarcophagus is a rare type. Painted clay and stone sarcophagi are known from western Asia Minor, the most distinctive being the Lycian types that began in the sixth century, some of which had explicitly historical reliefs.[43] Five roughly contemporary (dated from 550 to 330) examples of relief sarcophagi are known in Cyprus.[44] These are also varied in their appearance. What makes the Sidonian sarcophagi stand out from their Phoenician predecessors is how they seemingly reject the anthropoid form initiated by Tabnit and Eshmunazar. The Satrap Sarcophagus, possibly the earliest of the four, is anthropoid in its interior, suggesting it marks the transition from the old type to the new. Further, the Sidonian sarcophagi make no hint of the religious roles it is clear those kings played, and they do not draw on the same symbols of kingship seen on Sidonian coin reverses. We cannot prove, of course, that the relief sarcophagi belonged to Sidonian kings—they all lack inscriptions—but their ostentation and entombment in the same nekropolis as Tabnit suggest as much. Possibly a hundred years on from the arrival of the anthropoid type, the kings sought other ways to distinguish themselves.[45] Perhaps the change came with the rise of the new dynasty of Ba'alshillem.[46]

A few preliminary points must be made here. The relief sarcophagi cannot be used to reconstruct top-down trends in Phoenician or even Sidonian art. Rather, these monuments make sense in light of other Sidonian monumental art that likewise aggregates disparate iconography in a few styles, incorporating elements from Greek, Persian, and Egyptian art, besides Phoenician. Accordingly, they are not evidence of the Hellenization of Sidon any more than the so-called tribune of Eshmun (see Figure 30, Plates 12 and 13). Yes, each relief sarcophagus has elements derived from Greek art and architecture, and, yes, it is entirely likely that the artists who made them were Greek trained (most would say, simply, Greek).[47] But the sarcophagi are not objects that would be found in Greek nekropoleis, and they have nothing to do with Greek burial practices. It is strange to think that looking Hellenic or assimilating Hellenic funerary rights could be thought their goal, as each would fail miserably. However odd and individualized they seem, the relief and anthropoid sarcophagi as a whole relate to one another, casting some doubt on the idea that the Alexander Sarcophagus stood apart from the group in its desire to promote the new world order established by the Macedonian conquest.[48] If indeed it is the last of the Sidonian royal sarcophagi, it is especially important to relate the Alexander Sarcophagus to what came before it. I will expand on these ideas below.

While the recognition of Alexander on its large battle scene has leant the work its lasting nickname, the majority opinion has long favored the idea that the tomb was built for the client king Abdalonymos of Sidon.[49] Almost nothing is known of the historical Abdalonymos aside from a dedication made by his son on Kos. He is associated with a character in a classical allegorical tale set only sometimes in Sidon. In Quintus Curtius's version (4.1.15–26; cf. Just. *Epit.* 11.10.8), Abdalonymos was appointed king of Sidon by Alexander following the battle of Issos in 333. Abdalonymos is sometimes said to have died at the Battle of Gaza in 312, although some claim to see in numismatic evidence a reign that lasted at least to 306/5. Each of these claims is speculation, and the inconsistency in the stories casts further doubt on the historicity of this tale—Abdalonymos is absent from Arrian, his name is misspelled by Diodoros (17.46.6–17.47), who also sets the story in Tyre, and Plutarch (*Mor.* 340d) puts him in Paphos. No Phoenician sources can confirm his identity. It is entirely possible that Abdalonymos is mainly a literary construct, though his name makes a convenient stand-in for the Sidonian king appointed by Alexander.

The finer disputes of the tomb's date are related to style, the association of one pedimental scene with the 320 murder of Perdikkas (see Plate 20), and the idea that the work was made during Abdalonymos's lifetime and displayed in the

Sidonian court.[50] Largely because it does not betray the style of Lysippos, the tomb's Alexander is thought to be his earliest extant portrait (see Plate 18). Accordingly, the work is usually dated to the late third or fourth quarter of the fourth century. Like many of the other widely accepted arguments for the date of the sarcophagus, this one is problematic. It is likely that a number of Alexander portrait types existed in this period. More to the point, the Alexander, other supposed portraits, and Persians on the sarcophagus can have similar "idealized" facial features, many of which seem related to coin images of Herakles.[51] The dynamic figure in Greek costume on the long-side hunt is sometimes called an Alexander portrait as well (see Plate 19, left), but the identification is not secure because he has facial similarities to other figures and lacks distinguishing attributes.

A clear connection to Greek art comes from compositional similarities between the long-side battle scene and the Alexander Mosaic, specifically the left area of the mosaic where a Persian is being skewered by Alexander as he charges into the battle on horseback (see Plate 18). The mosaic was laid in Pompeii's House of the Faun in circa 100. It likely shows the battle of Issos in 333 and has been persuasively interpreted as a version of a now-lost painting by Philoxenos of Eretria commissioned by Alexander's general Kassander (Pliny *HN* 35.110). The sarcophagus must date sometime after the painting was made, circa 334–324.[52] Stewart notes the important differences between the mosaic and the sarcophagus. In the former, the Persian is already stabbed and flails helplessly.[53] In the Sidonian tomb, he is not yet impaled and leaps off his fallen horse while brandishing his sword at Alexander. The head of Alexander in the sarcophagus's battle scene is rather unlike the one on the mosaic that is bare and fierce. The leonine headgear on the tomb—a cap—differs also from the images on Alexander's own Herakles tetradrachms where the god wears a toothless skin set well back on his head, knotted below the chin. The sarcophagus lion helmet is closer to a Herakles sculpture type known from the fifth century that shows up on Lycian coins in the early fourth century and, later in the century, on some Macedonian ones.[54]

Connections to Macedonians and Macedonian historical art encourage the idea that at least some of the scenes on the sarcophagus are historical as well. Some art historians are keen to view nearly the entire monument in biographical terms. Others take a more conservative view and prefer to see glimpses of recent events.[55] The long-side battle scene with Alexander is generally thought to show Issos because of its apparent similarities to the now-lost painting of Philoxenos, although the arrangement of its composition between the Alexander group at far left and the so-called Antigonos Monopthalmos at far right is baroque: dense, frenetic, and visually complicated.[56] The association of one of the pediments with Perdikkas's assassination is more tentative (see Plate 20). All the figures in this area are in Greek costume: at center, a man dressed in a tunic is being killed by two armed soldiers; at left, a youth holds up another dead man; and at right, a bearded man wearing a fillet, purple chiton, and muscle cuirass moves to kill another man attempting to crawl out of the scene. It does seem possible that this is a depiction of the mutiny leading to Perdikkas's murder in Egypt (Diod. Sic. 18.36.2–5).[57] It is also possible that we are seeing something different or more generic here.

It is important to place the sarcophagus in the context of Sidonian history as well. Only in circa 350 had Tennes and others revolted. While Diodoros's account of the repercussions of the revolt is theatrical (Diod. Sic. 16.41–45), there is reason to believe that Sidon was sacked by Artaxerxes in circa 345. Alexander arrived shortly after Issos. Sidon wisely opened its gates to the Macedonian forces (Arr. *Anab.* 2.15.6), an event marked by the replacement of its autonomous coin issues with Alexander's (monogrammed SI).[58] Sidonian forces are said to have assisted Alexander in the siege of Tyre (Arr. *Anab.* 2.16–24; Curt. 4.2.6–4.4.18; Diod. Sic. 17.40–46). Once Phoenicia was conquered, a number of political arrangements are recorded during Alexander's lifetime. The last of these arrangements places the Phoenician cities under the control of the Syrian satrap (Arr. *Anab.* 4.7.2). Even this relative stability was short lived, as chaos erupted upon Alexander's death in 323. Control of Sidon changed six times in the quarter century that followed. If we are correct in interpreting the sarcophagus's historical cues, and date the tomb to the last quarter of the fourth century, the tomb was created in a charged postcolonial or neocolonial moment in which Sidonians found themselves negotiating near-constant changes of political realities. As in their previous colonial situation, this one did not bring large numbers of foreigners into Phoenicia. But it is not uncommon for scholars, following on the visual rhetoric of the diadochoi and Arrian's account of the Sidonian attitude toward Alexander's conquests (*Anab.* 2.15.6), to frame the sarcophagus in terms of Sidon's liberation and to thus see Abdalonymos likewise celebrating Alexander and the events that brought both to power.

The large sarcophagus (more than 3.0×1.5 m) was made in two blocks of Pentelic marble, once richly painted and further embellished with metal attachments.[59] Like the Ionic temples it and the Mourning Women Sarcophagus evoke, it is covered in sculpture: four horizontal friezes, two pediments, and an elaborate roof program fashioned as an entablature, as seen in Plate 17. The roof itself is scaled. Its ridge and gutters are adorned with eagles and female heads, the latter presumably deities and usually identified as Atargatis. Horned griffins guard the long sides, and lions the four corners. The lower part of the roof has moldings, ovolo and dentils, above a frieze of vines, lesbian kymation, and astragal (see Plate 20). The friezes on the body of the sarcophagus are likewise framed by moldings. At the top are an elaborate meander, ovolo with egg and dart, and astragal with bead and reel. Below the horizontal friezes we find more moldings, from the top, astragal, lesbian kymation, torus with guilloche, scotia, and a larger torus with guilloche. A meander-ovolo-astragal pattern is found also on the upper moldings of the "tribune"/altar/Aštart-throne base in the Eshmun complex at Bostan esh-Sheikh; the lower moldings are similar, too (see Plate 13).[60] It is possible the same workshop executed these and a number of other monumental marble works. We can see in the roof program a general conceptual tie to the early Sidonian sarcophagi that used Egyptian symbols of protection, such as Tabnit's winged Isis, and had inscribed warnings about violating the body.

The major friezes show standard Near Eastern and Greek scenes, two hunts and two battles, respectively. But for the short-side hunt, which shows only figures in Persian dress (see Plate 17), each frieze has figures clad in Greek and Persian costume as well as nudes.[61] Military equipment is at times deliberately ahistorical. Both the heavy infantry and figures in Persian dress can carry hoplite shields, not the Macedonian *sarissai* seen on the Alexander Mosaic or Persian bows and short spears.[62] On the short-side battle scene, one of the figures in Persian dress carries a Greek hoplite shield painted inside with a remarkable image of a figure bowing before the enthroned Achaemenid king (see Plates 21 and 22).[63] The painted image can be compared to the audience scene on the Satrap Sarcophagus. In the battles, "Greeks" and "Persians" fight one another. In the long-side hunt (see Plate 19), which evokes a Persian paradeisos—perhaps in reference to the one in Sidon (Diod. Sic. 16.41.5)—they participate side by side, as seen also on the Lycian and Mourning Women sarcophagi. The pediments show mostly soldiers. The one above the panther hunt shows the clash of figures in Greek and Persian dress. The pediment above the battle frieze is the so-called murder of Perdikkas (see Plate 20). The scene has thematic echoes in the Lycian sarcophagus's murder of Kaineus. In Near Eastern art, a hero or ruler killing a bound enemy is seen in Assyrian reliefs, Achaemenid cylinder seals, metal bowls, and elsewhere, although these are only general parallels.[64] It is not clear, then, if the pediments are thematically balanced in the same way as the friezes.

The carving is very deep and confident, and the emotional intensity of the figures is notable, as on the pediment where the murderer of "Perdikkas" locks eyes with the soldier at his right (see Plate 20). Throughout the fighting is passionate, with the Persian soldiers and hunters sometimes winning. The style of carving is generally Greek but hard to pin down more specifically. Close stylistic analysis has led to the suggestion that the artists came either from the Ionian or the Rhodian regional school. Others argue that the stocky bodies are stylistically indebted to Attic sculpture, while the emotional intensity follows on the work of the Parian sculptor Skopas.[65] Alexander is the only figure who may be unambiguously identified on the friezes, but the figure in Persian costume at the center of the hunt is so prominent in the composition that association between him and the entombed is natural (see Plate 19). In the other relief sarcophagi the relationship between the entombed and the figures also appears to be general or indirect.

The tomb's consistent treatment in handbooks of Greek art and studies of Alexander mean that many different readings have been made since its discovery, some nuanced, many openly colonial in their outlook: Alexander von Gräve's influential publication of 1970 is pointedly Hellenocentric; others see the tomb as a manifestation of Alexander's practice of delegating power and pursuing a policy of cultural fusion;[66] and still others see instead an allegory of the perennial struggle of East and West in which all non-Greeks (Phoenicians, Persians) are barbaroi and all non-barbaroi (Macedonians, Hellenes) are Greeks.[67] Challenges to the idea that Abdalonymos commissioned the sarcophagus are few. The historian Waldemar Heckel has recently revived the idea (rejected by Stewart and others) that the tomb's occupant was instead another Alexander appointee, the Persian governor of Babylon Mazday (Mazaeus in Curt. 5.1.44). Like von Gräve, although with different particular arguments, Heckel seeks to read the work "as a historical document" in which a straightforward interpretation of costume figures prominently.[68] Whereas trousers surely signal that certain figures are non-Hellenic, these authors go so far as to claim that the figure on the center of the long end's hunt, and repeated in the center of the short-end battle, *is* Abdalonymos or Mazday (see Plate 19).

The idea that Phoenician elites wore Persian garb has support from the other Sidonian relief sarcophagi, other sculpture such as the Umm el-'Amed and Yehawmilk reliefs, and coins, the last, we recall, sometimes explicitly appropriating Achaemenid iconography (see Figures 19; 33, left; and 37, right).[69] Some scholars find it hard to believe that a ruler put into power by Alexander or Hephaistion would fail to separate himself visually from Persians. Others think the Macedonian client king was being nostalgic.[70] It is not easy to relate the imagery of ceremonial religious attire to hunting or battle, however, or to the Persian cavalry dress seen on the sarcophagus. Quasi-historical interpretations such as these fail to account for the complexity of the relationship between representation and history, but they do remind us that costume is an important part of how the sarcophagus's visual program worked. Alexander's garb in the battle scene suggests the monument is delicately balancing accord and opposition. He wears a costume of Persian origin called in Greek the chitōniskos cheiridōtos, previously mentioned in connection with the different depictions of Memnon in vase painting (see Chapter 3). The garment has long sleeves and a double girdle that creates a long overfall (see Plate 18).[71] Alexander's purple cloak, bare legs, painted footwear (*krēpides*), and lion-scalp helmet separate him from his foe, but it is hard to ignore how his garment, and that of several other Greek figures, is formally identical to that of the Persians he battles or hunts beside. That the chitōniskos cheiridōtos was adopted by Greeks and Macedonians generations earlier does not lessen the interesting visual rhyme made by the sleeved *chitōnes*.[72] There is even a hint of a false sleeve in the fold of Alexander's flying cloak. At the same time, these similarities heighten dissonance in the contrast of bare legs versus trousers. The Persian figures' blue eyes and pale skin, the latter signaling to Greeks that Persians lacked andragathia, set them still further apart (see Plates 21 and 22).[73] What those traits mean in a Sidonian context is unclear, but they are deliberate. Even the horses are physically distinguished, with those bearing Persians having tightly wrapped forelocks. In these elements the tomb seems overtly concerned with ethnic and physical differences.

These examples show that, while the sarcophagus's visual conventions and style are Greek, it retains dizzying visual ambiguity. Both have been exploited by modern scholars to fit the tomb to particular, often mutually exclusive, interpretations of its intentions. There is a tendency in these interpretations to ignore how vision—reception—is something socially and contextually coded.[74] Stewart is one of the few to focus clearly on the work's reception. He imagines that the sarcophagus was made during Abdalonymos's lifetime and displayed in the Sidonian court. References to Alexander were political, an acknowledgment of the ruler who guaranteed his power. The Greek and Near Eastern program functioned together as a visually seductive apparatus meant to appeal to Macedonian and local visitors. Pointed historical references to Issos and the murder of the treacherous Perdikkas strengthened this connection, whereas the Near Eastern hunting and battle scenes spoke to local priorities and symbols of power. These episodes are not contradictory in Stewart's reading. Rather, they speak to the fluidity of identity.

Stewart's approach to the sarcophagus employs a dialectical method. Although it is not his aim, his reception-driven approach is a useful starting point for viewing the sarcophagus in a postcolonialist lens. A few methods suggest themselves, all of which follow on the idea that the patron of the work of art had an intimate understanding of the conventions of Greek art and how it would be received by both Macedonian and local audiences. The sarcophagus seems to be a hybrid in multiple senses, consciously mixing different artistic and social traditions to articulate a new, subjective identity in reaction to its historical and physical context. To Greeks and Macedonians, the sarcophagus narrates struggle and, ultimately, conquest, whereas to Sidonians it narrates metamorphosis. Yet beyond the murder of "Perdikkas," the sarcophagus seems to forego any critique of the Macedonian hegemony, past or present, as one might expect in such explicit colonial situations. Bearing that in mind, it is harder to imagine how its program would redeem the political or cultural situation of the Sidonian subaltern. We might prefer to see the tomb as an expression of the "double ideals" associated with double consciousness.[75] In this framing, the tomb is an articulation of independent, warring (literally, in this case) ideals, with its patron caught somewhere in between.

It records a historical moment when the Sidonians find themselves needing, once again, to negotiate political, cultural, and perhaps even psychological conflict. Thus, through the tomb, the Sidonians are demonstrating their mastery at code switching, doing so in part to ingratiate themselves to their latest masters.

Both characterizations seem unsatisfactory and, ultimately, somewhat colonialist. In each the sarcophagus is a kind of celebration of the latest episode of Sidon's marginalization. The readings hinge on the idea that what we see in the Alexander Sarcophagus does not relate to its context—to earlier sarcophagi or to the visual strategies found in contemporary Sidonian art. They are also hard to reconcile with the sarcophagus's loudly triumphant tone, which suggests to me the tomb was a celebration of Sidonian identity most of all. I believe that we should pay more attention to the sarcophagus's capacity for subversion. It is possible that, in the eyes of the Sidonian elite, the tomb's mixed program was not a compromise, nor a way to flatter Macedonians at court, but an inverted kind of strategic essentialism.[76] Rather than defensively presenting Sidonian identity in terms of its conquerors past and present, the tomb visually constructs artificial "Persians" and "Greeks" in order to negate them both. What it says in political terms is a statement that could not be understood by non-Sidonian audiences. In this scenario, the tomb's negotiation of the colonial encounter is much more sophisticated even while it follows earlier precedents. Other art from early Hellenistic Sidon—the child statues, reliefs, and "tribune"/altar/Aštart throne (see Figures 27, 29, and 30)—share with the Alexander Sarcophagus the complex visual language of Sidonian elites. These examples, along with the later bilingual stele from the Kerameikos, show how familiar iconography and style might be used to construct imagery discernible only to a culturally conditioned, Phoenician audience. If in fact the Alexander Sarcophagus anticipated an audience of Sidonians as well as Greeks, Macedonians, and Persians, these skills might be put to use to subtly deconstruct the power of the Achaemenids and Alexander's successors, who, despite their military prowess, were unable to maintain order in the region.

Where do these possibilities leave us? While I think it is possible to interpret the Alexander Sarcophagus through hybridity, if in doing so we also read it as a celebration of Greek art and culture, we perpetuate the colonialist discourse, which, in addition to being unpalatable, is illogical. While one could make the case that hybridity is always doomed to reify the hegemony, one needs to make that case here, and I do not feel it fits the evidence. Some would argue that hybridity, like other postcolonial theories, is applicable to the ancient Mediterranean only if we continue to view it in eighteenth- or nineteenth-century terms, when the study of antiquity and modern thought more or less merged for the first time. I disagree. But we are too likely, I believe, to see hybridity as an active way of forging quasi-Greek identity and to ignore its capacity, or desire, for (in)difference.

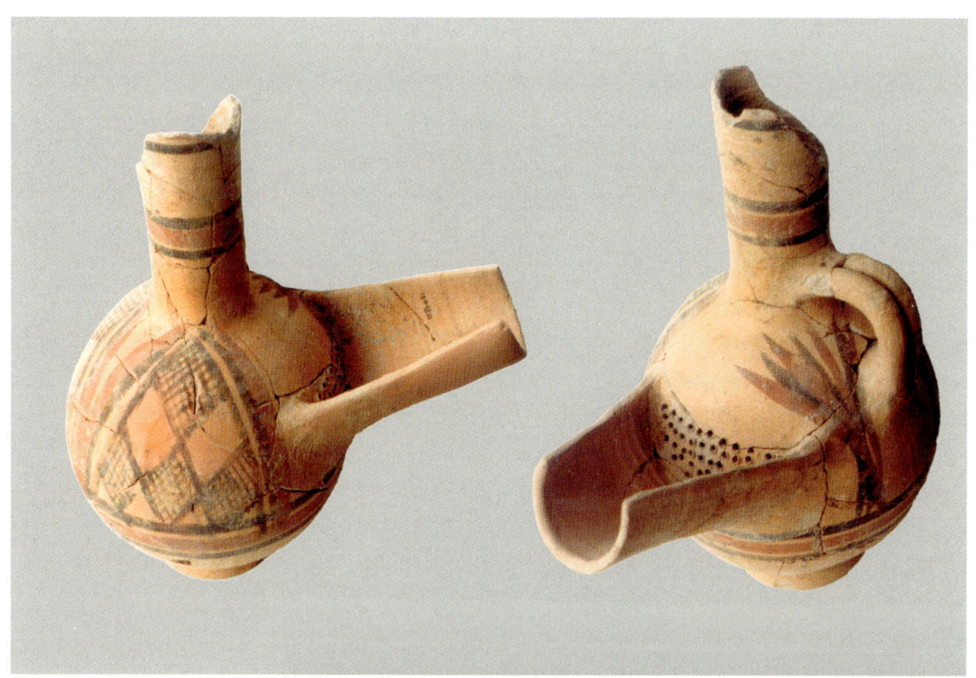

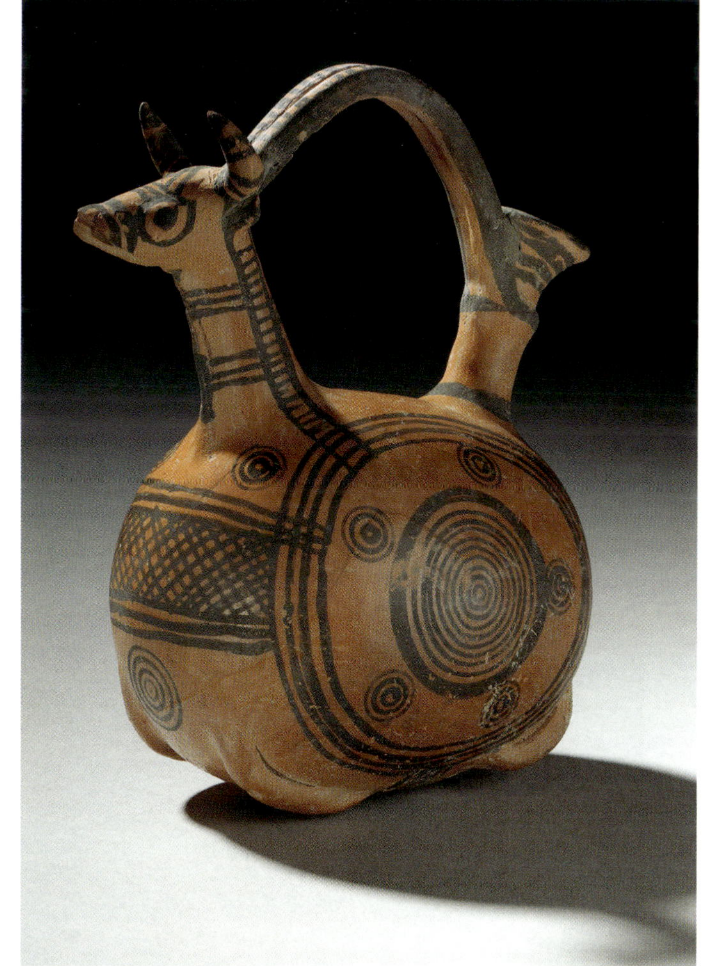

Plate 1. Top: Bichrome strainer jug from Tel Dor, early 9th c. Tel Dor no. 190089, L17313. Ceramic. Est. ht. 0.30 m. Photo: The Tel Dor Project. Bottom: Cypro-Archaic I black-on-red zoomorphic askos from Kourion, 750–600. London, British Museum 1896,0201.195. Ceramic. Ht. 0.19–0.22 m. Photo: © The Trustees of the British Museum.

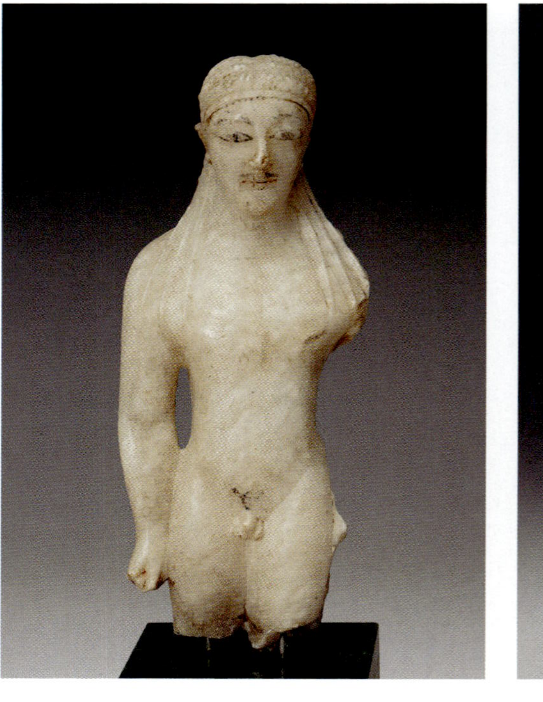
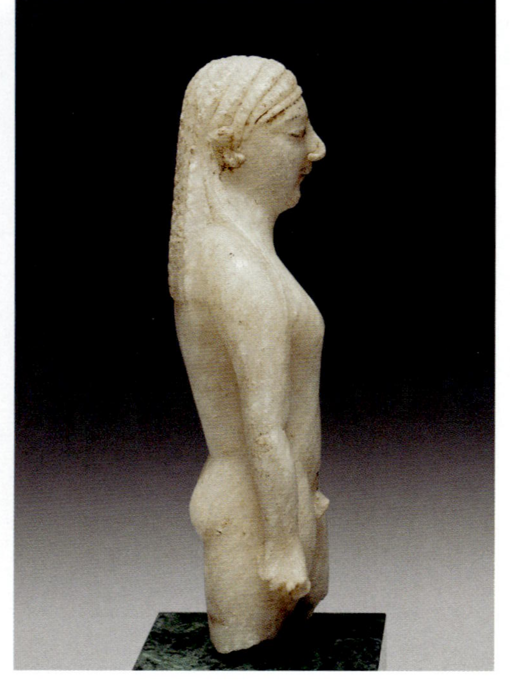
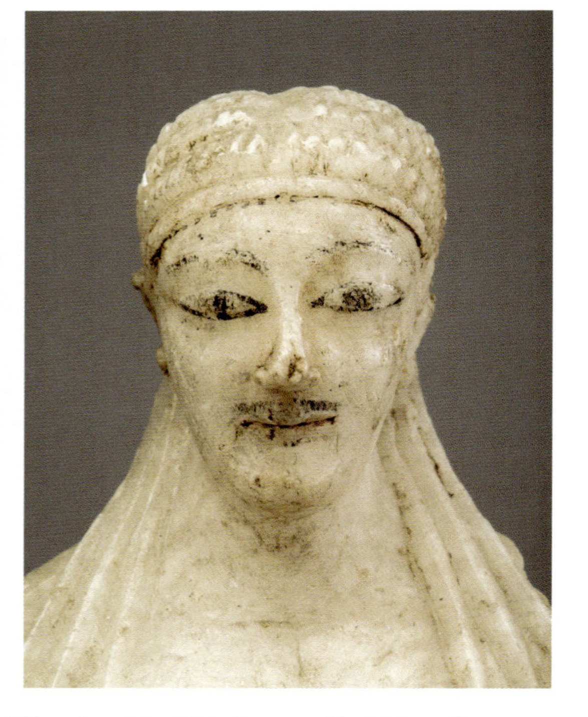

Plate 2. Kouros with painted features from Naukratis, 575–500. Moscow, Pushkin State Museum of Fine Arts I 1a 3000. Gypsum. Ht. 1.75 m. Photo: Pushkin State Museum of Fine Arts.

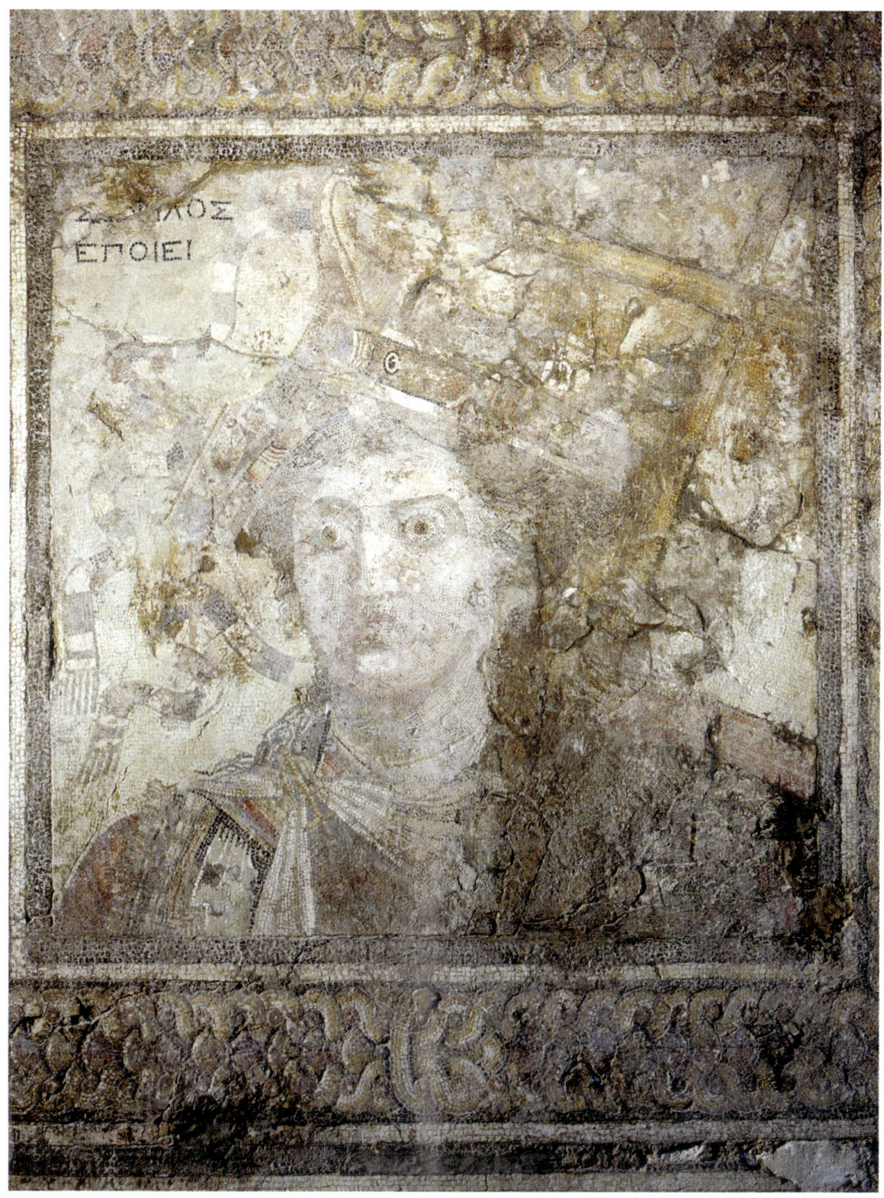

Plate 3. Mosaic said to be from Tell Timai (Thmuis) signed by Sōphilos, ca. 200. Alexandria, Graeco-Roman Museum 21739. Various materials. 2.77×2.61 m. Photo: Werner Forman/Universal Images Group/Getty Images.

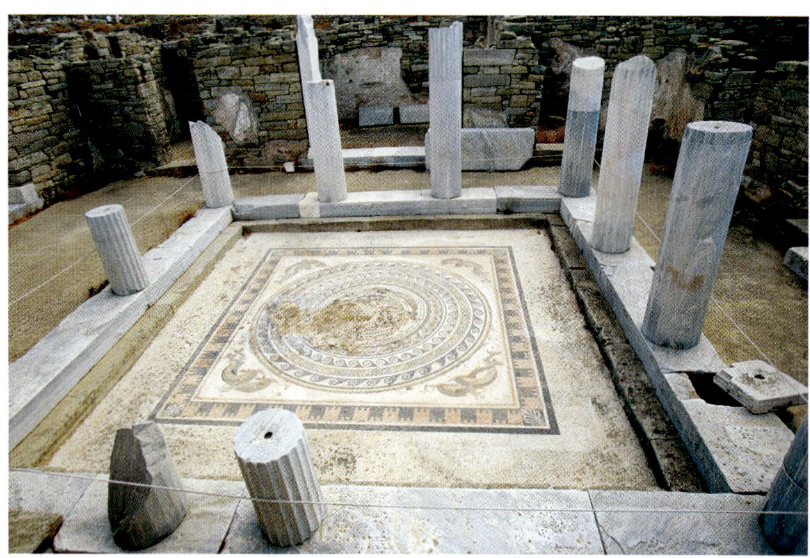

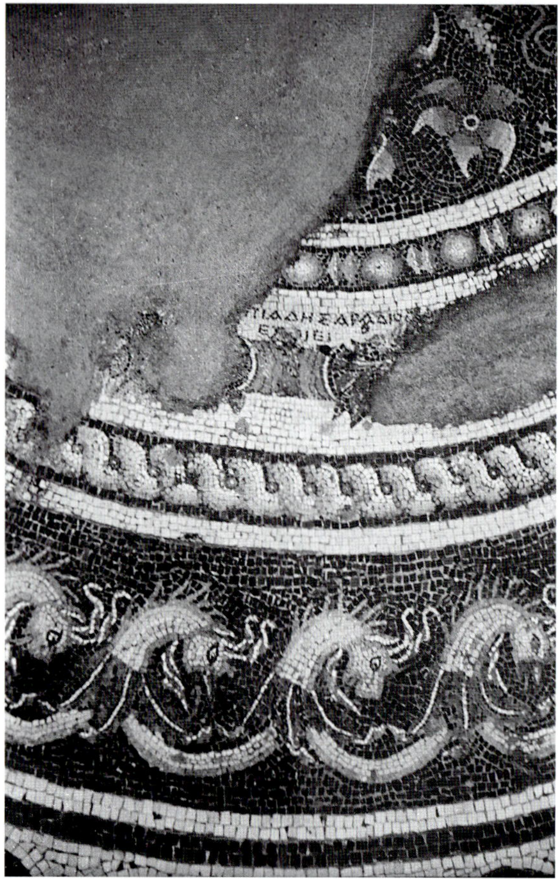

Plate 4. Top: peristyle mosaic in the House of the Dolphins, Delos, ca. 100. Various materials. Est. 5.5×5.5 m. Photo: age fotostock/Alamy. Bottom: detail of artist's signature. Photo: courtesy École française d'Athènes.

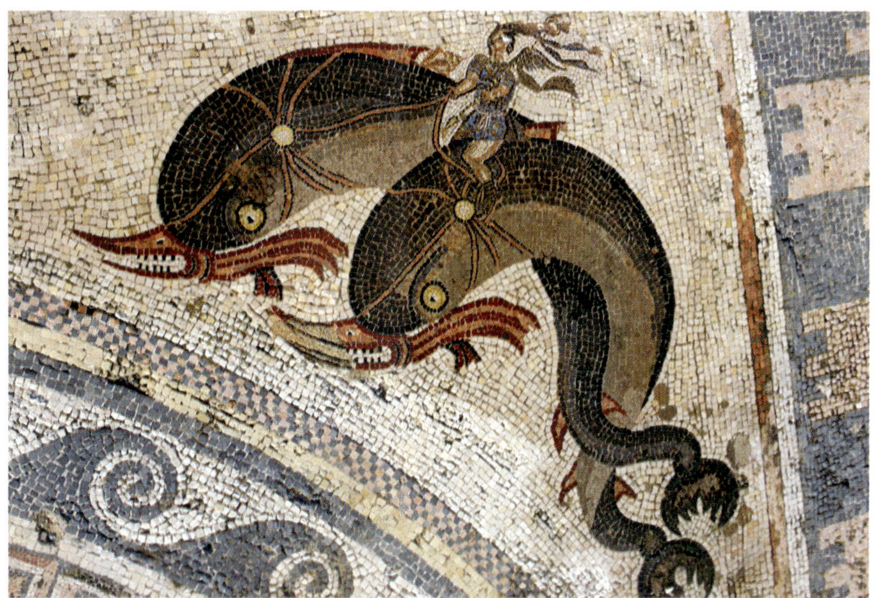

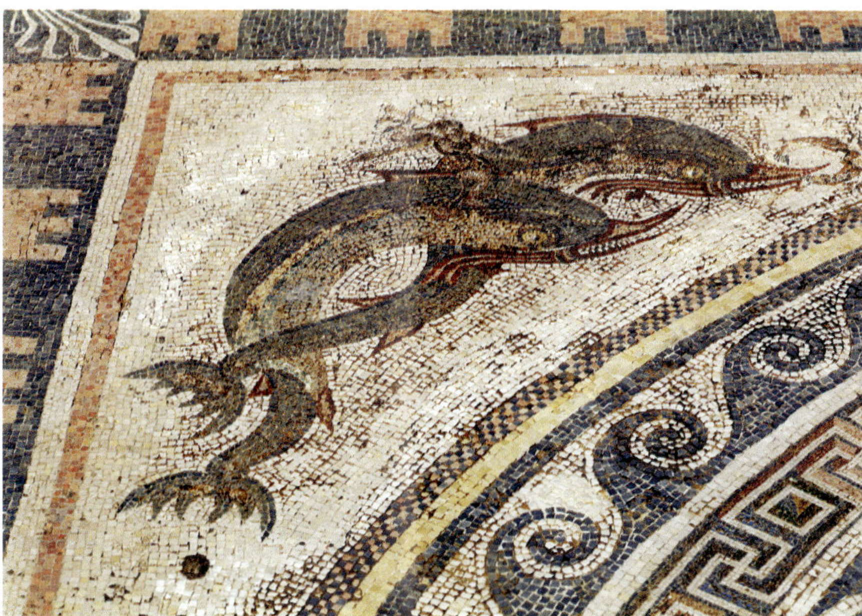

Plate 5. Top: detail of Plate 4. Photo: IML Image Group Ltd./Alamy. Bottom: detail of Plate 4. Photo: age fotostock/Alamy.

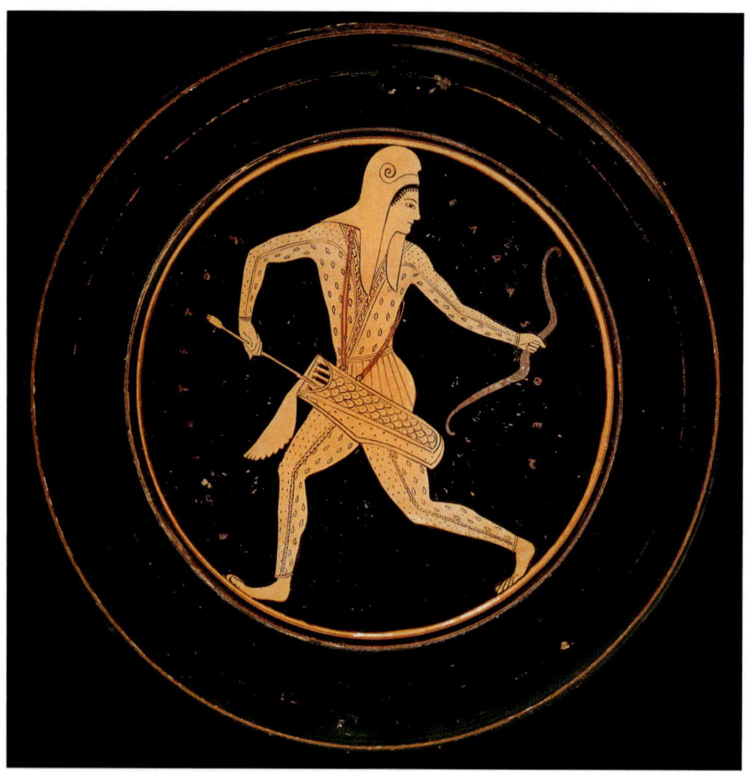

Plate 6. Attic red-figure plate from Vulci signed by Epiktetos, 520–500. London, British Museum GR 1837.6–9.59. Ceramic. Diam. 0.19 m. Photo: © The Trustees of the British Museum.

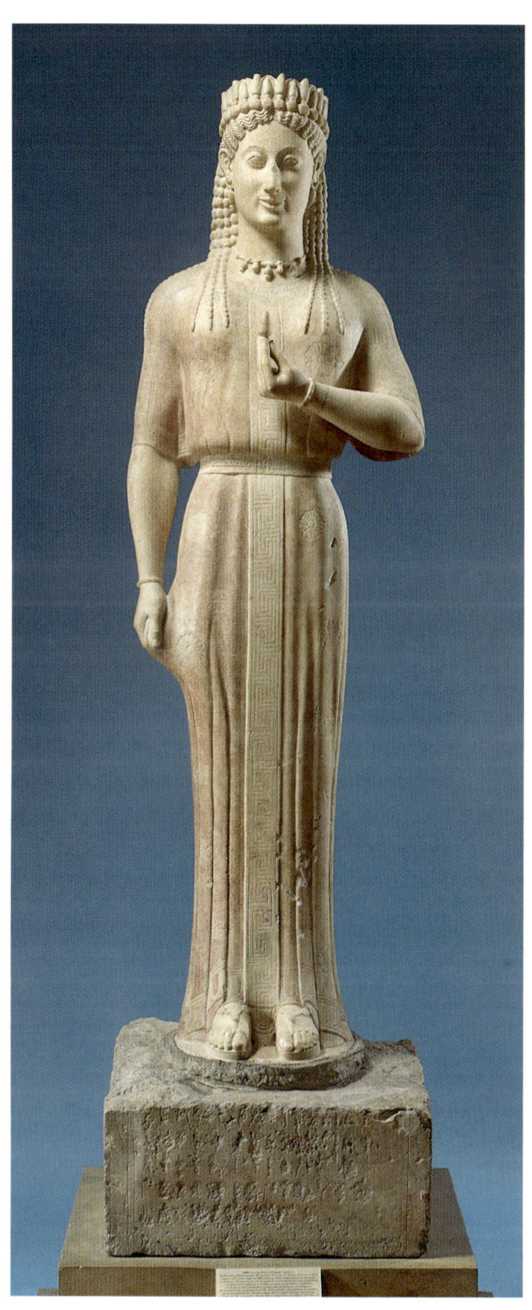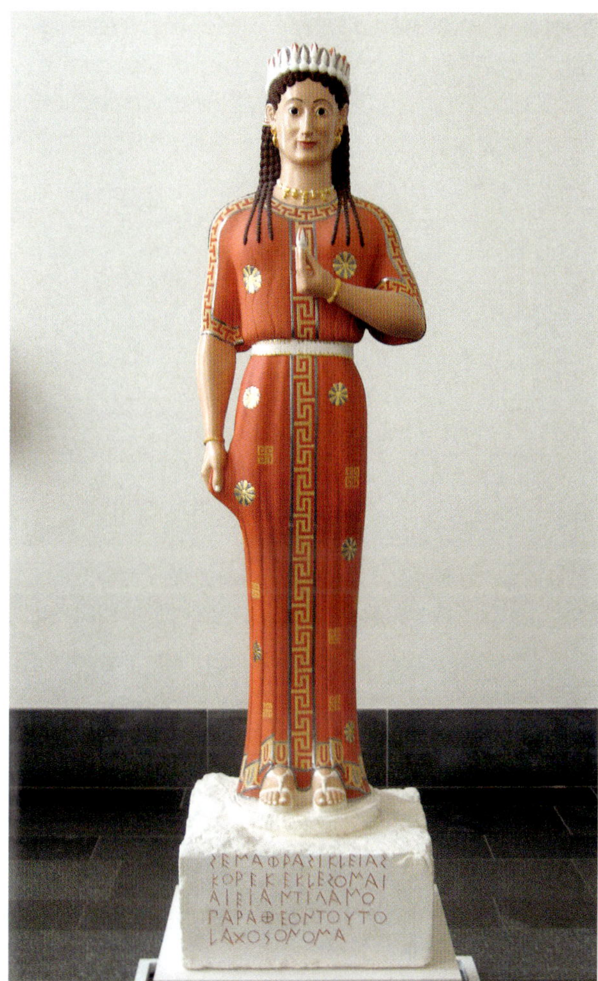

Plate 7. Left: grave marker of Phrasikleia from Attika, ca. 540. Athens, National Museum 4889. Photo: National Archaeological Museum, Athens, C. and M. Mauzy. Marble. Ht. 1.18 m. Right: painted reconstruction of the same by Vinzenz Brinkmann and Ulrike Koch-Brinkmann. Photo: Marcus Cyron, available under the terms of the GNU Free Documentation License.

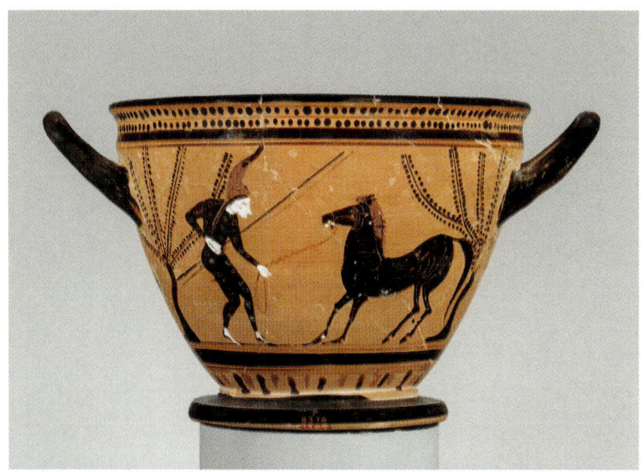

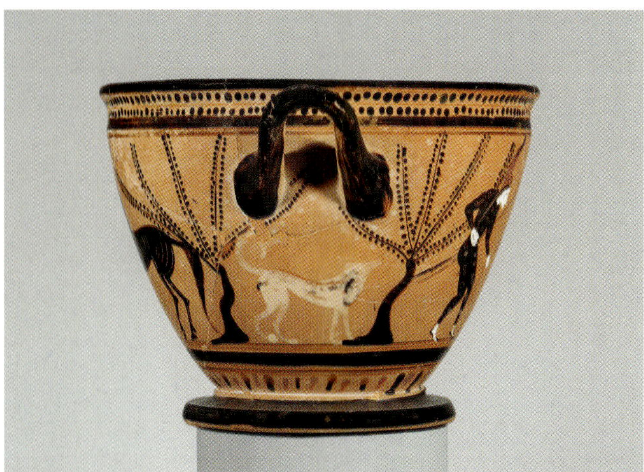

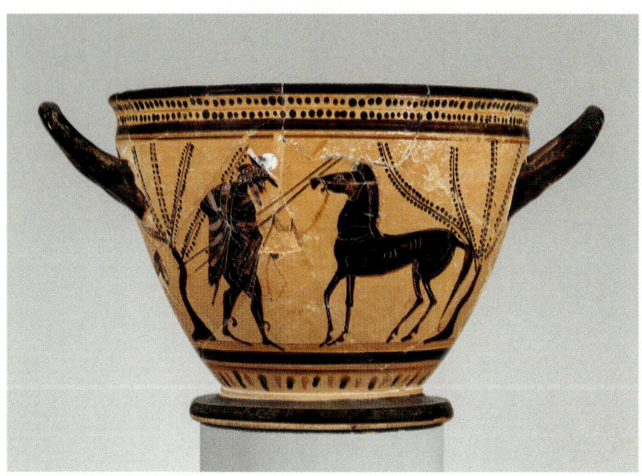

Plate 8. Attic black-figure skyphos attr. to the Durand Painter, 510–500. Boston, Museum of Fine Arts 99.524. Ceramic. Ht. 0.17 m. Photo: Museum of Fine Arts, Boston.

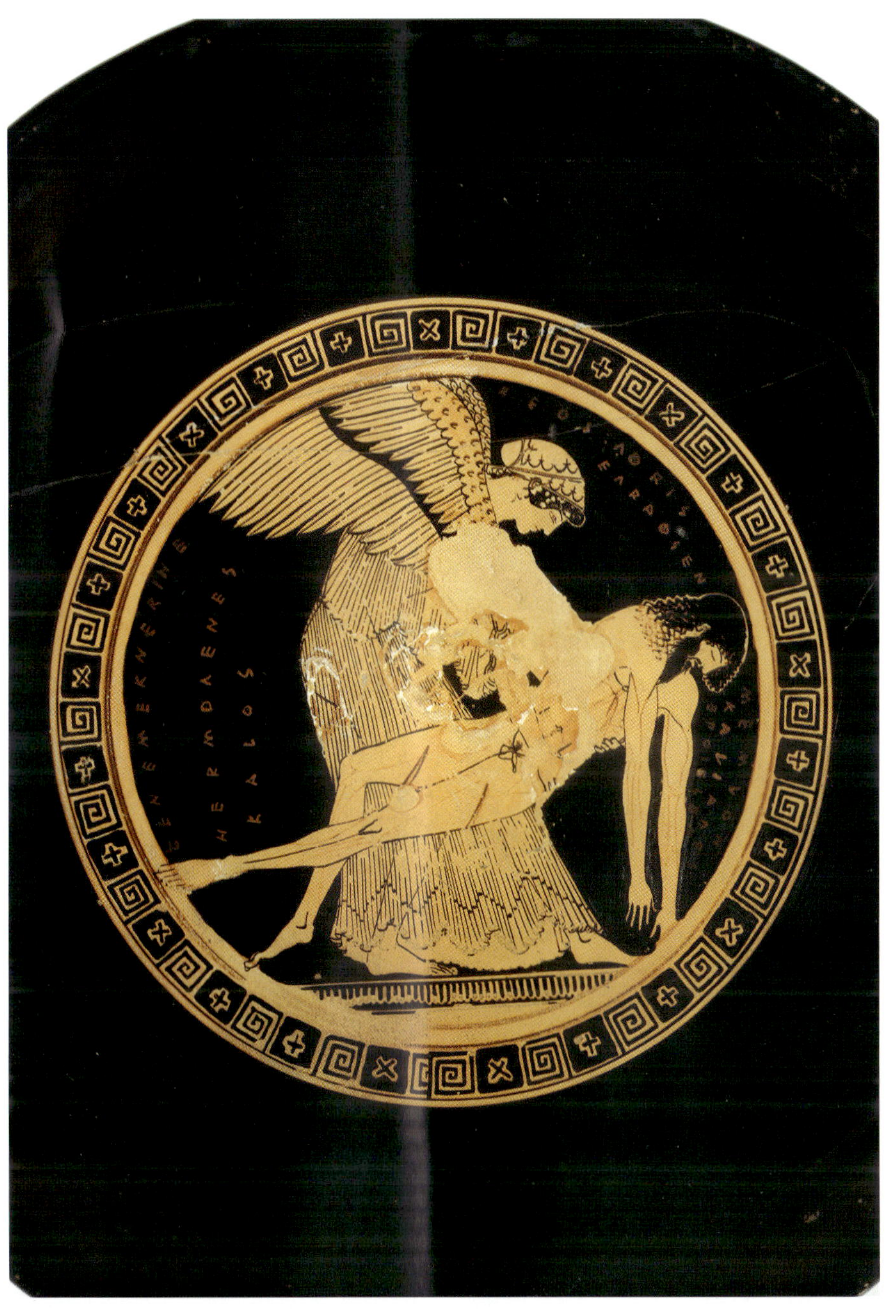

Plate 9. Interior of Athenian red-figure cup signed by Douris as painter and Kalliades as potter, 490–480. Paris, Louvre G 115. Diam. 0.26 m. Photo: Art Resource, N.Y.

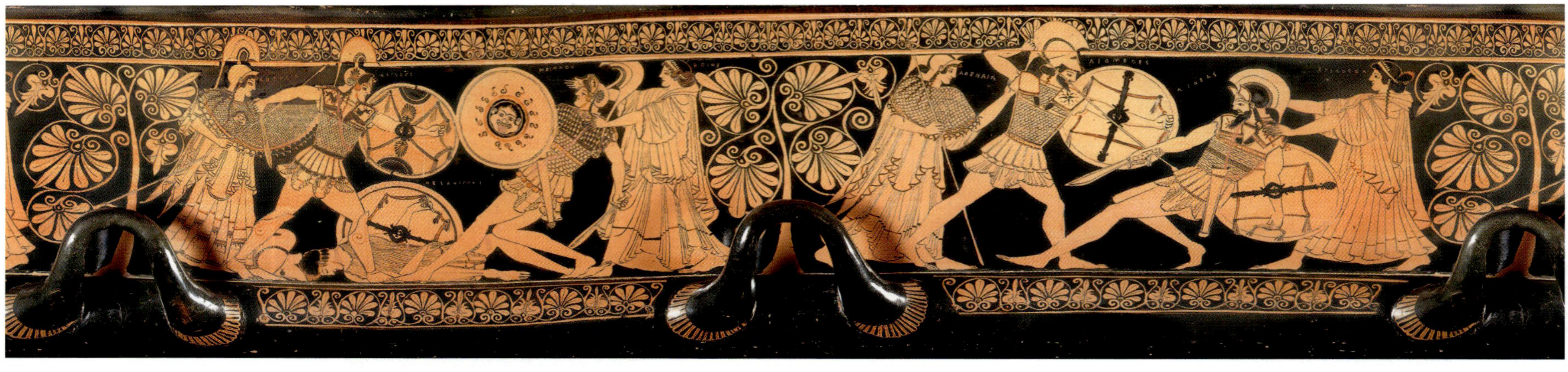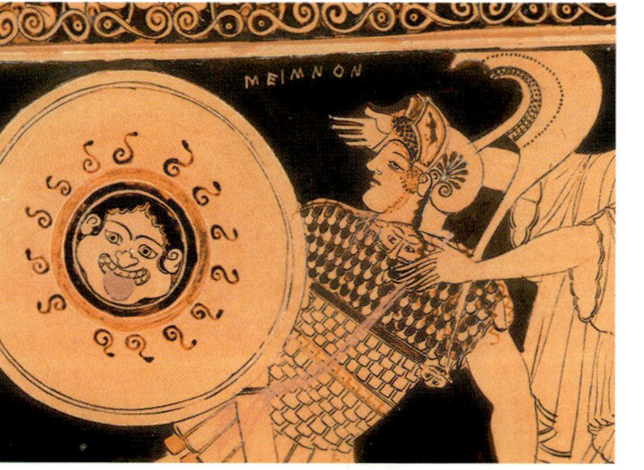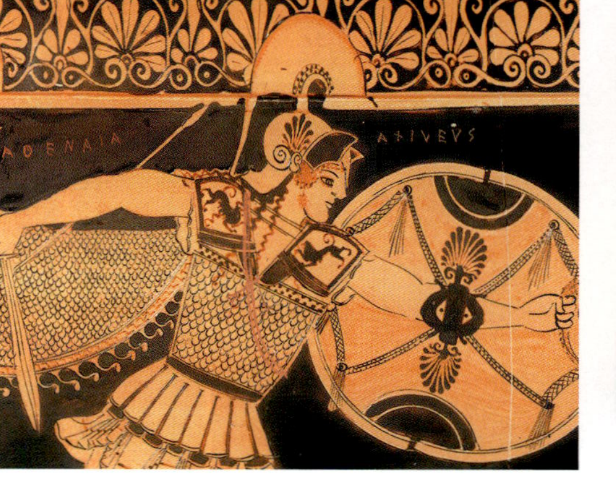

Plate 10. Top: stitched photographs with detail of Athenian red-figure calyx krater said to be from Vulci attr. to the Tyszkiewicz Painter, 490–480. Bottom: details of Achilles and Memnon. Boston, Museum of Fine Arts 97.368. Ceramic. Ht. 0.45 m. Photo: Museum of Fine Arts, Boston.

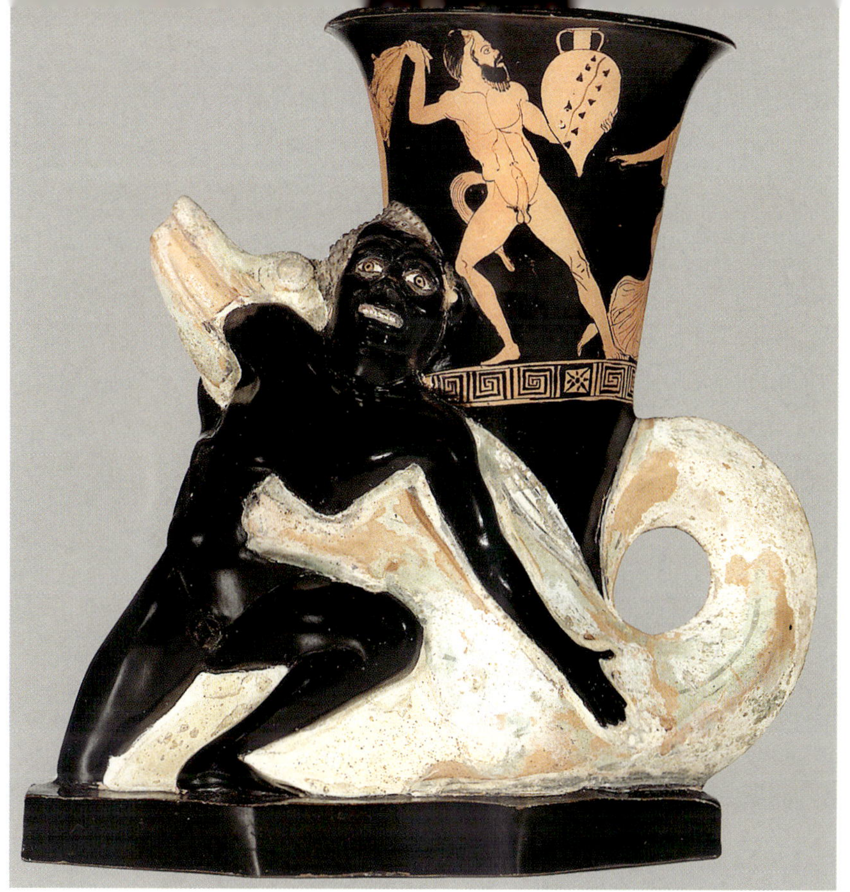

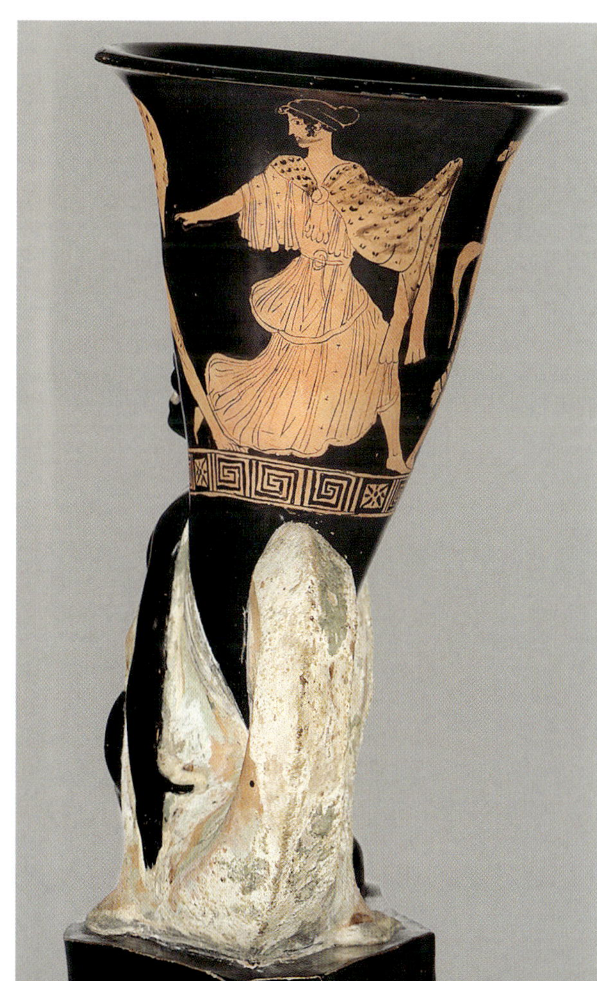

Plate 11. Attic red-figure plastic horn on a base attr. to the Manner of the Sotades Painter, 460. Boston, Museum of Fine Arts 98.881. Ceramic. Ht. 0.24 m. Photo: Museum of Fine Arts, Boston.

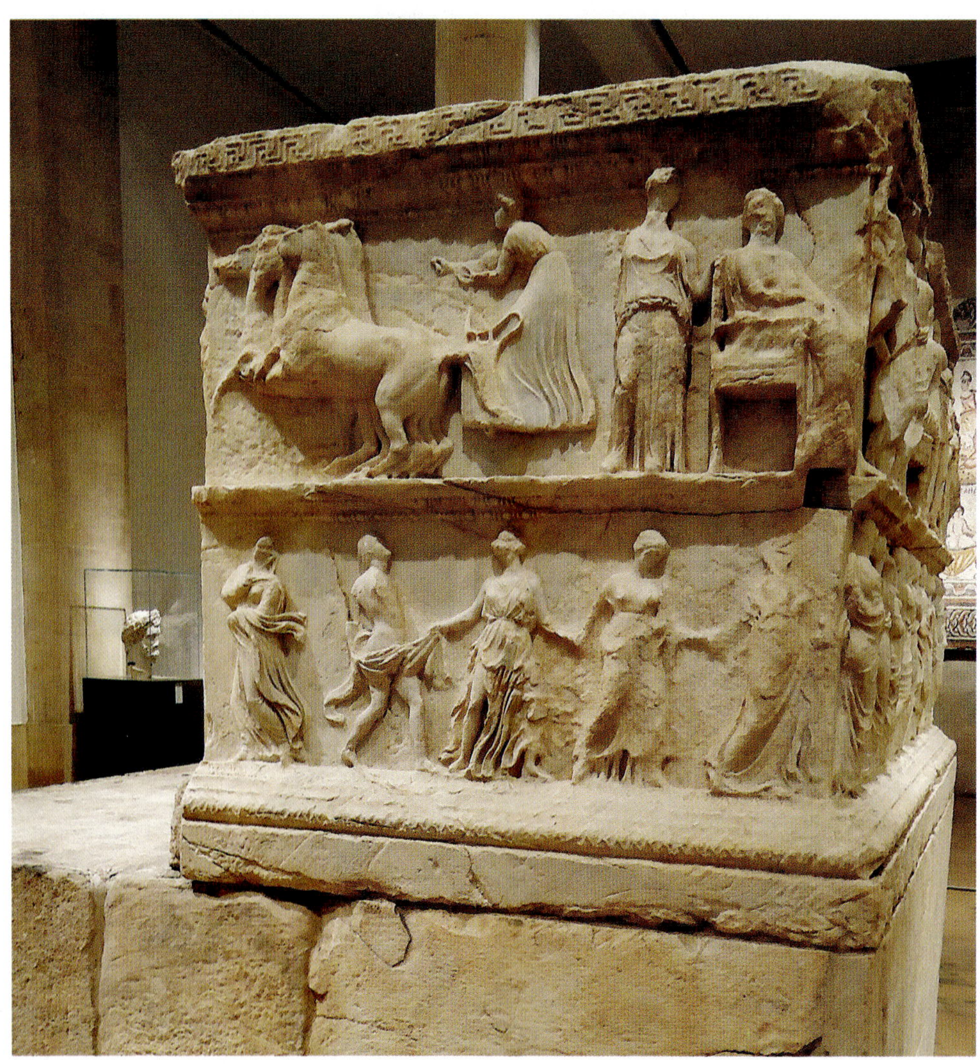

Plate 12. Front-side view of the so-called tribune (altar) from Bostan esh-Sheikh, probably late 4th c. Marble on limestone foundation. Beirut, National Museum 2080. Ht. 2.4 m. Photo: author's own.

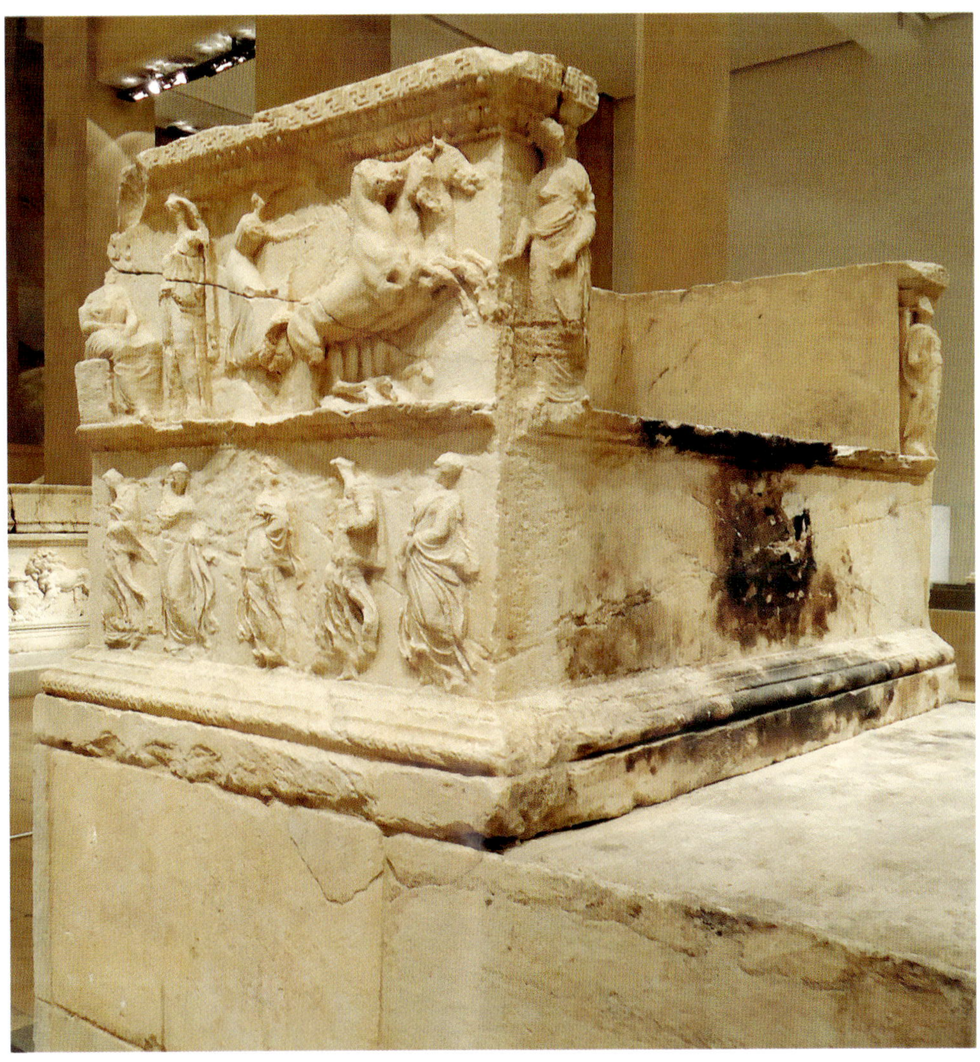

Plate 13. Side-back view of the so-called tribune (altar) from Bostan esh-Sheikh (compare Plate 12). Photo: author's own.

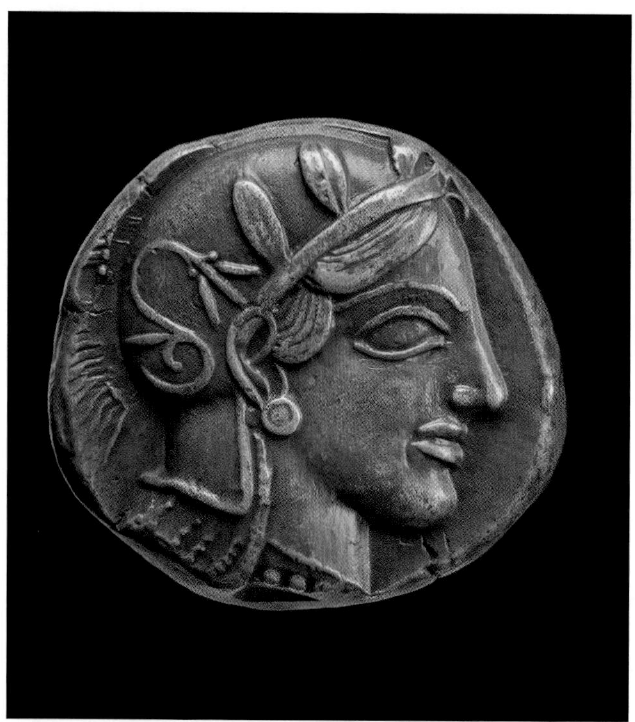

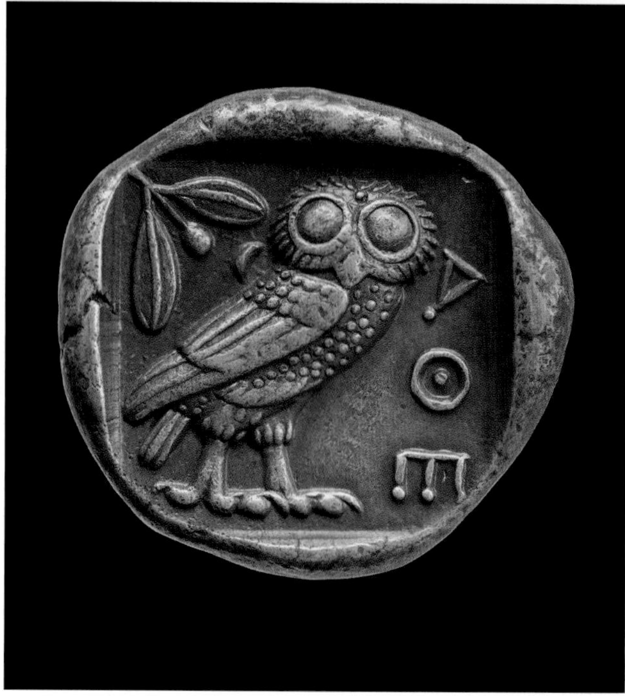

Plate 14. Classical Athenian tetradrachm, 450–405. Obverse: laureate Athena; reverse: olive branch, owl, moon, and Greek inscription. London, British Museum 1920,0805.317. Silver. 17.15 gr. Photo: © The Trustees of the British Museum.

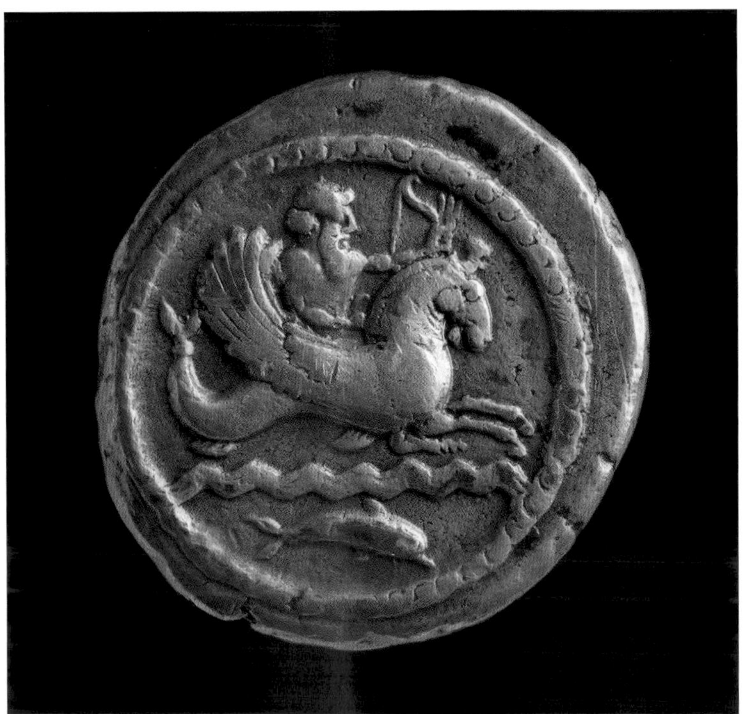

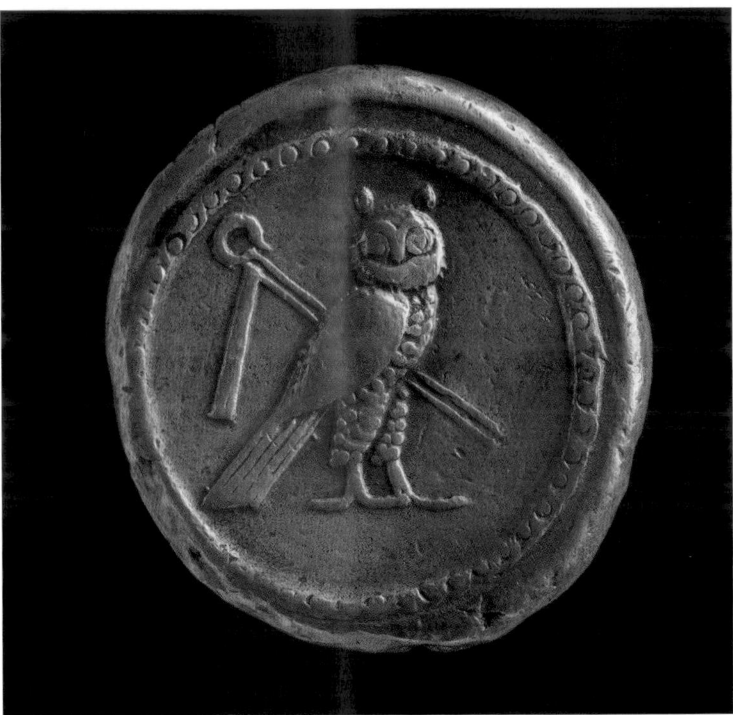

Plate 15. Silver coin minted in Tyre. Obverse: deity on a winged sea horse over a dolphin; reverse: owl, scepter, and flail, ca. 360–350. Silver. 13.6 gr. London, British Museum 1906,0713.1. Photo: © The Trustees of the British Museum.

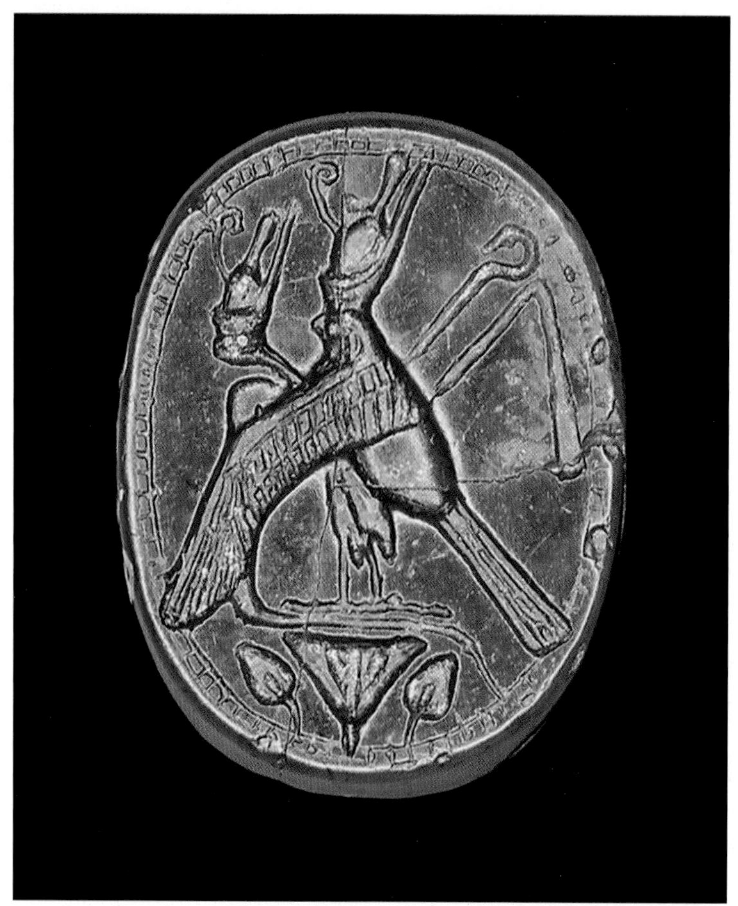

Plate 16. Persian-period seal from Tharros (Sardinia). Double-crowned falcon protecting uraeus with double crown standing on lotus with buds at the side. Behind the falcon are the crook and flail. London, British Museum ANE 133538. Green jasper. 1.45 × 1.10 cm. Photo: © The Trustees of the British Museum.

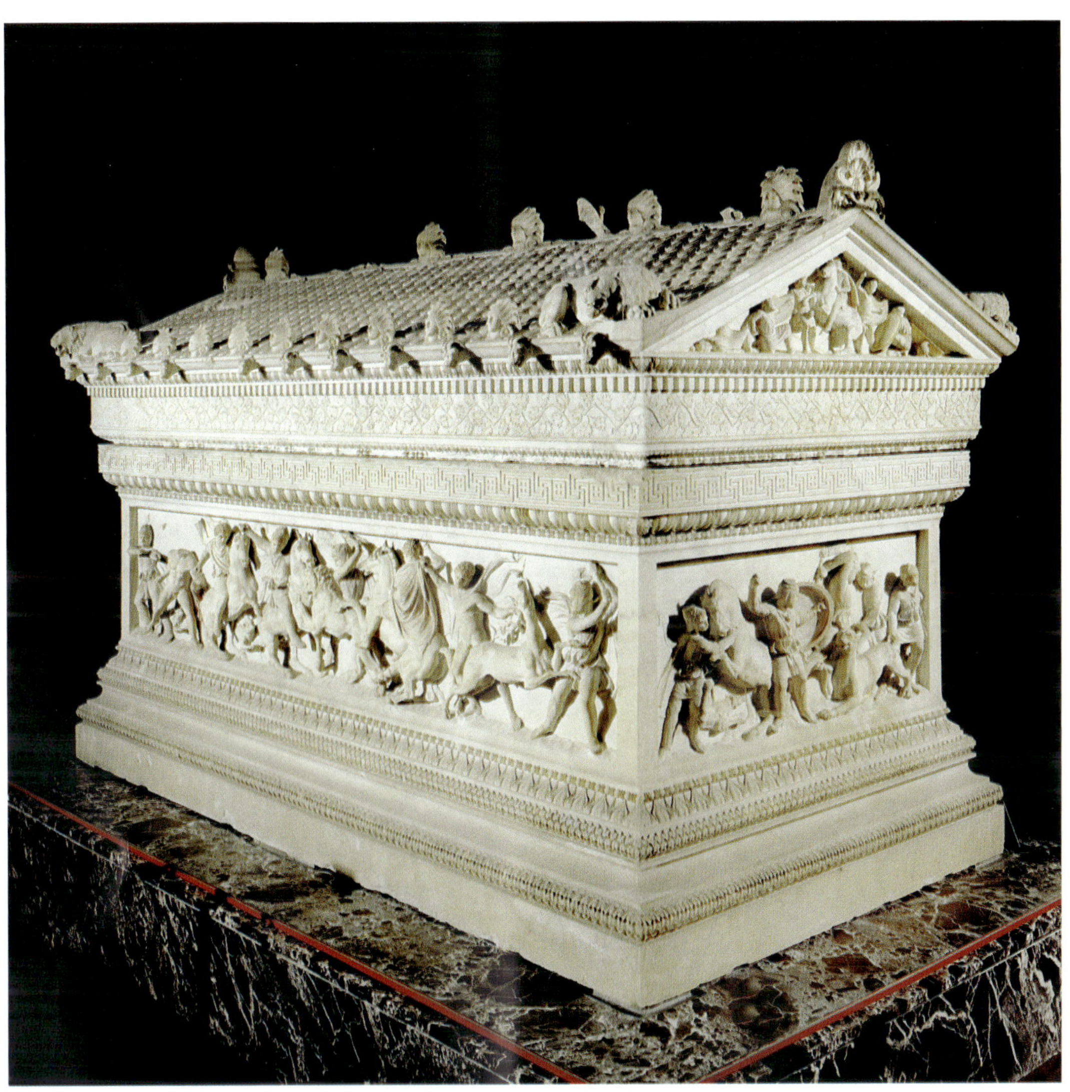

Plate 17. Alexander Sarcophagus. ʿAyaa nekropolis near Sidon, later 4th c. Istanbul, Archaeological Museum 370. Marble. Ht. 1.70 m; ht. of friezes 0.58 m. Photo: Art Resource, N.Y.

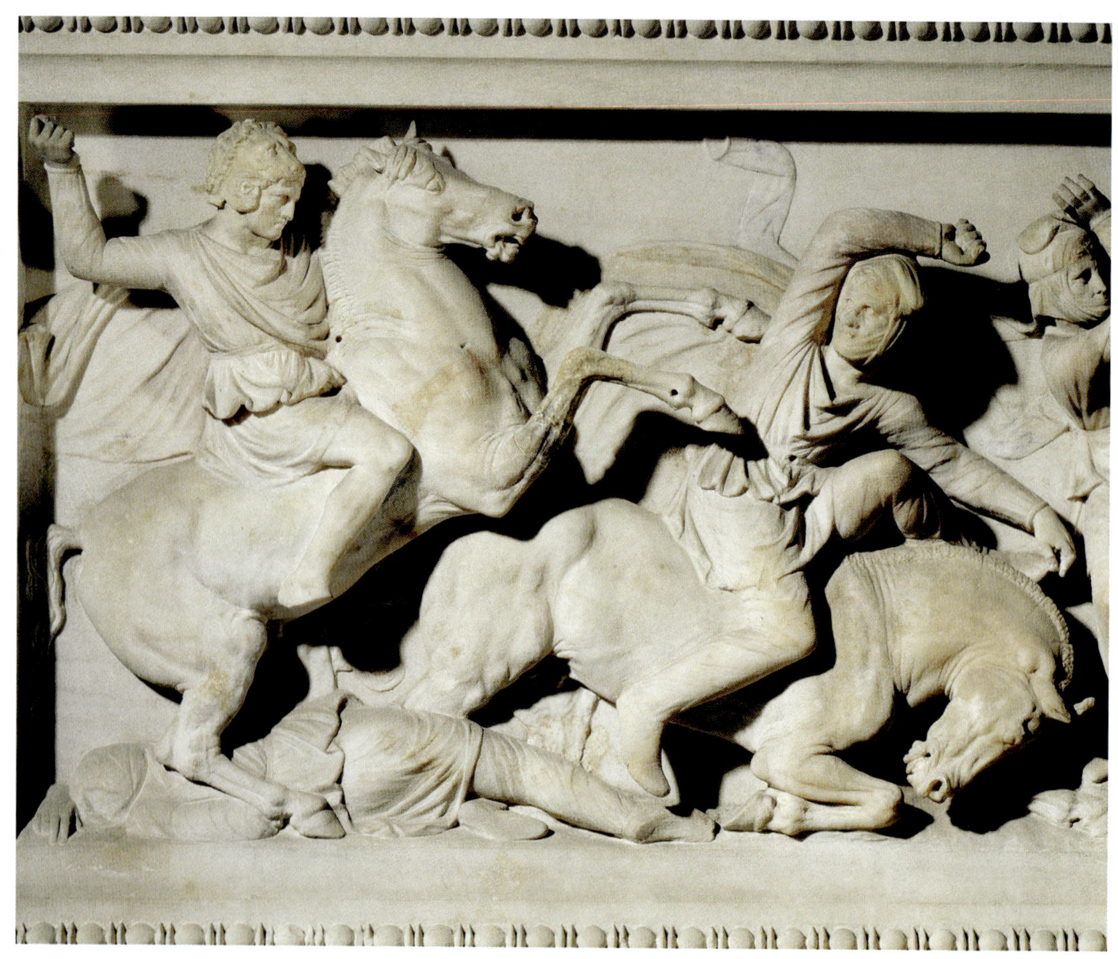

Plate 18. Detail of Alexander Sarcophagus: left side of the long-side battle scene. ʿAyaa nekropolis near Sidon, later 4th c. Istanbul, Archaeological Museum 370. Marble. Ht. 1.70 m; ht. of friezes 0.58 m. Photo: Art Resource, N.Y.

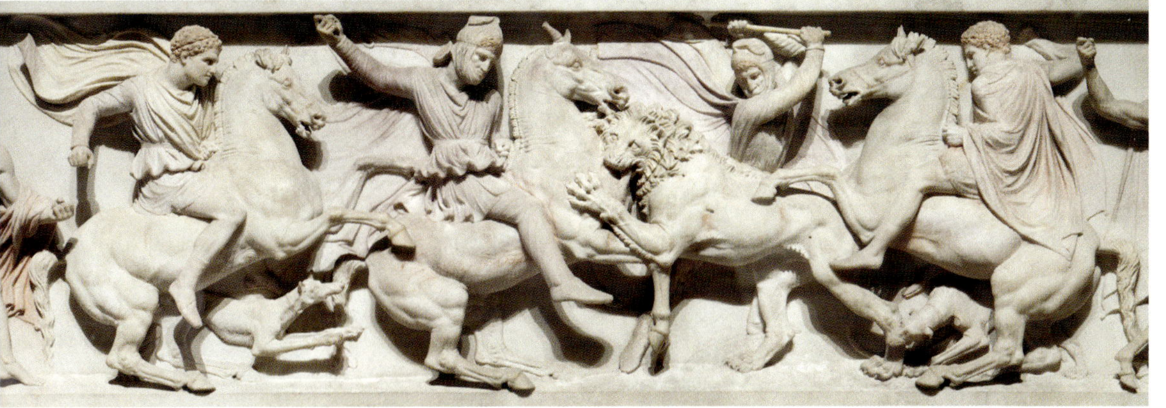

Plate 19. Detail of Alexander Sarcophagus: lion hunt. ʿAyaa nekropolis near Sidon, later 4th c. Istanbul, Archaeological Museum 370. Marble. Ht. 1.70 m; ht. of friezes 0.58 m. Photo: Art Resource, N.Y.

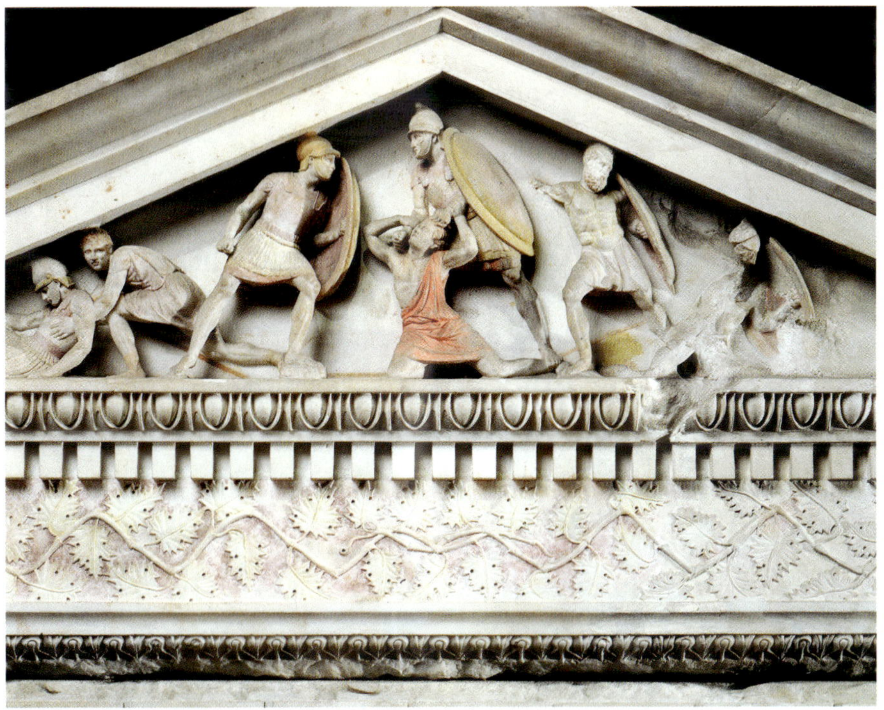

Plate 20. Detail of Alexander Sarcophagus: pediment. ʿAyaa nekropolis near Sidon, later 4th c. Istanbul, Archaeological Museum 370. Marble. Ht. 1.70 m; ht. of friezes 0.58 m. Photo: Art Resource, N.Y.

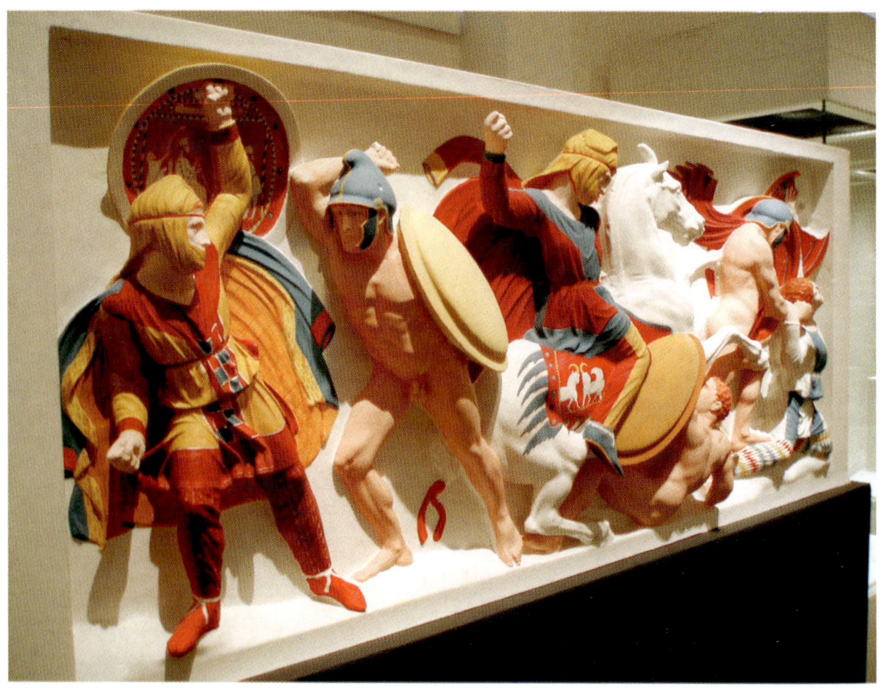

Plate 21. Painted reconstruction of Alexander Sarcophagus short-side battle scene by Vinzenz Brinkmann and Ulrike Koch-Brinkmann. Photo: Marsyas, available under the terms of the Creative Commons Attribution-Share Alike 2.5 Generic.

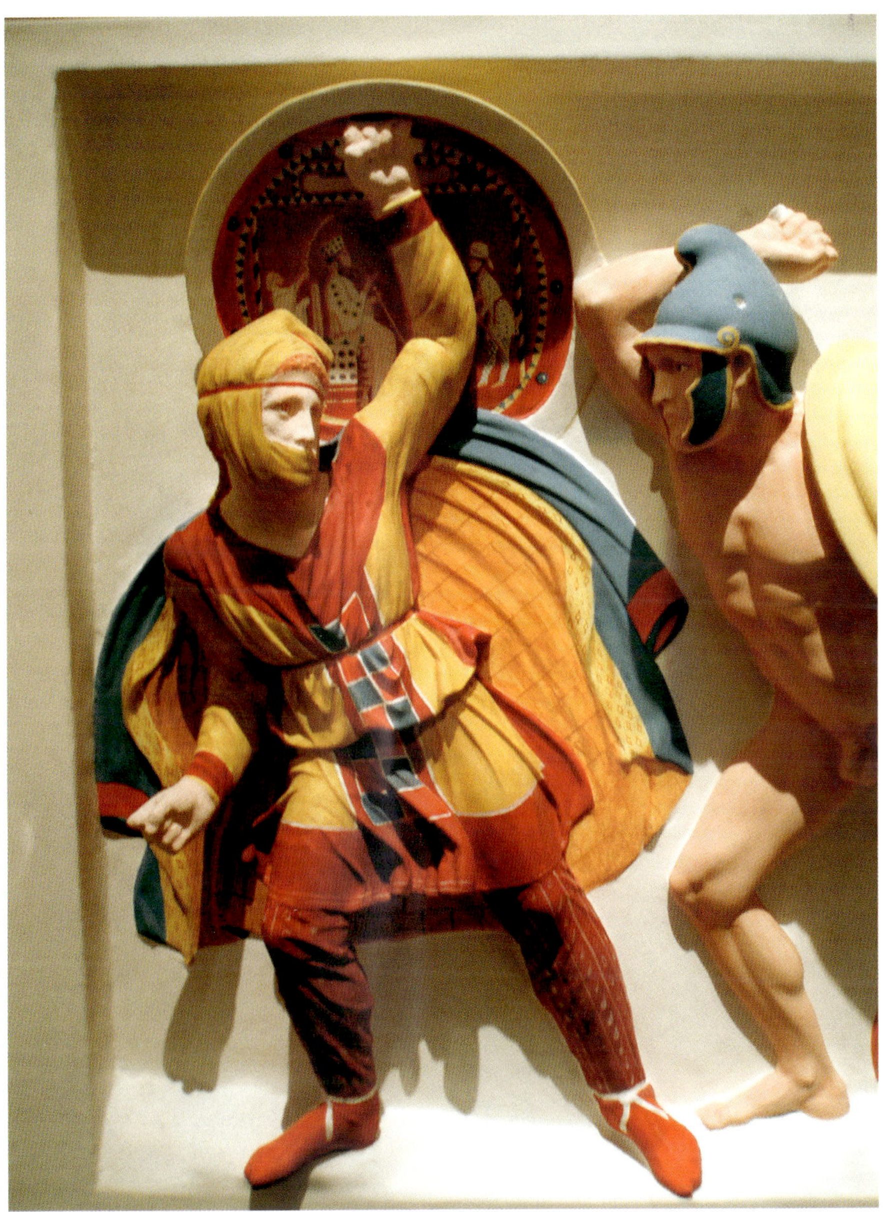

Plate 22. Detail of left side of painted reconstruction of Alexander Sarcophagus short-side battle scene by Vinzenz Brinkmann and Ulrike Koch-Brinkmann. Photo: Marsyas, available under the terms of the Creative Commons Attribution-Share Alike 2.5 Generic.

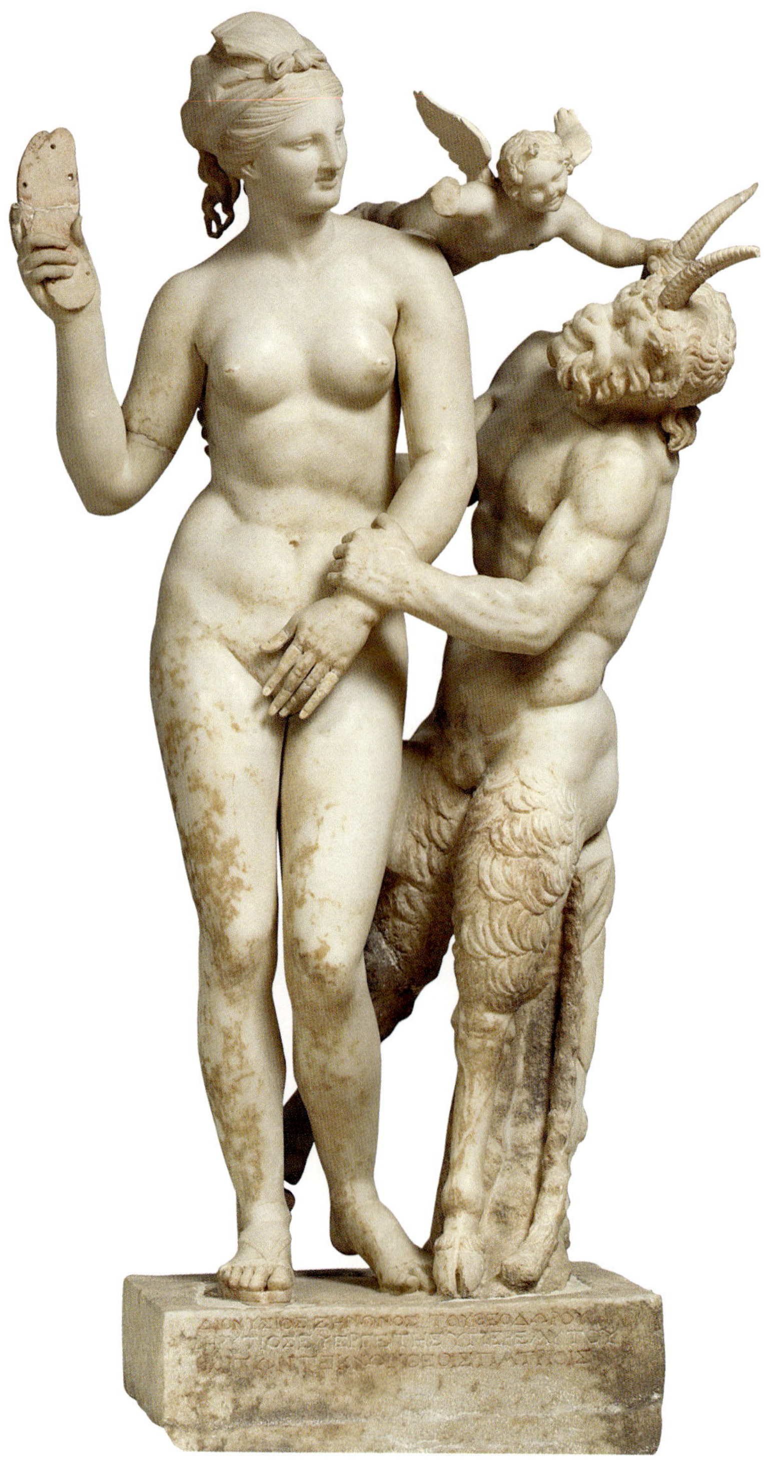

Plate 23. Group of Aphrodite, Eros, and Pan from Delos, ca. 100. Athens, National Museum 3335. Marble. Ht. 1.32 m without base. Photo: National Archaeological Museum, Athens, G. Patrikianos.

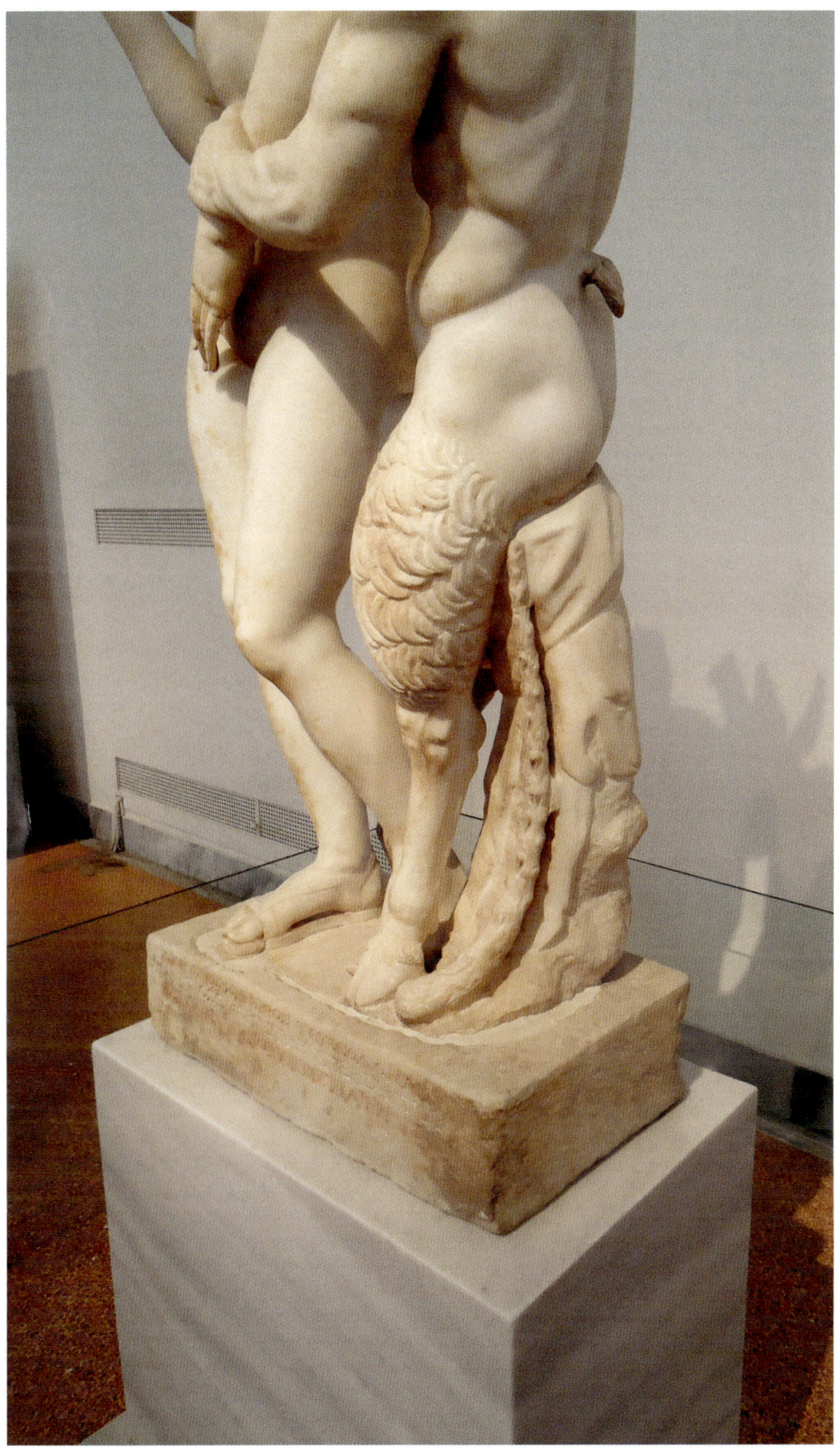

Plate 24. Detail of group of Aphrodite, Eros, and Pan from Delos (Plate 23). Photo: author's own.

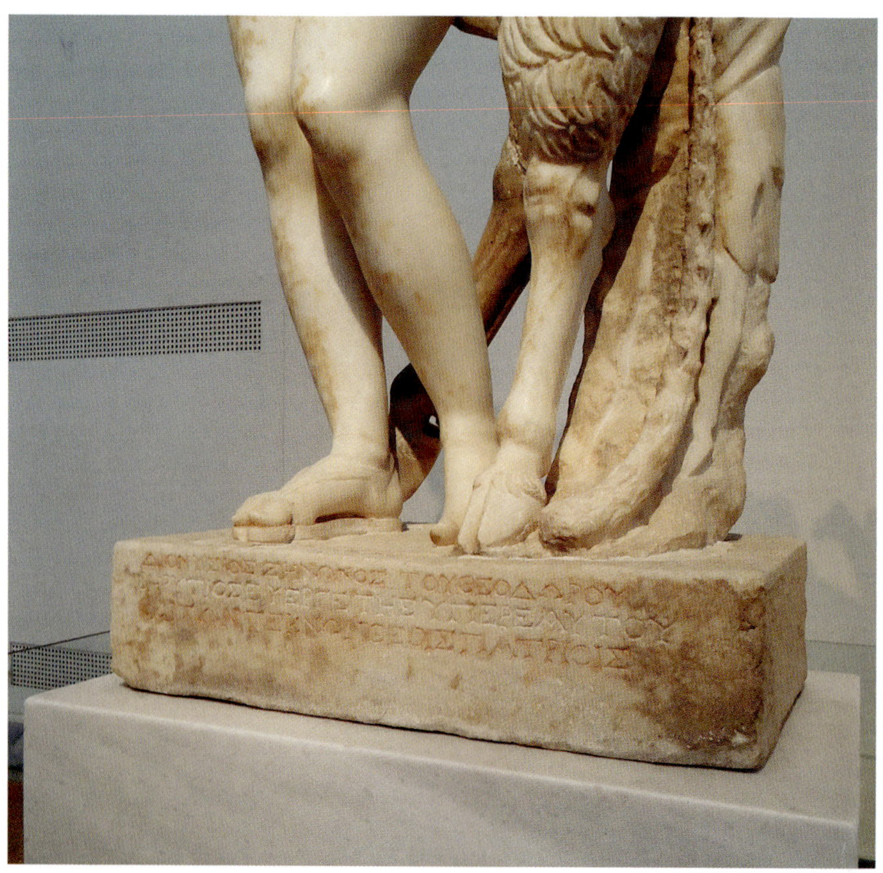

Plate 25. Detail of group of Aphrodite, Eros, and Pan from Delos (Plate 23). Photo: author's own.

Reading the Alexander Sarcophagus through a differential hybridity recognizes it as a monument of a "historically contingent hegemonic relationship,"[77] an expression of subaltern consciousness, not a celebration of Alexander's liberation and the arrival of Hellenism.[78] After all, Phoenicia and Sidon were not then free. This reading of the tomb suggests that it meant to deliberately destabilize the hegemony in a way that Macedonians (and modern scholars) were not likely to recognize because, once again, although external stimulus might have been necessary for the creation of this monument, the artwork expresses inward-looking ideas. Its main, if not only, intended viewers were elite Sidonians. We lack evidence anyone else would, or could, have seen it. Moreover, the sarcophagus was part of a funerary tradition that began two hundred years earlier. Although it seems to quote historical events, or the artworks that portrayed them, we must be cautious about relating the tomb to Alexander's conquest, an event prone to exaggeration in our source material (none of which is Phoenician). While it is quite possible to disagree that the tomb is ideologically subversive, the conversation must include this possibility.

Stockhammer has lamented that "hybridity as an epistemological concept has long been undertheorized."[79] To conclude, I would take that point a step farther, to suggest that hybridity's popularity has barely altered the traditional discourses of Greek and Phoenician art. The fashion for hybridity is reminiscent of the roles claimed for the Euboeans and Phoenicians in the transmission of Iron Age culture.[80] As I have shown here, it is easy to use hybridity in such a way as to perpetuate untenable ideas, notably those that present viewing neutrally, conflate observation with causation, and still wish to see a hybrid monument as an indicium of Hellenization. Scholars who see a positive, acculturating hybridity in works such as the Alexander Sarcophagus rely upon an ethnicity-image relationship that is Greek or Macedonian in its outlook, not Sidonian. One could make the argument that this hybridity is little more than a veneer of critical theory applied over a still-healthy teleology of acculturation, a disguise thrown on old ideologies with the power to reinvigorate cultural essentialism. It is understandable why many have rejected the term and what it stands for, choosing to focus instead on processes.[81] Still others favor the idea of entanglement.[82] The chief problem with this terminology is that it is not capable on its own of counteracting ancient or modern bias. If we do not change the way we think about the past, using a new term to point to it accomplishes little. It serves no purpose to use hybridity to valorize cultural heterogeneity because doing so is now fashionable.[83] The advantage of using postcolonial theory is to draw attention to approaches and debate them. Its benefit is how much it complicates what it is we think we see.

Admittedly we know very little about the artistic process anywhere in Phoenicia, either the role of artists or that of patrons. What we do know is that art was often aggregated, iconographically, thematically, and stylistically. This suggests that artist and patron played significant roles in Phoenician art. It is in this context that the Alexander Sarcophagus must be placed, whatever theories we choose or reject to interpret it. Whether some figures in Persian dress should be read as Sidonians is beside the point. In the context of the history of Sidonian funerary art, the Greek conventions found on one tomb are not so significant as to overpower precedent. Seen from a Sidonian perspective, the Alexander Sarcophagus's primary function was to display its owner's status within local terms rather than appease outsiders at court. (Of course, we have no direct evidence of any such court.) We do not need to rely on fragile historical associations, such as the identification of Abdalonymos as patron, to support this reading; the findspot suffices.

We will probably never recover the identity of the tomb's occupant. We cannot know the ethnicity of its sculptors, either, regardless of where we think they were trained. We would do well to remember that even if they were Rhodian or Ionian, the sculptors were working within a Sidonian tradition that lacks parallels elsewhere. On a small scale, the Sidonian sarcophagi might echo the Persian Apadana and, even, the Periklean building program, both of which employed nonlocal sculptors but nevertheless created works of art that express the priorities of their respective states. It is important to remember that, so far as we know, early Hellenistic Sidon was a site of only occasional meetings between merchants and ruling classes from different locales, not a place of intensive and ongoing contact between disparate people who found themselves suddenly forced to live side by side. In order to understand the role of Phoenician art in that kind of environment, we can turn to Delos.

Aphrodite in the Middle Ground

Hellenistic Delos was quite clearly a contact zone (see Map 2). I believe it was also a site of ongoing negotiations that constitutes a middle ground, something that is explicit in its art industry. Delos is the only Cycladic island with "sustained evidence" of Phoenician religious activity. Our extant evidence begins with a fourth-century Tyrian inscription and grows to include city-states as far north as Arwad, south to Ashkelon, and west to Carthage. Lipiński attributes Phoenician interest in Delos to the role it played in maritime trade.[84] In 166 Delos was declared by Roman decree a free port in the possession of Athens. From that time until its sacks by Mithradates (88) and by pirates (69) trading activity truly boomed, making Delos a center of commerce that attracted Greeks, Cypriots, various Near Easterners, Egyptians, Persians, Arabs, and others, with the largest foreign group, one with a clearly discernible impact on art and architecture, coming from Italy (and who, it should be noted, referred to themselves collectively as "Italians").[85] It is from precisely this period that Phoenicians become most visible in the fabric of Delian life, as attested by the establishment of residential groups and the many inscriptions naming Phoenicians as participants in the Delian games, in religious activities, and in acts of patronage.[86] The small Cycladic island (reaching a maximum of 5×1.3 km) might have had as many as twenty thousand to thirty thousand residents in this period of peak activity. People from different regions interacted with one another to a significant extent, motivated to intermarry and to exploit the free port for profit and by a "desire for self-ostentation."[87] Although sacred to Apollo, Delos was home to many other cults, some of which were established by non-Greeks, with temples to Egyptian, Jewish, and Levantine gods. Certainly religion was very important to economic networks.[88] Inscriptions make it clear that a variety of grouping strategies were in play, from those that emphasize large regions (notably, the Italians) to those that are expressed only through patronymics. Notable is the Phoenician approach that is defined civically, and, within that designation, could be narrowed further by religion.

The middle ground is a heuristic historical theory that was first articulated by Richard White in his 1991 book, *The Middle Ground*. The theory is postcolonial insofar as it rejects acculturation and resistance as the only outcomes of contact. White developed it as a way to understand the French-Algonquian alliance in the Great Lakes region of the seventeenth to early nineteenth centuries. He seeks to explore the trajectory of the relationship between Europeans and Indians from one of complete alienation to something "mutually comprehensible."[89] A few things about middle ground theory are important to bear in mind. It is not interchangeable with the idea of the contact zone, although frequent, even daily, contact is a prerequisite. The middle ground is created by a set of relationships, negotiations, and accommodations that must be constantly reinforced in order to survive and can fail even as contact is ongoing. Because not all culture contact produces the middle ground, it cannot be used to describe all contact any more than it describes all negotiations (recalling hybridity's specificity).[90] A contact zone is something physical and conceptual; the middle ground is a process built and rebuilt over time, requiring constant inventions that may only later be represented as convention.[91] While the middle ground may require some adjusting of expectations, it is not about common ground or compromise (despite how it is often used). According to White, the middle ground is full of fundamental, sometimes even willful, misunderstandings as people appeal to one another according to what they perceive to be true about their beliefs and practices.[92] Tactful negotiation might require accepting a pretense that seems, to one party, plainly false.[93] Misunderstandings can, however, be fertile for creating new meanings and behaviors that exist exclusively in the context of the middle ground.

At the heart of White's work is the idea that the middle ground results only from very particular historical circumstances in which two or more parties are truly interdependent and motivated to negotiate. In such a context, therefore, mediation was not only a necessary, important act; it was also a major source of power.[94] Understanding, even if not terribly authentic, was something to be used to personal advantage, perhaps especially within one's own society.[95] Nevertheless, it is important to distinguish the powerful role of mediation from coercion. The middle ground cannot exist if one participant truly has the power to dominate the other. Alliance is the goal across economic, political, social, and cultural spheres. An advantage of middle ground theory, although it seems simple to say, is that it does not concern itself excessively with precontact events. In that way, middle ground theory can be applied to what we observe rather than to presuppose what we lack—and here I am thinking of Phoenician art especially.

A helpful illustration of White's theory comes from his presentation of the contact between Jesuits and Indian refugees. A missionary named Father Claude-Jean Allouez was initially regarded with suspicion by Algonquians, but, after surviving a harsh winter and giving presents to the needy, Allouez was welcomed as a *manitou*, or "other-than-human-person," who could protect and assist them.[96] His god was recognized as powerful, and Allouez was asked to teach them how to honor this "great manitou" Jesus. When Allouez tried to explain to a group of Mascoutens that he was not a manitou but rather the manitou's servant, they reportedly did not really understand him but nevertheless reassured him that they now had "knowledge of the true God." Over time, and with repeated contact and hardships, Indians became less impressed with the Jesus manitou, many doubting his power and his servants outright. It is easy to see how much misunderstanding fueled this interaction, carrying the relationship with Allouez and his god from alienation to a desire to accommodate and thence to rejection. The special status of Jesus was not disputed, however, but, as a great manitou, he was not living up to his description by Jesuits. More than one former manitou would be subject to dismissal or violence as he failed to understand or provide what Indians wanted in return.

Hellenistic Delos is certainly not the type of environment that White envisioned for his theory, and it is doubtful that this same kind of doubled and prolonged misunderstanding would occur between the different people active there. As Fernand Braudel has put it, the Mediterranean itself can be understood as "exchange," so at least some familiarity with the customs of others was to be expected.[97] Yet middle ground theory fits well the interdependence of foreigners on the island as well as the idea that negotiation and mediation brought power. White's theory has made its mark elsewhere in classical Mediterranean studies, notably in the work of Irad Malkin, a historian specializing in Iron Age colonization.[98] In a 2005 essay

Malkin explores the middle ground in the context of a wider discussion of the myriad deployments of Herakles foundation myths in western Sicily. One of Malkin's intriguing examples is an Archaic inscription found at Poggioreale.[99] It is a dedication to Herakles written in the Dorian dialect and using the alphabet of nearby Selinous. It is not clear if the inscription was in the chora of Greek Selinous or in the eastern Elymian territory settled by Phoenician speakers. Herakles is, of course, a Greek hero with ties to Phoenician Melqart in terms of his physical strength and, we think, his appearance in art. The gods are sometimes so close that it can be difficult for modern scholars to distinguish them visually or, because of the translation of the names of Phoenician gods in Greek, in inscriptions.

Malkin raises the question, "Was this [inscription] an extension of a Greek Herakles from Selinous, or was it a Melqart (written in Greek) protecting his territory vis-à-vis the Greeks?"[100] Possibly exploiting the fluidity of Herakles-Melqart was the point of the dedication. Malkin later asks, "Or was [the god] perhaps both—a mediating figure acceptable to Elymians, Greeks, and Phoenicians?"[101] A reading of the god in this inscription as simultaneously Herakles and Melqart is appealing, if only hypothetical. The colonization of Sicily provides the right environment for this kind of reception-driven approach, suggesting it would be much more difficult, even ahistorical, to argue against the inscription's capacity for bilingualism. But is the Sicilian Herakles-Melqart truly operating in the middle ground in White's conception of the theory? Appropriately, in Sicily there was no central authority, and the groups coming into contact might have had only limited previous experience with one another, although certainly not to the degree of the French and Algonquian. Yet Sicily fails to provide an environment of total interdependence paralleling the violently disposed Algonquian and the French who were desperate for peace and economic stability.[102] It seems very difficult to find many or *any* good parallels to White's middle ground test case in the first millennium Mediterranean, in which interaction among certain peoples—merchants, sailors, and so forth—was commonplace.

Some who admire the concept question whether the middle ground as a process can be separated from the physical space of the Great Lakes Region.[103] Others, such as Malkin, have played with it more freely. In his well-received recent book on network theory, *A Small Greek World*, Malkin explains: "Middle grounds, in this book, characterize regional clusters of networks where Greeks founded colonies or lived in *emporia* and mixed settlements."[104] This interweaving of middle ground and network theory suggests that Malkin explores the concept in a looser fashion, as one of many variations on both theories. What he values in the middle ground is the idea of a balance of power that encourages, "role playing . . . a kind of imprecise double mirror reflection [that] creates a 'third' civilization that is

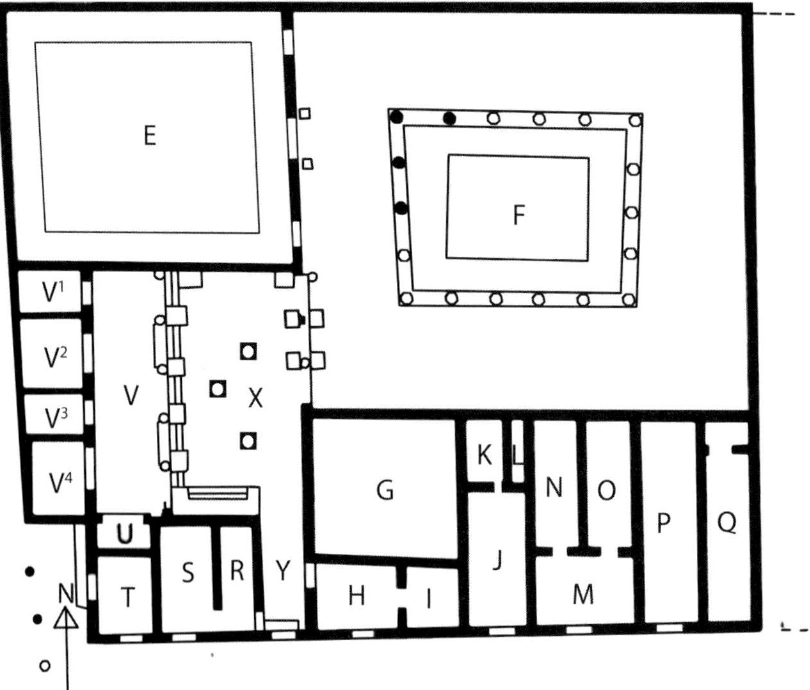

Figure 39. Plan of the final phase of the Poseidoniasts' clubhouse at Delos. Plan redrawn by Sveta Matskevich after Bruneau and Ducat 1983, fig. 63.

neither purely native nor entirely colonial imported."[105] While this characterization recalls hybridity's third space, I maintain that it is important to distinguish the two theories, as hybridity is a theory suited for unequal relationships—hierarchies—whereas the middle ground requires that no party has the upper hand. Its relationships and negotiations are horizontal.

The under-life-sized Hellenistic sculptural group known as the Sandal Slapper or the Slipper Slapper offers us an opportunity to explore a middle ground negotiation in art (see Plates 23–25).[106] It was found in the lake quarter of Delos in a complex identified by Greek inscription (Figure 39):

ΤΟ ΚΟΙΝΟΝ ΒΗΡΥΤΙΩΝ ΠΟΣΕΙΔΩΝΙΑΣΤΩΝ ΕΜΠΟΡΩΝ ΚΑΙ ΝΑΥΚΛΗΡΩΝ ΚΑΙ ΕΓΔΟΧΕΩΝ ΤΟΝ ΟΙΚΟΝ ΚΑΙ ΤΗΝ ΣΤΟΑΝ ΚΑΙ ΤΑ ΧΡΗΣΤΗΡΙΑ ΘΕΟΙΣ ΠΑΤΡΙΟΙΣ ΑΝΕΘΗΚΕΝ

Club of the Poseidoniasts of Berytos, merchants, shippers, and warehousemen set up the building, the stoa, and the oracles for our ancestral gods.[107]

The Poseidoniasts were part of a broader phenomenon of sacred and secular merchant groups or "clubs" established on Delos and elsewhere in the Mediterranean, which consisted of people brought together by common interests that arose outside of extant state structures.[108] Clubs combined economic, religious, and social activities. Familiar Phoenician onomastic practices indicate that "Poseidon," especially since he seems to be one of the group's "ancestral gods," or *theoi patrioi*, might be the name used here for "Ba'al" the Phoenician sky god—although it is difficult to be certain.[109] The formula naming merchants, shippers, and warehousemen from Beirut is found in several dedications inside the building. Although it belongs to an explicitly Beiruti group composed of residents of Delos, the complex's plan is loosely comparable to the earlier "building with the children friezes" from the Eshmun complex at Bostan esh-Sheikh (see Figure 28).[110] The similarity might indicate that the plan stems from a broadly Phoenician design, but it might be merely coincidental. At the same time, a mercantile group with a religious association has Greek and Italian parallels, and the courtyard design of the complex itself has Italian precedents.[111] The complex measured fourteen hundred square meters in its largest iteration. It has been studied recently in detail by Monica Trümper, who shows that the final, third phase of the structure had two courtyards ("E" and "F"), four small rooms on the south side, and a sanctuary with an entrance room ("X"), colonnaded antechamber ("V"), and four shrines ("V1–4").[112] It was loaded with statuary: marble cult images and other religious dedications, twelve portraits of Greeks and Romans, and a number of terracottas.

The entrance room "X" was accessible from a narrow passage from the street and from the connecting courtyard "F." An inscription with the name Zeno son of Dionysios was found in this entrance room as part of a dedication to his theoi patrioi.[113] A number of portrait statues and altars were once placed there, but now only their bases survive. Rooms "V2" and "V3" are thought to be dedicated to the club's theoi patrioi. According to an inscribed statue base, Poseidon was honored in room "V2." Most agree that room "V3" would have honored Aphrodite/Aštart. Charles Picard's original publication suggested that room "V4" was dedicated to the third member of the so-called Berytian Triad, Herakles/Melqart; later publications following his rationale have suggested Eshmun. The argument reflects outdated thinking about Phoenician religion, and Philippe Bruneau rightly argued against it. He believed that the "V4" shrine never held a cult statue. Trümper suggests it contained a bench for cult offerings.[114] Room "V1" was dedicated to Roma, as was one of the altars in room "X," demonstrating again this group's ties to Italy and underscoring the kind of mixing that was a part of Delian life.[115] More ties between the Poseidoniasts and Italians are recorded. One Marcus Miniatus paid for part of the construction of the Poseidoniasts' complex, which also contained an honorific dedication to one Gn. Octavius, consul in 87 BCE.[116]

The Roma statue in room "V1" is thought to date to circa 130–110. It is draped conservatively in chiton and himation and preserved to a height of 1.54 m. It is one of—if not *the*—earliest surviving depictions of the goddess and is the only known statue of Roma on the island.[117] Its inscribed base secures the attribution and makes clear that it was dedicated on behalf of the club by Mnaseas, son of a Dionysios. The signature is of an Athenian sculptor who is identified as a son of Melas. The sculptor's name is reconstructed to Menandros, although it does not appear that the signature is original to the Roma dedication.[118] The statue overlooks a black and white checker mosaic. The design, although known elsewhere on Delos, might be another conscious nod to the Italian Peninsula.[119] Other than Roma and the Slipper Slapper, the other preserved statuary in the complex includes a Herakles epitrapezios, a Herakles table support (?), a seated goddess statuette, a Hekateion, a nymph (once with a satyr, Pan, or perhaps Poseidon), and an Aphrodite of the Arles type.[120]

We can compare the appearance of Roma in the Poseidoniasts' complex to cult of the Lares Compitales that was widespread on the island from the late second century BCE. Domestic paintings in the houses of competaliasts show sacrificial scenes according to the Roman fashion (togate and with head covered) as well as the Greek (wearing himation and wreathed), with inscriptions in Greek and in Latin. Houses of competaliasts also had paintings of Hermes and Herakles or their attributes. One painting shows three magistrates sacrificing in a Greek fashion and identified in Latin THEOGIPIASON, Theog(enes), Hip(. . .), and Iason.[121] It appears that the cult of the lares had "changed on foreign ground."[122] It had connections to the one in Italy in its administration and also diverged from it by worshipping other gods and sacrificing in the Greek manner. While most household dedications on Delos were to Greek gods, in the lares cult we see a wider range of connections between groups and across social strata. Clearly it was not only the Poseidoniasts or other associations that were participating in what appear to be religious admixtures. There is evidence of individual Greeks and Italians using the Egyptian and Syrian sanctuaries on the island as well.[123] It is possible to see in this evidence the creativity and negotiations characteristic of the middle ground.

The quarters on the south side of the Poseidoniast complex were constructed a bit later than the courtyard and shrines, in around 110 BCE. In this section, three nude or seminude female statues are thought to have once stood, the nymph/satyr group, Arles Aphrodite, and Slipper Slapper.[124] The Slipper Slapper group was found near its base in a basement room "N," presumably having fallen from the lavishly decorated dining room above it (see Plates 23–25).[125] The work is dated to circa 100 according to its inscription, which begins with the typical formula of name, patronyms, and toponym:

ΔΙΟΝΥΣΙΟΣ ΖΗΝΩΝΟΣ ΤΟΥ ΘΕΟΔΩΡΟΥ ΒΗΡΥΤΙΟΣ ΕΥΕΡΓΕΤΗΣ ΥΠΕΡ
ΕΑΥΤΟΥ ΚΑΙ ΤΩΝ ΤΕΚΝΩΝ ΘΕΟΙΣ ΠΑΤΡΙΟΙΣ

Dionysios son of Zeno son of Theodoros of Berytos, benefactor, on behalf
of himself and his children to his ancestral gods.[126]

Altogether, Dionysios was a named patron four times in the club, here, on another statue base, and in inscriptions for the south and west colonnades of courtyard "F," confirming that he was a major benefactor.[127] The name of Zeno, son of
likely the same Dionysios, shows up on two statue bases, the aforementioned inscription in room "X" and on a statue base for Poseidon.[128] What we see in this
complex is similar to what Birgit Tang has observed in houses at Delos: mixed
Greek, Italian, and other features that cannot be sorted into distinct types and do
not in themselves reveal the identity of those who used the space. As in the House
of the Dolphins, but eclipsing it in complexity, here Greek inscriptions play a critical
role in tying various patrons, artists, and works of art to Phoenicians.

The complex's main courtyard was an important space for circulation of different people. The rooms leading off it—those dedicated to the ancestral gods—
are an extension of this circulatory space and thus become a site for the active
engagement with, and crafting of identity for, mixed audiences. Here, as elsewhere
in the Hellenistic world, we must understand that what was on view in such spaces
addressed multiple audiences, in this case at minimum Beiruti, Italian, and perhaps also Athenian.[129] Code switching is evident even in the name of the club, and
it seems possible that Roma, whose altar was in room "V" and whose statue was
in the adjoining shrine "V1," was honored as one of the theoi patrioi.[130] Certainly
Roma added to the Poseidoniasts' prestige. While Trümper has argued that spaces
in Delian houses were often multifunctional, meaning that a sharp private/public
divide might be misleading, it is clear that some areas of this complex were more
public than others.[131] If the intended placement of the Slipper Slapper was in the
room above its basement findspot, it was in a more intimate space, one that seems
designed for a group of about fifteen diners.

The Slipper Slapper group shows an unusual trio: Aphrodite holding her sandal, Pan holding onto to her, and Eros flying overhead grasping one of Pan's horns
(see Plate 23). The group's Aphrodite quotes the late Classical Aphrodite of Knidos by Praxiteles, while reversing the position of the prototype's arms and swap-
ping the Knidia's robe for the eponymous sandal (Figures 40 and 41).[132] The
meaning of the Slipper Slapper is debated and hinges on the relative stress one
places on its reference to the Knidia, on its context, or on its seemingly humorous
content. The group measures 1.55 meters tall. It is sculpted in Parian marble and
inserted into a small, inscribed base. It cannot be accused of being a favorite of art

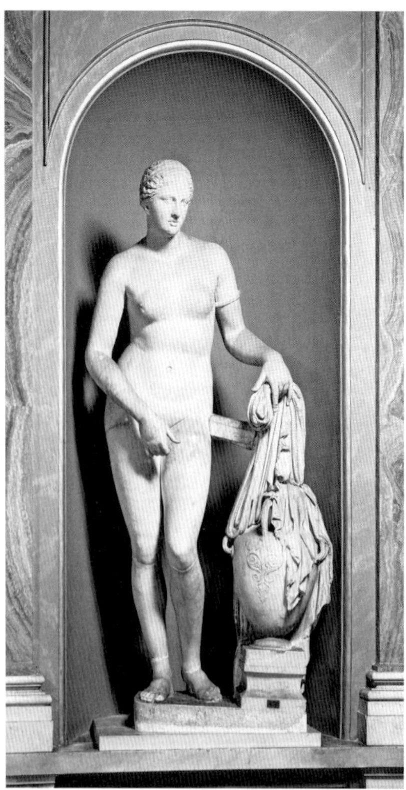

Figure 40. Vatican version of the Aphrodite from Knidos, original ca. 350. Vatican Museum 812. Marble. Ht. 2.04 m. Photo: Art Resource, N.Y.

history, and a number of scholars have taken pleasure in disdaining it or pointing out that it inspired no imitations.[133] The limited delight in this piece has discouraged full consideration of what makes the work important. In fact the Slipper Slapper is rather sophisticated in its visual constructions and at least as clever as the Knidia from which it draws.[134]

The Slipper Slapper goddess is very similar in pose and proportion to the Vatican copy of the Knidia (Figure 40).[135] Despite their mirrored arm positions, they are arranged in the same contrapposto. Both Aphrodites put weight on their right legs, the left legs bent inward with motion implied by trailing feet. In the Knidia this action is interpreted as a sign of modesty, as Aphrodite hastens to press her knees together, perhaps in reaction to an observer. Their facial features are similar, and their heads are both directed to their left, although the Slipper Slapper turns more sharply and tips her head slightly forward. The Slipper Slapper goddess's hairstyle and pudica pose are, however, much closer to the Capitoline Venus (Figure 41).[136] Both cover their genital areas with the left hand, for the Slipper Slapper the one closest to Pan. This is another apparent gesture of *aidos,* "modesty," but one about which there is some speculation concerning Aphrodite's intent, whether it is to conceal or draw attention to herself.[137] Whatever the answer, it is

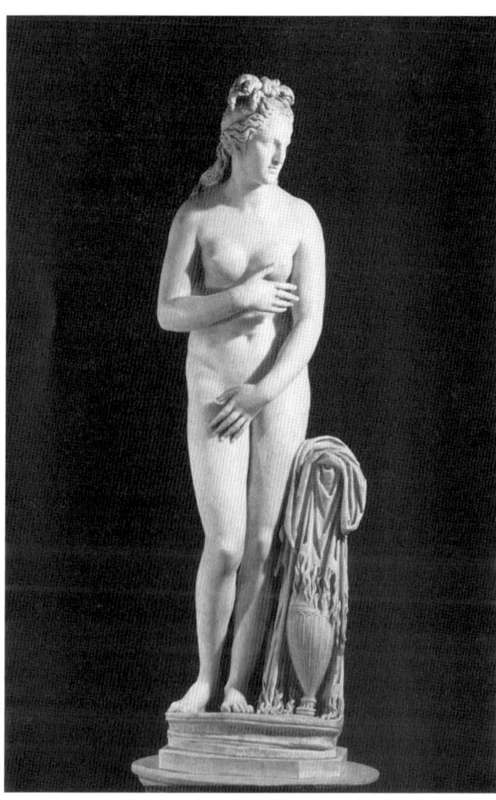

Figure 41. Venus from the Capitoline Museum, date of prototype uncertain. Rome, Capitoline Museum 409. Marble. Ht. 1.93 m. Photo: Art Resource, N.Y.

important to remember that the Slipper Slapper is the earliest extant example of this pose in Hellenistic sculpture.

The contraction of her right side is balanced by her upraised and bent arm with which she holds the sandal removed from her trailing foot. She stands before the observer nude but for her knotted scarf and right sandal, on which she puts her weight. Her hair is sculpted in long waves parted at center, with girlish curls hanging out from behind her head covering. The straps of her upraised sandal were once added in metal; those on her right sandal are instead sculpted. Traces of reddish-brown paint are visible on the notched soles of the sandals and on her hair, as well as on the hair of Eros and Pan.[138] Color was surely used elsewhere in the usual places, at least on her nipples, which are also incised, and on her leftward-turned head, picking out her delicate features and hair covering. Most often this Aphrodite is understood as brandishing her sandal at Pan in order to fight off his unwanted sexual advances. Eros, for his part, seems bemused by the feeble attempts of the unsophisticated suitor, though his pose is ambiguous. He grasps Pan's horn either to bring him closer to his mother or to shove Pan away. He is attached to Aphrodite's left shoulder. He flies over her, diagonally through the center of the group and toward the frontal viewer. Eros is very small relative to the other figures, rendered as an infant with appropriately diminutive wings. His right arm is missing from just above the elbow, though enough is preserved to understand that it was once bent. His head tilts to his right, toward Aphrodite. He is laughing. The group is self-contained, with Aphrodite and Eros turned toward Pan. But while Pan's head is tilted back, and his face is pointed lustily at the goddess, neither Aphrodite nor Eros looks directly back at him. Eros looks out to us, the viewers, inviting us into the scene. Aphrodite looks past, rather than at, Pan, a formal device familiar from Praxitelean works.[139]

If he were standing fully upright, Pan's head might reach a little over Aphrodite's shoulder. His dual nature is explicit in the alternating emphasis on his caprine and human features. His horns are long and curve only slightly. Only his right ear is preserved; it is large and pricked up. Pan leans around Eros to gain a better view of the goddess's face. His muscular back would pass for a young man's were it not for the small tail visible from the side. Pan's shaggy fur starts only below the buttocks.[140] His left hoof rests on the ground to balance out the group. Pan's genitals are damaged, but his reaction to this close encounter with Aphrodite is plain in his smiling face and taut muscles.

Pan has always seemed difficult to understand in this group. He is shown seated fully on top of a stump draped by an animal skin identified as a sheepskin by excavators (see Plate 24). The skin lets us know that Pan has taken effort to make himself comfortable; he has been at rest some time and cheerfully kicks up his back leg behind the goddess. Pan's lagobolon is leaning up against the stump, too, further emphasizing that he is in repose in his milieu, the wilderness. A close look at Pan suggests that he is not the sexual aggressor here. Rather, it appears that Aphrodite has disrobed and approached Pan. Is it *she* who seduces *him*? Perhaps so. This is not a struggle: for all of his taut musculature, Pan is in no danger of moving Aphrodite's arm against her will.[141] Bearing this in mind, we can correctly interpret the actions of Aphrodite. Her trailing leg does not indicate she is running or turning away from Pan but instead shows that she is caressing the back of his hoof with her nude foot (see Plate 25).[142]

Given that Aphrodite appears to have approached Pan in a state of undress, the raised sandal could be read as an equally sexual gesture. G. W. Elderkin was surely correct that Aphrodite is not brandishing her sandal here so much as displaying it.[143] Elderkin saw the Slipper Slapper as a representation of a Phoenician erotic goddess, possibly one with punning ties to Aphrodite Pandemos and Aphrodite Epitragia ("on the goat"). Of course, Aphrodite is shown elsewhere with a sandal, which she sometimes throws at Eros when he is naughty.[144] Others have suggested the sandal makes reference to prostitution, and the practice, although it is unclear how widespread, of prostitutes putting nails on the bottom of the sole to spell out in the dust *akolouthe*, "follow."[145] Still others associate the sandal with the name Ba'alat, the honorific title for goddesses such as Ba'alat Gebal, who is honored in the Yehawmilk stele and, as simply "Ba'alat," on the Batnoam sarcophagus (see Figures 19 and 20).[146] Some speculate that Ba'alat is close enough to the name of a type of Greek sandal, *blautē*, that it is returning here in a form brought on by misunderstanding or creative wordplay.[147] However much these readings seem appropriate in the circumstances of the middle ground, it is difficult to reconcile them with the learned patronage of a Poseidoniast. Yet it is still possible to acknowledge the important sexual nature of the sandal in representations of fertility goddesses, with which, like the Knidia, Dionysios might have been personally familiar. We see hints of the action's lasting importance in later Hellenistic and Roman works that show the goddess removing or holding her left sandal. Others show her in a similar pose holding her breast band, the *strophion* (Figure 42). In some examples of the latter, such as the one illustrated here, she is paired with Eros.[148]

Regardless of how erotic the sandal might be, the statue's inscription and findspot suggest that it is unwise to cleave the religious from the secular or to see

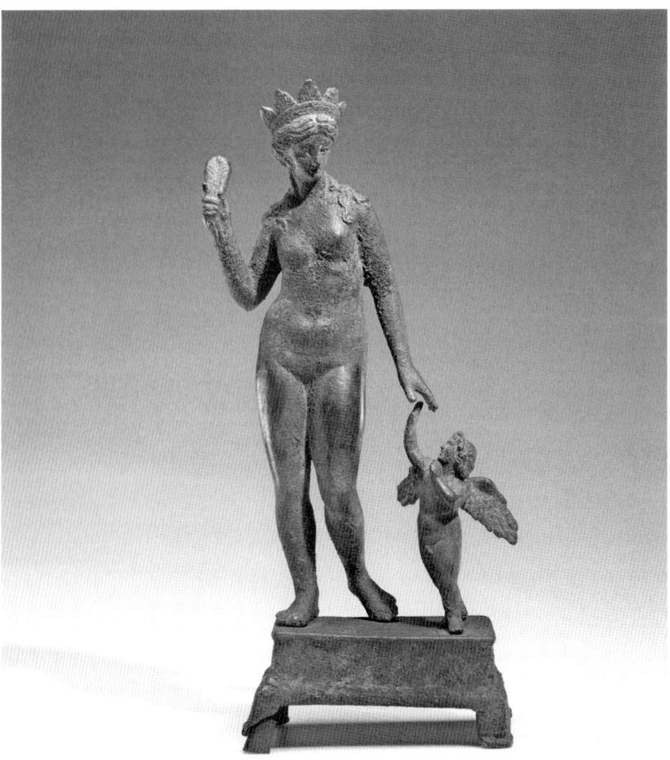

Figure 42. Bronze statuette of Aphrodite and Eros on a base thought to be from Egypt, 2nd to 1st c. Malibu, J. Paul Getty Museum 57.AB.7. Bronze. Ht. 0.28 m. Photo: digital image courtesy of the Getty's Open Content Program.

the work as merely pornographic.[149] This group was meant to be flattering, in which case any interpretation that assumes the Pan is farcical is inadequate. The inscription makes clear that the image was a votive, one that, although referencing Praxiteles's Knidia, was dedicated to the gods of the patron's forefathers in Beirut. As I mentioned above with regard to the shrine "V3" (Figure 39), one of these ancestral gods was almost certainly Aštart, Aphrodite's popular Levantine counterpart and one precedent for her nudity in art. Aštart—who is thought to be related to Akkadian Ishtar and Hebrew ʿAshtarot (less often in the singular)—was the most important female deity in the Near East of the first millennium.[150] Like Aphrodite, she had many iterations: sometimes acting as a war goddess, as in the treaty of Esarhaddon of circa 676, at other times as a fertility goddess; the Queen of Heaven, Aštart Shemayim; or the counterpart of El, the storm god Baʿal (with whom Zeus was associated in addition to Poseidon), Baʿal-Hammon, or Melqart.[151]

As has already been seen, Aštart was an important deity in Tyre, Byblos, Sidon, and Umm el-ʿAmed, Sidon being where the mother of Eshmunazar II was her priestess.[152] Her Shemayim cult was expanded when Delos became a major center of religious activity beginning in the third century. We have good, albeit circumstantial, evidence that Beirut once had a sanctuary dedicated to Aštart.[153] Some seven hundred terracotta figurines of a goddess standing with outstretched arms were found in the salvage excavations in Beirut's harbor area. An inscribed bowl was found, too, although in topsoil, with a dedication to the goddess. These finds are dated to the Hellenistic period by excavators.[154] City coins with images of the goddess extend into the third century, further strengthening the idea that an important civic sanctuary to Aštart was in Beirut during the lifetime of Dionysios's forefathers, if not during his own.[155] Like many of the known or surmised sites of Aštart temples in Phoenicia, the likely Beirut site was connected to the sea.

The club was held together explicitly through the worship of Poseidon, whatever god its members understood Poseidon to represent. Perhaps it included also Baʿal's female counterpart Aštart, who is sometimes called his "name," as in line 18 of the Eshmunazar sarcophagus, where she is Aštart-Name-of-Baʿal. It is for this reason that the Slipper Slapper goddess can be understood as a representation of Aštart, although I wish to emphasize again that what representation means in this and other scenarios is really rather complicated. It certainly does not mean, of course, that the reference to the Knidia was accidental or ignorant. Quite the contrary. It is appropriate, however, to frame this group in terms of its contextual reception—as a product of the middle ground. Stewart has shown that a key characteristic of artistic production in Delos from 166 to 88 was the creation of new sculptural types through collaborations of Athenian artists and non-Greek patrons.[156] The Slipper Slapper group must be read as the product of the same type of collaborations that generated the Roma as well as the famous Republican portraits of C. Ofellius Ferus and the so-called Pseudo-Athlete.[157]

Though their visual conventions strike us as unusual, even at times distasteful, these works were expensive, skillfully carved, and, in the case of the portraits, popular. They remind us that the art of Hellenistic Delos did not strive for sameness. Instead it was an amplification of both similarities and differences in which the wealthy competed through benefaction as well as personal aggrandizement (compare the kouros). The island was a wonderfully creative environment in which patrons and artists were generating completely new types from a selective and creative recombination of features. It is hard to image how the Pseudo-Athlete or the Slipper Slapper might have been invented anywhere else. As has been argued recently for the Aphrodite of Melos, the goddess of the Slipper Slapper can be understood as a "selective vision of the past" made "to serve as a model for the present,"[158] one that emphasizes the antiquity of the patron's ancestral goddess through this version of her. When we look at what the work does, rather than overreact to its Classical referent, the Slipper Slapper has the potential to function as a statue of Aštart. By implication, to a Phoenician like Dionysios, so did the Knidia.

Studies of Aštart-Aphrodite *interpretatio* (parallelism) are prevalent. Yet, as Stephanie Budin has shown, Aštart-Aphrodite syncretisms were neither "inevitable" nor exclusive.[159] Even if Greeks had a tendency to equate a number of Levantine deities with Aphrodite, it does not follow that the reverse was always the case. We must be cautious when dealing with the visual representation of gods, too. Images that scholars traditionally associate with Aštart are varied, from the "naked goddess" (see Figure 5) to breastfeeding figures to a goddess on horseback, an enthroned goddess, and an empty throne (see Figure 29).[160] Although it is far from certain that all of these were, in fact, representations of Aštart—or that the name Aštart referred to the same goddess in all contexts over time—it is clear enough that some of these images have more resonance with Aphrodite imagery than others. Aštart and Aphrodite—and also Inanna-Ishtar, Isis, and Atargatis— were not indistinguishable.[161] Nor was Aphrodite merely some kind of clone of these Eastern deities.

Delos is one place where we find direct evidence that the names Aphrodite, Aštart, and Isis could be used to refer to the same goddess with a cult of the *euploia*, or "good voyage" (*IDelos* 2132).[162] Isis reminds us that these goddesses sometimes had the role of kourotrophos. Perhaps this is how Eros fits the Slipper Slapper group, as another sign of sexual desire and its link to primordial fertility. Readings of this figure might include Eros as Protogenos (Hes. *Theog.* 116–22), Horus the Child/Harpokrates as the child of Isis (again *IDelos* 2132), or the so-called young Ba'al Hammon.[163] We might think of the goddess of the Slipper Slapper as a "permutation" of Aštart, a goddess whom Corinne Bonnet has shown to be critical to the commercial expansion of Hellenistic Delos.[164] The repeated formula of these Poseidoniasts—merchants, shippers, and warehousemen—demonstrates how maritime commerce also united the group, a force that we have already seen sometimes encouraged Phoenicians to act collectively. Here we find another likely reason the reference to the Knidia was so explicit: she was the image on Knidos, itself a free port since 126, for the cult of the *euploia*. Like the popular Egyptianizing cults of Isis Pelagia and Isis Euploia, Aphrodite Euploia is especially appropriate on the island and in this building.[165]

It is possible to read Pan in terms of Phoenician maritime religion as well. There are a few credible ways in which a goat-horned deity fits this context. The clearest, albeit general, point of connectivity is found in Ba'al-Hammon, who, in his various cognates, was an important ram-horned deity in the Near East, Cyprus, Egypt, and some other western Mediterranean sites, especially Carthage. His consort is a fertility goddess, usually Tanit.[166] Of course the word "Ba'al" like "Ba'alat" is sometimes or perhaps always an honorific title, one that means "lord" or "master," and can refer to a number of different deities.[167] As the god Melqart is sometimes referred to as the Ba'al Ṣūr or "Lord of Tyre," we should not be too quick to say that the ram-horned god *was* Ba'al-Hammon or that "Ba'al-Hammon" always referred to the same god.[168] Nevertheless, the association between ramheaded and ram-horned deities with Ba'al/Zeus-Hammon is strong. A purchased inscription dated to 222 said to come from Umm el-'Amed offers evidence of the worship of Aštart and Hammon in the same sacred space.[169] At the sanctuary of Deir el-Qal'a outside Beirut is another iteration of Ba'al, identified in Greek inscriptions as *balmarkōs/odēs* apparently from *bʿl mrqd*.[170] Ba'al Marqod was associated with fertility, thunder, and rain, and at the same site there is a dedication to Zeus-Amon. Although these are all admittedly loose connections, and while bearing in mind that no such connections may have been intended, it is imperative to attempt to understand the reception of Pan's pairing with the goddess of the Slipper Slapper in deliberate religions terms—as one of the ancestral gods honored in the accompanying inscription.

It is here that we can come full circle, by retuning one last time to the Knidia. The precise motivation for that statue's double reaction, turning stage left happily, but cautiously, and shielding or indicating her genitals from or to some intrusion stage right, has always been hard to pin down (see Figure 40). Because the Slipper Slapper is the first known quotation of the Knidia, some speculate that Dionysios had seen her in person. (Recall how the painted audience scene on the Alexander Sarcophagus in Plates 21 and 22 suggests that artist was familiar with Achaemenid art.)[171] If that impossible-to-prove speculation was true, we can imagine what Dionysios might have thought encountering the Knidia, and how he, as a Beiruti, might have understood what drew her gaze to her left: her divine consort. The

Slipper Slapper can be understood as a Phoenician or at least Beiruti interpretation of the same sexual encounter in a fashion encouraged by this middle ground, even if we cannot know whether Dionysios was specific when he commissioned the statue or whether he only received the group in that fashion.

The Delos statue seems to celebrate the fertility of goddess and god, female and male, culture and nature, a divine couple of many names and progenitor of the world itself, as represented by the baby Eros. It draws further on the power of the prototype, situating patron and gods together in the context of maritime livelihood. In both White's and Malkin's understanding, there is a craftiness to negotiations in the middle ground. In Hellenistic Delos, there is evidence that people explored connectivity, as when the names Aphrodite, Aštart, and Isis appear in the same dedication, or in the development of the Roma cult. While no one would claim that Aphrodite was always Isis on Delos, there were roles and contexts where their names, at least, were equally applicable to the same goddess. We are faced with a challenge when trying to characterize the Slipper Slapper's use of the Knidia. Certainly Dionysios's goddess is appropriating the Knidia's form and, as I have argued, Aphrodite's euploia cult, while recontextualizing her romantic encounter.

How should we characterize these appropriations and changes? Middle ground theory will not answer this question for us. It can help us tease out possibilities, however. One possibility is that we are witnessing a kind of creative misunderstanding, in which a Phoenician patron's attempts to signal urbanity results in a grouping that displays his ignorance of Greek art, religion, and taste. This seems quite unlikely, as Hellenistic Delos was a site of contact that encouraged sophisticated patronage, from the mosaics in the House of the Dolphins to the Italian portraits to the dedications in the Poseidoniasts' complex itself. Public displays drove competition and, as they piled up, they encouraged greater creativity.[172] A much more likely possibility, and one that is hinted at by other dedications in the complex to the goddess Roma, is that Dionysios knew well what he was doing, and exploited the felicitous proximity of Aštart, Aphrodite, and Isis; Ba'al/Hammon and Pan; and, perhaps, Harpokrates and Eros, to create a translation in multiple senses, one that is unexpected but perfectly appropriate in this setting.

The differences between these readings boil down to the extent of Dionysios's familiarity with Hellenism, the elasticity of art and religion on Delos, the attitude of the artist, and how we understand the statue's function within the quarters of the Poseidoniasts' complex. I have speculated already about the first, and we have seen some solid evidence of the connectivity of religion on the island. As to the third issue, the perspective of the maker, we must assume that he intended his work to be pleasing, just as, in making contemporary portraits of Italians, Greek-trained artists intended to flatter their patrons—never mind our reaction to the result.[173] Sheila Dillon and Elizabeth Baltes have shown persuasively the extent to which "stylistic novelty" was prized on Delos as a way "to achieve and maintain status and identity, to stand out from the crowd" and to showcase the virtuosity of the sculptor if a patron was rich enough to afford a good one.[174] Although I detect greater creativity in composition than style, the point is important. The more dedications piled up, the greater the incentive for patrons and top artists to show off through changes to well-established types.

The Slipper Slapper is surely operating in a similar fashion. If competition drove stylistic changes in public portraits, appropriating a famous work of art and changing its composition in a clubhouse was another avenue for self-promotion. After all, the Slipper Slapper is a very fine and expensive work of art paid for by a major patron. To dismiss it as a bawdy genre piece is to willfully misunderstand the work and its religious and social value. That the goddess looked like the Knidia but functioned as part of a group—perhaps Aštart-Baʿal/Hammon-Harpokrates—must have been the point. As with the Alexander Sarcophagus, we should understand this work as an example of Phoenician sculpture, in this case, Beiruti, in addition to Greek sculpture. While this is of course only a label of academic convenience, it matters very much to the conversation about these and other objects produced by contact. We should note that even in the middle ground, no one on Delos was interested in doing away with Aštart or Isis in favor of Aphrodite. In a parallel way, huge numbers of public portraits did not encourage sameness. Instead, contact, patronage, and artistic rivalries created an environment where a work such as the Slipper Slapper made sense. It is not a subtle monument, which must have made it all that much more effective.

Phoenician Art, Conundrums, and Definitions

The Alexander Sarcophagus and the Slipper Slapper could not have come about without artists trained in Greek sculpture workshops, but Phoenician patronage was equally critical to how each piece functioned. Greek art, manufacturing technique, and iconography *and* Phoenician art, religion, and patronage were required. The anthropoid sarcophagi belong to this discussion, too. They show explicitly how Greek and Phoenician visual art were not the only important precedents to their invention. These observations underscore how theories of mixing, collaboration, and contact can help us to understand them, to do more than just point to the fact of their mixture or to avoid colonialist views that dismiss their appropriations as mere mimicry of superior artistic traditions.[175]

Hybridity offers insights into how the Alexander Sarcophagus might have functioned. It is illogical to, on the one hand, read this work as a cultural fusion, one made perhaps in emulation of Alexander's policies, and, on the other hand, read this work's negotiations as a triumph of the Greek world order. Hybridity theory underscores how such negotiations did not aim to valorize the displacement of Sidonian identity in favor of a new Hellenic one. Instead, the tomb might be a subversive statement about contemporary events. It is also possible, however, that we have overreacted to its portrait of Alexander, leading us to assume, falsely, that the work's primary function was to respond to contemporary politics. The Slipper Slapper has likewise suffered from our strong reaction to what in it is familiar, the Knidia. Middle ground theory clarifies how the Slipper Slapper came to be in the Poseidoniasts' complex while freeing the work from dismissive attitudes about its "distasteful" modification of the prototype (the latter never an issue for the Alexander Sarcophagus). The Slipper Slapper might be understood as a material manifestation of the middle ground of Delos, a work rich with potential functions and connections while at the same time rather particular in its ambitious.

These case studies have shown that it is possible to add to the corpus of Phoenician art sculptures treated primarily in scholarship as Greek art made in Phoenician contexts. One result of the prevailing approach is that such works are almost never read together, and are not discussed alongside other works of Phoenician sculpture, such as the famous child statues and Aštart thrones. (We know most about the sculptural production of Sidon thanks to the excavation of its cemeteries as well as the Eshmun sanctuary.) Yet the inclusion of these more famous works produced by contact is critical to future discussions of Phoenician art in the second half of the first millennium in order for us to talk more seriously about what was in fact a robust Phoenician tradition of monumental religious sculpture. It might be that there is no connection between the child statues and the Eros of the Slipper Slapper group, as, after all, these are two discrete types tied to two different city-states, and only certain people within them. Likewise, the identification of all the sculptured thrones with Aštart is not guaranteed. There is a variety of representational strategies in Persian and Hellenistic Phoenician sculpture, but the association between these artworks, Phoenicia, and Phoenicians is explicit. We do a disservice to Greek sculpture of the same periods when we deemphasize its variety or dismiss the uncanonical (as with Syracuse).

We can move from these case studies to new working definitions of Phoenician art. It seems helpful at this point to iterate what Phoenician art is not. I have argued that some of the supposed eclecticism of Phoenician art is exaggerated by the very fact that we have overattributed works produced in the later Iron Age—the carved ivories, metal bowls, tridacna shells, and so on presented in previous chapters—to Phoenician manufacture at a time when the very existence of a meaningful Phoenician identity is suspect and when our evidence suggests increasingly that "Phoenician" works were created and used in a variety of Mediterranean locations. So, although the point might seem obvious, a key criterion for the idea of a

Phoenician art history is the existence of Phoenicia. Deciding what that means is no simple exercise, despite the long-standing scholarly interest in this issue. It seems there must be some evidence of a regional identity maintained by social-religious practices that are interconnected and recognizably different from neighboring people.

While "Phoenicia" might be a convenient way to refer to the homeland of some occupants of Pithekoussai or "Phoenician" might be applied to the makers of the alphabet that would be adopted by Greeks, I have argued that the earliest one can point to an explicit Phoenician collective identity is the late sixth to fifth centuries. Of course, many would disagree with this claim, even those who think that Moscati's *I Fenici* exhibit essentially created the current idea of a Mediterranean-wide Phoenician culture. The most important point is to approach the issue with methodological rigor, to show, not simply tell, that Phoenicia and Phoenicianism are valid entities. A lingering question is whether or not—or when—to leave the Phoenician mainland in this pursuit. I am generally in favor of the idea, since from the fifth century there are some connections demonstrated in the material and textual records: the distribution of anthropoid sarcophagi (and their possible forerunners in Cyprus), the popularity of Tanit, the Carthaginian embassies to Tyre, and so forth. Further, the west is understudied by Hellenists, who tend to focus on the eastern Mediterranean in the Classical and Hellenistic periods until the rise of Rome.[176] So long as we approach the idea of Phoenician art in the Mediterranean with some sort of clear criteria, there is no reason to exclude the western Mediterranean in favor of a falsely cohesive mainland tradition.

Yet it remains difficult to characterize even the mainland corpus. An independent, mobile people fond of portable objects is not disposed to homogeneity in its art. Although somewhat disrupted by *I Fenici*, earlier scholarship's emphasis on Phoenician art's unoriginality lingers, proving that essentialism, diffusion, and eclecticism can coexist in Phoenician studies. One cannot help but notice in the study of Phoenician art that the professional has succeeded the amateur but the methods and conclusion have remained uncomfortably similar.[177] Whereas Greece and its art are autonomous and authentic, are we to suppose that Phoenicia was a culture of appropriation, its art always and only a mixture? Recent studies of Phoenician sculpture by, for example, Lembke at ʻAmrit have emphasized the social meaning of art rather than attending to the impossible and unsatisfying task of dissecting all of its influences.[178] It is also possible to point to certain genres of art that are found only in Phoenicia, such as sculpted thrones. Yet, as an academic category, Phoenician art history suffers a crisis of originality reminiscent of the appropriation anxieties of (post)modernism.[179] Phoenician art history is itself a conundrum of mixing, and I do not think it is possible to change that picture by claiming that a homogenous Phoenician artistic style ever existed. The question of Phoenician art's originality is, however, an important one. It will be addressed in the Conclusion.

Conclusion

This book has been investigating select examples of Greek and Phoenician art, sometimes resulting directly from the interaction of Greeks and Phoenicians or their artistic traditions. Many other examples of art resulting from Mediterranean connectivity come to mind readily and raise questions of their own. Take for instance works of pottery that respond to the Athenian exports found throughout the Mediterranean and Black Sea regions (and sometimes beyond) in the fifth and fourth centuries. Whether or not we characterize these items in Phoenicia as "imitations" of Athenian pottery, as I have sometimes done myself, is significant.[1] But is the Phoenician response to an Athenian cup that itself imitates some features of a Persian metal bowl necessarily "unoriginal"? Posing this kind of question always generates more, such as what precisely was appealing in the "original" pot—the object itself, its contents, its function, or its social capital—and to what extent any of these options depend upon an understanding or even awareness of the original objects' makers and intentions.

It is my aim in this Conclusion to take on two topics, albeit briefly, that speak to these questions. I begin by asking what role is played by originality in our interpretation of the arts of contact and use these reflections to continue to characterize Phoenician art and challenge the idea that Greek art was somehow sui generis. Then we turn back to the idea introduced in Chapter 1 of art as a quasi-autonomous system. Doing so opens up some interesting avenues for future study of art outside culture history, an important prospect for those boundary objects that resist existing taxonomies. Lastly, I revisit the book's starting principles and suggest objectives for future Greek and Phoenician art histories.

Originalities

I wish to pursue further the idea of originality in art through two of its interrelated qualities, origins and creativity. One reason origins are contested is because they hold the keys to authority. In the nineteenth century, a major goal of scholarship was to disaggregate the parts of an object in order to determine who was responsible for what.[2] Such taxonomies of course continue in the ongoing process of classification that employs and builds upon the established systems. Even this basic act of art history in effect entails high stakes, since, as Patrice Rankine points out, "the inventor retains first claims."[3] Rankine's statement has two implications for this book. First, the recognition of originality or its absence is when the creative value of an object is assessed; this scholarly enterprise can be divorced from or directly contrasted with the values of ancient makers and observers. Second, the training of scholars has an enormous impact on their judgment of objects, whether or not in our case they emphasize classical or Near Eastern priorities and whether or not theory is a foregrounded part of the process.

Take, for example, the artist signature. There is a remarkable number of signatures in Greek art compared to Egyptian art, for example, even though most works went unsigned.[4] In traditional views of Greek art a signature points to an individual and raises the status of the artist and his object. The signature is thought to simultaneously accompany the rise of the individual in late Archaic society and foreground the idea of the creative genius in Western art. Signatures in Greek art turn up mostly in three genres: on certain pots (e.g., Boiotian, Attic) beginning in the seventh century; on some statues beginning in the sixth century (maybe earlier); and on some gems from the Archaic, Classical, and Hellenistic periods.[5] The chronological and geographical distributions of signatures are erratic, however, which argues against the idea that the signature is an expression of individualism born in the late Archaic Greek polis.[6] While some signatures accompany works of great creativity or skill, such was not always the case, as is evident in pot painting and at least one low-quality mosaic mentioned in Chapter 2 (see Table 1).[7]

Although it is tempting to conflate the artistic signature with a declaration of originality, existing evidence cannot support the idea. But signatures do underscore artistic agency. It is possible to reject the idea that the signature heralds the rise of the individual even while acknowledging that the status of artistry changed from the seventh century—when signatures appear on the Euthykartides statue base and, perhaps, on the Aristonothos krater—to the end of the Hellenistic period, when the Arwadi artist Asklepiadēs signed his mosaic in the House of the Dolphins.[8] We know that Greeks themselves were interested in the history of artists, beginning at least in the early Hellenistic period when Douris of Samos, one of Pliny's sources, wrote his books on painting and metalwork.[9] Yet the signature reminds us again how training, here, whether or not we subscribe to the cult of the artist (or of the polis), colors our reaction to the evidence.[10] We can cite clear examples of signed Greek art that cannot live up to the expectations put on it by the Western tradition.

The preceding case studies have shown that originality is a, if not the, key issue used to separate our conceptions of Greek and Phoenician art. The practice is prejudicial and all the more questionable when we recall that such determinations are often made by Greek archaeologists and art historians. I have emphasized especially the extent to which Hellenization has effectively obliterated the idea of a Phoenician art industry after 500 right along with the possibility of originality in Phoenician art. Of course this problem is not restricted to the second half of the first millennium, as artworks from the Iron Age attributed to Phoenicians can be presented as equally derivative thanks to the Assyrian or Egyptian iconography and style used to identify them. Phoenician art has also been dubbed eclectic, but I think that idea is somewhat inapt owing to problems of attribution in the creation of a Phoenician art history, problems that should call into question the validity of the very concepts "Phoenicia" and "Phoenicians." I have argued that Iron Age "Phoenician art" is not eclectic—it just *isn't*, at least not at this stage of research. While it is possible to argue that "Greek art" did not yet exist in the Archaic period, as Hellas was very much still "in the making,"[11] it is undeniable that there are works of Archaic art, notably the kouros and the architectural orders, that imply a sort of artistic cohesion among some of those we call Greeks.

The juxtaposition of the treatment of originality in Greek and Phoenician art is illuminating. So, too, is turning the idea of originality and reproduction back on Greek art itself.[12] On the one hand, we can note that the kouros was an "endlessly repeatable schema"[13] in which each part always referred to the whole. On the other, the kouros' originality in the sense of its origin was always on display because it also "endlessly" repeated its referent, whether we understand that referent as the kouros type or as Egyptian elite statuary or both. Innovation, when it did occur, needed to be contextually correct, whether we mean the invention of monumental stone statuary itself or the attention paid to individual characteristics in any one kouros.[14]

Two examples of ancient attitudes toward the origins of Greek statuary come to mind in this context, albeit from very different perspectives. One describes how the emperor Tiberias was forced by popular demand to return a beloved Lysippan Apoxyomenos to public view in Rome despite having supplied a marble copy to take its place, possibly the well-known one now in the Vatican (Pliny *HN* 34.62).[15] We must be content to study the copy, however, and we do so "in light of its adaptation of Polykleitan proportions, *contrapposto*, and movement." Kenneth Lapatin points out that these were not the qualities that motivated Tiberias to remove the "original bronze" statue and fueled the public's demand for its restoration.[16] For "although the statue did not originate in Rome but had been taken previously from Greece or Asia Minor, the Roman populace nonetheless had assimilated the figure into their own history."[17] Another is the story of Antenor's

Tyrannicides statue group, said to have been captured in the Athenian agora by Xerxes and carted away to Susa. There it was recaptured by Alexander or a diadoch and restored to Athens where Kritios's version apparently still stood (Arr. *Anab.* 3.16.7–8; Paus. 1.8.5; Pliny *HN* 34.70). If such a thing ever occurred, one can only imagine the impression given by the twin pairs, one visibly Archaic in its presentation of heroism, the other, especially if we follow Stewart's argument, in what had been a brand-new, sober style meant to declare the new world order established by the Athenian victory in and recovery from the Persian Wars. (Never mind that Athens's independence was drawn permanently to a close by the very Macedonian conquest that led to the "original" statue's return.)

Originality, then, is yet another deeply subjective idea. While we can try to disaggregate arts of contact to understand their constituent parts, we will always stop the process only where we define the original element. Origins are important in Greek art, as for Greeks the ideal was nearly always in the past. If we are to push the question of origins hard in Greek art, however, we will inevitably end up elsewhere, most often in Asia Minor, the Levant, or Egypt. Contemplation of origins can be fruitful, as I have shown through readings of the kouros, the Slipper Slapper, and Phoenician coins, or merely disorienting, as are the many portable luxury objects associated carelessly with "Phoenicians." Study of those Iron Age portable objects shows just how much the act of disaggregation can be distorted by ideology, dulling both terminology and evidence to the point of incoherence.

Origins are problematic in the interpretation of picture mosaics, too. I have argued that a misguided sense of the genre's origins only in Greek painting and Greek pebble floors has contributed to the false idea of the picture mosaic as an indicium of Hellenization. Rather, I believe that the genre was one way of signaling participation in the Mediterranean sociocultural scene, similar to what Morris has called Mediterraneanization. Yet, it is not so satisfying to call works like the picture mosaic material expressions of Mediterraneanization.[18] The term is "cumbersome."[19] And, like similar network theories, it is also frustrating in that it emphasizes interconnections without full regard for the agency of artist, patron, or art object. Mediterraneanization does not necessarily ask why receptivity is greater or lesser or simply different in different cases. It cannot explain the very important differences in the way that the kouros and the picture mosaic emphasize or not their artistic ancestry. Ideologically driven interest in origins can also lead to misinterpretation. I have argued as much for the kouros, the Slipper Slapper, and the Alexander Sarcophagus, albeit for different, if reliably Hellenocentric, reasons. In most scholarship semiotic readings have focused principally on the nudity of the kouros, a priority that speaks to the type's perceived role in the Western tradition. Whereas statuary came from Egypt, the thinking goes, the nude body of the kouros was a rejection of its original Egyptianness. Yet it is possible to argue the opposite using the very same visual cues, namely, the sculpted male body. The kouros in my reading is not concerned with Hellenism, certainly not in an effort to declare its superiority over Egyptianism. Instead, the kouros celebrates the privilege of elite males among fellow Hellenes to claim some of Egypt's social status.

In the Slipper Slapper, the referent to the Knidia is critical, but it has been used to dismiss the work as a tasteless genre piece that falls short of the original. More careful consideration of the reference, however, can help us understand what the statue does. In referencing the Knidia, the Slipper Slapper becomes a part of the cult of euploia and creatively completes Praxiteles's narrative in terms meaningful to Beirutis operating in a middle ground. This reading of the group allows us to reintegrate it into the broader discourse of art and patronage of Hellenistic Delos, enriching our understanding of both. Its creative power is not dissimilar to the more famous, if also sometimes disdained, portraits of Italians from the island. The portrait on the Alexander Sarcophagus has encouraged scholars to treat the work as though it were made by a lesser diadoch, thereby emphasizing its strategic use of Macedonian imagery. The advantage of using postcolonial theory to read the tomb is that it forces us to consider how small a part that portrait, and the apparent reference to the lost painting of Philoxenos, played overall. This sarcophagus was made to address an elite Sidonian audience, as were its predecessors. Hybridity theory opens up the work to a number of new interpretations and reminds us that a Sidonian tomb is a different type of object from a painting commissioned by one of Alexander's generals or a coin minted by a diadoch making a claim to his empire.

The Phoenician coins and anthropoid sarcophagi have their own originalities. Both put their reactions and appropriations in the foreground, the Tyrian owls pointing to, at minimum, Athens and Egypt, and, when paired with the archer riding the winged sea horse, also to Persia. The anthropoid sarcophagi, too, have multiple origins, in type (Egyptian), style (Greek), and iconography (Egyptian and Greek). As with the child statues and altar/Eshmun "tribune," no attempt is made in the coins or tombs to modify these referents. Clearly quite the opposite, which suggests that an important element of Phoenician art, both elite sculpture and middling civic coins, was to signal its awareness of the artistic traditions with which its observers, patrons, and artists were in contact. Perhaps here we can find a conceptual thread between Phoenician and Greek art in that both looked backward even while they innovated. The Alexander Sarcophagus can be understood as a particularly lavish response to the same social values.

According to the terminology I explore in Chapter 2, the Slipper Slapper, the sarcophagi (including the Alexander Sarcophagus), the Umm el-'Amed and Eshmun complex reliefs and sculpture, and Phoenician coins draw closely together the ideas of emulation and appropriation. It might be preferable to understand the many aggregations made plain in Phoenician art as appropriations, but doing so feels more defensive than illuminating. Alternately, it is possible to conceive of these ideas as points on a continuum, emphasizing the differences between wholesale appropriation and imitation. But I think it worth considering seriously whether or not we are capable of distinguishing emulation from appropriation in ancient art. Our own biases seem likely to overwhelm the evidence, but perhaps these ideas are simply not that different in a more fundamental way.

Art's Agency

In Chapter 1, I pointed out a few methods that frame art as a social agent, even while cautioning there are many other valid approaches to object study. One of these was articulated in the work of Alois Riegl, among other turn-of-the-century art historians, especially through his theory of the "will to art," or Kunstwollen. To be sure, Kunstwollen is not an easy concept, and it suffers further from its relationship with formalism, a practice deeply wedded to the theory of style and dependent upon ideological classification. That being said, I believe we can still find in Kunstwollen "critically suggestive" ideas about art's affectiveness, recalling Bernal's ongoing contributions to Greek social history.[20] Kunstwollen simultaneously advocates for the more familiar understanding of a rational art that responds to its context and for the less familiar idea of art's quasi-autonomy, always striving to express the ideal Zeitgeist.[21] Kunstwollen offers an alternate route around the problem of cultural relativism. While we cannot view an Aštart throne as a Phoenician did, we can still see that it is sculpture and not an unworked stone. From that basic premise we can ask of the sculpture what it wanted to do.

The question of "what objects want" connects Kunstwollen to the currently popular anthropological approach to art explored by Chris Gosden (from whom I borrow the phrase), Bruno Latour, and others, Alfred Gell most of all. Gell's art agency posits art objects as extensions of people, their makers or owners—what is called distributed personhood. The process of making is driven by a chain of agents that ends with the viewer. It moves from what Gell calls the artist to index and prototype to recipient, or what we can call the maker, the point of reference (what is being represented), the object itself (and all of its connections), and, finally, the viewer whom the object affects.[22] The point of reference can itself be an art object, a key idea in the discussion of art produced by contact. It is also possible to plot the patron before the artist, as I have suggested a few times throughout this book. Patronage was certainly important in Near Eastern art, but nevertheless the object depends on the artist's agency.

On its face, art agency seems to better fit some objects than others. Distributed personhood is easy to understand in portraits (especially photographs), elite gift exchange, or monumental objects that put the skilled work of the artist on display, such as the altar/Eshmun "tribune," Alexander Sarcophagus, or Slipper Slapper. But it works also for mass-produced or mechanically produced objects like coins, as it is concerned with how relationships are made material and how objects affect their users. The points of reference in Phoenician coins are social, from city-state to its patron deity to its king to the individual who manipulates the coin in his or her hand. The pursuit of origins for any given object is likely to arrive at one or more points of reference that are themselves the result of a disorderly chain of agents and their inferences, a knot of connections between ever more ancient or distant people and their observations, aspirations, and creative capacities. The replications and recursions are limitless, rendering the totality of an object's inferences unknowable.

Yet Gell's approach does not concern systems. Gell was not interested in writing sociologies of art in the tradition of Bourdieu with its emphasis on institutions of production, reception, and circulation. Rather, art agency concerns the social nexus. One advantage is that it eschews essentialism. It is good at talking about how objects make people behave and getting at what people believed about the point of reference and its agents. Put differently, art agency explores how an object affects a viewer's belief about how and why the object came to be. In art agency, we find a way or a reminder to question perhaps the biggest assumption about Phoenician receptivity to Greek art, namely, that what Phoenicians wanted was fundamentally *aesthetic*. For Gell the emphasis on aesthetics is a Western preoccupation,[23] one that can be tied to the problem of proceeding from Boasian, reified culture. Here I will emphasis that the East/West language Gell is using does not map onto Phoenician/Greek. Instead, what he is getting at, and what I hope this book shows, is that conflating Greek art with the Western tradition is a distortion of history resulting from the reversal of cause and effect.

One shortcoming from the perspective of art history is art agency's relative indifference to the artist, although Gell does not argue for the outright autonomy of art.[24] Riegl's Kunstwollen was likewise less concerned or unconcerned with individual artists, which was both its strength as a theory written first for a disparaged and anonymous late antique art and its weakness for those interested in the idea of artistic creativity, for whom the point of reference may be relatively unimportant. As Whitney Davis has argued, although it is rich with possibility, Gell's approach to art as index can take us further away than we wish to be from the *history* of art.[25] The limited, often contentious, engagement by classical art history with theory is in part in reaction to such approaches that are more processual or systemic than historical. Gell's work is very provocative, inspiring an impressive amount of admiration, critique, and, at times, scorn.[26] Yet art agency reminds us that there is clear benefit to exploring methods beyond culture history. If the goal of a study is to learn about production and circulation, it must use theories that explore systems.[27] Likewise, if we are aiming to understand human behaviors, agency theories are needed (this is where hybridity properly fits). If we want meaning, semiotic-symbolic theories fit. And so on. Culture history is poorly equipped to speak to these interests. Each time we scale up analysis, from individual to family to tribe to city-state and beyond, we lose accuracy. What makes culture an especially difficult concept in the first-millennium Mediterranean is the extent of connectivity and the often rapid pace of social and political change. Both of these factors, connectivity and rapid change, make it problematic to approach art only through cultural categories. Even though we might wish to compare and contrast Greek and Phoenician art broadly, I find it helpful to try, insofar as any of us are able, to first ask particular objects what it is that they "wanted" before tying them to sometimes overbearing cultural labels. As Riegl's Kunstwollen suggests, it is possible to move from art to broader ideas like culture.

That theories "travel" between and within disciplines is not novel,[28] and examples of a desire to tie art agency and art history are growing even while tensions remain.[29] Art agency encourages fresh approaches to the relationships between Greek and Phoenician art, both their similarities and their disjunctions. Further, the problematic carved ivories and metal bowls that form the basis of Phoenician art history might be meaningfully reconstituted through the theoretical approach to their agencies. Indeed, these works seem especially suited to Gell's influential writing on the "technology of enchantment."[30] In this work, Gell proposes that art is a technical system in which greater formal complexity creates a greater sense of awe or enchantment. A theory of affectiveness can be used to explore virtuoso objects, even without requiring an understanding of the ethnic or cultural identity of individual makers. In this case we seem to have a theory, if a very complex one, that fits our imperfect evidence.

Greek and Phoenician Objectives

We began with Herodotos and the idea that Europe and Asia are "historically determined rather than essential" ideas.[31] It seems a fine place to close. While there is a general trend toward deconstruction in history writing,[32] one that is certainly evident in this book, I hope it is not the main idea readers take away. Rather, I would like to end with a few objectives that follow from Herodotos's proem and the four "principles and aims" given at the outset of the book.

(1) Given that the first principle of this study was *barbarians matter*, the first objective is to continue to work toward producing scholarship that *rejects the idea that Greece and "the East" are axiomatic*. The same goes for the very ideas "the West" and "the East." Doing so requires us to acknowledge that essential, I would say racial, ideals underpin the conception of Greek and Phoenician and that both conceptions are Hellenocentric. We cannot write their art histories without bringing along some of this ideological baggage, even though I have tried to distinguish between good and bad use of the terms. (The same problems dog the use of "koine." Not only is it openly Hellenocentric, it also threatens to present the Hellenistic period as cohesively Greekish.) While it would be fair to ask why, if these collectivities are so poorly drawn, we continue to use them, I will confess that I am not yet ready to abandon either term. Instead, I feel that we must come to terms with our terms, recognizing that Greeks and Phoenicians are useful fictions for the enterprise of writing Mediterranean art history, that of the Greeks from around the beginning of the first millennium BCE, that of the Phoenicians perhaps only from about 500 years later. It is a good idea for us to grow more comfortable with inconsistency, to agree that history is supposed to become increasingly complicated as we deepen our understanding of it. Even while participating in rationalist exercises—when producing archaeological catalogues, for example—I want to advocate for more experimental approaches. My hope is for Greek art and Phoenician art to remain contested spaces.

(2) To follow from the second principle, *proper use of theory is our responsibility*, I propose that *we endeavor to make regular use of critical theory* even though for most of us theory will never constitute the subject matter of our work. Of course, there are ways to use theory poorly that discourage its embrace by the field of Greek art history. Yet I continue to find strange the frequent complaints concerning the use of inaccessible jargon from classical scholars who are committed to subjects completely inaccessible to nonspecialists. I am convinced that the greater danger is in using theoretical concepts without attendant theorizing. The differences between acculturation and the alternatives I explore here are not merely superficial corrections to terminology. Nor do they threaten knowledge. Fundamental and open-ended debate signals confidence and encourages thought.[33] No analytical vocabulary can fully circumscribe the complexity of studying the past, but it is possible to encourage changes in the way we think by changing the way we gather and characterize the evidence.

We are at a point in Greek art history where it is less important to say what things were than to study the arguments for and against interpretations of what they did. Objectivism, I contend, is not only an impossible pursuit; it is also not always trying hard enough. Thinking anew about terms and approaches can be very fruitful when it allows us to reconsider their implications. Take Antonaccio's point that the now-popular use of hybridity "may be an unnecessary tool of analysis for Greek culture(s), if we accept [the idea] of cultures as open systems, constantly shifting."[34] Attentive use of critical terminology gives us the power to reflect and thence avoid reinscribing traditional hierarchies (which is my major complaint about current use of hybridity).[35] Put simply, while only a very few scholars will ever be theorists, all of us should aim to use critical theory well.

(3)–(4) As Zainab Bahrani reminds us, comparative studies are neither new nor necessarily forward-looking.[36] Bearing her caution in mind, the third and fourth principles concerning comparative study—*contact makes critical contributions to the expressions of identity in Mediterranean art* and *art is where we might learn the most about collective identity, especially Phoenician*—are where the last two objectives must come home to roost. The objectives here, then, are that *in studies of art produced by contact, we must reject the premise that the artistic traditions are axiomatic,* and, therefore, *we must seek appropriate strategies to understand how the resulting artworks came to be and how they functioned.* One of the persistent problems of Phoenician art, through its many references to arts and cultures more familiar, is that it coaxes us into thinking we understand it.[37] Greek art is still more seductive, however, to Anglo-American and European scholars who have grown up on the idea that we are somehow still operating in the Greek tradition.

Even if we move to new terms to better reflect our interests—ancient Mediterranean studies, for example—they do not do us any good as proxies for the very ways of thinking we are trying to leave behind. Whatever our interventions, we will never grow immune to institutional epistemologies.[38] I do not foresee in the near future Hellenists denying the privileged role of Greece in the foundation of Western civilization.[39] These tensions contribute quite a lot to what makes Greek art history interesting to me in the first place, and I doubt that feeling is rare. So our goals must be smaller. Here I hope to have encouraged new ideas by leaving the subject of Greek-Phoenician arts of contact "open and un-finished."[40] I do so precisely because it is not easy to be vigilant of institutional frameworks, terminology, and so forth, and, at the same time, say something that does not reinforce just those things. Of course we do not all need to be engaged in an unending discourse about the discourse of art history—that would be quite tedious. But neither can we pretend conversations that do not interest us do not matter. Even if it is not the subject of our particular research, it is our responsibility to work out a point of view on what art is, what a Greek is, what a Phoenician is or is not, what culture is, and so forth. Our feelings on the subject are part of what we do, evident in our work and especially in the classroom. Put another way, we must not leave theory up to the theorists alone.

I claimed at the outset of this book that it is easy to confuse what is simple, best, or correct with what we value. Grappling with historiography and theory does not make that idea less true. But a refusal to value critical theory at all is self-deceptive. I agree that in art history the "stakes are always in part philosophical and theoretical, and never wholly empirical."[41] The problems with a sensible, Occam's razor approach to writing art history are thus further exposed. The history of the art of contact, then, is not so much a history of facts and events as it an exploration of what we value about the past. Awareness of and critical engagement with those values are fundamental to what we do.

Notes

Introduction

Note to epigraph: Herodotos, *Histories*, proem (Hdt. 1.1.1–1.5.4), trans. after Godley 1963 with minor revisions. The abbreviations for all ancient sources follow those used in *The Oxford Classical Dictionary*, third rev. ed. (Hornblower and Spawforth 2003).

1. Immerwahr 1956 and Węcowski 2004 offer compelling discussions of the proem's structure. Węcowski includes the critical bibliography.

2. Cretans.

3. Węcowski 2004, 152. L. Mitchell (2007, especially 29) shows that other discussions of Hellenes and Barbarians were not lacking in self-criticism.

4. Of course, according to the "learned Persians," the Greeks overreact by abducting two different Asian women, Europa and Medea, before truly overreacting by invading Troy for Helen.

5. Węcowski 2004, especially 150–51.

6. Rood 2010, here 45 and 46 (my emphasis).

7. Purcell (2013, 377–83) addresses the question of the Mediterranean's "eastern boundary."

8. S. Martin 2007. See also S. Martin 2014b; Shalev and Martin 2012; Stewart and Martin 2003, 2005.

9. See, e.g., Mairs 2012b. The term has been taken to task by those working in the western Mediterranean as well (e.g., Dietler and López-Ruiz 2009).

10. The now classic, if debated, text concerning art and anthropological agency is Gell 1998. Rampley (2005) offers a practical primer of Gell. Examples of recent applications in ancient art are found in Osborne and Tanner 2007.

11. Terminological precision and critique play critical roles in some important recent publications, such as Dusinberre 2013; Gunter 2009; Riva and Vella 2006.

12. The definition by Hornblower in the *Oxford Classical Dictionary* (Hornblower and Spawforth 2003), s.v. "Hellenism, Hellenization," provides an introduction to the topic from a classicist's point of view. It can be compared to the more recent and nuanced approaches in Mairs 2006, 2012b, and 2014.

13. And which distinguish both from the powerful kingdoms of the Near East: Malkin 2005a, 245–46; cf. Demand 2006.

14. See especially Boardman 1993, 1999; Burkert 1992, 2004; Coleman and Walz 1997; T. Dunbabin 1957; Élayi 1988b; Kaschnitz von Weinberg 1944, 1961; Kropp 2013; Kuhrt and Sherwin-White 1987; M. Miller 1997; S. Morris 1992; Whitmarsh and Thomson 2013. For ethnicity and identity, see especially Adam-Veleni and Stefani 2012; Bonfante 2011; J. Hall 1997, 2002; Hodos 2006; S. Jones 1997; Malkin 2001a; Shennan 1989; Waldbaum 1997. For culture, acculturation, hybridity and creolization, and their critiques, see especially Bhabha 1994; Brah and Coombes 2000; Hurwit 1979; Langin-Hooper 2013a; Rowe 1998; Stockhammer 2012; Van

Pelt 2013; Webster 2001; Werbner and Modood 1997; and R. J. C. Young 1990, 1994, 1995, 2001, 2003.

15. Prag and Quinn 2013b, 7. On the price paid by Punic and Phoenician studies, see Bonnet 2015; Vella 1996.

16. Another point remarked upon by Prag and Quinn (2013b, 7). See Purcell 2013. I use Punes here as a noun for Punic people: Prag 2014, 11–12.

17. Mediterranean studies following in the footsteps of the *Annales* school have become increasingly popular in the past twenty-five or so years. Arguably the trend in classical studies started with Horden and Purcell 2000 and is still important, notably, in Broodbank 2013. Many of these texts are histories. In archaeology, see especially I. Morris 2003, 2005.

18. For similar views on the ability of art history to negotiate a new path in classical studies, see *Arethusa* 43 (2), 2010. For a good overview of early trends in Greek-Phoenician studies, see T. Dunbabin 1957, especially 35–36.

19. See Vout 2012. On the negotiation between ancient and modern ways of thinking about art, see especially Tanner 2006. Tanner (2006, 156–204) addresses the social status of the artist.

20. Keesling (2003, 43–46, 55–59, 90–92, 108), for example, addresses the interpretation of Athenian akropolis dedications by *banausoi,* "laborers."

21. The classic essay on "art" versus "object" is Fried 1967.

22. See Porter 2010. Compare to Goldhill and Osborne 1994, 7.

23. Osborne 2010, though I do not follow Osborne's conclusions about ancient artists.

24. Sayre 2002, xi. Compare to the idea of "expressive symbolism" in Tanner 2006, defined on 20–21.

25. Throughout the text all dates are BCE unless noted.

26. An approach taken also by Hoffman 1997.

27. Burkert 1984, 1992; Gunter 2009; M. Miller 1997; S. Morris 1992.

28. There are too many scholars to mention individuals here. Instead, see Bondì et al. 2009; the *Dizionario enciclopedico della civiltà fenicia*: http://www.decf-cnr.org/.

29. See Gruen (2011, 116–22) for a recounting of the evidence. On the origin of the term "phoinix," see, e.g., W. Röllig 1983a and b.

30. Prag 2006, 4 with bibliography.

31. A comparison can be made with biblical studies. See Faust 2006.

32. In prehistory, see especially Hodder and Hutson 2003; Renfrew 2009. Symbol cognition: Renfrew and Scarre 1998. Memory: Alcock 2002; Van Dyke and Alcock 2003. Marconi 2013 addresses both. State formation: Routledge 2013. A good summary of theoretical and critical perspectives in classical studies up to the late 1990s can be found in Falkner et al. 1999 and Cohen 2000, 3–20.

33. As S. Morris 1992, xxii: "The most important thing I learned from this book was how modern attitudes shape our view of the past, often blatantly in cross-cultural contact, where they form a major impediment to understanding intimacy between East and West." And as Alcock and Osborne 2012b, 4: "Archaeological theory is about making the assumptions explicit."

34. See, e.g., Münch and Smelser 1992.

35. And, as Whitley (2010, 460) points out, so is art itself. The bibliography on style in art is vast. See Conkey and Hastorf 1990 (archaeology); Elsner 2010b (critical); Gombrich 1968 (critical); B. Lang 1987 (critical); Neer 2010a, 1–19 ("an apology"); Schapiro 1994 (a collection of essays from arguably the most articulate advocate of style).

36. Baxandall 1985.

37. Middle-range theory was developed and popularized by the sociologist Robert Merton in 1949 in *Social Theory and Social Structure*: "Sociological Theories of the Middle Range," 39–53.

In archaeology, it is associated especially with Lewis Binford, beginning with his 1977 introduction to the volume *For Theory Building in Archaeology.*

38. Dyson 1993, 198.

39. See Patrik (1985) who interrogates the idea of the "archaeological record."

40. The guiding text for this section is Gell 1998 and the large bibliography responding to his work and the idea of art agency. Support for employing multiple perspectives can be found in Hodder and Hutson 2003.

Chapter 1

1. Burkert 2004, 123.

2. Cultural distinctiveness is a theme frequently examined and questioned in the work of Uehlinger: Keel and Uehlinger 1998; Suter and Uehlinger 2005; Uehlinger 2000. Similar points were made by Hoffman 1997. See also Ulf 2009.

3. Shipley et al. 2006, s.v. "acculturation." The quoted text concerns Celtic identity.

4. See Dougherty and Kurke 2003.

5. Dougherty and Kurke 2003, 1–2.

6. Gunter 2009, 61–70 for an overview.

7. As underscored by van Dommelen and López-Bertran 2013, 278–79.

8. Shipley et al. 2006, s.v. "culture."

9. J. Hall (2004, 36) commented on this point.

10. Geertz 1973, 14.

11. See J. Clifford 1988 and J. Hall 2004, which I follow here along with Dyson 1981, 1993, 2006. A concise and insightful overview can be found in Sahlins 1999.

12. E.g., Benedict 1989; Boas 1940; Kroeber 1948.

13. Trouillot 2003. Another important critique of culture is in Kuper 1999.

14. Trouillot 2003, 102.

15. Whitley 2013, 410.

16. Trouillot 2003, 99–101.

17. See Dyson 2006; Snodgrass 1987; Trigger 1989a.

18. Weber 1978 [1922]. Much modern thinking about cultural groups stems from the work of Weberian anthropologists such as Clifford Geertz (1973), with his notion of cultures as symbol systems, and Fredrik Barth (1966, 1969), with his idea that an understanding of boundaries is necessary to understand ethnicity. See also Hutchinson and Smith 1996; R. Jones 2009; and S. Smith 2003. Of secondary importance in classical studies, especially, is Pierre Bourdieu's idea that political and symbolic negotiation produce culture through what he calls *habitus*: Bourdieu 1993.

19. I. Morris 2005, especially 30–31. See also Barth 1969; Finley 1973 (updated with a new introduction in 1999).

20. See especially Hodder 1982, 1992, 2012; Hodder and Hutson 2003.

21. Snodgrass 1987; Wiseman 1983. The global *Journal of Field Archaeology* was established at Boston University in 1974. New archaeology continues to be relevant with many diverse practitioners as it reacts to systems and middle-range theories (among others), as well as its sustained critique in postprocessualism, contra Courbin (1988), who concludes that new archaeology was a failed experiment without paying attention to its development (as noted by Trigger 1989b).

22. Dyson 1993, 198. Of course, art and archaeology are not the only impacted areas. See Benjamin 1988.

23. Bintliff 2013, 1216. A similar comment was made by I. Morris already in 1994, especially 4. See also D. Miller 2005.

24. Renfrew 1980.

25. J. Hall 2004, 39. This kind of put-down is not new, nor is it restricted to classical archaeology. In 1999 Michael Sahlins (1999, 399) pointed out, "Transatlantic working misunderstandings of the culture concept are still about what they were nearly half a century ago when George Peter Murdock and Raymond Firth debated the issue in the pages of the *American Anthropologist*." Writing in 1951, Murdock accused his British counterparts of being stuck in the 1920s.

26. See especially Boardman 1995a, 1999 (published originally in 1964); Burkert 1992, 2004; West 1997.

27. In Anglo-American scholarship, see: Gunter 2009; Hoffman 1997; Langdon 1989, 1993, 1997, 2008; I. Morris 2000; S. Morris 1992; Whitley 1991, 2001, 102–33. See also Brisart 2011; Rollinger and Schnegg 2014; Rollinger and Ulf 2004.

28. Bates and Plog 1991, 4.

29. See Sewell 1996a and b, 1999, 2005. Beck et al. (2007) and Bolender (2010) aim to use Sewell's interest in events and social transformation in the field of archaeology. See also Swidler 1986 for another perspective on the dynamic relationship between culture and behavior.

30. For the idea of material culture as an active force, see Hodder 1982.

31. A summary is presented in Renfrew and Bahn 2005, s.v. "Phenomenological Archaeology."

32. Greek culture and Greek art are subject frequently to this kind of presumptuous empathy. For example, continuity between Greece (ancient and modern) and the United States was central to the early 1990s exhibition entitled *The Greek Miracle*: Buitron-Oliver et al. 1992. The presumption that early Greek visuality was identical to our own: Papalexandrou 2010.

33. A recent criticism of systems (network) theory and its lack of emphasis on agency: Walsh 2014, especially 70.

34. Progress is a common theme to many theories of culture change by classical scholars, as in Burkert's conception of Orientalizing, where the Near East helps to generate Greek high culture: Burkert 1992. Accident or chance is a theme common to Boasian theories of culture change, summarized conveniently in Trigger 1989a, 151–52.

35. While it is true that many groups were interested in the idea of Hellenization, their interest was largely self-interest: Greeks commenting on the relative "Greekness" of their neighbors; the Greek-speaking author, Jason of Cyrene, of 2 Maccabees calling Jewish enemies (the Greeks) barbaroi; and so on. See Gruen 2001; 2 Macc 2:21 (enemies as barbarians), 4:10, 4:13, 4:15, 6:9, 11:24.

36. Whitley 2001, xxiii quoted in Squire 2010a, 140–41.

37. Wiley and Philips 1958, 2, quoted in Renfrew 1980, 295. See also Nichols et al. 2003; Renfrew et al. 2004.

38. Including: Appadurai 1986; Basu 2013; Hicks and Beaudry 2010; Knappett 2005; Tilley et al. 2006; van Dommelen and Knapp 2010.

39. And, in doing so, hope to avoid the study of made objects through grand narrative history (Marxist, structuralist, and so on). Compare to the employment of "material culture" in American studies, where "decorative arts" or "minor arts" might have once been used.

40. D. Miller (2005) offers a lucid introduction to materiality.

41. This issue is frequently discussed, as is the tension between art (especially "primitive art"), art history, and anthropology: Basu 2013; Gell 1998; Yonan 2011.

42. Kopytoff 1986, 67.

43. Compare to Ingold's discussions of making (2000, 2013) and Bourdieu's habitus (1977).

44. Compare to Strathern (1990) on the idea that artifacts "contain events."

45. Duke University, for example, has a Department of Art, Art History and Visual Studies, each area of which is perceived as a distinct entity. Visual culture and visual studies: Elkins 2003; Pinney 2006; Davis 2011. Visual culture and material culture: P. Stewart 2014.

46. An idea found in Riegl's category of "haptic" versus "optic" art (1893). While the expression of art is not only visual, as Tanner (1992; 2006, 20–21; 2010a, 269–70) points out, there is a lot more to the visual realm of a given culture than what we would call art. One distinction is functional; objects with a "cognitive" function cannot be grouped meaningfully with art. Rather, Tanner, following Parsons and Weber, would have us distinguish art according to its "expressive symbolism."

47. Compare to literature and intertextuality, although I do not believe works of art are themselves texts. Alcock and Osborne (2012a, especially 466–67) make several similar points with no little emphasis on the transcendence of art in their introduction to Vout 2012.

48. "Social Lives" is a modification of the title of Appadurai (1986), *The Social Life of Things*. Further comparison can be made with the problems of Kopienkritik: Junker and Stähli 2008; Vout 2012.

49. Contra S. Scott 2006. "Age value" and "historical value" are more Rieglisms (1982, original 1903).

50. D. Miller 2005. Strathern (1990) explores relationships between objects and context. Yonan 2011 comments on the extent to which art history has not engaged or been engaged by material culture but comes to rather different conclusions, advocating social art history and emphasizing meaning.

51. Or even if art history is not to one's tastes: S. Scott 2006.

52. Donahue 2013, 1.

53. Donahue 2013, 2015; Donahue and Fullerton 2003; Osborne and Tanner 2007; Tanner 1994, 2006, 1–11. A mid-century perspective with some of the same criticisms: Seltman 1948. See also Elsner 2007; Falkner et al. 1999; de Grummond 1996; Marchand 1996; Ridgway 1994, 2005; Shanks 1996; and several contributions to Smith and Plantzos 2012.

54. Lapatin 2003.

55. Pliny: Isager 1991 and 2003. In the latter, Isager draws out connections to Giorgio Vasari. Murphy (2004) concentrates on Pliny's imperial teleologies.

56. See Potts 2000 for a provocative discussion of Winckelmann and his legacy. Harloe (2013) takes on his often contentious early reception. The study of vase painting also took off in the eighteenth century with the publication of Sir William Hamilton's private collection: Oakley 2009, here 601.

57. A helpful overview is Podro 1982, 98–116.

58. The contribution of Morelli to modern art history was quite significant: Kurtz 1985a, 240–41.

59. Furtwängler 1893, trans. Strong 1895. Beard (2003) has shown that the English edition was substantially revised.

60. Wollheim 1973 in reference to Morelli.

61. Kurtz 1985a and b. Oakley (2009, 606–7) argues that Beazley's method drew from other scholars, but I still believe it accurate to characterize his approach as Morellian.

62. Beazley 1956 and 1963.

63. An apt descriptor borrowed from Oakley 2009, 606.

64. Beazley's approach and its critics are summarized by Sparkes 1996, 90–113. Recent work has contributed provocative analyses about various topics relating to pottery, especially concerning feasting and the symposion, many of which are indebted to François Lissarague's 1987 *Un flot d'images* (published in English in 1990): Berlin 1993; Crielaard 1999; Lynch 2011; Neer 2002; Topper 2012. The prioritization of workshop identification continues, however, in both the *CVA* series and the Beazley online archive (http://www.beazley.ox.ac.uk).

65. It has been instrumental in my work on Greek pottery in southern Phoenicia: S. Martin 2007, 2014a; Stewart and Martin 2005.

66. Whitley 1997; rebutted in Oakley 1998. See also Oakley 1999.

67. Very different approaches to painted vases can be found in Bérard et al. 1989 (which eschews the artist); Vickers 1985; Vickers and Gill 1994. Vickers and Gill advocate for craft over connoisseurship by emphasizing excessively the pots' metal prototypes. Ways of looking at Greek pottery: Stansbury-O'Donnell 1999; Steiner 2007.

68. There are, of course, plenty of examples of the deleterious effects of attribution, when connoisseurship leads to illicit collecting of antiquities. On the antiquities trade, archaeological ethics, and the ease with which even good intentions can encourage illicit collecting and destruction of cultural heritage: Brodie et al. 2006; Gill and Chippindale 1993; Kersel 2012a and b; Muscarella 2000; Renfrew 2000.

69. A helpful introduction to the concept can be found in Pächt 1963.

70. Podro 1982, 97.

71. See Elsner 2006 for Riegl bibliography. Riegl was influential for another Austrian historian, Ernst Gombrich (1909–2001). Gombrich's *Story of Art* (1950) and *Art and Illusion* (1961) are masterworks, but Riegl's influence is most explicit in 1979's *The Sense of Order*.

72. Compare the theme of the moral decline of Rome after conquering Greece: Gros 1978.

73. Yet his major works were translated into English very late: M. Iverson 1993; Olin 1992; Podro 1982, 71–97. *Spätrömische Kunstindustrie* was translated by Winkes in 1985. *Stilfragen* was translated in 1992 by Kain.

74. See, especially, Bailey 2005; Chua and Elliott 2013; Gell 1998; Gosden 2005 (cf. W. Mitchell 1996, 2004); Hoskins 1998; Joyce and Lopiparo 2005; Lesure 2005. But see also Knappett 2005, especially 11–34.

75. Gunter 2009, 91–95.

76. Neer 2005, most of all. For archaeology, the essays in Conkey and Hastorff's 1990 *The Uses of Style in Archaeology* remain important. See also Lang 1987; Sackett 1977. Davis (2011, 75–119) discusses the relationship and differences between form/formalism and style/stylistic analysis.

77. Some still see in classical archaeology a fundamental difference from classical art history, since the former is concerned with the entirety of material culture and the latter studies art: Donahue 2013, especially 2.

78. Vase painting is a good example of a genre with specialists who are trained in various subfields and who self-identify as art historians or as archaeologists, all while relying fundamentally on style. Robertson (1949 and 1963) was a vase-painting specialist who employed the Beazleyan method and eloquently identified himself as an art historian.

79. Boardman 1974, 1985a and b, 1987, 1989, 1995a and b, 1998, 1999 (the book's fourth edition), 2003, 2016 (the book's fifth edition); Cook 1960, 1972; Robertson 1959, 1975, 1981, 1992; Wagner and Boardman 2003.

80. Still true since argued by Renfrew in 1980.

81. See Salles 1995 and van Dongen 2010 for the geographic and conceptual aspects of the term "Phoenicia."

82. Rainey 2001, especially 57.

83. Attempts have been made to emend Ps.-Skylax's confused text: Galling 1938, 1963; Shipley 2011.

84. Very little is known about the political arrangement of this area. Even the seat of the governor is uncertain.

85. Other inconclusive links between Canaan/ite and Phoenicia/n: some second-century BCE coins of Beirut are inscribed in Phoenician "Canaan" (Bordreuil 1988, 304–9; Hill 1910, l–li, 52, no. 5; Millar 1983, 56). Euseb. *Praep. evang.* 1.10.39, quoting Philo of Byblos, makes a

mythical link between a person named Chna who changes his name to Phoinix. The grammarian Herodian claims Chna was the original name of Phoenicia (Lentz 7.32–8.8).

86. Quinn et al. 2014, here 186, with extensive bibliography on this and related texts.

87. Heliodoros 10.41.4. Emesa, the now-notorious Syrian city of Homs and hometown of Elagabalus, was part of the Roman province of Syria Phoenike. See Millar 1993, 300–309. On the complexities of identity in Heliodoros, see Whitmarsh 1998.

88. Contra Rainey 2001.

89. Aubet 1993; Niemeyer 2000.

90. Gilboa 2001; Riis 1970.

91. Myriandos/Myriandros: Hdt. 4.38 (where it is described as near Phoenicia); Ps.-Skylax 102 (it is located in Cilicia but identified as Phoenician); Xen. *An.* 1.4.6 (it is Phoenician). Ashkelon: Élayi 1982. The main Phoenician source is the sarcophagus of Eshmunazar II, discussed in Chapters 2 and 4.

92. Shalev and Martin 2011.

93. Briend and Humbert 1980; Gal 1992. The identification of these sites as Phoenician is based in part on ceramics. The evidence is not conclusive. For the study of the Hellenistic Galilee concerned with a ware identified as Phoenician semi-fine (distinguished as a local product, unlike Phoenician bichrome), see Berlin 1997a, b, and c.

94. The date and means of transmission of the Phoenician alphabet into Greece is often discussed and rarely agreed upon: Lipiński 1997; especially, Sass 2005.

95. Summarized in Amadasi Guzzo and Röllig 1995.

96. *ANET* 25–29; Joseph. *AJ* 8.55; Joseph. *Ap.* 1.106–7. The bullae of Kedesh included some Phoenician inscriptions, but most are in Greek: Herbert 2003.

97. Amadasi Guzzo 1995, 19. Hackett 2008 offers a good overview of the Phoenician language. Inscriptions are collected in the *KAI, ICO,* and *CIS.*

98. James Whitley in a forthcoming essay, "The Material Entanglements of Writing Things Down," in *Theoretical Approaches to the Archaeology of Ancient Greece,* edited by Lisa Nevett.

99. See, e.g., O'Connor 1977. Many inscriptions are found in southern Asia Minor: Lipiński 1997; Markoe 2000, 108–9, fig. 31. In subsequent periods some Phoenician speakers and scribes must have had command of other languages, especially Aramaic, to communicate with their overseers and neighbors. Briant (2002, 507–8) describes the central Persian administration's reliance on local scribes to translate official documents composed in Persian and Aramaic.

100. This story is told in Vella 2010 and 2014. Book-length studies on Phoenicia and Phoenicians now abound. To cite only a very few: Aubet 1993; Contenau 1949; Grainger 1991 (just Hellenistic Phoenicia; critiqued in Macadam 1993); Harden 1962; Krings 1995; Lipiński 1987, 2015; Markoe 2000; Moscati 1968; Peckham 2014; Quinn and Vella 2014; Woolmer 2011. Recent book-length studies that engage Phoenicia, in addition to those cited below, include: Brown and Feldman 2014; Cheng and Feldman 2007; Curtis and Reade 1995; Feldman 2002, 2006, 2014; Frankfort 1996 (the text's annotated fifth edition); Gunter 2009; Hoffman 1997; S. Morris 1992; Ornan 2005b; Sader 2005; Sasson 2001; Vlassopoulous 2013. Book-length studies and key articles on Phoenician art include Brown 1991, 1992; Clermont-Ganneau 1880; Gubel 2000; Markoe 1990b; Perrot and Chipiez 1885; I. Winter 2010 (select essays). Museum exhibition catalogues include Adam-Veleni and Stefani 2012; Doumet-Serhal 2013; Fontan and Le Meaux 2007; Langdon 1993; *Liban, l'autre rive*; Moscati 1988b; Peters 2004. See also Aruz et al. 2014, which, although not focused in name on Phoenicians, follows a similar approach as Moscati 1988b.

101. Riva and Vella 2006, 4–10. The Cypriot bowls were looted perhaps from Kourion and are now part of the Cesnola collection. Ivories followed soon after, beginning with the 1847 discovery of a cache at Nimrud.

102. Helbig 1876; Vella 2010, 22–23, with bibliography.

103. Some ivories are dated earlier, however, to the ninth century. Only the Ahiram sarcophagus from Byblos must date earlier. The sarcophagus was found alongside a carved ivory plaque showing a griffin and lion attacking a bull. It is sometimes dated as early as the thirteenth century: Frankfort 1996, 263–64, fig. 305. Its relief looks similar to some of the Megiddo ivories, such as the "Celebration" ivory, which dates to the twelfth century. The inscription is dated to the tenth century. See Frankfort 1996, 271–72, figs. 317–18; cf. fig. 316. Color image: Markoe 2000, pl. 5.

104. Barnett 1967 and 1974; Layard 1853. See also Falsone 1988. The standard publication of the bowls is Markoe 1985. See also Matthäus 1985, 1999; Riva and Vella 2006, 4–10.

105. Frankfort 1996, 328–29, fig. 391.

106. "Egyptianizing": Barrett 2011; Markoe 1990a.

107. E.g., C. Herrmann 1994.

108. The most critical analytical publications are: Cinquatti 2015; G. Herrmann 2000; I. Winter 1976; and G. Herrmann and I. Winter's contributions to Suter and Uehlinger 2005. The first to attempt a division of the ivories by region according to style was Poulsen 1912. Some (all?) so-called "Phoenician" ivories were made outside mainland Phoenicia. In Samaria, unworked ivory was found with finished products: Crowfoot and Crowfoot 1938; Crowfoot et al. 1957. Bronze bowl from Kefar Veradim: Koller 2012 with bibliography.

109. Perrot and Chipiez 1885. Compare to Clermont-Ganneau (1880) who explores the relationship between Phoenician and Greek iconography and mythology. Cypriot art: Coldstream 1986.

110. Among others, Moscati 1968, 1972a, 1974, 1977, 1980, 1982, 1986, 1988a and b, 1989, 1990a and b, 1992, 1993, 1996; Moscati et al. 1997; Moscati and Bondì 1986; Moscati and Uberti 1981, 1988.

111. Hodos 2006, 12.

112. Vella 2014, 25.

113. Suro 1988.

114. Wolff 1993. Similar: Brown 1992; Harden 1962; Markoe 2000.

115. Suro 1988.

116. The sequence was developed relatively recently owing to the lack of controlled excavations of urban areas. The excavation of Sarepta and some probes at Tyre have allowed for the creation of a typology: W. Anderson 1990 with bibliography; Bikai 1978. The refinement of the bichrome sequence still depends on southern sites, notably Tell Abu Hawam, Tell Keisan, and Tel Dor: Gilboa 2005; Gilboa and Sharon 2003; Lehmann 1996, 1998.

117. Culican 1976 and Stern 1976 offer the traditional view of masks, which is summarized in Brown 1992, 18–20. Note that Brown states that most masks are found in graves; in southern Phoenicia, at least, this is not necessarily the case. Pregnant female figurines are summarized in Pritchard 1988, especially 50–52.

118. Markoe 2000, 164–65, figs. 67 and 168; Moscati 1988c; Reese and Sease 1993, 2004; Savio 2004; Stucky 1974. Painted eggs (from Egyptian, north African, and, perhaps, Syrian ostriches) were common in Punic burials from the seventh to the second century. The eggs were cut in different ways to serve a variety of functions. The tridacna mollusk was imported from the Indian Ocean. Some 120 carved shells are known (Reese and Sease 2004, 29; Stucky 1974 catalogues the ninety that were known to him). I am aware of only one from the Phoenician mainland, found in Byblos: Reese and Sease 2004, 30. Those with provenance come from as far west as Italy and as far east as Iran, with the most coming from the Aegean (Lindos, Samos), Mesopotamia, and Naukratis (Stucky 1974, 10–11). They are thought to date to the mid-late seventh century and were perhaps made in a single workshop (alternatives to Phoenician manufacture are cited and dismissed in Stucky 1974, 88). A number of both objects come from the art market.

119. Such as Markoe 2000, 158–59. A similar suggestion is made by I. Jenkins (2000, 173) regarding Cypriot figurines.

120. Which seems to distinguish the interpretations of Phoenician art from, for example, the study of now-lost monumental Greek painting (such as Stansbury-O'Donnell 1989, 1990). Although see the damning perspective of Croce (1966, 500–501, quoted in Elsner 2010a, 291–92), which denies the possibility of producing critical ancient history altogether: "the history of ancient Greek painting is just a tissue of vain words."

121. Beirut: Curvers and Stuart 2004; Élayi and Sayegh 1998, 2000. Byblos: Dunand 1937–73; Élayi 2009; Jidejian 1968. Sarepta: W. Anderson 1988; Khalifeh 1988; Koehl 1985; Pritchard 1975, 1978, 1988. Sidon: Doumet-Serhal 2013, and see the bibliography at http://www.sidon excavation.com/index.php/publications; Dunand 1970, 1973; Élayi 1989; Hamdi Bey and Reinach 1892; Jidejian 1971; Macridy-Bey 1902. Tyre: Aubet 2004, 2010; Aubet et al. 2014; Bikai et al. 1996; Chéhab 1983–86. Umm el-'Amed: Dunand and Duru 1962.

122. Contra Markoe 2000, 143, among many others.

123. Quinn 2005, here 390–91, following S. Hall (1990), who takes a structuralist approach to identity.

124. Some of which are known elsewhere, as in studies of Hellenistic Babylon (Holt 1999; Langin-Hooper 2007, 2013a and b; Mairs 2006, 2014) or "Greco-Persian" art (Boardman 1995a; Gates 2002; Root 1985).

125. Although exceptions can be found, such as the sixth-century terracotta plaque showing a sphinx from Puig des Molins, Ibiza that bears a strong resemblance to the ivory sphinx from Nimrud in Figure 4 (Moscati 1988b, 721, no. 808).

126. See, e.g., T. Dunbabin 1957.

127. Bronze Age antecedents: S. Morris 1992, 1997. Persistence of Greek receptivity into the fourth century: M. Miller 1997, 2000.

128. See the discussion in Whitley 2013.

129. Romantic perceptions of the East (Mesopotamia): Bohrer 2003.

130. For example, Renan's 1864 publication of Phoenician inscriptions in *Mission de Phénicie* led to the development of the *Corpus Inscriptionum Semiticarum* (*CIS*).

131. P. Miller 1988, here 206. Vernant as art historian: Neer 2010b. See also: Lissarrague and Schnapp 2000.

132. Translated into English in 1988.

133. See also Niemeier 2001; Niemeyer 2003; Rollinger and Schnegg 2014; Rollinger and Ulf 2004.

134. Burkert's text was published in English in 1992. Riva and Vella 2006 has further bibliography. It must be pointed out that West's interest in Greek–Near Eastern contact is clear earlier on: West 1971.

135. Riva and Vella 2006, 1. Brisart (2011, 55–56) defends use of the term as indicative of Greek perceptions, casting Orientalizing as Greek self-fashioning. I. Winter (1995, 253) makes similar comments.

136. As Osborne 2006, 154.

137. Riva and Vella 2006, 1, my emphasis. The quotation is borrowed from another context. In the introduction to the text, Riva and Vella explain the reasons for the conference. While "researching cultural interaction and change in Etruria and Sardinia . . . [i]t became clear that the 'Orient' was often brought in by scholars intent on explaining change in both places, a veritable metaphorical bazaar, with its opulence and sophistication, that purportedly had a lasting impact on western Mediterranean communities." The idea that Phoenicians are a solution to the Orientalizing problem comes up in several papers and despite Purcell's (2006, 25) cogent plea to avoid doing so.

138. As Purcell 2006, 23.

139. Whitley 2010, 460.

140. Whitley 2013, 410 his emphasis.

141. As called for by Hoffman (2008, 552) in her review of Riva and Vella 2006. The state of Etruscan studies is outlined in Nagy et al. 2008 and accompanying papers.

142. J. Hall 2002, 107. S. Morris (1992, 367) considers Orientalizing in "reverse."

143. Hornblower and Spawforth 2003, s.v. "Hellenism, Hellenization." No entries on Hellenization (or Romanization) appear in the first or second editions (1949 and 1970).

144. Droysen 1877. In the very large Droysen and Hellenismus bibliography, see especially Bichler 1983; Canfora 1987; Funck 1996; Momigliano 1955, 1970. An important cognate is *hellēnisti*: "to understand Greek" (Xen. *An.* 7.6.9); "in the Greek language" (Pl. *Ti.* 21e); "in the Greek fashion" (Luc. *Scyth.* 3). The term could refer to speaking the koine, as opposed to Attic: *POxy.* 1012.17.

145. Prag and Quinn 2013b, 5–7, here 5.

146. Momigliano 1975.

147. E.g., E. Hall 1989, 5.

148. In reference to the *Il.* 2.867's description of Karians as *barbarophōnoi.* Cf. Hdt. 8.20, 9.43, both in reference to the Persians.

149. The term is used by Hellanikos of Mytilene (4 *FGrHist* 71a), who describes Thracians living on Lemnos who had become *mixellēnes.* In the Hellenistic period, Polybios (1.67.7) uses the term to describe some mercenaries working in the service of the Carthaginians.

150. Not, apparently, a Greek-barbarian mixture, or *Verschmelzung.* J. Hall (2002, 171) notes another term, *meixobarbaros*, in Eur. *Phoen.* 138. Antigone, speaking to a tutor, describes Tydeus (an Aitolian) as meixobarbaros.

151. The context of this passage is discussed by Malkin (2001b), who points out that the people considered Greek in these regions—including the Amphilochian Argives—are the relatively "familiar" inhabitants of colonies. Malkin explicitly connects colonization to Hellenization in Thucydides.

152. Thucydides is the first to use the verb "hellēnizein" and is the only known author to employ it in the fifth century.

153. Thuc. 2.68.5 is discussed by Hornblower (1984, 246, with bibliography), who suggests either translation may apply. The second translation is supported by Malkin (2001b, 196), who offers this more polished version: "Adopting the Ambracians' language, they became Hellenes." I am not convinced, however, that in this passage we can say that "Hellenized" refers to a change of ethnicity or identity, as Malkin's translation of the line implies. Rather, I see that the Argives are being contrasted to other Amphilochians.

154. Twice (8.6.6, 14.2.28) Strabo derides Thucydides (1.3.3) for missing or misconstruing the reference in Homer to barbarophōnoi (*Il.* 2.867).

155. As Malkin (2001c, 12–13) has pointed out, most of us are predisposed to binary (structuralist and Straussian) thinking, which suggests, to me, that almost any kind of linear model is too easily turned into an evolution between poles.

156. And of course barbaros was not the only term used for non-Greeks. The Spartans, for example, used *xenoi,* "foreigners": Hdt. 9.11.2.

157. And not just among barbaroi: Herodotos (1.57) explains that the Athenians, as descendants of the Pelasgians, must have learned to speak Greek when they *became* Hellenes: R. Thomas 2001, especially 222–25. It should be noted, however, that Herodotos does not use hellēnizein in this passage. Instead he says that the Pelasgians learned a different tongue.

158. Likewise we would not consider Themistokles less Greek because he spoke some Persian: Thuc. 4.137.

159. Multi- and bi-lingualism were not uncommon in the ancient Mediterranean: Adams 2003; Mairs 2012a; Mullen and James 2012.

160. S. Jones (1997, xii) defines ethnic identity as "that aspect of a person's self-conceptualization which results from identification with a broader group in opposition to others on the basis of perceived culturation differentiation and/or common descent." Cf. Goudriaan 1988; J. Hall 1997, especially 19–26; Herbert 2003, especially 320–21; Malkin 2001a. Introductions to primordialist and instrumentalist views of ethnicity: Siapkas 2003 (critically reviewed by Luraghi 2005).

161. Greeks acknowledged heroes as progenitors of non-Hellenes. The Persian eponymous founder, Perses, was presented by envoys as the son of the Argive hero Perseus: Hdt. 7.150. Cf. E. Hall (1989, 80) for a possible reference to this story in Aesch. *Pers.* 79–80.

162. Malkin 2001c, 3.

163. Gruen (2001, 365) in reference to Jewish self-perception vis-à-vis perceptions of Hellenes. Cf. M. Miller 2005, 85, where, in the context of competing ideas about the Greek legitimacy of immigrant founding fathers, cities might claim they were the "most Greek" by "modulating the definition of 'Greek' to suit circumstances."

164. Pauly-Wissowa, s.v. "Hellenization: Culture," column 101.

165. A helpful introduction to the problems of understanding culture contact is found in Campbell 2003 and Strathern 1990, both concerning European interpretation of first contact scenarios. Compare to Malkin 2011; Pratt 1992; White 2011.

166. An interpretation disputed by Papadopoulos (1997, 2011). See also Sherratt and Sherratt 1993, although they put too much stock in the "ethnicity of language."

167. Contact zones: Pratt 1991, 1992.

168. Indeed, much contact was not amicable. The book of Joel 3.4–6 claims that Sidonians and Tyrians were selling Jews as slaves to Greeks; compare Ez 27.13, where "Iavan" (probably Ionian) ships carry men and metals as cargo. When Alexander besieged and sacked Tyre, he sold most of its population into slavery. And, of course, Greeks regularly enslaved conquered people, again demonstrating how violent encounters could provoke cultural exchange.

169. Campbell 2003, s.v. "Models of Culture Contact."

170. Kroeber 1948, 425.

171. Shipley et al. 2006, s.v. "acculturation"; Winthrop 1991, 82–83. While it is understandable why acculturation can be considered a stage in a process of assimilation (M. Gordon 1964), some postcolonial studies have co-opted the term's political implications, extending its analytical efficacy in a manner similar to hybridity and creolization theories.

172. Hornblower and Spawforth 2003, s.v. "Hellenism, Hellenization," my emphasis.

173. Siapkas 2003, 1–5.

174. Language is surely one reason a Euboean interred with Levantine goods is not considered acculturated. The same logic is not used for Phoenicians. Resistance to Hellenism in the Near East: Eddy 1961.

175. Quinn 2003, 29. A provocative discussion of Romanization in the Galilee can be found in Berlin 2002. Shortcomings of "commonsense" approaches to archaeology are introduced in Johnson 2010, 1–11.

Chapter 2

1. Purcell 2006, 23–24, here 24.

2. Third edition = Richter 1970. "Kouros" was first used in 1895 by Vassilis Leonardos: Ridgway 1993, 61–62. The first major study of the type is Déonna 1909.

3. Hurwit 1985, 191.

4. Brüggemann 2007, tables 3–4, maps 2–3, 5.

5. The religious component of the kouros—and most of Greek art—is often underplayed: e.g., Levin (1964, 27), who says Egyptian statuary was religious, Greek statuary "primarily aesthetic." To a remarkable extent, the current discourse on the kouros in Anglo-American scholarship concerns the kouros as a grave marker, a role it played especially in Athens.

6. A brief and accessible summary of Gombrich's treatment of the kouros can be found in Squire 2011, 32–68.

7. Critiques are numerous: e.g., Beard 1985.

8. Squire 2011, 62 regarding history more generally. Squire 2012, 482, in reference to the way the kouros is interpreted versus the interpretation of Egyptian modes of representation.

9. Havelock 1995, 140–41.

10. Tanner 2001, 257, regarding the kouros. Mendoza 2015, especially 407, has a convenient list of similarities between Greek and Egyptian art.

11. Mack 1996, 31. Compare to Hurwit (1985, 186) regarding the Doric order: "The Egyptian experience, in other words, stimulated an architectural declaration of originality." And sculpture: "Egyptian influence made Greek sculpture not less original but more so." See also Gunter 2009, 64; Shapiro 1996.

12. Cook 1959, 120, on survival rates of the Panathenaic amphora, which he estimates at 0.25 percent. The estimate must be used cautiously: Bresson and Callataÿ 2013; Snodgrass 1983, especially 21–22 (on marble); A. Stewart 1997, 63–64.

13. Brüggemann 2007, 93–94.

14. Keesling 2003, 97–121.

15. Ducat 1971.

16. Cyrene: Goodchild et al. 1966–67. Magna Graecia: Luni 2007. Naukratis: I. Jenkins 2001. A limestone nude youth similar to the kouros type comes from Idalion; a kouros was found at Marion: I. Jenkins 2001, 170–71, 177, fig. 9.

17. This so-called Apollo stands at 0.8 m: Coldstream 2003, 283–84, fig. 91; Boardman 2006, 1–3, fig. 1.

18. A. Stewart 1986, 66.

19. As on a Parian amphora from Melos: Boardman 1998, 111, fig. 250.

20. Brüggemann 2007, table 2. Apollo versus human identification: A. Stewart 1986 and Brüggemann 2007, 95–98, 121–24, with bibliography. Recently Keesling (2003, 124, 149–58, 199–203) revived the idea that the Athenian acropolis korai show Athenas on the grounds of the extended arm found on all but six examples, a gesture associated with but not exclusive to cult statues. See also Ridgway 1993, 66–67.

21. Essential to Mack 1996, 6–7; A. Stewart 1986 offers a more judicious view.

22. A. Stewart 1986, 63. Whether or not the Archaic smile comes from Egyptian art, and from what period, is debated, but Mendoza (2015, 409–10) lays out the likely scenario that Greeks saw Saïte and Middle Kingdom sculpture in the delta with a similar smile. To some, the smile on Saïte statuary lacks the kouros's joyfulness: Davis 1981, 63, but see the comparison in Grace 1942, 353, figs. 3 and 4, 355, figs. 5 and 7. Lawrence (1927, 66, citing "Dr. H. R. Hall") suggests, fantastically, that it was Egyptian sculptors who adopted the smile from Greek ones in the later sixth century.

23. Tanner 2001, 264. Compare A. Stewart (1997, 63–70), who emphasizes the theme of tragic loss in Attic funerary kouroi.

24. A. Stewart 1986, 64–65.

25. Kurtz and Boardman 1970, 148.

26. Neer 2010a, 41, with bibliography.

27. A. Stewart 1997, 65–67, although most histories deemphasize or deny the sexual appeal of male nudity in Greek art. As Havelock (1995, 140) remarked, critically: "The develop-

ment of the male nude in Greek art then is construed as evidence of an ever more expressive humanity in which sexuality plays virtually no role." Compare Plato *Resp.* 474e.

28. Richter 1970, 30–58, nos. 1–30, figs. 25–131 (Sounion Group); 75–79, nos. 63–85, figs. 208–72 (Tenea-Volomandra Group); 90–112, nos. 86–134, figs. 273–390 (Melos Group).

29. Hurwit 2007a, 274, mentions this idea in passing.

30. Fowler 1984; Hurwit 2007a, n. 38; Neer 2002, 16 (the *poikilion ethos*). Color: Brinkmann 2007d; Brinkmann and Primavesi 2003; Kaltsas 2002, 49; Richter 1970, 10; Stager 2012.

31. D'Onofrio 2012.

32. Brinkmann 2007e; Brinkmann and Primavesi 2003, no. 352; Ferrari 2002, 116; Hurwit 2007a, 267–68, 275; Kyrieleis 1996, 23–26, 45–46, 65–67; A. Stewart 1997, 65. Similar features are painted on miniatures: I. Jenkins 2001, 168–70. Richter 1970, 155–56, nos. 124a–c, figs. 616–27, discusses clothed statues of the kouros type.

33. As Kyrieleis 1996, 87–101.

34. As on a cuirassed torso from the Athenian akropolis: Brinkmann 2007a.

35. E.g., Klein 1904, 146–47. Thera kouros: Richter 1970, 69–70, no. 49, figs. 178–83.

36. Ridgway 1993, 30. It is not clear what Ridgway means here except that the idea of action is tied to her understanding of the kouros as walking. Further discussion of action: A. Stewart 1986, 1990, 109–10, and Spivey 1996, 43.

37. Bianchi 1990, 76–77.

38. With the addition of attributes (the bow), the kouros likely represented Apollo. The Naxians dedicated a kouros-type Apollo on Delos in ca. 600: Ridgway 1993, 61–62, 72. Meskell (2001) argues monumentality can make the divine tangible.

39. And following the pioneering study of proportions by Erik Iverson (1957): Guralnick 1970, 1978, 1985. On the second canon, which is less consistent than often claimed, see the summary of previous scholarship by Robins (1994, 31–56) and discussion of the late period (160–64, 256–57).

40. And so we find the relationship expressed as "Greek Kouroi and Egyptian Methods" (the title of a note by Ridgway 1966) or "Die *Bildidee* der monumentalen männlichen Statue wurde wohl unmittelbar aus Ägypten nach Griechenland *importiert*, zusammen mit den *technischen Fertigkeiten* der Marmorbearbeitung, die zur Umsetzung dieser Bildidee unerläßlich waren" (Vorster 2002, 127 my emphasis).

41. Davis 1981, 64; Robins 1994, 160–63, here 259: "The grid was not, then, a straightjacket that forced all figures to be identical. When a figure differs from slightly ideal proportions, it is not because it was produced by a bad draftsman but because there was room for some variation."

42. Carter and Steinberg 2010. This study does not prove the independent, internal development of the kouros, however. Although Davis (1981) follows Guralnick, he explains how the proportional system and stance of Egyptian art could operate independently. Shapiro (1996) compares the development of regional identities to dialects.

43. Grace 1942, especially 351–53, figs. 2–3. Convenient overviews of Kushite and Saïte sculpture in relation to Greek sculpture: Mendoza 2015, 408–10; Russmann 2010.

44. Boardman 1967, 108. Compare the nineteenth-century perspectives reported by Gunter 2009, 62. This interpretation of the kouros is nearly ubiquitous.

45. Comparison can be made to literature of this period produced in the Hellenistic courts: Platt 2010, especially 199.

46. The following discussion owes much to the comprehensive treatment in K. Dunbabin 1999, 5–17 (on pebble mosaics), 18–37 (tessellation); see also, Donderer 1989 and 2008; K. Dunbabin 1979; Ling 1998; Westgate 2012. The earliest known pattern floor dates to the eighth century. It was found in the West Phrygian House at Gordion: R. S. Young 1965. Pebble mosaics appear in Spain as early as the seventh century: Fernández-Galiano 1982. Other early

decorative pavements are found in North Africa, some with figuration, such as the famous early third-century sign of Tanit from a threshold at Kerkouane: K. Dunbabin 1999, 101–2, fig. 100; Fantar 1966, 1978, 1984, 506–8, pls. 52–55; and see also Wilson 2013.

47. Daszewski 1985, 73–86; Tsakirgis 1989, 413–15; contra Salzmann 1982. See also K. Dunbabin 1979, 270–72 ("irregular technique" mosaics), 274–75 (pebble and tessellated mosaics). So-called transitional floors (e.g., the Shatby stag hunt) are found in both eastern and western sites in the third century, but Morgantina, the site that has produced the earliest archaeologically datable tessellated mosaics, notably lacks pebble ones. Delos has some interesting combinations of pebble, chip, and tessellated mosaics: Tang 2005, 47.

48. Alexandria: Daszewski 1985; contra K. Dunbabin 1994 and 1999, 23; Ling 1998. Sicily: Levi 1947; Phillips 1960; contra Salzmann 1982; von Boeselager 1983, especially 26–30; Tsakirgis 1989.

49. Tsakirgis 1989, no. 3. Date: Tsakirgis 1989, 413 contra Salzmann 1982, 61. Iconography: Phillips 1960. The specially cut stones seen in the Ganymede mosaic can be interpreted as forerunners to *opus sectile,* as K. Dunbabin 1979, 272–73.

50. K. Dunbabin 1979, 277. See Joyce (1979, 258) on the appearance of lead strips in specific regions. They are used in Athens, Pergamon, Delos, and Alexandria but not, apparently, in Malta, Sicily, or Italy. The dark ground seems to be indebted to red-figure vase painting: Ling 1998, 23; Lydakes 2004, 212–16, fig. 171.

51. Bruneau 1967. Daszewski (1985, 23–25) discusses this text at length. Turfa and Steinmayer (1999) offer a detailed study of the ship.

52. Simpson 1996, 224–41. The event is dated between the beginning of Ptolemy III's reign (246) and the date of the Canopus Decree *OGI* 56 (239/8) that mentions the relief efforts.

53. Daszewski (1985, 24) suggests that the idea of mosaic decorating a ship was considered novel.

54. Westgate 2002. The floors from Pergamon date no earlier than the first half of the second century, however, relatively late in the development of tessellation.

55. Pollitt 1990, 220–22. Sosos's most famous works are known through copies. *Asarōtos oikos*: Donderer 1989, 63, A16, pl. 13. Drinking doves: Bruneau 1972, 29, pl. A2; Pernice 1938, pls. 64–67. Good color images of both: Andreae 2003, 46–51, 161–75.

56. For example, the "Casa del Fauno" workshop: Meyboom 1977.

57. Edgar 1931, no. 59665; corrections in Koenen 1971. Paradeigma: Bruneau 1980; Bruneau 1984.

58. Thmuis mosaic signed ΣΩΦΙΛΟΣ ΕΠΟΙΕΙ, Alexandria, Graeco-Roman Museum of Alexandria inv. no. 21739: Andreae 2003, 27–38; Daszewski 1985, 142–58, pls. A, 32, 42a; Donderer 1989, 79–80, A39, pl. 25. Both this and the unsigned Thmuis mosaic with the same subject (Alexandria, Graeco-Roman Museum of Alexandria inv. no. 21736), are discussed in Daszewski 1996; Friedman 2011, 14–19; Kuttner 1999.

59. Dunbabin 1999, 24–25. Daszewski (1985, 146–58) proposed the identification with Berenike II.

60. Dunbabin 1999, 25.

61. Shatby hunt, third century: Daszewski 1985, cat. no. 2, 75–78, 103–10, 180–81, pls. 4–7, 10–12; Dunbabin 1999, 23–24, figs. 22–24. Alexandria dog and wrestlers, second half of the second century: Hawass 2002, Bibliotheca Alexandria Archaeology Museum 858 (wrestlers) and 859 (dog), 51–54. See also the opus vermiculatum border fragment, Bibliotheca Alexandria Archaeology Museum 11: Hawass 2002, 53.

62. Sosos: Donderer 1989, 63, A16, pl. 13; Pliny *HN* 36.184.

63. A helpful summary of mosaic subjects: Pollitt 1990, 212–13.

64. Ling (1989, especially 34–48) makes the convincing argument that black and white floors are a major Italian contribution.

65. Contra Salzmann 1982.

66. Burkert 2004, 123.

67. Hurwit 2015, especially 3–4, fig. 1; Richter 1970, 53, no. 16 = Delos Museum no. A728 from Delos, made of Naxian marble and signed by one Euthykartides as maker and dedicator. Euthykartides's signature is one of the earliest sculptor's signatures extant. Because only the feet of the statue remain, we cannot be certain this was a kouros. One kore from the Ptoion is signed (Richter 1968, 26–27, no. 2, figs. 29–30 = Athens, National Museum 2), and might be earlier than Euthykartides's, and a signature appears on the seated female in the Genelaos dedication; in both cases the signatures appear on their garments (as with Nikandre): Osborne 2010, 247, n. 34. By the time Phrasikleia was made, the artist signature—Aristiōn of Paros— had moved to a less prominent position, the side of the base (see Plate 7).

68. Richter 1970, 49–50, nos. 12a and b, figs. 78–83, 91, 92; A. Stewart 1990, 109, 112.

69. Guralnick (1978, 462) following, among others, the sentiments of Déonna 1909; compare Cook 1967. The Daidalic theory of early Greek art: R. Jenkins 1936; refuted thoroughly by S. Morris 1992.

70. Guralnick 1978, 463. Ridgway (1968) suggests that Greeks apprenticed in Egyptian stone workshops. The idea that pattern books existed is weak according to Carter and Steinberg 2010.

71. I. Morris 1997.

72. Symposion: Topper 2012. Kouros: e.g., S. Morris (1992, 240–41) downplays the significance of Egyptian art to Greek art.

73. Cook 1967, 25, in response to Carpenter. Carpenter (1960, 8; cf. 16) says that Greeks "were moved to emulation" by impressive Egyptian statuary and later (1960, 13) uses the term "derivative" in a nonjudgmental way. Hurwit (1985, 185) calls the Doric order an emulation of Egyptian architecture, though he maintains Greeks would have come up with it eventually, regardless of contact with Egypt. I disagree with Hurwit's insistence that the schematic kouros was a "critique" of Egyptian naturalism: Hurwit 1985, 194; see also Fullerton 2000, 60. Compare Cook (1967, 25): "It seems to me that for reasons of style there can have been no direct influence of Egyptian sculpture on Greek in the seventh century and that no Greek sculptor of that time shows any sign of having observed an Egyptian statue." Cook was not alone in this kind of thinking: Anthes 1963; Kranz 1972. Origins and symbolism of the Doric order: Barletta 2001, 54–83; M. Jones 2002.

74. E.g., Grace 1942. Cook 1967 makes a similar suggestion about "indirect transmission." A comparable argument is made by Markoe (1990a) regarding Cypriot Egyptianizing statuary. Sader (2010) discusses motif transmission according to material excavated in the Phoenician mainland, notably the Tyre al-Bass cemetery. Gunter (2009, especially 64) comments on the idea of Phoenician influence on Greek art in, e.g., Pater 1910.

75. Cook 1967.

76. On imports, see Boardman 1999, 111–17; Gunter 2009, 141; Pendlebury 1930 updated and expanded by Skon-Jedele 1994.

77. Levin 1964, 26, figs. 17–18, pl. 9.

78. Until they were removed by Amasis: Hdt. 2.152–54. This period of Egyptian dominance was ended by the Babylonians: Fantalkin 2006, 202–4. Further discussion of Greeks in Egypt before the founding of Naukratis: Davis 1981, 67–68.

79. Inscribed stelai: Masson 1978. Abu Simbel graffiti: Bernard and Masson 1957; Boardman 1999, 115–17, figs. 134–35. The earliest artistic depiction of Greeks (Ionians) in Egyptian art dates to the fourteenth century, in the tomb of Amenophis III: Demetriou 2012, 106 with bibliography. See also Raaflaub 2004a.

80. Haider 2004.

81. Hdt. 2.178–79. The foundation date for Naukratis is disputed. The earliest Greek pottery at the site was thought to date to the late seventh century, but Venit (1988) wishes to push

it back to ca. 660. The official charter was granted later by Amasis (r. 570-26). Demetriou (2012, especially 110–11); Fantalkin 2006 (202–4); and I. Jenkins (2001, 164) summarize the evidence and debates.

82. Hurwit (1985, 179–202) spells out the evidence and connections. Some evidence of monumental stone work in Corinth dates early (in the last quarter of the eighth century) relative to the traditional understanding of Greeks coming into Egypt ca. 664, suggesting either that some experiments in stone architecture predated Egyptian contact or that Greeks were in Egypt earlier: Hurwit 1985, 181. Bietak 2001 includes a range of perspectives on the extent of Egyptian influence.

83. Tanner 2003, 115.

84. S. Morris (1997, 64) regarding Orientalizing pottery: "How on earth do we tell who dedicated, or was buried with, which artifacts—whether they were citizens or foreigners, male or female, wealthy or humble?" Compare Osborne (2011, 108) regarding the represented body itself: "Can we tell, then, when we look at a sculpted figure or figure painted on a pot, whether we are looking at a citizen body?"

85. I. Jenkins 2001.

86. Compare Webb 1978 regarding faience objects.

87. For example, Kroisos is not a Greek name but invokes the famous Lydian king: Osborne 2011, 108–11. Neer (2010a, 28) suggests Kroisos might belong to the Alkmaionid clan, which had Lydian ties.

88. A. Stewart (1997, 24–42) discusses nakedness (he prefers the term's neutrality over the more charged "nudity"). See also Osborne 2007, 2011, especially 27–54; Thuc. 1.6. Nudity in classical art: Bonfante 1989; Hallett 2005; Himmelmann 1990; Hurwit 2007b. Compare to Koloski-Ostrow and Lyons 1997.

89. A. Stewart 1997, 24–25. Supporting this idea are the negative views of the naked male body in Egyptian art "as a uniform of defeat and humiliation" seen in representations of foes, both dead and alive, from the Narmer Palette into the Late Period: Goelet 1993, 20. It is also used in some representations of male laborers. On the positive side are representations of prepubescent children of all classes. Horus the Child (Harpokrates) is, for example, regularly shown naked but for his headgear. While there are examples of adult males represented naked in Egyptian Old Kingdom art, royal, adult males do not seem to appear naked. It is possible that naked images found in royal tombs were once clothed or show Osiris, whose nudity is explained by his religious roles: Goelet 1993, 23–24. Ridgway (1993, 71, 74) has suggested that the nudity of kouroi might be derived from Egyptian statuary, but it seems unlikely that it could have come from representations of kings that Greeks would have seen (though some Old Kingdom tombs seem to have been opened for visitors in the Saïte period: Grace 1942, 351). Hurwit (2007a) points out that the oft-cited "nude" *ka* statue of Hor (W. Smith 1998, 97, fig. 172) was belted and once likely kilted. Old Kingdom reliefs show the production of naked statues for funerary rights. See W. Smith (1998, 72, fig. 136) for an example of a nude wood statuette, identified as an "uncircumcised youth."

90. A. Stewart 1997, 40.

91. A. Stewart (1997, 24–25, fig. 14) shows a belted but otherwise naked charioteer from Olympia that dates to ca. 800–750.

92. A. Stewart 1997, 24, 26, 239 (ancient sources) contra Bonfante 1989, 552–53. Stewart suggests that athletic nudity at the Olympic games might date as much as a century later.

93. Osborne 2011, 37–41.

94. Guralnick seems to have anticipated these points when she suggested the naturalism of some kouroi hid their "essential modularity": Guralnick 1978, 469.

95. Trans. Neer 2010a, 33–36; Pollitt 1974, 263–69.

96. Carpenter 1960, 27.

97. As Osborne 2011, 111: "Kouroi are surely products of projection [of ideals] rather than observation."

98. Hurwit 1985, 194, n. 102; Kenfield 1973; Shanks 1999, 119–20, fig. 3.25; Snodgrass 1993.

99. Mack 1996, 133–36.

100. Mack 1996, 137.

101. The symbolic body: e.g., R. Smith 2007, 108.

102. As also in life, although one of Jenkins' Cypriot statuettes wears a wig and a kilt (2001, fig. 1). Some other kouroi were clothed as well, and it seems like special pleading to claim that clothing excludes these examples from the typological group in order to make it more cohesive in its "opposition" to Egyptian statuary.

103. Carpenter 1960, 4.

104. Carpenter 1960, 15.

105. Hurwit 1985, 188–90. See also Carpenter 1960, 16.

106. Kenfield 1973. Hurwit 1985, n. 102, makes the same tentative suggestion.

107. D'Onofrio 2012. Kenfield (1973, 152–55, figs. 10–12) suggests the sphyrelaton from Dreros might foreshadow this process but only in a general way.

108. Davis 1981.

109. "Lady of Auxerre," Paris, Musée de Louvre 3098: A. Stewart 1990, 107–8, pls. 27–28. "Nikandre" kore, Athens, National Museum 1: A. Stewart 1990, 108, pls. 34–35.

110. Boardman 1967, 2006; Brisart 2011; Grace 1942; Gunter 2009.

111. Daszewski 1985, 10, 12. The idea that the tholoi floors were tessellated and not pebbled comes from both Daszewski 1985, 13–14, and Bruneau 1980.

112. K. Dunbabin 1999, 38

113. K. Dunbabin 1999, 43.

114. As noted by Westgate 2000a, 273, n. 74.

115. Bruneau 1972, 111, n. 2; Hurwit 2015, 64–70; Westgate 2000a, 272; and see also K. Dunbabin (1999, 269–78). *Pergamon*, garland frieze and borders with trompe l'oeil inscription ΗΦΑΙΣΤΙΩΝ ΕΠΟΙΕΙ, Berlin, Pergamonmuseum inv. no. 70: Andreae 2003, 44–47; Donderer 1989, 64, A17, pl. 14; Kawerau and Wiegand 1930, 53–61, pls. 17–19, figs. 27–38; Kriseleit 2000, 17–23, figs. 8–15. *Delos*, geometric mosaic in the Sanctuary of the Syrian Gods signed ΑΝΤΑΙΟΣ ΑΙΣΧΡΙΩΝΟΣ ΕΠΟΙΕΙ: Bruneau 1972, 225–26, no. 195, figs. 156–59; Donderer 1989, 55, A4, pl. 4. *Delos*, H. Dolphin peristyle mosaic signed [ΑΣΚΛΕ]ΠΙΑΔΗΣ ΑΡΑΔΙΟ[Σ] ΕΠΟΙΕΙ: Bruneau 1972, no. 210, 235–39, figs. 168–75, pl. B.1–2; Donderer 1989, 56, A6, pl. 6. *Athens*, fragmentary monochrome centauromachy with partial signature [. . .] ΩΝ ΕΠΟ[ΙΕΙ or ΗΣΕΝ]: Donderer 1989, 80, A41, pl. 26:1; Salzmann 1982, 30, 86–87, no. 20, pl. 41:1. *Pella*, stag hunt signed ΓΝΩΣΙΣ ΕΠΟΗΣΕΝ: Andreae 2003, 22–24; Donderer 1989, 58, A9, pl. 7:2; Salzmann 1982, 12, 19, 28–29, 107, 108, no. 103, pl. 29, color pls. 101:2–6, 102:1, 2. *Thmuis*, personification mosaic signed ΣΩΦΙΛΟΣ ΕΠΟΙΕΙ, Alexandria, Graeco-Roman Museum of Alexandria inv. no. 21739: Andreae 2003, 27–38; Daszewski 1985, 142–58, pls. A, 32, 42a; Donderer 1989, 79–80, A39, pl. 25. *Pompeii*, comedic scenes in marble frames from the "Villa of Cicero" signed ΔΙΟΣΚΟΥΡΙΔΗΣ ΣΑΜΙΟΣ ΕΠΟΙΗΣΕ, Naples, Museo Nazionale inv. nos. 9985 and 9987: Andreae 2003, 219–26; Donderer 1989, 59–61, A11, pl. 9; Pernice 1938, pls. 70–71. *Segesta*, highly fragmentary monochrome? mosaic signed [Δ]ΙΟΝΥΣΙΟΣ [Η]ΡΑΚΛΕΙΔΟΥ [ΑΛΕΞ]ΑΝΔΡΕΥΣ Ε[ΠΟΙΕΙ]: Donderer 2008, 44–45, A5, pl. 4:1; K. Dunbabin 1999, 273, n. 23; Pinna and Sfligiotti 1991, 906–8, pl. 289:1. *Euesperides*, tessellated threshold mosaic dating to 325–260 signed either ΕΥΚ[ΛΕΙΔ]Α ΕΡΓ[ΟΝ] "work of Eukleidēs" or, as the excavators prefer, ΕΥΚ[ΑΙΡ]Α ΕΡΓ[ΟΙΣ] "good fortune in your affairs": Donderer 2008, 48, A8; Wilson 2003, 1656, fig. 8; Wilson 2006, 143, figs. 2, 5. The most systematic studies of signatures and other epigraphic data for mosaicists are Donderer's (1989, 2008). He includes more examples from mosaics of disputed, but possibly preimperial, date.

116. Bruneau 1972, 232, fig. 166 (plan) and 111–12, fig. 175 (inscription).

117. In addition to Bruneau 1972, see Tang 2005, 45–48 for an overview of the Delos mosaics.

118. Prevalence of the Doric order: Tang 2005, 34.

119. Bruneau 1972, no. 209, 235, fig. 167; cf. 71. Bruneau speculated that the other Delos mosaicist, Antaios, was Syrian because his signature was found in the Sanctuary of Syrian Gods. He rightly admits that without an ethnic the idea has no real basis. Appearances of the "sign of Tanit" in the eastern Mediterranean post-500 indicate she was more popular there than the inscriptional evidence suggests: Benigni 1975; Bordreuil 1987; Chollot 1975; Cintas 1968–69; Dothan 1974 (which lists all the finds up to its publication); Dunand and Duru 1962: 175, E20–21, pl. 67; Hvidberg-Hansen 1979 (textual study); Korr 1981 (on objects from Egyptian Thebes); Linder 1973; Lipiński 1995, 62–64, 199–215, 423–26, 440–46; Lipiński 2015, 63–94; Pritchard 1982; Sader 1992, no. 13 (a possible Tanit theophoric from Tyre); Sader 2005 and 2010 ("pseudo-ankhs"); Stieglitz 1990. A Tanit epithet on an inscription from Carthage is *blbnn*, (probably) "of Lebanon," and suggests eastern origins could be important in colonial conceptions of the goddess: Quinn 2005, 395–96. Succinct remarks on the spelling of Tanit/Tinnit are in Christian 2013, n. 2.

120. Brown (1991, 123–31) has a good overview of the literature regarding the elements and origins of the motif. See also Doak 2015, 61–66; Lipiński 1995, 206–15, Lipiński 2015, 90–94; Mettinger 1995, 111–12; Moscati 1972b, 1979, 1988b, 113–15; Colette Picard 1968; Sader 2010.

121. Brown 1991, 124, contra Linder 1973. See, for example, the stele from Carthage Tanit II showing the motif under the crescent and disk (motifs sometimes associated with Ba'al-Hammon) and inscribed in Punic "To our lady, to Tanit . . . and to our lord, to Ba'al Hammon, that which was vowed" (Stager and Wolff 1984, 46, left).

122. Fantar 1966, followed by K. Dunbabin 1999, 33, and Tang 2005, 53. Other examples of the motif on Delos are found on oil lamps: Bruneau 1965, 106, nos. 4524–28, pl. 27.

123. Leading some to assume that the motif here indicates the homeowners were Carthaginians in particular, as Lipiński 2004, 168.

124. Christian 2013, 193, with bibliography. Examples of grave stelai showing the "sign of Tanit" and a dolphin or prow of the ship can be found conveniently in Moscati 1988b, 615, no. 184 (from Carthage); 619, no. 207 (from Cirta, Algeria). A ship's prow and the "sign of Tanit" are found also on the obverse and reverse, respectively, of a Hellenistic lead weight from Tyre, Musée du Louvre AO 7017.

125. Casson 1995, 94–96, figs. 103–5. See also Woolmer 2012. According to Hdt. 3.37, Phoenician ships of his era carried statues or figureheads on their bows.

126. Franks 2014.

127. Hdt. 8.10. Whitehead 1987, 179. The pairing of dolphins and caducei in the context of maritime power is also a feature of the Thmuis personifications/portraits; both are found on the side of the female figure's ship headdress along with sea serpents. These features are difficult to see in photographs: Friedman 2011, 14–19, figs. 3.1.1–3.1.6; Oppen de Ruiter 2015, 63, pl. 3.12, for a clear, detailed photograph of the unsigned Thmuis mosaic.

128. Nitschke 2013.

129. Brown 1991, 131–34. Good examples of the caduceus on Hellenistic (and later) stelai are found at Cirta now in the Costa collection in the Louvre: Bertrandy and Sznycer 1987.

130. Pollitt 1990, 216. The only house with an explicit thematic program is the House of the Masks: Bruneau 1972, 156–69, figs. 55–79, pl. A:3–4.

131. The precise date of monumental painting's invention is debated, but it was certainly a feature of Greek art by the fifth century when Polygnotos completed his famous works in Athens and Delphi: Paus. 10.25–31; Pemberton 1988; Robertson 1959, 34–51 and 1975, 49–56. Bronze

Age painted floors: Hirsch 1977. There are newly discovered painted floors at Tell Kabri in modern Israel: Cline et al. 2011. Pliny *HN* 35.15 dismisses the idea that painting was invented in Egypt six thousand years before his day. Probably his objection is to the very early date, not to the idea that painting was known first in Egypt.

132. Westgate 1997–98; 2000b; 2002.

133. Replication and emulation: Gaifman 2006.

134. Here we should remember that Egyptian hieroglyphs are "miniature images." The term for hieroglyph also means sign and representation: Hurwit 1990, 180. The walking kouros or kouros as a representation of the "'hieroglyph' of walking": Ridgway 1993, 31–32, here 31. The idea is tied to her interpretation of the early kouros as a dynamic Apollo. The Egyptian hieroglyph for walking was a pair of parted lower legs, suggesting that the Egyptian prototypes were not only representing walking visually but using it as a linguistic sign as well.

135. A. Stewart 2008b. Herm as the successor to the kouros: Osborne 1985, especially 52–53, and, recently, Quinn 2007.

136. The name Lyre-Player Group was coined by Porada (1956), and the group was published by Buchner and Boardman 1966; see also Boardman 1990.

137. An especially intriguing seal was recently excavated from Monte Vetrano, modern Salerno. The seal is associated by its excavators with an early seventh-century tomb but was found out of context, unfortunately: Cerchiai and Nava 2008–9; Węcowski 2014, 148–49.

138. Buchner and Boardman 1966 claimed a north Syrian origin for these seals on the basis of their large numbers there, as well as their material and style. Other sites of manufacture have been suggested, such as Rhodes (Porada 1956, 192) and Phoenicia (Dusinberre 2005, 43–44). Huelva seal: Serrano Pichardo et al. 2012.

139. Helpful summary: Hodos 2006, 66–70.

140. Much Athenian pottery was made for markets beyond Athens, but at least some pots had specific social functions at their site of production that were likely to be different from their use in new contexts: Dietler 2010; Dietler and López-Ruiz 2009; Schmidt and Stähli 2012; Walsh 2014. In other words, although it was very popular, Athenian pottery of the late Archaic and Classical eras was not *on the whole* an art produced by contact.

141. General overview of Phoenician sculpture: Caubet et al. 2002.

142. Wallinga 1987, 47–48.

143. Date: Quack 2011.

144. Buhl 1983 argues a workshop in Giza or Saqqara was the likely source. It is also possible these were interred in an unfinished state (as were several of the anthropoid sarcophagi): Buhl 1959; Caubet et al. 2002, 101–11; Élayi 1988a; Élayi and Haykal 1996; Ferron 1993; Frede et al. 2000–2002; Kukahn 1955; Lembke 2001.

145. Although inscriptions indicate that the inviolate body was clearly important to Phoenician royalty, mummification is not common in Phoenician burials. Tabnit's is the only secure example, but some attempt at the preservation of soft tissue is found in several others: Dixon 2013, especially 547–53. Hamdi Bey and Reinach 1892, 401–10, includes an analysis of Tabnit's remains and his skull in comparison to other "Semitic" examples—a telling snapshot of late nineteenth-century perspectives. Gras et al. 1991 is a short overview.

146. Tabnit sarcophagus = *KAI* 13, Istanbul Archaeological Museum 800: Lembke 2001, 121, no. 1, pl. 17. Unidentified female, usually called a queen: Lembke 2001, 122, no. 3. It is often said this female is mummified, too, but the evidence is not certain. Her sarcophagus and several others had wooden planks and iron rings similar to what were found in Tabnit's sarcophagus. These elements are familiar from the Egyptian "opening of the mouth" ceremony, but it is not clear how they were used in Phoenicia: Dixon 2013, 552–53; Élayi and Haykal 1996, 50 and 56; Hamdi Bey and Reinach 1892, 14.

147. Eshmunazar II sarcophagus = *KAI* 14, Paris, Louvre AO 4806: Lembke 2001, 121, no. 2, pl. 17.

148. Remaining examples come from sites on Cyprus (eight) or lack provenance (ten). A few are found in Egypt and in the west—Malta, Solontum, Cadiz: Lembke 2001, 5–25, 50–55, 79–81. Maria Aubet believes that the recently excavated Tyre al-Bass cemetery was for common folk, so it possible this picture will change with the discovery of an elite cemetery in Tyre: Abousamra and Lemaire 2013, 2014; Aubet 2004, 2010; Aubet et al. 2014; Sader 1991, 1992, 2005, 2010.

149. Lembke 2001, 91–92, discusses polychromy. An anthropoid sarcophagus from Amathos in the Cesnola collection has a *shin* on the foot of its lid: Teixidor 1976, 68, no. 28.

150. A group from Arwad is made in terracotta and basalt. It is unclear where these fall in the sequence of events, though some scholars, such as Lembke (2001, 43–44, 49, 84), believe they belong to an intermediate period between the looted objects ca. 525 and the start of marble examples in Sidon in ca. 480. The latter Lembke attributes to established Greek workshops. While it is plausible, even likely, that marble examples postdate the Persian Wars, for the most part this reconstruction of events is fragile and cannot be taken too seriously. Examples are known also in other materials, such as limestone and gypsum: Lembke 2001, 82–85.

151. Because of the persistence of their imagery directly or indirectly in other media: Lembke 2001, 54; Stager 2005, 435.

152. Summarized in Nitschke 2007, 80.

153. Hamdi Bey and Reinach 1892, esp. 149–52, no. 11, pl. 42:11; Lembke 2001, 122–23, nos. 5–6.

154. Hamdi Bey and Reinach 1892, esp. 147–49, no. 3, pl. 42:3.

155. Another source of inspiration seems to be Hellenistic grave reliefs from Asia Minor. Cypriot sculptural elements have also been detected, and the relief sarcophagus in the Cesnola collection from Amathos should be mentioned in this context: New York, Metropolitan Museum of Art 74.51.2453. See Lembke 2001, 82–24, 136–38.

156. As Lembke 2001, especially 104–10. Pro-Greek arguments are summarized in Hermary 1987. Élayi has been a long, outspoken supporter of Phoenician manufacture: Élayi 1988a.

157. Nitschke 2007, 74–86.

158. The stylistic elements used to date the sarcophagi are just as likely to reflect workshop practices as chronological change.

159. Ridgway (1966, 70) suggests technical differences might be at play in the amount of stone removed, but still maintains the Greek "propensity" toward naturalism was a factor, too.

160. Dietler 2005, 2010.

Chapter 3

1. Whitley 1997, 43, regarding theory implicit in Beazley's connoisseurship.

2. A theme in Gunter 2009; Prag and Quinn 2013a.

3. Recalling Weber's *Idealtypus*, or "ideal types": Weber 1978. The classical study of "imagined communities" is by B. Anderson (1983), now in its second edition (2006). See Stockhammer 2013, 12–14, for a discussion of taxonomic purity.

4. A recent discussion of the meanings of Hellenism and Hellenistic (or "Hellenistics") can be found in Prag and Quinn 2013b, 3–10; Van Dommelen and López-Bertran 2013, 276–79.

5. As Sancisi-Weerdenburg 2001, 323: "How were Greeks seen by others, in particular by their Near Eastern neighbors? I wish we knew."

6. As Momigliano 1975.

7. The text of Philo of Byblos is imperial in date but presented as a translation of Sanchuniathon who was thought to have lived before or during the Trojan War: Eissfeldt 1952a and b. The structure of Philo's text suggests his earlier sources did not predate the Hellenistic period: Millar 1983, 64.

8. See S. Sherratt 2010.

9. Hurwit 1990.

10. Greek and Phoenician city-states seem to bear a resemblance that might or might not be coincidental (compare Murray 2000 and Raaflaub 2004b). The choice to call both poleis has been criticized (Redford 1992, 267), however, so here I use "polis" to refer only to Greek city-states.

11. The Greek polis began to develop in the seventh century (as J. Hall 1997). Some see the appearance of the god Melqart as one indication of the rise of the Phoenician city-state in the eleventh or tenth century: Malkin 2005a, 241–42.

12. Burkert (1992, 1), for example, argues that Greeks became "aware of their own identity as separate from that of the 'Orient' when they succeeded in repelling the attacks of the Persian empire." See also Malkin 2001c, 7–9.

13. J. Hall 1997, 47–48. For a more recent treatment of the role of competition in ethnicity, see Faust 2006.

14. As demonstrated in M. Miller 1997. See also Shapiro 2009.

15. Wallinga 1987, 2005.

16. Wallinga speculates they made up the bulk of the rowers. If the navy was composed of three hundred triremes, he estimates an astonishing number of rowers would have been required—between eighteen thousand and fifty-one thousand (1987, 70).

17. Meiggs and Lewis 1988, 24.

18. After Salamis, Phoenician ships were dedicated at Sounion, Isthmia, and Salamis (Hdt. 8.121.1). S. Morris (1992, 289–90) sees in this evidence a pronounced confrontation (superiority over "the chief Eastern opponent at sea"), whereas I see these examples as more isolated incidents. Euripides's *Phoenissae* of ca. 408 was, however, a barbarizing send-up of Thebes's betrayal that played upon its Kadmian origins: E. Hall 1989, 115–16. On Punes and Phoenicians in the Greek conception of the oikoumenē, see Romm 1992, 18–22, 126–27, 148.

19. A term I first heard Quinn use—and also "Phoenicianisms" (plural)—in her Miriam Balmuth lectures at Tufts University, delivered in spring 2012. Bondì (2014) opts for "Phoenicity." On Lebanese identity and modern Phoenicianism, see Kaufman 2004.

20. Barth 1969. Hutchinson and Smith 1996 is a valuable overview of the term and the evolution of its use.

21. J. Hall 2007, especially 49–53. Some, such as Snodgrass (1980, especially 25–26, 42–44), approach the polis-ethnos relationship more in terms of organization.

22. This example is borrowed from the helpful online *Lexicon of Greek Personal Names.*

23. Here I follow closely McInerney 2001, especially 56–57. For Herodotos and ethnicity, see Konstan 2001; R. Thomas 2001. Territory (nationalization) and ethnos: A. D. Smith 1986. Politics: J. Hall 1997; Morgan 2002 (and for colonization).

24. Faust (2006) offers a structuralist approach; Morgan 2002, especially 101; Morgan 2009, especially 11–12.

25. J. Hall 2002, 172–228.

26. S. Jones 2007, 48. Ethnicity is nonetheless archaeologically retrievable: Bentley and Maschner 2008, 4–5; S. Jones 1997, 2007 contra J. Hall 1997. Ethnicity and style: Gates 2002; Gunter 2009, 91–95; Hurwit 1979; Pasztory 1989; Ucko 1989.

27. See Vernant 1983. One can find "race" used even to translate ethnos alongside other, less charged, translations, such as "tribe," "people," and "nation." For example, in Macaulay's

1890 translation of Herodotos, "race" appears in book 1 as a translation of ethnos: τὰ ἔθνεα βάρβαρα = "Barbarian races" (1.4.4; see also 1.56.2); genos: Κροῖσος ἦν Λυδὸς γένος = "Croesus was Lydian by race" (1.6.1; see also 1.31.2); τὸ Ἑλληνικὸν = "Hellenic race" (e.g., 1.4.4); and so on. On nineteenth-century nationalism's relationship to classical antiquity, see Whitmarsh 2011.

28. Genetic groups do exist, but the boundaries between genetic groups are blurred and their racial designations are arbitrary. Moreover, the use of race in the humanities and social sciences is *always* arbitrary, typically having little or nothing to do with genetics and much to do with appearance. A recent summary of genomics and race can be found in Hochschild et al. 2012, 83–112. A. D. Smith (1986, especially 2) discusses the relationship between modern and nineteenth-century scholarship.

29. McCoskey 2012, 9 including brief bibliography on race and classical identity.

30. A critique made by Bernal but found in plenty of other scholarship. Prag (2006, 3) cites some egregious examples from scholarship on ancient Sicily and discusses the ancient sources.

31. Rankine 2011, 40–41.

32. Osborne 1996; Routledge 2013.

33. On the Second Sophistic and ethnicity, see Kemezis 2014 with bibliography.

34. Hellenic genealogy: J. Hall 1997, 42–44, fig. 1. Dialects: J. Hall 1997, 143–81; 2007, 56. On the question of Roman ethnic prejudice, see Gruen 2013.

35. Panhellenism and sanctuaries: J. Hall 2002, 125–71; Morgan 1993. Scott (2010) also grounds his discussion of Panhellenism in the context of the sanctuary, but the implications are quite far-reaching. He argues that Panhellenism was largely an invention of Rome (compare Alcock 2002, 36–98). L. Mitchell (2007), in contrast, believes Panhellenism is a part of Greek identity before the Persian Wars, from the sixth century. The Hellēnion sanctuary at Naukratis (Hdt. 2.178) might be an early expression of Panhellenism.

36. See Sznycer 1978. Important points are made in Prag 2006, 4–7; 2014.

37. For example, Stern 1993.

38. Contrary to what is sometimes claimed, in biblical texts the Phoenicians are not described as a people. Sometimes "Canaanite" is used but without meaning precisely a national group; sometimes it means trader, not unlike the use of "Phoenician" in Homer.

39. Markoe 2000; Tubb 1998. Each writes about his subject in the Bronze and Iron ages (*Canaanites* begins in the eighth millennium; *Phoenicians* in the late Bronze Age) and concludes in the second half of the first millennium (*Phoenicians* stops in 64 BCE). The books cover the same region, although *Canaanites* also includes the Transjordan and Israel. See also Peckham (2014), who explicitly calls eleventh- to tenth-century Canaan the "origin" of Phoenicians, and Röllig 1983b.

40. This section follows closely the excellent histories of ethnicity and race studies in J. Hall 1997, 1–2 and McCoskey 2012, 1–34, respectively. See also McCoskey 2003, 2006; Skinner 2012; Tuplin 1999, 2007. On the exceptional qualities of Greek art, see now Hurwit 2015, 11–32.

41. See the recent and provocative treatment of this topic in Orrells et al. 2011, here 4. Frederickson 2003 is a helpful introduction to the history of racism.

42. See Sewell 1996b, 247–48, on sociology as a teleology.

43. I borrow the sense of "character" as a quasi-racial or essentialist term from J. Hall 1997, 1.

44. Montagu trained with Boas while at Columbia. Montagu 1997 is the work's sixth edition and has been updated with scientific data (genetic, anthropological) disputing the theory of race.

45. His approach is now understood as "constructivism" for its emphasis on ethnicity as a social process rather than a fixed or primordial component of a culture. Especially critical is Barth 1969. Geertz 1973 is another key text, although its focus is specifically culture. There are several other terms used to describe different views about ethnicity. Wimmer 2008 offers a lucid summary.

46. The bibliography is immense. Of particular importance are Cohen 2000; Dover 1978; Gruen 2005, 2011.

47. McCoskey 2003.

48. Identity: Antonaccio 2009 (and for ethnicity); Meskell 2001; Knapp 2014. Memory and national identity: Gillis 1996. On the fatigue with identity studies, see S. Hall 2000 and Mairs 2010.

49. There are, of course, exceptions to this simple timeline, notably A. Sherwin-White 1967 and Helm 1988. Tuplin 1999 and Isaac 2004 were among the first major publications of the current wave of interest in racism and ethnic prejudice.

50. As, for example, Jared Diamond's 1997 Pulitzer Prize-winning bestseller *Guns, Germs and Steel: The Fates of Human Societies*, published by W.W. Norton.

51. Lieberman 2010.

52. On the 2010 Census form, for example, Hochschild et al. (2012, 4–6, fig. 1.1) count 126 possible combinations of "origin" and "race;" there are sixty-three ways to express "race" alone.

53. A fourth volume responding to his critics appeared in 2001. McCoskey 2012, 171–85, provides a compact overview of *Black Athena* and its reception. The bibliography is very large. Especially useful are Berlinerblau 1999; Lefkowitz and Rogers 1996; Orrells et al. 2011; R. J. C. Young 1994.

54. Snowden 1983. Momigliano and Burkert would seem to offer still more intellectual companionship for Bernal, as all three challenge Hellenocentrism while promoting external (Near Eastern or African) contributions to Greek civilization: Momigliano 1975; Burkert 1984, 1992, 2004.

55. See Coleman and Walz 1997.

56. McCoskey 2006; Snowden 1983; Tanner 2010b, especially 15–18; Thompson 1989. On blackness in late antiquity: Starks 2011.

57. *Aithiops* is "burnt face" in Greek, hardly a compliment. One can compare the name to "Huron" from the French *hure* meaning "bristly or ugly head": Bitterli 1989, 93.

58. See Romm 1992, 49–60; Skinner 2012, 95–99; Snowden 1970, 1997.

59. Dee 2004, 160. In *Il.* 5.499–505 the Achaeans "become white" from the dust raised by galloping horses. Barry 2011 considers the meanings of white stone in Roman statuary.

60. *Il.* 20.44–6; 22.25–36; 22.131–37; compare Hdt. 2.152, where "bronze men" means armed Hellenes.

61. E.g., Xen. *Ages.* 1.28. Lape (2010) argues that gender and race were intertwined in Athenian thinking. Color and gender: Eaverly 2013.

62. Athens, National Museum 4889; see Brinkmann 2007c, 32; Brinkmann et al. 2010. Brinkmann was a student of Volkmar von Gräve, who published the Alexander Sarcophagus (von Graeve 1970).

63. A recent treatment of this topic from the perspective of American history can be found in Painter 2010. A sensitive treatment of Winckelmann's legacy with respect to color can be found in Stager 2012, especially 15.

64. Tanner 2003, 116.

65. Whitmarsh 2011, 211, in reference to Droysen.

66. According to Lefkowitz and Rogers 1996, sixty-eight review articles of *Black Athena* had appeared by 1993.

67. While the nineteenth century may mark the start of "scientific" (pseudo-quantitative) racism, it is quite possible to place its origin earlier, in the fourteenth and fifteenth centuries (as Frederickson 2003, 6) or even in Greco-Roman antiquity (as Isaac 2004).

68. One source of inspiration was Cyrus Gordon (Bernal 1987, 416–19), eighteen of whose publications are listed in Bernal's bibliography. Gordon was a linguist who held some controversial, so-called diffusionist views (as Stengel 2000). Notably, he argued on the basis of the Bat Creek, Tennessee, and Paraíba, Brazil, inscriptions, both widely recognized as fakes, that Iron Age Jews and Phoenicians colonized the Americas: C. Gordon 1968; see also C. Gordon 1971. Cross 1968 and Mainfort and Kwas 1991, 1993 demolish both inscriptions' authenticity.

69. However different the aims, conclusions, and reception, in Bernal's and Snowden's work Afrocentrists found much to admire: a past free of skin-color prejudice and the revelation of a powerful black African diaspora at the very heart of classical antiquity, centuries before some thought the idea of "blackness" emerged.

70. Bernal's open embrace of Afrocentrism was especially infuriating to scholars such as Mary Lefkowitz, who considered Afrocentrism's incursions into the academy a serious threat to intellectual integrity, a point of view informed by her personal experiences as a faculty member at Wellesley College. See Lefkowitz's 1996 *Not Out of Africa*, which began as a review article on *Black Athena*. See also Bernal's uncharitable 1996 review and Lefkowitz's 1996 response. Lefkowitz 2009 details a feud with Wellesley colleague and professor of Africana studies Tony Martin, including Martin's suit against Lefkowitz for libel. Martin's version of events can be found in his controversial 1993 book, *The Jewish Onslaught: Despatches* [sic] *from the Wellesley Battlefront* (Dover, Mass.: Majority Press).

71. Berlinerblau 1999, especially part 2.

72. The phrase "culture war" was revived in American politics by Pat Buchanan at the 1992 Republican National Convention: "My friends, this election is about more than who gets what. It is about who we are. It is about what we believe and what we stand for as Americans. There is a religious war going on in this country for the soul of America. It is a cultural war as critical to the kind of nation we shall be as the Cold War itself, for this war is for the soul of America." See the full transcript at Buchanan 1992.

73. Frederickson 2003, 151.

74. R. J. C. Young 1994, 156, cited in McCoskey 2012, 176. On the overlap between racism and cultural difference, "cultural essentialism," and "culturalism," see Frederickson 2003, 3–7.

75. McCoskey 2003; Trouillot 2003, 105: "Today there is more conceptual confusion about race among anthropologists than there was at the beginning of the last century."

76. And elsewhere. Compare Lape (2010) to Harrison (1998), who has a similar argument regarding the Parthenon, although she frames it in terms of ethnicity. A good summary of Greek sources about the East can be found in Isaac 2004, 257–303; see also Eliav-Feldon et al. 2009. Kennedy et al. 2013 combines the sources in translation.

77. Isaac 2004, set out most clearly on 33–38.

78. See, conveniently, *ANET* figs. 2–8, 25, 43, 93, 95, 97–98, 100–102, 123.

79. Pointed out in Osborne 2010, 246.

80. On the meaning of mimesis before Plato, see the classic treatment by Keuls (1978) in which she argues that the term meant "dramatic enactment" and only later came to be used in reference to the visual arts; compare Neer 1995, 121, after Else 1958. Halliwell (2002, 22, n. 53) warns that the evidence is too scant to know for certain the meaning of mimesis in the Archaic and early Classical periods, but he nonetheless calls Keuls's claim "untenable."

81. *HN* 34.55; Pollitt 1990, 75. Compare to "seeing as" and "seeing in": Wollheim 1980.

82. We should not mistake naturalism as the goal of Greek (or other) art, however, as Pollitt 1972, xiii: "It would be idle to deny that a development in the direction of a more naturalistic representation of anatomy, drapery and the like, is a *fact* of Greek art; whether it was always its

aim is more doubtful." Representation and mimesis: Frigg and Hunter 2010; Gombrich 1960; Goodman 1968.

83. Mattusch 1988: 143–45; Overbeck 1868, 103–7, nos. 550–91.

84. Myron's cow: A. Stewart 1990, 48, 255–57 (T43). See Squire 2010b for a recent treatment of the epigrams. Painting and verisimilitude: Pliny *HN* 35.67–72 (Parrhasios), *HN* 35.140 (Ktesilas).

85. Statues of even the well-known Miltiades and Themistokles that stood in the Prytaneion were given new, Roman and Thracian, identities: Mattusch 2006, 228.

86. A. Stewart 2008a, 39, after Roland Barthes's "reality effect."

87. Pliny (*HN* 35.153) reports that the artist's brother Lysistratos invented the practice of working from plaster life masks "from the surface [of the body] itself" (*e facie ipsa*). Lysistratos: Palagia 2006, 263; Pollitt 1990, 104. A. Stewart (1990, 34) mentions live models. The female model appears in connection with anecdotes about the Knidia (e.g., Plato *Anth. Gr.* 16.160; Ath. 13.590d–e), but the historicity of such evidence is unclear. Sources for Alexander's portraits are gathered in A. Stewart 1990, 72–78; 1993.

88. Mattusch 2006, 227–28, though I note that even the general idea of recasting is contested by a number of Greek art historians. See Rolley 1999, 406–10.

89. Poseidippos 142A–B; recently discussed in Prauscello 2006. In addition to Gutzwiller 1998 on Hellenistic epigrams, see Gutzwiller 2002 on Poseidippos and sculpture. Allegory and personification: A. C. Smith 2011. Kairos: A. Stewart 1990, 187–88, 292 (T127), fig. 555; Tanner 2006, 180–82, fig. 4.5.

90. Attic red-figure plate from Vulci signed by Epiktetos, 520–500. London, British Museum GR 1837.6–9.59.

91. Interior of Athenian red-figure cup signed by Douris as painter and Kalliades as potter, 490–480. Paris, Louvre G 115.

92. Tanner 2003, 121.

93. Athenian red-figure calyx krater said to be from Vulci att. to the Tyszkiewicz Painter, 490–480. Boston, Museum of Fine Arts 97.368.

94. Ethiopian attendants: *LIMC* "Memnon" no. 6; cf. nos. 5, 7–10, all of which date to 540–500. Attic red-figure calyx krater showing Memnon in Oriental dress battling Amazons, attributed to the Painter of London E489, Copenhagen, National Museum 8 286 (147) = *LIMC* "Memnon" no. 11. Though she can be marked as foreign by her clothing, Andromeda is sometimes also shown with Ethiopian servants, as on an Athenian red-figure hydria from Vulci from ca. 450, London, British Museum 1843.11-3.24.

95. Attic red-figure plastic horn on a base attr. to the Manner of the Sotades Painter, 460. Boston, Museum of Fine Arts 98.881.

96. M. Miller 2000.

97. Boardman 1982; *LIMC* "Amazones," "Alexandros," "Andromeda"; Raeck 1981; Von Bothmer 1957. Cf. Euphronios's krater of 510–500 showing Amazons dressed as hoplites and in patterned trousers, Arezzo, Museo Civico 1465: Woodford 1993, fig. 79 = *LIMC* "Amazones" no. 64; Paris: Castriota 1992, 106. Cf. Eur. *Tro.* 990–95.

98. *LIMC* "Kadmos;" M. Miller 2005, 79–84, figs. 12–16.

99. E.g., Kadmos fighting the serpent on coins of Tyre: Hill 1910, 142, 280–81, 293, 295.

100. See Perrot and Chipiez 1885; Rawlinson 1889; Renan 1864.

101. Vella 2014, 29.

102. Vella (2014, 34–35) notes a particularly egregious example in Harden 1962, 218: "The Phoenician, though he possessed an artistic bent, was less interested in art for its own purposes than for the price he could get for it abroad."

103. "Elusive" is the term used by Vella 1996.

104. Falsone 1988. North Syria: I. Winter 1988.

105. Ivories: Pritchard 1988, 112–13, no. 20 (fragment of ivory? container); 113, no. 25, figs. 29–30 (fragments of ivory nude female with headdress); 113–14, no. 26, figs. 29–30 (ivory plaque of female head); 114, no. 28, fig. 31 (half of ivory filial); 114, nos. 29–30, figs. 29, 31 (ivory knobs); 115, no. 33, fig. 31 (bone or ivory amulet with human figure); 115, no. 34, fig. 31 (ivory die). Bowls: Pritchard 1988, 106, no. 40, fig. 46 is a bronze miniature bowl/cup. There are no vessels made in gold or silver.

106. Niemeyer 2003, 204; Vella 2010, 23–24; Vella 2014, 36.

107. Markoe 2003, 210, cited in Vella 2010, 25.

108. Summarized in Vella 2010, 24–25.

109. Feldman 2014, especially 21–41, 113–16; Cinquatti 2015 has similar arguments. Feldman takes an important step beyond those, such as Muhly (1985), who have expressed doubts about our ability to distinguish between Phoenician imports and their imitations. See also Feldman 2002, 2006 on the "International Style."

110. Compare Gunter 2009, 160–64, on "artisans and mobility."

111. The most lucid counterargument can be found in Irene Winter's extensive work on the ivories. These appear as part of the collected essays in I. Winter 2010. "Phoenician" art in Etruria: Coldstream 1982.

112. Feldman 2014, 61–63 (here 63), fig. 2.9. Taste: Bourdieu 1984.

113. Vella 2010, 28.

114. That is to say, the situation recalls some of the points made by Papadopoulos 1997's article "Phantom Euboians" and its 2011 successor.

115. W. Anderson 1990. The phrase "incipient Phoenician culture" appears in Gilboa 1999, 1. Bichrome production ends in the ninth century, Cypro-Phoenician black-on-red ends in the seventh, and red slip follows shortly thereafter.

116. See the essays in the special issue of the *Bulletin of the American Schools of Oriental Research,* vol. 279 (1990), edited by Patricia Bikai.

117. Abousamra and Lemaire 2013; Bikai 1978; Bikai et al. 1996; Chéhab 1983–86; Gubel 1983; Sader 1991, 1992.

118. See, e.g., Gubel 1983, 25–26.

119. Aubet 2004, 2010; Aubet et al. 2014.

120. Association of the shrine with Tanit rests precariously on an inscribed ivory plaque from the sanctuary seemingly describing the offering of a statue to Tanit-Aštart (reg. no. 4125): Pritchard 1982; Pritchard 1988, 7–8, figs. 1:1, 4:1. For the date, see Pritchard 1988, 54.

121. Dunand 1937–73. Markoe (2000, 202–3) summarizes the evidence.

122. In the Tale of Wenamun (*ANET* 25–29) Byblos controls the cedar trade, and Byblos is the only Phoenician city-state listed in the approximately contemporary onomasticon of Amenenope: Gardiner 1968, 150, no. 257.

123. Ahiram sarcophagus: Beirut, National Museum 2086 = *KAI* 1; Frankfort 1996, 271–72, figs. 317–18; Markoe 2000, pl. 5 (color image). Storm god: Paris, Musée du Louvre AO 22247; Markoe 2000, 152, fig. 58. Tyre relief: Beirut, National Museum; Gubel 1983, 28–29, fig. 2 (Gubel and others refer to this work incorrectly as a statuette). The Osorkon statue (Paris, Musée du Louvre AO 9502) was purchased along with a fragment of a second statue. The Phoenician inscription on the better preserved statue indicates it was dedicated to Ba'alat Gebal: Markoe 2000, 37, fig. 3.

124. Many of the al-Bass stelai were lost to looting: Sader 2005b, 15–16.

125. Similar stelai were found at 'Achziv, a site with ties to Tyre: Dixon 2013, 71–74; Sader 2005b, 16. Dixon (2013, conclusions summarized on 568–70) has shown that mortuary practices were varied in all classes before the Persian period.

126. Curvers and Stuart 2004; Élayi and Sayegh 1998, 2000.

127. One figurine was made in limestone. It is not clear that the rectangular foundations next to the deposit were for a temple: Kaoukabani 1973; *Kharayeb*; Oggiano 2015a and b.

128. Dunand 1944–45, 1946–48; Dunand and Saliby 1985; Lembke 2004. The deity honored here is not known, but archaeological evidence has been used to argue for Melqart and, more recently, Eshmun.

129. Nitschke 2007, 56–59.

130. van Dongen 2010, 474–77, contra Markoe 1990b.

131. Sharon 1987, especially 27–28.

132. Discussed in the preceding and following chapters, respectively.

133. Traces of color are found on carved ivories also (Reiche et al. 2013), although, again, the connection to Phoenicia is unclear. A brief summary of monumental painting and painted objects can be found in Amadasi Guzzo 1988.

134. Recent experiments recreating the dying process suggest it was incredibly labor intensive—and produced an apparently permanent stench. Ruscillo (2005) conducted her experiments using *murex trunculus* from Crete. She found that processed wool produces the darkest black-purple. Another recent study is from the Thessaloniki toumba: Veropoulidou et al. 2008.

135. Stucky 1984, 1993a and b most of all.

136. Lembke 2001 and 2004.

137. Especially Élayi 1988b, critiqued in Salles 1991.

138. Jigoulov 2010, reviewed in Martin 2012.

139. Nitschke 2007, 2011, 2015.

140. Stager 2005.

141. Tanner 2003, 116; Vella 2014, 28–29. Of course other factors were in play in the conception of Mediterranean history during this period, notably the gradual weakening of the Ottoman Empire and European colonialism: Held 1997.

142. Peckham 2014, 559.

143. Skinner 2012, 86.

144. Gunter 2009, especially 53–54, 61–70; van Dommelen 1998a, 17–24.

145. van Dongen 2010, 471.

146. Phoenician religion: Brody 1998, 2005; R. Clifford 1990; Peckham 1987; Ribichini 1988.

147. See, conveniently, Markoe 2000, 39.

148. Compare van Dommelen 1998a and b, 2002 regarding Punic identities in Sardinia.

149. Bolender 2010, 11 in reference to time periods but equally applicable in most every case to Phoenician history.

Chapter 4

1. Greek and trans. after A. Godley 1963, with changes.

2. P. Smith et al. 2013; Stager and Wolf 1984; Xella et al. 2013.

3. "Phoenician" was derived apparently from a (vague, etic) regional name with little concern for ethnic or other precision: Prag 2006, 2014; I. Winter 1995. Compare to Frankenstein 1979, 288 quoted in S. Morris 1992, 124; Patzek 1996.

4. In addition to Prag 2006, 2014 and I. Winter 1995: Lipiński 1992; Mazza et al. 1988 (a source book without commentary). Jigoulov 2010, 9–15, outlines the standard approaches. Xella 1995a and b review cuneiform and biblical sources. Scandone 1995 reviews the Egyptian sources.

5. Baslez and Briquel-Chatonnet 2003; Grainger 1991.

6. Because Punic is similar to Tyrian and Sidonian, its relatively large number of inscriptions is critical to our understanding of the language. The inscriptions are collected in the *KAI, ICO,* and *CIS.* An overview can be found in Bonnet and Niehr 2010, 27–35. See *ANET* (passim), Cooke 1903, and Gibson 1982 for English translations.

7. Friedrich et al. 1999.

8. On the dating of Phoenician scripts, see Peckham 1968; Röllig 1983a.

9. Jigoulov (2010, 39–70) surveys the Persian period inscriptions. Dixon (2013, especially 168–87) includes the Persian and Hellenistic funerary inscriptions together.

10. Benz 1972; Israel 1995.

11. Prag (2006, 24–26) and Sznycer (1978) survey the evidence. See also the appendix to Macadam 1993, 341–44. There are a few examples of toponyms as personal names. See Amadasi Guzzo 2013 regarding the translation of *ṣdnm* as "Sidon" not "Sidonian," which I follow throughout this chapter.

12. Paris, Musée du Louvre AO 22368: Caubet et al. 2002, 82–83; Markoe 2000, 117, fig. 34. The main part of the stele was discovered by accident; the lower right-hand corner, which is in Beirut, was excavated by Dunand near the temples.

13. *KAI* 10, trans. after Gibson 1982, 93–99.

14. Disk: Hölbl 1989, especially 325; Ornan 2005a; Vella 2000, 38–39.

15. Vance 1994, 10.

16. As, e.g., on a relief of Xerxes from Persepolis: Shahbazi 1992, fig. 49.

17. As Jigoulov 2010, 46. Further discussion of Egyptian "influence" in Phoenician religion, art, and architecture: Taylor 1993; P. Wagner 1980.

18. Remains of an Achaemenid fortress have been found in Byblos: Jidejian 1968, 93.

19. *KAI* 14, line 18: Gibson 1982, 113. From Byblos itself comes a funerary inscription of an unnamed king, possibly Shiptibaʿal III, that might reference *mdy,* "the Medes" (*KAI* 9, line 3: Cross 1979, 43).

20. Beirut, National Museum = *KAI* 11, trans. Gibson 1982, 99–100. On the funerary practice described here, see Dixon 2013, 178–79. As Azabaʿal's father was not a king, some see signs of dynastic changes at Byblos: Jigoulov 2010, 47–48.

21. Compare the sarcophagus from Sidon now in Paris, Musée du Louvre AO 4969.

22. Istanbul Archaeological Museum 800 = Lembke 2001, 121, no. 1, pl. 17. Trans. of *KAI* 13 after Gibson 1982, 101–5, with minor changes.

23. See also *KAI* 9.

24. Paris, Louvre AO 4806 = Lembke 2001, 121, no. 2, pl. 17.

25. Trans. of *KAI* 14 after Gibson 1982, 105–14, with minor changes.

26. Summaries of the finds from both sites in this period can be found in Stern 2001.

27. See the full commentary in S. Martin 2007, 288–91, though my ideas about the date have since changed. The high chronology was recently advocated in Élayi and Élayi 2004, 600–11. See also Cooke 1903 (low chronology); Galling 1963; Peckham 1968, 78–84; Kelly 1987 (various middle chronologies).

28. However, Dixon (2013, 547–53) points out that while the preservation of his body is remarkable, it does indicate that Sidonian mummification (e.g., leaving the organs within the body cavity) is not identical to the preparation of the body in Egyptian mummification.

29. Some interpret the first line of the inscription as evidence that Eshmunazar died at the age of 14 (as Cooke 1903, 38): *byrḥ bl bšnt ʿsr wʾrbʿ* 14 *lmlky mlk ʾšmnʿzr mlk ṣdnm,* "In the month of Bul, in the fourteenth year of the reign of king Eshmunazar, king of Sidon."

30. Dunand 1970, 1973; Macridy-Bey 1902; Stucky 1984, 1993b, 1997; Stucky et al. 2005.

31. Élayi 2006.

32. Beirut, National Museum: Dunand 1965. Translation after Gibson 1982, 114–16, with minor changes.

33. Nearly one hundred fragments or statues in all: Stucky 1993a, 29–38, 83–92, nos. 98–158 23–35. Nitschke (2007, 146–50) summarizes the scholarship. Cypriot type: Beer 1994.

34. They were found in a canal near the sanctuary: Dunand 1965.

35. As made clear by several copies of a foundation inscription; see *CIS* 4. Eshmunazar II also claimed to have erected a temple at the site in his sarcophagus inscription *KAI* 14.

36. As argued persuasively by Nitschke 2007, 121–24.

37. Stucky 1997, 923; Stucky et al. 2005, 165–66.

38. Problems of chronology in the Eshmun complex are numerous, but I think it is reasonable to date this structure and the adjacent one to the late Persian to Hellenistic periods. To my eyes, the children in the friezes look mid-fourth to later fourth century, and, as pointed out by Nitschke (2007, 128), one female figure has a melon hairstyle (a style that begins only after the mid-fourth century).

39. *KAI* 17 = Bloch-Smith 2014, 190; Doumet-Serhal 1998, 26; Gibson 1982, 116–18. See also Delcor 1983; Gubel 1987, 37–84.

40. Ridgway 1997, 213. Beirut, National Museum 2080.

41. Nitschke 2007, 133–34, contra Stucky 1984. Ridgway (1997, 211–15, pls. 55a–c) concludes that, while the altar's friezes are eclectic, they do not need to be down-dated to the late Hellenistic period.

42. The often tortured attempts to connect the Apollo figure to Eshmun or to the sanctuary are surveyed in Nitschke 2007, 139–42. See also Dunand 1983.

43. Beirut, National Museum 2067. Kawkabani 2003.

44. Vorster 1983, who was aware only of the child statues in the National Museum in Beirut. Now see Bobou 2015.

45. Stucky 1993b, nos. 69–76, 81–92.

46. Vella 2000.

47. Dunand and Duru 1962 (who contest that this site should be associated with the Hammon of Josh 19: 24–31, but see *KAI* 19); Kamlah 2008; Michelau 2014; Nitschke 2011; Renan 1864, 695–749 (the site's first exploration); Vella 2000.

48. Lipiński 1995, 272–73. See Amadasi Guzzo 1991 for a fuller consideration of the meaning of Milk ʿAštart.

49. Colonnaded hall: Dunand and Duru 1962, 29–34, figs. 4–7, pls. 5:1, 12.

50. Dunand and Duru 1962, 143–45, nos. 1–2, M 440 and M 539, pls. 28:1 and 29:4.

51. Nitschke 2011, 95.

52. Dunand and Duru 1962, 145–46, no. 4, M 305, pl. 27:1.

53. Dunand and Duru 1962, 168–69, E 33 and E 34, pl. 67. Pl. 87:1 shows a smaller throne found in Renan's campaign. Its exact findspot is not known.

54. Beirut, National Museum: Doumet-Serhal 1998, no. 25, 171; Dunand and Duru 1962, 156a, M 436, pl. 30.

55. Trans. after Dunand and Duru 1962, 116, M 435, 193, no. 14, pl. 31:1.

56. Such as ʿAmrit. Markoe 1990a discusses the type in Cyprus.

57. Nitschke 2011, 97–98.

58. Clermont-Ganneau and Clermont-Ganneau 1902; Dunand and Duru 1962, 160–67, pls. 38:2, 38:6, 77, 78:1–2, 79, 80:1–2, 81:1, 82:1–2, 84:3, 85:1, 88 bis:1–3. Recently discussed in Annan 2013; Michelau 2014; Nitschke 2011, 98–99.

59. Caubet et al. 2002 (funerary); Doumet-Serhal 1998 (votive); Dunand and Duru 1962, 165–66 (both).

60. Maes 1991; Markoe 2000, 120–21, fig. 35. If we interpret the male figures as priests, we should ask if the female stelai show priestesses: Annan 2013, 54.

61. Stele of Baʿalyaton, Copenhagen, Ny Carlsberg Glyptotek 1835 = Clermont-Ganneau and Clermont-Ganneau 1902 = Dunand and Duru 1962, 160–61, no. 1, 187–88, no. 5, pl. 77.

Inscribed: *z mṣbt skr bʿlytn bn bʿlytn hr[b]*, "this is the commemorative stele of Baʿalyaton son of Baʿalyaton the chief" (Phoenician and trans. after Michelau 2014, 82).

62. Stele of Baʿalshamar, Beirut, National Museum 2072 = Dunand and Duru 1962, 165 no. 9, 194–95, no. 16, pl. 88 bis: 1. Kausia: Saatsoglou-Paliadeli 1993; Michelau 2014, 83, n. 24. Another stele, very fragmentary, also seems to show a male in Greek sacrificial attire: stele of ʿAbdʿa[don?], Paris, Musée du Louvre AO 4402 = Dunand and Duru 1962, 164 no. 3, 190 no. 10, pl. 79:2. Inscribed: *z mṣbt skr šm ʿbdʿ[dn] bn ʿbdrbt ʾ. . n . . ššt . rt .*, "this is the commemorative stele set up by ʿAbdʿa[don?] son of ʿAbdrabat . . ."

63. Translation after Michelau 2014, 82.

64. Beirut, National Museum 2071 and 2075 = Dunand and Duru 1962, 165, nos. 10–11, pl. 88 bis: 2–3.

65. See Oggiano 2015a and b.

66. A commemorative inscription for Diotimos son of Dionysios of Sidon, victor in the chariot race of the Nemean games: Bonnet 2015, 260–65, 342–43. Some believe that this Diotimos is a descendant of Abdalonymos, King of Sidon whose son [. . .]timos is named in a fourth-century dedication on Kos: Habicht 2007; *SEG* 36.758.

67. Paris, Musée du Louvre AO 4827. Trans. of *KAI* 60 and *IG* II–III2, 2946, after Gibson 1982, 148–51, and McLaughlin 2001, 43, with minor changes. In this context "marzeah" seems to mean a festival: Gibson 1982, 149; McLaughlin 2001, 44.

68. Gibson 1982, 148–49.

69. Diopeithes, "obeying Zeus," correlates to *šmʿbʿl*, "Baʿal has heard": Gibson 1982, 150, n. 2.

70. Such as *KAI* 19, line 8, which dates to 222: Gibson 1982, 118–21.

71. Gibson 1982, 150; Lipiński 2004, 171.

72. Boiy 2007, 21, 39; Jigoulov 2010, 64; Lipiński 2004, 171–72; McLaughlin 2001, 43, n. 136.

73. Baslez and Briquel-Chatonnet 2003. Evidence of Phoenician kings ceases by the mid-third century: Grainger 1991, 55–66.

74. *CIS* I, 115, pl. 21:23, no. 120 = *KAI* 54: Stager 2005; Tribulato 2013.

75. I follow the most recent dating in Tribulato 2013, 461.

76. Greek, Phoenician, and trans. after Stager 2005, 429 with minor changes.

77. Stager 2005, 431.

78. Tribulato 2013, 466–70.

79. Tribulato (2013) offers a different, consistently symbolic reading of the imagery that nevertheless notes its use of Athenian (she says "Greek") style with Near Eastern/Levantine meaning.

80. Greek and translation after Tribulato (2013, 463), which I follow because of her extended, careful study of the epigram. Stager (2005, 436) offers a slightly different translation: "I left Phoenicia and I, a body, am buried in this land."

81. Prag 2006, 21–24, 26–28; cf. Edwards 1979, 87–113.

82. See Lipiński 2004, 169–76, for a summary of the evidence.

83. Greek and trans. after Gaselee 1969 with minor changes.

84. Fragments are preserved in Eus. *Praep. evang.*, who was using Porphyry's excerpts (= *FGrHist* 790). Attridge and Oden 1981; Baumgarten 1981; Eissfeldt 1952a and b (regarding the supposed source of Philo's "translation," Sanchuniathon); Millar 1983, 64.

85. E.g., van Dommelen 1998b.

86. Sommer 2010, 115.

87. Hdt. 1.94 says coins were invented in Lydia in the seventh century. The earliest known coins in the Mediterranean are ninety-three electrum pieces that use the Milesian standard found in the excavations of the Temple of Artemis at Ephesos. See Kraay 1964, 1976; Kurke 1999, 6–7; T. Martin 1996; Price 1983; Schaps 2004, 93–110.

88. Carradice 1995, 25.

89. The Laureion mines were opened under Peisistratos, but only later was a major new vein discovered.

90. Arist. *Av.* 1106–8 trans. Kennedy 1883. The question of when the owls were first minted is not settled, but a date in the last quarter of the sixth century is widely accepted: Kraay 1976, 60–63; Kroll and Waggoner 1984. Attending this debate is the question of how much the minting of the owls represented a self-conscious break with the earlier *Wappenmünzen*, a triumph of the middling/polis identity over the earlier tyrants: Shapiro 1993, 223.

91. Imitation Athenian owls were found and produced in many areas, such as Philistia: Gitler and Tal 2006.

92. The coins are consistent after their design is settled in the earliest issues: Shapiro 1993, 218, 223–24; the coin in fig. 6 shows an example of the owl facing left. Shapiro (1993, 224, n. 33) notes one other instance when the owls face left, on a special series of decadrachms issued in 490–486.

93. According to Shapiro (1993, 216–17), the owl becomes an explicit symbol of Athens in the third quarter of the sixth century. In the late sixth century, it becomes synonymous with its sanctuary.

94. Carradice 1995, 40. Although the Laureion mine would close in 413 and minting slowed for a time, the owls were revived in the fourth century. The basic design lasted until around the mid-third century and was reinterpreted in the so-called New Style coins of the second century.

95. Circulation: Kraay 1964, 80–82; 1976, 60–63. Purity: Kurke 1999, 302–3.

96. Kurke 1999, 311–12.

97. Jigoulov 2010, 71–73.

98. Carradice 1987.

99. Only folk etymology connects Darius to the coinage's name, however: Alram 1994.

100. Wallinga 1987, 71–72.

101. Jigoulov 2010, 101.

102. Schaps 2004, 106.

103. Other cities followed, although their mints are much less well known: Élayi and Élayi 1993, 11–13. The governor of the Transeuphrates, it is worth noting, did not mint coins as did the governors of Samaria and Judea. The so-called Mazday issues seem to be the exception. The following discussion of Phoenician coinage is much indebted to the close study of Jigoulov 2010, 71–112.

104. Élayi and Élayi 2009, 330, 334, no. 61.

105. Élayi and Élayi 1993, 386; Jigoulov 2010, 107.

106. Jigoulov 2010, 74. Tyre, for example, also minted ⅛ Attic drachms and Attic didrachms: Jigoulov 2010, 97. Arwad standard: Betlyon 1982 contra Millar 1983, 67–68. Byblos minted some of its earliest coins on the Attic standard; subsequent issues used the Phoenician standard. Only one early Byblian coin minted on the Attic standard was known to Betlyon (1982, 13–14, 52–59, 86–88, 111–13, 138).

107. According to Xen. *An.* 1.3.21, a daric equaled a month's pay for standard infantry in the Persian army.

108. Dusinberre 2013, 72; Wallinga 1987, 72.

109. Kurke 1999; I. Morris 1996, 1997.

110. Briant 2002, 214; Carradice 1987.

111. Kurke 1999, 304, n. 11.

112. On these points, see Kurke 1999, 12, 47.

113. Gubel 1992, 1993, the latter critiqued in Jigoulov 2010, 61–63.

114. Jigoulov 2010, 76–78.

115. Jigoulov 2010, 79–82.

116. Overviews of Sidonian coinage: Betlyon 1982; Élayi and Élayi 2004; Jigoulov 2010, 82–97.

117. Jigoulov 2010, 101. Although surely more coins will turn up with further excavation, we cannot mistake the lack of evidence as only an accident of preservation. It appears that Persian imperial coinage did not circulate in this area.

118. Alram 1994; Carradice 1987.

119. *IG* II2 141; Rhodes and Osborne 1993, 86–91. See Nitschke 2007, 86–90, concerning 'Abdaštart's modern epithet "Philhellene."

120. Diod. Sic. 16.43; Grainger 1991, 26–30.

121. Diod. Sic. 16.40–46. In his description of the "Tennes Rebellion," Diod. Sic. 16.41.1 describes Tripolis as the seat of a pan-Phoenician council including, apparently, Arwad, Sidon, and Tyre. Later, in 16.44.6, Diodoros mentions another pan-Phoenician meeting. Maier (1994, 323 with bibliography) is reluctant to see the latter as a standing assembly and prefers instead the idea that they were "ad hoc delegations formed in an emergency." A similar interpretation may suit the *presbeis* of Tyre (Arr. *Anab.* 2.15.6–7). Others disagree: Markoe 2000, 87. As did the "Satraps' Revolt" of 366–360 (Weiskopf 1989), the "Tennes Rebellion" extended beyond Phoenicia to include Cyprus. For the possible involvement of Judah in the latter revolt, see Barag 1966.

122. Jigoulov 2010, 85.

123. Dusinberre 2013, 72–76, fig. 41.

124. On the use of Achaemenid motifs on other coinage: Gitler 2000.

125. Élayi and Élayi 2009; Hill 1910, 126–43; Jigoulov 2010, 97–98.

126. Élayi and Élayi 2009, 259 and 264; Gubel 1992, pl. 4.

127. Nitschke 2013, 261–64.

128. Nitschke 2013, 264.

129. Élayi and Élayi 2009, 253–58; Jigoulov 2010, 98.

130. There is, of course, a good deal of variation in the execution of these features. The major change in the representation of the owl comes with the change in standard in the fourth century. These later owls are more stylized: Élayi and Élayi 2009, 257.

131. Sometimes the hieroglyphs have small ear tufts. Owl hieroglyphs have several variations, with some facing left, and so on.

132. Élayi and Élayi 2009, 258 gathers the sources. The dolphin might also be an appropriation: Jigoulov 2010, 98.

133. Schmitz 2009.

134. See, conveniently, *ANET*, fig. 160.

135. And on one stele showing El from Egypt: Élayi and Élayi 2009, 258.

136. Boardman 2003, 39–42, pls. 7–8, 50; Gubel 1992, pl. 2:4–6. They appear also on seals as attributes of deities, such as Osiris. Note that on some Tyrian coins, the position of the crook and flail is mirrored (see, e.g., Élayi and Élayi 2009, pl. 15; see also pl. 25:808, where the crook appears in the field and without the flail).

137. The silver owls were not the only Athenian owls to appear in fifth-century Phoenicia. Imports of owl skyphoi are well documented at least in southern Phoenicia, where archaeologists have much more frequently reached fifth-century levels than on the mainland. The type dates to the middle quarters of that century, just when the mainland cities began minting coins: *Agora* 12, 86–87; *Agora* 30, 63–64 with extensive references; F. Johnson 1955; Stewart and Martin 2005, 83.

138. The closest natural corollaries to the Tyrian owl are the eagle owl (cf. Ps 102:7a, Isa 34:11, Zeph 2:14), long-eared owl, scops owl (*Otus scops* or *Otus brucei*), and brown fish owl

(*Ketupa zeylonensis*). All have ear tufts and are native to this region. See Gilbert 2002, 67, table 1.2, cited in Schmitz 2009, 53–54, for a complete list of owls inhabiting this area. Élayi and Élayi (2009, 254–55) present a slightly more narrow and literal interpretation of the Tyrian owl species than mine. Athena's owl is inspired by the *Athene noctua,* or little owl.

139. Élayi and Élayi 2009, 255.

140. Élayi and Élayi 2009, 330–34. Byblos's navy is not mentioned in Herodotos, so it usually assumed to have none at this time. Diod. Sic. 11.71 and Thuc. 1.110 (the only Phoenician victory recorded in these sources) discuss the suppression of the revolt of Inaros in Egypt in which the Phoenician fleet clashed with the Athenian one led by Kimon. The number of Phoenician ships in the Persian navy, again according to Greek sources, ranged between eighty and three hundred ships: Élayi and Élayi 2009, 333, following, e.g., Hdt. 7.89.1. The number of participants from Phoenicia might have been far greater at any given time if Wallinga (1987, 70) is correct that Phoenicians constituted the majority of rowers early on. The size of the Persian fleet reached its peak before 480 with twelve hundred triremes: Hdt. 7.89.1; Diod. Sic. 11.3.7.

141. Acquaro 1988, 466.

142. See Briant 2002, 487–88.

143. A pre-Roman estimate derived from the analysis of its bedrock: Markoe 2000, 68.

144. Boyes 2012, 42. The dispute is described in Strabo 16.2.22.

145. Hill 1910, 293, no. 488, pl. 35:1. Discussed in terms of identity in Herbert 2003, 323.

146. Hill 1910, 277, no. 409, pl. 33:6; 266, no. 447; 284, no. 440, pl. 34:5; 290, no. 470; pl. 44:8.

147. M. Scott 2010.

148. Which differs in important ways from the economic status of Phoenicia under the Assyrians: Elat 1991.

149. Ray 1987, 79 quoted in Manning 2010, 25. This did not prevent periodic revolts in Egypt either, of course.

150. Renfrew 1986, 7–8.

151. M. Miller (1997, 251–56) argues that although these "Perserie" were initially the concern of the elite including the state, they were downgraded and "democratized" by the Peloponnesian Wars.

152. The sharp divide between the Archaic and Classical periods had already been challenged by Snodgrass (1980), and I. Morris (2000) has explored this idea more recently in some depth.

153. Quinn 2005, 403.

154. Ca. 365–350 several city-states begin minting coins on the Attic standard, including Sidon, Arwad, and Tyre (the precise date of Tyre's shift is disputed). Arwad's abandonment of the Persian standard in favor of the Attic is brief also.

155. Aubet 1993. Stager and Wolff (1984) explore the connections between population increase and child sacrifice in the period called, in the tophet excavations, Tanit II.

156. The Ma'agen Michael shipwreck of ca. 400 illustrates this point well. According to its excavators, the ship was constructed at Karystos, Euboea, and was heavy with Cypriot material—pottery vessels and various raw building materials such as rocks and clay—when it ran aground near Tel Dor: Linder and Kahanov 2003.

157. Summarized in van Alfen 2002, 316–18. A possible alternate source of timber for Greeks is Rough Cilicia, a region with many geographical parallels to mainland Phoenicia: Blanton 2000, especially 7. Cf. Clark 2005, which focuses on the cultural aspects of exchange.

158. van Alfen 2002, 292. Van Alfen offers the data lacking in the otherwise provocative 1993 essay by Sherratt and Sherratt.

159. van Alfen 2002, table 1.

160. van Alfen 2002, 277.

161. It can be difficult to distinguish cause and effect: Sherratt and Sherratt 1993.

162. As was suggested already in Sherratt and Sherratt 1991.

Chapter 5

1. Grainger 1991, 51, cited in Nitschke 2011, 87.

2. Coombes and Brah 2000, 1.

3. As several scholars have argued (Dietler and López-Ruiz 2009; Stein 2005), it is not necessary to restrict the use of these theories to scenarios that are unambiguously colonial. Rather, the colonial encounter describes a new proximity resulting from sustained contact between people previously geographically separated. It is understood as a cross-cultural phenomenon. Stein 2005, 1–3, discusses the terminology.

4. Portions of this chapter draw on two essays written for other contexts: S. Martin 2014b and a forthcoming essay in *Theoretical Approaches to the Archaeology of Ancient Greece*, edited by Lisa Nevett.

5. The critical texts concerning Seleukia and Babylonia are Sherwin-White and Kuhrt 1993 and Mairs 2014, respectively. Manning (2010, 49–54) offers a judicious overview of colonialism and Ptolemaic Egypt.

6. Turfa and Steinmayer 1999.

7. Wescoat 1989.

8. Antonaccio 2003, 65. Ancient sources sometimes point out the decadence of the western Greeks, e.g., Polyb. 8.37. Paestum has, however, long been an accepted part of discussion of Greek architecture.

9. Gandhi 1998; R. J. C. Young 2001, 2003. Hodos (2006) takes a practical approach. Malkin (2004) argues that Greek history has something to offer to postcolonialism as well.

10. See Barrett 2011; Knapp 2008; Langin-Hooper 2007, 2013a and b; van Dommelen 1998a, 2005, 2006, 2011. Receptivity and reciprocity have had some traction in recent studies of Cypriot art and archaeology. Sometimes the focus is on hybridity, as in an article by Derek Counts that seeks to remove from the Master of the Lion iconography "the baggage of culturally defined labels": Counts 2008: 23; cf. J. Gordon 2012. Reciprocity has been a major theme in literary and social study of Greece: Dougherty and Kurke 2003; Gill et al. 1998; M. Miller 1997.

11. Champion 1990 cited in Bolender 2010, 3. Beck et al. (2007) and Bolender (2010) distinguish the history of events from what they call, after Sewell (1996a and b, 2005), "eventful archaeology."

12. The critical essay is Spivak 1988a; see now R. Morris 2010. Gramsci's subaltern: M. Green 2002. The most famous post-Gramscian scholar is Stuart Hall, who is known especially for his reception theory of encoding/decoding (S. Hall 1973).

13. Kuhrt and Sherwin-White 1987; Sherwin-White and Kuhrt 1993.

14. Network theory is another: Knappett 2013; Latour 2005.

15. Bhabha 1994 as discussed in Antonaccio 2003, 59–61.

16. The bibliography on hybridity is immense. Helpful introductions can be found in Burke 2009; Stockhammer 2012; Werbner and Modood 1997; R. J. C. Young 1995. "Creolization" and "mestizaje" are popular, too. Although some believe these terms have little place in the discussion of material culture, both "creole" and "mestizo" were used in social and racial ways before being employed in linguistics and language: compare Antonaccio 2003, 60; Fabre 2002; J. Webster 2001. "Syncretism" (Plut. *Mor.* 2.490b) is another used, yet fraught, term. C. Stewart 1999 argues that it is nonetheless useful.

17. Recently: Çakmak 2009; Kouremenos et al. 2011; Langin-Hooper 2013a (critical); Nitschke 2007.

18. Warren 1884 offers a fascinating snapshot of late nineteenth-century scholarship's etymologies of the term.

19. Hybrid animals in Greek art: Padgett 2003.

20. Antonaccio 2003, 60.

21. R. J. C. Young 1995, 9.

22. C. Stewart 1999, 40.

23. Papastergiadis 1997.

24. Coombes and Brah 2000, 2.

25. Stockhammer 2012, 46.

26. But see Antonaccio 2009 for hybridity between peers.

27. Stockhammer 2013, 12–14.

28. See the many examples of "purely" and "wholly" Greek in Spier 1992 (gems) or Boardman 1967, 108 (borrowings from the East).

29. C. Stewart 1999, 55.

30. Langin-Hooper 2013a, 109.

31. Moreiras 1999, 374, my emphasis, regarding gender, ethnicity, and other essentializing categories that hybridity aims to upend. Feldman 2006, 63, makes a similar point.

32. Jiménez outlines these concerns, as here (2011, 114): "The problem of seeing hybridity as a result of contacts in multicultural scenarios is that it reproduces the creation of a classificatory grid that is closely linked to the notion of cultural purity."

33. Latour 2005; Said 1993, xxv.

34. As Manning 2010, 3.

35. C. Stewart 1999, 56.

36. Millar 1983 is the key essay.

37. R. J. C. Young 1995, 25.

38. Istanbul, Archaeological Museum 370. The main publications are Hamdi Bey and Reinach 1892; Schefold 1968, with photographs by Max Seidel; and the monograph by von Gräve = von Graeve 1970. Note the reviews: Ridgway 1969 (on Schefold) and Havelock 1972 (on von Graeve 1970). See also Charbonneaux et al. 1973, 237, figs. 248–50; Ferron 1993; Ridgway 1990, 37–45; A. Stewart 1993, 294–306; F. Winter 1912.

39. The cemetery at 'Ain al-Hilweh, "sweet water spring," produced a large number of anthropoid sarcophagi and is accordingly sometimes interpreted as a royal nekropolis, too. (The name 'Ain al-Hilweh is now also used for the largest Palestinian refugee site in Lebanon.)

40. Each has at least one monograph, the most recent being Fleischer and Schiele 1983 (Mourning Women); Kleemann 1958 (Satrap); Langer-Karrenbrock 2000 (Lycian, a publication of her 1990 Ph.D. thesis); Schmidt-Dounas 1985 (Lycian). Ferron 1993 and Houser 1998 discuss all four, although Houser's focus is the Alexander Sarcophagus.

41. Matters of chronology are discussed in detail in Ferron 1993, 250–61, and Ridgway 1997, 173–74.

42. A. Stewart 1990, 171, 182, 193–95, figs. 466–67, 539, 588–94.

43. Kjeldsen and Zahle 1975; Özer (2014); Stucky 1993a. See also: Childs 1978.

44. Three from Amathos and one each from Golgoi and Soli. All are presented alongside the Sidonian examples in Ferron 1993.

45. Nitschke 2007, 101.

46. The chronology of the Sidonian kings is debated. The date of Ba'alshillem's dynasty depends in part on how the dedication for his son at the Eshmun sanctuary at Bostan esh-Sheikh is dated (see Figure 27). According to Élayi's latest calculations, the Ba'alshillem dynasty arose in ca. 450 (Élayi 2006; see also Dunand 1975–76). Gibson (1982, 114–15) down-dates the Ba'alshillem inscription to ca. 400. A late fifth-century date for the Satrap sarcophagus could fit either scenario.

47. Compare to R. Smith (1981, here 29), who argues that Italian portraits were made by Greek artists and that, indeed, there were "*no* top Roman artists or portraitists."

48. As Houser 1998.

49. Comprehensive treatment of sources and scholarship can be found in A. Stewart 1993, 290–306, 422–23, figs. 101–6 (Kos inscription: 296, n. 11 = *SEG* 36.758). Brief, updated remarks can be found in A. Stewart 2014, 258–60, fig. 155.

50. The argument in favor of display depends on Anatolian and Egyptian practices (A. Stewart 1993, 298), although Achaemenid tombs and the tombs at 'Amrit are better comparanda. Other Phoenician evidence is underused in this discussion. The image on the Kerameikos bilingual stele shows the display of the body, and a Hellenistic relief from Tyre (Beirut, National Museum 22544) shows an anthropoid sarcophagus likewise laid out on a bier: Lembke 2001, 54; Stager 2005, 435.

51. Portraits: A. Stewart 1993, 304; von Graeve 1970, 134–36; F. Winter 1912. A. Stewart (1993, 306) suggests that the Herakles coins relate to the battle-scene Alexander, but I find them similar to other figures as well.

52. A. Stewart 1993, 130–50, lays out the different arguments concerning the mosaic and the painting.

53. A. Stewart 1993, 299–300.

54. A. Stewart 1993, 305. The earliest example of the type is on the Athenian treasury at Delphi of ca. 490.

55. Biographical/historical readings of varying degree: Heckel 2006; Messerschmidt 1989; Pollitt 1986, 38–45; A. Stewart 1990, 193–95; A. Stewart 1993, 294–306; von Graeve 1970. Charbonneaux et al. 1973, 237, and Ridgway 1990, 37–45 are more skeptical.

56. As Charbonneaux et al. 1973, 237: "The influence of historical painting, for example the Alexander mosaic . . . will not suffice to explain this far-reaching change of mood and attitude."

57. von Graeve (1970, 138–42) made this association.

58. von Graeve 1970, 127–28.

59. Much of which has now faded: Brinkmann 2007b; Piening 2007.

60. Nitschke 2007, 134. Meander moldings are rare in this period, yet they are on the Alexander Sarcophagus and the other tombs found with it as well as the "tribune." Others have tied the altar to the Mourning Women sarcophagus: Ferron 1993, 250–61; Stucky 1984.

61. Although battle scenes are commonplace in some Near Eastern art, there is no evidence of them at this time in Phoenicia. The terms "Greek" and "Persian" are common names used to signal typical Greek artistic conventions: chiton, chlamys, and nudity as Hellenic, trousers (*anaxyrides* in Greek) and the felt hat (*tiara*) as Persian; cf. Hdt. 7.61–62.

62. Cf. Euphronios's krater of 510–500 showing Amazons dressed as hoplites and in patterned trousers, Arezzo, Museo Civico 1465 = *LIMC* "Amazones" no. 64.

63. Brinkmann 2007d, figs. 284–87, 296–97. Compare to another painted shield held by a Greek, figs. 299–300.

64. Frankfort 1996, figs. 122, 346, 353, 392–93; cf. 441.

65. Frel 1971 (Ionian, Rhodian); Pollitt 1986, 43, and T. Webster 1966, 38 (Attic, "post-Praxitelean"); A. Stewart 1993, 295 (Attic, Skopas).

66. E.g., Messerschmidt 1989, 82–92.

67. Schefold 1968, for example, emphasizes the tomb's nonhistorical aspects.

68. Heckel 2006, here 386; A. Stewart 1993, especially 298–306, figs. 101–6. See also von Graeve 1970, 125, n. 30.

69. Phoenicians wear robes in Neo-Assyrian reliefs. See, conveniently, Markoe 2000, 38, fig. 4 (tributary in palace of Ashurnasirpal); 41, fig. 5 (Ithoba'al supervising tribute on the Balawat gates).

70. As von Graeve (1970, 156–57) suggests.

71. M. Miller 1997, 156–65.

72. Some readings misunderstand Alexander's clothing as deliberately Medizing, an adoption of Persian dress following his victory over Darius: e.g., F. Winter 1912, 15, contra von Graeve 1970, 148–49.

73. According to Brinkmann (2007b, 161), the natural color of marble was never used for white, although it appears that the background of the reliefs was not painted.

74. Papalexandrou 2010; W. Davis 2011, part 3: "What Is Cultural About Vision?"

75. Allen 2002, here 218. Double consciousness was first articulated by W. E. B. Du Bois in reference to African Americans in an 1897 issue of the *Atlantic Monthly*, in an essay entitled "Strivings of the Negro People." The now-classic treatment is in Du Bois 1903, "Of Our Spiritual Strivings" (in *The Soul of Black Folk*), which makes reference to "two warring ideals in one dark body." See the collected readings in Du Bois 1996; Gilroy 1993.

76. Strategic essentialism: Spivak 1988b. I have altered her meaning here, and she has since recanted her original idea: Brohi 2014.

77. Moreiras 1999, 398, addresses modern cultural hybridity.

78. See the "fantasy of difference" in Bhabha 1994, 108.

79. Stockhammer 2013, 23.

80. Papadapoulos 1997, 2011; van Dongen 2010.

81. Nederveen Pieterse 2001.

82. In the Mediterranean, Dietler (1998, 2010) and Hodder (especially 2012) are the most frequently cited scholars on the archaeology of entanglement, but their approaches are dissimilar. Dietler is interested in entanglement as a theory of cultural mixture, whereas Hodder focuses on what he calls "human-thing" relationships. Stockhammer 2012 following N. Thomas 1991 makes use of the term "entanglement" as well.

83. C. Stewart 1999, 41.

84. Lipiński 2004, 166–69, here 166.

85. According to Strabo 14.5.2, the commercial slave trade was especially robust. Rauh (1993, 44–46) considers Syrian and Phoenician participation in the slave trade. Delos was attracting foreign businessman from the fourth or third century, but from 167 that activity increased, and the pace of urbanization quickened: Lipiński 2004, 166–69, Zarmakoupi 2013. See Baslez 1987 on Phoenicians in economic centers of the Aegean.

86. Lipiński 2004, 166–67, surveys the evidence.

87. Tang 2005, 177.

88. Rauh 1993.

89. White 2011, xxv. See also Bitterli 1989, 87–108, especially the case study on French missionaries in Canada.

90. Deloria 2006, 15.

91. White 2011, 52.

92. White 2011, 52; compare Burkert 2004, 5. A recent treatment of the idea of borrowing and misunderstanding can be found in Török 2011, 27–40.

93. White 2011, 26.

94. White 2011, 33–34.

95. White 2011, 87, 103.

96. White 2011, 7–10, 25–27.

97. Braudel 1995; Broodbank 2013; Horden and Purcell 2000.

98. Malkin 1994, 2001a, 2002, 2004, 2005a, b, and c, 2011. See also Antonaccio 2013.

99. *SEG* 19, no. 615, dating to the late seventh or early sixth century.

100. Malkin 2005a, 252.

101. Malkin 2005a, 252.

102. White 2011, 14.

103. Such as Deloria 2006.

104. Malkin 2011, 47–48.

105. Malkin 2011, 46.

106. Athens National Museum 3335, 1.32 m without base: Bruneau and Ducat 1983, 72–75, no. 57, figs. 46–48; Bulard 1906; Charbonneaux et al. 1973, 316, 321, fig. 353; Marquardt 1995, 227–36, no. 1, pl. 23: 3–4; Pollitt 1986, 130–31, fig. 138; Ridgway 2000, 147–49; Squire 2011, 109–14, fig. 39, pl. 8; A. Stewart 1990, 226–27, figs. 831, 834. Marquardt (1995, 236–44, nos. 2–11, pls. 24:1–2) collects other Pan-Aphrodite types.

107. *IDelos* 1774 = Ascough et al., no. 5977. Complex originally published by Charles Picard in 1921. Important updates are in Bruneau 1978; Bruneau and Ducat 1983, 174–78, no. 57, figs. 46, 48; Meyer 1988; Trümper 2002.

108. The term "club" comes from Baslez 1977, 210–12.

109. E.g., Stager 2005, especially 429–30. Compare *IDelos* 1519. Lipiński (1995, 116–20; 2004, 168) is cautious about associating Poseidon with any one Phoenician god.

110. As has the Sanctuary of the Syrian Gods on Delos: Stucky 1997, 923; Stucky et al. 2005, 165–66.

111. Tang 2005, especially 63–65, explains the impact of Italian traditions on the urban character of Delos.

112. Trümper 2002.

113. *IDelos* 1789.

114. Bruneau 1978, 171–75; Trümper 2002, especially 318, 327, fig. 32. See also Apicella 2012, 187–88.

115. The altar is dated ca. 130-125. It is inscribed with the name of another Dionysios, this one identifying himself as a son of Sosipater: *IDelos* 1779 = Ascough et al., no. 227.

116. Marcus Minatius: *IDelos* 1520 = Ascough et al., no. 224. Gn. Octavius = *IDelos* 1782 = Ascough et al., no. 228. A man named Philostratos from Ashkelon but with Neapolitan citizenship paid for a portico in the Agora of the Italians in 153/2 or 149/8: *IDelos* 1718 (see also *IDelos* 1719, 1724); Tang 2005, 63–64.

117. Cults to Roma grew up in the eastern Mediterranean as an independent practice, not in emulation of Roman or Italian ones. Evidence of her cult in Italy is lacking before Hadrian: Beard et al. 1998, 158–60.

118. E115 = *IDelos* 1778 = Ascough et al., no. 226: Marcadé 1969, 128–33, pl. 65. The signature was truncated when the original block was moved. The entire inscription above the signature was a later addition: Charles Picard 1921, 59–61. The same Mnaseas paid for a stoa in the club, as well, in ca. 150 = *IDelos* 1773 and another sculpture in the temenos of Dionysos, Hermes, and Pan southwest of the theater that dates to 110/109: Bruneau and Ducat 1983, 249, no. 116c, plan VI. Controversy surrounds the chronology of the Roma cult and the statue. The particular date of Roma's introduction to the complex has little bearing on the interpretation of the Slipper Slapper statue, however. Here I follow Trümper 2002, which has an extensive discussion of the statue and its location; fig. 11 is a drawing of the base.

119. Bruneau 1972, 143–45, no. 40, fig. 38.

120. The statuary, including terracottas, is catalogued in Kreeb 1988, 21–29, 105–19. Marble statues are discussed in Marcadé 1969, 386–96, pls. 25, 43, 50, 53, 59, 62; Charles Picard 1921, 35, 56–62, 67–70, 121–25, figs. 28, 49–53, 58, 60–61, 96, 99–102. Sanders 2001, 44–49, concerns dedicatory inscriptions. Nonnos (*Dion.* books 41–43) writes of the foundation of Beirut with the story of nymph Beroë—who, in one version of the story, is the daughter of Aphrodite and Adonis—and of her wooing by Poseidon and Dionysos.

121. Tang 2005, 55, 56, house DelN26. For bilingualism at Delos, see Adams 2003, 642–86.

122. Tang 2005, 53–55, here 55.

123. E.g., Bruneau 1970, 472.

124. Only the Slipper Slapper was found in this section, however. The other two were found in the peristyle court (Figure 39 "F"): Charles Picard 1921, 123, 124, n. 1.

125. There is evidence of a vermiculatum mosaic in this area, perhaps once signed: Bruneau 1972, 144, 146, nos. 42–43, fig. 40; Charles Picard 1921, 119–20. Colonnettes, architectonic moldings, and colored stucco were also found in the basements: black paneling, fragments of green foliage on a blue ground, and yellow and red courses (Charles Picard 1921, 120–21, fig. 98). The strut between Pan's right leg and Aphrodite's left was painted blue in an effort to have it blend in to its background. My thanks to Adrian Stähli for bringing this information to my attention.

126. *IDelos* 1783 = Ascough et al., no. 225. My translation.

127. Colonnades: *IDelos* 1772, 1785.

128. *IDelos* 1788, 1789.

129. One dedication in the complex was paid in part by Athenians: *IDelos* 1780.

130. Some support comes from the inscription itself, which speaks of Roma's goodwill to the club and to the homeland.

131. Trümper 1998.

132. Havelock 1995; A. Stewart 1990, 177–78, figs. 503–5.

133. E.g., when Pollitt (1986, 130) calls it "technically crude but amusing."

134. Havelock 1995, 56–57, 104–5; Martin 2014b.

135. Rome, Vatican Museums 812, also known as the "Venus Colonna": A. Stewart 1990, 177–78, figs. 503–4. This work is 2.04 m, so another important difference between it and the Slipper Slapper is in its scale.

136. Rome, Capitoline Museum 409: Havelock 1995, 74–80, fig. 18.

137. Seaman 2004, 551–57; A. Stewart 1997, 96–106.

138. Bulard (1906, 611–12) reports other colors that are no longer visible: black to delineate the bark of the tree trunk and a gray-blue line to pick out the contours of the animal skin. The strut once connecting Pan's left arm to Aphrodite was painted "sky blue."

139. A point also noted in Squire 2011, 113.

140. There is a good deal of variety in representations of Pan. In art he can be shown fully as a goat or as a human with diminutive horns or at the stages in between: *LIMC* "Pan" especially "Pan and Aphrodite/Eros." In Plato *Cra.* 408d, he is described as "smooth" in his upper body, rough and caprine below.

141. Squire 2011, 113. Havelock 1995, 56, includes similar comments about Aphrodite's "friendly" reaction. See also Charles Picard 1935, 13–14.

142. Havelock (1995, 56) sees Pan's back leg moving in to caress Aphrodite's ankle.

143. Elderkin (1941) believed the sandal was turned around the wrong way for a good slap. This positioning of the sandal works best from a formal perspective.

144. As *LIMC* "Aphrodite" no. 516. A marble fragment of a hand holding a sandal from Samos thought to date to the second-century CE is more similar: Jantzen and Megow 1977, 189–90, pl. 89. In a bronze statuette from the eastern slope of the Athenian akropolis, Aphrodite stands holding a sandal: Athens National Museum 7406 = *LIMC* "Aphrodite" 62, no. 515 = Marinatos 1923, fig. 1.

145. Budin (2006, 2008) disputes the existence of sacred prostitution in the Mediterranean; compare Ath. 572e.

146. Zernecke 2013 after Charles Picard 1921, 121–22.

147. Fauth 1985–86 offers alternate interpretations of the sandal. In one bilingual inscription from Byblos, Aštart the Great Goddess and Ba'alat Gebal are presented as equivalents: Bonnet 1996, 21.

148. Bronze statuette of Aphrodite and Eros on a base thought to be from Egypt, second to first c., J. Paul Getty Museum 57.AB.7. See also the Venus of Hinzerath (Rheinisches

Landesmuseum Trier 1935, 107), on which sandals are added in silver. I thank Heather Sharpe for this parallel and for her help identifying the strophion.

149. As Charles Picard 1935, 13 insists. Squire (2011, 114) likewise emphasizes that it is religious, whereas Beard and Henderson (2001, 139–41) want to read the religious and secular aspects separately.

150. Bahrani 1996; Budin 2003; Fitzmyer 1966, 287.

151. Cic. *Nat. D.* 3.42; Hdt. 1.105; Philo *ap.* Eus. *Praep. evang.* 1.10.31. A sober and short overview of the evidence can be found in Bonnet and Pirenne-Delforge 1999, 257–60. Stager (2005, 439–40) offers a more maximal view. Aštart's prominence in Phoenicia: Baurain and Bonnet 1992, 67; Röllig 1992. Associations with Asherah of the sea and Tanit in Canaanite religion: Brody 1998, 26–33. Westward expansion of Ishtar/Aphrodite: Paus. 1.14.7.

152. Ackerman (2013) discusses Phoenician priestesses in the mainland and colonies.

153. Bloch-Smith 2014, 184–85, summarizes the evidence.

154. Curvers and Stuart 2004, 253; Élayi 2010, 166; Élayi and Sayegh 1998, 224; Élayi and Sayegh 2000, 267; Sader 1998, 205.

155. Bloch-Smith (2014, 191) suggests that the peak of Phoenician Aštart worship was in the fifth and fourth centuries and tapered off in the third and second.

156. A. Stewart 1979. This is not to say that the artist of the Slipper Slapper was necessarily Athenian and not Delian. Some propose an "Oriental" sculptor: Moreno 1994, 680–92, fig. 827.

157. Hafner (1954, 73) suggests both portraits were made by the same artist.

158. Kousser 2005, 248.

159. Budin 2004, here 136.

160. E.g., Barrett 2011, 157–87, on "Oriental Aphrodite."

161. Bonnet 1996; Budin 2004; and Bonnet and Pirenne-Delforge 1999 address the goddesses' relationship head on and call for more careful and precise language to describe it. Budin argues that only on Cyprus were Aphrodite and Aštart the same goddess. It is in practice quite difficult to distinguish the iconography of the Near Eastern goddess contra, e.g., Cornelius 2004.

162. Found in Serapieion C. Relationships between Aštart, Aphrodite, and Ishtar are treated in the edited volume Sugimoto 2014. The association of Aštart and Isis is known from the Iron Age, perhaps as early as 700: Abousamra and Lemaire 2013, 156–57. Bordreuil (1998) associates Ba'alat Gebal with Aštart but under the "influence" of Hathor and Isis (compare the Yehawmilk stele, Figure 19). A stele from Memphis (*KAI* 48.2) dated to the second or first century BCE is dedicated to Isis, Aštart, and other gods on behalf of the votary's wife and sons. See also Moyer 2011, 142–207, concerning the introduction of the Egyptian cults to Delos.

163. Harpokrates as the "young" Ba'al-Hammon is known in Hellenistic Carthage: Tang 2005, 101.

164. "Permutation" is taken from the 2013 issue of *Die Welt des Orients* edited by Schmitt and Christian. Bonnet 1996, especially 87–89; Bruneau 1970. Aštart (Palestinian Astarte Ourania) is named in Greek in the dedicatory inscriptions by Ashkelonites *IDelos* 1719 (dedicated by the aforementioned Philostratos) and *IDelos* 2305 (Palestinian Astarte Aphrodite Ourania). See also *IDelos* 2101 and 2132. So-called double deities: Xella 1990.

165. Isis Euploia = *IDelos* 2153. See Barrett 2011, especially 438; Corso 2007, 233–34, n. 34. Phoenician maritime cults: Brody 1998, 2005, 2008; Christian 2013; Raban and Kahanov 2003.

166. The major study is Xella 1991, especially 34–42, for the eastern evidence of the god. See also Bordreuil 1986, 1987; Lipiński 1995, 251–64.

167. While Xella 1991 treats the sources, Pardee's 1993 review points out his inability to resolve the etymological issues fully.

168. Some even go so far as to claim that this god "makes the transition to the images of Pan popular in the Hellenistic period": Hermary and Mertens 2014, 240–42, here 241, nos. 321–25. See also Buchholz 1991.

169. *KAI* 19. Xella (1991, 31–42) claims that references to Ba'al Hammon are not found in the eastern Mediterranean after the sixth century, but this inscription should challenge the idea that the Hammon cult was somehow irrelevant there. It describes the dedication of a portico in the temple of Hammon in the twenty-sixth year of Ptolemy. It is not clear that the Tanit and Hammon cults were connected, however. Bloch-Smith (2014, 187) suggests that the two gods were merely "temple-mates" rather than a pair.

170. Lipiński 1995, 115–16; Renan 1864, 352–53. Bonnet 1991 explores the idea that Tanit is Aštart's "little sister" at Deir el-Qal'a, while noting that their relationship is complex.

171. Brinkmann 2007b, 159.

172. Dillon and Baltes 2013.

173. Contra R. Smith 1981.

174. Dillon and Baltes (2013, 239) after Schultz (2009, 76), the latter concerning sculpture in fourth-century Epidauros.

175. Bhabha 1984 and 1994 treat the confusion of mimesis and mimicry.

176. Prag and Quinn 2013b.

177. An idea borrowed from Paul Crossley with respect to architectural history. From a lecture on "The Myth of the Gothic Cathedral," given on March 7, 2013, in the History of Art & Architecture Department at Boston University.

178. Lembke 2004.

179. E.g., Crimp 1985; Krauss 1986.

Conclusion

1. E.g., Stewart and Martin 2005, 90.

2. Gunter 2009, 62.

3. Rankine 2011, 41.

4. See now Hurwit 2015.

5. Osborne 2010, 242. In practice, in some genres such as gems, it can be difficult or impossible to know who is named, artist or patron, unless an explicit formula is used. Signatures on other genres, including architecture, monumental painting, and metal work are discussed in Hurwit 2015.

6. Osborne 2010 (following Osborne 1996) contra Neer 2002.

7. See Beazley 1989, 54.

8. Tanner 2006, 158, 173–75, 191–200.

9. The interest in artists is clear in the writings of Douris and his contemporary Xenokrates, even if Douris was a "sensational chronicler": Pollitt 1990, 75.

10. As, e.g., Routledge 2013. In the study of Greek art, Rhys Carpenter and Brunilde Ridgway (his student) have written the most pointed critiques of the idea of artistic genius.

11. As Osborne 1996.

12. Original versus copy is the most common subject (Gaifman 2006; Junker and Stähli 2008; Ridgway 1984), but there are also many studies of related topics such as collaboration (Goodlett 1989) and simulation (Vernant 1990).

13. Hurwit 2007a, 273.

14. Tanner 2006, 182–90.

15. Rome, Vatican, Museo Pio-Clementino 1185, thought to date to the first century CE after the bronze by Lysippos of ca. 320. See Isager 1991 on the theme of *origo* in Pliny.

16. Lapatin 2010, 262.

17. Lapatin 2010, 262.

18. I. Morris 2003, 2005.

19. Whitley 2013, 421.

20. Podro 1982, 97.

21. An idea that appealed to Nazis from whose ideologies it can no longer be fully separated, especially when it comes to Greek art: Elsner 2010a, 296–97.

22. Davis 2007; Ma 2013, 298–99, following Davis.

23. Gell 1998, 3; cf. Gell 1995.

24. Thomas's introduction to Gell 1998, viii; I. Winter 2007, 44. See also Porter 2010.

25. Davis 2007.

26. The bibliography is very large. See Bowden 2004; Chua and Elliott 2013; Layton 2003; Osborne and Tanner 2007.

27. See Gell 1998, 10–11.

28. See especially Bal 2002.

29. Rampley 2005; Whitley 2012.

30. Gell 1992.

31. Rood 2010, 46.

32. Also commented on in Prag and Quinn 2013b, 4.

33. As Neer (2005) has argued also for connoisseurship.

34. Antonaccio 2003, 71 invoking the work of Sewell.

35. Mattos 2014, 260.

36. Most recently Bahrani 2013, 516.

37. Cf. Mattos 2014, 261 in reference to Maya, Aztec, and Inca monumental architecture.

38. Spivak 1988b, 15; R. J. C. Young 1990.

39. Similar observations are made by Elsner 2010a, 290.

40. Sewell (1996a, 878) theorizing the Bastille as a series of socially transformative events.

41. Elsner 2010a, 291 made in reference to the study of Greek art.

Works Cited

The abbreviations for all ancient sources follow those used in *The Oxford Classical Dictionary*, third rev. ed.

Abousamra, G. and A. Lemaire. 2013. "Astarte in Tyre According to New Iron Age Funerary Stelae." In *Permutations of Astarte*, ed. R. Schmitt and M. Christian, 153–57. Die Welt des Orients 43. Göttingen: Vandenhoeck und Ruprecht.

Abousamra, G. and A. Lemaire. 2014. *Nouvelles stèles funeraires phéniciennes*. Beirut: Kutub.

Ackerman, S. 2013. "The Mother of Eshmunazor, Priest of Astarte: A Study of Her Cultic Role." In *Permutations of Astarte*, ed. R. Schmitt and M. Christian, 158–78. Die Welt des Orients 43. Göttingen: Vandenhoeck und Ruprecht.

Acquaro, E. 1988. "Coins." In *The Phoenicians*, ed. Sabatino Moscati, 464–73. Milan: Bompiani.

Adam-Veleni, P. and E. Stefani, eds. 2012. *Greeks and Phoenicians at the Mediterranean Crossroads*. Archaeological Museum of Thessaloniki 15. Trans. T. Papakostas. Thessaloniki: Hellenic Ministry of Culture and Tourism.

Adams, J. 2003. *Bilingualism and the Latin Language*. Cambridge: Cambridge University Press.

Agora 12 = Sparkes, B. A. and L. Talcott. 1970. *Black and Plain Pottery of the 6th, 5th and 4th Centuries B.C.* Agora 12. Princeton: American School of Classical Studies at Athens.

Agora 30 = Moore, M. B. 1997. *Attic Red-Figured and White Ground Pottery*. Agora 30. Princeton: American School of Classical Studies at Athens.

Alcock, S. 2002. *Archaeologies of the Greek Past: Landscape, Monuments, and Memories*. Cambridge: Cambridge University Press.

Alcock, S. and R. Osborne, eds. 2012a. *Classical Archaeology*. Second ed. Malden, Mass.: Wiley-Blackwell.

Alcock, S. and R. Osborne. 2012b. "Introduction." In *Classical Archaeology*, ed. S. Alcock and R. Osborne, 1–10. Second ed. Malden, Mass.: Wiley-Blackwell.

Allen, E., Jr. 2002. "Du Boisian Double Consciousness: The Unsustainable Argument." *Massachusetts Review* 43 (2): 217–53.

Alram, M. 1994. "Daric." *Encyclopædia Iranica*, vol. 7, 36–40. London: Routledge and Kegan Paul.

Amadasi Guzzo, M. G. 1988. "Painting." In *The Phoenicians*, ed. S. Moscati, 448–55. Milan: Bompiani.

Amadasi Guzzo, M. G. 1991. "Tanit-ʿŠTRT e Milk-ŠTRT: Ipotesi." *Orientalia* 60: 82–91.

Amadasi Guzzo, M. G. 1995. "Les inscriptions." In *La civilisation phénicienne et punique: Manuel de recherche*, ed. V. Krings, 19–30. Leiden: Brill.

Amadasi Guzzo, M. G. 2013. "'Re dei Sidonii?.'" In *Ritual, Religion and Reason: Studies in the Ancient World in Honour of Paolo Xella*, ed. O. Loretz et al., 257–65. Münster: Ugarit.

Amadasi Guzzo, M. G. and W. Röllig. 1995. "La langue." In *La civilisation phénicienne et punique: Manuel de recherche*, ed. V. Krings, 185–92. Leiden: Brill.

Anderson, B. 2006. *Imagined Communities: Reflections on the Origin and Spread of Nationalism*. Rev. ed. London: Verso.

Anderson, W. 1988. *Sarepta I: The Late Bronze and Iron Age Strata of Area II,Y: The University of Pennsylvania Excavations at Sarafand, Lebanon*. Beirut: Département des publications de l'Université libanese.

Anderson, W. 1990. "The Beginnings of Phoenician Pottery: Vessel Shape, Style, and Ceramic Technology in the Early Phases of the Phoenician Iron Age." *Bulletin of the American Schools of Oriental Research* 279: 35–54.

Andreae, B. 2003. *Antike Bildmosaiken*. Mainz: Philipp von Zabern.

ANET = Pritchard, J. 1969. *Ancient Near Eastern Texts Relating to the Old Testament*. Third ed. Princeton: Princeton University Press.

Annan, B. 2013. "'Parce qu'il a entendu sa voix, qu'il le bénisse': Représentations d'orants et d'officiants dans les sanctuaires hellénistiques d'Oumm el-'Amed (Liban)." *Histoire de l'Art* 73: 39–50.

Anthes, R. 1963. "Affinity and Difference Between Egyptian and Greek Sculpture and Thought in the Seventh and Sixth Centuries B.C." *Proceedings of the American Philosophical Society* 107: 60–81.

Antonaccio, C. 2003. "Hybridity and the Cultures Within Greek Culture." In *The Cultures Within Ancient Greek Culture: Contact, Conflict, Collaboration*, ed. C. Dougherty and L. Kurke, 57–74. Cambridge: Cambridge University Press.

Antonaccio, C. 2009. "(Re)defining Ethnicity: Culture, Material Culture, and Identity." In *Visual Culture and Social Identity in the Ancient Mediterranean*, ed. S. Hales and T. Hodos, 32–53. Cambridge: Cambridge University Press.

Antonaccio, C. 2013. "Networking the Middle Ground? The Greek Diaspora, Tenth to Fifth Century BC." In *Archaeology and Cultural Mixture,* ed. W. van Pelt, 237–51. Archaeological Review from Cambridge 28. Cambridge: Department of Archaeology, University of Cambridge.

Apicella, C. 2012. "Le culte d'Apollon à Sidon ou les modalités d'intégration d'un die étranger." In *Les représentations des dieux des autres*, ed. C. Bonnet, A. Declercq, and I. Slobodzianek, 177–92. Caltanissetta: Sciascia.

Appadurai, A., ed. 1986. *The Social Life of Things: Commodities in Cultural Perspective*. Cambridge: Cambridge University Press.

Aruz, J., S. Graff, and Y. Rakic, eds. 2014. *Assyria to Iberia at the Dawn of the Classical Age*. New York: Metropolitan Museum of Art.

Ascough, R., P. Harland, and J. Kloppenborg. *Associations in the Greco-Roman World*. Accessed May 17, 2016. http://www.philipharland.com/greco-roman-associations/.

Attridge, H. and R. Oden, Jr. 1981. *Philo of Byblos: The Phoenician History*. Washington, D.C.: Catholic Biblical Association of America.

Aubet, M. 1993. *The Phoenicians and the West: Politics, Colonies, and Trade*. Cambridge: Cambridge University Press.

Aubet, M. 2004. *The Phoenician Cemetery of Tyre-al Bass: Excavations 1997–1999*. Beirut: Direction Générale des Antiquités.

Aubet, M. 2010. "The Phoenician Cemetery of Tyre." *Near Eastern Archaeology* 73 (2/3): 144–55.

Aubet, M., F. Nuñez, and L. Trelliso. 2014. *The Phoenician Cemetery of Tyre-al Bass II: Archaeological Seasons, 2002–2005*. Beirut: Direction Générale des Antiquités.

Bahrani, Z. 1996. "The Hellenization of Ishtar: Nudity, Fetishism, and the Production of Cultural Differentiation in Ancient Art." *Oxford Art Journal* 19 (2): 3–16.

Bahrani, Z. 2013. "Regarding Art and Art History." *Art Bulletin* 95 (4): 516–17.

Bailey, D. 2005. *Prehistoric Figurines: Representation and Corporeality in the Neolithic.* London: Routledge.

Bal, M. 2002. *Travelling Concepts in the Humanities: A Rough Guide.* Toronto: University of Toronto Press.

Barag, D. 1966. "The Effects of the Tennes Rebellion on Palestine." *Bulletin of the American Schools of Oriental Research* 183: 6–12.

Barletta, B. 2001. *The Origins of the Greek Architectural Orders.* Cambridge: Cambridge University Press.

Barnett, R. 1967. "Layard's Nimrud Bronzes and Their Inscriptions." *Eretz-Israel* 8: 1*–6*.

Barnett, R. 1974. "The Nimrud Bowls in the British Museum." *Rivista di studi fenici* 2: 11–33.

Barrett, C. 2011. *Egyptianizing Figurines from Delos: A Study in Hellenistic Religion.* Leiden: Brill.

Barry, F. 2011. "A Whiter Shade of Pale: Relative and Absolute White in Roman Sculpture and Architecture." In *Revival and Invention: Sculpture Through Its Material Histories*, ed. S. Clerbois and M. Droth, 31–62. New York: Peter Lang.

Barth, F. 1966. *Models of Social Organization.* London: Royal Anthropological Institute.

Barth, F., ed. 1969. *Ethnic Groups and Boundaries: The Social Organization of Culture Difference. Results of a Symposium Held at the University of Bergen, 23rd to 26th February 1967.* London: Allen and Unwin.

Baslez, M.-F. 1977. *Rechérches sur les conditions de pénétration et de diffusion des religions orientales à Délos (iie–ier s. avant notre ère).* Paris: École normale supérieure de jeunes filles.

Baslez, M.-F. 1987. "Le rôle et la place des Phéniciens dans la vie économique des ports de l'Égée." In *Phoenicia and the East Mediterranean in the First Millennium B.C.*, ed. E. Lipiński, 267–85. Leuven: Peeters.

Baslez, M.-F. and F. Briquel Chatonnet. 2003. "Les Phéniciens dans les royaumes hellénistiques d'Orient (323–55)." In *L'orient méditerranéen de la mort d'Alexandre au 1er siècle avant notre ère*, ed. M.-T. Le Dinahet, 197–212. Nantes: Éditions du Temps.

Basu, P. 2013. "Material Culture: Ancestries and Trajectories in Material Culture Studies." In *Handbook of Sociocultural Anthropology*, ed. J. Carrier and D. Gewertz, 370–90. Oxford: Berg.

Bates, D. and F. Plog. 1991. *Human Adaptive Strategies.* New York: McGraw-Hill.

Baumgarten, A. 1981. *The Phoenician History of Philo of Byblos: A Commentary.* Leiden: E. J. Brill.

Baurain, C. and C. Bonnet. 1992. *Les Phéniciens: Marins des trois continents.* Paris: A. Colin.

Baxandall, M. 1985. *Patterns of Intention: On the Historical Explanation of Pictures.* New Haven: Yale University Press.

Beard, M. 1985. "Reflections on 'Reflections on the Greek Revolution.'" *Archaeological Review from Cambridge* 4 (2): 207–14.

Beard, M. 2003. "Mrs. Arthur Strong, Morelli, and the Troopers of Cortés." In *Ancient Art and Its Historiography*, ed. A. Donohue and M. Fullerton, 148–70. Cambridge: Cambridge University Press.

Beard, M. and J. Henderson. 2001. *Classical Art: From Greece to Rome.* Oxford: Oxford University Press.

Beard, M., J. North, and S. Price. 1998. *Religions of Rome. Vol. 1: A History.* Cambridge: Cambridge University Press.

Beazley, J. 1956 [1928]. *Attic Black-figure Vase-Painters.* Oxford: Clarendon Press.

Beazley, J. 1963 [1942]. *Attic Red-figure Vase-Painters.* Oxford: Clarendon Press.

Beazley, J. 1989. "Potter and Painter in Ancient Athens." In *Greek Vases: Lectures*, ed. D. Kurtz, 39–59. Oxford: Clarendon Press.

Beck, R., Jr., D. Bolender, J. Brown, and T. Earle. 2007. "Eventful Archaeology: The Place of Space in Structural Transformation." *Current Anthropology* 48 (6): 833–60.

Beer, C. 1994. *Temple-Boys: A Study of Cypriote Votive Sculpture.* Jonsered: Paul Åströms.

Benedict, R. 1989 [1934]. *Patterns of Culture.* Boston: Houghton Mifflin.

Benigni, G. 1975. "Il 'segno di Tanit' in Oriente." *Rivista di studi fenici* 3: 17–18.

Benjamin, A., ed. 1988. *Post-structuralist Classics.* London: Routledge.

Bentley, R. and H. Maschner. 2008. "Introduction: On Archaeological Theories." In *Handbook of Archaeological Theories*, ed. R. Bentley, H. Maschner, and C. Chippindale, 1–8. Lanham, Md.: Altamira Press.

Benz, F. 1972. *Personal Names in the Phoenician and Punic Inscriptions: A Catalog, Grammatical Study and Glossary of Elements.* Rome: Biblical Institute Press.

Bérard, C. et al. 1989. *A City of Images: Iconography and Society in Ancient Greece.* Princeton: Princeton University Press.

Berlin, A. 1993. "Italian Cooking Vessels and Cuisine from Tel Anafa." *Israel Exploration Journal* 43: 35–44.

Berlin, A. 1997a. *Tel Anafa II, i, The Hellenistic and Roman Pottery: The Plain Wares.* Ed. S. Herbert. Journal of Roman Archaeology suppl. 10, II, i; Kelsey Museum Fieldwork Series. Ann Arbor: Kelsey Museum.

Berlin, A. 1997b. "Between Large Forces: Palestine in the Hellenistic Period." *Biblical Archaeologist* 60: 2–51.

Berlin, A. 1997c. "From Monarchy to Markets: The Phoenicians in Hellenistic Palestine." *Bulletin of the American Schools of Oriental Research* 306: 75–88.

Berlin, A. 2002. "Romanization and Anti-Romanization in Pre-Revolt Galilee." In *The First Jewish Revolt: Archaeology, History, and Ideology*, ed. A. Berlin and J. Overman, 57–73. London: Routledge.

Berlinerblau, J. 1999. *Heresy in the University: The* Black Athena *Controversy and the Responsibilities of American Intellectuals.* New Brunswick, N.J.: Rutgers University Press.

Bernal, M. 1987. *Black Athena: The Afroasiatic Roots of Classical Civilization. Vol. 1: The Fabrication of Ancient Greece 1785–1985.* New Brunswick, N.J.: Rutgers University Press.

Bernal, M. 1991. *Black Athena: The Afroasiatic Roots of Classical Civilization. Vol. 2: The Archaeological and Documentary Evidence.* New Brunswick, N.J.: Rutgers University Press.

Bernal, M. 1996. Review of *Not Out of Africa: How Afrocentrism Became an Excuse to Teach Myth as History*, by Mary Lefkowitz. *Bryn Mawr Classical Review*, April 5, 1996.

Bernal, M. 2001. *Black Athena Writes Back: Martin Bernal Responds to His Critics*, ed. D. Moore. Durham, N.C.: Duke University Press.

Bernal, M. 2006. *Black Athena: The Afroasiatic Roots of Classical Civilization. Vol. 3: The Linguistic Evidence.* New Brunswick, N.J.: Rutgers University Press.

Bernard, A. and O. Masson. 1957. "Les inscriptions grecques d'Abou-Simbel." *Revue des études grecques* 70: 1–46.

Bertrandy, F. and M. Sznycer. 1987. *Les stèles puniques de Constantine.* Musée du Louvre, Département des antiquités orientales. Paris: Éditions de la Réunion des Musées Nationaux.

Betlyon, J. 1982. *The Coinage and Mints of Phoenicia: The Pre-Alexandrine Period.* Chico, Calif.: Scholars Press.

Bhabha, H. 1984. "Of Mimicry and Man: The Ambivalence of Colonial Discourse." *October* 28: 125–33.

Bhabha, H. 1994. *The Location of Culture.* London: Routledge.

Bianchi, R. 1990. "Egyptian Metal Statuary of the Third Intermediate Period (Circa 1070–656 B.C.), from Its Egyptian Antecedents to Its Samian Examples." In *Small Bronze Sculpture from the Ancient World: Papers Delivered at a Symposium Organized by the Departments of Antiquities and Antiquities Conservation and Held at the J. Paul Getty Museum, March 16–19, 1989*, 61–84. Malibu: J. Paul Getty Museum.

Bichler, R. 1983. *"Hellenismus." Geschichte und Problematik eines Epochenbegriffs*. Darmstadt: Wissenschaftliche Buchgesellschaft.

Bietak, M., ed. 2001. *Archaische griechische Tempel und Altägypten*. Vienna: Österreichischen Akademie der Wissenschaften.

Bikai, P. 1978. *The Pottery of Tyre*. Warmister: Aris and Phillips.

Bikai, P., W. Fulco, and J. Marchand. 1996. *Tyre: The Shrine of Apollo*. Amman: National Press.

Binford, L. 1977. "General Introduction." In *For Theory Building in Archaeology: Essays on Faunal Remains, Aquatic Resources, Spatial Analysis, and Systemic Modeling*, ed. L. Binford, 1–10. New York: Academic Press.

Bintliff, J. 2013. "Archaeological Theory: Back to the Future?" *Antiquity* 87 (338): 1214–16.

Bitterli, U. 1989. *Cultures in Conflict: Encounters Between European and Non-European Cultures, 1492–1800*. Trans. R. Robertson. Stanford: Stanford University Press.

Blanton, R. 2000. *Hellenistic, Roman and Byzantine Settlement Patterns of the Coast Lands of Western Rough Cilicia*. BAR International Series 879. Oxford: Archaeopress.

Bloch-Smith, E. 2014. "Archaeological and Inscriptional Evidence for Phoenician Astarte." In *Transformation of a Goddess: Ishtar—Astarte—Aphrodite*, ed. D. Sugimoto, 167–94. Orbis Biblicus et Orientalis 263. Göttingen: Vandenhoeck und Ruprecht.

Boardman, J. 1967. *Pre-Classical: From Crete to Archaic Greece*. Middlesex: Penguin.

Boardman, J. 1974. *Athenian Black Figure Vases, a Handbook*. London: Thames and Hudson.

Boardman, J. 1982. "Herakles, Theseus, and Amazons." In *The Eye of Greece: Studies in the Art of Athens*, ed. D. Kurtz and B. Sparkes, 1–28. Cambridge: Cambridge University Press.

Boardman, J. 1985a. *Athenian Red Figure Vases: The Archaic Period, a Handbook*. London: Thames and Hudson.

Boardman, J. 1985b. *Greek Sculpture: The Archaic Period, a Handbook*. London: Thames and Hudson.

Boardman, J. 1987. *Greek Sculpture: The Classical Period, a Handbook*. London: Thames and Hudson.

Boardman, J. 1989. *Athenian Red Figure Vases: The Classical Period, a Handbook*. London: Thames and Hudson.

Boardman, J. 1990. "The Lyre-Player Group of Seals: An Encore." *Archäologischer Anzeiger* 1990: 1–17.

Boardman, J. 1993. *Classical Art in Eastern Translation: A Lecture Delivered at the Ashmolean Museum, Oxford, on 27th May, 1993*. Oxford: Leopard's Head Press.

Boardman, J. 1995a. *The Diffusion of Classical Art in Antiquity*. Princeton: Princeton University Press.

Boardman, J. 1995b. *Greek Sculpture: The Late Classical Period and Sculpture in Colonies and Overseas*. London: Thames and Hudson.

Boardman, J. 1998. *Early Greek Vase Painting: 11th–6th Centuries BC, a Handbook*. London: Thames and Hudson.

Boardman, J. 1999 [1964]. *The Greeks Overseas: Their Early Colonies and Trade*. Fourth ed. London: Thames and Hudson.

Boardman, J. 2003. *Classical Phoenician Scarabs: A Catalogue and Study*. Oxford: Archaeopress.

Boardman, J. 2006. "Sources and Models." In *Greek Sculpture: Function, Materials, and Techniques in the Archaic and Classical Periods*, ed. O. Palagia, 1–31. Cambridge: Cambridge University Press.

Boardman, J. 2016 [1964]. *Greek Art*. Fifth ed. London: Thames and Hudson.

Boas, F. 1940. *Race, Language and Culture*. New York: Macmillan.

Bobou, O. 2015. *Children in the Hellenistic World: Statues and Representation*. Oxford: Oxford University Press.

Bohrer, F. 2003. *Orientalism and Visual Culture: Imagining Mesopotamia in Nineteenth-Century Europe.* Cambridge: Cambridge University Press.

Boiy, T. 2007. *Between High and Low: A Chronology of the Early Hellenistic Period.* Frankfurt am Main: Antike.

Bolender, D., ed. 2010. *Eventful Archaeologies: New Approaches to Social Transformation in the Archaeological Record.* Albany: State University of New York Press.

Bondì, S. 2014. "Phoenicity, Punicities." In *The Punic Mediterranean: Identities and Identification from Phoenician Settlement to Roman Rule,* ed. J. Quinn and N. Vella, 58–68. Cambridge: Cambridge University Press.

Bonfante, L. 1989. "Nudity as Costume in Classical Art." *American Journal of Archaeology* 93: 543–70.

Bonfante, L., ed. 2011. *The Barbarians of Ancient Europe: Realities and Interactions.* Cambridge: Cambridge University Press.

Bonnet, C. 1991. "Tinnit, soeur cadette d'Astarté? A propos des cultes de Deir el-Qal'a près de Beyrouth." *Die Welt des Orients* 22: 73–84.

Bonnet, C. 1996. *Astarté: Dossier documentaire et perspectives historiques.* Rome: Consiglio nazionale delle ricerche.

Bonnet, C. 2015. *Les enfants de Cadmos: Le paysage religieux de la Phénicie hellénistique.* Paris: De Boccard.

Bonnet, C., and H. Niehr. 2010. *Religionen in der Umwelt des Alten Testaments 2: Phönizier, Punier, Aramäer.* Stuttgart: Kohlhammer.

Bonnet, C. and V. Pirenne-Delforge. 1999. "Deux déesses en interaction: Astarté et Aphrodite dans le monde égéen." In *Les syncrétismes religieux dans le monde Méditerranéen antique: Actes du Colloque International en l'honneur de Franz Cumont à l'occasion du cinquantième anniversaire de sa mort. Rome, Academia Belgica, 25–27 septembre 1997,* ed. C. Bonnet and A. Motte, 249–73. Brussels: Brepols.

Bordreuil, P. 1986. "Attestations inédites de Melqart, Baal Hammon et Baal Saphon à Tyr." In *Religio Phoenicia: Acta colloquii Namurcensis habiti diebus 14 et 15 mensis Decembris anni 1984,* ed. C. Bonnet, E. Lipiński, and P. Marchetti, 82–86. Namur: Société des études classiques.

Bordreuil, P. 1987. "Tanit du Liban." In *Phoenicia and the East Mediterranean in the First Millennium B.C.: Proceedings of the Conference Held in Leuven from the 14th to the 16th of November 1985,* ed. E. Lipiński, 80–82. Leuven: Peeters.

Bordreuil, P. 1988. "Du Carmel à l'Amanus, notes de toponymie phénicienne II." In *Géographie historique au Proche-Orient: Syrie, phénicie, arabie, grecques, romaines, byzantines. Actes de la table ronde de Valbonne, 16–18 septembre 1985,* ed. P.-L. Gatier, B. Helly, and J.-P. Rey-Coquais, 301–14. Paris: Centre national de la recherche scientifique.

Bourdieu, P. 1977 [1972]. *Outline of a Theory of Practice.* Cambridge: Cambridge University Press.

Bourdieu, P. 1984. *Distinction: A Social Critique of the Judgment of Taste.* Trans. R. Nice. Cambridge, Mass.: Harvard University Press.

Bourdieu, P. 1993. *The Field of Cultural Production.* New York: Columbia University Press.

Bowden, R. 2004. "A Critique of Alfred Gell on *Art and Agency.*" *Oceania* 74 (4): 309–24.

Boyes, P. 2012. "'The King of the Sidonians': Phoenician Ideologies and the Myth of the Kingdom of Tyre-Sidon." *Bulletin of the American Schools of Oriental Research* 365: 33–44.

Brah, A. and A. Coombes, eds. 2000. *Hybridity and Its Discontents: Politics, Science, Culture.* London: Routledge.

Braudel, F. 1995. *The Mediterranean and the Mediterranean World in the Age of Philip II.* Trans. S. Reynolds. Second ed. Berkeley: University of California Press.

Bresson, A. and F. de Callataÿ. 2013. "The Greek Vase Trade: Some Reflections about Scale, Value and Market." *Pottery Markets in the Ancient Greek World (8th–1st centuries B.C.),* ed. A. Tsingarida and D. Viviers, 21–24. Brussels: CReA-Patrimoine.

Briant, P. 2002. *From Cyrus to Alexander: A History of the Persian Empire*. Winona Lake, Ind.: Eisenbrauns.

Briend, J. and J.-B. Humbert. 1980. *Tell Keisan (1971–1976): Une cité phénicienne en Galilée*. Fribourg: Éditions universitaires.

Brinkmann, V. 2007a. "Armor on the Naked Skin? The Early Classical 'Cuirass-Torso' from the Athenian Acropolis." In *Gods in Color: Painted Sculpture of Classical Antiquity*, ed. V. Brinkmann, 100–105. Munich: Stiftung Archäologie Glyptothek Munich.

Brinkmann, V. 2007b. "The Blue Eyes of the Persians: The Colored Sculpture of the Time of Alexander and the Hellenistic Period." In *Gods in Color: Painted Sculpture of Classical Antiquity*, ed. V. Brinkmann, 150–67. Munich: Stiftung Archäologie Glyptothek Munich.

Brinkmann, V. 2007c. "The Coloring of Archaic and Early Classical Sculpture." In *Gods in Color: Painted Sculpture of Classical Antiquity*, ed. V. Brinkmann, 29–44. Munich: Stiftung Archäologie Glyptothek Munich.

Brinkmann, V., ed. 2007d. *Gods in Color: Painted Sculpture of Classical Antiquity*. Munich: Stiftung Archäologie Glyptothek Munich.

Brinkmann, V. 2007e. "The Nude Marble Colossus from Samos." In *Gods in Color: Painted Sculpture of Classical Antiquity, 2008*, ed. V. Brinkmann, 66–69. Munich: Stiftung Archäologie Glyptothek Munich.

Brinkmann, V., U. Koch-Brinkmann, and H. Piening. 2010. "Das Grabmal der Phrasikleia." In *Bunte Götter: Die Farbigkeit antiker Skulptur. Eine Ausstellung der Antikensammlung, Staatliche Museen zu Berlin in Kooperation mit der Liebieghaus-Skulpturensammlung, Frankfurt am Main, und der Stiftung Archäologie, München, im Pergamonmuseum auf der Museumsinsel Berlin, 13. Juli–3. Oktober 2010*, ed. V. Brinkmann, 76–83. Munich: Hirmer.

Brinkmann, V. and O. Primavesi. 2003. *Polychromie der archaischen und frühklassischen Skulptur*. Munich: Biering und Brinkmann.

Brisart, T. 2011. *Un art citoyen: Recherches sur l'orientalisation des artisanats en Grèce proto-archaïque*. Brussels: Académie royale de Belgique.

Brodie, N. et al., eds. 2006. *Archaeology, Cultural Heritage, and the Antiquities Trade*. Gainesville: University Press of Florida.

Brody, A. 1998. *"Each Man Cried Out to His God": The Specialized Religion of Canaanite and Phoenician Seafarers*. Atlanta: Scholars Press.

Brody, A. 2005. "Further Evidence of the Specialized Religion of Phoenician Seafarers." In *Terra Marique: Studies in Art History and Marine Archaeology in Honor of Anna Marguerite McCann on the Receipt of the Gold Medal of the Archaeological Institute of America*, ed. J. Pollini, 177–82. Oxford: Oxbow.

Brody, A. 2008. "The Specialized Religions of Ancient Mediterranean Seafarers." *Religion Compass* 2: 1–11.

Brohi, N. 2014. "Herald Exclusive: In Conversation with Gayatri Spivak." *Dawn News*, December 23, 2014.

Broodbank, C. 2013. *The Making of the Middle Sea: A History of the Mediterranean from the Beginning to the Emergence of the Classical World*. Oxford: Oxford University Press.

Brown, B. and M. Feldman, eds. 2014. *Critical Approaches to Ancient Near Eastern Art*. Boston: De Gruyter.

Brown, S. 1991. *Late Carthaginian Child Sacrifice and Sacrificial Monuments in Their Mediterranean Context*. Sheffield: Sheffield Academic Press.

Brown, S. 1992. "Perspectives on Phoenician Art." *Biblical Archaeologist* 55: 6–24.

Brüggemann, N. 2007. "Kontexte und Funktionen von Kouroi im archaischen Griechenland." In *Kore und Kouros: Weihegaben für die Götter*, ed. M. Meyer and N. Brüggemann, 93–226. Vienna: Phoibos.

Bruneau, P. 1965. *Les lampes*. Exploration archéologique de Délos 26. Paris: De Boccard.

Bruneau, P. 1967. "Le sens de ἀβακίσκοι (Athénée V, 207 C) et l'invention de l'*opus tessella-tum*." *Revue des études grecques* 80: 325–30.

Bruneau, P. 1970. *Recherches sur les cultes de Délos à l'époque hellénistique et à l'époque impériale.* Paris: De Boccard.

Bruneau, P. 1972. *Les mosaïques.* Exploration archéologique de Délos 29. Paris: De Boccard.

Bruneau, P. 1978. "Les cultes de l'établissement des Poseidoniastes de Bérytos à Délos." In *Hommages à Maarten J. Vermaseren: Recueil d'études offert par les auteurs de la série Études préliminaires aux religions orientales dans l'Empire romain à Maarten J. Vermaseren à l'occasion de son soixantième anniversaire le 7 avril 1978,* ed. M. de Boer and T. Edridge, 160–90. Leiden: Brill.

Bruneau, P. 1980. "Un devis de pose de mosaïques: Le papyrus Cairo Zen. 59665." In Στήλη: τόμος εἰς μνήμην Νικολάου Κοντολέοντος, ed. K. Schefold and J. Pouilloux, 134–43. Athens: Σωματείο φίλων του Νικολάου Κοντολέοντος.

Bruneau, P. 1984. "Les mosaïstes antiques avaient-ils des cahiers de modèles?" *Revue archéologique* 2: 241–72.

Bruneau, P. and J. Ducat. 1983. *Guide de Délos.* Third ed. Paris: De Boccard.

Buchanan, P. 1992. "The Election Is About Who We Are." *Vital Speeches of the Day* 58 (23): 712–15.

Buchholz, H.-G. 1991. "Der Gott Hammon und Zeus Ammon auf Zypern." *Mitteilungen des Deutschen Archäologischen Instituts Athenische Abteilung* 106: 85–128.

Buchner, G. and J. Boardman. 1966. "Seals from Ischia and the Lyre-Player Group." *Jahrbuch des Deutschen Archäologischen Instituts* 81: 1–62.

Budin, S. 2003. *The Origin of Aphrodite.* Bethesda, Md.: CDL Press.

Budin, S. 2004. "A Reconsideration of the Aphrodite-Ashtart Syncretism." *Numen* 51 (2): 95–145.

Budin, S. 2006. "Sacred Prostitution in the First Person." In *Prostitutes and Courtesans in the Ancient World,* ed. C. Faraone and L. McClure, 77–92. Madison: University of Wisconsin Press.

Budin, S. 2008. *The Myth of Sacred Prostitution in Antiquity.* New York: Cambridge University Press.

Buhl, M.-L. 1959. "The Late Egyptian Anthropoid Stone Sarcophagi." Ph.D. diss., Københavns universitet.

Buhl, M.-L. 1983. "L'origine des sarcophages anthropoïdes phéniciens en pierre." In *Atti del I congresso internazionale di studi fenici e punici: Roma, 5–10 novembre 1979, Vol. 1,* 199–202. Rome: Consiglio nazionale delle ricerche.

Buitron-Oliver, D. et al. 1992. *The Greek Miracle: Classical Sculpture from the Dawn of Democracy, the Fifth Century B.C.* Washington, D.C.: National Gallery of Art.

Bulard, M. 1906. "Aphrodite, Pan et Éros: Groupe en marbre." *Bulletin de Correspondance Hellénique* 30: 610–31.

Burke, P. 2009. *Cultural Hybridity.* Oxford: Polity Press.

Burkert, W. 1984. *Die orientalisierende Epoche in der griechischen Religion und Literatur.* Heidelberg: Carl Winter.

Burkert, W. 1992. *The Orientalizing Revolution: Near Eastern Influence on Greek Culture in the Early Archaic Age.* Cambridge, Mass.: Harvard University Press.

Burkert, W. 2004. *Babylon, Memphis, Persepolis: Eastern Contexts of Greek Culture.* Cambridge, Mass.: Harvard University Press.

Çakmak, L. 2009. "Mixed Signals: Androgyny, Identity, and Iconography on the Graeco-Phoenician Sealings from Tel Kedesh, Israel." Ph.D. diss., University of Michigan.

Campbell, I. 2003. "The Culture of Culture Contact: Refractions from Polynesia." *Journal of World History* 14 (1): 63–86.

Canfora, L. 1987. *Ellenismo.* Rome: Laterza.

Carpenter, R. 1960. *Greek Sculpture: A Critical Review.* Chicago: University of Chicago Press.

Carradice, I. 1987. "The 'Regal' Coinage of the Persian Empire." In *Coinage and Administration in the Athenian and Persian Empires: The Ninth Oxford Symposium on Coinage and Monetary History*, ed. I. Carradice, 73–95. BAR International Series 343. Oxford: BAR.

Carradice, I. 1995. *Greek Coins.* London: British Museum Press.

Carter, J. 1985. *Greek Ivory-Carving in the Orientalizing and Archaic Periods.* New York: Garland.

Carter, J. and L. Steinberg. 2010. "Kouroi and Statistics." *American Journal of Archaeology* 114 (1): 103–28.

Casson, L. 1995. *Ships and Seamanship in the Ancient World.* Baltimore: Johns Hopkins University Press.

Castriota, D. 1992. *Myth, Ethos, and Actuality: Official Art in Fifth-Century B.C. Athens.* Madison: University of Wisconsin Press.

Caubet, A., É. Fontan, and E. Gubel. 2002. *Art phénicien, la sculpture de tradition phénicienne.* Musée du Louvre, Département des antiquités orientales. Paris: Réunion des musées nationaux.

Champion, T. 1990. "Medieval Archaeology and the Tyranny of the Historical Record." In *From the Baltic to the Black Sea: Studies in Medieval Archaeology*, ed. D. Austin and L. Alcock, 79–95. London: Unwin Hyman.

Charbonneaux, J., R. Martin, and F. Villard. 1973. *Hellenistic Art: 330–50 B.C.* London: Thames and Hudson.

Chéhab, M. 1983–86. *Fouilles de Tyr: La nécropole* 1–3. Bulletin du Musée de Beyrouth 33–36. Paris: Librairie d'Amérique et d'Orient.

Cheng, J. and M. Feldman, eds. 2007. *Ancient Near Eastern Art in Context: Studies in Honor of Irene J. Winter.* Leiden: Brill.

Cerchiai, L. and M. Nava. 2008–9. "Uno scarabeo del 'Lyre-Player Group' da Monte Vetrano (Salerno)." *AION: Annali dell'Istituto Universitario Orientale di Napoli* 15–16: 101–8.

Childs, W. 1978. *The City-Reliefs of Lycia.* Princeton: Princeton University Press.

Chollot, M. 1975. "Étude de deux modèles de barques en terre cuite pêchées en mer." *Cahiers d'archéologie subaquatique* 4: 83–89.

Christian, M. 2013. "Phoenician Maritime Religion: Sailors, Goddess Worship, and the Grotta Regina." In *Permutations of Astarte*, ed. R. Schmitt and M. Christian, 179–205. Die Welt des Orients 43. Göttingen: Vandenhoeck und Ruprecht.

Chua, L. and M. Elliott, eds. 2013. *Distributed Objects: Meaning and Mattering After Alfred Gell.* New York: Berghahn.

Cinquatti, A. 2015. "Question of Style: The Use of Qualitative and Quantitative Methods to Assess the Significance of First Millennium BCE Ivory Carving Traditions." *Altorientalische Forschungen* 42: 46–58.

Cintas, P. 1968–69. "Le signe 'de Tanit': Interprétations d'un symbole." *Archéologie vivante* 1: 4–10.

CIS = 1881–1952. *Corpus Inscriptionum Semiticarum.* Paris: Klincksieck.

Clark, J., ed. 2005. *Archaeological Perspectives on the Transmission and Transformation of Culture in the Eastern Mediterranean.* Oxford: Oxbow.

Clermont-Ganneau, Ch. 1880. *Études d'archéologie orientale: L'imagerie phénicienne et la mythologie iconologique chez les grecs. 1re partie: La coupe phénicienne de Palestrina.* Paris: E. Leroux.

Clermont-Ganneau, Ch. and M. Clermont-Ganneau. 1902. "La stèle phénicienne d'Oumm el-'Aouamid." *Revue archéologique* 40: 200–207.

Clifford, J. 1988. *The Predicament of Culture: Twentieth-Century Ethnography, Literature, and Art.* Cambridge, Mass.: Harvard University Press.

Clifford, R. 1990. "Phoenician Religion." *Bulletin of the American Schools of Oriental Research* 279: 55–64.

Cline, E., A. Yasur-Landau, and N. Goshen. 2011. "New Fragments of Aegean-Style Painted Plaster from Tel Kabri, Israel." *American Journal of Archaeology* 115 (2): 245–61.

Cohen, B., ed. 2000. *Not the Classical Ideal: Athens and the Construction of the Other in Greek Art*. Leiden: Brill.

Coldstream, J. 1982. "Greeks and Phoenicians in the Aegean." In *Phönizier im Westen: Die Beiträge des Internationalen Symposiums über 'Die phönizische Expansion im westlichen Mittelmeerraum' in Köln vom 24. bis 27. April 1979*, ed. H. Niemeyer, 261–75. Mainz: Philipp von Zabern.

Coldstream, J. 1986. *The Originality of Ancient Cypriot Art*. Lecture Series. Nicosia: Cultural Foundation of the Bank of Cyprus.

Coldstream, J. 2003. *Geometric Greece*. Second ed. London: Routledge.

Coleman, J. and C. Walz, eds. 1997. *Greeks and Barbarians: Essays on the Interactions Between Greeks and Non-Greeks in Antiquity and the Consequences for Eurocentrism*. Bethesda, Md.: CDL Press.

Conkey, M. and C. Hastorf, eds. 1990. *The Uses of Style in Archaeology*. Cambridge: Cambridge University Press.

Contenau, G. 1949. *La civilisation phénicienne*. Paris: Payot.

Cook, R. 1959. "Die Bedeutung der bemalten Keramik für den griechischen Handel." *Jahrbuch des Deutschen Archäologischen Instituts* 74: 114–23.

Cook, R. 1960. *Greek Painted Pottery*. London: Methuen.

Cook, R. 1967. "Origins of Greek Sculpture." *Journal of Hellenic Studies* 87: 24–32.

Cook, R. 1972. *Greek Art: Its Development, Character and Influence*. London: Weidenfeld and Nicolson.

Cooke, G. 1903. *A Text-Book of North-Semitic Inscriptions: Moabite, Hebrew, Phoenician, Aramaic, Nabataean, Palmyrene, Jewish*. Oxford: Clarendon.

Coombes, A. and A. Brah. 2000. "Introduction: The Conundrum of 'Mixing.'" In *Hybridity and Its Discontents: Politics, Science, Culture*, ed. A. Brah and A. Coombes, 1–16. London: Routledge.

Cornelius, I. 2004. *The Many Faces of the Goddess: The Iconography of the Syro-Palestinian Goddesses Anat, Astarte, Qedeshet, and Asherah c. 1500–1000 BCE*. Orbis Biblicus et Orientalis 204. Göttingen: Vandenhoeck und Ruprecht.

Corso, A. 2007. *The Art of Praxiteles II: The Mature Years*. Rome: L'erma di Bretschneider.

Counts, D. 2008. "Master of the Lion: Representation and Hybridity in Cypriote Sanctuaries." *American Journal of Archaeology* 112 (1): 3–27.

Courbin, P. 1988 [1982]. *What Is Archaeology? An Essay on the Nature of Archaeological Research*. Trans. P. Bahn. Chicago: University of Chicago Press.

Crielaard, J. 1999. "Early Iron Age Greek Pottery in Cyprus and North Syria: A Consumption-Oriented Approach." In *The Complex Past of Pottery: Production, Circulation and Consumption of Mycenaean and Greek Pottery*, ed. J. Crielaard, V. Stissi, and G. van Wijngaarden, 261–90. Amsterdam: Gieben.

Crimp, D. 1985. "Appropriating Appropriation." In *Theories of Contemporary Art*, ed. R. Hertz, 157–63. Upper Saddle River, N.J.: Prentice Hall.

Croce, B. 1966 [1937]. "History, Chronicle, and Pseudo-History." In *Philosophy, Poetry, History: An Anthology of Essays*, 497–508. Trans. C. Sprigge. London: Oxford University Press.

Cross, F., Jr. 1968. "The Phoenician Inscription from Brazil: A Nineteenth-Century Forgery." *Orientalia* 37 (4): 437–60.

Cross, F., Jr. 1979. "A Recently Published Phoenician Inscription of the Persian Period from Byblos." *Israel Exploration Journal* 29: 40–44.

Crowfoot, J. and G. Crowfoot. 1938. *Early Ivories from Samaria*. London: Palestine Exploration Fund.

Crowfoot, J., G. Crowfoot, and K. Kenyon. 1957. *The Objects from Samaria*. London: Palestine Exploration Fund.

Culican, W. 1976. "Some Phoenician Masks and Other Terracottas." *Berytus* 24: 47–87.

Curtis, J. and J. Reade, eds. 1995. *Art and Empire: Treasures from Assyria in the British Museum*. New York: Metropolitan Museum of Art.

Curvers, H. and B. Stuart. 2004. "Beirut Central District Archaeology Project 1994–2003." In *Decade: A Decade of Archaeology and History in the Lebanon*, ed. C. Doumet-Serhal, 248–65. Beirut: Lebanese British Friends of the National Museum.

Daszewski, W. 1985. *Corpus of Mosaics from Egypt 1: Hellenistic and Early Roman Period*. Mainz: Philipp von Zabern.

Daszewski, W. 1996. "From Hellenistic Polychromy of Sculptures to Roman Mosaics." In *Alexandria and Alexandrianism*, ed. K. Hamma, 141–54. Malibu: J. Paul Getty Museum.

Davis, W. 1981. "Egypt, Samos, and the Archaic Style in Greek Sculpture." *Journal of Egyptian Archaeology* 67: 61–81.

Davis, W. 2007. "Abducting the Agency of Art." In *Art's Agency and Art History*, ed. R. Osborne and J. Tanner, 199–219. Oxford: Blackwell.

Davis, W. 2011. *A General Theory of Visual Culture*. Princeton: Princeton University Press.

Dee, J. 2004. "Black Odysseus, White Caesar: When Did 'White People' Become 'White'?" *Classical Journal* 99: 157–67.

de Grummond, N., ed. 1996. *Encyclopedia of the History of Classical Archaeology*. Westport, Conn.: Greenwood Press.

Delcor, M. 1983. "Les trônes d'Astarté." In *Atti del I congresso internazionale di studi fenici e punici: Roma, 5–10 novembre 1979*, 777–87. Rome: Consiglio nazionale delle ricerche.

Deloria, P. 2006. "What Is the Middle Ground, Anyway?" *William and Mary Quarterly* 63 (1): 15–22.

Demand, N. 2006. *A History of Ancient Greece in Its Mediterranean Context*. Cornwall-on-Hudson, N.Y.: Sloan.

Demetriou, D. 2012. *Negotiating Identity in the Ancient Mediterranean: The Archaic and Classical Greek Multiethnic Emporia*. Cambridge: Cambridge University Press.

Déonna, W. 1909. *Les "Apollons archaïques": Étude sur le type masculin de la statuaire greque du VIe siècle avant notre ère*. Geneva: Georg.

Dietler, M. 1998. "Consumption, Agency, and Cultural Entanglement: Theoretical Implications of a Mediterranean Colonial Encounter." In *Studies in Culture Contact: Interaction, Culture Change, and Archaeology*, ed. J. Cusick, 288–315. Carbondale: Southern Illinois University Press.

Dietler, M. 2005. *Consumption and Colonial Encounters in the Rhône Basin of France: A Study of Early Iron Age Political Economy*. Lattes: Association pour le développement de l'archéologie en Languedoc-Roussillon.

Dietler, M. 2010. *Archaeologies of Colonialism: Consumption, Entanglement, and Violence in Ancient Mediterranean France*. Berkeley: University of California Press.

Dietler, M. and C. López-Ruiz, eds. 2009. *Colonial Encounters in Ancient Iberia: Phoenician, Greek, and Indigenous Relations*. Chicago: University of Chicago Press.

Dillon, S. and E. Baltes. 2013. "Honorific Practices and the Politics of Space on Hellenistic Delos: Portrait Statue Monuments Along the Dromos." *American Journal of Archaeology* 117 (2): 207–46.

Dixon, H. 2013. "Phoenician Mortuary Practice in the Iron Age I–III (ca. 1200–ca. 300 BCE) Levantine 'Homeland.'" Ph.D. diss., University of Michigan.

Dizionario enciclopedico della civiltà fenicia: http://www.decf-cnr.org/.

Doak, B. 2015. *Phoenician Aniconism in Its Mediterranean and Ancient Near Eastern Contexts.* Atlanta: SBL Press.

Donahue, A. 2013. "History and the Historian of Classical Art." *Journal of Art Historiography* 9: 1–19.

Donahue, A. 2015. "The Historiography of Greek and Roman Art and Architecture." In *Oxford Handbook of Greek and Roman Art and Architecture,* ed. C. Marconi, 440–54. Oxford: Oxford University Press.

Donahue, A. and M. Fullerton, eds. 2003. *Ancient Art and Its Historiography.* Cambridge: Cambridge University Press.

Donderer, M. 1989. *Die Mosaizisten der Antike und ihre wirtschaftliche und soziale Stellung: Eine Quellenstudie.* Erlangen: Universitätsbund.

Donderer, M. 2008. *Die Mosaizisten der Antike II: Epigraphische Quellen–Neufunde und Nachträge.* Erlangen: Universitätsbund Erlangen-Nürnberg.

D'Onofrio, A. 2012. "*Kouroi* e opliti: Sulle tracce della *charis* maschile." In *L'olpe Chigi: Storia di un agalma, Atti del convegno internazionale, Salerno 3–4 giugno 2010,* ed. E. Mugione (curator) with A. Benincasa, 135–49. Paestum (Salerno): Pandemos.

Dothan, M. 1974. "A Sign of Tanit from Tel 'Akko." *Israel Exploration Journal* 24: 44–49.

Dougherty, C. and L. Kurke, eds. 2003. *The Cultures Within Ancient Greek Culture: Contact, Conflict, Collaboration.* Cambridge: Cambridge University Press.

Doumet-Serhal, C., ed. 1998. *Stones and Creed: 100 Artefacts from Lebanon's Antiquity.* London: Lebanese British Friends of the National Museum.

Doumet-Serhal, C. 2013. *Sidon: 15 Years of Excavations.* Beirut: Lebanese British Friends of the National Museum.

Dover, K. 1978. *Greek Homosexuality.* Cambridge, Mass.: Harvard University Press.

Droysen, J. 1877. *Geschichte des Hellenismus.* Gotha: F. A. Perthes.

Du Bois, W. 1996. *The Oxford W. E. B. Du Bois Reader.* Ed. E. Sundquist. New York: Oxford University Press.

Ducat, J. 1971. *Les kouroi du Ptoion: Le sanctuaire d'Apollon Ptoieus à l'époque archaïque.* Paris: De Boccard.

Dunand, M. 1937–73. *Fouilles de Byblos.* Paris: P. Geuthner.

Dunand, M. 1944–45. "Les sculptures de la favissa du temple d'Amrit." *Bulletin du Musée de Beyrouth* 7: 99–107.

Dunand, M. 1946–48. "Les sculptures de la favissa du temple d'Amrit (suite)." *Bulletin du Musée de Beyrouth* 8: 81–107.

Dunand, M. 1965. "Nouvelles inscriptions phéniciennes du temple d'Echmoun à Bostan ech-Cheikh, près Sidon." *Bulletin du Musée de Beyrouth* 18: 105–9.

Dunand, M. 1970. "La statuaire de la favissa du temple d'Echmoun à Sidon." In *Archäologie und Altes Testament, Festschrift für Kurt Galling,* ed. A. Kuschke and E. Kutsch, 61–67. Tübingen: Mohr.

Dunand, M. 1973. "Le temple d'Echmoun à Sidon: Essai de chronologie." *Bulletin du Musée de Beyrouth* 26: 7–25.

Dunand, M. 1975–76. "Les rois de Sidon au temps des Perses." *Mélanges de l'Université Saint-Joseph* 49: 489–500.

Dunand, M. 1983. "L'iconographie d'Echmoun dans son temple sidonien." In *Atti del I congresso internazionale di studi fenici e punici: Roma, 5–10 novembre 1979,* 515–19. Rome: Consiglio nazionale delle ricerche.

Dunand, M. and R. Duru. 1962. *Oumm el-'Amed, une ville de l'époque hellénistique aux échelles de Tyr.* Paris: Librairie d'amérique et d'orient et Maisonneuve.

Dunand, M. and N. Saliby. 1985. *Le temple d'Amrith dans la pérée d'Aradus.* Paris: Librairie orientaliste Paul Geuthner.

Dunbabin, K. 1979. "Technique and Materials of Hellenistic Mosaics." *American Journal of Archaeology* 83: 265–77.

Dunbabin, K. 1994. "Early Pavement Types in the West and the Invention of Tessellation." In *Fifth International Colloquium on Ancient Mosaics: Held at Bath, England, on September 5–12, 1987*, ed. P. Johnson, R. Ling, and D. Smith, 26–40. Ann Arbor, Mich.: Journal of Roman Archaeology.

Dunbabin, K. 1999. *Mosaics of the Greek and Roman World*. Cambridge: Cambridge University Press.

Dunbabin, T. 1957. *The Greeks and Their Eastern Neighbours: Studies in the Relations Between Greece and the Countries of the Near East in the Eighth and Seventh Centuries B.C.* London: Society for the Promotion of Hellenic Studies.

Dusinberre, E. 2005. *Gordion Seals and Sealings: Individuals and Society*. Philadelphia: University of Pennsylvania Museum of Archaeology and Anthropology.

Dusinberre, E. 2013. *Empire, Authority, and Autonomy in Achaemenid Anatolia*. Cambridge: Cambridge University Press.

Dyson, S. 1981. "A Classical Archaeologist's Response to the 'New Archaeology.'" *Bulletin of the American Schools of Oriental Research* 242: 7–13.

Dyson, S. 1993. "From New to New Age Archaeology: Archaeological Theory and Classical Archaeology—A 1990s Perspective." *American Journal of Archaeology* 97: 195–206.

Dyson, S. 2006. *In Pursuit of Ancient Pasts: A History of Classical Archaeology in the Nineteenth and Twentieth Centuries*. New Haven: Yale University Press.

Eaverly, M. 2013. *Tan Men/Pale Women: Color and Gender in Archaic Greece and Egypt. A Comparative Approach*. Ann Arbor: University of Michigan Press.

Eddy, S. 1961. *The King Is Dead: Studies in Near Eastern Resistance to Hellenism, 334–31 B.C.* Lincoln: University of Nebraska Press.

Edgar, C. 1931. *Catalogue général des antiquités égyptiennes du musée du Caire. Vol. IV, Nos. 59532–59800: Zenon papyri*. Service des antiquités de l'Égypte. Cairo: Institut français d'archéologie orientale.

Edwards, R. 1979. *Kadmos the Phoenician: A Study in Greek Legends and the Mycenaean Age*. Amsterdam: A. M. Hakkert.

Eissfeldt, O. 1952a. *Sanchunjaton von Berut und Ilumilku von Ugarit*. Halle (Saale): Max Niemeyer.

Eissfeldt, O. 1952b. *Taautos und Sanchunjaton*. Berlin: Akademie.

Elat, M. 1991. "Phoenician Overland Trade Within the Mesopotamian Empires." In *Ah, Assyria . . . : Studies in Assyrian History and Ancient Near Eastern Historiography Presented to Hayim Tadmor*, ed. M. Cogan and I. Eph'al, 21–35. Jerusalem: Hebrew University Magnes Press.

Élayi, J. 1982. "Studies in Phoenician Geography During the Persian Period." *Journal of Near Eastern Studies* 41 (2): 83–110.

Élayi, J. 1988a. "Les sarcophages phéniciens d'époque perse." *Iranica Antiqua* 23: 275–322.

Élayi, J. 1988b. *Pénétration grecque en Phénicie sous l'empire perse*. Nancy: Presses universitaires de Nancy.

Élayi, J. 1989. *Sidon, cité autonome de l'empire perse*. Paris: Idéaphane.

Élayi, J. 2006. "An Updated Chronology of the Reigns of Phoenician Kings During the Persian Period (539–333 BCE)." *Transeuphratène* 32: 11–43.

Élayi, J. 2009. *Byblos, cité sacrée (8e–4e s. av. J.-C.)*. Paris: Gabalda.

Élayi, J. 2010. "An Unexpected Archaeological Treasure: The Phoenician Quarters in Beirut City Center." *Near Eastern Archaeology* 73: 156–68.

Élayi, A. and J. Élayi. 1993. *Trésors de monnaies phéniciennes et circulation monétaire (Ve–IVe s. av. J. C.)*. Transeuphratène suppl. 1. Paris: Gablda.

Élayi, J. and A. Élayi. 2004. *Le monnayage de la cité phénicienne de Sidon à l'époque perse (Ve–IVe siècles avant J.-C.)*. Paris: Gabalda.

Élayi, J. and A. Élayi. 2009. *The Coinage of the Phoenician City of Tyre in the Persian Period (5th–4th cent. BCE)*. Leuven: Peeters.

Élayi, J. and M. Haykal. 1996. *Nouvelles découvertes sur les usages funéraires des Phéniciens d'Arwad*. Transeuphratène suppl. 4. Paris: Gabalda.

Élayi, J. and H. Sayegh, eds. 1998. *Un quartier du port phénicien de Beyrouth au Fer III–Perse: Les objets*. Transeuphratène suppl. 6. Paris: Gabalda.

Élayi, J. and H. Sayegh. 2000. *Un quartier du port phénicien de Beyrouth au Fer III–Perse: Archéologie et histoire*. Transeuphratène suppl. 7. Paris: Gabalda.

Elderkin, G. 1941. "The Hero on a Sandal." *Hesperia* 10: 381–87.

Eliav-Feldon, M., B. Isaac, and J. Ziegler, eds. 2009. *The Origins of Racism in the West*. Cambridge: Cambridge University Press.

Elkins, J. 2003. *Visual Studies: A Skeptical Introduction*. New York: Routledge.

Else, G. 1958. "'Imitation' in the Fifth Century." *Classical Philology* 53: 73–90.

Elsner, J. 2006. "From Empirical Evidence to the Big Picture: Some Reflections on Riegl's Concept of *Kunstwollen*." *Critical Inquiry* 32: 741–66.

Elsner, J. 2007. "Archéologie classique et histoire de l'art en Grande-Bretagne." *Perspective* 2: 231–42.

Elsner, J. 2010a. "Myth and Chronicle: A Response to the Values of Art." *Arethusa* 43 (2): 289–307.

Elsner, J. 2010b. "Style." In *Critical Terms for Art History*, ed. R. Nelson and R. Shiff, 98–109. Second ed. Chicago: University of Chicago Press.

Fabre, T. 2002. "Metaphors for the Mediterranean: Creolization or Polyphony?" *Mediterranean Historical Review* 17 (1): 15–24.

Falkner, T., N. Felson, and D. Konstan. 1999. *Contextualizing Classics: Ideology, Performance, Dialogue: Essays in Honor of John J. Peradotto*. Lanham, Md.: Rowman and Littlefield.

Falsone, G. 1988. "Phoenicia as a Bronzeworking Centre in the Iron Age." In *Bronzeworking Centres of Western Asia, c. 1000–539 B.C.*, ed. J. Curtis, 227–50. London: Kegan Paul International.

Fantalkin, A. 2006. "Identity in the Making: Greeks in the Eastern Mediterranean During the Iron Age." In *Naukratis: Greek Diversity in Egypt. Studies on East Greek Pottery and Exchange in the Eastern Mediterranean*, ed. A. Villing and U. Schlotzhauer, 199–208. London: British Museum.

Fantar, M. 1966. "Pavimenta Punica et signe dit de Tanit dans les habitations de Kerkouane." In *Studi magrebini* 1, 57–65. Naples: Istituto universitario orientale.

Fantar, M. 1978. "Les pavements puniques." *Dossiers de l'archéologie* 31: 6–11.

Fantar, M. 1984. *Kerkouane: Une cité punique du Cap-Bon*. Tunis: Institut national d'archéologie et d'art.

Faust, A. 2006. *Israel's Ethnogenesis: Settlement, Interaction, Expansion and Resistance*. London: Equinox.

Fauth, W. 1985–86. "Aphrodites Pantoffel und die Sandale der Hekate." *Grazer Beiträge* 12–13: 193–211.

Feldman, M. 2002. "Luxurious Forms: Redefining a Mediterranean 'International Style,' 1400–1200 B.C.E." *Art Bulletin* 84 (1): 6–29.

Feldman, M. 2006. *Diplomacy by Design: Luxury Arts and an "International Style" in the Ancient Near East, 1400–1200 BCE*. Chicago: University of Chicago Press.

Feldman, M. 2014. *Communities of Style: Portable Luxury Arts, Identity, and Collective Memory in the Iron Age Levant*. Chicago: University of Chicago Press.

Fernández-Galiano, D. 1982. "New Light on the Origins of Floor Mosaics." *Antiquaries Journal* 62: 235–44.

Ferrari, G. 2002. *Figures of Speech: Men and Maidens in Ancient Greece*. Chicago: University of Chicago Press.

Ferron, J. 1993. *Sarcophages de Phénicie: Sarcophages a scènes en relief*. Paris: Geuthner.

FGrHist = Jacoby, F., ed. 1923– . *Fragmente der griechischen Historiker*. Berlin: Weidmann (et al.).

FHG = Müller, K., ed. 1841–1938. *Fragmenta historicorum graecorum*. Paris: A. Firmin Didot.

Finley, M. 1973. *The Ancient Economy*. Berkeley: University of California Press.

Fitzmyer, J. 1966. "The Phoenician Inscription from Pyrgi." *Journal of the American Oriental Society* 86 (3): 285–97.

Fleischer, R. and W. Schiele. 1983. *Der Klagefrauensarkophag aus Sidon*. Tübingen: E. Wasmuth.

Fontan, É. and H. Le Meaux. 2007. *La Méditerranée des Phéniciens de Tyr à Carthage*. Paris: Somogy.

Fowler, B. 1984. "The Archaic Aesthetic." *American Journal of Philology* 105 (2): 119–49.

Frankenstein, S. 1979. "The Phoenicians in the Far West: A Function of Neo-Assyrian Imperialism." In *Power and Propaganda: A Symposium on Ancient Empires*, ed. M. Larsen, 263–94. Copenhagen: Akademisk Forlag.

Frankfort, H. 1996. *The Art and Architecture of the Ancient Orient*. Fifth ed. New Haven: Yale University Press.

Franks, H. 2014. "Traveling, in Theory: Movement as Metaphor in the Ancient Greek Andron." *Art Bulletin* 96 (2): 156–69.

Frede, S., S. Grallert, and H. Richter. 2000–2002. *Die phönizischen anthropoiden Sarkophage*. Mainz: Von Zabern.

Frederickson, G. 2003. *Racism: A Short History*. Princeton: Princeton University Press.

Frel, J. 1971. "The Rhodian Workshop of the Alexander Sarcophagus." *Istanbuler Mitteilungen* 21: 121–24.

Fried, M. 1967. "Art and Objecthood." *Artforum* 5: 12–23.

Friedman, Z. 2011. *Ship Iconography in Mosaics: An Aid to Understanding Ancient Ships and Their Construction*. BAR International Series 2202. Oxford: Archaeopress.

Friedrich, J., W. Röllig, and M. G. Amadasi Guzzo. 1999. *Phönizisch-punische Grammatik*. Rome: Pontificio istituto biblico.

Frigg, R. and M. Hunter. 2010. *Beyond Mimesis and Convention: Representation in Art and Science*. New York: Springer.

Fullerton, M. 2000. *Greek Art*. Cambridge: Cambridge University Press.

Funck, B., ed. 1996. *Hellenismus: Beiträge zur Erforschung von Akkulturation und politischer Ordnung in den Staaten des hellenistischen Zeitalters: Akten des Internationalen Hellenismus-Kolloquiums, 9.–14. März 1994 in Berlin*. Tübingen: J. C. B. Mohr.

Furtwängler, A. 1893. *Meisterwerke der griechischen Plastik: Kunstgeschichtliche Untersuchungen*. Leipzig: Giesecke und Devrient. Trans. in 1895 by E. Strong as *Masterpieces of Greek Sculpture: A Series of Essays on the History of Art*. London: W. Heinemann.

Gaifman, M. 2006. "Statue, Cult and Reproduction." *Art History* 29 (2): 258–79.

Gal, Z. 1992. "Hurbat Rosh Zayit and the Early Phoenician Pottery." *Levant* 24: 173–86.

Galling, K. 1938. "Die syrisch-palästinische Küste nach der Beschreibung bei Pseudo-Skylax." *Zeitschrift des deutschen Palästina-Vereins* 61: 66–96.

Galling, K. 1963. "Eschmunazar und der Herr der Könige." *Zeitschrift des deutschen Palästina-Vereins* 79: 140–51.

Gandhi, L. 1998. *Postcolonial Theory: A Critical Introduction*. New York: Columbia University Press.

Gardiner, A. 1968. *Ancient Egyptian Onomastica*. Oxford: Oxford University Press.

Gaselee, S. 1969. *Achilles Tatius: Leucippe and Clitophon*. Loeb Classical Library 45. Cambridge, Mass.: Harvard University Press.

Gates, J. 2002. "The Ethnicity Name Game: What Lies Behind 'Graeco-Persian'?" *Ars Orientalis* 32: 105–32.

Geertz, C. 1973. *The Interpretation of Cultures*. New York: Basic Books.

Gell, A. 1992. "The Technology of Enchantment and the Enchantment of Technology." In *Anthropology, Art and Aesthetics*, ed. J. Coote and A. Shelton, 40–63. Oxford: Clarendon Press.

Gell, A. 1995. "On Coote's 'Marvels of Everyday Vision.'" *Social Analysis: The International Journal of Social and Cultural Practice* 38: 18–31.

Gell, A. 1998. *Art and Agency: An Anthropological Theory*. Foreword by N. Thomas. Oxford: Oxford University Press.

Gibson, J. 1982. *Textbook of Syrian Semitic Inscriptions. Vol. III: Phoenician Inscriptions Including Inscriptions in the Mixed Dialect of Arslan Tash*. Oxford: Clarendon Press.

Gilbert, A. 2002. "The Native Fauna of the Ancient Near East." In *A History of the Animal World in the Ancient Near East*, ed. B. J. Collins, 3–75. Leiden: Brill.

Gilboa, A. 1999. "The Dynamics of Phoenician Bichrome Pottery: A View from Tel Dor." *Bulletin of the American Schools of Oriental Research* 316: 1–22.

Gilboa, A. 2001. "Southern Phoenicia During Iron Age I–IIA in the Light of the Tel Dor Excavations: The Evidence of Pottery." Ph.D. diss., Hebrew University, Jerusalem.

Gilboa, A. 2005. "Sea Peoples and Phoenicians Along the Southern Phoenician Coast—A Reconciliation: An Interpretation of Šikila (SKL) Material Culture." *Bulletin of the American Schools of Oriental Research* 337: 47–78.

Gilboa, A. and I. Sharon. 2003. "An Archaeological Contribution to the Early Iron Age Chronological Debate: Alternative Chronologies for Phoenicia and Their Effects on the Levant, Cyprus, and Greece." *Bulletin of the American Schools of Oriental Research* 332: 7–80.

Gill, C., N. Postlethwaite, and R. Seaford. 1998. *Reciprocity in Ancient Greece*. Oxford: Oxford University Press.

Gill, D. and C. Chippindale. 1993. "Material and Intellectual Consequences of Esteem for Cycladic Figurines." *American Journal of Archaeology* 97: 601–59.

Gillis, J., ed. 1996. *Commemorations: The Politics of National Identity*. Princeton: Princeton University Press.

Gilroy, P. 1993. *The Black Atlantic: Modernity and Double Consciousness*. Cambridge, Mass.: Harvard University Press.

Gitler, H. 2000. "Achaemenid Motifs in the Coinage of Ashdod, Ascalon and Gaza from the Fourth Century BC." *Transeuphratène* 20: 73–87.

Gitler, H. and O. Tal. 2006. *The Coinage of Philistia of the Fifth and Fourth Centuries BC: A Study of the Earliest Coins of Palestine*. Milan: Ennere.

Godley, A., ed. and trans. 1963. *Herodotus: History*. Loeb Classical Library 117–20. Cambridge, Mass.: Harvard University Press.

Goldhill, S. and R. Osborne, eds. 1994. *Art and Text in Ancient Greek Culture*. Cambridge: Cambridge University Press.

Goelet, O. 1993. "Nudity in Ancient Egypt." *Source: Notes on the History of Art. Essays on Nudity in Antiquity in Memory of Otto Brendel* 12 (2): 20–31.

Gombrich, E. 1950. *The Story of Art*. London: Phaidon Press.

Gombrich, E. 1960. *Art and Illusion: A Study in the Psychology of Pictorial Representation*. New York: Pantheon Books.

Gombrich, E. 1968. "Style." In *International Encyclopedia of the Social Sciences* 15, ed. D. Sills, 352–61. New York: Macmillan.

Gombrich, E. 1979. *The Sense of Order: A Study in the Psychology of Decorative Art*. Oxford: Phaidon.

Goodchild, R., J. Pedley, and D. White. 1966–67. "Recent Discoveries of Archaic Sculpture at Cyrene." *Libya Antiqua* 3–4: 179–98.

Goodlett, V. 1989. "Collaboration in Greek Sculpture: The Literary and Epigraphical Evidence." Ph.D. diss., New York University.

Goodman, N. 1968. *Languages of Art: An Approach to a Theory of Symbols*. Indianapolis: Bobbs-Merrill.

Gordon, C. 1968. "The Canaanite Text from Brazil." *Orientalia* 37 (4): 425–36.

Gordon, C. 1971. *Before Columbus: Links Between the Old World and Ancient America*. New York: Crown.

Gordon, J. 2012. "Between Alexandria and Rome: A Postcolonial Archaeology of Cultural Identity in Hellenistic and Roman Cyprus." Ph.D. diss., University of Cincinnati.

Gordon, M. 1964. *Assimilation in American Life: The Role of Race, Religion, and National Origins*. New York: Oxford University Press.

Gosden, C. 2005. "What Do Objects Want?" *Journal of Archaeological Method and Theory* 12: 193–211.

Goudriaan, K. 1998. *Ethnicity in Ptolemaic Egypt*. Amsterdam: J. C. Gieben.

Grace, F. 1942. "Observations on Seventh-Century Sculpture." *American Journal of Archaeology* 46: 341–59.

Grainger, J. 1991. *Hellenistic Phoenicia*. Oxford: Clarendon Press.

Gras, M., P. Rouillard, and J. Teixidor. 1991. "The Phoenicians and Death." *Berytus* 39: 127–76.

Green, M. 2002. "Gramsci Cannot Speak: Presentations and Interpretations of Gramsci's Concept of the Subaltern." *Rethinking Marxism* 14 (3): 1–24.

Gros, P. 1978. "Vie et mort de l'art hellénistique selon Vitruve et Pline." *Revue des études latines* 56: 289–313.

Gruen, E. 2001. "Jewish Perspectives on Greek Culture and Ethnicity." In *Ancient Perceptions of Greek Ethnicity*, ed. I. Malkin, 347–73. Washington, D.C.: Center for Hellenic Studies.

Gruen, E., ed. 2005. *Cultural Borrowings and Ethnic Appropriations in Antiquity*. Stuttgart: Franz Steiner.

Gruen, E. 2011. *Rethinking the Other in Antiquity*. Princeton: Princeton University Press.

Gruen, E. 2013. "Did the Romans Have an Ethnic Identity?" In *Culture, Identity and Politics in the Ancient Mediterranean World: Papers from a Conference in Honour of Erich Gruen*, ed. P. Burton, 1–17. Canberra: Australasian Society for Classical Studies.

Gubel, E. 1983. "Art in Tyre During the First and Second Iron Age: A Preliminary Survey." In *Sauvons Tyr/Histoire Phénicienne*, ed. E. Gubel, E. Lipiński, and B. Servais-Soyez, 23–52. Leuven: Peeters.

Gubel, E. 1987. *Phoenician Furniture: A Typology Based on Iron Age Representations with Reference to the Iconographical Context*. Leuven: Peeters.

Gubel, E. 1992. "La glyptique et la genèse de l'iconographie monétaire phénicienne." In *Numismatique et histoire économique phéniciennes et puniques: Actes du Colloque tenu à Louvain-la-Neuve, 13–16 mai 1987*, 1–11. Louvain: Université Catholique de Louvain.

Gubel, E. 1993. "The Iconography of Inscribed Phoenician Glyptic." In *Studies in the Iconography of Northwest Semitic Inscribed Seals*, ed. B. Sass and C. Uehlinger, 101–29. Fribourg-Göttingen: Vandenhoeck und Ruprecht.

Gubel, E. 2000. "Multicultural and Multimedial Aspects of Early Phoenician Art, c. 1200–675 BCE." In *Images as Media: Sources for the Cultural History of the Near East and the Eastern Mediterranean. 1st Millennium BCE*, ed. C. Uehlinger, 185–214. Fribourg: University Press.

Gunter, A. 2009. *Greek Art and the Orient*. Cambridge: Cambridge University Press.

Guralnick, E. 1970. "Kouroi and the Egyptian Canon: A Study of Proportions." Ph.D. diss., University of Chicago.

Guralnick, E. 1978. "Proportions of Kouroi." *American Journal of Archaeology* 82: 461–72.

Guralnick, E. 1985. "Profiles of Kouroi." *American Journal of Archaeology* 89: 399–409.

Gutzwiller, K. 1998. *Poetic Garlands: Hellenistic Epigrams in Context.* Berkeley: University of California Press.

Gutzwiller, K. 2002. "Posidippus on Statuary." In *Il papiro di Posidippo un anno dopo: Atti del convegno internazionale di studi, Firenze 13–14 giugno 2002*, ed. G. Bastianini and A. Casanova, 41–60. Florence: Istituto papirologico G. Vitelli.

Habicht, C. 2007. "Neues zur hellenistischen Geschichte von Kos." *Chiron* 37: 123–52.

Hackett, J. 2008. "Phoenician." In *The Ancient Languages of Syria-Palestine and Arabia*, ed. R. Woodard, 82–102. Cambridge: Cambridge University Press.

Hafner, G. 1954. *Späthellenistische Bildnisplastik: Versuch einer landschaftlichen Gliederung.* Berlin: Gebr. Mann.

Haider, P. 2004. "Kontakte zwischen Griechen und Ägyptern und ihre Auswirkungen auf die archaisch-griechische Welt." In *Griechische Archaik: Interne Entwicklungen—Externe Impulse*, ed. R. Rollinger and C. Ulf, 447–91. Berlin: Akademie.

Hall, E. 1989. *Inventing the Barbarian: Greek Self-Definition Through Tragedy.* Oxford: Oxford University Press.

Hall, J. 1997. *Ethnic Identity in Greek Antiquity.* Cambridge: Cambridge University Press.

Hall, J. 2002. *Hellenicity: Between Ethnicity and Culture.* Chicago: University of Chicago Press.

Hall, J. 2004. "Culture, Cultures and Acculturation." In *Griechische Archaik: Interne Entwicklungen—Externe Impulse*, ed. R. Rollinger and C. Ulf, 35–50. Berlin: Akademie.

Hall, J. 2007. "Polis, Community, and Ethnic Identity." In *The Cambridge Companion to Archaic Greece*, ed. H. Shapiro, 40–60. Cambridge: Cambridge University Press.

Hall, S. 1973. "Encoding and Decoding in the Television Discourse." *Stencilled Occasional Paper 7.*

Hall, S. 1990. "Cultural Identity and Diaspora." In *Identity: Community, Culture, Difference*, ed. J. Rutherford, 222–37. London: Lawrence and Wishart.

Hall, S. 2000. "Who Needs 'Identity'?" In *Identity: A Reader*, ed. P. Du Gay, J. Evans, and P. Redman, 15–30. London: SAGE.

Hallett, C. 2005. *The Roman Nude: Heroic Portrait Statuary 200 B.C.–A.D. 300.* Oxford: Oxford University Press.

Halliwell, S. 2002. *The Aesthetics of Mimesis: Ancient Texts and Modern Problems.* Princeton: Princeton University Press.

Hamdi Bey, O. and T. Reinach. 1892. *Une nécropole royale à Sidon: Fouilles de Hamdy Bey.* Paris: Leroux.

Harden, D. 1962. *The Phoenicians.* London: Thames and Hudson.

Harloe, K. 2013. *Winckelmann and the Invention of Antiquity: History and Aesthetics in the Age of Altertumswissenschaft.* New York: Oxford University Press.

Harrison, E. 1998. "Hellenic Identity and Athenian Identity in the Fifth Century B.C." In *Cultural Differentiation and Cultural Identity in the Visual Arts*, ed. S. Barnes and W. Melion, 41–61. Washington, D.C.: National Gallery of Art.

Hartog, F. 1988. *The Mirror of Herodotus: The Representation of the Other in the Writing of History.* Trans. J. Lloyd. Berkeley: University of California Press.

Havelock, C. 1972. Review of *Der Alexandersarkophag und seine Werkstatt*, by Volkmar von Graeve. *American Journal of Archaeology* 76 (1): 98–99.

Havelock, C. 1995. *The Aphrodite of Knidos and Her Successors: A Historical Review of the Female Nude in Greek Art.* Ann Arbor: University of Michigan Press.

Hawass, Z. 2002. *Bibliotheca Alexandria: The Archaeology Museum.* Cairo: Supreme Council of Antiquities.

Heckel, W. 2006. "Mazaeus, Callisthenes and the Alexander Sarcophagus." *Historia: Zeitschrift für Alte Geschichte* 55: 385–96.

Helbig, W. 1876. "Cenni sopra l'arte fenicia (Lettera di W. Helbig al sig. senatore G. Spano)." *Annali dell'Instituto di corrispondenza archeologia* 48: 197–257.

Held, D. 1997. "Shaping Eurocentrism: The Uses of Greek Antiquity." In *Greeks and Barbarians: Essays on the Interactions Between Greeks and Non-Greeks in Antiquity and the Consequences for Eurocentrism*, ed. J. Coleman and C. Walz, 255–72. Bethesda, Md.: CDL Press.

Helm, P. 1988. "Races and Physical Types in the Classical World." In *Civilization of the Ancient Mediterranean: Greece and Rome*, vol. 1, ed. M. Grant and R. Kitzinger, 137–54. New York: Scribner's.

Herbert, S. 2003. "Excavating Ethnic Strata: The Search for Hellenistic Phoenicians in the Upper Galilee of Israel." In *100 Years of American Archaeology in the Middle East: Proceedings of the American Schools of Oriental Research Centennial Celebration, Washington, D.C., April 2000*, ed. D. Clark and V. Matthews, 319–29. Boston: American Schools of Oriental Research.

Herbert, S. 2003. "The Hellenistic Archives from Tel Kedesh (Israel) and Seleucia-on-the-Tigris (Iraq)." *Bulletin of the University of Michigan Museums of Art and Archaeology* 15: 65–86.

Hermary, A. 1987. "Statuettes, sarcophages et stèles décorées." In *La nécropole d'Amathonte. Tombes 113–367*, ed. V. Karageorghis, O. Picard, and C. Tytgat, 55–75. Nicosia: École française d'Athènes.

Hermary, A. and J. Mertens. 2014. *The Cesnola Collection of Cypriot Art: Stone Sculpture.* New York: Metropolitan Museum of Art.

Herrmann, C. 1994. *Ägyptische Amulette aus Palästina/Israel, mit einem Ausblick auf ihre Rezeption durch das Alte Testament.* Orbis Biblicus et Orientalis 138. Göttingen: Universitätsverlag Freiburg Schweiz, Vandenhoeck und Ruprecht.

Herrmann, G. 2000. "Ivory Carving of First Millennium Workshops, Traditions and Diffusion." In *Images as Media: Sources for the Cultural History of the Near East and the Eastern Mediterranean. 1st Millennium BCE*, ed. C. Uehlinger, 267–82. Fribourg: University Press.

Hicks, D. and M. Beaudry, eds. 2010. *The Oxford Handbook of Material Culture Studies.* Oxford: Oxford University Press.

Hill, G. 1910. *Catalogue of the Greek Coins of Phoenicia.* London: British Museum.

Himmelmann, N. 1990. *Ideale Nacktheit in der griechischen Kunst.* Berlin: W. de Gruyter.

Hirsch, E. 1977. *Painted Decoration on the Floors of Bronze Age Structures on Crete and the Greek Mainland.* Göteberg: P. Åström.

Hochschild, J., V. Weaver, and T. Burch. 2012. *Creating a New Racial Order: How Immigration, Multiracialism, Genomics, and the Young Can Remake Race in America.* Princeton: Princeton University Press.

Hodder, I. 1982. *Symbols in Action: Ethnoarchaeological Studies of Material Culture.* Cambridge: Cambridge University Press.

Hodder, I. 1992. *Theory and Practice in Archaeology.* London: Routledge.

Hodder, I. 2012. *Entangled: An Archaeology of the Relationships Between Humans and Things.* Malden, Mass.: Wiley-Blackwell.

Hodder, I. and S. Hutson. 2003. *Reading the Past: Current Approaches to Interpretation in Archaeology.* Third ed. Cambridge: Cambridge University Press.

Hodos, T. 2006. *Local Responses to Colonization in the Iron Age Mediterranean.* London: Routledge.

Hoffman, G. 1997. *Imports and Immigrants: Near Eastern Contacts with Iron Age Greece.* Ann Arbor: University of Michigan Press.

Hoffman, G. 2008. Review of *Debating Orientalization: Multidisciplinary Approaches to Change in the Ancient Mediterranean*, by Corinna Riva and Nicholas C. Vella. *American Journal of Archaeology* 112 (3): 551–52.

Hölbl, G. 1989. "Ägyptische Kunstelemente im phönikischen Kulturkreis des 1. Jahrtausends v. Chr.: Zur Methodik ihrer Verwendung." *Orientalia* 58: 318–25.

Holt, F. 1999. *Thundering Zeus: The Making of Hellenistic Bactria.* Berkeley: University of California Press.

Horden, P. and N. Purcell. 2000. *The Corrupting Sea: A Study of Mediterranean History.* Malden, Mass.: Blackwell.

Hornblower, S. 1984. Review of *"Hellenismus": Geschichte und Problematik eines Epochenbegriffs,* by Reinhold Bichler. *Classical Review* n.s. 34 (2): 245–47.

Hornblower, S. and A. Spawforth, eds. 2003. *The Oxford Classical Dictionary.* Third ed. Oxford: Oxford University Press.

Hoskins, J. 1998. *Biographical Objects: How Things Tell the Stories of People's Lives.* New York: Routledge.

Houser, C. 1998. "The 'Alexander Sarcophagus' of Abdalonymus: A Hellenistic Monument from Sidon." In *Regional Schools in Hellenistic Sculpture: Proceedings of an International Conference Held at the American School of Classical Studies at Athens, March 15–17, 1996,* ed. O. Palagia and W. Coulson, 281–91. Oxford: Oxbow Books.

Hurwit, J. 1979. "The Dendra Octopus Cup and the Problem of Style in the Fifteenth Century Aegean." *American Journal of Archaeology* 83: 413–26.

Hurwit, J. 1985. *The Art and Culture of Early Greece, 1100–480 B.C.* Ithaca: Cornell University Press.

Hurwit, J. 1990. "The Words in the Image: Orality, Literacy, and Early Greek Art." *Word and Image* 6 (2): 180–97.

Hurwit, J. 2007a. "The Human Figure in Early Greek Sculpture and Vase Painting." In *The Cambridge Companion to Archaic Greece,* ed. H. Shapiro, 265–86. Cambridge: Cambridge University Press.

Hurwit, J. 2007b. "The Problem with Dexileos: Heroic and Other Nudities in Greek Art." *American Journal of Archaeology* 111: 35–60.

Hurwit, J. 2015. *Artists and Signatures in Ancient Greece.* Cambridge: Cambridge University Press.

Hutchinson, J. and A. Smith, eds. 1996. *Ethnicity.* Oxford: Oxford University Press.

Hvidberg-Hansen, F. 1979. *La déesse TNT: Une étude sur la religion canaanéo-punique.* Copenhagen: G. E. C. Gad.

ICO = Guzzo Amadasi, M. G. 1976. *Le iscrizioni fenicie e puniche delle colonie in occidente.* Rome: Istituto di studi del Vicino Oriente, Università di Roma.

IDelos = *Inscriptions de Délos.* 1926–72. 7 vols. Paris: H. Champion.

Immerwahr, H. 1956. "Aspects of Historical Causation in Herodotus." *Transaction of the American Philological Association* 87: 241–80.

Ingold, T. 2000. "On Weaving a Basket." In *The Perception of the Environment: Essays on Livelihood, Dwelling and Skill,* ed. T. Ingold, 339–48. London: Routledge.

Ingold, T. 2013. *Making: Anthropology, Archaeology, Art and Architecture.* New York: Routledge.

Isaac, B. 2004. *The Invention of Racism in Classical Antiquity.* Princeton: Princeton University Press.

Isager, J. 1991. *Pliny on Art and Society: The Elder Pliny's Chapters on the History of Art.* Odense: Odense University Press.

Isager, J. 2003. "*Humanissima ars*: Evaluation and Devaluation in Pliny, Vasari and Baden." In *Ancient Art and Its Historiography,* ed. A. Donahue and M. Fullerton, 48–68. Cambridge: Cambridge University Press.

Israel, F. 1995. "L'onomastique et la prosopographie." In *La civilisation phénicienne et punique: Manuel de recherche*, ed. V. Krings, 215–21. Leiden: Brill.

Iverson, E. 1957. "The Egyptian Origin of the Archaic Greek Canon." *Mitteilungen des Deutschen Archäologischen Instituts, Abteilung Kairo* 15: 134–47.

Iverson, M. 1993. *Alois Riegl: Art History and Theory*. Cambridge, Mass.: MIT Press.

Jantzen, U., and W.-R. Megow. 1977. "Eine Zisterne im Stadtgebiet von Samos." *Mitteilungen des Deutschen Archäologischen Instituts, Athenische Abteilung* 92: 171–95.

Jenkins, I. 2000. "Cypriot Limestone Sculpture from Cnidus." In *Periplous: Papers on Classical Art and Archaeology Presented to Sir John Boardman*, ed. G. Tsetskhladze, A. Prag, and A. Snodgrass, 153–62. London: Thames and Hudson.

Jenkins, I. 2001. "Archaic Kouroi in Naucratis: The Case for Cypriot Origin." *American Journal of Archaeology* 105: 163–79.

Jenkins, R. 1936. *Dedalica: A Study of the Dorian Plastic Art in the Seventh Century B.C.* Cambridge: Cambridge University Press.

Jidejian, N. 1968. *Byblos Through the Ages*. Beirut: Dar el-Machreq.

Jidejian, N. 1971. *Sidon Through the Ages*. Beirut: Dar el-Machreq.

Jigoulov, V. 2010. *The Social History of Achaemenid Phoenicia: Being a Phoenician, Negotiating Empires*. London: Equinox.

Jiménez, A. 2011. "Pure Hybridism: Late Iron Age Sculpture in Southern Iberia." In *Postcolonial Archaeologies*, ed. P. van Dommelen, 102–23. World Archaeology 43. Abingdon: Routledge.

Johnson, F. 1955. "A Note on Owl Skyphoi." *American Journal of Archaeology* 59: 119–24.

Johnson, M. 2010. *Archaeological Theory: An Introduction*. Second ed. Malden, Mass.: Wiley-Blackwell.

Jones, M. 2002. "Tripods, Triglyphs, and the Origin of the Doric Frieze." *American Journal of Archaeology* 106 (3): 353–90.

Jones, R. 2009. "Categories, Borders and Boundaries." *Progress in Human Geography* 33 (2): 174–89.

Jones, S. 1997. *The Archaeology of Ethnicity: Constructing Identities in the Past and Present*. London: Routledge.

Jones, S. 2007. "Discourses of Identity in the Interpretation of the Past." In *The Archaeology of Identities: A Reader*, ed. T. Insoll, 44–58. London: Routledge.

Joyce, J. 1979. "Form, Function and Technique in the Pavements of Delos and Pompeii." *American Journal of Archaeology* 83: 253–63.

Joyce, R. and J. Lopiparo. 2005. "Postscript: Doing Agency in Archaeology." *Journal of Archaeological Method and Theory* 12 (4): 365–74.

Junker, K. and A. Stähli, eds. 2008. *Original und Kopie: Formen und Konzepte der Nachahmungen in der antiken Kunst, Akten des Kolloquiums in Berlin 17.–19. Februar 2005*. Wiesbaden: Reichert.

KAI = Donner, H. and W. Röllig, eds. 1966–2002. *Kanaanäische und aramäische Inschriften*. 3 vols. Wiesbaden: Otto Harrassowitz.

Kaltsas, N. 2002. *Sculpture in the National Archaeological Museum, Athens*. Los Angeles: J. Paul Getty Museum.

Kamlah, J. 2008. "Die Bedeutung der phönizischen Tempel von Umm el-Amed für die Religionsgeschichte der Levante in vorhellenistischer Zeit." In *Israeliten und Phönizier: Ihre Beziehungen im Spiegel der Archäologie und der Literatur des Alten Testaments und seiner Umwelt*, ed. M. Witte and J. Diehl, 125–64. Göttingen: Vandenhoeck und Ruprecht.

Kaoukabani, I. 1973. "Rapport préliminaire sur les fouilles de Kharayeb: 1969–1970." *Bulletin du Musée de Beyrouth* 26: 41–59.

Kaschnitz von Weinberg, G. 1944. *Die mittelmeerischen Grundlagen der antiken Kunst*. Frankfurt am Main: Vittorio Klostermann.

Kaschnitz von Weinberg, G. 1961. *Die eurasischen Grundlagen der antiken Kunst.* Frankfurt am Main: Vittorio Klostermann.

Kaufman, A. 2004. *Reviving Phoenicia: The Search for Identity in Lebanon.* London: I. B. Tauris.

Kawerau, G. and T. Wiegand. 1930. *Die Paläste der Hochburg.* Altertümer von Pergamon 5:1. Berlin: Staatliche Museen zu Berlin.

Kawkabani, I. 2003. "La pseudo-tribune d'Echmoun d'après un témoignage oculaire." *Archaeology and History in Lebanon* 18: 120–28.

Keel, O. and C. Uehlinger. 1998. *Gods, Goddesses, and Images of God in Ancient Israel.* Minneapolis: Fortress Press.

Keesling, C. 2003. *The Votive Statues of the Athenian Akropolis.* Cambridge: Cambridge University Press.

Kelly, T. 1987. "Herodotus and the Chronology of the Kings of Sidon." *Bulletin of the American Schools of Oriental Research* 268: 39–56.

Kemezis, A. 2014. "Greek Ethnicity and the Second Sophistic." In *A Companion to Ethnicity in the Ancient Mediterranean*, ed. J. McInerney, 390–404. Malden, Mass.: Wiley-Blackwell.

Kenfield, J., III. 1973. "The Sculptural Significance of Early Greek Armour." *Opuscula Romana* 9: 149–56.

Kennedy, B. 1883. *The Birds of Aristophanes: The Greek Text as Performed by Members of the University at the Theatre Royal, Cambridge, November, 1883.* Cambridge: Macmillan and Bowes.

Kennedy, R., C. Sydnor Roy, and M. Goldman, eds. 2013. *Race and Ethnicity in the Classical World: An Anthology of Primary Sources in Translation.* Indianapolis: Hackett.

Kersel, M. 2012a. "The Power of the Press: The Effects of Press Releases and Popular Magazines on the Antiquities Trade." In *Archaeology, Bible, Politics, and the Media,* ed. E. Meyers and C. Meyers, 73–83. Winona Lake, Ind.: Eisenbrauns.

Kersel, M. 2012b. "The Value of a Looted Object—Stakeholder Perceptions in the Antiquities Trade." In *The Oxford Handbook of Public Archaeology*, ed. R. Skeates, C. McDavid, and J. Carman, 253–72. Oxford: Oxford University Press.

Keuls, E. 1978. *Plato and Greek Painting.* Leiden: Brill.

Khalifeh, I. 1988. *Sarepta II: The Late Bronze and Iron Age Periods of Area II, X: The University Museum of the University of Pennsylvania Excavations at Sarafand, Lebanon.* Beirut: Département des publications de l'Université libanese.

Kharayeb = Chéhab, M. 1951–52; 1953–54. *Les terres cuites de Kharayeb.* Paris: Maisonneuve.

Kjeldsen, K. and J. Zahle. 1975. "Lykische Gräber: Ein vorläufiger Bericht." *Archäologischer Anzeiger* 1975: 312–50.

Kleeman, I. 1958. *Der Satrapen-Sarkophag aus Sidon.* Berlin: Gebr. Mann.

Klein, W. 1904. *Geschichte der griechischen Kunst. Vol. 1: Die griechische Kunst bis Myron.* Leipzig: Veit.

Knapp, A. 2008. *Prehistoric and Protohistoric Cyprus: Identity, Insularity, and Connectivity.* Oxford: Oxford University Press.

Knapp, A. 2014. "Mediterranean Archaeology and Ethnicity." In *A Companion to Ethnicity in the Ancient Mediterranean*, ed. J. McInerney, 34–49. Malden, Mass.: Wiley-Blackwell.

Knappett, C. 2005. *Thinking Through Material Culture: An Interdisciplinary Perspective.* Philadelphia: University of Pennsylvania Press.

Knappett, C., ed. 2013. *Network Analysis in Archaeology: New Approaches to Regional Interaction.* Oxford: Oxford University Press.

Koehl, R. 1985. *Sarepta III: The Imported Bronze and Iron Age Wares from Area II, X: The University Museum of the University of Pennsylvania Excavations at Sarafand, Lebanon.* Beirut: Librarie orientale.

Koenen, L. 1971. "Bemerkungen zu P. Cairo Zenon 59665: Verlegen eines Mosaikfussbodens." *Zeitschrift für Papyrologie und Epigraphik* 8: 276–77.

Koller, A. 2012. "The *Kos* in the Levant: Thoughts on Its Distribution, Function, and Spread from the Late Bronze to the Iron Age II." In *The Ancient Near East in the 12th–10th Centuries BCE, Culture and History*, ed. G. Galil et al., 269–90. Münster: Ugarit.

Koloski-Ostrow, A. and C. Lyons, eds. 1997. *Naked Truths: Women, Sexuality, and Gender in Classical Art and Archaeology*. London: Routledge Press.

Konstan, D. 2001. "*To Hellenikon Ethnos*: Ethnicity and the Construction of Ancient Greek Identity." In *Ancient Perceptions of Greek Ethnicity*, ed. I. Malkin, 29–50. Washington, D.C.: Center for Hellenic Studies.

Kopytoff, I. 1986. "The Cultural Biography of Things: Commoditization as Process." In *The Social Life of Things: Commodities in Cultural Perspective*, ed. A. Appadurai, 64–91. Cambridge: Cambridge University Press.

Korr, C. 1981. "Evidence of the Sign of the Goddess Tanit in the Theban Region of Egypt." *Israel Exploration Journal* 31: 95–96.

Kouremenos, A., S. Chandrasekaran, and R. Rossi, eds., with J. Boardman (foreword). 2011. *From Pella to Gandhara: Hybridisation and Identity in the Art and Architecture of the Hellenistic East*. BAR International Series 2221. Oxford: Archaeopress.

Kousser, R. 2005. "Creating the Past: The Vénus de Milo and the Hellenistic Reception of Classical Greece." *American Journal of Archaeology* 109 (2): 227–50.

Kraay, C. 1964. "Hoards, Small Change and the Origin of Coinage." *Journal of Hellenic Studies* 84: 76–91.

Kraay, C. 1976. *Archaic and Classical Greek Coins*. London: Methuen.

Kranz, P. 1972. "Frühe griechische Sitzfiguren—Zum Problem der Typenbildung und des orientalischen Einflusses in der frühen griechischen Rundplastik." *Mitteilungen des Deutschen Archäologischen Instituts, Athenische Abteilung* 87: 1–55.

Krauss, R. 1986. *The Originality of the Avant-Garde and Other Modernist Myths*. Cambridge, Mass.: MIT Press.

Kreeb, M. 1988. *Untersuchungen zur figürlichen Ausstattung delischer Privathäuser*. Chicago: Ares.

Krings, V., ed. 1995. *La civilisation phénicienne et punique: Manuel de recherche*. Leiden: Brill.

Kriseleit, I. 2000. *Antike Mosaiken*. Mainz: Philipp von Zabern.

Kroeber, A. 1948. *Anthropology: Race, Language, Culture, Psychology, Prehistory*. New York: Harcourt, Brace.

Kroll, J. and N. Waggoner. 1984. "Dating the Earliest Coins of Athens, Corinth and Aegina." *American Journal of Archaeology* 88: 325–40.

Kropp, A. 2013. *Images and Monuments of Near Eastern Dynasts: 100 BC–AD 100*. Oxford: Oxford University Press.

Kuhrt, A. and S. Sherwin-White, eds. 1987. *Hellenism in the East: The Interaction of Greek and Non-Greek Civilizations from Syria to Central Asia After Alexander*. Berkeley: University of California Press.

Kukahn, E. 1955. *Anthropoide Sarkophage in Beyrouth und die Geschichte dieser sidonischen Sarkophagkunst*. Berlin: Mann.

Kuper, A. 1999. *Culture: The Anthropologists' Account*. Cambridge, Mass.: Harvard University Press.

Kurke, L. 1999. *Coins, Bodies, Games, and Gold: The Politics of Meaning in Archaic Greece*. Princeton: Princeton University Press.

Kurtz, D. 1985a. "Beazley and the Connoisseurship of Greek Vases." In *Greek Vases in the J. Paul Getty Museum*, 2: 237–50. Malibu: J. Paul Getty Museum.

Kurtz, D., ed. 1985b. *Beazley and Oxford*. Oxford: Oxford University Committee for Archaeology.

Kurtz, D. and J. Boardman. 1970. *Greek Burial Customs*. London: Thames and Hudson.

Kuttner, A. 1999. "Hellenistic Images of Spectacle, From Alexander to Augustus." In *The Art of Ancient Spectacle*, ed. B. Bergmann and C. Kondoleon, 97–123. Washington, D.C.: National Gallery of Art.

Kyrieleis, H. 1996. *Der grosse Kuros von Samos*. Samos 10. Bonn: R. Habelt.

Lang, B., ed. 1987. *The Concept of Style*. Ithaca: Cornell University Press.

Langdon, S. 1989. "The Return of the Horse-Leader." *American Journal of Archaeology* 93 (2): 185–201.

Langdon, S., ed. 1993. *From Pasture to Polis: Art in the Age of Homer*. Columbia: University of Missouri Press.

Langdon, S., ed. 1997. *New Light on a Dark Age: Exploring the Culture of Geometric Greece*. Columbia: University of Missouri Press.

Langdon, S. 2008. *Art and Identity in Dark Age Greece, 1100–700 B.C.E.* Cambridge: Cambridge University Press.

Langer-Karrenbrock, M.-T. 2000. *Der lykische Sarkophag aus der Königsnekropole von Sidon*. Münster: LIT.

Langin-Hooper, S. 2007. "Social Networks and Cross-Cultural Interaction: A New Interpretation of the Female Terracotta Figurines of Hellenistic Babylon." *Oxford Journal of Archaeology* 26: 145–65.

Langin-Hooper, S. 2013a. "Problematizing Typology and Discarding the Colonialist Legacy: Approaches to Hybridity in the Terracotta Figurines of Hellenistic Babylonia." In *Archaeology and Cultural Mixture*, ed. W. van Pelt, 95–113. Archaeological Review from Cambridge 28. Cambridge: Department of Archaeology, University of Cambridge.

Langin-Hooper, S. 2013b. "Terracotta Figurines and Social Identities in Hellenistic Babylonia." In *Critical Approaches to Ancient Near Eastern Art*, ed. M. Feldman and B. Brown, 451–79. Berlin: De Gruyter.

Lapatin, K. 2003. "The Fate of Plate and Other Precious Materials: Towards a Historiography of Ancient Greek Minor (?) Arts." In *Ancient Art and Its Historiography*, ed. A. Donahue and M. Fullerton, 69–91. Cambridge: Cambridge University Press.

Lapatin, K. 2010. "The 'Art' of Politics." *Arethusa* 43 (2): 253–65.

Lape, S. 2010. *Race and Citizen Identity in the Classical Athenian Democracy*. Cambridge: Cambridge University Press.

Latour, B. 2005. *Reassembling the Social: An Introduction to Actor-Network-Theory*. Oxford: Oxford University Press.

Lawrence, A. 1927. *Later Greek Sculpture and Its Influence on East and West*. New York: Harcourt, Brace.

Layard, A. 1853. *A Second Series of the Monuments of Nineveh; Including Bas-Reliefs from the Palace of Sennacherib and Bronzes from the Ruins of Nimroud. From Drawings Made on the Spot, During a Second Expedition to Assyria*. London: John Murray.

Layton, R. 2003. *"Art and Agency*: A Reassessment." *Journal of the Royal Anthropological Institute* 9 (3): 447–64.

Lefkowitz, M. 1996. *Not Out of Africa: How Afrocentrism Became an Excuse to Teach Myth as History*. New York: Basic Books.

Lefkowitz, M. 1996. "Lefkowitz on Bernal on Lefkowtiz." A response to Martin Bernal's 1996 review of *Not Out of Africa: How Afrocentrism Became an Excuse to Teach Myth as History*, by Mary Lefkowitz. *Bryn Mawr Classical Review*, April 19, 1996.

Lefkowitz, M. 2009. *History Lesson: A Race Odyssey*. New Haven: Yale University Press.

Lefkowitz, M. and G. Rogers, eds. 1996. *Black Athena Revisited*. Chapel Hill: University of North Carolina Press.

Lehmann, G. 1996. *Untersuchungen zur späten Eisenzeit in Syrien und Libanon: Stratigraphie und Keramikformen zwischen ca. 720 bis 300 v. Chr.* Münster: Ugarit.

Lehmann, G. 1998. "Trends in the Local Pottery Development of the Late Iron Age and Persian Period in Syria and Lebanon, ca. 700 to 300 B.C." *Bulletin of the American Schools of Oriental Research* 311: 7–37.

Lembke, K. 2001. *Phönizische anthropoide Sarkophage.* Mainz am Rhein: Philipp von Zabern.

Lembke, K. 2004. *Die Skulpturen aus dem Quellheiligtum von Amrit: Studie zur Akkulturation in Phönizien.* Mainz am Rhein: Philipp von Zabern.

Lentz = Lentz, A. 1867–70. *Herodiani technici reliquiae.* Leipzig: Teubner.

Lesure, R. 2005. "Linking Theory and Evidence in an Archaeology of Human Agency: Iconography, Style, and Theories of Embodiment." *Journal of Archaeological Method and Theory* 12: 237–55.

Levi, D. 1947. *Antioch Mosaic Pavements.* Princeton: Princeton University Press.

Levin, K. 1964. "The Male Figure in Egyptian and Greek Sculpture of the Seventh and Sixth Centuries B.C." *American Journal of Archaeology* 68: 13–28.

Lexicon of Greek Personal Names. British Academy for the Humanities and Social Sciences. Accessed July 2, 2014. http://www.lgpn.ox.ac.uk/index.html.

Liban, l'autre rive = Liban, l'autre rive: Exposition présentée à l'Institut du monde arabe du 27 octobre 1998 au 2 mai 1999. 1998. Paris: Flammarion.

Lieberman, B. 2010. "'Ethnic Cleansing' Versus Genocide?" In *The Oxford Handbook of Genocide Studies,* ed. D. Bloxham and A. Moses, 42–60. Oxford: Oxford University Press.

LIMC = Lexicon Iconographicum Mythologiae Classicae. 1981–2009. Zurich: Artemis.

Linder, E. 1973. "A Cargo of Phoenicio-Punic Figurines." *Archaeology* 26: 182–87.

Linder, E. and Y. Kahanov. 2003. *The Ma'agan Mikhael Ship: The Recovery of a 2400-Year-Old Merchantman. Final Report.* Jerusalem: Israel Exploration Society and University of Haifa.

Ling, R. 1998. *Ancient Mosaics.* London: British Museum Press.

Lipiński, E., ed. 1987. *Phoenicia and the East Mediterranean in the First Millennium B.C.: Proceedings of the Conference Held in Leuven from the 14th to 16th of November 1985.* Leuven: Peeters.

Lipiński, E. 1992. "Auteurs classiques." In *Dictionnaire de la civilisation phénicienne et punique,* ed. E. Lipiński, 49–52. Turnhout: Brepols.

Lipiński, E. 1995. *Dieux et déesses de l'univers phénicien et punique.* Leuven: Peeters.

Lipiński, E. 1997. *Semitic Languages: Outline of a Comparative Grammar.* Leuven: Peeters.

Lipiński, E. 2004. *Itineraria Phoenicia.* Leuven: Peeters.

Lipiński, E. 2015. *Peuples de la mer, phéniciens, puniques: Études d'épigraphie et d'histoire méditerranéenne.* Leuven: Peeters.

Lissarrague, F. 1990. *The Aesthetics of the Greek Banquet: Images of Wine and Ritual.* Princeton: Princeton University Press.

Lissarrague, F. and A. Schnapp. 2000. "Tradition und Erneuerung in der klassischen Archäologie in Frankreich." In *Klassische Archäologie: Eine Einführung,* ed. A. Borbein, T. Hölscher, and P. Zanker, 365–82. Berlin: Dietrich Reimer.

Luni, M. 2007. *I Greci in Adriatico nell'età dei kouroi.* Urbino: QuattroVenti.

Luraghi, N. 2005. "Messenian Ethnicity." *Classical Review* 55 (2): 572–73.

Lydakes, S. 2004. *Ancient Greek Painting and Its Echoes in Later Art.* Los Angeles: J. Paul Getty Museum.

Lynch, K. 2011. *The Symposium in Context: Pottery From a Late Archaic House Near the Athenian Agora.* Hesperia suppl. 46. Princeton: American School of Classical Studies, Athens.

Ma, J. 2013. *Statues and Cities: Honorific Portraits and Civic Identity in the Hellenistic World.* Oxford: Oxford University Press.

Macadam, H. 1993. "Phoenicians at Home, Phoenicians Abroad: John D. Grainger, *Hellenistic Phoenicia*, 1991." *Topoi* 3: 321–44.

Macaulay, G. 1890. *The History of Herodotus*. New York: Macmillan.

Mack, R. 1996. "Ordering the Body and Embodying Order: The Kouros in Archaic Greek Society." Ph.D. diss., University of California, Berkeley.

Macridy-Bey, T. 1902. "Le temple d'Echmoun à Sidon (Fouilles exécutées par le Musée Impérial Ottoman)." *Revue Biblique* 11: 489–515.

Maes, A. 1991. "Le costume phénicien des stèles d'Umm el-'Amed." In *Phoenicia and the Bible: Proceedings of the Conference Held at the University of Leuven on the 15th and 16th of March 1990*, ed. E. Lipiński, 209–30. Leuven: Peeters.

Maier, F. 1994. "Cyprus and Phoenicia." In *The Cambridge Ancient History, Vol. 6: The Fourth Century B.C.*, second ed., ed. D. Lewis et al., 297–336. Cambridge: Cambridge University Press.

Mainfort, R., Jr. and M. Kwas. 1991. "The Bat Creek Stone: Judeans in Tennessee?" *Tennessee Anthropologist* 16 (1): 1–19.

Mainfort, R., Jr. and M. Kwas. 1993. "The Bat Creek Fraud: A Final Statement." *Tennessee Anthropologist* 18 (2): 87–93.

Mairs, R. 2006. "Ethnic Identity in the Hellenistic Far East." Ph.D. diss., University of Cambridge.

Mairs, R. 2010. "An 'Identity Crisis'? Identity and Its Discontents in Hellenistic Studies." In *Bollettino di Archeologia On Line* special issue, 2010, 55–62. Accessed May 17, 2016. http://www.bollettinodiarcheologiaonline.beniculturali.it/documenti/generale/5_MAIRS.pdf.

Mairs, R. 2012a. "Bilingualism." In *The Encyclopedia of Ancient History*, ed. R. Bagnall et al. Malden, Mass.: Wiley-Blackwell.

Mairs, R. 2012b. "Hellenization." In *The Encyclopedia of Ancient History*, ed. R. Bagnall et al. Malden, Mass.: Wiley-Blackwell.

Mairs, R. 2014. *The Hellenistic Far East: Archaeology, Language, and Identity in Greek Central Asia*. Berkeley: University of California Press.

Malkin, I. 1994. *Myth and Territory in the Spartan Mediterranean*. Cambridge: Cambridge University Press.

Malkin, I., ed. 2001a. *Ancient Perceptions of Greek Ethnicity*. Washington, D.C.: Center for Hellenic Studies.

Malkin, I. 2001b. "Greek Ambiguities: Between 'Ancient Hellas' and 'Barbarian Epirus.'" In *Ancient Perceptions of Greek Ethnicity*, ed. I. Malkin, 187–212. Washington, D.C.: Center for Hellenic Studies.

Malkin, I. 2001c. "Introduction." In *Ancient Perceptions of Greek Ethnicity*, ed. I. Malkin, 1–28. Washington, D.C.: Center for Hellenic Studies.

Malkin, I. 2002. "A Colonial Middle Ground: Greek, Etruscan, and Local Elites in the Bay of Naples." In *The Archaeology of Colonialism*, ed. C. Lyons and J. Papadopoulos, 151–81. Los Angeles: Getty Research Institute.

Malkin, I. 2004. "Postcolonial Concepts and Ancient Greek Colonization." *Modern Language Quarterly* 65 (3): 341–64.

Malkin, I. 2005a. "Herakles and Melqart: Greeks and Phoenicians in the Middle Ground." In *Cultural Borrowings and Ethnic Appropriations in Antiquity*, ed. E. Gruen, 238–58. Stuttgart: F. Steiner.

Malkin, I., ed. 2005b. *Mediterranean Paradigms and Classical Antiquity*. London: Routledge.

Malkin, I. 2005c. "Networks and the Emergence of Greek Identity." In *Mediterranean Paradigms and Classical Antiquity*, ed. I. Malkin, 56–74. London: Routledge.

Malkin, I. 2011. *A Small Greek World: Networks in the Mediterranean*. Oxford: Oxford University Press.

Manning, J. 2010. *The Last Pharaohs: Egypt under the Ptolemies, 305–30 BC*. Princeton: Princeton University Press.

Marcadé, J. 1969. *Au musée de Délos: Étude sur la sculpture hellénistique en ronde bosse découverte dans l'île*. Paris: De Boccard.

Marchand, S. 1996. *Down from Olympus: Archaeology and Philhellenism in Germany, 1750–1970*. Princeton: Princeton University Press.

Marconi, C. 2013. "Mirror and Memory: Images of Ritual Actions in Greek Temple Decoration." In *Heaven on Earth: Temples, Ritual, and Cosmic Symbolism in the Ancient World*, ed. D. Ragavan, 425–46. Chicago: University of Chicago Press.

Marinatos, S. 1923. "En Symplegma Aphroditis, Panos kai Erotos Progensesteron tou ek Delou." *Archaiologikon Deltion* 8: 175–81 (Greek).

Markoe, G. 1985. *Phoenician Bronze and Silver Bowls from Cyprus and the Mediterranean*. Berkeley: University of California Press.

Markoe, G. 1990a. "Egyptianizing Male Votive Statuary from Cyprus: A Reexamination." *Levant* 22: 111–22.

Markoe, G. 1990b. "The Emergence of Phoenician Art." *Bulletin of the American Schools of Oriental Research* 279: 13–26.

Markoe, G. 2000. *Phoenicians*. Berkeley: University of California Press.

Markoe, G. 2003. "Phoenician Metalwork Abroad: A Question of Export or On-Site Production?" In *ΠΛΟΕΣ Sea Routes: Interconnections in the Mediterranean 16th–6th C. BC. Proceedings of the International Symposium Held at Rethymnon, Crete in September 29th–October 2nd 2002*, ed. N. Stampolidis and V. Karageorghis, 209–16. Athens: University of Crete and A. G. Leventis Foundation.

Marquardt, N. 1995. *Pan in der hellenistischen und kaiserzeitlichen Plastik*. Bonn: Habelt.

Martin, S. 2007. "'Hellenization' and Southern Phoenicia: Reconsidering the Impact of Greece Before Alexander." Ph.D. diss., University of California, Berkeley.

Martin, S. 2012. Review of *The Social History of Achaemenid Phoenicia: Being a Phoenician, Negotiating Empires*, by Vadim Jigoulov. *Review of Biblical Literature*. http://www.bookreviews.org.

Martin, S. 2014a. "'East Greek' and Greek Imported Pottery of the First Millennium B.C.E." In *The Smithsonian Institution Excavation at Tell Jemmeh, Israel 1970–1990*, ed. D. Ben-Shlomo and G. Van Beek, 749–75. Washington, D.C.: Smithsonian Institution Scholarly Press.

Martin, S. 2014b. "Ethnicity and Representation." In *Blackwell Companion to Ethnicity in the Ancient Mediterranean*, ed. J. McInerney, 356–75. Oxford: Blackwell.

Martin, T. 1996. "Why Did the Greek *Polis* Originally Need Coins?" *Historia: Zeitschrift für Alte Geschichte* 45 (3): 257–83.

Masson, O. 1978. *Carian Inscriptions from North Saqqara and Buhen*. London: Egypt Exploration Society.

Matthäus, H. 1985. *Metallgefässe und Gefässuntersätze der Bronzezeit, der geometrischen und archaischen Periode auf Cypern*. Munich: C. H. Beck.

Matthäus, H. 1999. "The Greek Symposion and the Near East. Chronology and Mechanisms of Cultural Transfer." In *Proceedings of the XVth International Congress of Classical Archaeology, Amsterdam, July 12–17, 1998: Classical Archaeology Towards the Third Millennium; Reflections and Perspectives*, ed. R. Docter and E. Moormann, 256–60. Amsterdam: Allard Pierson Museum.

Mattos, C. 2014. "Whither Art History? Geography, Art Theory, and New Perspectives for an Inclusive Art History." *Art Bulletin* 96 (3): 259–64.

Mattusch, C. 1988. *Greek Bronze Statuary: From the Beginnings Through the Fifth Century B.C.* Ithaca: Cornell University Press.

Mattusch, C. 2006. "Archaic and Classical Bronzes." In *Greek Sculpture: Function, Materials, and Techniques in the Archaic and Classical Periods*, ed. O. Palagia, 208–42. Cambridge: Cambridge University Press.

Mazza, F., S. Ribichini, and P. Xella. 1988. *Fonti classiche per la civiltà fenicia e punica*. Rome: Consiglio nazionale delle ricerche.

McCoskey, D. 2003. "By Any Other Name? Ethnicity and the Study of Ancient Identity." *Classical Bulletin* 79 (1): 93–109.

McCoskey, D. 2006. "Naming the Fault in Question: Theorizing Racism Among the Greeks and Romans." *International Journal of the Classical Tradition* 13 (2): 243–67.

McCoskey, D. 2012. *Race: Antiquity and Its Legacy*. Oxford: Oxford University Press.

McInerney, J. 2001. "Ethnos and Ethnicity in Early Greece." In *Ancient Perceptions of Greek Ethnicity*, ed. I. Malkin, 51–73. Cambridge, Mass.: Harvard University Press.

McLaughlin, J. 2001. *The Marzeah in the Prophetic Literature: References and Allusions in Light of the Extra-Biblical Evidence*. Leiden: Brill.

Meiggs, R. and D. Lewis. 1988. *A Selection of Greek Historical Inscriptions to the End of the Fifth Century B.C.* Rev. ed. Oxford: Clarendon.

Mendoza, B. 2015. "Egyptian Connections with the Larger World: Greece and Rome." In *A Companion to Ancient Egyptian Art*, ed. M. Hartwig, 399–422. Chichester: Wiley-Blackwell.

Merton, R. 1949. *Social Theory and Social Structure: Toward the Codification of Theory and Research*. Glencoe, Ill.: Free Press.

Meskell, L. 2001. "Archaeologies of Identity." In *Archaeological Theory Today*, ed. I. Hodder, 187–213. Cambridge: Polity Press.

Messerschmidt, W. 1989. "Historische und ikonographische Untersuchungen zum Alexandersarkophag." *Boreas* 12, 64–92.

Mettinger, T. 1995. *No Graven Image? Israelite Aniconism in Its Ancient Near Eastern Context*. Stockholm: Almquist and Wiskell International.

Meyboom, P. 1977. "I mosaici pompeiani con figure di pesci." *Mededeelingen van het Nederlands Historisch Instituut te Rome* 39: 49–93.

Meyer, H. 1988. "Zur Chronologie des Poseidoniastenhauses in Delos." *Mitteilungen des Deutschen Archäologischen Instituts, Athenische Abteilung* 103: 203–20.

Michelau, H. 2014. "Hellenistische Stelen mit Kultakteuren aus Umm el-'Amed." *Zeitschrift des Deutschen Palästina-Vereins* 130 (1): 77–95.

Millar, F. 1983. "The Phoenician Cities: A Case-Study of Hellenisation." *Proceedings of the Cambridge Philological Society* 209: 55–71.

Millar, F. 1993. *The Roman Near East, 31 BC–AD 337*. Cambridge, Mass.: Harvard University Press.

Miller, D. 2005. "Materiality: An Introduction." In *Materiality*, ed. D. Miller, 1–50. Durham, N.C.: Duke University Press.

Miller, M. 1997. *Athens and Persia in the Fifth Century B.C.: A Study in Cultural Receptivity*. Cambridge: Cambridge University Press.

Miller, M. 2000. "The Myth of Bousiris: Ethnicity and Art." In *Not the Classical Ideal: Athens and the Construction of the Other in Greek Art*, ed. B. Cohen, 413–42. Leiden: Brill.

Miller, M. 2005. "Barbarian Lineage in Classical Greek Mythology and Art: Pelops, Danaos and Kadmos." In *Cultural Borrowings and Ethnic Appropriations in Antiquity*, ed. E. Gruen, 68–89. Stuttgart: F. Steiner.

Miller, P. 1998. "The Classical Roots of Poststructuralism: Lacan, Derrida, and Foucault." *International Journal of the Classical Tradition* 5 (2): 204–25.

Mitchell, L. 2007. *Panhellenism and the Barbarian in Archaic and Classical Greece*. Swansea: Classical Press of Wales.

Mitchell, W. 1996. "What Do Pictures Really Want?" *October* 77: 71–82.

Mitchell, W. 2004. *What Do Pictures Want? The Lives and Loves of Images.* Chicago: University of Chicago Press.

Momigliano, A. 1955. "Genesi storica e funzione attuale del concetto di ellenismo." In *Contributo alla storia degli studi classici*, 165–93. Rome: Edizioni di Storia e letteratura.

Momigliano, A. 1970. "J. G. Droysen Between Greeks and Jews." *History and Theory* 9 (2): 139–53.

Momigliano, A. 1975. *Alien Wisdom: The Limits of Hellenization.* Cambridge: Cambridge University Press.

Montagu, A. 1997 [1942]. *Man's Most Dangerous Myth: The Fallacy of Race.* Sixth ed. Walnut Creek, Calif.: Altamira Press.

Moreiras, A. 1999. "Hybridity and Double Consciousness." *Cultural Studies* 13 (3): 373–407.

Moreno, P. 1994. *Scultura ellenistica.* Rome: Istituto poligrafico e Zecca dello Stato, Libreria dello Stato.

Morgan, C. 1993. "The Origins of Panhellenism." In *Greek Sanctuaries: New Approaches*, ed. N. Marinatos and R. Hägg, 18–44. New York: Routledge.

Morgan, C. 2002. "Ethnicity: The Example of Achaia." In *Gli Achei e l'identità etnica degli Achei d'Occidente: Atti del convegno internazionale di studi, Paestum (Salerno), 23–25 febbraio 2001*, ed. E. Greco, 95–116. Tekmeria 3. Salerno: Pandemos.

Morgan, C. 2009. "Ethnic Expression on the Early Iron Age and Early Archaic Greek Mainland. Where Should We Be Looking?" In *Ethnic Constructs in Antiquity: The Role of Power and Tradition*, ed. T. Derks and N. Roymans, 11–36. Amsterdam: Amsterdam University Press.

Morris, I., ed. 1994. *Classical Greece: Ancient Histories and Modern Archaeologies.* Cambridge: Cambridge University Press.

Morris, I. 1996. "The Strong Principle of Equality and the Archaic Origins of Greek Democracy." In *Dēmokratia: A Conversation on Democracies, Ancient and Modern,* ed. J. Ober and C. Hedrick, 19–48. Princeton: Princeton University Press.

Morris, I. 1997. "The Art of Citizenship." In *New Light on a Dark Age: Exploring the Culture of Geometric Greece*, ed. S. Langdon, 9–43. Columbia: University of Missouri Press.

Morris, I. 2000. *Archaeology as Cultural History: Words and Things in Iron Age Greece.* Oxford: Blackwell.

Morris, I. 2003. "Mediterraneanization." *Mediterranean Historical Review* 18 (2): 30–55.

Morris, I. 2005. "Mediterraneanization." In *Mediterranean Paradigms and Classical Antiquity*, ed. I. Malkin, 30–55. London: Routledge.

Morris, R., ed. 2010. *Can the Subaltern Speak? Reflections on the History of an Idea.* New York: Columbia University Press.

Morris, S. 1992. *Daidalos and the Origins of Greek Art.* Princeton: Princeton University Press.

Morris, S. 1997. "Greek and Near Eastern Art in the Age of Homer." In *New Light on a Dark Age: Exploring the Culture of Geometric Greece*, ed. S. Langdon, 56–71. Columbia: University of Missouri Press.

Moscati, S. 1968. *The World of the Phoenicians.* New York: Frederick A. Praeger.

Moscati, S. 1972a. *I fenici e Cartagine.* Turin: Unione tipografico-editrice torinese.

Moscati, S. 1972b. "L'origine del 'segno di Tanit.'" In *Rendiconti dell'Accademia nazionale dei Lincei: Classe di scienze morali, storiche, critiche e filologiche*, 27, 371–74. Rome: Accademia nazionale dei Lincei.

Moscati, S. 1974. *Problematica della civiltà fenicia.* Rome: Consiglio nazionale delle ricerche.

Moscati, S. 1977. *I cartaginesi in Italia.* Milan: Mondadori.

Moscati, S. 1979. "Tanit in Fenicia." *Rivista di studi fenici* 7: 143–44.

Moscati, S. 1980. *Il mondo punico.* Turin: UTET.

Moscati, S. 1982. *L'enigma dei Fenici.* Milan: A. Mondadori.

Moscati, S. 1986. *L'arte della Sardegna punica*. Milan: Jaca Book.

Moscati, S. 1988a. *L'arte della Sicilia punica*. Milan: Jaca Book.

Moscati, S., ed. 1988b. *I Fenici* (= *The Phoenicians*). Milan: Bompiani.

Moscati, S. 1988c. "Ostrich Eggs." In *The Phoenicians*, ed. S. Moscati, 456–63. Milan: Bompiani.

Moscati, S. 1989. *L'ancora d'argento: Colonie e commerci fenici tra Oriente e Occidente*. Milan: Jaca Book.

Moscati, S. 1990a. *L'arte dei Fenici*. Milan: Fabbri.

Moscati, S. 1990b. *Techne: Studi sull'artigianato fenicio*. Rome: Università degli studi di Roma, Dipartimento di storia.

Moscati, S. 1992. *La stele puniche in Italia*. Rome: Istituto poligrafico e Zecca dello Stato, Libreria dello Stato.

Moscati, S. 1993. *Nuovi studi sull'identità fenicia*. Rome: Accademia nazionale dei Lincei.

Moscati, S. 1996. *Artigianato a Monte Sirai*. Rome: Università degli studi di Roma.

Moscati, S. et al. 1997. *La penetrazione fenicia e punica in Sardegna: Trent'anni dopo*. Rome: Accademia nazionale dei Lincei.

Moscati, S. and S. Bondì. 1986. *Italia punica*. Milan: Rusconi.

Moscati, S. and M. Uberti. 1981. *Scavi a Mozia, le stele*. Rome: Consiglio nazionale delle ricerche.

Moscati, S. and M. Uberti. 1988. *Testimonianze fenicio-puniche a Oristano*. Rome: Accademia nazionale dei Lincei.

Moyer, I. 2011. *Egypt and the Limits of Hellenism*. Cambridge: Cambridge University Press.

Muhly, J. 1985. "Phoenicia and the Phoenicians." In *Biblical Archaeology Today: Proceedings of the International Congress on Biblical Archaeology, Jerusalem, April 1984*, ed. J. Amitai, 177–91. Jerusalem: Israel Exploration Society.

Mullen, A. and P. James, eds. 2012. *Multilingualism in the Graeco-Roman Worlds*. Cambridge: Cambridge University Press.

Münch, R. and N. Smelser, eds. 1992. *Theory of Culture*. Berkeley: University of California Press.

Murphy, T. 2004. *Pliny the Elder's* Natural History: *The Empire in the Encyclopedia*. Oxford: Oxford University Press.

Murray, O. 2000. "What Is Greek About the Polis?" In *Polis and Politics: Studies in Ancient Greek History*, ed. P. Flensted-Jensen, T. Nielsen, and L. Rubinstein, 231–44. Copenhagen: Museum Tusculanum Press.

Muscarella, O. 2000. *The Lie Became Great: The Forgery of Ancient Near Eastern Cultures*. Groningen: Styx.

Nagy, H., L. Bonfante, and J. Whitehead. 2008. "Searching for Etruscan Identity." *American Journal of Archaeology* 112 (3): 413–17.

Nederveen Pieterse, J. 2001. "Hybridity, So What? The Anti-Hybridity Backlash and the Riddles of Recognition." *Theory, Culture and Society* 18 (2–3): 219–45.

Neer, R. 1995. "The Lion's Eye: Imitation and Uncertainty in Attic Red-Figure." *Representations* 51: 118–53.

Neer, R. 2002. *Style and Politics in Athenian Vase-Painting: The Craft of Democracy, ca. 530–460 B.C.E.* Cambridge: Cambridge University Press.

Neer, R. 2005. "Connoisseurship and the Stakes of Style." *Critical Inquiry* 32: 1–26.

Neer, R. 2010a. *The Emergence of the Classical Style in Greek Sculpture*. Chicago: University of Chicago Press.

Neer, R. 2010b. "Jean-Pierre Vernant and the History of the Image." *Arethusa* 43 (2): 181–95.

Nichols, D., R. Joyce, and S. Gillespie. 2003. "Is Archaeology Anthropology?" In *Archaeology Is Anthropology*, ed. S. Gillespie et al., 3–13. Arlington, Va.: American Anthropological Association.

Niemeier, W.-D. 2001. "Archaic Greeks in the Orient: Textual and Archaeological Evidence." *Bulletin of the American Schools of Oriental Research* 332: 11–32.

Niemeyer, H. 2000. "The Early Phoenician City-States on the Mediterranean: Archaeological Elements for Their Description." In *A Comparative Study of Thirty City-state Cultures: An Investigation*, ed. M. Hansen, 89–115. Copenhagen: Royal Danish Academy of Sciences and Letters.

Niemeyer, H. 2003. "On Phoenician Art and Its Role in Trans-Mediterranean Interconnections." In *ΠΛΟΕΣ Sea Routes: Interconnections in the Mediterranean 16th–6th C. BC. Proceedings of the International Symposium Held at Rethymnon, Crete in September 29th–October 2nd 2002*, ed. N. Stampolidis and V. Karageorghis, 201–8. Athens: University of Crete and A. G. Leventis Foundation.

Nitschke, J. 2007. "Perceptions of Culture: Interpreting Greco-Near Eastern Hybridity in the Phoenician Homeland." Ph.D. diss., University of California, Berkeley.

Nitschke, J. 2011. "'Hybrid' Art, Hellenism and the Study of Acculturation in the Hellenistic East: The Case of Umm el-'Amed in Phoenicia." In *From Pella to Gandhara. Hybridisation and Identity in the Art and Architecture of the Hellenistic East*, ed. A. Kouremenos, S. Chandrasekaran, and R. Rossi with J. Boardman (foreword), 87–104. BAR International Series 2221. Oxford: Archaeopress.

Nitschke, J. 2013. "Interculturality in Image and Cult in the Hellenistic East: Tyrian Melqart Revisited." In *Shifting Social Imaginaries in the Hellenistic Period: Narrations, Practices, and Images*, ed. E. Stavrianopoulou, 253–82. Leiden: Brill.

Nitschke, J. 2015. "What Is Phoenician About Phoenician Material Culture in the Hellenistic Period?" In *La Phénicie hellénistique: Actes du colloque international de Toulouse (18–20 février 2013)*, ed. J. Aliquot and C. Bonnet, 207–38. Topoi suppl. 13. Lyon: Maison de l'Orient et de la Méditerranée-Jean Pouilloux.

Oakley, J. 1998. "Why Study a Greek Vase-Painter? A Response to Whitley's 'Beazley as Theorist.'" *Antiquity* 72: 209–13.

Oakley, J. 1999. "'Through a Glass Darkly' I: Some Misconceptions About the Study of Greek Vase-Painting." In *Proceedings of the XVth International Congress of Classical Archaeology, Amsterdam, July 12–17, 1998*, ed. R. Docter and E. Moorman, 286–90. Amsterdam: Allard Pierson Museum.

Oakley, J. 2009. "State of the Discipline: Greek Vase Painting." *American Journal of Archaeology* 113: 599–627.

O'Connor, M. 1977. "The Rhetoric of the Kilamuwa Inscription." *Bulletin of the American Schools of Oriental Research* 226: 15–29.

Oggiano, I. 2015a. "Le sanctuaire de Kharayeb et l'évolution de l'imagerie phénicienne dans l'arrière-pays de Tyr." In *La Phénicie hellénistique: Actes du colloque international de Toulouse (18–20 février 2013)*, ed. J. Aliquot and C. Bonnet, 239–66. Topoi suppl. 13. Lyon: Maison de l'Orient et de la Méditerranée-Jean Pouilloux.

Oggiano, I. 2015b. "The Question of 'Plasticity' of Ethnic and Cultural Identity: The Case Study of Kharayeb." In *Cult and Ritual on the Levantine Coast and Its Impact on the Eastern Mediterranean Realm: Proceedings of the International Symposium, Beirut 2012*, ed. A.-M. Maïla-Afeiche, 507–28. Beirut: Ministère de la culture, Direction Générale des antiquités.

Olin, M. 1992. *Forms of Representation in Alois Riegl's Theory of Art*. University Park: Pennsylvania State University Press.

Oppen de Ruiter, B. 2015. *Berenice II Euergetis: Essays in Early Hellenistic Queenship*. New York: Palgrave Macmillan.

Ornan, T. 2005a. "A Complex System of Religious Symbols: The Case of the Winged Disc in Near Eastern Imagery of the First Millennium BCE." In *Crafts and Images in Contact: Studies on*

Eastern Mediterranean Art of the First Millennium BCE, ed. C. Suter and C. Uehlinger, 207–41. Fribourg: Academic Press.

Ornan, T. 2005b. *The Triumph of the Symbol: Pictorial Representations of Deities in Mesopotamia and the Biblical Image Ban*. Orbis Biblicus et Orientalis 213. Göttingen: Vandenhoeck und Ruprecht.

Orrells, D., G. Bhambra, and T. Roynon. 2011. *African Athena: New Agendas*. Oxford: Oxford University Press.

Osborne, R. 1985. "The Erection and Mutilation of the Hermai." *Proceedings of the Cambridge Philological Society* 31: 47–73.

Osborne, R. 1996. *Greece in the Making, 1200–479 BC*. London: Routledge.

Osborne, R. 1997. "Men Without Clothes: Heroic Nakedness and Greek Art." *Gender and History* 9 (3): 504–28.

Osborne, R. 2006. "W(h)ither Orientalization." In *Debating Orientalization: Multidisciplinary Approaches to Change in the Ancient Mediterranean*, ed. C. Riva and N. Vella, 153–58. London: Equinox.

Osborne, R. 2010. "The Art of Signing in Ancient Greece." *Arethusa* 43 (2): 231–51.

Osborne, R. 2011. *The History Written on the Classical Greek Body*. Cambridge: Cambridge University Press.

Osborne, R. and J. Tanner, eds. 2007. *Art's Agency and Art History*. Oxford: Blackwell.

Overbeck, J. 1868. *Die antiken Schriftquellen zur Geschichte der bildenden Künste bei den Griechen*. Leipzig: W. Engelmann.

Özer, E. 2014. "A Typological Suggestion Concerning Hellenistic and Roman Lycian Sarcophagi." *CEDRUS* 11: 75–87.

Pächt, O. 1963. "Art Historians and Art Critics, VI: Alois Riegl." *Burlington Magazine* 105: 188–93.

Padgett, M. 2003. *The Centaur's Smile: The Human Animal in Early Greek Art*. New Haven: Yale University Press.

Painter, N. 2010. *The History of White People*. New York: W. W. Norton.

Palagia, O., ed. 2006. *Greek Sculpture: Function, Materials, and Techniques in the Archaic and Classical Periods*. New York: Cambridge University Press.

Papadopoulos, J. 1997. "Phantom Euboians." *Journal of Mediterranean Archaeology* 10 (2): 191–219.

Papadopoulos, J. 2011. "'Phantom Euboians'—A Decade On." *Euboea and Athens: Proceedings of a Colloquium in Memory of Malcolm B. Wallace, Athens 26–27 June 2009*, ed. J. Tomlinson, M. Wallace, and D. Rupp, 113–33. Toronto: Canadian Institute in Greece/Institut canadien en Grèce.

Papalexandrou, N. 2010. "Are There Hybrid Visual Cultures? Reflections on the Orientalizing Phenomena in the Mediterranean of the Early First Millennium BCE." In *Theorizing Cross-Cultural Interaction Among the Ancient and Early Medieval Mediterranean, Near East and Asia*, ed. M. Canepa. *Ars Orientalis* 38: 31–48.

Papastergiadis, N. 1997. "Tracing Hybridity in Theory." In *Debating Cultural Hybridity: Multi-Cultural Identities and the Politics of Anti-Racism*, ed. P. Werbner and T. Modood, 257–81. London: Zed Books.

Pardee, D. 1993. Review of *Baal Hammon: Recherches sur l'identité et l'histoire d'un dieu phénico-punique*, by Paolo Xella. *Journal of the American Oriental Society* 113 (1): 116–17.

Pasztory, E. 1989. "Identity and Difference: The Uses and Meanings of Ethnic Styles." In *Cultural Differentiation and Cultural Identity in the Visual Arts*, ed. S. Barnes and W. Melion, 15–38. Washington, D.C.: National Gallery of Art.

Pater, W. 1910. "The Beginnings of Greek Sculpture I: The Heroic Age of Greek Art." In *Greek Studies: A Series of Essays*, 187–223. London: Macmillan.

Patrik, L. 1985. "Is There an Archaeological Record?" *Advances in Archaeological Method and Theory* 8: 27–62.

Patzek, B. 1996. "Griechen und Phöniker in homerischer Zeit: Fernhandel und der orientalische Einfluss auf die frühgriechische Kultur." *Münstersche Beiträge zur antiken Handelsgeschichte* 15 (2): 1–32.

Pauly-Wissowa = Cancik, H. and H. Scheider, eds. 2002– . *Brill's New Pauly: Encyclopaedia of the Ancient World*. Leiden: Brill.

Peckham, B. 1968. *The Development of the Late Phoenician Scripts*. Cambridge, Mass.: Harvard University Press.

Peckham, B. 1987. "Phoenicia and the Religion of Israel: The Epigraphic Evidence." In *Ancient Israelite Religion: Essays in Honor of Frank Moore Cross*, ed. P. Miller, P. Hanson, and S. McBride, 79–99. Philadelphia: Fortress Press.

Peckham, B. 2014. *Phoenicia: Episodes and Anecdotes from the Ancient Mediterranean*. Winona Lake, Ind.: Eisenbrauns.

Pemberton, E. 1988. "The Beginning of Monumental Painting in Ancient Greece." In *Studia Pompeiana et Classica in Honor of Wilhelmina F. Jashemski*, vol. 2, ed. R. Curtis, 181–97. New Rochelle, N.Y.: A. D. Caratzas.

Pendlebury, J. 1930. *Aegyptiaca: A Catalogue of Egyptian Objects in the Aegean Area*. Cambridge: Cambridge University Press.

Pernice, E. 1938. *Die hellenistische Kunst in Pompeji VI: Pavimente und figürliche Mosaiken*. Berlin: De Gruyter.

Perrot, G. and C. Chipiez. 1885. *History of Art in Phoenicia and Its Dependencies*. London: Chapman and Hall.

Peters, S. 2004. *Hannibal ad portas: Macht und Reichtum Karthagos*. Karlsruhe: Badisches Landesmuseum.

Phillips, K. 1960. "Subject and Technique in Hellenistic-Roman Mosaics: A Ganymede Mosaic from Sicily." *Art Bulletin* 42: 243–62.

Picard, Charles. 1921. *L'établissement des Poseidoniastes de Bérytos*. Exploration archéologique de Délos 6. Paris: De Boccard.

Picard, Charles. 1935. "Observations sur les sculptures bérytiennes de Délos." *Berytus* 2: 11–24.

Picard, Colette. 1968. "Genèse et évolution des signes de la bouteille et de Tanit à Carthage." In *Studi magrebini* 2, 77–88. Naples: Istituto universitario orientale.

Piening, H. 2007. "A Colorful Legacy: The Colorants of the 'Alexander-Sarcophagus' in Istanbul." In *Gods in Color: Painted Sculpture of Classical Antiquity*, ed. V. Brinkmann, 168–71. Munich: Stiftung Archäologie Glyptothek Munich.

Pinney, C. 2006. "Four Types of Visual Culture." In *Handbook of Material Culture*, ed. C. Tilley et al., 131–45. London: SAGE.

Platt, V. 2010. "Art History in the Temple." *Arethusa* 43 (2): 197–213.

Podro, M. 1982. *The Critical Historians of Art*. New Haven: Yale University Press.

Pollitt, J. 1972. *Art and Experience in Classical Greece*. Cambridge: Cambridge University Press.

Pollitt, J. 1974. *The Ancient View of Greek Art: Criticism, History, and Terminology*. New Haven: Yale University Press.

Pollitt, J. 1986. *Art in the Hellenistic Age*. Cambridge: Cambridge University Press.

Pollitt, J. 1990. *The Art of Ancient Greece: Sources and Documents*. Cambridge: Cambridge University Press.

Porada, E. 1956. "A Lyre Player from Tarsus and His Relations." In *The Aegean and the Near East: Studies Presented to Hetty Goldman on the Occasion of Her Seventy-Fifth Birthday*, ed. S. Weinberg, 185–211. Locus Valley, N.Y.: J. J. Augustin.

Porter, J. 2010. "Why Art Has Never Been Autonomous." *Arethusa* 43 (2): 165–80.

Potts, A. 2000. *Flesh and the Ideal: Winckelmann and the Origins of Art History*. New Haven: Yale University Press.

Poulsen, F. 1912. *Der Orient und die frühgriechische Kunst*. Leipzig: Teubner.

Prag, J. 2006. "'Poenus plane est'—But Who Were the 'Punickes'?" *Papers of the British School at Rome* 74: 1–37.

Prag, J. 2014. "*Phoinix* and *Poenus*: Usage in Antiquity." In *The Punic Mediterranean: Identities and Identification from Phoenician Settlement to Roman Rule*, ed. J. Quinn and N. Vella, 11–23. Cambridge: Cambridge University Press.

Prag, J. and J. Quinn. 2013a. *The Hellenistic West: Rethinking the Ancient Mediterranean*. Cambridge: Cambridge University Press.

Prag, J. and J. Quinn. 2013b. "Introduction." In *The Hellenistic West: Rethinking the Ancient Mediterranean*, ed. J. Prag and J. Quinn, 1–13. Cambridge: Cambridge University Press.

Pratt, M. 1991. "Arts of the Contact Zone." *Profession*: 33–40.

Pratt, M. 1992. *Imperial Eyes: Travel Writing and Transculturation*. London: Routledge.

Prauscello, L. 2006. "Sculpted Meanings, Talking Statues: Some Observations on Posidippus 142.12 A–B (=XIX G–P) ΚΑΙ ΕΝ ΠΡΟΘΥΡΟΙΣ ΘΗΚΕ ΔΙΔΑΣΚΑΛΙΗΝ." *American Journal of Philology* 127 (4): 511–23.

Price, M. 1983. "Thoughts on the Beginning of Coinage." In *Studies in Numismatic Method Presented to Philip Grierson*, ed. C. Brooke, B. Stewart, J. Pollard, and T. Volk, 1–10. Cambridge: Cambridge University Press.

Pritchard, J. 1975. *Sarepta, a Preliminary Report on the Iron Age: Excavations of the University Museum of the University of Pennsylvania, 1970–72*. Philadelphia: University Museum, University of Pennsylvania.

Pritchard, J. 1978. *Recovering Sarepta, a Phoenician City: Excavations at Sarafand, Lebanon, 1969–1974, by the University Museum of the University of Pennsylvania*. Princeton: Princeton University Press.

Pritchard, J. 1982. "The Tanit Inscription from Sarepta." In *Phönizier im Westen: Die Beiträge des Internationalen Symposiums über "Die phönizische Expansion im westlichen Mittelmeerraum" in Köln vom 24. bis 27. April 1979*, ed. H. Niemeyer, 83–92. Mainz: Philipp von Zabern.

Pritchard, J. 1988. *Sarepta IV: The Objects from Area II, X: The University Museum of the University of Pennsylvania Excavations at Sarafand, Lebanon*. Beirut: Département des publications de l'Université libanese.

Purcell, N. 2006. "Orientalizing: Five Historical Questions." In *Debating Orientalization: Multidisciplinary Approaches to Change in the Ancient Mediterranean*, ed. C. Riva and N. Vella, 21–30. London: Equinox.

Purcell, N. 2013. "On the Significance of East and West in Today's 'Hellenistic' History: Reflections on Symmetrical Worlds, Reflecting Through World Symmetries." In *The Hellenistic West: Rethinking the Ancient Mediterranean*, ed. J. Prag and J. Quinn, 367–90. Cambridge: Cambridge University Press.

Quack, J. 2011. "Zum Datum der persischen Eroberung Ägyptens unter Kambyses." *Journal of Egyptian History* 4: 228–46.

Quinn, J. 2003. "Roman Africa?" *Digressus* suppl. 1: 7–34.

Quinn, J. 2005. "The Cultures of the Tophet: Identification and Identity in the Phoenician Diaspora." In *Cultural Borrowings and Ethnic Appropriations in Antiquity*, ed. E. Gruen, 388–413. Stuttgart: Franz Steiner.

Quinn, J. 2007. "Herms, Kouroi and the Political Anatomy of Athens." *Greece and Rome* 54: 82–105.

Quinn, J., N. McLynn, R. Kerr, and D. Hadas. 2014. "Augustine's Canaanites." *Papers of the British School at Rome* 82: 175–97.

Quinn, J. and N. Vella, eds. 2014. *The Punic Mediterranean: Identities and Identification from Phoenician Settlement to Roman Rule.* Cambridge: Cambridge University Press.

Raaflaub, K. 2004a. "Archaic Greek Aristocrats as Carriers of Cultural Interaction." In *Commerce and Monetary Systems in the Ancient World: Means of Transmission and Cultural Interaction*, ed. R. Rollinger, C. Ulf, and K. Schnegg, 197–217. Stuttgart: Franz Steiner.

Raaflaub, K. 2004b. "Zwischen Ost und West: Phönizische Einflüsse auf die griechische Polisbildung?" In *Griechische Archaik: Interne Entwicklungen—Externe Impulse*, ed. R. Rollinger and C. Ulf, 271–89. Berlin: Akademie.

Raban, A. and Kahanov, Y. 2003. "Clay Models of Phoenician Vessels in the Hecht Museum at the University of Haifa, Israel." *International Journal of Nautical Archaeology* 32 (1): 61–72.

Raeck, W. 1981. *Zum Barbarenbild in der Kunst Athens im 6. und 5. Jahrhundert v. Chr.* Bonn: R. Habelt.

Rainey, A. 2001. "Herodotus' Description of the East Mediterranean Coast." *Bulletin of the American Schools of Oriental Research* 321: 57–63.

Rampley, M. 2005. "Art History and Cultural Difference: Alfred Gell's Anthropology of Art." *Art History* 28 (4): 524–51.

Rankine, P. 2011. "Black Apollo? Martin Bernal's *Black Athena: The Afroasiatic Roots of Classical Civilization*, Volume iii, and Why Race Still Matters." In *African Athena: New Agendas*, ed. D. Orrells, G. Bhambra, and T. Roynon, 40–55. Oxford: Oxford University Press.

Rauh, N. 1993. *The Sacred Bonds of Commerce: Religion, Economy, and Trade Society at Hellenistic Roman Delos, 166–87 B.C.* Amsterdam: J. C. Gieben.

Rawlinson, G. 1889. *History of Phoenicia.* London: Longmans, Green.

Ray, J. 1987. "Egypt: Dependence and Independence (425–343 B.C.)." In *Achaemenid History, Vol. 1: Sources, Structures and Synthesis. Proceedings of the Groningen 1983 Achaemenid History Workshop*, ed. H. Sancisi-Weerdenburg, 79–95. Leiden: Nederlands Instituut voor het Nabije Oosten.

Redford, D. 1992. *Egypt, Canaan, and Israel in Ancient Times.* Princeton: Princeton University Press.

Reese, D. and C. Sease. 1993. "Some Previously Unpublished Engraved Tridacna Shells." *Journal of Near Eastern Studies* 52: 109–28.

Reese, D. and C. Sease. 2004. "Additional Unpublished Engraved Tridacna and Anadara Shells." *Journal of Near Eastern Studies* 63: 29–41.

Reiche, I. et al. 2013. "Discovering Vanished Paints and Naturally Formed Gold Nanoparticles on 2800 Years Old Phoenician Ivories Using SR-FF-MicroXRF with the Color X-ray Camera." *Analytical Chemistry* 85 (12): 5857–66.

Renan, E. 1864. *Mission de Phénicie.* Paris: Imprimerie impériale.

Renfrew, C. 1980. "The Great Tradition Versus the Great Divide: Archaeology as Anthropology?" *American Journal of Archaeology* 84: 287–98.

Renfrew, C. 1986. "Introduction: Peer Polity Interaction and Socio-Political Change." In *Peer Polity Interaction and Socio-Political Change*, ed. C. Renfrew and J. Cherry, 1–18. Cambridge: Cambridge University Press.

Renfrew, C. 2000. *Loot, Legitimacy and Ownership: The Ethical Crisis in Archaeology.* London: Duckworth.

Renfrew, C. 2009. *Prehistory: The Making of the Human Mind.* New York: Modern Library.

Renfrew, C. and P. Bahn, eds. 2005. *Archaeology: The Key Concepts.* London: Routledge.

Renfrew, C., C. Gosden, and E. DeMarrais. 2004. "Introduction: Art as Archaeology and Archaeology as Art." In *Substance, Memory, and Display: Archaeology and Art*, ed. C. Renfrew, C. Gosden, and E. DeMarrais, 1–6. Cambridge: McDonald Institute for Archaeological Research.

Renfrew, C. and C. Scarre, eds. 1998. *Cognition and Material Culture: The Archaeology of Symbolic Storage.* Cambridge: McDonald Institute for Archaeological Research.

Rhodes, P. and R. Osborne. 2003. *Greek Historical Inscriptions 404–323 BC.* Oxford: Oxford University Press.

Ribichini, S. 1988. "Beliefs and Religious Life." In *The Phoenicians,* ed. S. Moscati, 104–25. Milan: Bompiani.

Richter, G. 1968. *Korai, Archaic Greek Maidens: A Study of the Development of the Kore Type in Greek Sculpture.* London: Phaidon.

Richter, G. 1970. *Kouroi, Archaic Greek Youths: A Study of the Development of the Kouros Type in Greek Sculpture.* Third ed. With I. Richter. London: Phaidon.

Ridgway, B. 1966. "Greek Kouroi and Egyptian Methods." *American Journal of Archaeology* 70: 68–70.

Ridgway, B. 1969. Review of *Der Alexander-Sarkophag,* by Karl Schefold. *American Journal of Archaeology* 73: 482.

Ridgway, B. 1984. *Roman Copies of Greek Sculpture: The Problem of the Originals.* Jerome Lectures 15. Ann Arbor: University of Michigan Press.

Ridgway, B. 1990. *Hellenistic Sculpture I: The Styles of ca. 331–200 B.C.* Madison: University of Wisconsin Press.

Ridgway, B. 1993. *The Archaic Style in Greek Sculpture.* Second ed. Chicago: Ares.

Ridgway, B. 1994. "The Study of Classical Sculpture at the End of the 20th Century." *American Journal of Archaeology* 98: 759–72.

Ridgway, B. 1997. *Fourth-Century Styles in Greek Sculpture.* Madison: University of Wisconsin Press.

Ridgway, B. 2000. *Hellenistic Sculpture II: The Styles of ca. 200–100 B.C.* Madison: University of Wisconsin Press.

Ridgway, B. 2005. "The Study of Greek Sculpture in the Twenty-First Century." *Proceedings of the American Philosophical Society* 149: 63–71.

Riegl, A. 1893. *Stilfragen: Grundlegungen zu einer Geschichte der Ornamentik.* Berlin: G. Siemens. Trans. by E. Kain in 1992 as *Problems of Style: Foundations for a History of Ornament,* ed. D. Castriota. Princeton: Princeton University Press.

Riegl, A. 1901. *Die spätrömische Kunstindustrie nach den Funden in Österreich-Ungarn.* Vienna: Österreichischen Staatsdruckerei. Trans. by R. Winkes in 1985 as *Late Roman Art Industry.* Rome: G. Bretschneider.

Riegl, A. 1982. "The Modern Cult of Monuments: Its Character and Its Origin." Trans. K. Forster and D. Ghirardo. *Oppositions* 25: 21–51.

Riis, P. 1970. *Sukas I: The North-East Sanctuary and the First Settling of Greeks in Syria and Palestine.* Copenhagen: Munksgaard.

Riva, C. and N. Vella, eds. 2006. *Debating Orientalization: Multidisciplinary Approaches to Change in the Ancient Mediterranean.* London: Equinox.

Roberston, M. 1949. *Why Study Greek Art? An Inaugural Lecture Delivered at University College, London on 31st January 1949.* London: H. K. Lewis.

Robertson, M. 1959. *Greek Painting.* Geneva: Skira.

Robertson, M. 1963. *Between Archaeology and Art History.* Oxford: Clarendon Press.

Robertson, M. 1975. *A History of Greek Art.* Cambridge: Cambridge University Press.

Robertson, M. 1981. *A Shorter History of Greek Art.* Cambridge: Cambridge University Press.

Robertson, M. 1992. *The Art of Vase-Painting in Classical Athens.* Cambridge: Cambridge University Press.

Robins, G. 1994. *Proportion and Style in Ancient Egyptian Art.* Austin: University of Texas Press.

Rolley, C. 1999. *La sculpture grecque 2: La période classique.* Paris: Picard.

Röllig, W. 1983a. "The Phoenician Language: Remarks on the Present State of Research." In *Atti del I congresso internazionale di studi fenici e punici: Roma, 5–10 novembre 1979*, 375–85. Rome: Consiglio nazionale delle ricerche.

Röllig, W. 1983b. "On the Origin of the Phoenicians." *Berytus* 31: 79–93.

Röllig, W. 1992. "Asia Minor as a Bridge Between East and West: The Role of the Phoenicians and Aramaeans in the Transfer of Culture." In *Greece Between East and West, 10th–8th Centuries BC: Papers of the Meeting at the Institute of Fine Arts, New York University, March 15–16th, 1990*, ed. G. Kopcke and I. Tokumaru, 93–102. Mainz am Rhein: Philipp von Zabern.

Rollinger, R. and K. Schnegg, eds. 2014. *Kulturkontakte in antiken Welten, Vom Denkmodell zum Fallbeispiel: Proceedings des internationalen Kolloquiums aus Anlass des 60. Geburtstages von Christoph Ulf, Innsbruck, 26. bis 30. Januar 2009.* Leuven: Peeters.

Rollinger, R. and C. Ulf, eds. 2004. *Griechische Archaik: Interne Entwicklungen—Externe Impulse.* Berlin: Akademie.

Romm, J. 1992. *The Edges of the Earth in Ancient Thought: Geography, Exploration, and Fiction.* Princeton: Princeton University Press.

Rood, T. 2010. "Herodotus' Proem: Space, Time, and the Origins of International Relations." *ARIADNE* 16: 43–74.

Root, M. 1985. "The Parthenon Frieze and the Apadana Reliefs at Persepolis: Reassessing a Programmatic Relationship." *American Journal of Archaeology* 89: 103–20.

Routledge, B. 2013. *Archaeology and State Theory: Subjects and Objects of Power.* London: Bloomsbury Academic.

Rowe, J., ed. 1998. *"Culture" and the Problem of the Disciplines.* New York: Columbia University Press.

Ruscillo, D. 2005. "Reconstructing *Murex* Royal Purple and Biblical Blue in the Aegean." In *Archaeomalacology: Molluscs in Former Environments of Human Behaviour*, ed. D. Bar-Yosef Meyer, 99–106. Oxford: Oxbow.

Russmann, E. 2010. "Late Period Sculpture." In *A Companion to Ancient Egypt*, ed. A. Lloyd, 944–69. Malden, Mass.: Wiley-Blackwell.

Saatsoglou-Paliadeli, C. 1993. "Aspects of Ancient Macedonian Costume." *Journal of Hellenic Studies* 113: 122–47.

Sackett, J. 1977. "The Meaning of Style in Archaeology: A General Model." *American Antiquity* 42: 369–80.

Sader, H. 1991. "Phoenician Stelae from Tyre." *Berytus* 39: 101–26.

Sader, H. 1992. "Phoenician Stelae from Tyre." *Studi epigrafici e linguistici sul Vicino Oriente antico* 9: 53–79.

Sader, H. 1998. "Phoenician Inscriptions from Beirut." In *Ancient Egyptian and Mediterranean Studies in Memory of William A. Ward*, ed. L. Lesko, 203–13. Providence: Brown University, Department of Egyptology.

Sader, H. 2005. *Iron Age Funerary Stelae from Lebanon.* Barcelona: Universidad Pompeu Fabra.

Sader, H. 2010. "Phoenician 'Popular Art': Transmission, Transformation, and Adaptation of Foreign Motifs in the Light of Recent Archaeological Evidence from Lebanon." In *Interkulturalität in der Alten Welt: Vorderasien, Hellas, Ägypten und die vielfältigen Ebenen des Kontakts*, ed. R. Rollinger et al., 23–40. Wiesbaden: Harrassowitz.

Sahlins, M. 1999. "Two or Three Things That I Know About Culture." *Journal of the Royal Anthropological Institute* 5: 399–421.

Said, E. 1993. *Culture and Imperialism.* New York: Vintage.

Said, E. 2003. *Orientalism.* With preface and afterword. New York: Vintage.

Salles, J.-F. 1991. "Du bon et du mauvais usage des Phéniciens." *Topoi* 1: 48–70.

Salles, J.-F. 1995. "Phénicie." In *La civilisation phénicienne et punique: Manuel de recherche*, ed. V. Krings, 553–82. Leiden: Brill.

Salzmann, D. 1982. *Untersuchungen zu den antiken Kieselmosaiken*. Berlin: Mann.

Sancisi-Weerdenburg, H. 2001. "*Yaunā* by the Sea and Across the Sea." In *Ancient Perceptions of Greek Ethnicity*, ed. I. Malkin, 323–46. Washington, D.C.: Center for Hellenic Studies.

Sanders, H. 2001. "Sculptural Patronage and the Houses of Late Hellenistic Delos." Ph.D. diss., University of Michigan.

Sass, B. 2005. *The Alphabet at the Turn of the Millennium: The West Semitic Alphabet ca. 1150–850 BCE, The Antiquity of the Arabian, Greek and Phrygian Alphabets*. Tel Aviv: Emery and Claire Yass Publications in Archaeology.

Sasson, J., ed. 2001. *Civilizations of the Ancient Near East*. 4 vols. Peabody, Mass.: Hendrickson.

Savio, G. 2004. *Le uova di struzzo dipinte nella cultura punica*. Madrid: Real Academia de la historia.

Sayre, H. 2002. *Writing About Art*. Fourth ed. Upper Saddle River, N.J.: Prentice Hall.

Scandone, G. 1995. "Les sources égyptiennes." In *La civilisation phénicienne et punique: Manuel de recherche*, ed. V. Krings, 57–63. Leiden: Brill.

Schapiro, M. 1994. *Theory and Philosophy of Art: Style, Artist, and Society*. New York: George Braziller.

Schaps, D. 2004. *The Invention of Coinage and the Monetization of Ancient Greece*. Ann Arbor: University of Michigan Press.

Schefold, K. 1968. *Der Alexander-Sarkophag*. Frankfurt am Main: Propyläen.

Schmidt, S. and A. Stähli, eds. 2012. *Vasenbilder im Kulturtransfer: Zirkulation und Rezeption griechischer Keramik im Mittelmeerraum*. Corpus Vasorum Antiquorum, Germany, vol. 5. Munich: C. H. Beck.

Schmidt-Dounas, B. 1985. *Der lykische Sarkophag aus Sidon*. Tübingen: E. Wasmuth.

Schmitz, P. 2009. "The Owl in Phoenician Mortuary Practice." *Journal of Ancient Near Eastern Religions* 9: 51–85.

Schultz, P. 2009. "Accounting for Agency at Epidauros: A Note on *IG* IV² 102 AI–BI and the Economies of Style." In *Structure, Image, Ornament: Architectural Sculpture in the Greek World*, ed. P. Schultz and R. von den Hoff, 70–78. Oxford: Oxbow.

Scott, M. 2010. *Delphi and Olympia: The Spatial Politics of Panhellenism in the Archaic and Classical Periods*. Cambridge: Cambridge University Press.

Scott, S. 2006. "Art and the Archaeologist." *World Archaeology* 38 (4): 628–43.

Seaman, K. 2004. "Retrieving the Original Aphrodite of Knidos." *Rendiconti dell'Accademia nazionale dei Lincei: Classe di scienze morali, storiche, critiche e filologiche* 9 (15): 531–94.

Seltman, C. 1948. *Approach to Greek Art*. London: Studio.

Serrano Pichardo, L. et al. 2012. "Scaraboid Seal of the 'Lyre-Player Group' at the Huelva Museum." In *Actas do V Encontro de arqueologia do sudoeste peninsular (Almodôvar, Portugal, 18–20 November 2010)*, 279–88. Almodôvar: Câmara Municipal de Almodôvar.

Sewell, W., Jr. 1996a. "Historical Events as Transformations of Structures: Inventing Revolution at the Bastille." *Theory and Society* 25 (6): 841–81.

Sewell, W., Jr. 1996b. "Three Temporalities: Toward an Eventful Sociology." In *The Historic Turn in the Human Sciences*, ed. T. McDonald, 245–80. Ann Arbor: University of Michigan Press.

Sewell, W., Jr. 1999. "The Concept(s) of Culture." In *Beyond the Cultural Turn: New Directions in the Study of Society and Culture*, ed. V. Bonnell and L. Hunt, 35–61. Berkeley: University of California Press.

Sewell, W., Jr. 2005. *Logics of History: Social Theory and Social Transformation*. Chicago: University of Chicago Press.

Shahbazi, S. 1992. "CLOTHING ii: In the Median and Achaemenid Periods." In *Encyclopaedia Iranica* 5, 723–37. London: Routledge and Kegan Paul.

Shalev, Y. and S. Martin. 2012. "Crisis as Opportunity: Phoenician Urban Renewal After the Babylonians." *Transeuphratène* 41: 81–100.

Shanks, M. 1996. *Classical Archaeology of Greece: Experiences of the Discipline.* London: Routledge.

Shanks, M. 1999. *Art and the Greek City State: An Interpretive Archaeology.* Cambridge: Cambridge University Press.

Shapiro, H. 1993. "From Athena's Owl to the Owl of Athens." In *Nomodeiktes: Greek Studies in Honor of Martin Ostwald*, ed. R. Rosen and J. Farrell, 213–24. Ann Arbor: University of Michigan Press.

Shapiro, H. 1996. "Tradizioni regionali, botteghe e stili d'arte." In *I Greci: Storia, cultura, arte, società*, vol. 2.1, ed. S. Settis, 1181–1207. Turin: Einaudi.

Shapiro, H. 2009. "The Invention of Persia in Classical Athens." In *The Origins of Racism in the West*, ed. M. Eliav-Feldon, B. Isaac, and J. Ziegler, 57–87. Cambridge: Cambridge University Press.

Sharon, I. 1987. "Phoenician and Greek Ashlar Construction Techniques at Tel Dor, Israel." *Bulletin of the American Schools of Oriental Research* 267: 21–42.

Shennan, S., ed. 1989. *Archaeological Approaches to Cultural Identity.* London: Hyman.

Sherratt, S. 2010. "Greeks and Phoenicians: Perceptions of Trade and Traders in the Early First Millennium BC." In *Social Archaeologies of Trade and Exchange*, ed. A. Bauer and A. Agbe-Davies, 119–42. Walnut Creek, Calif.: Left Coast Press.

Sherratt, S. and A. Sherratt. 1991. "From Luxuries to Commodities: The Nature of Mediterranean Bronze Age Trading Systems." In *Bronze Age Trade in the Mediterranean: Papers Presented at the Conference Held at Rewley House, Oxford, in December 1989*, ed. N. Gale, 351–86. Jonsered: P. Åström.

Sherratt, S. and A. Sherratt. 1993. "The Growth of the Mediterranean Economy in the Early First Millennium BC." *World Archaeology* 24 (3): 361–78.

Sherwin-White, A. 1967. *Racial Prejudice in Imperial Rome.* Cambridge: Cambridge University Press.

Sherwin-White, S. and A. Kuhrt. 1993. *From Samarkhand to Sardis: A New Approach to the Seleucid Empire.* Berkeley: University of California Press.

Shipley, G. 2011. *Pseudo-Skylax's Periplous: The Circumnavigation of the Inhabited World.* Exeter: Bristol Phoenix Press.

Shipley, G. et al., eds. 2006. *The Cambridge Dictionary of Classical Civilization.* Cambridge: Cambridge University Press.

Siapkas, J. 2003. *Heterological Ethnicity: Conceptualizing Identities in Ancient Greece.* Uppsala: Uppsala Universitet.

Simpson, R. 1996. *Demotic Grammar in the Ptolemaic Sacerdotal Decrees.* Oxford: Ashmolean Museum.

Skinner, J. 2012. *The Invention of Greek Ethnography: From Homer to Herodotus.* Oxford: Oxford University Press.

Skon-Jedele, N. 1994. "Aigyptiaka: A Catalogue of Egyptian and Egyptianizing Objects Excavated from Greek Archaeological Sites, ca. 1100–525 B.C., with Historical Commentary." Ph.D. diss., University of Pennsylvania.

Smith, A. C. 2011. *Polis and Personification in Classical Athenian Art.* Leiden: Brill.

Smith, A. D. 1986. *The Ethnic Origins of Nations.* Oxford: Blackwell.

Smith, P., L. Stager, J. Greene, and G. Avishai. 2013. "Age Estimations Attest to Infant Sacrifice at the Carthage Tophet." *Antiquity* 87: 1191–1207.

Smith, R. 1981. "Greeks, Foreigners, and Roman Republican Portraits." *Journal of Roman Studies* 71: 24–38.

Smith, R. 2007. "Pindar, Athletes, and the Early Greek Statue Habit." In *Pindar's Poetry, Patrons and Festivals*, ed. S. Hornblower and C. Morgan, 83–139. Oxford: Oxford University Press.

Smith, S. 2003. *Wretched Kush: Ethnic Identities and Boundaries in Egypt's Nubian Empire*. London: Routledge.

Smith, T. and D. Plantzos, eds. 2012. *A Companion to Greek Art*. Oxford: Wiley-Blackwell.

Smith, W. 1998. *The Art and Architecture of Ancient Egypt*. New Haven: Yale University Press.

Snodgrass, A. 1980. *Archaic Greece: The Age of Experiment*. London: J. M. Dent.

Snodgrass, A. 1983. "Heavy Freight in Archaic Greece." In *Trade in the Ancient Economy*, ed. P. Garnsey, K. Hopkins, and C. Whittaker, 16–26. Berkeley: University of California Press.

Snodgrass, A. 1987. *An Archaeology of Greece: The Present State and Future Scope of a Discipline*. Berkeley: University of California Press.

Snodgrass, A. 1993. "Four Last Songs." *Classical Review* 43: 376–77.

Snowden, F. 1970. *Blacks in Antiquity: Ethiopians in the Greco-Roman Experience*. Cambridge, Mass.: Harvard University Press.

Snowden, F. 1983. *Before Color Prejudice: The Ancient View of Blacks*. Cambridge, Mass.: Harvard University Press.

Snowden, F. 1997. "Greeks and Ethiopians." In *Greeks and Barbarians: Essays on the Interactions Between Greeks and Non-Greeks in Antiquity and the Consequences for Eurocentrism*, ed. J. Coleman and C. Walz, 103–26. Bethesda, Md.: CDL Press.

Sommer, M. 2010. "Shaping Mediterranean Economy and Trade: Phoenician Cultural Identities in the Iron Age." In *Material Culture and Social Identities in the Ancient World*, ed. S. Hales and T. Hodos, 114–37. Cambridge: Cambridge University Press.

Sparkes, B. 1996. *The Red and the Black: Studies in Greek Pottery*. London: Routledge.

Spier, J. 1992. *Ancient Gems and Finger Rings: Catalogue of the Collection*. Malibu, Calif.: J. Paul Getty Museum.

Spivak, G. 1988a. "Can the Subaltern Speak?" In *Marxism and the Interpretation of Culture*, ed. C. Nelson and L. Grossberg, 271–313. Urbana: University of Illinois Press.

Spivak, G. 1988b. "Subaltern Studies: Deconstructing Historiography." In *Selected Subaltern Studies*, ed. R. Guha and G. Spivak, 3–32. New York: Oxford University Press.

Spivey, N. 1996. *Understanding Greek Sculpture: Ancient Meanings, Modern Readings*. New York: Thames and Hudson.

Squire, M. 2010a. "Introduction: The Art of Art History in Greco-Roman Antiquity." *Arethusa* 43 (2): 133–63.

Squire, M. 2010b. "Making Myron's Cow Moo? Ecphrastic Epigram and the Poetics of Simulation." *American Journal of Philology* 131 (4): 589–634.

Squire, M. 2011. *The Art of the Body: Antiquity and Its Legacy*. London: I. B. Tauris.

Squire, M. 2012. "Classical Archaeology and the Contexts of Art History." In *Classical Archaeology*, ed. S. Alcock and R. Osborne, 468–500. Second ed. Malden, Mass.: Wiley-Blackwell.

Stager, J. 2005. "'Let No One Wonder at This Image': A Phoenician Funerary Stele in Athens." *Hesperia* 74: 427–49.

Stager, J. 2012. "The Embodiment of Color in Ancient Mediterranean Art." Ph.D. diss., University of California, Berkeley.

Stager, L. and S. Wolff. 1984. "Child Sacrifice at Carthage: Religious Rite or Population Control?" *Biblical Archaeology Review* 10: 30–51.

Stansbury-O'Donnell, M. 1989. "Polygnotos's *Iliupersis*: A New Reconstruction." *American Journal of Archaeology* 93: 203–15.

Stansbury-O'Donnell, M. 1990. "Polygnotos's *Nekyia*: A Reconstruction and Analysis." *American Journal of Archaeology* 94: 213–35.

Stansbury-O'Donnell, M. 1999. *Pictorial Narrative in Ancient Greek Art*. Cambridge: Cambridge University Press.

Starks, J., Jr. 2011. "Was Black Beautiful in Vandal Africa?" In *African Athena: New Agendas*, ed. D. Orrells, G. Bhambra, and T. Roynon, 239–57. Oxford: Oxford University Press.

Stein, G., ed. 2005. *The Archaeology of Colonial Encounters: Comparative Perspectives*. Santa Fe: School of American Research Press.

Steiner, A. 2007. *Reading Greek Vases*. Cambridge: Cambridge University Press.

Stengel, M. 2000. "The Diffusionists Have Landed." *Atlantic Monthly* 285 (1): 35–61.

Stern, E. 1976. "Phoenician Masks and Pendants." *Palestine Exploration Quarterly* 108: 109–18.

Stern, E. 1993 "The Many Masters of Dor, Part 1: When Canaanites Became Phoenician Sailors." *Biblical Archaeology Review* 19 (1): 22–31.

Stern, E. 2001. *Archaeology of the Land of the Bible. Vol. II: The Assyrian, Babylonian, and Persian Periods, 732–332 BCE*. New York: Doubleday.

Stewart, A. 1979. *Attika: Studies in Athenian Sculpture of the Hellenistic Age*. London: Society for the Promotion of Hellenic Studies.

Stewart, A. 1986. "When Is a Kouros Not an Apollo? The Tenea 'Apollo' Revisited." In *Corinthiaca: Studies in Honor of Darrell A. Amyx*, ed. M. Del Chiaro, 54–70. Columbia: University of Missouri Press.

Stewart, A. 1990. *Greek Sculpture: An Exploration*. New Haven: Yale University Press.

Stewart, A. 1993. *Faces of Power: Alexander's Image and Hellenistic Politics*. Berkeley: University of California Press.

Stewart, A. 1997. *Art, Desire, and the Body in Ancient Greece*. Cambridge: Cambridge University Press.

Stewart, A. 2008a. *Classical Greece and the Birth of Western Art*. Cambridge: Cambridge University Press.

Stewart, A. 2008b. "The Persian and Carthaginian Invasions of 480 B.C.E. and the Beginning of the Classical Style: Part 1, The Stratigraphy, Chronology, and Significance of the Acropolis Deposits; Part 2, The Finds from Other Sites in Athens, Attica, Elsewhere in Greece, and on Sicily; Part 3, The Severe Style: Motivations and Meaning." *American Journal of Archaeology* 112: 377–412, 581–615.

Stewart, A. 2014. *Art in the Hellenistic World*. Cambridge: Cambridge University Press.

Stewart, A. and S. Martin. 2003. "Hellenistic Discoveries at Tel Dor (Israel)." *Hesperia* 72 (2): 121–45.

Stewart, A. and S. Martin. 2005. "Attic Imported Pottery at Tel Dor, Israel: An Overview." *Bulletin of the American Schools of Oriental Research* 337: 79–94.

Stewart, C. 1999. "Syncretism and Its Synonyms: Reflections on Cultural Mixture." *Diacritics* 29 (3): 40–62.

Stewart, P. 2014. "Art-Archaeology: The Materiality of Classical Art History." Unpublished lecture. Accessed December 1, 2014. https://www.academia.edu/6961613/Art-Archaeology _The_Materiality_of_Classical_Art_History.

Stieglitz, R. 1990. "Die Göttin Tanit im Orient." *Antike Welt* 21 (2): 106–9.

Stockhammer, P., ed. 2012. *Conceptualizing Cultural Hybridization: A Transdiciplinary Approach*. Berlin: Springer.

Stockhammer, P. 2013. "From Hybridity to Entanglement, From Essentialism to Practice." In *Archaeology and Cultural Mixture*, ed. W. van Pelt, 11–28. Archaeological Review from Cambridge 28. Cambridge: Department of Archaeology, University of Cambridge.

Strathern, M. 1990. "Artefacts of History: Events and the Interpretation of Images." In *Culture and History in the Pacific*, ed. J. Siikala, 25–44. Helsinki: Finnish Anthropological Society.

Stucky, R. 1974. *The Engraved Tridacna Shells.* Dédalo 19. São Paulo: Museu de arqueologia e etnologia, Universidade de São Paulo.

Stucky, R. 1984. *Tribune d'Echmoun: Ein griechischer Reliefzyklus des 4. Jahrhunderts v. Chr. in Sidon.* Basel: Vereinigung der Freunde antiker Kunst.

Stucky, R. 1993a. "Lykien—Karien—Phönizien: Kulturelle Kontakte zwischen Kleinasien und der Levante während der Perserherrschaft." In *Akten des II. internationalen Lykien-Symposions: Wien, 6.–12. Mai 1990,* ed. J. Borchhardt and G. Dobesch, 261–68. Vienna: Österreichische Akademie der Wissenschaften.

Stucky, R. 1993b. *Die Skulpturen aus dem Eschmun-Heiligtum bei Sidon: Griechische, römische, kyprische und phönizische Statuen und Reliefs vom 6. Jahrhundert vor Chr. bis zum 3. Jahrhundert nach Chr.* Basel: Vereinigung der Freunde antiker Kunst.

Stucky, R. 1997. "Le bâtiment aux frises d'enfants du sanctuaire d'Echmoun à Sidon." *Topoi* 7: 915–27.

Stucky, R., S. Stucky, A. Loprieno, H-P. Mathys, and R. Wachter. 2005. *Das Eschmun-Heiligtum von Sidon: Architektur und Inschriften.* Basel: Vereinigung der Freunde antiker Kunst.

Sugimoto, D., ed. 2014. *Transformation of a Goddess: Ishtar—Astarte—Aphrodite.* Orbis Biblicus et Orientalis 263. Göttingen: Vandenhoeck und Ruprecht.

Suro, R. 1988. "A Neglected Civilization Gets Its Due in Venice." *New York Times,* March 15, 1988.

Suter, C. and C. Uehlinger, eds. 2005. *Crafts and Images in Contact: Studies on Eastern Mediterranean Art of the First Millennium BCE.* Orbis Biblicus et Orientalis 210. Fribourg: Academic Press.

Swidler, A. 1986. "Culture in Action: Symbols and Strategies." *American Sociological Review* 51 (2): 273–86.

Sznycer, M. 1978. "L'emploi des termes 'phénicien,' 'punique,' 'néopunique' (problèmes de méthodologie)." In *Atti del secondo congresso internazionale di linguistica camito-semitica: Firenze, 16–19 aprile 1974,* ed. P. Fronzaroli, 261–68. Florence: Istituto di linguistica e di lingue orientali.

Tang, B. 2005. *Delos, Carthage, Ampurias: The Housing of Three Mediterranean Trading Centres.* Rome: L'Erma di Bretschneider.

Tanner, J. 1992. "Art as Expressive Symbolism: Civic Portraits in Classical Athens." *Cambridge Archaeological Journal* 2: 167–90.

Tanner, J. 1994. "Shifting Paradigms in Classical Art History." *Antiquity* 68: 650–55.

Tanner, J. 2001. "Nature, Culture and the Body in Classical Greek Religious Art." *World Archaeology* 33 (2): 257–76.

Tanner, J. 2003. "Finding the Egyptian in Early Greek Art." In *Ancient Perspectives on Egypt,* ed. R. Matthews and C. Roemer, 115–43. London: UCL Press, Institute of Archaeology.

Tanner, J. 2006. *The Invention of Art History in Ancient Greece: Religion, Society and Artistic Rationalisation.* Cambridge: Cambridge University Press.

Tanner, J. 2010a. "Aesthetics and Art History Writing in Comparative Historical Perspective." *Arethusa* 43 (2): 267–88.

Tanner, J. 2010b. "Introduction to the New Edition, Race and Representation in Ancient Art: *Black Athena* and After." In *The Image of the Black in Western Art 1,* ed. D. Bindman, H. Gates, Jr., and K. Dalton, 1–39. Cambridge, Mass.: Belknap Press.

Taylor, G. 1993. *Yahweh and the Sun: Biblical and Archaeological Evidence for Sun Worship in Ancient Israel.* Sheffield: JSOT Press.

Teixidor, J. 1976. "The Phoenician Inscriptions of the Cesnola Collection." *Metropolitan Museum Journal* 11: 55–70.

Thomas, N. 1991. *Entangled Objects: Exchange, Material Culture, and Colonialism in the Pacific.* Cambridge, Mass.: Harvard University Press.

Thomas, R. 2001. "Ethnicity, Genealogy, and Hellenism in Herodotus." In *Ancient Perceptions of Greek Ethnicity*, ed. I. Malkin, 213–33. Washington, D.C.: Center for Hellenic Studies.

Thompson, L. 1989. *Romans and Blacks*. Norman: University of Oklahoma Press.

Tilley, C. et al. 2006. *Handbook of Material Culture*. London: SAGE.

Topper, K. 2012. *The Imagery of the Athenian Symposium*. Cambridge: Cambridge University Press.

Török, L. 2011. *Hellenizing Art in Ancient Nubia, 300 BC–AD 250, and Its Egyptian Models: A Study in "Acculturation."* Leiden: Brill.

Tribulato, O. 2013. "Phoenician Lions: The Funerary Stele of the Phoenician Shem/Antipatros." *Hesperia* 82: 459–86.

Trigger, B. 1989a. *A History of Archaeological Thought*. Cambridge: Cambridge University Press.

Trigger, B. 1989b. Review of *What Is Archaeology? An Essay on the Nature of Archaeological Research*, by Paul Courbin, trans. Paul Bahn. *Canadian Journal of Archaeology* 13: 237–39.

Trouillot, M.-R. 2003. *Global Transformations: Anthropology and the Modern World*. New York: Palgrave Macmillan.

Trümper, M. 2002. "Das Sanktuarium des 'Établissement des Poseidoniastes de Bértyos' in Delos: Zur Baugeschichte eines griechischen Vereinsheiligtums." *Bulletin de Correspondance Hellénique* 126: 265–330.

Tsakirgis, B. 1989. "The Decorated Pavements of Morgantina I: The Mosaics." *American Journal of Archaeology* 93: 395–416.

Tubb, J. 1998. *Canaanites*. Peoples of the Past 2. Norman: University of Oklahoma Press.

Tuplin, C. 1999. "Greek Racism? Observations on the Character and Limits of Greek Ethnic Prejudice." In *Ancient Greeks West and East*, ed. G. Tsetskhladze, 47–75. Leiden: Brill.

Tuplin, C. 2007. "Racism in Classical Antiquity? Three Opinions." *Ancient West and East* 6: 327–58.

Turfa, J. and A. Steinmayer, Jr. 1999. "The *Syracusia* as a Giant Cargo Vessel." *International Journal of Nautical Archaeology* 28 (2): 105–25.

Ucko, P. 1989. "Foreword." In *Archaeological Approaches to Cultural Identity*, ed. S. Shennan, ix–xx. London: Hyman.

Uehlinger, C. 2000. *Images as Media: Sources for the Cultural History of the Near East and the Eastern Mediterranean. 1st Millennium BCE*. Fribourg: University Press.

Ulf, C. 2009. "Rethinking Cultural Contacts." *Ancient West and East* 8: 81–132.

van Alfen, P. 2002. "Pant'agatha: Commodities in Levantine-Aegean Trade During the Persian Period, 6–4th c. B.C." Ph.D. diss., University of Texas at Austin.

van Dommelen, P. 1998a. *On Colonial Grounds: A Comparative Study of Colonialism and Rural Settlement in First Millennium BC West Central Sardinia*. Leiden: Faculty of Archaeology, University of Leiden.

van Dommelen, P. 1998b. "Punic Persistence: Colonialism and Cultural Identities in Roman Sardinia." In *Cultural Identity in the Roman Empire*, ed. R. Laurence and J. Berry, 25–48. London: Routledge.

van Dommelen, P. 2002. "Ambiguous Matters: Colonialism and Local Identities in Punic Sardinia." In *The Archaeology of Colonialism*, ed. C. Lyons and J. Papadopoulos, 121–47. Los Angeles: Getty Research Institute.

van Dommelen, P. 2005. "Colonial Interactions and Hybrid Practices: Phoenician and Carthaginian Settlement in the Ancient Mediterranean." In *The Archaeology of Colonial Encounters: Comparative Perspectives*, ed. G. Stein, 109–41. Santa Fe: School of American Research Press.

van Dommelen, P. 2006. "The Orientalizing Phenomenon: Hybridity and Material Culture in the Western Mediterranean." In *Debating Orientalization: Multidisciplinary Approaches to Change in the Ancient Mediterranean*, ed. C. Riva and N. Vella, 135–52. London: Equinox.

van Dommelen, P., ed. 2011. *Postcolonial Archaeologies*. World Archaeology 43. Abingdon: Routledge.

van Dommelen, P. and A. Knapp, eds. 2010. *Material Connections in the Ancient Mediterranean: Mobility, Materiality and Mediterranean Identities*. London: Routledge.

van Dommelen, P. and M. López-Bertran. 2013. "Hellenism as Subaltern Practice: Rural Cults in the Punic World." In *The Hellenistic West: Rethinking the Ancient Mediterranean*, ed. J. Prag and J. Quinn, 273–99. Cambridge: Cambridge University Press.

van Dongen, E. 2010. "'Phoenicia': Naming and Defining a Region in Syria-Palestine." In *Interkulturalität in der alten Welt: Vorderasien, Hellas, Ägypten und die vielfältigen Ebenen des Kontakts*, ed. R. Rollinger et al. 471–88. Wiesbaden: Harrassowitz.

Van Dyke, R. and S. Alcock, eds. 2003. *Archaeologies of Memory*. Malden, Mass.: Blackwell.

Van Pelt, W., ed. 2013. *Archaeology and Cultural Mixture*. Archaeological Review from Cambridge 28. Cambridge: Department of Archaeology, University of Cambridge.

Vance, D. 1994. "Literary Sources for the History of Palestine and Syria: The Phoenician Inscriptions, Part I." *Biblical Archaeologist* 57: 2–19.

Vella, N. 1996. "Elusive Phoenicians." *Antiquity* 70 (268): 245–50.

Vella, N. 2000. "Defining Phoenician Religious Space: "Oumm el-'Amed Reconsidered." *Ancient Near Eastern Studies* 37: 27–55.

Vella, N. 2010. "'Phoenician' Metal Bowls: Boundary Objects in the Archaic Period." *Bollettino di Archeologia On Line* special issue, 22–37. Accessed May 17, 2016. http://www.bollettinodi archeologiaonline.beniculturali.it/documenti/generale/5_VELLA.pdf.

Vella, N. 2014. "The Invention of the Phoenicians: On Object Definition, Decontextualization and Display." In *The Punic Mediterranean: Identities and Identification from Phoenician Settlement to Roman Rule*, ed. J. Quinn and N. Vella, 24–41. Cambridge: Cambridge University Press.

Venit, M. 1988. *Greek Painted Pottery from Naukratis in Egyptian Museums*. Winona Lake, Ind.: Eisenbrauns.

Vernant, J.-P. 1983. *Myth and Thought Among the Greeks*. London: Routledge and Kegan Paul.

Vernant, J.-P. 1990. *Figures, idoles, masques*. Paris: Julliard.

Veropoulidou, R., S. Andreou, and K. Kotsakis. 2008. "Small Scale Purple-Dye Production in the Bronze Age of Northern Greece: The Evidence from the Thessaloniki Toumba." In *Purpureae Vestes II: Vestidos, Textiles y Tintes. Estudios sobre la producción de bienes de consumo en la Antigüedad*, ed. C. Alfaro and L. Karali, 171–80. Valencia: Universitat de València.

Vickers, M. 1985. "Artful Crafts: The Influence of Metalwork on Athenian Painted Pottery." *Journal of Hellenic Studies* 105: 108–28.

Vickers, M. and D. Gill. 1994. *Artful Crafts: Ancient Greek Silverware and Pottery*. Oxford: Clarendon Press.

Vlassopoulos, K. 2013. *Greeks and Barbarians*. Cambridge: Cambridge University Press.

von Boeselager, D. 1983. *Antike Mosaiken in Sizilien: Hellenismus und römische Kaiserzeit, 3. Jahrhundert v. Chr.–3. Jahrhundert n. Chr.* Rome: Giorgio Bretschneider.

Von Bothmer, D. 1957. *Amazons in Greek Art*. Oxford: Clarendon Press.

von Graeve, V. 1970. *Der Alexandersarkophag und seine Werkstatt*. Berlin: Gebr. Mann.

Vorster, C. 1983. *Griechische Kinderstatuen*. Cologne: Wasmuth.

Vorster, C. 2002. "Früharchaische Plastik." In *Die Geschichte der antiken Bildhauerkunst 1: Frühgriechische Plastik*, ed. P. Bol et al., 97–132. Mainz am Rhein: Philipp von Zabern.

Vout, C. 2012. "Putting the Art into Artifact." In *Classical Archaeology*, ed. S. Alcock and R. Osborne, 442–67. Second ed. Malden, Mass.: Wiley-Blackwell.

Wagner, C. and J. Boardman. 2003. *A Collection of Classical and Eastern Intaglios, Rings and Cameos*. Oxford: Archaeopress.

Wagner, P. 1980. *Der ägyptische Einfluss auf die phönizische Architektur*. Bonn: R. Habelt.

Waldbaum, J. 1997. "Greeks *in* the East or Greeks *and* the East? Problems in the Definition and Recognition of Presence." *Bulletin of the American Schools of Oriental Research* 305: 1–17.

Wallinga, H. 1987. "The Ancient Persian Navy and Its Predecessors." In *Achaemenid History, Vol. 1: Sources, Structures and Synthesis. Proceedings of the Groningen 1983 Achaemenid History Workshop*, ed. H. Sancisi-Weerdenburg, 47–77. Leiden: Nederlands Instituut voor het Nabije Oosten.

Wallinga, H. 2005. *Xerxes' Greek Adventure: The Naval Perspective*. Leiden: Brill.

Walsh, J. 2014. *Consumerism in the Ancient World: Imports and Identity Construction*. London: Routledge.

Warren, M. 1884. "On the Etymology of Hybrid (Lat. Hybrida)." *American Journal of Philology* 5 (4): 501–2.

Webb, V. 1978. *Archaic Greek Faience: Miniature Scent Bottles and Related Objects from East Greece, 650–500 B.C.* Warminster: Aris and Phillips

Weber, M. 1978 [1922]. *Economy and Society: An Outline of Interpretive Sociology*, ed. G. Roth and C. Wittich. Berkeley: University of California Press.

Webster, J. 2001. "Creolizing the Roman Provinces." *American Journal of Archaeology* 105 (2): 209–25.

Webster, T. 1966. *The Art of Greece: The Age of Hellenism*. New York: Crown.

Węcowski, M. 2004. "The Hedgehog and the Fox: Form and Meaning in the Prologue of Herodotus." *Journal of Hellenic Studies* 124: 143–64.

Węcowski, M. 2014. *The Rise of the Greek Aristocratic Banquet*. Oxford: Oxford University Press.

Weiskopf, M. 1989. *The So-Called "Great Satraps' Revolt," 366–360 B.C.: Concerning Local Instability in the Achaemenid Far West*. Stuttgart: F. Steiner.

Werbner, P. and T. Modood, eds. 1997. *Debating Cultural Hybridity: Multi-Cultural Identities and the Politics of Anti-Racism*. London: Zed Books.

Wescoat, B., ed. 1989. *Syracuse, the Fairest Greek City: Ancient Art from the Museo Archeologico Regionale 'Paolo Orsi'*. Rome: De Luca edizioni d'arte.

West, M. 1971. *Early Greek Philosophy and the Orient*. Oxford: Clarendon Press.

West, M. 1997. *The East Face of Helicon: West Asiatic Elements in Greek Poetry and Myth*. Oxford: Clarendon Press.

Westgate, R. 1997–98. "Greek Mosaics in their Architectural and Social Context." *Bulletin of the Institute of Classical Studies* 42: 93–115.

Westgate, R. 2000a. "*Pavimenta atque emblemata vermiculata*: Regional Styles in Hellenistic Mosaic and the First Mosaics at Pompeii." *American Journal of Archaeology* 104: 255–75.

Westgate, R. 2000b. "Space and Decoration in Hellenistic Houses." *The Annual of the British School at Athens* 95: 391–426.

Westgate. R. 2002. "Hellenistic Mosaics." In *The Hellenistic World: New Perspectives*, ed. D. Ogden, 221–51. Swansea: The Classical Press of Wales.

Westgate, R. 2012. "Mosaics." In *A Companion to Greek Art*, ed. T. Smith and D. Plantzos, 186–99. Oxford: Wiley-Blackwell.

White, R. 2011 [1991]. *The Middle Ground: Indians, Empires, and Republics in the Great Lakes Region, 1650–1815*. Cambridge: Cambridge University Press.

Whitehead, I. 1987. "The Periplous." *Greece and Rome* 34: 178–85.

Whitley, J. 1991. *Style and Society in Dark Age Greece: The Changing Face of a Pre-Literate Society 1100–700 BC*. Cambridge: Cambridge University Press.

Whitley, J. 1997. "Beazley as Theorist." *Antiquity* 71 (271): 40–7.

Whitley, J. 2001. *The Archaeology of Ancient Greece*. Cambridge: Cambridge University Press.

Whitley, J. 2010. Review of *Greek Art and the Orient,* by Anne Gunter; *Art and Identity in Dark Age Greece, 1100–700 B.C.E.*, by Susan Langdon; and *Art and Society in Cyprus from the Bronze Age into the Iron Age,* by Joanna Smith. *Cambridge Archaeological Journal* 20 (3): 460–63.

Whitley, J. 2012. "Agency in Greek Art." In *A Companion to Greek Art,* ed. T. Smith and D. Plantzos, 579–95. Oxford: Wiley-Blackwell.

Whitley, J. 2013. "The Cretan Orientalizing: A Comparative Perspective." In *Kreta in der geometrischen und archaischen Zeit,* ed. W. Niemeier, O. Pillz, and I. Kaiser, 409–26. Munich: Hirmer.

Whitmarsh, T. 1998. "The Birth of a Prodigy: Heliodorus and the Genealogy of Hellenism." In *Studies in Heliodorus,* ed. R. Hunter, 93–124. Cambridge: Cambridge Philological Society.

Whitmarsh, T. 2011. "Hellenism, Nationalism, Hybridity: The Invention of the Novel." In *African Athena: New Agendas,* ed. D. Orrells, G. Bhambra, and T. Roynon, 210–24. Oxford: Oxford University Press.

Whitmarsh, T. and S. Thomson, eds. 2013. *The Romance Between Greece and the East.* Cambridge: Cambridge University Press.

Wiley, G. and P. Phillips. 1958. *Method and Theory in American Archaeology.* Chicago: University of Chicago Press.

Wilson, A. 2003. "Une cité grecque de Libye: Fouilles d'Euhésperidès (Benghazi)." *Comptes rendus de l'Académie des inscriptions et belles-lettres* 147 (4): 1648–75.

Wilson, A. 2006. "New Light on a Greek City: Archaeology and History at Euesperides." In *Cirenaica: Studi, scavi e scoperte. Atti del X Convegno di Archeologia cirenaica, Chieti 24–26 novembre 2003,* ed. E. Fabbricotti and O. Menozzi, 141–52. BAR International Series 1488. Oxford: John and Erica Hedges.

Wilson, A. 2013. "Trading Across the Syrtes: Euesperides and the Punic world." In *The Hellenistic West: Rethinking the Ancient Mediterranean,* ed. J. Prag and J. Quinn, 120–56. Cambridge: Cambridge University Press.

Wimmer, A. 2008. "The Making and Unmaking of Ethnic Boundaries: A Multilevel Process Theory." *American Journal of Sociology* 113 (4): 970–1022.

Winter, F. 1912. *Der Alexandersarkophag aus Sidon.* Strassburg: K. J. Trübner.

Winter, I. 1976. "Phoenician and North Syrian Ivory Carving in Historical Context: Questions of Style and Distribution." *Iraq* 38: 1–22.

Winter, I. 1988. "North Syria as a Bronzeworking Centre in the Early First Millennium B.C.: Luxury Commodities at Home and Abroad." In *Bronzeworking Centres of Western Asia, c. 1000–539 B.C.,* ed. J. Curtis, 193–225. London: Kegan Paul International.

Winter, I. 1995. "Homer's Phoenicians: History, Ethnography, or Literary Trope? (A Perspective on Early Orientalism)." In *The Ages of Homer: A Tribute to Emily Townsend Vermeule,* ed. J. Carter and S. Morris, 247–71. Austin: University of Texas Press.

Winter, I. 2005. "Establishing Group Boundaries: Toward Methodological Refinement in the Determination of Sets as a Prior Condition to the Analysis of Cultural Contact and/or Innovation in First Millennium BCE Ivory Carving." In *Crafts and Images in Contact: Studies on Eastern Mediterranean Art of the First Millennium BCE,* ed. C. Suter and C. Uehlinger, 23–42. Fribourg: Academic Press.

Winter, I. 2007. "Agency Marked, Agency Ascribed: The Affective Object in Ancient Mesopotamia." In *Art's Agency and Art History,* ed. R. Osborne and J. Tanner, 42–69. Oxford: Blackwell.

Winter, I. 2010. *On Art in the Ancient Near East. Vol. I: Of the First Millennium BCE.* Leiden: Brill.

Winthrop, R., ed. 1991. *Dictionary of Concepts in Cultural Anthropology.* New York: Greenwood Press.

Wiseman, J. 1983. "Conflicts in Archaeology: Education and Practice." *Journal of Field Archaeology* 10: 1–9.

Wolff, S. 1993. Review of *The Phoenicians*, ed. Sabatino Moscati. *Israel Exploration Journal* 43 (4): 276–79.

Wollheim, R. 1973. "Giovanni Morelli and the Origins of Scientific Connoisseurship." In *On Art and Mind: Essays and Lectures*, 177–201. London: Allen Lane.

Wollheim, R. 1980. *Art and Its Objects.* Second ed. Cambridge: Cambridge University Press.

Woodford, S. 1993. *The Trojan War in Ancient Art.* Ithaca: Cornell University Press.

Woolmer, M. 2011. *Ancient Phoenicia: An Introduction.* London: Bristol Classical Press.

Woolmer, M. 2012. "'Ornamental' Horns on Phoenician Warships." *Levant* 44 (2): 238–52.

Xella, P. 1990. "'Divinités doubles' dans la monde phénico-punique." *Semitica* 39: 167–75.

Xella, P. 1991. *Baal Hammon: Recherches sur l'identité et l'histoire d'un dieu phénico-punique.* Rome: Consiglio nazionale delle richerche.

Xella, P. 1995a. "Les sources cunéiforms." In *La civilisation phénicienne et punique: Manuel de recherche*, ed. V. Krings, 39–56. Leiden: Brill.

Xella, P. 1995b. "La Bible." In *La civilisation phénicienne et punique: Manuel de recherche*, ed. V. Krings, 64–72. Leiden: Brill.

Xella, P. et al. 2013. "Phoenician Bones of Contention." *Antiquity* 87 (338): 1199–1207.

Yonan, M. 2011. "Toward a Fusion of Art History and Material Culture Studies." *West 86th* 18 (2): 232–48.

Young, R. J. C. 1990. *White Mythologies: Writing History and the West.* London: Routledge.

Young, R. J. C. 1994. "Egypt in America: *Black Athena*, Racism and Colonial Discourse." In *Racism, Modernity and Identity: On the Western Front*, ed. A. Rattansi and S. Westwood, 150–69. Cambridge: Polity Press.

Young, R. J. C. 1995. *Colonial Desire: Hybridity in Theory, Culture, and Race.* London: Routledge.

Young, R. J. C. 2001. *Postcolonialism: An Historical Introduction.* Oxford: Blackwell.

Young, R. J. C. 2003. *Postcolonialism: A Very Short Introduction.* Oxford: Oxford University Press.

Young, R. S. 1965. "Early Mosaics at Gordion." *Expedition* 7: 4–13.

Zarmakoupi, M. 2013. "The Quartier du Stade on Late Hellenistic Delos: A Case Study of Rapid Urbanization (Fieldwork Seasons 2009–2010)." *ISAW Papers* 6: n.p.

Zernecke, A. 2013. "The Lady of the Titles: The Lady of Byblos and the Search for Her 'True Name.'" In *Permutations of Astarte*, ed. R. Schmitt and M. Christian, 226–42. Die Welt des Orients 43. Göttingen: Vandenhoeck und Ruprecht.

Index

Acknowledgments

Thanks are owed to the staff, faculty, and students of the Departments of History of Art, AHMA, NES, and Classics at Berkeley, as well as a number of faculty members in the Department of Art at Southeast Missouri State University, where I taught from 2009 to 2011, and Boston University's Department of History of Art & Architecture, where I wrote this book. I would like to thank Marian Feldman, who helped initiate this project and who has been a steady presence in its writing, and my mentor at BU, Fred Kleiner. I am particularly indebted to Andrew F. Stewart (who has been a generous mentor over the years) and Christopher H. Hallett from Berkeley's History of Art; Professor Erich S. Gruen from History, now emeritus; and Ilan Sharon from the Institute of Archaeology at the Hebrew University, Jerusalem.

Preliminary research in Israel was supported by the staff at the C.O.N.R.A.D./ Mizgaga Museum at Nahsholim and by its curator, Bracha Guz-Zilberstein. At the Hebrew University I thank the library staff of the Institute of Archaeology. I am grateful also for support of Ayelet Gilboa of the University of Haifa, Ephraim Stern of Hebrew University (now emeritus), and my colleagues from the Tel Dor excavations, particularly Sveta Matskevich (who is responsible for the drawings, plans, and maps in this book) and Yiphtah Shalev. At the William F. Albright Institute of Archaeological Research I thank the library, housing, and office staff and fellows in residence, as well as the director during my tenure there (2003–2005), Seymour Gitin. I would also like to thank the staff, directors, and members of the Kenyon Institute (Jerusalem) for hosting me at various points in the research process. Research in Greece and Israel was funded by the Samuel H. Kress Foundation, the William F. Albright Institute of Archaeological Research, the Brittan Fund via the Department of Classics at Berkeley, the History of Art Department at Berkeley, the Berkeley Graduate Division, and a Getty Collaborative Research Award (PI, Andrew Stewart).

Writing was supported by a grant from the Mabelle McLeod Lewis Memorial Fund, the Grants and Research Funding Committee at Southeast Missouri State University, a Faculty Travel Award from the Office of the Associate Dean for Research and Outreach at Boston University, the Boston University Center for the

Humanities, the National Endowment for the Humanities, the American School of Classical Studies at Athens, and the American Research Institute in Turkey. Thanks are owed to my research assistants, Bronwen Manning-Rozenblum (Albright intern) and Angelica Bradley (BU). Finally, I thank my family, friends, and colleagues for their support, for coping with the demands imposed by the academic lifestyle, and for cheering me along the way. Marian Feldman, Janling Fu, Jeffrey Hurwit, Kathleen Lynch, Oswyn Murray, Helen Sader, Philip Schmitz, Marek Weçowski, and James Whitley have read chapter drafts or generously shared with me unpublished material. I thank Josette Élayi for her helpful comments on the study of Tyrian coins. I must mention in particular Jessica Nitschke and Nicholas Hudson, with whom I have worked for many years and who were especially important in the writing phase of the project (via RAD). I am also deeply in debt to Jo Crawley Quinn and an anonymous reviewer, who made great efforts to help me shape and correct the manuscript.

Finally, special thanks are owed to Deborah Blake, Hannah Blake, and Erica Ginsburg at the University of Pennsylvania Press for their patience and editorial guidance. Image and licensing fees were generously paid by the Art History Publications Initiative, funded by the Andrew W. Mellon Foundation. A preparatory essay for part of Chapter 3 appeared in the *Blackwell Companion to Ethnicity in the Ancient Mediterranean*, edited by Jeremy McInerney, as "Representation and Ethnicity" (Oxford: Blackwell, 2014). A final word of thanks to readers of the book for enduring my incursions into their areas of research. The text is both broad in scope and selective in examples. It no doubt falls short relative to the expertise and depth of interest of many in its attempt to understand Greek and Phoenician art from a few different angles. I thank them for their patience.